# Webster's Notebook Dictionary

Created in Cooperation with the Editors of
Merriam-Webster

FEDERAL
STREET
PRESS

A Division of Merriam-Webster, Incorporated
Springfield, Massachusetts

# Contents

This 2018 edition published by
Federal Street Press,
A Division of Merriam-Webster, Incorporated
P.O. Box 281
Springfield, MA 01102

Federal Street Press books are available for bulk purchase for
sales promotion and premium use. For details write the manager of
special sales, Federal Street Press, P.O. Box 281, Springfield, MA 01102

ISBN 13   978-1-59695-056-6

Printed in Canada

2nd printing   Webcom, Toronto, ON   6/2018

# Preface

This new dictionary is unique in many respects. While small in size, it contains more than 19,000 words that represent the very core of the language. It is intended to serve as a quick reference for spelling, hyphenation, and meaning of the words in everyday use. Conciseness of presentation necessarily requires special treatment of entries, and this book has a number of special features all its own.

Entry words appear in **boldface type** with raised periods to indicate where they can be hyphenated at the end of a line in writing. Words that begin an entry paragraph are **main entry words** and are followed by definitions or cross-references to related entries.

> **aard·vark** . . . : ant-eating African mammal
> **abroad** . . . **1**: over a wide area **2** : outside one's country
> **ate** *past of* EAT

**Variant spellings** of bold words are shown following a comma.

> **blond, blonde** . . . **1** : fair in complexion

Labels indicating a word's grammatical function in the sentence **(part of speech)** are shown as abbreviations in italics after the bold word.

> **cam·era** *n* : box with a lens for taking pictures . . .
> **cam·ou·flage** *vb* : hide by disguising . . .
> **can·did** *adj* **1** : frank **2** : not posed . . .
> — **can·did·ly** *adv* . . .

Within an entry paragraph, derived words with the same spelling but a different part of speech are represented by a **swung dash** and are provided with their own definitions.

> **di·rect** *vb* **1** : address **2** : cause to move or to follow a certain course . . .
> ∼ *adj* **1** : leading to or coming from a point without deviation or interruption . . .

Derived words are run on undefined at the end of the entry when their meanings are self-evident from the definitions preceding. This treatment allows for the saving of space to permit many more words to be entered and at the same time shows word relationships.

> **ex·haust** *vb* **1** : draw out or develop completely **2** : use up . . .
> ∼ *n* : waste steam or gas from an engine . . . — **ex·haus·tion** *n*
> — **ex·haus·tive** *adj*

Main entries with the same spelling but not derived from one another are entered separately, marked with a superscript numeral.

> [1]**file** *n* : tool for smoothing or sharpening . . .
> [2]**file** *vb* **1** : arrange in order **2** : enter or record officially . . .
> [3]**file** *n* : row of persons or things one behind the other

Plurals of nouns, principal parts of verbs, and comparative and superlative forms of adjectives (and adverbs) are know as **inflected forms.** Those formed by the regular addition of a suffix (such as *-s, -ed, -ing, -er, -est*) are well-known regular formations and are not shown in this dictionary. Inflections formed by an internal change in the spelling of the word (or no change) are shown inside parentheses. For nouns, the forms shown will be plurals (*pl*); for verbs, the forms shown will be past tense (*past*) and past participle (*past part*). The past and past participle are separated by a semicolon. If variant spellings are shown for any inflected form, that spelling is set off by a slash (/).

> **grow** *vb* **grew; grown 1** : come into existence and develop to maturity
> **knife** *n* **knives** : sharp blade with a handle . . .
> [1]**lie** *vb* **lay; lain 1** : be in, rest in, or assume a horizontal position . . .

**moose** *n* **moose** : large heavy-antlered deer
**prove** *vb* **proved; proved/prov·en 1** : test by experiment or by a standard . . .

When a particular sense of a word is used in a special way, such as used only in the plural form, that information is indicated after the sense number.

> **re·fresh·ment** *n* **1** : act of refreshing **2** *pl* : light meal

If at a particular sense the form of the inflection is unique or not regularly formed, that information is also provided.

> **an·ten·na** *n* **1** *pl* **an·ten·nae** : one of the long slender paired sensory organs on the head of an arthropod **2** *pl* **an·ten·nas** : metallic device for sending or receiving radio waves
> **young** *adj* **1** : being in the first or an early stage of life . . . ∼ *n* **young** : persons or animals that are young
> **up** *adv* **1** : in or to a higher position or level . . . ∼ *vb* **1 up; upped** : act abruptly **2 upped; upped** : move or cause to move upward . . .

In the first example, the form of the plural is different for each of the two noun senses and is therefore shown. In the second example, the plural form for the noun sense is unchanged. In the third example, the verb inflections for the past tense are different for each of these two verb senses.

To show the range of entries on a page, **guide words** appear at the top, indicating the first main entry word and the last main entry word on that page.

Common **abbreviations**, including those used in this book, are shown in a separate section immediately following the dictionary proper.

# Abbreviations

Most of these abbreviations are shown in one form only. Variation in use of periods, in kind of type, and in capitalization is frequent and widespread (as mph, MPH, m.p.h., Mph)

**abbr** abbreviation
**AD** in the year of our Lord
**adj** adjective
**adv** adverb
**AK** Alaska
**AL, Ala** Alabama
**alt** alternate, altitude
**a.m., A.M.** before noon
**Am, Amer** America, American
**amt** amount
**anon** anonymous
**ans** answer
**Apr** April
**AR** Arkansas
**Ariz** Arizona
**Ark** Arkansas
**assn** association
**asst** assistant
**atty** attorney
**Aug** August
**ave** avenue
**AZ** Arizona

**BC** before Christ
**bet** between
**bldg** building
**blvd** boulevard
**Br, Brit** Britain, British
**bro** brother
**bros** brothers
**bu** bushel

**c** carat, cent, centimeter, century, chapter, cup
**C** Celsius, centigrade
**CA, Cal, Calif** California
**Can, Canad** Canada, Canadian
**cap** capital, capitalize, capitalized
**Capt** captain
**ch** chapter, church
**cm** centimeter
**co** company, county
**CO** Colorado
**COD** cash on delivery, collect on delivery
**col** column
**Col** colonel, Colorado
**Colo** Colorado
**conj** conjunction
**Conn** Connecticut
**cpu** central processing unit
**ct** cent, court
**CT** Connecticut
**cu** cubic
**CZ** Canal Zone

**d** penny
**DC** District of Columbia
**DDS** doctor of dental surgery
**DE** Delaware
**Dec** December
**Del** Delaware
**dept** department
**DMD** doctor of dental medicine
**doz** dozen
**Dr** doctor
**DST** daylight saving time

**E** east, eastern, excellent
**ea** each
**e.g.** for example
**Eng** England, English
**esp** especially
**etc** et cetera

**f** false, female, forte
**F** Fahrenheit
**FBI** Federal Bureau of Investigation
**Feb** February
**fem** feminine
**FL, Fla** Florida
**fr** father, from
**Fri** Friday
**ft** feet, foot, fort

**g** gram
**G** good
**Ga, GA** Georgia
**gal** gallon
**GB** gigabyte
**gen** general
**geog** geographic, geographical, geography
**gm** gram
**gov** governor
**govt** government
**gt** great
**GU** Guam

**HI** Hawaii
**hr** hour
**HS** high school
**ht** height
**Ia, IA** Iowa
**ID** Idaho
**i.e.** that is
**IL, Ill** Illinois
**in** inch
**IN** Indiana
**inc** incorporated
**Ind** Indian, Indiana
**interj** interjection
**intrans** intransitive

**Jan** January
**jr, jun** junior

**Kan, Kans** Kansas
**KB** kilobyte
**kg** kilogram
**km** kilometer
**KS** Kansas
**Ky, KY** Kentucky

**l** left, liter
**La, LA** Louisiana
**lb** pound
**Lt** lieutenant
**ltd** limited

**m** male, meter, mile
**MA** Massachusetts
**Maj** major
**Mar** March
**masc** masculine
**Mass** Massachusetts
**MB** megabyte
**Md** Maryland
**MD** doctor of medicine, Maryland
**Me, ME** Maine
**Mex** Mexican, Mexico
**mg** milligram
**MI, Mich** Michigan
**min** minute
**Minn** Minnesota
**Miss** Mississippi
**ml** milliliter
**mm** millimeter
**MN** Minnesota
**mo** month
**Mo, MO** Missouri
**Mon** Monday
**Mont** Montana
**mpg** miles per gallon
**mph** miles per hour
**MS** Mississippi
**mt** mount, mountain
**MT** Montana

**n** noun
**N** north, northern
**NC** North Carolina
**ND, N Dak** North Dakota
**NE** Nebraska, northeast
**Neb, Nebr** Nebraska
**Nev** Nevada
**NH** New Hampshire
**NJ** New Jersey
**NM, N Mex** New Mexico
**no** north, number
**Nov** November
**NV** Nevada
**NW** northwest
**NY** New York

**O** Ohio
**obj** object, objective
**Oct** October
**off** office
**OH** Ohio
**OK, Okla** Oklahoma
**OR, Ore, Oreg** Oregon
**oz** ounce, ounces

**p** page
**Pa, PA** Pennsylvania
**part** participle
**pat** patent
**Penn, Penna** Pennsylvania
**pg** page
**pk** park, peck
**pkg** package
**pl** plural
**p.m., P.M.** afternoon
**PO** post office
**poss** possessive
**pp** pages
**pr** pair
**PR** Puerto Rico
**prep** preposition
**pres** present, president
**prof** professor
**pron** pronoun
**PS** postscript, public school
**pt** pint, point
**PTA** Parent-Teacher Association
**PTO** Parent-Teacher Organization

**qt** quart

**r** right
**rd** road, rod
**recd** received
**reg** region, regular
**res** residence
**Rev** reverend
**RFD** rural free delivery
**RI** Rhode Island
**rpm** revolutions per minute
**RR** railroad
**RSVP** please reply
**rt** right
**rte** route

**S** south, southern
**Sat** Saturday
**SC** South Carolina
**sci** science
**Scot** Scotland, Scottish
**SD, S Dak** South Dakota
**SE** southeast

**sec** second
**Sept** September
**SI** International System of Units
**sing** singular
**so** south
**sq** square
**sr** senior
**Sr** sister
**SS** steamship
**st** state, street
**St** saint
**Sun** Sunday
**SW** southwest

**t** true
**tbs, tbsp** tablespoon
**TD** touchdown
**Tenn** Tennessee
**Tex** Texas
**Thurs, Thu** Thursday
**TN** Tennessee
**trans** transitive
**tsp** teaspoon
**Tues, Tue** Tuesday
**TX** Texas

**UN** United Nations
**US** United States
**USA** United States of America
**USSR** Union of Soviet Socialist Republics
**usu** usual, usually
**UT** Utah

**v** verb
**Va, VA** Virginia
**var** variant
**vb** verb
**VG** very good
**vi** verb intransitive
**VI** Virgin Islands
**vol** volume
**VP** vice president
**vs** versus
**vt** verb transitive
**Vt, VT** Vermont

**W** west, western
**WA, Wash** Washington
**Wed** Wednesday
**WI, Wis, Wisc** Wisconsin
**wk** week
**wt** weight
**WV, W Va** West Virginia
**WWW** World Wide Web
**WY, Wyo** Wyoming

**yd** yard
**yr** year

# A

[1]**a** *n* : 1st letter of the alphabet

[2]**a** *indefinite article* : one or some — used to indicate an unspecified or unidentified individual

**aard•vark** *n* : ant-eating African mammal

**aback** *adv* : by surprise

**ab•a•lo•ne** *n* : large edible shellfish

**aban•don** *vb* : give up without intent to reclaim — **aban•don** *n* — **aban•doned** *adj* — **aban•don•ment** *n*

**abase** *vb* : lower in dignity — **abase•ment** *n*

**abate** *vb* : decrease or lessen — **abate•ment** *n*

**ab•bess** *n* : head of a convent

**ab•bey** *n* : monastery or convent

**ab•bot** *n* : head of a monastery

**ab•bre•vi•ate** *vb* : shorten — **ab•bre•vi•a•tion** *n*

**ab•di•cate** *vb* : renounce — **ab•di•ca•tion** *n*

**ab•do•men** *n* 1 : body area between chest and pelvis 2 : hindmost part of an insect — **ab•dom•i•nal** *adj* — **ab•dom•i•nal•ly** *adv*

**ab•er•ra•tion** *n* : deviation or distortion — **ab•er•rant** *adj*

**abet** *vb* : incite or encourage — **abet•tor, abet•ter** *n*

**abey•ance** *n* : state of inactivity

**ab•hor** *vb* : hate — **ab•hor•rence** *n* — **ab•hor•rent** *adj*

**abide** *vb* 1 : endure 2 : remain, last, or reside

**abil•i•ty** *n* 1 : competence 2: natural aptitude

**ab•ject** *adj* : low in spirit or hope — **ab•jec•tion** *n* — **ab•ject•ly** *adv* — **ab•ject•ness** *n*

**ablaze** *adj or adv* : on fire

**able** *adj* 1 : having sufficient power, skill, or resources 2 : skilled or efficient — **ably** *adv*

**ab•lu•tion** *n* : washing of one's body

**ab•nor•mal** *adj* : deviating from the normal or average — **ab•nor•mal•i•ty** *n* — **ab•nor•mal•ly** *adv*

**aboard** *adv* : on, onto, or within a car, ship, or aircraft ∼ *prep* : on or within

**abode** *n* : residence

**abol•ish** *vb* : do away with — **ab•o•li•tion** *n*

**abom•i•na•ble** *adj* : thoroughly unpleasant or revolting

**abom•i•nate** *vb* : hate — **abom•i•na•tion** *n*

**ab•orig•i•nal** *adj* 1 : original 2 : primitive

**ab•orig•i•ne** *n* : original inhabitant

**abort** *vb* : terminate prematurely — **abor•tion** *n* — **abor•tive** *adj*

**abound** *vb* : be plentiful

**about** *adv* : around ∼ *prep* 1 : on every side of 2 : on the verge of 3 : having as a subject

**above** *adv* : in or to a higher place ∼ *prep* 1 : in or to a higher place than 2 : more than

**above•board** *adv or adj* : without deception

**abrade** *vb* : wear away by rubbing — **abra•sion** *n* — **abra•sive** *adj* — **abra•sive•ly** *adv*

**abreast** *adv or adj* 1 : side by side 2 : up to a standard or level

**abridge** *vb* : shorten or condense — **abridg•ment, abridge•ment** *n*

**abroad** *adv or adj* 1 : over a wide area 2 : outside one's country

**abrupt** *adj* 1 : sudden 2 : so quick as to seem rude — **abrupt•ly** *adv*

**ab•scess** *n* : collection of pus surrounded by inflamed tissue — **ab•scessed** *adj*

**ab•scond** *vb* : run away and hide

**ab•sent** *adj* : not present ∼ **ab•sent** *vb* : keep oneself away — **ab•sence** *n* — **ab•sen•tee** *n*

**ab•sent•mind•ed** *adj* : unaware of one's surroundings or action — **ab•sent•mind•ed•ly** *adv* — **ab•sent•mind•ed•ness** *n*

**ab•so•lute** *adj* 1 : pure 2 : free from restriction 3 : definite — **ab•so•lute•ly** *adv*

**ab•so•lu•tion** *n* : remission of sins

**ab•solve** *vb* : set free of the consequences of guilt

**ab•sorb** *vb* 1 : suck up or take in as a sponge does 2 : engage (one's attention) — **ab•sor•ben•cy** *n* — **ab•sor•bent** *adj or n* — **ab•sorb•ing** *adj* — **ab•sorp•tion** *n* — **ab•sorp•tive** *adj*

**ab•stain** *vb* : refrain from doing something — **ab•stain•er** *n* — **ab•sten•tion** *n* — **ab•sti•nence** *n*

**ab•ste•mi•ous** *adj* : sparing in use of food or drink — **ab•ste•mi•ous•ly** *adv* — **ab•ste•mi•ous•ness** *n*

**ab•stract** *adj* 1 : expressing a quality apart from an object 2 : not representing something specific ∼ *n* : summary ∼ *vb* 1 : remove or separate 2 : make an abstract of — **ab•stract•ly** *adv* — **ab•stract•ness** *n* — **ab•strac•tion** *n*

**ab•surd** *adj* : ridiculous or unreasonable — **ab•sur•di•ty** *n* — **ab•surd•ly** *adv*

**abun•dant** *adj* : more than enough — **abun•dance** *n* — **abun•dant•ly** *adv*

**abuse** *vb* 1 : misuse 2 : mistreat 3 : attack with words ∼ *n* 1 : corrupt practice 2 : improper use 3 : mistreatment 4 : coarse and insulting speech — **abus•er** *n* — **abu•sive** *adj* — **abu•sive•ly** *adv* — **abu•sive•ness** *n*

**abut** *vb* : touch along a border — **abut•ter** *n* — **abut•ment** *n*

**abys•mal** *adj* 1 : immeasurably deep 2 : wretched — **abys•mal•ly** *adv*

**abyss** *n* : immeasurably deep gulf

**acad•e•my** *n* 1 : private high school 2 : society of scholars or artists — **ac•a•dem•ic** *adj or n* — **ac•a•dem•i•cal•ly** *adv*

**ac•cede** *vb* 1 : become a party to an agreement 2 : express approval 3 : enter upon an office

**ac•cel•er•ate** *vb* 1 : bring about earlier 2 : speed up — **ac•cel•er•a•tion** *n* — **ac•cel•er•a•tor** *n*

**ac•cent** *n* 1 : distinctive manner of pronunciation 2 : prominence given to one syllable of a word 3 : mark (as ´, `, ˆ) over a vowel in writing or printing to indicate pronunciation ∼ *vb* : emphasize — **ac•cen•tu•al** *adj* — **ac•cen•tu•ate** *vb* — **ac•cen•tu•a•tion** *n*

**ac•cept** *vb* 1 : receive willingly 2 : agree to — **ac•cept•abil•i•ty** *n* — **ac•cept•able** *adj* — **ac•cep•tance** *n*

**ac•cess** *n* : capability or way of approaching — **ac•ces•si•bil•i•ty** *n* — **ac•ces•si•ble** *adj*

**ac•ces•so•ry** *n* 1 : nonessential addition 2 : one guilty of aiding a criminal — **ac•ces•so•ry** *adj*

**ac•ci•dent** *n* 1 : event occurring by chance or unintentionally 2 : chance — **ac•ci•den•tal** *adj* — **ac•ci•den•tal•ly** *adv*

**ac•claim** *vb or n* : praise — **ac•cla•ma•tion** *n*

**ac•cli•mate** *vb* : acclimatize — **ac•cli•ma•tion** *n*

**ac•cli•ma•tize** *vb* : accustom to a new climate or situation — **ac•cli•ma•ti•za•tion** *n*

**ac•co•lade** *n* : expression of praise

**ac•com•mo•date** *vb* 1 : adapt 2 : provide with something needed 3 : hold without crowding — **ac•com•mo•da•tion** *n*

**ac•com•pa•ny** *vb* 1 : go or occur with 2 : play supporting music — **ac•com•pa•ni•ment** *n* — **ac•com•pa•nist** *n*

**ac•com•plice** *n* : associate in crime

**ac•com•plish** *vb* : do, fulfill, or bring about — **ac•com•plished** *adj* — **ac•com•plish•er** *n* — **ac•com•plish•ment** *n*

**ac•cord** *vb* 1 : grant 2 : agree ∼ *n* 1 : agreement 2 : willingness to act — **ac•cor•dance** *n* — **ac•cor•dant** *adj*

**ac•cord•ing•ly** *adv* : consequently

**according to** *prep* 1 : in conformity with 2 : as stated by

**ac•cor•di•on** *n* : keyboard instrument with a bellows and reeds ∼ *adj* : folding like an accordion bellows — **ac•cor•di•on•ist** *n*

**ac•cost** *vb* : approach and speak to esp. aggressively

**ac•count** *n* 1 : statement of business transactions 2 : credit arrangement with a vendor 3 : report 4 : worth 5 : sum deposited in a bank ∼ *vb* : give an explanation — **ac•count•able** *adj* — **ac•count•abil•i•ty** *n* — **ac•coun•tant** *n*

**ac•cou•tre•ment, ac•cou•ter•ment** *n* 1 : accessory item — usu. pl. 2 : identifying characteristic

**ac•cred•it** *vb* 1 : approve officially 2 : attribute — **ac•cred•i•ta•tion** *n*

**ac•crue** *vb* : be added by periodic growth — **ac•cru•al** *n*

**ac•cu•mu•late** *vb* : collect or pile up — **ac•cu•mu•la•tion** *n*

**ac•cu•rate** *adj* : free from error — **ac•cu•ra•cy** *n* — **ac•cu•rate•ly** *adv* — **ac•cu•rate•ness** *n*

**ac•cursed, ac•curst** *adj* 1 : being under a curse 2 : damnable

**ac•cuse** *vb* : charge with an offense — **ac•cu•sa•tion** *n* — **ac•cused** *n* — **ac•cus•er** *n*

**ac•cus•tom** *vb* : make familiar through use or experience

**ace** *n* : one that excels

**acer•bic** *adj* : sour or biting in temper, mood, or tone

**acet•amin•o•phen** *n* : pain reliever

**ac•e•tate** *n* : fabric or plastic derived from acetic acid

**ace•tic acid** *n* : acid found in vinegar

**ache** *vb* 1 : suffer a dull persistent pain 2 : yearn — **ache** *n*

**achieve** *vb* : gain by work or effort — **achieve•ment** *n* — **achiev•er** *n*

**ac•id** *adj* 1 : sour or biting to the taste 2 : sharp in manner 3 : of or relating to an acid ∼ *n* : sour water-soluble chemical compound that reacts with a base to form a salt — **acid•ic** *adj* — **acid•i•fy** *vb* — **acid•i•ty** *n* — **ac•id•ly** *adv*

**ac•knowl•edge** *vb* 1 : admit as true 2 : admit the authority of 3 : express thanks for — **ac•knowl•edg•ment** *n*

**ac•me** *n* : highest point

**ac•ne** *n* : skin disorder marked esp. by pimples

**acorn** *n* : nut of the oak

**acous•tic** *adj* : relating to hearing or sound — **acous•ti•cal** *adj* — **acous•ti•cal•ly** *adv*

**acous•tics** *n sing or pl* 1 : science of sound 2 : qualities in a room that affect how sound is heard

**ac•quaint** *vb* 1 : inform 2 : make familiar — **ac•quain•tance** *n* — **ac•quain•tance•ship** *n*

**ac•qui•esce** *vb* : consent or submit — **ac•qui•es•cence** *n* — **ac•qui•es•cent** *adj* — **ac•qui•es•cent•ly** *adv*

**ac•quire** *vb* : gain — **ac•qui•si•tion** *n* — **ac•qui•si•tive** *adj*

**ac•quit** *vb* 1 : pronounce not guilty 2 : conduct (oneself) usu. well — **ac•quit•tal** *n*

**acre** *n* 1 *pl* : lands 2 : 4840 square yards — **acre•age** *n*

**ac•rid** *adj* : sharp and biting — **acrid•i•ty** *n* — **ac•rid•ly** *adv* — **ac•rid•ness** *n*

**ac•ri•mo•ny** *n* : harshness of language or feeling — **ac•ri•mo•ni•ous** *adj* — **ac•ri•mo•ni•ous•ly** *adv*

**ac•ro•bat** *n* : performer of tumbling feats — **ac•ro•bat•ic** *adj*

**across** *adv* : to or on the opposite side ∼ *prep* 1 : to or on the opposite side of 2 : on so as to cross

**acryl•ic** *n* 1 : plastic used for molded parts or in paints 2 : synthetic textile fiber

**act** *n* 1 : thing done 2 : law 3 : main division of a play ∼ *vb* 1 : perform in a play 2 : conduct oneself 3 : operate 4 : produce an effect — **ac•tive** *adj or n* — **ac•tive•ly** *adv* — **ac•tor** *n* — **ac•tress** *n*

**ac•tion** *n* 1 : legal proceeding 2 : manner or method of performing 3 : activity 4 : thing done over a period of time or in stages 5 : combat 6 : events of a literary plot 7 : operating mechanism

**ac•ti•vate** *vb* : make active or reactive — **ac•ti•va•tion** *n*

**ac•tiv•i•ty** *n* 1 : quality or state of being active 2 : what one is actively doing

**ac•tu•al** *adj* : really existing — **ac•tu•al•i•ty** *n* — **ac•tu•al•iza•tion** *n* — **ac•tu•al•ize** *vb* — **ac•tu•al•ly** *adv*

**ac•tu•ary** *n* : one who calculates insurance risks and premiums — **ac•tu•ar•i•al** *adj*

**acu•men** *n* : mental keenness

**acu•punc•ture** *n* : treatment by puncturing the body with needles — **acu•punc•tur•ist** *n*

**acute** *adj* 1 : sharp 2 : containing less than 90 degrees 3 : mentally alert 4 : severe — **acute•ly** *adv* — **acute•ness** *n*

**ad** *n* : advertisement

**ad•age** *n* : old familiar saying

**ad•a•mant** *adj* : insistent — **ad•a•mant•ly** *adv*

**adapt** *vb* : adjust to be suitable for a new use or condition — **adapt•abil•i•ty** *n* — **adapt•able** *adj* — **ad•ap•ta•tion** *n* — **adap•ter** *n* — **adap•tive** *adj*

**add** *vb* 1 : join to something else so as to increase in amount 2 : say further 3 : find a sum — **ad•di•tion** *n* — **ad•di•tion•al** *adj*

**ad•der** *n* 1 : poisonous European snake 2 : No. American snake

**ad•dict** *n* : one who is psychologically or physiologically dependent (as on a drug) ∼ *vb* : cause to become an addict — **ad•dic•tion** *n* — **ad•dic•tive** *adj*

**ad•di•tive** *n* : substance added to another

**ad•dle** *vb* : confuse

**ad•dress** *vb* 1 : direct one's remarks to 2 : mark an address on ∼ *n* 1 : formal speech 2 : place where a person may be reached or mail may be delivered

**adept** *adj* : highly skilled — **adept•ly** *adv* — **adept•ness** *n*

**ad•e•quate** *adj* : good or plentiful enough — **ad•e•qua•cy** *n* — **ad•e•quate•ly** *adv*

**ad•here** *vb* 1 : remain loyal 2 : stick fast — **ad•her•ence** *n* — **ad•her•ent** *adj or n*

**ad•he•sion** *n* : act or state of adhering

**ad•he•sive** *adj* : tending to adhere ∼ *n* : adhesive substance

**adieu** *n* : farewell

**ad•ja•cent** *adj* : situated near or next

**ad•jec•tive** *n* : word that serves as a modifier of a noun — **ad•jec•ti•val** *adj* — **ad•jec•ti•val•ly** *adv*

**ad•join** *vb* : be next to

**ad•journ** *vb* : end a meeting — **ad•journ•ment** *n*

**ad•ju•di•cate** *vb* : settle judicially — **ad•ju•di•ca•tion** *n*

**ad•junct** *n* : something joined or added but not essential

**ad•just** *vb* : fix, adapt, or set right — **ad•just•able** *adj* — **ad•just•er, ad•jus•tor** *n* — **ad•just•ment** *n*

**ad–lib** *vb* : speak without preparation — **ad–lib** *n or adj*

**ad•min•is•ter** *vb* 1 : manage 2 : give out esp. in doses — **ad•min•is•tra•ble** *adj*

**ad•min•is•tra•tion** *n* 1 : process of managing 2 : persons responsible for managing — **ad•min•is•tra•tive** *adj* —

**ad•min•is•tra•tive•ly** *adv* — **ad•min•is•tra•tor** *n*
**ad•mi•ra•ble** *adj* : worthy of admiration — **ad•mi•ra•bly** *adv*
**ad•mi•ral** *n* : commissioned officer in the navy ranking next below a fleet admiral
**ad•mire** *vb* : have high regard for — **ad•mi•ra•tion** *n* — **ad•mir•er** *n* — **ad•mir•ing•ly** *adv*
**ad•mis•si•ble** *adj* : that can be permitted — **ad•mis•si•bil•i•ty** *n*
**ad•mis•sion** *n* **1** : act of admitting **2** : admittance or a fee paid for this **3** : acknowledgment of a fact
**ad•mit** *vb* **1** : allow to enter **2** : permit **3** : recognize as genuine — **ad•mit•ted•ly** *adv* — **ad•mit•tance** *n*
**ad•mix•ture** *n* **1** : thing added in mixing **2** : mixture
**ad•mon•ish** *vb* : rebuke — **ad•mon•ish•ment** *n* — **ad•mo•ni•tion** *n* — **ad•mon•i•to•ry** *adj*
**ado** *n* **1** : fuss **2** : trouble
**ado•be** *n* : sun-dried building brick
**ad•o•les•cence** *n* : period of growth between childhood and maturity — **ad•o•les•cent** *adj or n*
**adopt** *vb* **1** : take (a child of other parents) as one's own child **2** : take up and practice as one's own — **adop•tion** *n*
**adore** *vb* **1** : worship **2** : be extremely fond of — **ador•able** *adj* — **ador•ably** *adv* — **ad•o•ra•tion** *n*
**adorn** *vb* : decorate with ornaments — **adorn•ment** *n*
**adrift** *adv or adj* **1** : afloat without motive power or moorings **2** : without guidance or purpose
**adroit** *adj* : dexterous or shrewd — **adroit•ly** *adv* — **adroit•ness** *n*
**adult** *adj* : fully developed and mature ~ *n* : grown-up person — **adult•hood** *n*
**adul•ter•ate** *vb* : make impure by mixture — **adul•ter•a•tion** *n*
**adul•tery** *n* : sexual unfaithfulness of a married person — **adul•ter•er** *n* — **adul•ter•ess** *n* — **adul•ter•ous** *adj*
**ad•vance** *vb* **1** : bring or move forward **2** : promote **3** : lend ~ *n* **1** : forward movement **2** : improvement **3** : offer ~ *adj* : being ahead of time — **ad•vance•ment** *n*
**ad•van•tage** *n* **1** : superiority of position **2** : benefit or gain — **ad•van•ta•geous** *adj* — **ad•van•ta•geous•ly** *adv*
**ad•vent** *n* **1** *cap* : period before Christmas **2** : a coming into being or use
**ad•ven•ture** *n* **1** : risky undertaking **2** : exciting experience — **ad•ven•tur•er** *n* — **ad•ven•ture•some** *adj* — **ad•ven•tur•ous** *adj*
**ad•verb** *n* : word that modifies a verb, an adjective, or another adverb — **ad•ver•bi•al** *adj* — **ad•ver•bi•al•ly** *adv*
**ad•ver•sary** *n* : enemy or rival — **ad•ver•sary** *adj*
**ad•verse** *adj* : opposing or unfavorable — **ad•verse•ly** *adv* — **ad•ver•si•ty** *n*
**ad•ver•tise** *vb* : call public attention to — **ad•ver•tise•ment** *n* — **ad•ver•tis•er** *n* — **ad•ver•tis•ing** *n*
**ad•vice** *n* : recommendation with regard to a course of action
**ad•vis•able** *adj* : wise or prudent — **ad•vis•abil•i•ty** *n*
**ad•vise** *vb* : give advice to — **ad•vis•abil•i•ty** *n* — **ad•vis•able** *adj* — **ad•vis•er, ad•vis•or** *n* — **ad•vise•ment** *n*
**ad•vi•so•ry** *adj* : having power to advise
**ad•vo•cate** *n* : one who argues or pleads for a cause or proposal ~ *vb* : recommend — **ad•vo•ca•cy** *n*
**ae•gis** *n* : protection or sponsorship
**aer•ate** *vb* : supply or impregnate with air — **aer•a•tion** *n* — **aer•a•tor** *n*
**ae•ri•al** *adj* : inhabiting, occurring in, or done in the air ~ *n* : antenna
**aer•o•bic** *adj* : using or needing oxygen
**aer•o•bics** *n sing or pl* : exercises that produce a marked increase in respiration and heart rate
**aero•dy•nam•ics** *n* : science of bodies in motion in a gas — **aero•dy•nam•ic** *adj* — **aero•dy•nam•i•cal•ly** *adv*
**aero•nau•tics** *n* : science dealing with aircraft — **aero•nau•ti•cal** *adj*
**aero•sol** *n* **1** : liquid or solid particles suspended in a gas **2** : substance sprayed as an aerosol
**aero•space** *n* : earth's atmosphere and the space beyond — **aero•space** *adj*
**aes•thet•ic** *adj* : relating to beauty — **aes•thet•i•cal•ly** *adv* — **aes•thet•ics** *n*
**af•fa•ble** *adj* : easy to talk to — **af•fa•bil•i•ty** *n* — **af•fa•bly** *adv*
**af•fair** *n* : something that relates to or involves one
[1]**af•fect** *vb* : assume for effect — **af•fec•ta•tion** *n*
[2]**affect** *vb* : produce an effect on
**af•fect•ed** *adj* **1** : pretending to some trait **2** : artificially assumed to impress — **af•fect•ed•ly** *adv*
**af•fect•ing** *adj* : arousing pity or sorrow — **af•fect•ing•ly** *adv*
**af•fec•tion** *n* : kind or loving feeling — **af•fec•tion•ate** *adj* — **af•fec•tion•ate•ly** *adv*
**af•fi•da•vit** *n* : sworn statement
**af•fil•i•ate** *vb* : become a member or branch — **af•fil•i•ate** *n* — **af•fil•i•a•tion** *n*
**af•fin•i•ty** *n* : close attraction or relationship
**af•firm** *vb* : assert positively — **af•fir•ma•tion** *n*
**af•fir•ma•tive** *adj* : asserting the truth or existence of something ~ *n* : statement of affirmation or agreement
**af•flict** *vb* : cause pain and distress to — **af•flic•tion** *n*
**af•flu•ence** *n* : wealth — **af•flu•ent** *adj*
**af•ford** *vb* **1** : manage to bear the cost of **2** : provide
**af•front** *vb or n* : insult
**af•ghan** *n* : crocheted or knitted blanket
**aflame** *adj or adv* : flaming
**afloat** *adj or adv* : floating
**afoot** *adv or adj* **1** : on foot **2** : in progress
**afraid** *adj* : filled with fear
**afresh** *adv* : anew
**af•ter** *adv* : at a later time ~ *prep* **1** : behind in place or time **2** : in pursuit of ~ *conj* : following the time when ~ *adj* **1** : later **2** : located toward the back
**af•ter•life** *n* : existence after death
**af•ter•math** *n* : results
**af•ter•noon** *n* : time between noon and evening
**af•ter•thought** *n* : later thought
**af•ter•ward, af•ter•wards** *adv* : at a later time
**again** *adv* **1** : once more **2** : on the other hand **3** : in addition
**against** *prep* **1** : directly opposite to **2** : in opposition to **3** : so as to touch or strike
**ag•ate** *n* : quartz with bands or masses of various colors
**age** *n* **1** : length of time of life or existence **2** : particular time in life (as majority or the latter part) **3** : quality of being old **4** : long time **5** : period in history ~ *vb* : become old or mature — **age•less** *adj*
**aged** *adj* **1** : old **2** : allowed to mature
**agen•da** *n* : list of things to be done
**agent** *n* **1** : means **2** : person acting or doing business for another — **agen•cy** *n*
**ag•gra•vate** *vb* **1** : make more severe **2** : irritate — **ag•gra•va•tion** *n*
**ag•gre•gate** *adj* : formed into a mass ~ *vb* : collect into a mass ~ *n* **1** : mass **2** : whole amount
**ag•gres•sion** *n* **1** : unprovoked attack **2** : hostile behavior — **ag•gres•sor** *n* — **ag•gres•sive** *adj* — **ag•gres•sive•ly** *adv* — **ag•gres•sive•ness** *n*
**ag•grieve** *vb* **1** : cause grief to **2** : inflict injury on
**ag•ile** *adj* : able to move quickly and easily — **agil•i•ty** *n*
**ag•i•tate** *vb* **1** : shake or stir back and forth **2** : excite or trouble the mind of **3** : try to arouse public feeling — **ag•i•ta•tion** *n* — **ag•i•ta•tor** *n*
**ag•nos•tic** *n* : one who doubts the existence of God
**ago** *adj or adv* : earlier than the present
**agog** *adj* : full of excitement
**ag•o•nize** *vb* : suffer mental agony — **ag•o•niz•ing•ly** *adv* — **ag•o•ny** *n*
**agree** *vb* **1** : be of the same opinion **2** : express willingness **3** : get along together **4** : be similar **5** : be appropriate, suitable, or healthful — **agree•able** *adj* — **agree•able•ness** *n* — **agree•ably** *adv* — **agree•ment** *n*
**ag•ri•cul•ture** *n* : farming — **ag•ri•cul•tur•al** *adj* — **ag•ri•cul•tur•ist, ag•ri•cul•tur•al•ist** *n*
**aground** *adv or adj* : on or onto the bottom or shore
**ahead** *adv or adj* **1** : in or toward the front **2** : into or for the future **3** : in a more advantageous position
**ahead of** *prep* **1** : in front or advance of **2** : in excess of
**aid** *vb* : provide help or support ~ *n* : help
**aide** *n* : helper
**AIDS** *n* : serious disease of the human immune system
**ail** *vb* **1** : trouble **2** : be ill — **ail•ment** *n*
**aim** *vb* **1** : point or direct (as a weapon) **2** : direct one's efforts ~ *n* **1** : an aiming or the direction of aiming **2** : object or purpose — **aim•less** *adj* — **aim•less•ly** *adv* — **aim•less•ness** *n*
**air** *n* **1** : mixture of gases surrounding the earth **2** : melody **3** : outward appearance **4** : artificial manner **5** : compressed air **6** : travel by or use of aircraft **7** : medium of transmission of radio waves ~ *vb* **1** : expose to the air **2** : broadcast — **air•borne** *adj*
**air–condition** *vb* : equip with an apparatus (**air conditioner**) for filtering and cooling the air
**air•craft** *n* (**air•craft**) : craft that flies
**air force** *n* : military organization for conducting warfare by air
**air•lift** *n* : a transporting of esp. emergency supplies by aircraft — **air•lift** *vb*
**air•line** *n* : air transportation system — **air•lin•er** *n*
**air•mail** *n* : system of transporting mail by airplane — **air•mail** *vb*
**air•plane** *n* : fixed-wing aircraft heavier than air
**air•port** *n* : place for landing aircraft and usu. for receiving passengers
**air•tight** *adj* : tightly sealed to prevent flow of air
**air•waves** *n pl* : medium of transmission of radio waves
**airy** *adj* **1** : delicate **2** : breezy
**aisle** *n* : passage between sections or rows
**ajar** *adj or adv* : partly open
**akin** *adj* **1** : related by blood **2** : similar in kind
**al•a•bas•ter** *n* : white or translucent mineral
**alac•ri•ty** *n* : cheerful readiness
**alarm** *n* **1** : warning signal or device **2** : fear at sudden danger ~ *vb* **1** : warn **2** : frighten
**alas** *interj* — used to express unhappiness, pity, or concern
**al•be•it** *conj* : even though
**al•bum** *n* **1** : book for displaying a collection (as of photographs) **2** : collection of recordings
**al•bu•men** *n* **1** : white of an egg **2** : albumin
**al•bu•min** *n* : protein found in blood, milk, egg white, and tissues
**al•co•hol** *n* **1** : intoxicating agent in liquor **2** : liquor — **al•co•hol•ic** *adj or n* — **al•co•hol•ism** *n*
**al•cove** *n* : recess in a room or wall
**al•der•man** *n* : city official
**ale** *n* : beerlike beverage — **ale•house** *n*
**alert** *adj* **1** : watchful **2** : quick to perceive and act ~ *n* : alarm ~ *vb* : warn — **alert•ly** *adv* — **alert•ness** *n*
**al•fal•fa** *n* : cloverlike forage plant
**al•ga** *n* : any of a group of lower plants that includes seaweed — **al•gal** *adj*
**al•ge•bra** *n* : branch of mathematics — **al•ge•bra•ic** *adj* — **al•ge•bra•i•cal•ly** *adv*
**alias** *adv* : otherwise called ~ *n* : assumed name
**al•i•bi** *n* **1** : defense of having been elsewhere when a crime was committed **2** : justification ~ *vb* : offer an excuse
**alien** *adj* : foreign ~ *n* **1** : foreign-born resident **2** : extraterrestrial
**alien•ate** *vb* : cause to be no longer friendly — **alien•ation** *n*
**align** *vb* : bring into line — **align•er** *n* — **align•ment** *n*
**alike** *adj* : identical or very similar ~ *adv* : equally
**al•i•men•ta•ry** *adj* : relating to or functioning in nutrition
**al•i•mo•ny** *n* : money paid to a separated or divorced spouse
**alive** *adj* **1** : having life **2** : lively or animated
**al•ka•li** *n* : strong chemical base — **al•ka•line** *adj* — **al•ka•lin•i•ty** *n*
**all** *adj* **1** : the whole of **2** : greatest possible **3** : every one of ~ *adv* **1** : wholly **2** : so much **3** : for each side ~ *pron* **1** : whole number or amount **2** : everything or everyone
**Al•lah** *n* : God of Islam
**al•lay** *vb* **1** : alleviate **2** : calm
**al•lege** *vb* : assert without proof — **al•le•ga•tion** *n* — **al•leg•ed•ly** *adv*
**al•le•giance** *n* : loyalty
**al•le•go•ry** *n* : story in which figures and actions are symbols of general truths — **al•le•gor•i•cal** *adj*
**al•ler•gen** *n* : something that causes allergy — **al•ler•gen•ic** *adj*
**al•ler•gy** *n* : abnormal reaction to a substance — **al•ler•gic** *adj* — **al•ler•gist** *n*
**al•le•vi•ate** *vb* : relieve or lessen — **al•le•vi•a•tion** *n*
**al•ley** *n* **1** : place for bowling **2** : narrow passage between buildings
**al•li•ance** *n* : association
**al•li•ga•tor** *n* : large aquatic reptile related to the crocodiles
**al•lit•er•a•tion** *n* : repetition of initial sounds of words — **al•lit•er•a•tive** *adj*
**al•lo•cate** *vb* : assign — **al•lo•ca•tion** *n*
**al•lot** *vb* : distribute as a share — **al•lot•ment** *n*
**al•low** *vb* **1** : admit or concede **2** : permit — **al•low•able** *adj*
**al•low•ance** *n* **1** : allotted share **2** : money given regularly for expenses
**al•loy** *n* : metals melted together — **al•loy** *vb*
**all right** *adv or adj* **1** : satisfactorily **2** : yes **3** : certainly
**al•lude** *vb* : refer indirectly — **al•lu•sion** *n* — **al•lu•sive** *adj*
**al•lure** *vb* : entice ~ *n* : attractive power
**al•ly** *vb* : enter into an alliance — **al•ly** *n*
**al•ma•nac** *n* : annual information book
**al•mighty** *adj* : having absolute power
**al•most** *adv* : very nearly
**alms** *n* : charitable gift
**aloft** *adv* : high in the air
**alone** *adj* **1** : separated from others **2** : not including anyone or anything else — **alone** *adv*
**along** *prep* **1** : in line with the direction of **2** : at a point on or during ~ *adv* **1** : forward **2** : as a companion
**along•side** *adv or prep* : along or by the side
**alongside of** *prep* : alongside
**aloud** *adv* : so as to be heard
**al•pha•bet** *n* : ordered set of letters of a language — **al•pha•bet•i•cal, al•pha•bet•ic** *adj* — **al•pha•bet•i•cal•ly** *adv*
**al•pha•bet•ize** *vb* : arrange in alphabetical order — **al•pha•bet•iz•er** *n*
**al•ready** *adv* : by a given time
**al•so** *adv* : in addition
**al•tar** *n* : structure for rituals
**al•ter** *vb* : make different — **alter•a•tion** *n*
**al•ter•ca•tion** *n* : dispute
**al•ter•nate** *adj* **1** : arranged or succeeding by turns **2** : every other ~ *vb* :

occur or cause to occur by turns ~ *n* : substitute — **al•ter•nate•ly** *adv* — **al•ter•na•tion** *n*

**al•ter•na•tive** *adj* : offering a choice — **al•ter•na•tive** *n* — **al•ter•na•tive•ly** *adv*

**al•though** *conj* : even though

**al•ti•tude** *n* **1 :** distance up from the ground **2 :** angular distance above the horizon

**al•to** *n* : lower female choral voice

**al•to•geth•er** *adv* **1 :** wholly **2 :** on the whole

**al•tru•ism** *n* : concern for others — **al•tru•ist** *n* — **al•tru•is•tic** *adj* — **al•tru•is•ti•cal•ly** *adv*

**alu•mi•num** *n* : silver-white malleable ductile light metallic element

**al•ways** *adv* **1 :** at all times **2 :** forever

**am** *pres 1st sing of* BE

**amal•gam** *n* **1 :** mercury alloy **2 :** mixture

**amass** *vb* : gather

**am•a•teur** *n* **1 :** person who does something for pleasure rather than for pay **2 :** person who is not expert — **am•a•teur•ish** *adj* — **ama•teur•ism** *n*

**am•a•to•ry** *adj* : of or expressing sexual love

**amaze** *vb* : fill with wonder — **amaze•ment** *n* — **amaz•ing•ly** *adv*

**am•a•zon** *n* : tall strong woman — **am•a•zo•ni•an** *adj*

**am•bas•sa•dor** *n* : representative esp. of a government — **am•bas•sa•do•ri•al** *adj* — **am•bas•sa•dor•ship** *n*

**am•ber** *n* : yellowish fossil resin or its color

**am•bi•dex•trous** *adj* : equally skilled with both hands — **am•bi•dex•trous•ly** *adv*

**am•bi•ence, am•bi•ance** *n* : pervading atmosphere

**am•big•u•ous** *adj* : having more than one interpretation — **am•bi•gu•i•ty** *n*

**am•bi•tion** *n* : eager desire for success or power — **am•bi•tious** *adj* — **am•bi•tious•ly** *adv*

**am•ble** *vb* : go at a leisurely gait — **am•ble** *n*

**am•bu•lance** *n* : vehicle for carrying injured or sick persons

**am•bu•la•to•ry** *adj* **1 :** relating to or adapted to walking **2 :** able to walk about

**am•bush** *n* : trap by which a surprise attack is made from a place of hiding — **am•bush** *vb*

**amen** *interj* — used for affirmation esp. at the end of prayers

**ame•na•ble** *adj* : ready to yield or be influenced

**amend** *vb* **1 :** improve **2 :** alter in writing — **amend•ment** *n*

**amends** *n sing or pl* : compensation for injury or loss

**ame•ni•ty** *n* **1 :** agreeableness **2** *pl* **:** social conventions **3 :** something serving to comfort or accommodate

**ami•a•ble** *adj* : easy to get along with — **ami•a•bil•i•ty** *n* — **ami•a•bly** *adv*

**am•i•ca•ble** *adj* : friendly — **am•i•ca•bly** *adv*

**amino acid** *n* : nitrogen-containing acid

**am•mo•nia** *n* **1 :** colorless gaseous compound of nitrogen and hydrogen **2 :** solution of ammonia in water

**am•mu•ni•tion** *n* **1 :** projectiles fired from guns **2 :** explosive items used in war

**am•ne•sia** *n* : sudden loss of memory — **am•ne•si•ac, am•ne•sic** *adj or n*

**am•nes•ty** *n* : a pardon for a group — **am•nes•ty** *vb*

**amoe•ba** *n* : tiny one-celled animal that occurs esp. in water — **amoe•bic** *adj*

**amok** *adv* : in a violent or uncontrolled way

**among** *prep* **1 :** in or through **2 :** in the number or class of **3 :** in shares to each of

**am•o•rous** *adj* **1 :** inclined to love **2 :** being in love **3 :** indicative of love — **am•o•rous•ly** *adv* — **am•o•rous•ness** *n*

**am•or•tize** *vb* : get rid of (as a debt) gradually with periodic payments — **amor•ti•za•tion** *n*

**amount** *vb* **1 :** be equivalent **2 :** reach a total ~ *n* : total number or quantity

**am•per•sand** *n* : character & used for the word *and*

**am•phib•i•ous** *adj* **1 :** able to live both on land and in water **2 :** adapted for both land and water — **am•phib•i•an** *n*

**am•phi•the•ater** *n* : oval or circular structure with rising tiers of seats around an arena

**am•ple** *adj* **1 :** large **2 :** sufficient — **am•ply** *adv*

**am•pli•fy** *vb* : make louder, stronger, or more thorough — **am•pli•fi•ca•tion** *n* — **am•pli•fi•er** *n*

**am•pli•tude** *n* **1 :** fullness **2 :** extent of a vibratory movement

**am•pu•tate** *vb* : cut off (a body part) — **am•pu•ta•tion** *n* — **am•pu•tee** *n*

**am•u•let** *n* : ornament worn as a charm against evil

**amuse** *vb* **1 :** engage the attention of in an interesting and pleasant way **2 :** make laugh — **amuse•ment** *n*

**an** *indefinite article* : a — used before words beginning with a vowel sound

**anach•ro•nism** *n* : one that is chronologically out of place — **anach•ro•nis•tic** *adj*

**ana•gram** *n* : word or phrase made by transposing the letters of another word or phrase

**anal** *adj* : relating to the anus

**an•al•ge•sic** *n* : pain reliever

**anal•o•gy** *n* **1 :** similarity between unlike things **2 :** example of something similar — **an•a•log•i•cal** *adj* — **an•a•log•i•cal•ly** *adv* — **anal•o•gous** *adj*

**anal•y•sis** *n* **1 :** examination of a thing to determine its parts **2 :** a method of treatment of psychological problems — **an•a•lyst** *n* — **an•a•lyt•ic, an•a•lyt•i•cal** *adj* — **an•a•lyt•i•cal•ly** *adv*

**an•a•lyze** *vb* : make an analysis of

**an•ar•chism** *n* : theory that all government is undesirable — **an•ar•chist** *n or adj* — **an•ar•chis•tic** *adj*

**an•ar•chy** *n* : lack of government or order — **an•ar•chic** *adj* — **an•ar•chi•cal•ly** *adv* — **an•ar•chism** *n* — **an•ar•chist** *n or adj* — **an•ar•chis•tic** *adj*

**anath•e•ma** *n* **1 :** solemn curse **2 :** person or thing accursed or intensely disliked

**anat•o•my** *n* : science dealing with the structure of organisms — **an•a•tom•ic, an•a•tom•i•cal** *adj* — **an•a•tom•i•cal•ly** *adv* — **anat•o•mist** *n*

**an•ces•tor** *n* : one from whom an individual is descended

**an•ces•try** *n* **1 :** line of descent **2 :** ancestors — **an•ces•tral** *adj*

**an•chor** *n* **1 :** heavy device that catches in the sea bottom to hold a ship in place **2 :** anchorperson ~ *vb* : hold or become held in place by or as if by an anchor — **an•chor•age** *n*

**an•chor•per•son** *n* : news broadcast coordinator

**an•cho•vy** *n* : small herringlike fish

**an•cient** *adj* **1 :** having existed for many years **2 :** belonging to times long past — **an•cient** *n*

**and** *conj* — used to indicate connection or addition

**an•drog•y•nous** *adj* **1 :** having characteristics of both male and female **2 :** suitable for either sex

**an•ec•dote** *n* : brief story — **an•ec•dot•al** *adj*

**ane•mia** *n* : blood deficiency — **ane•mic** *adj*

**an•es•the•sia** *n* : loss of bodily sensation

**an•es•thet•ic** *n* : agent that produces anesthesia — **an•es•thet•ic** *adj* — **anes•the•tist** *n* — **anes•the•tize** *vb*

**an•eu•rysm, an•eu•rism** blood-filled bulge of a blood vessel

**anew** *adv* : over again

**an•gel** *n* : spiritual being superior to humans — **an•gel•ic, an•gel•i•cal** *adj* — **an•gel•i•cal•ly** *adv*

**an•ger** *n* : strong feeling of displeasure ~ *vb* : make angry

**an•gi•na** *n* : painful disorder of heart muscles — **an•gi•nal** *adj*

[1]**an•gle** *n* **1 :** figure formed by the meeting of 2 lines in a point **2 :** sharp corner **3 :** point of view ~ *vb* : turn or direct at an angle

[2]**angle** *vb* : fish with a hook and line — **an•gler** *n* — **an•gle•worm** *n* — **an•gling** *n*

**an•go•ra** *n* : yarn or cloth made from the hair of an Angora goat or rabbit

**an•gry** *adj* : feeling or showing anger — **an•gri•ly** *adv*

**an•guish** *n* : extreme pain or distress of mind — **an•guished** *adj*

**an•gu•lar** *adj* **1 :** having many or sharp angles **2 :** thin and bony — **an•gu•lar•i•ty** *n*

**an•i•mal** *n* **1 :** living being capable of feeling and voluntary motion **2 :** lower animal as distinguished from humans

**an•i•mate** *adj* : having life ~ *vb* **1 :** give life or vigor to **2 :** make appear to move — **an•i•mat•ed** *adj*

**an•i•ma•tion** *n* **1 :** liveliness **2 :** animated cartoon

**an•i•ma•tron•ic** : relating to an electrically animated mechanical figure

**an•i•mus** *n* : deep-seated hostility — **an•i•mos•i•ty** *n*

**an•ise** *n* : herb related to the carrot with aromatic seeds (**ani•seed** ) used in flavoring

**an•kle** *n* : joint or region between the foot and the leg — **an•kle•bone** *n*

**an•nals** *n pl* : chronological record of history — **an•nal•ist** *n*

**an•nex** *vb* : assume political control over (a territory) ~ *n* : added building — **an•nex•a•tion** *n*

**an•ni•hi•late** *vb* : destroy — **an•ni•hi•la•tion** *n*

**an•ni•ver•sa•ry** *n* : annual return of the date of a notable event or its celebration

**an•no•tate** *vb* : furnish with notes — **an•no•ta•tion** *n* — **an•no•ta•tor** *n*

**an•nounce** *vb* : make known publicly — **an•nounce•ment** *n* — **an•nounc•er** *n*

**an•noy** *vb* : disturb or irritate — **an•noy•ance** *n* — **an•noy•ing•ly** *adv*

**an•nu•al** *adj* **1 :** occurring once a year **2 :** living only one year — **an•nu•al** *n* — **an•nu•al•ly** *adv*

**an•nu•i•ty** *n* : amount payable annually or the right to such a payment

**an•nul** *vb* : make legally void — **an•nul•ment** *n*

**anom•a•ly** *n* : something abnormal or unusual — **anom•a•lous** *adj*

**anon•y•mous** *adj* : of unknown origin — **an•o•nym•i•ty** *n* — **anon•y•mous•ly** *adv*

**an•oth•er** *adj* **1 :** any or some other **2 :** one more ~ *pron* **1 :** one more **2 :** one different

**an•swer** *n* **1 :** something spoken or written in reply to a question **2 :** solution to a problem ~ *vb* **1 :** reply to **2 :** be responsible **3 :** be adequate — **an•swer•er** *n* — **an•swer•able** *adj*

**ant** *n* : small social insect — **ant•hill** *n*

**ant•ac•id** : agent that counteracts acidity

**an•tag•o•nize** *vb* : cause to be hostile — **an•tag•o•nism** *n* — **an•tag•o•nist** *n* — **an•tag•o•nis•tic** *adj*

**ant•arc•tic** *adj, often cap* : relating to the region near the south pole

**an•te•ced•ent** *n* : one that comes before — **an•te•ced•ent** *adj*

**an•te•lope** *n* : deerlike mammal related to the ox

**an•ten•na** *n* **1** *pl* **an•ten•nae :** one of the long slender paired sensory organs on the head of an arthropod **2** *pl* **an•ten•nas :** metallic device for sending or receiving radio waves

**an•them** *n* : song or hymn of praise or gladness

**an•thol•o•gy** *n* : literary collection

**an•thro•poid** *n* : large ape — **an•thro•poid** *adj*

**an•thro•pol•o•gy** *n* : science dealing with humans — **an•thro•po•log•i•cal** *adj* — **an•thro•pol•o•gist** *n*

**an•ti•bi•ot•ic** *n* : substance that inhibits harmful microorganisms — **an•ti•bi•ot•ic** *adj*

**an•ti•body** *n* : bodily substance that counteracts the effects of a foreign substance or organism

**an•tic** *n* : playful act ~ *adj* : playful

**an•tic•i•pate** *vb* **1 :** be prepared for **2 :** look forward to — **an•tic•i•pa•tion** *n* — **an•tic•i•pa•to•ry** *adj*

**an•ti•dote** *n* : remedy for poison

**an•ti•his•ta•mine** : drug for treating allergies and colds

**an•tip•a•thy** *n* : strong dislike

**an•ti•quat•ed** *adj* : out-of-date — **an•ti•quar•i•an** *n*

**an•tique** *adj* : very old or out-of-date — **an•tique** *n*

**an•tiq•ui•ty** *n* **1 :** ancient times **2** *pl* **:** relics of ancient times

**an•ti•sep•tic** *adj* : killing or checking the growth of germs — **an•ti•sep•tic** *n* — **an•ti•sep•ti•cal•ly** *adv*

**ant•ler** *n* : solid branched horn of a deer — **ant•lered** *adj*

**ant•onym** *n* : word of opposite meaning

**anus** *n* : the rear opening of the alimentary canal

**an•vil** *n* : heavy iron block on which metal is shaped

**anx•ious** *adj* **1 :** uneasy **2 :** earnestly wishing — **anx•ious•ly** *adv* — **anx•i•ety** *n*

**any** *adj* **1 :** one chosen at random **2 :** of whatever number or quantity ~ *pron* **1 :** any one or ones **2 :** any amount ~ *adv* : to any extent or degree

**any•body** *pron* : anyone

**any•how** *adv* **1 :** in any way **2 :** nevertheless

**any•more** *adv* : at the present time

**any•one** *pron* : any person

**any•place** *adv* : anywhere

**any•thing** *pron* : any thing whatever

**any•time** *adv* : at any time whatever

**any•way** *adv* : anyhow

**any•where** *adv* : in or to any place

**aor•ta** *n* : main artery from the heart — **aor•tic** *adj*

**apart** *adv* **1 :** separately in place or time **2 :** aside **3 :** to pieces

**apart•ment** *n* : set of usu. rented rooms

**ap•a•thy** *n* : lack of emotion or interest — **ap•a•thet•ic** *adj* — **ap•a•thet•i•cal•ly** *adv*

**ape** *n* : large tailless primate ~ *vb* : imitate

**apex** *n* : highest point

**aphid** *n* : small insect that sucks plant juices

**aph•ro•di•si•ac** *n* : substance that excites sexual desire

**apiece** *adv* : for each one

**apol•o•gize** *vb* : make an apology — **apol•o•get•ic** *adj* — **apol•o•get•i•cal•ly** *adv* — **apol•o•gist** *n*

**apol•o•gy** *n* **1 :** formal justification **2 :** expression of regret for a wrong

**apos•tle** *n* : disciple or advocate — **apos•tle•ship** *n* — **ap•os•tolic** *adj*

**apos•tro•phe** *n* : punctuation mark ’ to indicate the possessive case or the omission of a letter or figure

**apoth•e•cary** *n* : druggist

**ap•pall** *vb* : fill with horror or dismay

**ap•pa•ra•tus** *n* **1 :** equipment **2 :** complex machine or device

**ap•par•el** *n* : clothing

**ap•par•ent** *adj* **1 :** visible **2 :** obvious **3 :** having the appearance of being — **ap•par•ent•ly** *adv*

**ap•peal** *vb* **1 :** try to have a court case reheard **2 :** ask earnestly **3 :** have an attraction — **ap•peal** *n*

**ap•pear** *vb* **1 :** become visible or evident **2 :** come into the presence of someone **3 :** seem — **ap•pear•ance** *n*

**ap•pease** *vb* : pacify with concessions — **ap•pease•ment** *n*

**ap·pen·dec·to·my** *n* : surgical removal of the appendix

**ap·pen·di·ci·tis** *n* : inflammation of the appendix

**ap·pen·dix** *n* **1** : supplementary matter **2** : narrow closed tube extending from lower right intestine

**ap·pe·tite** *n* **1** : natural desire esp. for food **2** : preference

**ap·pe·tiz·er** *n* : food or drink to stimulate the appetite — **ap·pe·tiz·ing** *adj* — **ap·pe·tiz·ing·ly** *adv*

**ap·plaud** *vb* : show approval esp. by clapping

**ap·plause** *n* : a clapping in approval

**ap·ple** *n* : rounded fruit with firm white flesh

**ap·pli·ance** *n* : household machine or device

**ap·ply** *vb* **1** : place in contact **2** : put to practical use **3** : devote (one's) attention or efforts to something **4** : submit a request **5** : have reference or a connection — **ap·pli·ca·ble** *adj* — **ap·pli·ca·bil·i·ty** *n* — **ap·pli·cant** *n* — **ap·pli·ca·tion** *n* — **ap·pli·ca·tor** *n*

**ap·point** *vb* **1** : set or assign officially **2** : equip or furnish — **ap·poin·tee** *n* — **ap·point·ment** *n*

**ap·praise** *vb* : set value on — **ap·prais·al** *n* — **ap·prais·er** *n*

**ap·pre·ci·ate** *vb* **1** : value justly **2** : be grateful for **3** : increase in value — **ap·pre·cia·ble** *adj* — **ap·pre·cia·bly** *adv* — **ap·pre·ci·a·tion** *n* — **ap·pre·cia·tive** *adj*

**ap·pre·hen·sive** *adj* : fearful — **ap·pre·hen·sive·ly** *adv* — **ap·pre·hen·sive·ness** *n*

**ap·pren·tice** *n* : person learning a craft ~ *vb* : employ or work as an apprentice — **ap·pren·tice·ship** *n*

**ap·proach** *vb* **1** : move nearer or be close to **2** : make initial advances or efforts toward — **ap·proach** *n* — **ap·proach·able** *adj*

**ap·pro·pri·ate** *vb* **1** : take possession of **2** : set apart for a particular use ~ *adj* : suitable — **ap·pro·pri·ate·ly** *adv* — **ap·pro·pri·ate·ness** *n* — **ap·pro·pri·a·tion** *n*

**ap·prove** *vb* : accept as satisfactory — **ap·prov·al** *n*

**ap·prox·i·mate** *adj* : nearly correct or exact ~ *vb* : come near — **ap·prox·i·mate·ly** *adv* — **ap·prox·i·ma·tion** *n*

**April** *n* : 4th month of the year having 30 days

**apron** *n* : protective garment

**apropos of** *prep* : with regard to

**apt** *adj* **1** : suitable **2** : likely **3** : quick to learn — **apt·ly** *adv* — **apt·ness** *n*

**ap·ti·tude** *n* **1** : capacity for learning **2** : natural ability

**aquar·i·um** *n* : glass container for aquatic animals and plants

**aquat·ic** *adj* : of or relating to water — **aquat·ic** *n*

**aq·ue·duct** *n* : conduit for carrying running water

**ar·bi·trary** *adj* **1** : selected at random **2** : autocratic — **ar·bi·trari·ly** *adv* — **ar·bi·trari·ness** *n*

**ar·bi·trate** *vb* : settle a dispute as arbitrator — **ar·bi·tra·tion** *n*

**ar·bi·tra·tor** *n* : one chosen to settle a dispute

**ar·bor** *n* : shelter under branches or vines — **ar·bo·re·al** *adj*

**arc** *n* **1** : part of a circle **2** : bright sustained electrical discharge ~ *vb* : form an arc

**ar·cade** *n* : arched passageway between shops

**¹arch** *n* : curved structure spanning an opening ~ *vb* : cover with or form into an arch

**²arch** *adj* **1** : chief — usu. in combination **2** : mischievous — **arch·ly** *adv* — **arch·ness** *n*

**ar·chae·ol·o·gy, ar·che·ol·o·gy** *n* : study of past human life — **ar·chae·o·log·i·cal** *adj* — **ar·chae·ol·o·gist** *n*

**ar·cha·ic** *adj* : belonging to an earlier time — **ar·cha·i·cal·ly** *adv*

**arch·an·gel** *n* : angel of high rank

**arch·bish·op** *n* : chief bishop — **arch·bish·op·ric** *n*

**arch·di·o·cese** *n* : diocese of an archbishop

**ar·chery** *n* : shooting with bow and arrows — **ar·cher** *n*

**ar·chi·pel·a·go** *n* : group of islands

**ar·chi·tec·ture** *n* **1** : building design **2** : style of building **3** : manner of organizing elements — **ar·chi·tect** *n* — **ar·chi·tec·tur·al** *adj* — **ar·chi·tec·tur·al·ly** *adv*

**ar·chives** *n pl* : public records or their storage place — **archi·vist** *n*

**arch·way** *n* : passageway under an arch

**arc·tic** *adj* **1** : relating to the region near the north pole **2** : frigid

**ar·dent** *adj* : characterized by warmth of feeling — **ar·dent·ly** *adv*

**ar·dor** *n* : warmth of feeling

**ar·du·ous** *adj* : difficult — **ar·du·ous·ly** *adv* — **ar·du·ous·ness** *n*

**are** *pres 2d sing or pres pl of* BE

**ar·ea** *n* **1** : space for something **2** : amount of surface included **3** : region **4** : range covered by a thing or concept

**area code** *n* : 3-digit area-identifying telephone number

**are·na** *n* **1** : enclosed exhibition area **2** : sphere of activity

**ar·gue** *vb* **1** : give reasons for or against something **2** : disagree in words — **argu·able** *adj* — **ar·gu·ment** *n* — **ar·gu·men·ta·tive** *adj*

**ar·id** *adj* : very dry — **arid·i·ty** *n*

**arise** *vb* **arose; aris·en 1** : get up **2** : originate

**ar·is·toc·ra·cy** *n* : upper class — **aris·to·crat** *n* — **aris·to·crat·ic** *adj*

**arith·me·tic** *n* : mathematics that deals with numbers — **ar·ith·met·ic, ar·ith·met·i·cal** *adj*

**ark** *n* : big boat

**¹arm** *n* **1** : upper limb **2** : branch — **armed** *adj* — **arm·less** *adj*

**²arm** *vb* : furnish with weapons ~ *n* **1** : weapon **2** : branch of the military forces **3** *pl* : family's heraldic designs

**armed forces** *n pl* : military

**ar·mor** *n* : protective covering — **ar·mored** *adj*

**ar·mory** *n* : factory or storehouse for arms

**arm·pit** *n* : hollow under the junction of the arm and shoulder

**ar·my** *n* **1** : body of men organized for war esp. on land **2** : great number

**aro·ma** *n* : usu. pleasing odor — **ar·o·mat·ic** *adj*

**around** *adv* **1** : in or along a circuit **2** : on all sides **3** : near **4** : in an opposite direction ~ *prep* **1** : surrounding **2** : along the circuit of **3** : to or on the other side of **4** : near

**arouse** *vb* **1** : awaken from sleep **2** : stir up — **arous·al** *n*

**ar·raign** *vb* **1** : call before a court to answer to an indictment **2** : accuse — **ar·raign·ment** *n*

**ar·range** *vb* **1** : put in order **2** : settle or agree on **3** : adapt (a musical composition) for voices or instruments — **ar·range·ment** *n* — **ar·rang·er** *n*

**ar·ray** *vb* **1** : arrange in order **2** : dress esp. splendidly ~ *n* **1** : arrangement **2** : rich clothing **3** : imposing group

**ar·rest** *vb* **1** : stop **2** : take into legal custody — **ar·rest** *n*

**ar·rive** *vb* **1** : reach a destination, point, or stage **2** : come near in time — **ar·riv·al** *n*

**ar·ro·gant** *adj* : showing an offensive sense of superiority — **ar·ro·gance** *n* — **ar·ro·gant·ly** *adv*

**ar·ro·gate** *vb* : to claim without justification

**ar·row** *n* : slender missile shot from a bow — **ar·row·head** *n*

**ar·se·nic** *n* : solid grayish poisonous chemical element

**ar·son** *n* : willful or malicious burning of property — **ar·son·ist** *n*

**art** *n* **1** : skill **2** : branch of learning **3** : creation of things of beauty or works so produced **4** : ingenuity — **art·ful** *adj* — **art·ful·ly** *adv* — **art·ful·ness** *n* — **art·less** *adj* — **art·less·ly** *adv* — **art·less·ness** *n* — **art·ist** *n* — **ar·tis·tic** *adj* — **ar·tis·ti·cal·ly** *adv* — **ar·tis·try** *n*

**ar·te·rio·scle·ro·sis** *n* : hardening of the arteries — **ar·te·rio·scle·rot·ic** *adj or n*

**ar·tery** *n* **1** : tubular vessel carrying blood from the heart **2** : thoroughfare — **ar·te·ri·al** *adj*

**ar·thri·tis** *n* : inflammation of the joints — **ar·thrit·ic** *adj or n*

**ar·ti·cle** *n* **1** : distinct part of a written document **2** : nonfictional published piece of writing **3** : word (as *an, the*) used to limit a noun **4** : item or piece

**ar·tic·u·late** *adj* : able to speak effectively ~ *vb* **1** : utter distinctly **2** : unite by joints — **ar·tic·u·late·ly** *adv* — **ar·tic·u·late·ness** *n* — **ar·tic·u·la·tion** *n*

**ar·ti·fi·cial** *adj* **1** : man-made **2** : not genuine — **ar·ti·fi·ci·al·i·ty** *n* — **ar·ti·fi·cial·ly** *adv* — **ar·ti·fi·cial·ness** *n*

**ar·til·lery** *n* : large-caliber firearms

**ar·ti·san** *n* : skilled craftsman

**arty** *adj* : pretentiously artistic — **art·i·ly** *adv* — **art·i·ness** *n*

**as** *adv* **1** : to the same degree **2** : for example ~ *conj* **1** : in the same way or degree as **2** : while **3** : because **4** : though ~ *pron* — used after *same* or *such* ~ *prep* : in the capacity of

**as·bes·tos** *n* : fibrous incombustible mineral

**as·cen·dant** *n* : dominant position ~ *adj* **1** : moving upward **2** : dominant — **as·cen·dan·cy** *n*

**as·cent** *n* **1** : act of moving upward **2** : degree of upward slope

**as·cribe** *vb* : attribute — **as·crib·able** *adj* — **as·crip·tion** *n*

**¹ash** *n* : tree related to the olives

**²ash** *n* : matter left when something is burned — **ash·tray** *n*

**ashamed** *adj* : feeling shame — **asham·ed·ly** *adv*

**ash·en** *adj* : deadly pale

**ashore** *adv* : on or to the shore

**aside** *adv* **1** : toward the side **2** : out of the way

**aside from** *prep* **1** : besides **2** : except for

**as·i·nine** *adj* : foolish — **as·i·nin·i·ty** *n*

**ask** *vb* **1** : call on for an answer or help **2** : utter (a question or request) **3** : invite

**askance** *adv* **1** : with a side glance **2** : with lack of trust

**askew** *adv or adj* : out of line

**asleep** *adv or adj* **1** : sleeping **2** : numbed **3** : inactive

**as of** *prep* : from the time of

**as·par·a·gus** *n* : tall herb related to the lilies or its edible stalks

**as·pect** *n* **1** : way something looks to the eye or mind **2** : phase

**as·phalt** *n* : dark tarlike substance used in paving

**as·phyx·i·ate** *vb* : suffocate — **as·phyx·ia** *n* — **as·phyx·i·a·tion** *n*

**as·pire** *vb* : have an ambition — **as·pir·ant** *n* — **as·pi·ra·tion** *n*

**as·pi·rin** *n* : pain reliever

**ass** *n* **1** : long-eared animal related to the horse **2** : stupid person

**as·sail** *vb* : attack violently — **as·sail·able** *adj* — **as·sail·ant** *n*

**as·sas·si·nate** *vb* : murder esp. for political reasons — **as·sas·sin** *n* — **as·sas·si·na·tion** *n*

**as·sault** *n or vb* : attack

**as·say** *n* : analysis (as of an ore) to determine quality or properties — **as·say** *vb*

**as·sem·ble** *vb* **1** : collect into one place **2** : fit together the parts of

**as·sem·bly** *n* **1** : meeting **2** *cap* : legislative body **3** : a fitting together of parts — **as·sem·bly·man** *n* — **as·sem·bly·wom·an** *n*

**as·sent** *vb or n* : consent

**as·sert** *vb* **1** : declare **2** : defend — **as·ser·tion** *n* — **as·sert·ive** *adj* — **as·sert·ive·ness** *n*

**as·sess** *vb* **1** : impose (as a tax) **2** : evaluate for taxation — **as·sess·ment** *n* — **as·ses·sor** *n*

**as·set** *n* **1** *pl* : individually owned property **2** : advantage or resource

**as·sid·u·ous** *adj* : diligent — **as·si·du·i·ty** *n* — **as·sid·u·ous·ly** *adv* — **as·sid·u·ous·ness** *n*

**as·sign** *vb* **1** : transfer to another **2** : appoint to a duty **3** : designate as a task **4** : attribute — **as·sign·able** *adj* — **as·sign·ment** *n*

**as·sist** *vb* : help — **as·sist** *n* — **as·sis·tance** *n* — **as·sis·tant** *n*

**as·so·ci·ate** *vb* **1** : join in companionship or partnership **2** : connect in thought — **as·so·ci·ate** *n* — **as·so·ci·a·tion** *n*

**as·sort·ed** *adj* : consisting of various kinds

**as·sort·ment** *n* : assorted collection

**as·sume** *vb* **1** : take upon oneself **2** : pretend to have or be **3** : take as true — **as·sump·tion** *n*

**as·sure** *vb* **1** : give confidence or conviction to **2** : guarantee — **as·sur·ance** *n*

**as·ter·isk** *n* : a character * used as a reference mark or as an indication of omission of words

**as·ter·oid** *n* : small planet between Mars and Jupiter

**asth·ma** *n* : disorder marked by difficulty in breathing — **asth·mat·ic** *adj or n*

**astig·ma·tism** *n* : visual defect — **as·tig·mat·ic** *adj*

**as·ton·ish** *vb* : amaze — **as·ton·ish·ing·ly** *adv* — **as·ton·ish·ment** *n*

**as·tound** *vb* : fill with confused wonder — **as·tound·ing·ly** *adv*

**astray** *adv or adj* : off the right path

**astride** *adv* : with legs apart or one on each side ~ *prep* : with one leg on each side of

**as·trin·gent** *adj* : causing shrinking or puckering of tissues — **as·trin·gen·cy** *n* — **as·trin·gent** *n*

**as·trol·o·gy** *n* : prediction of events by the stars — **as·trol·o·ger** *n* — **as·tro·log·i·cal** *adj*

**as·tro·nau·tics** *n* : construction and operation of spacecraft — **as·tro·naut** *n* — **as·tro·nau·tic, as·tro·nau·ti·cal** *adj*

**as·tro·nom·i·cal** *adj* **1** : relating to astronomy **2** : extremely large

**as·tron·o·my** *n* : study of the celestial bodies — **as·tron·o·mer** *n*

**as·tute** *adj* : shrewd — **as·tute·ly** *adv* — **as·tute·ness** *n*

**asy·lum** *n* **1** : refuge **2** : institution for care esp. of the insane

**at** *prep* **1** — used to indicate a point in time or space **2** — used to indicate a goal **3** — used to indicate condition, means, cause, or manner

**ate** *past of* EAT

**athe·ist** *n* : one who denies the existence of God — **athe·ism** *n* — **athe·is·tic** *adj*

**ath·lete** *n* : one trained to compete in athletics

**ath·let·ics** *n sing or pl* : exercises and games requiring physical skill — **ath·let·ic** *adj*

**atlas** *n* : book of maps

**ATM** *n* : computerized machine for performing basic bank functions

**at·mo·sphere** *n* **1** : mass of air surrounding the earth **2** : surrounding influence — **at·mo·spher·ic** *adj* — **at·mo·spher·i·cal·ly** *adv*

**at·om** *n* **1** : tiny bit **2** : smallest particle of a chemical element that can exist alone or in combination

**atom•ic** adj **1** : relating to atoms **2** : nuclear

**at•om•iz•er** n : device for dispersing a liquid as a very fine spray

**atone** vb : make amends — **atone•ment** n

**atop** prep : on top of ∼ adv or adj : on, to, or at the top

**atri•um** n **1** : open central room or court **2** : heart chamber that receives blood from the veins

**atro•cious** adj : appalling or abominable — **atro•cious•ly** adv — **atro•cious•ness** n — **atroc•i•ty** n

**at•ro•phy** n : wasting away of a bodily part or tissue — **at•ro•phy** vb

**at•tach** vb **1** : seize legally **2** : bind by personalities **3** : join — **at•tach•ment** n

**at•ta•ché** : technical expert on a diplomatic staff

**at•tack** vb **1** : try to hurt or destroy with violence or words **2** : set to work on — n **1** : act of attacking **2** : fit of sickness

**at•tain** vb **1** : achieve or accomplish **2** : reach — **at•tain•abil•i•ty** n — **at•tain•able** adj — **at•tain•ment** n

**at•tempt** vb : make an effort toward — **at•tempt** n

**at•tend** vb **1** : handle or provide for the care of something **2** : accompany **3** : be present at **4** : pay attention — **at•ten•dance** n — **at•ten•dant** adj or n

**at•ten•tion** n **1** : concentration of the mind on something **2** : notice or awareness — **at•ten•tive** adj — **at•ten•tive•ly** adv — **at•ten•tive•ness** n

**at•test** vb : certify or bear witness — **at•tes•ta•tion** n

**at•tic** n : space just below the roof

**at•tire** vb : dress — **at•tire** n

**at•ti•tude** n **1** : posture or relative position **2** : feeling, opinion, or mood

**at•tor•ney** n : legal agent

**at•tract** vb **1** : draw to oneself **2** : have emotional or aesthetic appeal for — **at•trac•tion** n — **at•trac•tive** adj — **at•trac•tive•ly** adv — **at•trac•tive•ness** n

**at•tri•bute** n : inherent characteristic ∼ vb **1** : regard as having a specific cause or origin **2** : regard as a characteristic — **at•trib•ut•able** adj — **at•tri•bu•tion** n

**auc•tion** n : public sale of property to the highest bidder — **auc•tion** vb — **auc•tion•eer** n

**au•dac•i•ty** n : boldness or insolence — **au•da•cious** adj

**au•di•ble** adj : capable of being heard — **au•di•bly** adv

**au•di•ence** n **1** : formal interview **2** : group of listeners or spectators

**au•dio** adj : relating to sound or its reproduction ∼ n : television sound — **au•dio•vi•su•al** adj

**au•dit** vb : examine financial accounts — **au•dit** n — **au•di•tor** n

**au•di•tion** n : tryout performance — **au•di•tion** vb

**au•di•to•ri•um** n : room or building used for public performances

**au•di•to•ry** adj : relating to hearing

**au•ger** n : tool for boring

**aug•ment** vb : enlarge or increase — **aug•men•ta•tion** n

**au•gur** n : prophet ∼ vb : predict — **au•gu•ry** n

**Au•gust** n : 8th month of the year having 31 days

**aunt** n **1** : sister of one's father or mother **2** : wife of one's uncle

**au•ra** n **1** : distinctive atmosphere **2** : luminous radiation

**au•ral** adj : relating to the ear or to hearing

**au•ro•ra bo•re•al•is** n : display of light in the night sky of northern latitudes

**aus•pic•es** n pl : patronage and protection

**aus•pi•cious** adj : favorable

**aus•tere** adj : severe — **aus•tere•ly** adv — **aus•ter•i•ty** n

**au•then•tic** adj : genuine — **au•then•ti•cal•ly** adv — **au•then•tic•i•ty** n

**au•then•ti•cate** vb : prove genuine — **au•then•ti•ca•tion** n

**au•thor** n **1** : writer **2** : creator — **au•thor•ship** n

**au•thor•i•tar•i•an** adj : marked by blind obedience to authority

**au•thor•i•ta•tive** adj : being an authority — **au•thor•i•ta•tive•ly** adv — **au•thor•i•ta•tive•ness** n

**au•thor•i•ty** n **1** : expert **2** : right, responsibility, or power to influence **3** pl : persons in official positions

**au•tho•rize** vb : permit or give official approval for — **au•tho•ri•za•tion** n

**au•tism** n : mental disorder marked by impaired ability to communicate and form social relationships and by repetitive behavior patterns

**au•to** n : automobile

**au•to•bi•og•ra•phy** n : writer's own life story — **au•to•bi•og•ra•pher** n — **au•to•bio•graph•i•cal** adj

**au•toc•ra•cy** n : government by one person having unlimited power — **au•to•crat** n — **au•to•crat•ic** adj — **au•to•crat•i•cal•ly** adv

**au•to•graph** n : signature ∼ vb : write one's name on

**au•to•mate** vb : make automatic — **au•to•ma•tion** n

**au•to•mat•ic** adj **1** : involuntary **2** : designed to function without human intervention ∼ n : automatic device (as a firearm) — **au•to•mat•i•cal•ly** adv

**au•to•mo•bile** n : 4-wheeled passenger vehicle with its own power source

**au•to•mo•tive** adj : relating to automobiles

**au•ton•o•mous** adj : having independent existence or function — **au•ton•o•mous•ly** adv — **au•ton•o•my** n

**au•top•sy** n : medical examination of a corpse

**au•tumn** n : season between summer and winter — **au•tum•nal** adj

**aux•il•ia•ry** adj **1** : being a supplement or reserve **2** : accompanying a main verb form to express person, number, mood, or tense — **aux•il•ia•ry** n

**avail•able** adj **1** : usable **2** : accessible — **avail•abil•i•ty** n

**av•a•lanche** n : mass of sliding or falling snow or rock

**avenge** vb : take vengeance for — **aveng•er** n

**av•e•nue** n **1** : way of approach **2** : broad street

**av•er•age** adj **1** : being about midway between extremes **2** : ordinary ∼ vb **1** : be usually **2** : find the mean of ∼ n : mean

**averse** adj : feeling dislike or reluctance — **aver•sion** n

**avert** vb : turn away

**avi•a•tion** n : operation or manufacture of airplanes — **avi•a•tor** n

**av•id** adj **1** : greedy **2** : enthusiastic — **avid•i•ty** n — **av•id•ly** adv

**av•o•ca•do** n : tropical fruit with green pulp

**av•o•ca•tion** n : hobby

**avoid** vb **1** : keep away from **2** : prevent the occurrence of **3** : refrain from — **avoid•able** adj — **avoid•ance** n

**av•oir•du•pois** n : system of weight based on the pound of 16 ounces

**await** vb : wait for

**awake** vb (**awoke; awok•en**) : wake up — **awake** adj

**awak•en** vb : wake up

**award** vb : give (something won or deserved) ∼ n **1** : judgment **2** : prize

**aware** adj : having realization or consciousness — **aware•ness** n

**away** adv **1** : from this or that place or time **2** : out of the way **3** : in another direction **4** : from one's possession ∼ adj **1** : absent **2** : distant

**awe** n : respectful fear or wonder ∼ vb : fill with awe — **awe•some** adj — **awe•struck** adj

**aw•ful** adj **1** : inspiring awe **2** : extremely disagreeable **3** : very great — **aw•ful•ly** adv

**awk•ward** adj **1** : clumsy **2** : embarrassing — **awk•ward•ly** adv — **awk•ward•ness** n

**awl** n : hole-making tool

**aw•ning** n : window cover

**ax, axe** n : chopping tool

**ax•i•om** n : generally accepted truth — **ax•i•om•at•ic** adj

**ax•is** n : center of rotation — **ax•i•al** adj — **ax•i•al•ly** adv

**ax•le** n : shaft on which a wheel revolves

**aye** adv : yes ∼ n : a vote of yes

**aza•lea** n : rhododendron with funnel-shaped blossoms

**az•i•muth** n : horizontal direction expressed as an angle

**azure** n : blue of the sky — **azure** adj

# B

**b** n : 2d letter of the alphabet

**bab•ble** vb **1** : utter meaningless sounds **2** : talk foolishly or too much — **bab•ble** n — **bab•bler** n

**ba•bel** n : noisy confusion

**ba•boon** n : large Asian or African ape with a doglike muzzle

**ba•by** n : very young child ∼ vb : pamper — **baby** adj — **ba•by•hood** n — **ba•by•ish** adj

**ba•by–sit** vb : care for children while parents are away — **baby–sit•ter** n

**became** past of BECOME

**bac•ca•lau•re•ate** n : bachelor's degree

**bach•e•lor** n **1** : holder of lowest 4-year college degree **2** : unmarried man — **bach•e•lor•hood** n

**ba•cil•lus** n : rod-shaped bacterium — **bac•il•lary** adj

**back** n **1** : part of a human or animal body nearest the spine **2** : part opposite the front **3** : player farthest from the opponent's goal ∼ adv **1** : to or at the back **2** : ago **3** : to or in a former place or state **4** : in reply ∼ adj **1** : located at the back **2** : not paid on time **3** : moving or working backward **4** : not current ∼ vb **1** : support **2** : go or cause to go back **3** : form the back of — **back•ache** n — **back•er** n — **back•ing** n — **back•less** adj — **back•rest** n

**back•bone** n **1** : bony column in the back that encloses the spinal cord **2** : firm character

**back•drop** n : painted cloth hung across the rear of a stage

**back•gam•mon** n : board game

**back•ground** n **1** : scenery behind something **2** : sum of a person's experience or training

**back•hand** n : stroke (as in tennis) made with the back of the hand turned forward — **backhand** adj or vb — **back•hand•ed** adj

**back•lash** n : adverse reaction

**back•log** n : accumulation of things to be done — **backlog** vb

**back•pack** n : camping pack carried on the back ∼ vb : hike with a backpack — **back•pack•er** n

**back•slide** vb : lapse in morals or religious practice — **back•slid•er** n

**back•up** n : substitute

**back•ward, back•wards** adv **1** : toward the back **2** : with the back foremost **3** : in a reverse direction **4** : toward an earlier or worse state ∼ adj **1** : directed, turned, or done backward **2** : retarded in development — **back•ward•ness** n

**back•woods** n pl : remote or isolated place

**ba•con** n : salted and smoked meat from a pig

**bac•te•ri•um** n (**bac•te•ria**) : microscopic plant — **bac•te•ri•al** adj — **bac•te•ri•o•log•ic, bac•te•ri•o•log•i•cal** adj — **bac•te•ri•ol•o•gist** n — **bac•te•ri•ol•o•gy** n

**bad** adj **worse; worst 1** : not good **2** : naughty **3** : faulty **4** : spoiled — **bad** n or adv — **bad•ly** adv — **bad•ness** n

**bade** past of BID

**badge** n : symbol of status

**bad•ger** n : burrowing mammal ∼ vb : harass

**bad•min•ton** n : tennislike game played with a shuttlecock

**baf•fle** vb : perplex ∼ n : device to alter flow (as of liquid or sound) — **baf•fle•ment** n

**bag** n : flexible usu. closable container ∼ vb **1** : bulge out **2** : put in a bag **3** : catch in hunting

**ba•gel** n : hard doughnut-shaped roll

**bag•gage** n : traveler's bags and belongings

**bag•gy** adj : puffed out like a bag — **bag•gi•ness** n

**bag•pipe** n : musical instrument with a bag, a tube with valves, and sounding pipes — often pl.

¹**bail** n : container for scooping water out of a boat — **bail** vb — **bail•er** n

²**bail** n **1** : security given to guarantee a prisoner's appearance in court **2** : release secured by bail ∼ vb : bring about the release of by giving bail

**bai•liff** n **1** : British sheriff's aide **2** : minor officer of a U.S. court

**bail•out** n : rescue from financial distress

**bait** vb **1** : harass with dogs usu. for sport **2** : furnish (a hook or trap) with bait ∼ n : lure esp. for catching animals

**bake** vb : cook in dry heat esp. in an oven ∼ n : party featuring baked food — **bak•er** n — **bak•ery** n — **bake•shop** n

**bal•ance** n **1** : weighing device **2** : counteracting weight, force, or influence **3** : equilibrium **4** : that which remains ∼ vb **1** : compute the balance **2** : equalize **3** : bring into harmony or proportion — **bal•anced** adj

**bal•co•ny** n : platform projecting from a wall

**bald** adj **1** : lacking a natural or usual covering (as of hair) **2** : plain — **bald•ing** adj — **bald•ly** adv — **bald•ness** n

**bale** n : large bundle ∼ vb : pack in a bale — **bal•er** n

**bale•ful** adj **1** : deadly **2** : ominous

¹**ball** n **1** : rounded mass **2** : game played with a ball ∼ vb : form into a ball

²**ball** n : large formal dance — **ball•room** n

**bal•lad** n **1** : narrative poem **2** : slow romantic song — **bal•lad•eer** n

**bal•last** n : heavy material to steady a ship or balloon ∼ vb : provide with ballast

**bal•le•ri•na** n : female ballet dancer

**bal•let** n : theatrical dancing

**bal•loon** n : inflated bag ∼ vb **1** : travel in a balloon **2** : swell out — **bal•loon•ist** n

**bal•lot** n **1** : paper used to cast a vote **2** : system of voting ∼ vb : vote

**balmy** *adj* : gently soothing — **balm·i·ness** *n*

**ba·lo·ney** *n* : nonsense

**bal·sam** *n* **1** : aromatic resinous plant substance **2** : balsam-yielding plant — **bal·sam·ic** *adj*

**bam·boo** *n* : tall tropical grass with strong hollow stems

**ban** *vb* : prohibit ∼ *n* : legal prohibition

**ba·nal** *adj* : ordinary and uninteresting — **ba·nal·i·ty** *n*

**ba·nana** *n* : elongated fruit of a treelike tropical plant

**¹band** *n* **1** : something that ties or binds **2** : strip or stripe different (as in color) from nearby matter **3** : range of radio wavelengths ∼ *vb* **1** : enclose with a band **2** : unite for a common end — **band·ed** *adj* — **band·er** *n*

**²band** *n* **1** : group **2** : musicians playing together — **band·stand** *n*

**ban·dage** *n* : material used esp. in dressing wounds ∼ *vb* : dress or cover with a bandage

**ban·dan·na, ban·dana** *n* : large colored figured handkerchief

**ban·dit** *n* : outlaw or robber — **ban·dit·ry** *n*

**band·wag·on** *n* : candidate, side, or movement gaining support

**¹bang** *vb* : strike, thrust, or move usu. with a loud noise ∼ *n* **1** : blow **2** : sudden loud noise ∼ *adv* : directly

**²bang** *n* : fringe of short hair over the forehead — usu. pl. ∼ *vb* : cut in bangs

**ban·gle** *n* : bracelet

**ban·ish** *vb* **1** : force by authority to leave a country **2** : expel — **ban·ish·ment** *n*

**ban·is·ter** *n* **1** : upright support for a rail **2** : handrail

**ban·jo** *n* : stringed instrument with a drumlike body — **banjo·ist** *n*

**¹bank** *n* **1** : piled-up mass **2** : rising ground along a body of water **3** : sideways slope along a curve ∼ *vb* **1** : form a bank **2** : cover (as a fire) to keep inactive **3** : incline (an airplane) laterally

**²bank** *n* : tier of objects

**³bank** *n* **1** : money institution **2** : reserve supply ∼ *vb* : conduct business in a bank — **bank·book** *n* — **bank·er** *n* — **bank·ing** *n*

**bank·rupt** *n* : one required by law to forfeit assets to pay off debts ∼ *adj* **1** : legally a bankrupt **2** : lacking something essential — **bankrupt** *vb* — **bank·rupt·cy** *n*

**ban·ner** *n* : flag ∼ *adj* : excellent

**ban·quet** *n* : ceremonial dinner — **banquet** *vb*

**ban·shee** *n* : wailing female spirit that foretells death

**ban·tam** *n* : miniature domestic fowl

**ban·ter** *n* : good-natured joking — **banter** *vb*

**bap·tize** *vb* : administer baptism to — **bap·tism** *n* — **bap·tis·mal** *adj*

**bar** *n* **1** : long narrow object used esp. as a lever, fastening, or support **2** : barrier **3** : body of practicing lawyers **4** : wide stripe **5** : food counter **6** : place where liquor is served **7** : vertical line across the musical staff ∼ *vb* **1** : obstruct with a bar **2** : shut out **3** : prohibit — *prep* : excluding — **barred** *adj* — **bar·room** *n* — **bar·tend·er** *n*

**barb** *n* : sharp projection pointing backward — **barbed** *adj*

**bar·bar·ian** *adj* **1** : relating to people considered backward **2** : not refined — **barbarian** *n* — **bar·bar·ic** *adj*

**bar·ba·rous** *adj* **1** : lacking refinement **2** : mercilessly cruel — **bar·bar·ism** *n* — **bar·bar·i·ty** *n* — **bar·ba·rous·ly** *adv*

**bar·be·cue** *n* : gathering at which barbecued food is served ∼ *vb* : cook over hot coals or on a spit often with a highly seasoned sauce

**bar·ber** *n* : one who cuts hair

**bare** *adj* **1** : naked **2** : not concealed **3** : empty **4** : leaving nothing to spare **5** : plain ∼ *vb* : make or lay bare — **bare·foot, bare·foot·ed** *adv or adj* — **bare–hand·ed** *adv or adj* — **bare·head·ed** *adv or adj* — **bare·ly** *adv* — **bare·ness** *n*

**bare·back, bare·backed** *adv or adj* : without a saddle

**bare·faced** *adj* : open and esp. brazen

**bar·gain** *n* **1** : agreement **2** : something bought for less than its value ∼ *vb* **1** : negotiate **2** : barter

**barge** *n* : broad flat-bottomed boat ∼ *vb* : move rudely or clumsily — **barge·man** *n*

**bari·tone** *n* : male voice between bass and tenor

**¹bark** *vb* **1** : make the sound of a dog **2** : speak in a loud curt tone ∼ *n* : sound of a barking dog

**²bark** *n* : tough corky outer covering of a woody stem or root ∼ *vb* : remove bark or skin from

**bark·er** *n* : one who calls out to attract people to a show

**barn** *n* : building for keeping hay or livestock — **barn·yard** *n*

**barn·storm** *vb* : tour through rural districts giving performances

**ba·rom·e·ter** *n* : instrument for measuring atmospheric pressure — **baro·met·ric** *adj*

**bar·racks** *n sing or pl* : soldiers' housing

**bar·rel** *n* **1** : closed cylindrical container **2** : amount held by a barrel **3** : cylindrical part ∼ *vb* **1** : pack in a barrel **2** : move at high speed

**bar·ren** *adj* **1** : unproductive of life **2** : uninteresting — **bar·ren·ness** *n*

**bar·rette** *n* : clasp for a woman's hair

**bar·ri·cade** *n* : barrier — **barricade** *vb*

**bar·ri·er** *n* : something that separates or obstructs

**bar·ter** *vb* : trade by exchange of goods — **barter** *n*

**¹base** *n* **1** : bottom **2** : fundamental part **3** : beginning point **4** : supply source of a force **5** : compound that reacts with an acid to form a salt ∼ *vb* : establish — **base·less** *adj*

**²base** *adj* **1** : inferior **2** : contemptible — **base·ly** *adv* — **base·ness** *n*

**base·ball** *n* : game played with a bat and ball by 2 teams

**base·ment** *n* : part of a building below ground level

**bash** *vb* : strike violently ∼ *n* : heavy blow

**bash·ful** *adj* : self-conscious — **bash·ful·ness** *n*

**ba·sic** *adj* **1** : relating to or forming the base or essence **2** : relating to a chemical base — **ba·si·cal·ly** *adv* — **ba·sic·i·ty** *n*

**ba·sin** *n* **1** : large bowl or pan **2** : region drained by a river

**ba·sis** *n* **1** : something that supports **2** : fundamental principle

**bask** *vb* : enjoy pleasant warmth

**bas·ket** *n* : woven container — **bas·ket·ful** *n*

**bas·ket·ball** *n* : game played with a ball on a court by 2 teams

**¹bass** *n* : spiny-finned sport and food fish

**²bass** *n* **1** : deep tone **2** : lowest choral voice

**bas·set hound** *n* : short-legged dog with long ears

**bas·soon** *n* : low-pitched wind instrument

**bas·tard** *n* **1** : illegitimate child **2** : offensive person ∼ *adj* **1** : illegitimate **2** : inferior — **bas·tard·ize** *vb* — **bas·tardy** *n*

**¹baste** *vb* : sew temporarily with long stitches

**²baste** *vb* : moisten at intervals while cooking

**¹bat** *n* **1** : stick or club **2** : sharp blow ∼ *vb* : hit with a bat

**²bat** *n* : small flying mammal

**³bat** *vb* : wink or blink

**batch** *n* : quantity used or produced at one time

**bath** *n* **1** : a washing of the body **2** : water for washing the body **3** : liquid in which something is immersed **4** : bathroom **5** : large financial loss — **bath·robe** *n* — **bath·room** *n* — **bath·tub** *n*

**bathe** *vb* **1** : wash in liquid **2** : flow against so as to wet **3** : shine light over **4** : take a bath or a swim — **bath·er** *n*

**bat·tal·ion** *n* : military unit composed of a headquarters and two or more companies

**¹bat·ter** *vb* : beat or damage with repeated blows

**²batter** *n* : mixture of flour and liquid

**³batter** *n* : player who bats

**bat·tery** *n* **1** : illegal beating of a person **2** : group of artillery guns **3** : group of electric cells

**bat·ting** *n* : layers of cotton or wool for stuffing

**bat·tle** *n* : military fighting ∼ *vb* : engage in battle — **bat·tle·field** *n*

**bat·tle·ship** *n* : heavily armed ship of war

**bau·ble** *n* : a small ornament

**bawdy** *adj* : obscene or lewd — **bawd·i·ly** *adv* — **bawd·i·ness** *n*

**bawl** *vb* : cry loudly ∼ *n* : long loud cry

**¹bay** *adj* : reddish brown ∼ *n* : bay-colored animal

**²bay** *n* : European laurel

**³bay** *n* **1** : compartment **2** : area projecting out from a building and containing a window (**bay window**)

**⁴bay** *vb* : bark with deep long tones ∼ *n* **1** : position of one unable to escape danger **2** : baying of dogs

**⁵bay** *n* : body of water smaller than a gulf and nearly surrounded by land

**bay·ou** *n* : creek flowing through marshy land

**ba·zaar** *n* **1** : market **2** : fair for charity

**BB** *n* : small shot pellet

**be** *vb* was; were; been; am; is; are **1** : equal **2** : exist **3** : occupy a certain place **4** : occur ∼ *verbal auxiliary* — used to show continuous action or to form the passive voice

**beach** *n* : sandy shore of a sea, lake, or river ∼ *vb* : drive ashore — **beach·comb·er** *n*

**bea·con** *n* : guiding or warning light or signal

**bead** *n* : small round body esp. strung on a thread ∼ *vb* : form into a bead — **bead·ing** *n* — **beady** *adj*

**bea·gle** *n* : small short-legged hound

**beak** *n* : bill of a bird — **beaked** *adj*

**bea·ker** *n* **1** : large drinking cup **2** : laboratory vessel

**beam** *n* **1** : large long piece of timber or metal **2** : ray of light **3** : directed radio signals for the guidance of pilots ∼ *vb* **1** : send out light **2** : smile **3** : aim a radio broadcast

**bean** *n* : edible plant seed borne in pods

**¹bear** *n* **1** : large heavy mammal with shaggy hair **2** : gruff or sullen person — **bear·ish** *adj*

**²bear** *vb* (**bore; borne**) **1** : carry **2** : give birth to or produce **3** : endure **4** : press **5** : go in an indicated direction — **bear·able** *adj* — **bear·er** *n*

**beard** *n* **1** : facial hair on a man **2** : tuft like a beard ∼ *vb* : confront boldly — **beard·ed** *adj* — **beard·less** *adj*

**bear·ing** *n* **1** : way of carrying oneself **2** : supporting object or purpose **3** : significance **4** : machine part in which another part turns **5** : direction with respect esp. to compass points

**beast** *n* **1** : animal **2** : brutal person — **beast·li·ness** *n* — **beast·ly** *adj*

**beat** *vb* (**beat; beat·en/beat**) **1** : strike repeatedly **2** : defeat **3** : act or arrive before **4** : throb ∼ *n* **1** : single stroke or pulsation **2** : rhythmic stress in poetry or music ∼ *adj* : exhausted — **beat·er** *n*

**be·at·i·fy** *vb* : make happy or blessed — **be·atif·ic** *adj* — **be·at·i·fi·ca·tion** *n*

**be·at·i·tude** *n* : saying in the Sermon on the Mount (Matthew 5:3-12) beginning "Blessed are"

**beau·ty** *n* : qualities that please the senses or mind — **beau·te·ous** *adj* — **beau·te·ous·ly** *adv* — **beau·ti·fi·ca·tion** *n* — **beau·ti·fi·er** *n* — **beau·ti·ful** *adj* — **beau·ti·ful·ly** *adv* — **beau·ti·fy** *vb*

**bea·ver** *n* : large fur-bearing rodent

**be·cause** *conj* : for the reason that

**because of** *prep* : by reason of

**beck·on** *vb* : summon esp. by a nod or gesture

**be·come** *vb* became; become **1** : come to be **2** : be suitable — **be·com·ing** *adj* — **be·com·ing·ly** *adv*

**bed** *n* **1** : piece of furniture to sleep on **2** : flat or level surface ∼ *vb* : put or go to bed — **bed·room** *n* — **bed·spread** *n*

**bed·bug** *n* : wingless bloodsucking insect

**bed·ding** *n* **1** : sheets and blankets for a bed **2** : soft material (as hay) for an animal's bed

**bed·rid·den** *adj* : kept in bed by illness

**bed·rock** *n* : solid subsurface rock — **bedrock** *adj*

**¹bee** *n* : 4-winged honey-producing insect — **bee·hive** *n* — **bee·keep·er** *n* — **bees·wax** *n*

**²bee** *n* : neighborly work session

**beech** *n* : tree with smooth gray bark and edible nuts (**beech·nuts**) — **beech·en** *adj*

**beef** *n* : flesh of a steer, cow, or bull ∼ *vb* : strengthen — used with *up* — **beef·steak** *n*

**bee·line** *n* : straight course

**been** *past part of* BE

**beep** *n* : short usu. high-pitched warning sound — **beep** *vb* — **beep·er** *n*

**beer** *n* : alcoholic drink brewed from malt and hops — **beery** *adj*

**beet** *n* : garden root vegetable

**bee·tle** *n* : 4-winged insect

**be·fore** *adv* **1** : in front **2** : earlier ∼ *prep* **1** : in front of **2** : earlier than ∼ *conj* : earlier than

**be·fore·hand** *adv or adj* : in advance

**be·fud·dle** *vb* : confuse

**beg** *vb* : ask earnestly

**beg·gar** *n* : one that begs ∼ *vb* : make poor — **beg·gar·ly** *adj* — **beg·gary** *n*

**be·gin** *vb* be·gan; be·gun **1** : start **2** : come into being — **be·gin·ner** *n*

**be·grudge** *vb* **1** : concede reluctantly **2** : look upon disapprovingly

**be·guile** *vb* **1** : deceive **2** : amuse

**be·half** *n* : benefit

**be·have** *vb* : act in a certain way

**be·hav·ior** *n* : way of behaving — **be·hav·ior·al** *adj*

**be·head** *vb* : cut off the head of

**be·hind** *adv* : at the back ∼ *prep* **1** : in back of **2** : less than **3** : supporting

**be·hold** *vb* : see — **be·hold·er** *n*

**beige** *n* : yellowish brown — **beige** *adj*

**be·ing** *n* **1** : existence **2** : living thing

**be·lat·ed** *adj* : delayed

**belch** *vb* **1** : expel stomach gas orally **2** : emit forcefully — **belch** *n*

**be·lea·guer** *vb* **1** : besiege **2** : harass

**bel·fry** *n* : bell tower

**be·lief** *n* **1** : trust **2** : something believed

**be·lieve** *vb* **1** : trust in **2** : accept as true **3** : hold as an opinion — **be·liev·able** *adj* — **be·liev·ably** *adv* — **be·liev·er** *n*

**be·lit·tle** *vb* **1** : disparage **2** : make seem less

**bell** *n* : hollow metallic device that rings when struck ∼ *vb* : provide with a bell

**belle** *n* : beautiful woman

**bel·lig·er·ent** *adj* **1** : waging war **2** : aggressively asserting one's own will — **bel·lig·er·ence** *n* — **bel·lig·er·en·cy** *n* — **belligerent** *n*

**bel·low** *vb* : make a loud deep roar or shout — **bellow** *n*

**bel·lows** *n sing or pl* : device with sides that can be compressed to expel air

**bel·ly** *n* : abdomen ∼ *vb* : bulge

**be·long** *vb* **1** : be suitable **2** : be owned **3** : be a part of

**be·long·ings** *n pl* : possessions

**be·loved** *adj* : dearly loved — **beloved** *n*

**be·low** adv : in or to a lower place ~ prep : lower than

**belt** n 1 : strip (as of leather) worn about the waist 2 : endless band to impart motion 3 : distinct region ~ vb 1 : put a belt around 2 : beat soundly

**be·muse** vb : confuse

**bench** n 1 : long seat 2 : judge's seat 3 : court

**bend** vb (**bent; bent**) 1 : curve or cause a change of shape in 2 : turn in a certain direction ~ n 1 : act of bending 2 : curve

**be·neath** adv or prep : below

**bene·dic·tion** n : closing blessing

**bene·fac·tor** n : one who gives esp. charitable aid

**ben·e·fit** n 1 : something that does good 2 : help 3 : fund-raising event — **ben·efit** vb — **ben·e·fi·cial** adj — **ben·e·fi·cial·ly** adv — **ben·e·fi·cia·ry** n

**be·nev·o·lence** n 1 : charitable nature 2 : act of kindness — **be·nev·o·lent** adj — **be·nev·o·lent·ly** adv

**be·nign** adj 1 : gentle or kindly 2 : not malignant — **be·nig·ni·ty** n

**bent** n : aptitude or interest

**be·numb** vb : make numb esp. by cold

**be·queath** vb 1 : give by will 2 : hand down — **be·quest** n

**be·rate** vb : scold harshly

**be·reaved** adj : suffering the death of a loved one ~ n pl **bereaved** : one who is bereaved — **be·reave·ment** n

**be·ret** n : round soft visorless cap

**ber·ry** n : small pulpy fruit

**ber·serk** adj : acting out of control or insane — **berserk** adv

**berth** n 1 : place where a ship is anchored 2 : place to sit or sleep esp. on a ship 3 : job ~ vb : to bring or come into a berth

**be·seech** vb : entreat

**be·side** prep 1 : by the side of 2 : besides

**be·sides** adv 1 : in addition 2 : further to what has been said ~ prep 1 : other than 2 : in addition to

**be·siege** vb : lay siege to — **be·sieg·er** n

**best** adj, superlative of GOOD 1 : excelling all others 2 : most productive 3 : largest ~ adv superlative of WELL 1 : in the best way 2 : most ~ n : one that is best ~ vb : outdo

**bes·tial** adj 1 : relating to beasts 2 : brutish — **bes·ti·al·i·ty** n

**best man** n : chief male attendant at a wedding

**be·stow** vb : give — **be·stow·al** n

**bet** n 1 : something risked or pledged on the outcome of a contest 2 : the making of a bet ~ vb **bet; bet** 1 : risk (as money) on an outcome 2 : make a bet with

**be·tray** vb 1 : seduce 2 : report or reveal to an enemy by treachery 3 : abandon 4 : prove unfaithful to 5 : reveal unintentionally — **be·tray·al** n — **be·tray·er** n

**be·troth** vb : promise to marry — **be·troth·al** n — **be·trothed** n

**bet·ter** adj, comparative of GOOD 1 : more than half 2 : improved in health 3 : of higher quality ~ adv comparative of WELL 1 : in a superior manner 2 : more ~ n 1 : one that is better 2 : advantage ~ vb 1 : improve 2 : surpass — **bet·ter·ment** n

**bet·tor, bet·ter** n : one who bets

**be·tween** prep 1 : used to show two things considered together 2 : in the space separating 3 — used to indicate a comparison or choice ~ adv : in an intervening space or interval

**bev·el** n : slant on an edge ~ vb 1 : cut or shape to a bevel 2 : incline

**bev·er·age** n : drink

**be·ware** vb : be cautious

**be·wil·der** vb : confuse — **be·wil·der·ment** n

**be·witch** vb 1 : affect by witchcraft 2 : charm — **be·witch·ment** n

**be·yond** adv 1 : farther 2 : besides ~ prep 1 : on or to the farther side of 2 : out of the reach of 3 : besides

**bi·an·nu·al** adj : occurring twice a year — **bi·an·nu·al·ly** adv

**bi·as** n 1 : line diagonal to the grain of a fabric 2 : prejudice ~ vb : prejudice

**bib** n : shield tied under the chin to protect the clothes while eating

**Bi·ble** n 1 : sacred scriptures of Christians 2 : sacred scriptures of Judaism or another religion — **bib·li·cal** adj

**bib·li·og·ra·phy** n : list of writings on a subject or of an author — **bib·li·og·ra·pher** n — **bib·li·o·graph·ic** adj

**bi·cen·ten·ni·al** n : 200th anniversary — **bicentennial** adj

**bi·ceps** n : large muscle of the upper arm

**bick·er** vb or n : squabble

**bi·cus·pid** n : double-pointed tooth

**bi·cy·cle** n : 2-wheeled vehicle moved by pedaling ~ vb : ride a bicycle — **bi·cy·cler** n — **bi·cy·clist** n

**bid** vb **bade/bid; bid·den/bid** 1 : order 2 : invite 3 : express 4 : make a bid ~ n 1 : act of bidding 2 : buyer's proposed price — **bid·da·ble** adj — **bid·der** n

**bide** vb 1 : wait 2 : dwell

**bi·en·ni·al** adj 1 : occurring once in 2 years 2 : lasting 2 years — **biennial** n — **bi·en·ni·al·ly** adv

**bifocals** n pl : eyeglasses that correct for near and distant vision

**big** adj : large in size, amount, or scope — **big·ness** n

**big·a·my** n : marrying one person while still married to another — **big·a·mist** n — **big·a·mous** adj

**big·ot** n : one who is intolerant of others — **big·ot·ed** adj — **big·ot·ry** n

**big shot** n : important person

**big·wig** n : big shot

**bike** n : bicycle or motorcycle

**bi·ki·ni** n : woman's brief 2-piece bathing suit

**bile** n 1 : greenish liver secretion that aids digestion 2 : bad temper

**bi·lin·gual** adj : using 2 languages

**bilk** vb : cheat

**¹bill** n : jaws of a bird together with their horny covering ~ vb : caress fondly — **billed** adj

**²bill** n 1 : draft of a law 2 : list of things to be paid for 3 : printed advertisement 4 : piece of paper money ~ vb : submit a bill or account to

**bill·board** n : surface for displaying advertising bills

**bill·fold** n : wallet

**bil·liards** n : game of driving balls into one another or into pockets on a table

**bil·lion** n : 1000 millions — **billion** adj — **bil·lionth** adj or n

**bil·low** n 1 : great wave 2 : rolling mass ~ vb : swell out — **bil·lowy** adj

**billy goat** n : male goat

**bin** n : storage box

**bi·na·ry** adj : consisting of 2 things — **binary** n

**bind** vb 1 : tie 2 : obligate 3 : unite into a mass 4 : bandage — **bind·er** n — **binding** n

**binge** n : excessive indulgence

**bin·go** n : game of covering numbers on a card

**bin·oc·u·lar** adj : of or relating to both eyes ~ n : binocular optical instrument — usu. pl.

**bio·chem·is·try** n : chemistry dealing with organisms — **bio·chemi·cal** adj or n — **bio·chem·ist** n

**bio·de·grad·able** adj : able to be reduced to harmless products by organisms — **bio·de·grad·abil·i·ty** n — **bio·deg·ra·da·tion** n — **bio·de·grade** vb

**bi·og·ra·phy** n : written history of a person's life — **bi·og·ra·pher** n — **bi·o·graph·i·cal** adj

**bi·ol·o·gy** n : science of living beings and life processes — **bi·o·log·ic, bi·o·log·i·cal** adj — **bi·ol·o·gist** n

**bi·on·ic** adj : having normal biological capabilities enhanced by electronic or mechanical devices

**bio·phys·ics** n : application of physics to biological problems — **bio·phys·i·cal** adj — **bio·phys·i·cist** n

**bi·op·sy** n : removal of live bodily tissue for examination

**bi·par·ti·san** adj : involving members of 2 parties

**bi·ped** n : 2-footed animal

**birch** n : deciduous tree with close-grained wood — **birch, birch·en** adj

**bird** n : warm-blooded egg-laying vertebrate with wings and feathers — **bird·bath** n — **bird·house** n — **bird·seed** n

**bird's—eye** adj 1 : seen from above 2 : of a general or superficial nature

**birth** n 1 : act or fact of being born or of producing young 2 : origin — **birth·day** n — **birth·mark** n — **birth·place** n — **birth·rate** n — **birth·right** n

**bis·cuit** n : small bread made with leavening other than yeast

**bi·sect** vb : divide into 2 parts — **bi·sec·tion** n — **bi·sec·tor** n

**bish·op** n : clergy member higher than a priest

**bish·op·ric** n 1 : diocese 2 : office of bishop

**bi·son** n pl **bison** : large shaggy wild ox of central U.S.

**bis·tro** n : small restaurant or bar

**¹bit** n 1 : part of a bridle that goes in a horse's mouth 2 : drilling tool

**²bit** n 1 : small piece or quantity 2 : small degree

**bitch** n : female dog ~ vb : complain

**bite** vb **bit; bit·ten** 1 : to grip or cut with teeth or jaws 2 : dig in or grab and hold 3 : sting 4 : take bait ~ n 1 : act of biting 2 : bit of food 3 : wound made by biting — **bit·ing** adj

**bit·ten** past part of BITE

**bit·ter** adj 1 : having an acrid lingering taste 2 : intense or severe 3 : extremely harsh or resentful — **bit·ter·ly** adv — **bit·ter·ness** n

**bi·valve** n : animal (as a clam) with a shell of 2 parts — **bivalve** adj

**bi·zarre** adj : very strange — **bi·zarre·ly** adv

**blab** vb : talk too much

**black** adj 1 : of the color black 2 : having dark skin 3 : soiled 4 : lacking light 5 : wicked or evil 6 : gloomy ~ n 1 : black pigment or dye 2 : something black 3 : color of least lightness 4 : person of a dark-skinned race ~ vb : blacken — **black·ing** n — **black·ish** adj — **black·ly** adv — **black·ness** n

**black—and—blue** adj : darkly discolored from bruising

**black·ball** vb 1 : ostracize 2 : boycott — **blackball** n

**black·ber·ry** n : black or purple fruit of a bramble

**black·board** n : dark surface for writing on with chalk

**black·en** vb 1 : make or become black 2 : harm the reputation of

**black·head** n : small dark oily mass plugging the outlet of a skin gland

**black hole** n : invisible extremely massive celestial object

**black·jack** n 1 : flexible leather-covered club 2 : card game ~ vb : hit with a blackjack

**black·list** n : list of persons to be punished or boycotted — **blacklist** vb

**black·mail** n 1 : extortion by threat of exposure 2 : something extorted by blackmail — **blackmail** vb — **black·mail·er** n

**black·out** n 1 : darkness due to electrical failure 2 : brief fainting spell — **black out** vb

**black·smith** n : one who forges iron

**black·top** n : dark tarry material for surfacing roads — **blacktop** vb

**blad·der** n : sac into which urine passes from the kidneys

**blade** n 1 : leaf esp. of grass 2 : something resembling the flat part of a leaf 3 : cutting part of an instrument or tool — **blad·ed** adj

**blame** vb 1 : find fault with 2 : hold re-

sponsible or responsible for — **blam·able** adj — **blame** n — **blame·less** adj — **blame·less·ly** adv — **blame·worthy** adj

**bland** adj 1 : smooth in manner 2 : soothing 3 : tasteless — **bland·ly** adv — **bland·ness** n

**blank** adj 1 : showing or causing a dazed look 2 : lacking expression 3 : empty 4 : free from writing 5 : downright ~ n 1 : an empty space 2 : form with spaces to write in 3 : unfinished form (as of a key) 4 : cartridge with no bullet ~ vb : cover or close up — **blank·ly** adv — **blank·ness** n

**blan·ket** n 1 : heavy covering for a bed 2 : covering layer ~ vb : cover ~ adj : applying to a group

**blare** vb : make a loud harsh sound — **blare** n

**bla·sé** adj : indifferent to pleasure or excitement

**blas·pheme** vb : speak blasphemy — **blas·phem·er** n — **blas·phe·mous** adj — **blas·phe·my** n

**blast** n 1 : violent gust of wind 2 : explosion ~ vb : shatter by or as if by explosive — **blast off** vb : take off esp. in a rocket

**bla·tant** adj : offensively showy — **bla·tan·cy** n — **bla·tant·ly** adv

**¹blaze** n 1 : fire 2 : intense direct light 3 : strong display ~ vb : burn or shine brightly

**²blaze** n 1 : white stripe on an animal's face 2 : trail marker esp. on a tree ~ vb : mark with blazes

**bleach** vb : whiten — **bleach** n

**bleach·ers** n sing or pl : spectator stand without a roof

**bleak** adj 1 : desolately barren 2 : lacking cheering qualities — **bleak·ish** adj — **bleak·ly** adv — **bleak·ness** n

**bleary** adj : dull or dimmed esp. from fatigue

**bleat** n : cry of a sheep or goat or a sound like it — **bleat** vb

**bleed** vb 1 : lose or shed blood 2 : feel distress 3 : flow from a wound 4 : draw fluid from 5 : extort money from — **bleed·er** n

**blem·ish** vb : spoil by a flaw ~ n : noticeable flaw

**¹blench** vb : flinch

**²blench** vb : grow or make pale

**blend** vb 1 : mix thoroughly 2 : combine into an integrated whole — **blend** n — **blend·er** n

**bless** vb 1 : consecrate by religious rite 2 : invoke divine care for 3 : make happy — **bless·ed, blest** adj — **bless·ed·ly** adv — **bless·ed·ness** n — **bless·ing** n

**blew** past of BLOW

**blight** n 1 : plant disorder marked by withering or an organism causing it 2 : harmful influence 3 : deteriorated condition ~ vb : affect with or suffer from blight

**blimp** n : airship holding form by pressure of contained gas

**blind** adj 1 : lacking or quite deficient in ability to see 2 : not intelligently controlled 3 : having no way out ~ vb 1 : to make blind 2 : dazzle ~ n 1 : something to conceal or darken 2 : place of concealment — **blind·ly** adv — **blind·ness** n

**blind·fold** vb : cover the eyes of — **blindfold** n

**blink** vb 1 : wink 2 : shine intermittently ~ n : wink

**bliss** n 1 : complete happiness 2 : heaven or paradise — **bliss·ful** adj — **bliss·ful·ly** adv

**blis·ter** n 1 : raised area of skin containing watery fluid 2 : raised or swollen spot ~ vb : develop or cause blisters

**blithe** adj : cheerful — **blithe·ly** adv — **blithe·some** adj

**blitz** n 1 : series of air raids 2 : fast intensive campaign — **blitz** vb

**bliz·zard** n : severe snowstorm

**bloat** vb : swell

**blob** *n* : small lump or drop

**bloc** *n* : group working together

**block** *n* **1** : solid piece **2** : frame enclosing a pulley **3** : quantity considered together **4** : large building divided into separate units **5** : a city square or the distance along one of its sides **6** : obstruction **7** : interruption of a bodily or mental function ~ *vb* : obstruct or hinder

**block·ade** *n* : isolation of a place usu. by troops or ships — **block·ade** *vb* — **block·ad·er** *n*

**block·head** *n* : stupid person

**blond, blonde** *adj* **1** : fair in complexion **2** : of a light color — **blond, blonde** *n*

**blood** *n* **1** : red liquid that circulates in the heart, arteries, and veins of animals **2** : lifeblood **3** : line of descent from common ancestors — **blood·ed** *adj* — **blood·less** *adj* — **blood·stain** *n* — **blood·stained** *adj* — **blood·suck·er** *n* — **blood·suck·ing** *n* — **bloody** *adj*

**blood·hound** *n* : large hound with a keen sense of smell

**blood·mo·bile** *n* : truck for collecting blood from donors

**blood·shed** *n* : slaughter

**blood·shot** *adj* : inflamed to redness

**blood·thirsty** *adj* : eager to shed blood — **blood·thirst·i·ly** *adv* — **blood·thirst·i·ness** *n*

**bloom** *n* **1** : flower **2** : period of flowering **3** : fresh or healthy look ~ *vb* **1** : yield flowers **2** : mature — **bloomy** *adj*

**bloop·er** *n* : public blunder

**blos·som** *n or vb* : flower

**blot** *n* **1** : stain **2** : blemish ~ *vb* **1** : spot **2** : dry with absorbent paper — **blot·ter** *n*

**blotch** *n* : large spot — **blotch** *vb* — **blotchy** *adj*

**blouse** *n* : loose garment reaching from the neck to the waist

[1]**blow** *vb* **blew; blown 1** : move forcibly **2** : send forth a current of air **3** : sound **4** : shape by blowing **5** : explode **6** : bungle ~ *n* **1** : gale **2** : act of blowing — **blow·er** *n* — **blowy** *adj*

[2]**blow** *n* **1** : forcible stroke **2** *pl* : fighting **3** : calamity

**blow·out** *n* : bursting of a tire

**blow·torch** *n* : small torch that uses a blast of air

[1]**blub·ber** *n* : fat of whales

[2]**blubber** *vb* : cry noisily

**blud·geon** *n* : short club ~ *vb* : hit with a bludgeon

**blue** *adj* **1** : of the color blue **2** : melancholy ~ *n* : color of the clear sky — **blu·ish** *adj*

**blue·ber·ry** *n* : edible blue or blackish berry

**blue·bird** *n* : small bluish songbird

**blue jay** *n* : American crested jay

**blues** *n pl* **1** : depression **2** : music in a melancholy style

[1]**bluff** *adj* **1** : rising steeply with a broad flat front **2** : frank ~ *n* : cliff

[2]**bluff** *vb* : deceive by pretense ~ *n* : act of bluffing — **bluff·er** *n*

**blun·der** *vb* **1** : move clumsily **2** : make a stupid mistake ~ *n* : bad mistake

**blunt** *adj* **1** : not sharp **2** : tactless ~ *vb* : make dull — **blunt·ly** *adv* — **blunt·ness** *n*

**blur** *n* **1** : smear **2** : something perceived indistinctly ~ *vb* : cloud or obscure — **blur·ry** *adj*

**blurb** *n* : short publicity notice

**blurt** *vb* : utter suddenly

**blush** *n* : reddening of the face — **blush** *vb* — **blush·ful** *adj*

**blus·ter** *vb* **1** : blow violently **2** : talk or act with boasts or threats — **blus·ter** *n* — **blus·tery** *adj*

**boa** *n* **1** : a large snake (as the **boa con·stric·tor**) that crushes its prey **2** : fluffy scarf

**boar** *n* : male swine

**board** *n* **1** : long thin piece of sawed lumber **2** : flat thin sheet esp. for games **3** : daily meals furnished for pay **4** : official body ~ *vb* **1** : go aboard **2** : cover with boards **3** : supply meals to — **board·er** *n*

**board·walk** *n* : wooden walk along a beach

**boast** *vb* : praise oneself or one's possessions — **boast** *n* — **boast·er** *n* — **boast·ful** *adj* — **boast·ful·ly** *adv*

**boat** *n* : small vessel for traveling on water — **boat** *vb* — **boat·man** *n*

[1]**bob** *vb* **1** : move up and down **2** : appear suddenly

[2]**bob** *n* **1** : float **2** : woman's short haircut ~ *vb* : cut hair in a bob

**bob·bin** *n* : spindle for holding thread

**bob·ble** *vb* : fumble — **bobble** *n*

**bob·cat** *n* : small American lynx

**bob·sled** *n* : racing sled — **bobsled** *vb*

**bob·white** *n* : quail

[1]**bode** *vb* : indicate by signs

[2]**bode** *past of* BIDE

**bod·ice** *n* : close-fitting top of dress

**bodi·ly** *adj* : relating to the body ~ *adv* **1** : in the flesh **2** : as a whole

**body** *n* **1** : the physical whole of an organism **2** : human being **3** : main part **4** : mass of matter **5** : group — **bod·ied** *adj* — **bodi·less** *adj* — **body·guard** *n*

**bog** *n* : swamp ~ *vb* : sink in or as if in a bog — **bog·gy** *adj*

**bo·gey** *n* : someone or something frightening

**bog·gle** *vb* : overwhelm with amazement

**bo·gus** *adj* : fake

[1]**boil** *n* : inflamed swelling

[2]**boil** *vb* **1** : heat to a temperature (**boiling point**) at which vapor forms **2** : cook in boiling liquid **3** : be agitated — **boil** *n*

**boil·er** *n* : tank holding hot water or steam

**bois·ter·ous** *adj* : noisily turbulent — **bois·ter·ous·ly** *adv*

**bold** *adj* **1** : courageous **2** : insolent **3** : daring — **bold·ly** *adv* — **bold·ness** *n*

**boll** *n* : seed pod

**boll weevil** *n* : small grayish weevil that infests the cotton plant

**bo·lo·gna** *n* : large smoked sausage

**bol·ster** *n* : long pillow ~ *vb* : support

**bolt** *n* **1** : flash of lightning **2** : sliding bar used to fasten a door **3** : roll of cloth **4** : threaded pin used with a nut ~ *vb* **1** : move suddenly **2** : fasten with a bolt **3** : swallow hastily

**bomb** *n* : explosive device ~ *vb* : attack with bombs — **bomb·er** *n* — **bomb·proof** *adj*

**bom·bard** *vb* : attack with or as if with artillery — **bom·bard·ment** *n*

**bom·bast** *n* : pretentious language — **bom·bas·tic** *adj*

**bomb·shell** *n* **1** : bomb **2** : great surprise

**bona fide** *adj* **1** : made in good faith **2** : genuine

**bo·nan·za** *n* : something yielding a rich return

**bon·bon** *n* : piece of candy

**bond** *n* **1** *pl* : something that restrains **2** : uniting force **3** : obligation made binding by money **4** : interest-bearing certificate ~ *vb* **1** : insure **2** : cause to adhere — **bond·hold·er** *n*

**bond·age** *n* : slavery

**bonds·man** *n* : slave

**bone** *n* : skeletal material ~ *vb* : to free from bones — **bone·less** *adj* — **bony** *adj*

**bon·er** *n* : blunder

**bon·fire** *n* : outdoor fire

**bon·net** *n* : hat for a woman or infant

**bo·nus** *n* : extra payment

**boo** *n* : shout of disapproval — **boo** *vb*

**book** *n* **1** : paper sheets bound into a volume **2** : long literary work or a subdivision of one ~ *vb* : reserve — **book·case** *n* — **book·ish** *adj* — **book·let** *n* — **book·mark** *n* — **book·sell·er** *n* — **book·shelf** *n*

**book·ie** *n* : bookmaker

**book·keep·er** *n* : one who keeps business accounts — **book·keep·ing** *n*

**book·mak·er** *n* : one who takes bets — **book·mak·ing** *n*

[1]**boom** *n* **1** : long spar to extend the bottom of a sail **2** : beam projecting from the pole of a derrick

[2]**boom** *vb* **1** : make a deep hollow sound **2** : grow rapidly esp. in value ~ *n* **1** : booming sound **2** : rapid growth

**boo·mer·ang** *n* : angular club that returns to the thrower

**boon** *n* : benefit

**boor** *n* : rude person — **boor·ish** *adj*

**boost** *vb* **1** : raise **2** : promote — **boost** *n* — **boost·er** *n*

**boot** *n* **1** : covering for the foot and leg **2** : kick ~ *vb* : kick

**boo·tee, boo·tie** *n* : infant's knitted sock

**booth** *n* : small enclosed stall or seating area

**boot·leg** *vb* : make or sell liquor illegally — **bootleg** *adj or n* — **boot·leg·ger** *n*

**boo·ty** *n* : plunder

**booze** *vb* : drink liquor to excess ~ *n* : liquor — **booz·er** *n* — **boozy** *adj*

**bor·der** *n* **1** : edge **2** : boundary ~ *vb* **1** : put a border on **2** : be close

[1]**bore** *vb* **1** : pierce **2** : make by piercing ~ *n* : cylindrical hole or its diameter — **bor·er** *n*

[2]**bore** *past of* BEAR

[3]**bore** *n* : one that is dull ~ *vb* : tire with dullness — **bore·dom** *n*

**born** *adj* **1** : brought into life **2** : being such by birth

**borne** *past part of* BEAR

**bor·ough** *n* : incorporated town or village

**bor·row** *vb* **1** : take as a loan **2** : take into use

**bo·som** *n* : breast ~ *adj* : intimate — **bo·somed** *adj*

**boss** *n* : employer or supervisor ~ *vb* : supervise — **bossy** *adj*

**bot·a·ny** *n* : plant biology — **bo·tan·i·cal** *adj* — **bot·a·nist** *n* — **bot·a·nize** *vb*

**botch** *vb* : do clumsily — **botch** *n*

**both** *adj or pron* : the one and the other ~ *conj* — used to show each of two is included

**both·er** *vb* **1** : annoy or worry **2** : take the trouble — **bother** *n* — **both·er·some** *adj*

**bot·tle** *n* : container with a narrow neck and no handles ~ *vb* : put into a bottle

**bot·tle·neck** *n* : place or cause of congestion

**bot·tom** *n* **1** : supporting surface **2** : lowest part or place — **bottom** *adj* — **bot·tom·less** *adj*

**bot·u·lism** *n* : acute food poisoning

**bough** *n* : large tree branch

**bought** *past of* BUY

**boul·der** *n* : large rounded rock — **boul·dered** *adj*

**bou·le·vard** *n* : broad thoroughfare

**bounce** *vb* **1** : spring back **2** : make bounce — **bounce** *n* — **bouncy** *adj*

[1]**bound** *adj* : intending to go

[2]**bound** *n* : limit or boundary ~ *vb* : be a boundary of — **bound·less** *adj* — **bound·less·ness** *n*

[3]**bound** *adj* **1** : obliged **2** : having a binding **3** : determined **4** : incapable of failing

[4]**bound** *n* : leap ~ *vb* : move by springing

**bound·ary** *n* : line marking extent or separation

**boun·ty** *n* **1** : generosity **2** : reward — **boun·te·ous** *adj* — **boun·te·ous·ly** *adv* — **boun·ti·ful** *adj* — **boun·ti·ful·ly** *adv*

**bou·quet** *n* **1** : bunch of flowers **2** : fragrance

**bout** *n* **1** : contest **2** : outbreak

**bou·tique** *n* : specialty shop

**bo·vine** *adj* : relating to cattle — **bovine** *n*

[1]**bow** *vb* **1** : submit **2** : bend the head or body ~ *n* : act of bowing

[2]**bow** *n* **1** : bend or arch **2** : weapon for shooting arrows **3** : knot with loops **4** : rod with stretched horsehairs for playing a stringed instrument ~ *vb* : curve or bend — **bow·man** *n* — **bow·string** *n*

[3]**bow** *n* : forward part of a ship — **bow** *adj*

**bow·els** *n pl* **1** : intestines **2** : inmost parts

[1]**bowl** *n* : concave vessel or part — **bowl·ful** *n*

[2]**bowl** *n* : round ball for bowling ~ *vb* : roll a ball in bowling — **bowl·er** *n*

**bowl·ing** *n* : game in which balls are rolled to knock down pins

[1]**box** *n* : evergreen shrub — **box·wood** *n*

[2]**box** *n* **1** : container usu. with 4 sides and a cover **2** : small compartment ~ *vb* : put in a box

[3]**box** *n* : slap ~ *vb* **1** : slap **2** : fight with the fists — **box·er** *n* — **box·ing** *n*

**box·car** *n* : roofed freight car

**box office** *n* : theater ticket office

**boy** *n* : male child — **boy·hood** *n* — **boy·ish** *adj* — **boy·ish·ly** *adv* — **boy·ish·ness** *n*

**boy·cott** *vb* : refrain from dealing with — **boycott** *n*

**boy·friend** *n* **1** : male friend **2** : woman's regular male companion

**brace** *n* **1** : crank for turning a bit **2** : something that resists weight or supports **3** : punctuation mark { or } ~ *vb* **1** : make taut or steady **2** : invigorate **3** : strengthen

**brace·let** *n* : ornamental band for the wrist or arm

**brack·et** *n* **1** : projecting support **2** : punctuation mark [ or ] **3** : class ~ *vb* **1** : furnish or fasten with brackets **2** : place within brackets **3** : group

**brag** *vb* : boast — **brag** *n*

**brag·gart** *n* : boaster

**braid** *vb* : weave together ~ *n* : something braided

**braille** *n* : system of writing for the blind using raised dots

**brain** *n* **1** : organ of thought and nervous coordination enclosed in the skull **2** : intelligence ~ *vb* : smash the skull of — **brained** *adj* — **brain·less** *adj* — **brainy** *adj*

**braise** *vb* : cook (meat) slowly in a covered dish

**brake** *n* : device for slowing or stopping ~ *vb* : slow or stop by a brake

**bram·ble** *n* : prickly shrub

**bran** *n* : edible cracked grain husks

**branch** *n* **1** : division of a plant stem **2** : part ~ *vb* **1** : develop branches **2** : diverge — **branched** *adj*

**brand** *n* **1** : identifying mark made by burning **2** : mark of disgrace **3** : distinctive kind (as of goods from one firm) ~ *vb* : mark with a brand

**brand–new** *adj* : unused

**bran·dy** *n* : liquor distilled from wine

**brash** *adj* **1** : impulsive **2** : aggressively self-assertive

**brass** *n* **1** : alloy of copper and zinc **2** : outrageous confidence in oneself **3** : high-ranking military officers — **brassy** *adj*

**bras·siere** *n* : woman's undergarment to support the breasts

**brat** *n* : ill-behaved child — **brat·ti·ness** *n* — **brat·ty** *adj*

**bra·va·do** *n* : false bravery

**brave** *adj* : showing courage ~ *vb* : face with courage — **brave·ly** *adv* — **brav·ery** *n*

**brawl** *n* : noisy quarrel or violent fight — **brawl** *vb* — **brawl·er** *n*

**brawn** *n* : muscular strength — **brawny** *adj* — **brawn·i·ness** *n*

**bra·zen** *adj* **1** : made of brass **2** : bold — **bra·zen·ly** *adv* — **bra·zen·ness** *n*

**bra·zier** *n* : charcoal grill

**breach** *n* **1** : breaking of a law, obligation, or standard **2** : gap ~ *vb* : make a breach in

**bread** *n* : baked food made of flour ~ *vb* : cover with bread crumbs

**breadth** *n* : width

**bread•win•ner** *n* : wage earner
**break** *vb* **broke; bro•ken 1** : knock into pieces **2** : fail to fulfill or respect **3** : force a way into or out of **4** : exceed **5** : interrupt **6** : fail ~ *n* **1** : act or result of breaking **2** : stroke of good luck — **break•able** *adj or n* — **break•age** *n* — **break•er** *n* — **break in** *vb* **1** : enter by force **2** : interrupt **3** : train — **break out** *vb* **1** : erupt with force **2** : develop a rash
**break•down** *n* : physical or mental failure — **break down** *vb*
**break•fast** *n* : first meal of the day — **breakfast** *vb*
**breast** *n* **1** : milk-producing gland esp. of a woman **2** : front part of the chest
**breast•bone** *n* : bone connecting the ribs in front
**breath** *n* **1** : slight breeze **2** : air breathed in or out — **breath•less** *adj* — **breath•less•ly** *adv* — **breath•less•ness** *n* — **breathy** *adj*
**breathe** *vb* **1** : draw air into the lungs and expel it **2** : live **3** : utter
**breath•tak•ing** *adj* : exciting
**breech•es** *n pl* : trousers ending near the knee
**breed** *vb* **1** : give birth to **2** : propagate **3** : raise ~ *n* **1** : kind of plant or animal usu. developed by humans **2** : class — **breed•er** *n*
**breeze** *n* : light wind ~ *vb* : move fast — **breezy** *adj*
**brev•i•ty** *n* : shortness or conciseness
**brew** *vb* : make by fermenting or steeping — **brew** *n* — **brew•er** *n* — **brew•ery** *n*
**bri•ar** *var of* BRIER
**bribe** *vb* : corrupt or influence by gifts ~ *n* : something offered or given in bribing — **brib•able** *adj* — **brib•ery** *n*
**bric–a–brac** *n pl* : small ornamental articles
**brick** *n* : building block of baked clay — **brick** *vb* — **brick•lay•er** *n* — **brick•lay•ing** *n*
**bride** *n* : woman just married or about to be married — **brid•al** *adj*
**bride•groom** *n* : man just married or about to be married
**brides•maid** *n* : woman who attends a bride at her wedding
[1]**bridge** *n* **1** : structure built for passage over a depression or obstacle **2** : upper part of the nose **3** : compartment from which a ship is navigated **4** : artificial replacement for missing teeth ~ *vb* : build a bridge over — **bridge•able** *adj*
[2]**bridge** *n* : card game for 4 players
**bri•dle** *n* : headgear to control a horse ~ *vb* **1** : put a bridle on **2** : restrain **3** : show hostility or scorn
**brief** *adj* : short or concise ~ *n* : concise summary (as of a legal case) ~ *vb* : give final instructions or essential information to — **brief•ly** *adv* — **brief•ness** *n*
**brief•case** *n* : case for papers
[1]**bri•er** *n* : thorny plant
[2]**brier** *n* : heath of southern Europe
**bri•gade** *n* **1** : large military unit **2** : group organized for a special activity
**bright** *adj* **1** : radiating or reflecting light **2** : cheerful **3** : intelligent — **bright•en** *vb* — **bright•en•er** *n* — **bright•ly** *adv* — **bright•ness** *n*
**bril•liant** *adj* **1** : very bright **2** : splendid **3** : very intelligent — **bril•liance** *n* — **bril•lian•cy** *n* — **bril•liant•ly** *adv*
**brim** *n* : edge or rim ~ *vb* : be or become full — **brim•ful** *adj* — **brim•less** *adj* — **brimmed** *adj*
**brin•dled** *adj* : gray or tawny with dark streaks or flecks
**brine** *n* **1** : salt water **2** : ocean — **brin•i•ness** *n* — **briny** *adj*
**bring** *vb* **(brought; brought) 1** : cause to come with one **2** : persuade **3** : produce **4** : sell for — **bring•er** *n* — **bring about** *vb* : make happen — **bring up** *vb* **1** : care for and educate **2** : cause to be noticed
**brink** *n* : edge
**bri•quette, bri•quet** *n* : pressed mass (as of charcoal)
**brisk** *adj* **1** : lively **2** : invigorating — **brisk•ly** *adv* — **brisk•ness** *n*
**bris•ket** *n* : breast or lower chest of a quadruped
**bris•tle** *n* : short stiff hair ~ *vb* **1** : stand erect **2** : show angry defiance **3** : appear as if covered with bristles — **bris•tly** *adj*
**brit•tle** *adj* : easily broken — **brit•tle•ness** *n*
**broach** *n* : pointed tool (as for opening casks) ~ *vb* **1** : pierce (as a cask) to open **2** : introduce for discussion
**broad** *adj* **1** : wide **2** : spacious **3** : clear or open **4** : obvious **5** : tolerant in outlook **6** : widely applicable **7** : dealing with essential points — **broad•en** *vb* — **broad•ly** *adv* — **broad•ness** *n*
**broad•cast** *n* **1** : transmission by radio waves **2** : radio or television program ~ *vb* **1** : scatter or sow in all directions **2** : make widely known **3** : send out on a broadcast — **broad•cast•er** *n*
**broad–mind•ed** *adj* : tolerant of varied opinions — **broad–mind•ed•ly** *adv* — **broad–mind•ed•ness** *n*
**broad•side** *n* **1** : simultaneous firing of all guns on one side of a ship **2** : verbal attack
**broc•co•li** *n* : green vegetable akin to cauliflower
**bro•chure** *n* : pamphlet
**broil** *vb* : cook by radiant heat — **broil** *n*
**broil•er** *n* **1** : utensil for broiling **2** : chicken fit for broiling
[1]**broke** *past of* BREAK
[2]**broke** *adj* : out of money
**bro•ken** *adj* : imperfectly spoken — **bro•ken•ly** *adv*
**bro•ken•heart•ed** *adj* : overcome by grief or despair
**bro•ker** *n* : agent who buys and sells for a fee — **broker** *vb* — **bro•ker•age** *n*
**bron•chus** *n* : division of the windpipe leading to a lung — **bron•chi•al** *adj*
**bronze** *vb* : make bronze in color ~ *n* **1** : alloy of copper and tin **2** : yellowish brown — **bronzy** *adj*
**brooch** *n* : ornamental clasp or pin
**brood** *n* : family of young ~ *vb* **1** : sit on eggs to hatch them **2** : ponder ~ *adj* : kept for breeding — **brood•er** *n* — **brood•ing•ly** *adv*
[1]**brook** *vb* : tolerate
[2]**brook** *n* : small stream
**broom** *n* **1** : flowering shrub **2** : implement for sweeping — **broom•stick** *n*
**broth** *n* : liquid in which meat has been cooked
**broth•el** *n* : house of prostitutes
**broth•er** *n* **1** : male sharing one or both parents with another person **2** : kinsman — **broth•er•hood** *n* — **broth•er•li•ness** *n* — **broth•er•ly** *adj*
**broth•er–in–law** *n* **brothers–in–law** : brother of one's spouse or husband of one's sister or of one's spouse's sister
**brought** *past of* BRING
**brow** *n* **1** : eyebrow **2** : forehead **3** : edge of a steep place
**brow•beat** *vb* : intimidate
**brown** *adj* **1** : of the color brown **2** : of dark or tanned complexion ~ *n* : a color like that of coffee ~ *vb* : make or become brown — **brown•ish** *adj*
**browse** *vb* **1** : graze **2** : look over casually — **brows•er** *n*
**brows•er** *n* : computer program for accessing Web sites
**bruise** *vb* **1** : make a bruise on **2** : become bruised ~ *n* : surface injury to flesh
**brunch** *n* : late breakfast, early lunch, or combination of both
**bru•net, bru•nette** *adj* : having dark hair and usu. dark skin — **bru•net, brunette** *n*
[1]**brush** *n* **1** : small cut branches **2** : coarse shrubby vegetation
[2]**brush** *n* **1** : bristles set in a handle used esp. for cleaning or painting **2** : light touch ~ *vb* **1** : apply a brush to **2** : remove with or as if with a brush **3** : dismiss in an offhand way **4** : touch lightly — **brush up** *vb* : renew one's skill
**brush–off** *n* : curt dismissal
**brusque** *adj* : curt or blunt in manner — **brusque•ly** *adv*
**bru•tal** *adj* : like a brute and esp. cruel — **bru•tal•i•ty** *n* — **bru•tal•ize** *vb* — **bru•tal•ly** *adv*
**brute** *adj* **1** : relating to beasts **2** : unreasoning **3** : purely physical ~ *n* **1** : beast **2** : brutal person — **brut•ish** *adj*
**bub•ble** *vb* : form, rise in, or give off bubbles ~ *n* : globule of gas in or covered with a liquid — **bub•bly** *adj*
**buc•ca•neer** *n* : pirate
**buck** *n* **1** : male animal (as a deer) **2** : dollar ~ *vb* **1** : jerk forward **2** : oppose
**buck•et** *n* : pail — **buck•et•ful** *n*
**buck•le** *n* **1** : clasp (as on a belt) for two loose ends **2** : bend or fold ~ *vb* **1** : fasten with a buckle **2** : apply oneself **3** : bend or crumple
**buck•skin** *n* : soft leather (as from the skin of a buck) — **buckskin** *adj*
**buck•tooth** *n* : large projecting front tooth — **buck–toothed** *adj*
**buck•wheat** *n* : herb whose seeds are used as a cereal grain or the seeds themselves
**bud** *n* **1** : undeveloped plant shoot **2** : partly opened flower ~ *vb* **1** : form or put forth buds **2** : be or develop like a bud
**Bud•dhism** *n* : religion of eastern and central Asia — **Bud•dhist** *n or adj*
**bud•dy** *n* : friend
**budge** *vb* : move from a place
**bud•get** *n* **1** : estimate of income and expenses **2** : plan for coordinating income and expenses **3** : money available for a particular use — **budget** *vb or adj* — **bud•get•ary** *adj*
**buff** *n* **1** : yellow to orange yellow color **2** : enthusiast ~ *adj* : of the color buff ~ *vb* : polish
**buf•fa•lo** *n* : wild ox (as a bison)
[1]**buff•er** *n* : shield or protector
[2]**buffer** *n* : one that buffs
[1]**buf•fet** *n* : blow or slap ~ *vb* : hit esp. repeatedly
[2]**buf•fet** *n* : meal at which people serve themselves
**buf•foon** *n* : clown — **buf•foon•ery** *n*
**bug** *n* **1** : small usu. obnoxious crawling creature **2** : 4-winged sucking insect **3** : unexpected imperfection **4** : disease-producing germ **5** : hidden microphone ~ *vb* **1** : pester **2** : conceal a microphone in
**bug•gy** *n* : light carriage
**bu•gle** *n* : trumpetlike brass instrument — **bu•gler** *n*
**build** *vb* **(built; built) 1** : put together **2** : establish **3** : increase ~ *n* : physique — **build•er** *n*
**build•ing** *n* **1** : roofed and walled structure **2** : art or business of constructing buildings
**bulb** *n* **1** : large underground plant bud **2** : rounded or pear-shaped object — **bul•bous** *adj*
**bulge** *n* : swelling projecting part ~ *vb* : swell out
**bulk** *n* **1** : magnitude **2** : indigestible food material **3** : large mass **4** : major portion ~ *vb* : cause to swell or bulge — **bulky** *adj*
**bull** *n* : large adult male animal (as of cattle) ~ *adj* : male
**bull•dog** *n* : compact short-haired dog
**bull•doze** *vb* **1** : move or level with a tractor (**bull•doz•er**) having a broad blade **2** : force
**bul•let** *n* : missile to be shot from a gun — **bul•let•proof** *adj*
**bul•le•tin** *n* **1** : brief public report **2** : periodical
**bull•fight** *n* : sport of taunting and killing bulls — **bull•fight•er** *n*
**bull•frog** *n* : large deep-voiced frog
**bul•lion** *n* : gold or silver esp. in bars
**bull's–eye** *n* : center of a target
**bul•ly** *n* : one who hurts or intimidates others ~ *vb* : act like a bully toward
**bul•rush** *n* : tall coarse rush or sedge
**bul•wark** *n* **1** : wall-like defense **2** : strong support or protection
**bum** *vb* **1** : wander as a tramp **2** : get by begging ~ *n* : idle worthless person ~ *adj* : bad
**bum•ble•bee** *n* : large hairy bee
**bump** *vb* : strike or knock forcibly ~ *n* **1** : sudden blow **2** : small bulge or swelling — **bumpy** *adj*
[1]**bum•per** *adj* : unusually large
[2]**bump•er** *n* : shock-absorbing bar at either end of a car
**bump•kin** *n* : awkward country person
**bun** *n* : sweet biscuit or roll
**bunch** *n* : group ~ *vb* : form into a group — **bunchy** *adj*
**bun•dle** *n* **1** : several items bunched together **2** : something wrapped for carrying **3** : large amount ~ *vb* : gather into a bundle
**bun•ga•low** *n* : one-story house
**bun•gle** *vb* : do badly — **bungle** *n* — **bun•gler** *n*
**bun•ion** *n* : inflamed swelling of the first joint of the big toe
[1]**bunk** *n* : built-in bed that is often one of a tier ~ *vb* : sleep
[2]**bunk** *n* : nonsense
**bun•ker** *n* **1** : storage compartment **2** : protective embankment
**bun•ny** *n* : rabbit
[1]**bun•ting** *n* : small finch
[2]**bunting** *n* : flag material
**buoy** *n* : floating marker anchored in water ~ *vb* **1** : keep afloat **2** : raise the spirits of — **buoy•an•cy** *n* — **buoy•ant** *adj*
**bur, burr** *n* : rough or prickly covering of a fruit — **bur•ry** *adj*
**bur•den** *n* **1** : something carried **2** : something oppressive **3** : cargo ~ *vb* : load or oppress — **bur•den•some** *adj*
**bu•reau** *n* **1** : chest of drawers **2** : administrative unit **3** : business office
**bu•reau•cra•cy** *n* **1** : body of government officials **2** : unwieldy administrative system — **bu•reau•crat** *n* — **bu•reau•crat•ic** *adj*
**bur•geon** *vb* : grow
**bur•glary** *n* : forcible entry into a building to steal — **bur•glar** *n* — **bur•glar•ize** *vb*
**Bur•gun•dy** *n* : kind of table wine
**buri•al** *n* : act of burying
**bur•lap** *n* : coarse fabric usu. of jute or hemp
**bur•lesque** *n* **1** : witty or derisive imitation **2** : broadly humorous variety show ~ *vb* : mock
**bur•ly** *adj* : strongly and heavily built
**burn** *vb* **1** : be on fire **2** : feel or look as if on fire **3** : alter or become altered by or as if by fire or heat **4** : cause or make by fire ~ *n* : injury or effect produced by burning — **burn•er** *n*
**bur•nish** *vb* : polish
**burp** *n or vb* : belch
**bur•ro** *n* : small donkey
**bur•row** *n* : hole in the ground made by an animal ~ *vb* : make a burrow — **bur•row•er** *n*
**bur•si•tis** *n* : inflammation of a sac (**bur•sa** ) in a joint
**burst** *vb* **1** : fly apart or into pieces **2** : enter or emerge suddenly ~ *n* : sudden outbreak or effort
**bury** *vb* **1** : deposit in the earth **2** : hide
**bus** *n* : large motor-driven passenger vehicle ~ *vb* : travel or transport by bus
**bus•boy** *n* : waiter's helper
**bush** *n* **1** : shrub **2** : rough uncleared country **3** : a thick tuft or mat — **bushy** *adj*
**bush•el** *n* : 4 pecks
**bush•ing** *n* : metal lining used as a guide or bearing
**busi•ness** *n* **1** : vocation **2** : commercial or industrial enterprise **3** : personal

concerns — **busi·ness·man** n — **busi·ness·wom·an** n

¹**bust** n 1 : sculpture of the head and upper torso 2 : breasts of a woman

²**bust** vb 1 : burst or break 2 : tame ~ n 1 : punch 2 : failure

**bus·tle** vb : move or work briskly ~ n : energetic activity

**busy** adj 1 : engaged in action 2 : being in use 3 : full of activity ~ vb : make or keep busy — **busi·ly** adv

**busy·body** n : meddler

**but** conj 1 : if not for the fact 2 : that 3 : without the certainty that 4 : rather 5 : yet ~ prep : other than

**butch·er** n 1 : one who slaughters animals or dresses their flesh 2 : brutal killer 3 : bungler — **butcher** vb — **butch·ery** n

**but·ler** n : chief male household servant

¹**butt** vb : strike with a butt ~ n : blow with the head or horns

²**butt** n 1 : target 2 : victim

³**butt** vb : join edge to edge

⁴**butt** n : large end or bottom

**butte** n : isolated steep hill

**but·ter** n : solid edible fat churned from cream ~ vb : spread with butter — **but·ter·fat** n — **but·ter·milk** n — **but·tery** adj

**but·ter·cup** n : yellow-flowered herb

**but·ter·fly** n : insect with 4 broad wings

**but·ter·nut** n : edible nut of a tree related to the walnut or this tree

**but·ter·scotch** n : candy made from sugar, corn syrup, and water

**but·tocks** n pl : rear part of the hips

**but·ton** n 1 : small knob for fastening clothing 2 : buttonlike object ~ vb : fasten with buttons

**but·ton·hole** n : hole or slit for a button ~ vb : hold in talk

**but·tress** n 1 : projecting structure to support a wall 2 : support — **buttress** vb

**bux·om** adj : having a large bosom

**buy** vb (**bought; bought**) : purchase ~ n : bargain — **buy·er** n

**buzz** vb : make a low humming sound ~ n : act or sound of buzzing

**buz·zard** n : large bird of prey

**buzz·er** n : signaling device that buzzes

**buzz·word** n : word or phrase in current popular use

**by** prep 1 : near 2 : through 3 : beyond 4 : throughout 5 : no later than ~ adv 1 : near 2 : farther

**by·gone** adj : past — **bygone** n

**by·law, bye·law** n : organization's rule

**by·line** n : writer's name on an article

**by·pass** n : alternate route ~ vb : go around

**by–prod·uct** n : product in addition to the main product

**by·stand·er** n : spectator

**by·way** n : side road

**by·word** n : proverb

# C

**c** n : 3d letter of the alphabet

**cab** n 1 : light closed horse-drawn carriage 2 : taxi 3 : compartment for a driver — **cab·bie, cab·by** n — **cab·stand** n

**ca·bana** n : shelter at a beach or pool

**cab·bage** n : vegetable with a dense head of leaves

**cab·in** n 1 : private room on a ship 2 : small house 3 : airplane compartment

**cab·i·net** n 1 : display case or cupboard 2 : advisory council of a head of state — **cab·i·net·mak·er** n — **cab·i·net·mak·ing** n — **cab·i·net·work** n

**ca·ble** n 1 : strong rope, wire, or chain 2 : telegram sent through a cable under the sea 3 : bundle of electrical wires ~ vb : send a cablegram to

**ca·cao** n : So. American tree whose seeds (**cacao beans**) yield cocoa and chocolate

**cack·le** vb : make a cry or laugh like the sound of a hen — **cackle** n — **cack·ler** n

**cac·tus** n : drought-resistant flowering plant with scales or prickles

**ca·dav·er** n : dead body — **ca·dav·er·ous** adj

**cad·die, cad·dy** n : golfer's helper — **caddie, caddy** vb

**ca·det** n : student in a military academy

**ca·fé** n : restaurant

**caf·e·te·ria** n : self-service restaurant

**cage** n : box of wire or bars for confining an animal ~ vb : put or keep in a cage

**cake** n 1 : food of baked or fried usu. sweet batter 2 : compacted mass ~ vb 1 : form into a cake 2 : encrust

**ca·lam·i·ty** n : disaster — **ca·lam·i·tous** adj — **ca·lam·i·tous·ly** adv

**cal·cu·late** vb 1 : determine by mathematical processes 2 : judge — **cal·cu·la·ble** adj — **cal·cu·la·tion** n — **cal·cu·la·tor** n

**cal·cu·lat·ing** adj : shrewd

**cal·en·dar** n : list of days, weeks, and months

¹**calf** n calves : young cow or related mammal — **calf·skin** n

²**calf** n calves : back part of the leg below the knee

**cal·i·brate** vb : adjust precisely — **cal·i·bra·tion** n

**cal·is·then·ics** n sing or pl : stretching and jumping exercises — **cal·is·then·ic** adj

**call** vb 1 : shout 2 : summon 3 : demand 4 : telephone 5 : make a visit 6 : name — **call** n — **call·er** n — **call down** vb : reprimand — **call off** vb : cancel

**call·ing** n : vocation

**cal·li·ope** n : musical instrument of steam whistles

**cal·lous** adj 1 : thickened and hardened 2 : without apparent feelings ~ vb : make callous — **cal·los·i·ty** n — **cal·lous·ly** adv — **cal·lous·ness** n

**cal·lus** n : callous area on skin or bark ~ vb : form a callus

**calm** n 1 : period or condition of peace-fulness or stillness ~ adj : still or tranquil ~ vb : make calm — **calm·ly** adv — **calm·ness** n

**cal·o·rie** n : unit for measuring heat and energy value of food

**calves** pl of CALF

**cam** n : machine part that slides or rotates irregularly to transmit linear motion

**came** past of COME

**cam·el** n : large hoofed mammal of desert areas

**cam·eo** n : gem carved in relief

**cam·era** n : box with a lens for taking pictures — **cam·era·man** n

**cam·ou·flage** vb : hide by disguising — **camouflage** n

**camp** n 1 : place to stay temporarily esp. in a tent 2 : group living in a camp ~ vb : make or live in a camp — **camp·er** n — **camp·ground** n — **camp·site** n

**cam·paign** n : series of military operations or of activities meant to gain a result — **campaign** vb

**cam·pus** n : grounds and buildings of a college or school

¹**can** vb, (past **could**) 1 : be able to 2 : be permitted to by conscience or feeling 3 : have permission or liberty to

²**can** n : metal container ~ vb : preserve by sealing in airtight cans or jars — **can·ner** n — **can·nery** n

**ca·nal** n 1 : tubular passage in the body 2 : channel filled with water

**ca·nary** n : yellow or greenish finch often kept as a pet

**can·cel** vb 1 : cross out 2 : destroy, neutralize, or match the force or effect of — **cancel** n — **can·cel·la·tion** n — **can·cel·er, can·cel·ler** n

**can·cer** n 1 : malignant tumor that tends to spread 2 : slowly destructive evil — **can·cer·ous** adj — **can·cer·ous·ly** adv

**can·did** adj 1 : frank 2 : not posed — **can·did·ly** adv — **can·did·ness** n

**can·di·date** n : one who seeks an office or membership — **can·di·da·cy** n

**can·dle** n : tallow or wax molded around a wick and burned to give light — **can·dle·light** n — **can·dle·stick** n

**can·dy** n : food made from sugar ~ vb : encrust in sugar

**cane** n 1 : slender plant stem 2 : a tall woody grass or reed 3 : stick for walking or beating ~ vb 1 : beat with a cane 2 : weave or make with cane — **can·er** n

**ca·nine** adj : relating to dogs ~ n 1 : pointed tooth next to the incisors 2 : dog

**can·is·ter** n : cylindrical container

**can·ker** n : mouth ulcer — **can·ker·ous** adj

**can·ni·bal** n : human or animal that eats its own kind — **can·ni·bal·ism** n — **can·ni·bal·is·tic** adj — **can·ni·bal·ize** vb

**can·non** n : large heavy gun — **can·non·ball** n — **can·non·eer** n

**can·not** : can not — **cannot but** : be bound to

**ca·noe** n : narrow sharp-ended boat propelled by paddles — **canoe** vb — **ca·noe·ist** n

¹**can·on** n 1 : regulation governing a church 2 : authoritative list 3 : an accepted principle

²**canon** n : clergy member in a cathedral — **ca·non·i·cal** adj — **ca·non·i·cal·ly** adv

**can·on·ize** vb : recognize as a saint — **can·on·i·za·tion** n

**can·o·py** n : overhanging cover — **canopy** vb

**can't** : can not

**can·ta·loupe** n : muskmelon with orange flesh

**can·teen** n 1 : place of recreation for service personnel 2 : water container

**can·tor** n : synagogue official who sings liturgical music

**can·vas** n 1 : strong cloth orig. used for making tents and sails 2 : set of sails 3 : oil painting

**can·vass** vb : solicit votes, orders, or opinions from ~ n : act of canvassing — **can·vass·er** n

**can·yon** n : deep valley with steep sides

**cap** n 1 : covering for the head 2 : top or cover like a cap 3 : upper limit ~ vb 1 : provide or protect with a cap 2 : climax — **cap·ful** n

**ca·pa·ble** adj : able to do something — **ca·pa·bil·i·ty** n — **ca·pa·bly** adv

**ca·pac·i·ty** n 1 : ability to contain 2 : volume 3 : ability 4 : role or job ~ adj : equaling maximum capacity

¹**cape** n : point of land jutting out into water

²**cape** n : garment that drapes over the shoulders

**cap·il·lary** adj 1 : resembling a hair 2 : having a very small bore ~ n : tiny thin-walled blood vessel

¹**cap·i·tal** adj 1 : punishable by death 2 : being in the series A, B, C rather than a, b, c 3 : relating to capital 4 : excellent ~ n 1 : capital letter 2 : seat of government 3 : wealth 4 : total face value of a company's stock 5 : investors as a group — **cap·i·tal·ize** vb — **cap·i·tal·i·za·tion** n

²**capital** n : top part of a column

**cap·i·tal·ism** n : economic system of private ownership of capital — **cap·i·tal·ist** n or adj — **cap·i·tal·is·tic** adj

**cap·i·tol** n : building in which a legislature sits

**cap·size** vb : overturn

**cap·sule** n 1 : enveloping cover (as for medicine) 2 : small pressurized compartment for astronauts ~ adj : very brief or compact — **cap·su·lar** adj — **cap·su·lat·ed** adj

**cap·tain** n 1 : commander of a body of troops 2 : officer in charge of a ship 3 : commissioned officer in the navy ranking next below a rear admiral or a commodore 4 : commissioned officer (as in the army) ranking next below a major 5 : leader ~ vb : be captain of — **cap·tain·cy** n

**cap·tion** n 1 : title 2 : explanation with an illustration — **caption** vb

**cap·ti·vate** vb : attract and charm — **cap·ti·va·tion** n — **cap·ti·va·tor** n

**cap·tive** adj 1 : made prisoner 2 : confined or under control — **captive** n — **cap·tiv·i·ty** n

**cap·tor** n : one that captures

**cap·ture** n : seizure by force or trickery ~ vb : take captive

**car** n 1 : vehicle moved on wheels 2 : cage of an elevator

**car·a·mel** n 1 : burnt sugar used for flavoring and coloring 2 : firm chewy candy

**car·bo·hy·drate** n : compound of carbon, hydrogen, and oxygen

**car·bon** n 1 : chemical element occurring in nature esp. as diamond and graphite 2 : piece of carbon paper or a copy made with it

**car·bon·ate** vb : impregnate with carbon dioxide — **car·bon·ation** n

**car·cin·o·gen** n : agent causing cancer — **car·ci·no·gen·ic** adj

**card** n 1 : playing card 2 pl : game played with playing cards 3 : small flat piece of paper

**card·board** n : stiff material like paper

**car·di·ac** adj : relating to the heart

**car·di·nal** n 1 : official of the Roman Catholic Church 2 : bright red songbird

**cardinal number** n : number (as 1, 82, 357) used in counting

**car·di·ol·o·gy** n : study of the heart — **car·di·ol·o·gist** n

**care** n 1 : anxiety 2 : watchful attention 3 : supervision ~ vb 1 : feel anxiety or concern 2 : like 3 : provide care — **care·free** adj — **care·ful** adj — **care·ful·ly** adv — **care·ful·ness** n — **care·giv·er** n — **care·less** adj — **care·less·ly** adv — **care·less·ness** n

**ca·reer** n : vocation ~ vb : go at top speed

**ca·ress** n : tender touch ~ vb : touch lovingly or tenderly

**car·go** n : transported goods

**car·i·ca·ture** n : distorted representation for humor or ridicule — **caricature** vb — **car·i·ca·tur·ist** n

**car·na·tion** n : showy flower

**car·ni·val** n 1 : festival 2 : traveling enterprise offering amusements

**car·ni·vore** n : flesh-eating animal — **car·niv·o·rous** adj — **car·niv·o·rous·ly** adv — **car·niv·o·rous·ness** n

**car·ol** n : song of joy — **carol** vb — **car·ol·er, car·ol·ler** n

**car·ou·sel, car·rou·sel** n : merry-go-round

**car·pen·ter** n : one who builds with wood — **carpenter** vb — **car·pen·try** n

**car·pet** n : fabric floor covering ~ vb : cover with a carpet — **car·pet·ing** n

**car·riage** n 1 : conveyance 2 : manner of holding oneself 3 : wheeled vehicle

**car·rot** *n* : orange root vegetable

**car·ry** *vb* **1** : move while supporting **2** : hold (oneself) in a specified way **3** : support **4** : keep in stock **5** : reach to a distance **6** : win — **car·ri·er** *n* — **carry on** *vb* **1** : conduct **2** : behave excitedly — **carry out** *vb* : put into effect

**cart** *n* : wheeled vehicle ~ *vb* : carry in a cart — **cart·age** *n* — **cart·er** *n*

**car·ti·lage** *n* : elastic skeletal tissue — **car·ti·lag·i·nous** *adj*

**car·ton** *n* : cardboard box

**car·toon** *n* **1** : humorous drawing **2** : comic strip — **cartoon** *vb* — **car·toon·ist** *n*

**car·tridge** *n* **1** : tube containing powder and a bullet or shot for a firearm **2** : container of material for insertion into an apparatus

**carve** *vb* **1** : cut with care **2** : cut into pieces or slices — **carv·er** *n*

**cas·cade** *n* : small steep waterfall ~ *vb* : fall in a cascade

¹**case** *n* **1** : particular instance **2** : convincing argument **3** : inflectional form esp. of a noun or pronoun **4** : fact **5** : lawsuit **6** : instance of disease — **in case** : as a precaution — **in case of** : in the event of

²**case** *n* **1** : box **2** : outer covering ~ *vb* **1** : enclose **2** : inspect

**cash** *n pl* **cash 1** : ready money **2** : money paid at the time of purchase ~ *vb* : give or get cash for

**ca·shew** *n* : tropical American tree or its nut

**cash·ier** *n* : person who receives and records payments

**cash·mere** *n* : fine goat's wool or a fabric of this

**ca·si·no** *n* : place for gambling

**cas·ket** *n* : coffin

**cas·se·role** *n* : baking dish or the food cooked in this

**cas·sette** *n* : case containing magnetic tape

**cast** *vb* (**cast; cast**) **1** : throw **2** : deposit (a ballot) **3** : assign parts in a play **4** : mold ~ *n* **1** : throw **2** : appearance **3** : rigid surgical dressing **4** : actors in a play

**cast·er** *n* : small wheel on furniture

**cas·tle** *n* : fortified building

**ca·su·al** *adj* **1** : happening by chance **2** : showing little concern **3** : informal — **ca·su·al·ly** *adv* — **ca·su·al·ness** *n*

**ca·su·al·ty** *n* **1** : serious or fatal accident **2** : one injured, lost, or destroyed

**cat** *n* **1** : small domestic mammal **2** : related animal (as a lion) — **cat·like** *adj*

**cat·a·log, cat·a·logue** *n* **1** : list **2** : book containing a description of items ~ *vb* **1** : make a catalog of **2** : enter in a catalog — **cat·a·log·er, cat·a·logu·er** *n*

**cat·a·pult** *n* : device for hurling or launching — **catapult** *vb*

**ca·tas·tro·phe** *n* **1** : great disaster or misfortune **2** : utter failure — **cat·a·stroph·ic** *adj* — **cat·a·stroph·i·cal·ly** *adv*

**catch** *vb* **caught; caught 1** : capture esp. after pursuit **2** : trap **3** : detect esp. by surprise **4** : grasp **5** : get entangled **6** : become affected with or by **7** : seize and hold firmly ~ *n* **1** : act of catching **2** : something caught **3** : something that fastens **4** : hidden difficulty — **catch·er** *n*

**catch·ing** *adj* : infectious

**catchy** *adj* : likely to catch interest

**cat·e·chism** *n* : set of questions and answers esp. to teach religious doctrine

**cat·e·go·ry** *n* : group or class — **cat·e·go·ri·za·tion** *n* — **cat·e·go·rize** *vb*

**ca·ter** *vb* **1** : provide food for **2** : supply what is wanted — **ca·ter·er** *n*

**cat·er·cor·ner, cat·er·cor·nered** *adv or adj* : in a diagonal position

**cat·er·pil·lar** *n* : butterfly or moth larva

**ca·the·dral** *n* : principal church of a diocese

**Cath·o·lic** *n* : member of the Roman Catholic Church — **Ca·thol·i·cism** *n*

**cat·tle** *n pl* : domestic bovines — **cat·tle·man** *n*

**cat·ty** *adj* : mean or spiteful — **cat·ti·ly** *adv* — **cat·ti·ness** *n*

**Cau·ca·sian** *adj* : relating to the white race — **Caucasian** *n*

**caught** *past of* CATCH

**cau·li·flow·er** *n* : vegetable having a compact head of usu. white undeveloped flowers

**caulk** *vb* : make seams watertight — **caulk** *n* — **caulk·er** *n*

**cause** *n* **1** : something that brings about a result **2** : reason **3** : lawsuit **4** : principle or movement to support ~ *vb* : be the cause of — **caus·al** *adj* — **cau·sal·i·ty** *n* — **caus·al·ly** *adv* — **cau·sa·tion** *n* — **caus·ative** *adj* — **cause·less** *adj* — **caus·er** *n*

**caus·tic** *adj* **1** : corrosive **2** : sharp or biting — **caustic** *n*

**cau·tion** *n* **1** : warning **2** : care or prudence ~ *vb* : warn — **cau·tion·ary** *adj*

**cau·tious** *adj* : taking caution — **cau·tious·ly** *adv* — **cau·tious·ness** *n*

**cave** *n* : natural underground chamber — **cave in** *vb* : collapse

**cav·ern** *n* : large cave — **cav·ern·ous** *adj* — **cav·ern·ous·ly** *adv*

**cav·i·ar, cav·i·are** *n* : salted fish roe

**cav·i·ty** *n* **1** : unfilled place within a mass **2** : decay in a tooth

**CD** *n* : compact disc

**cease** *vb* : stop — **cease·less** *adj*

**ce·dar** *n* : cone-bearing tree with fragrant durable wood

**ceil·ing** *n* **1** : overhead surface of a room **2** : upper limit

**cel·e·brate** *vb* **1** : perform with appropriate rites **2** : honor with ceremonies **3** : praise highly — **cel·e·brant** *n* — **cel·e·bra·tion** *n* — **cel·e·bra·tor** *n*

**cel·e·brat·ed** *adj* : renowned

**ce·leb·ri·ty** *n* **1** : renown **2** : well-known person

**cel·ery** *n* : herb grown for crisp edible stalks

**ce·les·tial** *adj* **1** : relating to the sky **2** : heavenly

**cell** *n* **1** : small room **2** : tiny mass of protoplasm that forms the fundamental unit of living matter **3** : container holding an electrolyte for generating electricity — **celled** *adj*

**cel·lar** *n* : room or area below ground

**cel·lo** *n* : bass member of the violin family — **cel·list** *n*

**cell phone** *n* : portable cordless telephone

**cel·lu·lar** *adj* : relating to or consisting of cells

**Cel·sius** *adj* : relating to a thermometer scale on which the freezing point of water is 0° and the boiling point is 100°

**ce·ment** *n* **1** : powdery mixture of clay and limestone that hardens when wetted **2** : binding agent ~ *vb* : unite or cover with cement

**cem·e·tery** *n* : burial ground

**cen·sor** *n* : one with power to suppress anything objectionable (as in printed matter) ~ *vb* : be a censor of — **cen·so·ri·al** *adj* — **cen·sor·ship** *n*

**cen·sure** *n* : official reprimand ~ *vb* : find blameworthy — **cen·sur·able** *adj*

**cen·sus** *n* : periodic population count — **census** *vb*

**cent** *n* : monetary unit equal to ¹/₁₀₀ of a basic unit of value

**cen·ten·ni·al** *n* : 100th anniversary — **centennial** *adj*

**cen·ter** *n* **1** : middle point **2** : point of origin or greatest concentration **3** : region of concentrated population **4** : player near the middle of the team ~ *vb* **1** : place, fix, or concentrate at or around a center **2** : have a center — **cen·ter·piece** *n*

**cen·ti·grade** *adj* : Celsius

**cen·ti·me·ter** *n* : ¹/₁₀₀ meter

**cen·ti·pede** *n* : long flat many-legged arthropod

**cen·tral** *adj* **1** : constituting or being near a center **2** : essential or principal — **cen·tral·ly** *adv*

**cen·tral·ize** *vb* : bring to a central point or under central control — **cen·tral·i·za·tion** *n* — **cen·tral·iz·er** *n*

**cen·tri·fuge** *n* : machine that separates substances by spinning

**cen·tu·ry** *n* : 100 years

**ce·ram·ic** *n* **1** *pl* : art or process of shaping and hardening articles from clay **2** : product of ceramics — **ceramic** *adj*

**ce·re·al** *adj* : made of or relating to grain or to the plants that produce it ~ *n* **1** : grass yielding edible grain **2** : food prepared from a cereal grain

**cer·e·bel·lum** *n* : part of the brain controlling muscular coordination — **cer·e·bel·lar** *adj*

**ce·re·bral** *adj* **1** : relating to the brain, intellect, or cerebrum **2** : appealing to the intellect

**ce·re·brum** *n* : part of the brain that contains the higher nervous centers

**cer·e·mo·ny** *n* **1** : formal act prescribed by law, ritual, or convention **2** : prescribed procedures — **cer·e·mo·ni·al** *adj or n* — **cer·e·mo·ni·ous** *adj*

**cer·tain** *adj* **1** : settled **2** : true **3** : specific but not named **4** : bound **5** : assured ~ *pron* : certain ones — **cer·tain·ly** *adv* — **cer·tain·ty** *n*

**cer·tif·i·cate** *n* : document establishing truth or fulfillment

**cer·ti·fy** *vb* **1** : verify **2** : endorse — **cer·ti·fi·able** *adj* — **cer·ti·fi·ably** *adv* — **cer·ti·fi·ca·tion** *n* — **cer·ti·fi·er** *n*

**chafe** *vb* **1** : fret **2** : make sore by rubbing

**chain** *n* **1** : flexible series of connected links **2** *pl* : something that restrains **3** : linked series ~ *vb* : bind or connect with a chain

**chair** *n* **1** : seat with a back **2** : position of authority or dignity **3** : presiding officer ~ *vb* : act as presiding officer of — **chair·man** *n* — **chair·man·ship** *n* — **chair·wom·an** *n*

**chalk** *n* **1** : soft limestone **2** : chalky material used as a crayon ~ *vb* : mark with chalk — **chalky** *adj* — **chalk up** *vb* **1** : credit **2** : achieve

**chalk·board** *n* : blackboard

**chal·lenge** *vb* **1** : dispute **2** : invite or dare to act or compete — **challenge** *n* — **chal·leng·er** *n*

**cham·ber** *n* **1** : room **2** : enclosed space **3** : legislative meeting place or body **4** *pl* : judge's consultation room — **cham·bered** *adj*

**champ** *n* : champion

**cham·pagne** *n* : sparkling white wine

**cham·pi·on** *n* **1** : advocate or defender **2** : winning contestant ~ *vb* : protect or fight for — **cham·pi·on·ship** *n*

**chance** *n* **1** : element of existence that cannot be predicted **2** : opportunity **3** : probability **4** : risk **5** : raffle ticket ~ *vb* **1** : happen **2** : encounter unexpectedly **3** : risk — **chance** *adj*

**chan·de·lier** *n* : hanging lighting fixture

**change** *vb* **1** : make or become different **2** : exchange **3** : give or receive change for ~ *n* **1** : a changing **2** : excess from a payment **3** : money in smaller denominations **4** : coins — **change·able** *adj* — **change·less** *adj* — **chang·er** *n*

**chan·nel** *n* **1** : deeper part of a waterway **2** : means of passage or communication **3** : strait **4** : broadcast frequency ~ *vb* : make or direct through a channel

**chant** *vb* : sing or speak in one tone — **chant** *n* — **chant·er** *n*

**Cha·nu·kah** *var of* HANUKKAH

**cha·os** *n* : complete disorder — **cha·ot·ic** *adj* — **cha·ot·i·cal·ly** *adv*

¹**chap** *n* : fellow

²**chap** *vb* : dry and crack open usu. from wind and cold

**cha·pel** *n* : private or small place of worship

**chap·er·one, chap·er·on** : older person who accompanies young people at a social gathering ~ *vb* : act as chaperon at or for — **chap·er·on·age** *n*

**chap·lain** *n* : clergy member in a military unit or a prison — **chap·lain·cy** *n*

**chap·ter** *n* **1** : main book division **2** : branch of a society

**char·ac·ter** *n* **1** : letter or graphic mark **2** : trait or distinctive combination of traits **3** : peculiar person **4** : fictional person — **char·ac·ter·i·za·tion** *n* — **char·ac·ter·ize** *vb*

**char·ac·ter·is·tic** *adj* : typical ~ *n* : distinguishing quality — **char·ac·ter·is·ti·cal·ly** *adv*

**char·coal** *n* : porous carbon prepared by partial combustion

**charge** *vb* **1** : give an electric charge to **2** : impose a task or responsibility on **3** : command **4** : accuse **5** : rush forward in assault **6** : assume a debt for **7** : fix as a price ~ *n* **1** : excess or deficiency of electrons in a body **2** : tax **3** : responsibility **4** : accusation **5** : cost **6** : attack — **charge·able** *adj*

**char·i·ot** *n* : ancient 2-wheeled vehicle — **char·i·o·teer** *n*

**cha·ris·ma** *n* : special ability to lead — **char·is·mat·ic** *adj*

**char·i·ty** *n* **1** : love for mankind **2** : generosity or leniency **3** : alms **4** : institution for relief of the needy — **char·i·ta·ble** *adj* — **char·i·ta·ble·ness** *n* — **char·i·ta·bly** *adv*

**charm** *n* **1** : something with magic power **2** : appealing trait **3** : small ornament ~ *vb* : fascinate — **charm·er** *n* — **charm·ing** *adj* — **charm·ing·ly** *adv*

**chart** *n* **1** : map **2** : diagram ~ *vb* **1** : make a chart of **2** : plan

**char·ter** *n* **1** : document granting rights **2** : constitution ~ *vb* **1** : establish by charter **2** : rent — **char·ter·er** *n*

**chase** *vb* **1** : follow trying to catch **2** : drive away — **chase** *n* — **chas·er** *n*

**chasm** *n* : gorge

**chaste** *adj* **1** : abstaining from all or unlawful sexual relations **2** : modest or decent **3** : severely simple — **chaste·ly** *adv* — **chaste·ness** *n* — **chas·ti·ty** *n*

**chas·tise** *vb* **1** : punish **2** : censure — **chas·tise·ment** *n*

**chat** *n* : informal talk — **chat** *vb* — **chat·ty** *adj*

**chat·ter** *vb* **1** : utter rapidly succeeding sounds **2** : talk fast or too much — **chatter** *n* — **chat·ter·er** *n*

**chauf·feur** *n* : hired car driver ~ *vb* : work as a chauffeur

**cheap** *adj* **1** : not expensive **2** : shoddy — **cheap** *adv* — **cheap·en** *vb* — **cheap·ly** *adv* — **cheap·ness** *n*

**cheap·skate** *n* : stingy person

**cheat** *n* **1** : act of deceiving **2** : one that cheats ~ *vb* **1** : deprive through fraud or deceit **2** : violate rules dishonestly — **cheat·er** *n*

**check** *n* **1** : sudden stoppage **2** : restraint **3** : test or standard for testing **4** : written order to a bank to pay money **5** : ticket showing ownership **6** : slip showing an amount due **7** : pattern in squares or fabric in such a pattern **8** : mark placed beside an item noted ~ *vb* **1** : slow down or stop **2** : restrain **3** : compare or correspond with a source or original **4** : inspect or test for condition **5** : mark with a check **6** : leave or accept for safekeeping or shipment **7** : checker — **check in** *vb* : report one's arrival — **check out** *vb* : settle one's account and leave

¹**check·er** *n* : piece in checkers ~ *vb* : mark with different colors or into squares

²**checker** *n* : one that checks

**check·ers** *n* : game for 2 played on a checkerboard — **check·er·board** *n*

**check·mate** *vb* : thwart completely — **checkmate** *n*

**check•up** *n* : physical examination

**ched•dar** *n* : hard smooth cheese

**cheek** *n* **1** : fleshy side part of the face **2** : impudence — **cheeked** *adj* — **cheeky** *adj*

**cheer** *n* **1** : good spirits **2** : food and drink for a feast **3** : shout of applause or encouragement ~ *vb* **1** : give hope or courage to **2** : make or become glad **3** : urge on or applaud with shouts — **cheer•er** *n* — **cheer•ful** *adj* — **cheer•ful•ly** *adv* — **cheer•ful•ness** *n* — **cheer•lead•er** *n* — **cheer•less** *adj* — **cheer•less•ly** *adv* — **cheer•less•ness** *n*

**cheery** *adj* : cheerful — **cheer•i•ly** *adv* — **cheer•i•ness** *n*

**cheese** *n* : curd of milk usu. pressed and cured — **cheesy** *adj*

**chef** *n* : chief cook

**chem•i•cal** *adj* **1** : relating to chemistry **2** : working or produced by chemicals ~ *n* : substance obtained by chemistry — **chem•i•cal•ly** *adv*

**chem•ist** *n* : one trained in chemistry

**chem•is•try** *n* : science that deals with the composition and properties of substances

**che•mo•ther•a•py** *n* : use of chemicals in the treatment of disease — **che•mo•ther•a•peu•tic** *adj*

**cher•ish** *vb* : hold dear

**cher•ry** *n* : small fleshy fruit of a tree related to the roses or the tree or its wood

**cher•ub** *n* **1** *pl* **cher•u•bim** : angel **2** *pl* **cher•ubs** : chubby child — **che•ru•bic** *adj*

**chess** *n* : game for 2 played on a checkerboard — **chess•board** *n* — **chess•man** *n*

**chest** *n* **1** : boxlike container **2** : part of the body enclosed by the ribs and breastbone — **chest•ed** *adj*

**chest•nut** *n* : nut of a tree related to the beech or the tree

**chew** *vb* : crush or grind with the teeth ~ *n* : something to chew — **chew•able** *adj* — **chew•er** *n* — **chewy** *adj*

**chic** *n* : smart elegance of dress or manner ~ *adj* **1** : stylish **2** : currently fashionable

**chick** *n* : young chicken or bird

**chick•a•dee** *n* : small grayish American bird

**chick•en** *n* **1** : common domestic fowl or its flesh used as food **2** : coward

**chief** *n* : leader ~ *adj* **1** : highest in rank **2** : most important — **chief•dom** *n* — **chief•ly** *adv*

**child** *n* **chil•dren 1** : unborn or recently born person **2** : son or daughter — **child•bear•ing** *n or adj* — **child•birth** *n* — **child•hood** *n* — **child•ish** *adj* — **child•ish•ly** *adv* — **child•ish•ness** *n* — **child•less** *adj* — **child•less•ness** *n* — **child•like** *adj* — **child•proof** *adj*

**chili, chile, chil•li** *n* **1** : hot pepper **2** : spicy stew of ground beef, chilies, and beans

**chill** *vb* : make or become cold or chilly ~ *adj* : moderately cold ~ *n* **1** : feeling of coldness with shivering **2** : moderate coldness

**chilly** *adj* : noticeably cold — **chill•i•ness** *n*

**chime** *n* : set of tuned bells or their sound ~ *vb* : make bell-like sounds — **chime in** *vb* : break into or join in a conversation

**chim•ney** *n* **1** : passage for smoke **2** : glass tube around a lamp flame

**chimp** *n* : chimpanzee

**chim•pan•zee** *n* : small ape

**chin** *n* : part of the face below the mouth — **chin•less** *adj*

**chi•na** *n* **1** : porcelain ware **2** : domestic pottery

**chip** *n* **1** : small thin flat piece cut or broken off **2** : thin crisp morsel of food **3** : counter used in games **4** : flaw where a chip came off **5** : small slice of semiconductor containing electronic circuits ~ *vb* : cut or break chips from — **chip in** *vb* : contribute

**chip•munk** *n* : small striped ground-dwelling rodent

**chip•per** *adj* : lively and cheerful

**chi•ro•prac•tic** *n* : system of healing based esp. on manipulation of body structures — **chi•ro•prac•tor** *n*

**chirp** *n* : short sharp sound like that of a bird or cricket — **chirp** *vb*

**chis•el** *n* : sharp-edged metal tool ~ *vb* **1** : work with a chisel **2** : cheat — **chis•el•er** *n*

**chit•chat** *n* : casual conversation — **chitchat** *vb*

**chiv•al•ry** *n* **1** : system or practices of knighthood **2** : spirit or character of the ideal knight — **chi•val•ric** *adj* — **chiv•al•rous** *adj* — **chiv•al•rous•ly** *adv* — **chiv•al•rous•ness** *n*

**chive** *n* : herb related to the onion

**chlo•rine** *n* : chemical element that is a heavy strong-smelling greenish yellow irritating gas

**chlo•ro•phyll** *n* : green coloring matter of plants

**chock** *n* : wedge for blocking the movement of a wheel — **chock** *vb*

**chock–full** *adj* : full to the limit

**choc•o•late** *n* **1** : ground roasted cacao beans or a beverage made from them **2** : candy made of or with chocolate **3** : dark brown

**choice** *n* **1** : act or power of choosing **2** : one selected **3** : variety offered for selection ~ *adj* **1** : worthy of being chosen **2** : selected with care **3** : of high quality

**choir** *n* : group of singers esp. in church — **choir•boy** *n* — **choir•mas•ter** *n*

**choke** *vb* **1** : hinder breathing **2** : clog or obstruct ~ *n* **1** : a choking or sound of choking **2** : valve for controlling air intake in a gasoline engine

**cho•les•ter•ol** *n* : waxy substance in animal tissues

**choose** *vb* (**chose; cho•sen**) **1** : select after consideration **2** : decide **3** : prefer — **choos•er** *n* — **choosy** *adj*

**chop** *vb* **1** : cut by repeated blows **2** : cut into small pieces ~ *n* **1** : sharp downward blow **2** : small cut of meat often with part of a rib — **chop•per** *n*

**chop•py** *adj* **1** : rough with small waves **2** : jerky or disconnected — **chop•pi•ly** *adv* — **chop•pi•ness** *n*

**cho•ral** *adj* : relating to or sung by a choir or chorus or in chorus — **cho•ral•ly** *adv*

**cho•rale** *n* **1** : hymn tune or harmonization of a traditional melody **2** : chorus or choir

[1]**chord** *n* : harmonious tones sounded together

**chore** *n* **1** *pl* : daily household or farm work **2** : routine or disagreeable task

**cho•re•og•ra•phy** *n* : art of composing and arranging dances — **cho•reo•graph** *vb* — **cho•re•og•ra•pher** *n* — **cho•reo•graph•ic** *adj*

**cho•rus** *n* **1** : group of singers or dancers **2** : part of a song repeated at intervals **3** : composition for a chorus ~ *vb* : sing or utter together

**chose** *past of* CHOOSE

**cho•sen** *adj* : favored

[1]**chow** *n* : food

[2]**chow** *n* : thick-coated muscular dog

**chow•der** *n* : thick soup usu. of seafood and milk

**chris•ten** *vb* **1** : baptize **2** : name — **chris•ten•ing** *n*

**Chris•tian** *n* : adherent of Christianity ~ *adj* : relating to or professing a belief in Christianity or Jesus Christ — **Chris•tian•ize** *vb*

**Chris•ti•an•i•ty** *n* : religion derived from the teachings of Jesus Christ

**Christ•mas** *n* : December 25 celebrated as the birthday of Christ

**chro•mo•some** *n* : part of a cell nucleus that contains the genes — **chro•mo•som•al** *adj*

**chron•ic** *adj* : frequent or persistent — **chron•i•cal•ly** *adv*

**chron•i•cle** *n* : history ~ *vb* : record — **chron•i•cler** *n*

**chro•nol•o•gy** *n* : list of events in order of their occurrence — **chron•o•log•i•cal** *adj* — **chron•o•log•i•cal•ly** *adv*

**chub•by** *adj* : fat — **chub•bi•ness** *n*

[1]**chuck** *vb* **1** : tap **2** : toss ~ *n* **1** : light pat under the chin **2** : toss

[2]**chuck** *n* **1** : cut of beef **2** : machine part that holds work or another part

**chuck•le** *vb* : laugh quietly — **chuckle** *n*

**chum** *n* : close friend ~ *vb* : be chums — **chum•my** *adj*

**chump** *n* : fool

**chunk** *n* **1** : short thick piece **2** : sizable amount

**chunky** *adj* **1** : thickly built **2** : containing chunks

**church** *n* **1** : building esp. for Christian public worship **2** : whole body of Christians **3** : denomination **4** : congregation — **church•go•er** *n* — **church•go•ing** *adj or n* — **church•yard** *n*

**churn** *n* : container in which butter is made ~ *vb* **1** : agitate in a churn **2** : shake violently

**chute** *n* : trough or passage

**chutz•pah** *n* : nerve or insolence

**ci•der** *n* : apple juice

**ci•gar** *n* : roll of leaf tobacco for smoking

**cig•a•rette** *n* : cut tobacco rolled in paper for smoking

**cinch** *n* **1** : strap holding a saddle or pack in place **2** : sure thing — **cinch** *vb*

**cin•der** *n* **1** *pl* : ashes **2** : piece of partly burned wood or coal

**cin•e•ma** *n* : movies or a movie theater — **cin•e•mat•ic** *adj*

**cin•na•mon** *n* : spice from an aromatic tree bark

**ci•pher** *n* **1** : zero **2** : code

**cir•cle** *n* **1** : closed symmetrical curve **2** : cycle **3** : group with a common tie ~ *vb* **1** : enclose in a circle **2** : move or revolve around

**cir•cuit** *n* **1** : boundary **2** : regular tour of a territory **3** : complete path of an electric current **4** : group of electronic components — **cir•cuit•ry** *n*

**cir•cu•lar** *adj* **1** : round **2** : moving in a circle ~ *n* : advertising leaflet — **cir•cu•lar•i•ty** *n*

**cir•cu•late** *vb* : move or cause to move in a circle or from place to place or person to person — **cir•cu•la•tion** *n* — **cir•cu•la•to•ry** *adj*

**cir•cum•cise** *vb* : cut off the foreskin of — **cir•cum•ci•sion** *n*

**cir•cum•fer•ence** *n* : perimeter of a circle

**cir•cum•stance** *n* **1** : fact or event **2** *pl* : surrounding conditions **3** *pl* : financial situation — **cir•cum•stan•tial** *adj*

**cir•cum•vent** *vb* : get around esp. by trickery — **cir•cum•ven•tion** *n*

**cir•cus** *n* : show with feats of skill, animal acts, and clowns

**cite** *vb* **1** : summon before a court **2** : quote **3** : refer to esp. in commendation — **ci•ta•tion** *n*

**cit•i•zen** *n* : member of a country — **cit•i•zen•ry** *n* — **cit•i•zen•ship** *n*

**cit•rus** *n* : evergreen tree or shrub grown for its fruit (as the orange or lemon)

**city** *n* : place larger or more important than a town

**civ•ics** *n* : study of citizenship — **civ•ic** *adj*

**civ•il** *adj* **1** : relating to citizens **2** : polite **3** : relating to or being a lawsuit — **civ•il•ly** *adv*

**ci•vil•ian** *n* : person not in a military, police, or fire-fighting force

**ci•vil•i•ty** *n* : courtesy

**civ•i•lize** *vb* : raise from a primitive stage of cultural development — **civ•i•li•za•tion** *n* — **civ•i•lized** *adj*

**civil war** *n* : war among citizens of one country

**clad** *adj* : being covered

**claim** *vb* **1** : demand or take as the rightful owner **2** : maintain ~ *n* **1** : demand of right or ownership **2** : declaration **3** : something claimed — **claimant** *n*

**clair•voy•ant** *adj* : able to perceive things beyond the senses — **clair•voy•ance** *n* — **clairvoy•ant** *n*

**clam** *n* : bivalve mollusk

**clam•my** *adj* : being damp, soft, and usu. cool — **clam•mi•ness** *n*

**clam•or** *n* **1** : uproar **2** : protest — **clamor** *vb* — **clam•or•ous** *adj*

**clamp** *n* : device for holding things together — **clamp** *vb*

**clan** *n* : group of related families — **clan•nish** *adj* — **clan•nish•ness** *n*

**clan•des•tine** *adj* : secret

**clang** *n* : loud metallic ringing — **clang** *vb*

**clank** *n* : brief sound of struck metal — **clank** *vb*

**clap** *vb* **1** : strike noisily **2** : applaud ~ *n* **1** : loud crash **2** : noise made by clapping the hands

**clap•per** *n* : tongue of a bell

**clar•i•fy** *vb* : make or become clear — **clar•i•fi•ca•tion** *n*

**clar•i•net** *n* : woodwind instrument shaped like a tube — **clar•i•net•ist, clar•i•net•tist** *n*

**clar•i•ty** *n* : the quality of being clear

**clash** *vb* **1** : make or cause a clash **2** : be in opposition or disharmony ~ *n* **1** : crashing sound **2** : hostile encounter

**clasp** *n* **1** : device for holding things together **2** : embrace or grasp ~ *vb* **1** : fasten **2** : embrace or grasp

**class** *n* **1** : group of the same status or nature **2** : social rank **3** : course of instruction **4** : group of students ~ *vb* : classify — **class•less** *adj* — **class•mate** *n* — **class•room** *n*

**clas•sic** *adj* **1** : serving as a standard of excellence **2** : classical ~ *n* : work of enduring excellence and esp. of ancient Greece or Rome — **clas•si•cal** *adj* — **clas•si•cal•ly** *adv* — **clas•si•cism** *n* — **clas•si•cist** *n*

**clas•si•fied** *adj* : restricted for security reasons

**clas•si•fy** *vb* : arrange in or assign to classes — **clas•si•fi•ca•tion** *n* — **clas•si•fi•er** *n*

**clat•ter** *n* : rattling sound — **clat•ter** *vb*

**clause** *n* **1** : separate part of a document **2** : part of a sentence with a subject and predicate

**claus•tro•pho•bia** *n* : fear of closed or narrow spaces — **claus•tro•pho•bic** *adj*

**claw** *n* : sharp curved nail or naillike part of an animal ~ *vb* : scratch or dig — **clawed** *adj*

**clay** *n* : plastic earthy material — **clay•ey** *adj*

**clean** *adj* **1** : free from dirt or disease **2** : pure or honorable **3** : thorough ~ *vb* : make or become clean — **clean** *adv* — **clean•er** *n* — **clean•li•ness** *n* — **clean•ly** *adv* — **clean•ness** *n*

**cleanse** *vb* : make clean — **cleans•er** *n*

**clear** *adj* **1** : bright **2** : free from clouds **3** : transparent **4** : easily heard, seen or understood **5** : free from doubt **6** : free from restriction or obstruction ~ *vb* **1** : make or become clear **2** : go away **3** : free from accusation or blame **4** : explain or settle **5** : net **6** : jump or pass without touching ~ *n* : clear space or part — **clear** *adv* — **clear•ance** *n* — **clear•ly** *adv*

**clear•ing** *n* : land cleared of wood

[1]**cleave** *vb* : adhere

[2]**cleave** *vb* : split apart — **cleav•er** *n*

**clef** *n* : sign on the staff in music to show pitch

**cleft** *n* : crack

**clench** *vb* **1** : hold fast **2** : close tightly

**cler•gy** *n* : body of religious officials — **cler•gy•man** *n*

**cler•ic** *n* : member of the clergy

**cler•i•cal** *adj* **1** : relating to the clergy **2** : relating to a clerk or office worker

**clerk** *n* **1** : official responsible for record-keeping **2** : person doing general office work **3** : salesperson in a store — **clerk** *vb* — **clerk•ship** *n*

**clev•er** *adj* **1** : resourceful **2** : marked

by wit or ingenuity — **clev•er•ly** *adv* — **clev•er•ness** *n*

**cli•ché** *n* : trite phrase — **cli•chéd** *adj*

**click** *n* : slight sharp noise ~ *vb* : make or cause to make a click

**cli•ent** *n* **1** : person who engages professional services **2** : customer

**cli•en•tele** *n* : body of customers

**cliff** *n* : high steep face of rock

**cli•mate** *n* : average weather conditions over a period of years — **cli•mat•ic** *adj*

**cli•max** *n* : the highest point ~ *vb* : come to a climax — **cli•mac•tic** *adj*

**climb** *vb* **1** : go up or down by use of hands and feet **2** : rise ~ *n* : a climbing — **climb•er** *n*

**clinch** *vb* **1** : fasten securely **2** : settle **3** : hold fast or firmly — **clinch** *n* — **clinch•er** *n*

**cling** *vb* (**clung; clung**) **1** : adhere firmly **2** : hold on tightly

**clin•ic** *n* : facility for diagnosis and treatment of outpatients — **clin•i•cal** *adj* — **clin•i•cal•ly** *adv*

**clink** *vb* : make a slight metallic sound — **clink** *n*

**[1]clip** *vb* : fasten with a clip ~ *n* : device to hold things together

**[2]clip** *vb* **1** : cut or cut off **2** : hit ~ *n* **1** : clippers **2** : sharp blow **3** : rapid pace

**clip•per** *n* **1** *pl* : implement for clipping **2** : fast sailing ship

**clique** *n* : small exclusive group of people

**cloak** *n* **1** : loose outer garment **2** : something that conceals ~ *vb* : cover or hide with a cloak

**clob•ber** *vb* : hit hard

**clock** *n* : timepiece not carried on the person ~ *vb* : record the time of

**clock•wise** *adv or adj* : in the same direction as a clock's hands move

**clod** *n* **1** : lump esp. of earth **2** : dull insensitive person

**clog** *n* **1** : restraining weight **2** : thick-soled shoe ~ *vb* **1** : impede with a clog **2** : obstruct passage through **3** : become plugged up

**clone** *n* **1** : offspring produced from a single organism **2** : copy

**[1]close** *vb* **1** : shut **2** : cease operation **3** : terminate **4** : bring or come together ~ *n* : conclusion or end

**[2]close** *adj* **1** : confining **2** : secretive **3** : strict **4** : stuffy **5** : having little space between items **6** : fitting tightly **7** : near **8** : intimate **9** : accurate **10** : nearly even — **close** *adv* — **close•ly** *adv* — **close•ness** *n*

**clos•et** *n* : small compartment for household utensils or clothing

**clo•sure** *n* **1** : act of closing **2** : something that closes

**clot** *n* : dried mass of a liquid — **clot** *vb*

**cloth** *n* **1** : fabric **2** : tablecloth

**clothe** *vb* : dress

**clothes** *n pl* : clothing

**cloth•ing** *n* : covering for the human body

**cloud** *n* **1** : visible mass of particles in the air **2** : something that darkens, hides, or threatens ~ *vb* : darken or hide — **cloud•burst** *n* — **cloud•i•ness** *n* — **cloud•less** *adj* — **cloudy** *adj*

**clout** *n* **1** : blow **2** : influence ~ *vb* : hit forcefully

**clove** *n* : dried flower bud of an East Indian tree used as a spice

**clo•ver** *n* : leguminous herb with usu. 3-part leaves

**clown** *n* : funny costumed entertainer esp. in a circus ~ *vb* : act like a clown — **clown•ish** *adj* — **clown•ish•ly** *adv* — **clown•ish•ness** *n*

**cloy** *vb* : disgust with excess — **cloy•ing•ly** *adv*

**club** *n* **1** : heavy wooden stick **2** : playing card of a suit marked with a black figure like a clover leaf **3** : group associated for a common purpose ~ *vb* : hit with a club

**cluck** *n* : sound made by a hen — **cluck** *vb*

**clue** *n* : piece of evidence that helps solve a problem ~ *vb* : provide with a clue

**clump** *n* **1** : cluster **2** : heavy tramping sound ~ *vb* : tread heavily

**clum•sy** *adj* **1** : lacking dexterity, nimbleness, or grace **2** : tactless — **clum•si•ly** *adv* — **clum•si•ness** *n*

**clung** *past of* CLING

**clus•ter** *n* : group ~ *vb* : grow or gather in a cluster

**clutch** *vb* : grasp ~ *n* **1** : grasping hand or claws **2** : control or power **3** : coupling for connecting two working parts in machinery

**clut•ter** *vb* : fill with things that get in the way — **clutter** *n*

**coach** *n* **1** : closed 2-door 4-wheeled carriage **2** : railroad passenger car **3** : bus **4** : 2d-class air travel **5** : one who instructs or trains performers ~ *vb* : instruct or direct as a coach

**coal** *n* **1** : glowing fragment from a fire **2** : black solid mineral used as fuel — **coal•field** *n*

**co•ali•tion** *n* : temporary alliance

**coarse** *adj* **1** : composed of large particles **2** : rough or crude — **coarse•ly** *adv* — **coars•en** *vb* — **coarse•ness** *n*

**coast** *n* : seashore ~ *vb* : move without effort — **coast•al** *adj* — **coast•line** *n*

**coast•er** *n* **1** : one that coasts **2** : plate or mat to protect a surface

**coast guard** *n* : military force that guards or patrols a coast — **coast•guards•man** *n*

**coat** *n* **1** : outer garment for the upper body **2** : external growth of fur or feathers **3** : covering layer ~ *vb* : cover with a coat — **coat•ed** *adj* — **coat•ing** *n*

**coax** *vb* : move to action or achieve by gentle urging or flattery

**cob•bler** *n* **1** : shoemaker **2** : deep-dish fruit pie

**cob•web** *n* : network spun by a spider or a similar filament

**cock** *n* **1** : male fowl **2** : valve or faucet ~ *vb* **1** : draw back the hammer of a firearm **2** : tilt to one side — **cock•fight** *n*

**cock•eyed** *adj* **1** : tilted to one side **2** : slightly crazy

**cock•pit** *n* : place for a pilot, driver, or helmsman

**cock•roach** *n* : nocturnal insect often infesting houses

**cock•tail** *n* **1** : iced drink of liquor and flavorings **2** : appetizer

**cocky** *adj* : too confident in oneself — **cock•i•ly** *adv* — **cock•i•ness** *n*

**co•coa** *n* **1** : cacao **2** : powdered chocolate or a drink made from this

**co•co•nut** *n* : large nutlike fruit of a tropical palm (**coconut palm**)

**co•coon** *n* : case protecting an insect pupa

**cod** *n pl* **cod** : food fish of the No. Atlantic

**cod•dle** *vb* : pamper

**code** *n* **1** : system of laws or rules **2** : system of signals

**co•ed** *n* : female student in a coeducational institution — **coed** *adj*

**co•ed•u•ca•tion** *n* : education of the sexes together — **co•ed•u•ca•tion•al** *adj*

**co•erce** *vb* : force — **co•er•cion** *n* — **co•er•cive** *adj*

**cof•fee** *n* : drink made from the roasted and ground seeds (**coffee beans**) of a tropical shrub — **cof•fee•house** *n* — **cof•fee•pot** *n*

**cof•fin** *n* : box for burial

**cog** *n* : tooth on the rim of a gear — **cogged** *adj* — **cog•wheel** *n*

**cog•ni•zance** *n* : notice or awareness — **cog•ni•zant** *adj*

**co•hab•it** *vb* : live together as husband and wife — **co•hab•i•ta•tion** *n*

**co•here** *vb* : stick together — **co•he•sion** *n* — **co•he•sive** *adj* — **co•he•sive•ly** *adv* — **co•he•sive•ness** *n*

**co•her•ent** *adj* **1** : able to stick together **2** : logically consistent — **co•her•ence** *n* — **co•her•ent•ly** *adv*

**coil** *vb* : wind in a spiral ~ *n* : series of loops (as of rope)

**coin** *n* : piece of metal used as money ~ *vb* **1** : make (a coin) by stamping **2** : create — **coin•age** *n* — **coin•er** *n*

**co•in•cide** *vb* **1** : be in the same place **2** : happen at the same time **3** : be alike — **co•in•ci•dence** *n* — **co•in•ci•dent** *adj* — **co•in•ci•den•tal** *adj*

**co•la** *n* : carbonated soft drink

**col•an•der** *n* : perforated utensil for draining food

**cold** *adj* **1** : having a low or below normal temperature **2** : lacking warmth of feeling **3** : suffering from lack of warmth ~ *n* **1** : low temperature **2** : minor respiratory illness — **cold•ly** *adv* — **cold•ness** *n* — **in cold blood** : with premeditation

**cold–blood•ed** *adj* **1** : cruel or merciless **2** : having a body temperature that varies with the temperature of the environment

**cole•slaw** *n* : cabbage salad

**col•ic** *n* : sharp abdominal pain — **col•icky** *adj*

**col•i•se•um** *n* : arena

**col•lab•o•rate** *vb* **1** : work jointly with others **2** : help the enemy — **col•lab•o•ra•tion** *n* — **col•lab•o•ra•tor** *n*

**col•lapse** *vb* **1** : fall in **2** : break down physically or mentally **3** : fold down ~ *n* : breakdown — **col•laps•ible** *adj*

**col•lar** *n* : part of a garment around the neck ~ *vb* **1** : seize by the collar **2** : grab — **col•lar•less** *adj*

**col•lar•bone** *n* : bone joining the breastbone and the shoulder blade

**col•league** *n* : associate

**col•lect** *vb* **1** : bring, come, or gather together **2** : receive payment of ~ *adv or adj* : to be paid for by the receiver — **col•lect•ible, col•lect•able** *adj* — **col•lec•tive** *adj* — **col•lec•tive•ly** *adv* — **col•lec•tion** *n* — **col•lec•tor** *n*

**col•lege** *n* : institution of higher learning granting a bachelor's degree — **col•le•gian** *n* — **col•le•giate** *adj*

**col•lide** *vb* : strike together — **col•li•sion** *n*

**col•lie** *n* : large long-haired dog

**col•lu•sion** *n* : secret cooperation for deceit — **col•lu•sive** *adj*

**co•logne** *n* : perfumed liquid

**[1]co•lon** *n* : lower part of the large intestine — **co•lon•ic** *adj*

**[2]colon** *n* : punctuation mark : used esp. to direct attention to following matter

**col•o•nel** *n* : commissioned officer (as in the army) ranking below a general

**col•o•nize** *vb* **1** : establish a colony in **2** : settle — **col•o•ni•za•tion** *n* — **col•o•niz•er** *n*

**col•o•ny** *n* **1** : people who inhabit a new territory or the territory itself **2** : animals of one kind (as bees) living together — **co•lo•nial** *adj or n* — **col•o•nist** *n*

**col•or** *n* **1** : quality of visible things distinct from shape that results from light reflection **2** *pl* : flag **3** : liveliness ~ *vb* **1** : give color to **2** : blush — **col•or•fast** *adj* — **col•or•ful** *adj* — **col•or•less** *adj*

**col•or–blind** *adj* : unable to distinguish colors — **color blindness** *n*

**col•ored** *adj* **1** : having color **2** : of a race other than the white ~ *n* : colored person

**co•los•sus** *n* : something of great size or scope — **co•los•sal** *adj*

**colt** *n* : young male horse — **colt•ish** *adj*

**col•umn** *n* **1** : vertical section of a printed page **2** : regular feature article (as in a newspaper) **3** : pillar **4** : row (as of soldiers) — **co•lum•nar** *adj* — **col•um•nist** *n*

**co•ma** *n* : deep prolonged unconsciousness — **co•ma•tose** *adj*

**comb** *n* **1** : toothed instrument for arranging the hair **2** : crest on a fowl's head — **comb** *vb* — **combed** *adj*

**com•bat** *vb* : fight — **com•bat** *n* — **com•bat•ant** *n* — **com•bat•ive** *adj*

**com•bine** *vb* : join together ~ *n* **1** : association for business or political advantage **2** : harvesting machine — **com•bi•na•tion** *n*

**com•bust** *vb* : to catch fire — **com•bus•ti•bil•i•ty** *n* — **com•bus•ti•ble** *adj or n* — **com•bus•tion** *n*

**come** *vb* **came; come 1** : move toward or arrive at something **2** : reach a state **3** : originate or exist **4** : amount — **come clean** *vb* : confess — **come into** *vb* : acquire, achieve — **come off** *vb* : succeed — **come to** *vb* : regain consciousness — **come to pass** : happen — **come to terms** : reach an agreement

**come•back** *n* **1** : retort **2** : return to a former position — **come back** *vb*

**co•me•di•an** *n* **1** : comic actor **2** : funny person **3** : entertainer specializing in comedy

**co•me•di•enne** *n* : a woman who is a comedian

**com•e•dy** *n* **1** : an amusing play **2** : humorous entertainment

**com•et** *n* : small bright celestial body having a tail

**com•fort** *n* **1** : consolation **2** : well-being or something that gives it ~ *vb* **1** : give hope to **2** : console — **com•fort•able** *adj* — **com•fort•ably** *adv*

**com•fort•er** *n* **1** : one that comforts **2** : quilt

**com•ic** *adj* **1** : relating to comedy **2** : funny ~ *n* **1** : comedian **2** : sequence of cartoons — **com•i•cal** *adj*

**com•ing** *adj* : next

**com•ma** *n* : punctuation mark, used esp. to separate sentence parts

**com•mand** *vb* **1** : order **2** : control ~ *n* **1** : act of commanding **2** : an order given **3** : mastery **4** : troops under a commander — **com•man•dant** *n*

**com•man•deer** *vb* : seize by force

**com•mand•er** *n* **1** : officer commanding an army or subdivision of an army **2** : commissioned officer in the navy ranking below a captain

**com•mand•ment** *n* : order

**com•mem•o•rate** *vb* : celebrate or honor — **com•mem•o•ra•tion** *n* — **com•mem•o•ra•tive** *adj*

**com•mence** *vb* : start

**com•mence•ment** *n* **1** : beginning **2** : graduation ceremony

**com•mend** *vb* **1** : entrust **2** : recommend **3** : praise — **com•mend•able** *adj* — **com•men•da•tion** *n*

**com•ment** *n* : statement of opinion or remark — **comment** *vb*

**com•men•tary** *n* : series of comments

**com•men•ta•tor** *n* : one who discusses news

**com•merce** *n* : business

**com•mer•cial** *adj* : designed for profit or for mass appeal ~ *n* : broadcast advertisement — **com•mer•cial•ize** *vb* — **com•mer•cial•ly** *adv*

**com•mis•sary** *n* : store esp. for military personnel

**com•mis•sion** *n* **1** : order granting power or rank **2** : panel to judge, approve, or act **3** : the doing of an act **4** : agent's fee ~ *vb* **1** : confer rank or authority to or for **2** : request something be done

**com•mis•sion•er** *n* **1** : member of a commission **2** : head of a government department

**com•mit** *vb* **1** : turn over to someone for safekeeping or confinement **2** : perform or do **3** : pledge — **com•mit•ment** *n*

**com•mit•tee** *n* : panel that examines or acts on something

**com•mod•i•ty** *n* : article for sale

**com•mon** *adj* **1** : public **2** : shared by several **3** : widely known, found, or observed **4** : ordinary ~ *n* : community land — **com•mon•ly** *adv* — **in common** : shared together

**com•mon•place** *n* : cliché ~ *adj* : ordinary

**com•mon•wealth** *n* : state

**com•mo•tion** *n* : disturbance

**com·mu·ni·cate** *vb* 1 : make known 2 : transmit 3 : exchange information or opinions — **com·mu·ni·ca·ble** *adj* — **com·mu·ni·ca·tion** *n* — **com·mu·ni·ca·tive** *adj*

**Com·mu·nion** *n* : Christian sacrament of partaking of bread and wine

**com·mu·nism** *n* 1 : social organization in which goods are held in common 2 *cap* : political doctrine based on revolutionary Marxist socialism — **com·mu·nist** *n or adj, often cap* — **com·mu·nis·tic** *adj, often cap*

**com·mu·ni·ty** *n* : body of people living in the same place under the same laws

**com·mute** *vb* 1 : reduce (a punishment) 2 : travel back and forth regularly ~ *n* : trip made in commuting — **com·mu·ta·tion** *n* — **com·mut·er** *n*

**[1]com·pact** *adj* 1 : hard 2 : small or brief ~ *vb* : pack together ~ *n* 1 : cosmetics case 2 : small car — **com·pact·ly** *adv* — **com·pact·ness** *n*

**[2]com·pact** *n* : agreement

**compact disc** *n* : plastic-coated disc with laser-readable recorded music

**com·pan·ion** *n* 1 : close friend 2 : one of a pair — **com·pan·ion·able** *adj* — **com·pan·ion·ship** *n*

**com·pa·ny** *n* 1 : business organization 2 : group of performers 3 : guests 4 : infantry unit

**com·pare** *vb* 1 : represent as similar 2 : check for likenesses or differences ~ *n* : comparison — **com·pa·ra·ble** *adj* — **com·par·a·tive** *adj or n* — **com·par·a·tive·ly** *adv* — **com·par·i·son** *n*

**com·part·ment** *n* : section or room

**com·pass** *n* 1 : scope 2 : device for drawing circles 3 : device for determining direction

**com·pas·sion** *n* : pity — **com·pas·sion·ate** *adj*

**com·pat·i·ble** *adj* : harmonious — **com·pat·i·bil·i·ty** *n*

**com·pel** *vb* : cause through necessity

**com·pen·sate** *vb* 1 : offset or balance 2 : repay — **com·pen·sa·tion** *n* — **com·pen·sa·to·ry** *adj*

**com·pete** *vb* : strive to win — **com·pe·ti·tion** *n* — **com·pet·i·tive** *adj* — **com·pet·i·tive·ness** *n* — **com·pet·i·tor** *n*

**com·pe·tent** *adj* : capable — **com·pe·tence** *n* — **com·pe·ten·cy** *n*

**com·pile** *vb* : collect or compose from several sources — **com·pi·la·tion** *n* — **com·pil·er** *n*

**com·pla·cen·cy** *n* : unusual satisfaction with oneself — **com·pla·cent** *adj*

**com·plain** *vb* 1 : express grief, pain, or discontent 2 : make an accusation — **com·plain·ant** *n* — **com·plain·er** *n* — **com·plaint** *n*

**com·ple·ment** *n* 1 : something that completes 2 : full number or amount ~ *vb* : complete — **com·ple·men·ta·ry** *adj*

**com·plete** *adj* 1 : having all parts 2 : finished 3 : total ~ *vb* 1 : make whole 2 : finish — **com·plete·ly** *adv* — **com·plete·ness** *n* — **com·ple·tion** *n*

**com·plex** *adj* 1 : having many parts 2 : intricate ~ *n* : psychological problem — **com·plex·i·ty** *n*

**com·plex·ion** *n* : hue or appearance of the skin esp. of the face — **com·plex·ioned** *adj*

**com·pli·cate** *vb* : make complex or hard to understand — **com·pli·cat·ed** *adj* — **com·pli·ca·tion** *n*

**com·pli·ment** *n* 1 : flattering remark 2 *pl* : greeting ~ *vb* : pay a compliment to

**com·pli·men·ta·ry** *adj* 1 : praising 2 : free

**com·ply** *vb* : conform or yield — **com·pli·ance** *n* — **com·pli·ant** *n*

**com·po·nent** *n* : part of something larger ~ *adj* : serving as a component

**com·pose** *vb* 1 : create (as by writing) or put together 2 : calm 3 : set type — **com·pos·er** *n* — **com·po·si·tion** *n*

**com·pos·ite** *adj* : made up of diverse parts — **composite** *n*

**com·post** *n* : decayed organic fertilizing material

**com·po·sure** *n* : calmness

**[1]com·pound** *vb* 1 : combine or add 2 : pay (interest) on principal and accrued interest ~ *adj* : made up of 2 or more parts ~ *n* : something that is compound

**[2]com·pound** *n* : enclosure

**com·pre·hend** *vb* 1 : understand 2 : include — **com·pre·hen·si·ble** *adj* — **com·pre·hen·sion** *n* — **com·pre·hen·sive** *adj*

**com·press** *vb* : squeeze together ~ *n* : pad for pressing on a wound — **com·pres·sion** *n* — **com·pres·sor** *n*

**com·prise** *vb* 1 : contain or cover 2 : be made up of

**com·pro·mise** *vb* : settle differences by mutual concessions — **compromise** *n*

**com·pul·sion** *n* 1 : coercion 2 : irresistible impulse — **com·pul·sive** *adj* — **com·pul·so·ry** *adj*

**com·pute** *vb* : calculate — **com·pu·ta·tion** *n*

**com·put·er** *n* : electronic data processing machine — **com·put·er·i·za·tion** *n* — **com·put·er·ize** *vb*

**com·rade** *n* : companion — **com·rade·ship** *n*

**con·cave** *adj* : curved like the inside of a sphere — **con·cav·i·ty** *n*

**con·ceal** *vb* : hide — **con·ceal·ment** *n*

**con·cede** *vb* : grant

**con·ceit** *n* : excessively high opinion of oneself — **con·ceit·ed** *adj*

**con·ceive** *vb* 1 : become pregnant 2 : think of — **con·ceiv·able** *adj* — **con·ceiv·ably** *adv*

**con·cen·trate** *vb* 1 : gather together 2 : make stronger 3 : fix one's attention ~ *n* : something concentrated — **con·cen·tra·tion** *n*

**con·cen·tric** *adj* : having a common center

**con·cept** *n* : thought or idea

**con·cep·tion** *n* 1 : act of conceiving 2 : idea

**con·cern** *vb* 1 : relate to 2 : involve ~ *n* 1 : affair 2 : worry 3 : business — **con·cerned** *adj* — **con·cern·ing** *prep*

**con·cert** *n* 1 : agreement or joint action 2 : public performance of music — **con·cert·ed** *adj*

**con·cer·to** *n* : orchestral work with solo instruments

**con·ces·sion** *n* 1 : act of conceding 2 : something conceded 3 : right to do business on a property

**con·cil·i·a·to·ry** *adj* : doing what's necessary to gain goodwill

**con·cise** *adj* : said in few words — **con·cise·ly** *adv* — **con·cise·ness** *n* — **con·ci·sion** *n*

**con·clude** *vb* 1 : end 2 : decide — **con·clu·sion** *n* — **con·clu·sive** *adj* — **con·clu·sive·ly** *adv*

**con·coct** *vb* : prepare or devise — **con·coc·tion** *n*

**con·cord** *n* : agreement

**con·cor·dance** *n* 1 : agreement 2 : index of words — **con·cor·dant** *adj*

**con·course** *n* : open space where crowds gather

**con·crete** *adj* 1 : naming something real 2 : actual or substantial 3 : made of concrete ~ *n* : hard building material made of cement, sand, gravel, and water

**con·cur** *vb* : agree — **con·cur·rence** *n*

**con·cur·rent** *adj* : happening at the same time

**con·cus·sion** *n* 1 : shock 2 : brain injury from a blow

**con·demn** *vb* 1 : declare to be wrong, guilty, or unfit for use 2 : sentence — **con·dem·na·tion** *n*

**con·dense** *vb* 1 : make or become more compact 2 : change from vapor to liquid — **con·den·sa·tion** *n* — **con·dens·er** *n*

**con·de·scend** *vb* 1 : lower oneself 2 : act haughtily — **con·de·scen·sion** *n*

**con·di·ment** *n* : pungent seasoning

**con·di·tion** *n* 1 : necessary situation or stipulation 2 *pl* : state of affairs 3 : state of being ~ *vb* : put into proper condition — **con·di·tion·al** *adj* — **con·di·tion·al·ly** *adv*

**con·do·lence** *n* : expression of sympathy — usu. pl.

**con·do·min·i·um** *n* : individually owned apartment

**con·done** *vb* : overlook or forgive

**con·du·cive** *adj* : tending to help or promote

**con·duct** *n* 1 : management 2 : behavior ~ *vb* 1 : guide 2 : manage or direct 3 : be a channel for 4 : behave — **con·duc·tion** *n* — **con·duc·tive** *adj* — **con·duc·tiv·i·ty** *n* — **con·duc·tor** *n*

**cone** *n* 1 : scaly fruit of pine and related trees 2 : solid figure having a circular base and tapering sides

**con·fec·tion** *n* : sweet dish or candy — **con·fec·tion·er** *n*

**con·fed·er·ate** *adj* 1 : united in a league 2 *cap* : relating to the 11 southern states that seceded from the U.S. in 1860 and 1861 ~ *n* 1 : ally 2 *cap* : adherent of the Confederacy ~ *vb* : unite — **con·fed·er·a·cy** *n* — **con·fed·er·a·tion** *n*

**con·fer** *vb* 1 : give 2 : meet to exchange views — **con·fer·ee** *n* — **con·fer·ence** *n*

**con·fess** *vb* 1 : acknowledge or disclose one's misdeed, fault, or sin 2 : declare faith in — **con·fes·sion** *n* — **con·fes·sion·al** *n or adj*

**con·fes·sor** *n* 1 : one who confesses 2 : priest who hears confessions

**con·fet·ti** *n* : bits of paper or ribbon thrown in celebration

**con·fide** *vb* 1 : share private thoughts 2 : reveal in confidence — **con·fi·dant** *n*

**con·fi·dence** *n* 1 : trust 2 : certainty of one's nature or ability 3 : something confided — **con·fi·dent** *adj* — **con·fi·den·tial** *adj* — **con·fi·den·tial·ly** *adv* — **con·fi·dent·ly** *adv*

**con·fig·u·ra·tion** *n* : arrangement

**con·fine** *vb* 1 : restrain or restrict to a limited area 2 : imprison — **con·fine·ment** *n* — **con·fin·er** *n* — **con·fines** *n pl*

**con·firm** *vb* 1 : ratify 2 : verify 3 : admit as a full member of a church or synagogue — **con·fir·ma·tion** *n*

**con·fis·cate** *vb* : take by authority — **con·fis·ca·tion** *n* — **con·fis·ca·to·ry** *adj*

**con·flict** *n* 1 : war 2 : clash of ideas ~ *vb* : clash

**con·form** *vb* 1 : make or be like 2 : obey — **con·for·mi·ty** *n*

**con·front** *vb* : oppose or face — **con·fron·ta·tion** *n*

**con·fuse** *vb* 1 : make mentally uncertain 2 : jumble — **con·fu·sion** *n*

**con·geal** *vb* 1 : freeze 2 : become thick and solid

**con·ge·nial** *adj* : kindred or agreeable — **con·ge·ni·al·i·ty** *n*

**con·gest** *vb* : overcrowd or overfill — **con·ges·tion** *n* — **con·ges·tive** *adj*

**con·glom·er·ate** *adj* : made up of diverse parts ~ *vb* : form into a mass ~ *n* : diversified corporation — **con·glom·er·a·tion** *n*

**con·grat·u·late** *vb* : express pleasure to for good fortune — **con·grat·u·la·tion** *n* — **con·grat·u·la·to·ry** *adj*

**con·gre·gate** *vb* : assemble — **con·gre·ga·tion** *n* — **con·gre·ga·tion·al** *adj*

**con·gress** *n* : assembly of delegates or of senators and representatives — **con·gres·sio·nal** *adj* — **con·gress·man** *n* — **con·gress·wom·an** *n*

**co·ni·fer** *n* : cone-bearing tree — **co·nif·er·ous** *adj*

**con·ju·gate** *vb* : give the inflected forms of (a verb) — **con·ju·ga·tion** *n*

**con·junc·tion** *n* 1 : combination 2 : occurrence at the same time 3 : a word that joins other words together — **con·junc·tive** *adj*

**con·jure** *vb* 1 : summon by sorcery 2 : practice sleight of hand 3 : entreat — **con·jur·er, con·ju·ror** *n*

**con·nect** *vb* : join or associate — **con·nect·able** *adj* — **con·nec·tion** *n* — **con·nec·tive** *n or adj* — **con·nec·tor** *n*

**con·nive** *vb* 1 : pretend ignorance of wrongdoing 2 : cooperate secretly — **con·niv·ance** *n*

**con·nois·seur** *n* : expert judge esp. of art

**con·quer** *vb* : defeat or overcome — **con·quer·or** *n*

**con·quest** *n* 1 : act of conquering 2 : something conquered

**con·science** *n* : awareness of right and wrong

**con·sci·en·tious** *adj* : honest and hard-working — **con·sci·en·tious·ly** *adv*

**con·scious** *adj* 1 : aware 2 : mentally awake or alert 3 : intentional — **con·scious·ly** *adv* — **con·scious·ness** *n*

**con·se·crate** *vb* 1 : declare sacred 2 : devote to a solemn purpose — **con·se·cra·tion** *n*

**con·sec·u·tive** *adj* : following in order — **con·sec·u·tive·ly** *adv*

**con·sen·sus** *n* 1 : agreement in opinion 2 : collective opinion

**con·sent** *vb* : give permission or approval — **consent** *n*

**con·se·quence** *n* 1 : result or effect 2 : importance — **con·se·quent** *adj* — **con·se·quen·tial** *adj* — **con·se·quent·ly** *adv*

**con·ser·va·tive** *adj* 1 : disposed to maintain the status quo 2 : cautious — **con·ser·va·tism** *n* — **con·ser·va·tive** *n* — **con·ser·va·tive·ly** *adv*

**con·ser·va·to·ry** *n* : school for art or music

**con·serve** *vb* : keep from wasting ~ *n* : candied fruit or fruit preserves — **con·ser·va·tion** *n* — **con·ser·va·tion·ist** *n*

**con·sid·er** *vb* 1 : think about 2 : give thoughtful attention to 3 : think that — **con·sid·er·ate** *adj* — **con·sid·er·ation** *n*

**con·sid·er·able** *adj* 1 : significant 2 : noticeably large — **con·sid·er·a·bly** *adv*

**con·sign** *vb* 1 : transfer 2 : send to an agent for sale — **con·sign·ee** *n* — **con·sign·ment** *n* — **con·sign·or** *n*

**con·sist** *vb* 1 : be inherent — used with *in* 2 : be made up — used with *of*

**con·sis·ten·cy** *n* 1 : degree of thickness or firmness 2 : quality of being consistent

**con·sis·tent** *adj* : being steady and regular — **con·sis·tent·ly** *adv*

**[1]con·sole** *vb* : soothe the grief of — **con·so·la·tion** *n*

**[2]con·sole** *n* : cabinet or part with controls

**con·sol·i·date** *vb* : unite or compact — **con·sol·i·da·tion** *n*

**con·so·nant** *n* 1 : speech sound marked by constriction or closure in the breath channel 2 : letter other than *a, e, i, o,* and *u* — **con·so·nan·tal** *adj*

**con·spic·u·ous** *adj* : very noticeable — **con·spic·u·ous·ly** *adv*

**con·spire** *vb* : secretly plan an unlawful act — **con·spir·a·cy** *n* — **con·spir·a·tor** *n* — **con·spir·a·to·ri·al** *adj*

**con·sta·ble** *n* : police officer

**con·stant** *adj* 1 : steadfast or faithful 2 : not varying 3 : continually recurring ~ *n* : something unchanging — **con·stan·cy** *n* — **con·stant·ly** *adv*

**con·stel·la·tion** *n* : group of stars

**con·sti·pa·tion** *n* : difficulty of defecation — **con·sti·pate** *vb*

**con·stit·u·ent** *adj* 1 : component 2 : having power to elect ~ *n* 1 : component part 2 : one who may vote for a representative — **con·stit·u·en·cy** *n*

**con·sti·tute** *vb* 1 : establish 2 : be all or a basic part of

**con·sti·tu·tion** *n* 1 : physical composition or structure 2 : the basic law of an organized body or the document containing it — **con•sti•tu•tion•al** *adj* — **con•sti•tu•tion•al•i•ty** *n*

**con•strain** *vb* **1 :** compel **2 :** confine **3 :** restrain — **con•straint** *n*

**con•strict** *vb* **:** draw or squeeze together — **con•stric•tion** *n* — **con•stric•tive** *adj*

**con•struct** *vb* **:** build or make — **con•struc•tion** *n* — **con•struc•tive** *adj*

**con•strue** *vb* **:** explain or interpret

**con•sul** *n* **1 :** Roman magistrate **2 :** government commercial official in a foreign country — **con•sul•ar** *adj* — **con•sul•ate** *n*

**con•sult** *vb* **1 :** ask the advice or opinion of **2 :** confer — **con•sul•tant** *n* — **con•sul•ta•tion** *n*

**con•sume** *vb* **:** eat or use up — **con•sum•able** *adj* — **con•sum•er** *n*

**con•sump•tion** *n* **1 :** act of consuming **2 :** use of goods

**con•tact** *n* **1 :** a touching **2 :** association or relationship **3 :** connection or communication ~ *vb* **1 :** come or bring into contact **2 :** communicate with

**con•ta•gion** *n* **1 :** spread of disease by contact **2 :** disease spread by contact — **con•ta•gious** *adj*

**con•tain** *vb* **1 :** enclose or include **2 :** have or hold within **3 :** restrain — **con•tain•er** *n* — **con•tain•ment** *n*

**con•tam•i•nate** *vb* **:** soil or infect by contact or association — **con•tam•i•na•tion** *n*

**con•tem•plate** *vb* **:** view or consider thoughtfully — **con•tem•pla•tion** *n* — **con•tem•pla•tive** *adj*

**con•tem•po•ra•ne•ous** *adj* **:** contemporary

**con•tem•po•rary** *adj* **1 :** occurring or existing at the same time **2 :** of the same age — **con•tem•po•rary** *n*

**con•tempt** *n* **1 :** feeling of scorn **2 :** state of being despised **3 :** disobedience to a court or legislature — **con•tempt•ible** *adj*

**con•temp•tu•ous** *adj* **:** feeling or expressing contempt — **con•temp•tu•ous•ly** *adv*

**con•tend** *vb* **1 :** strive against rivals or difficulties **2 :** argue **3 :** maintain or claim — **con•tend•er** *n*

**[1]con•tent** *adj* **:** satisfied ~ *vb* **:** satisfy ~ *n* **:** ease of mind — **con•tent•ed** *adj* — **con•tent•ed•ly** *adv* — **con•tent•ed•ness** *n* — **con•tent•ment** *n*

**[2]con•tent** *n* **1** *pl* **:** something contained **2** *pl* **:** subject matter (as of a book) **3 :** essential meaning **4 :** proportion contained

**con•ten•tion** *n* **:** state of contending — **con•ten•tious** *adj* — **con•ten•tious•ly** *adv*

**con•test** *vb* **:** dispute or challenge ~ *n* **1 :** struggle **2 :** game — **con•test•able** *adj* — **con•tes•tant** *n*

**con•text** *n* **:** words surrounding a word or phrase

**con•ti•nent** *n* **:** great division of land on the globe — **con•ti•nen•tal** *adj*

**con•tin•gen•cy** *n* **:** possible event

**con•tin•gent** *adj* **:** dependent on something else ~ *n* **:** a quota from an area or group

**con•tin•u•al** *adj* **1 :** continuous **2 :** steadily recurring — **con•tin•u•al•ly** *adv*

**con•tin•ue** *vb* **1 :** remain in a place or condition **2 :** endure **3 :** resume after an intermission **4 :** extend — **con•tin•u•ance** *n* — **con•tin•u•ation** *n*

**con•tin•u•ous** *adj* **:** continuing without interruption — **con•ti•nu•ity** *n* — **con•tin•u•ous•ly** *adv*

**con•tort** *vb* **:** twist out of shape — **con•tor•tion** *n*

**con•tour** *n* **1 :** outline **2** *pl* **:** shape

**con•tra•band** *n* **:** illegal goods

**con•tract** *n* **:** binding agreement ~ *vb* **1 :** establish or undertake by contract **2 :** become ill with **3 :** make shorter — **con•trac•tion** *n* — **con•trac•tor** *n* — **con•trac•tu•al** *adj* — **con•trac•tu•al•ly** *adv*

**con•tra•dict** *vb* **:** state the contrary of — **con•tra•dic•tion** *n* — **con•tra•dic•to•ry** *adj*

**con•trap•tion** *n* **:** device or contrivance

**con•trary** *adj* **1 :** opposite in character, nature, or position **2 :** mutually opposed **3 :** unfavorable **4 :** uncooperative or stubborn — **con•trari•ly** *adv* — **con•trari•wise** *adv* — **contrary** *n*

**con•trast** *n* **1 :** unlikeness shown by comparing **2 :** unlike color or tone of adjacent parts ~ *vb* **1 :** show differences **2 :** compare so as to show differences

**con•tra•vene** *vb* **:** go or act contrary to

**con•trib•ute** *vb* **:** give or help along with others — **con•tri•bu•tion** *n* — **con•trib•u•tor** *n* — **con•trib•u•to•ry** *adj*

**con•trite** *adj* **:** repentant — **con•tri•tion** *n*

**con•trive** *vb* **1 :** devise or make with ingenuity **2 :** bring about — **con•triv•ance** *n* — **con•triv•er** *n*

**con•trol** *vb* **1 :** exercise power over **2 :** dominate or rule ~ *n* **1 :** power to direct or regulate **2 :** restraint **3 :** regulating device — **con•trol•la•ble** *adj* — **con•trol•ler** *n*

**con•tro•ver•sy** *n* **:** clash of opposing views — **con•tro•ver•sial** *adj*

**con•va•lesce** *vb* **:** gradually recover health — **con•va•les•cence** *n* — **con•va•les•cent** *adj or n*

**con•vec•tion** *n* **:** circulation in fluids due to warmer portions rising and colder ones sinking — **con•vec•tion•al** *adj* — **con•vec•tive** *adj*

**con•vene** *vb* **:** assemble or meet

**con•ve•nience** *n* **1 :** personal comfort or ease **2 :** device that saves work — **con•ve•nient** *adj* — **con•ve•nient•ly** *adv*

**con•vent** *n* **:** community of nuns

**con•ven•tion** *n* **1 :** agreement esp. between nations **2 :** large meeting **3 :** body of delegates **4 :** accepted usage or way of behaving — **con•ven•tion•al** *adj* — **con•ven•tion•al•ly** *adv*

**con•ver•sa•tion** *n* **:** an informal talking together — **con•ver•sa•tion•al** *adj*

**[1]con•verse** *vb* **:** engage in conversation — **con•verse** *n*

**[2]con•verse** *adj* **:** opposite — **con•verse** *n* — **con•verse•ly** *adv*

**con•vert** *vb* **1 :** turn from one belief or party to another **2 :** change ~ *n* **:** one who has adopted a religion — **con•ver•sion** *n* — **con•vert•er, con•ver•tor** *n* — **con•vert•ible** *adj*

**con•vert•ible** *n* **:** automobile with a removable top

**con•vex** *adj* **:** curved or rounded like the outside of a sphere — **con•vex•i•ty** *n*

**con•vey** *vb* **:** transport or transmit — **con•vey•ance** *n* — **con•vey•or** *n*

**con•vict** *vb* **:** find guilty ~ *n* **:** person in prison

**con•vic•tion** *n* **1 :** act of convicting **2 :** strong belief

**con•vince** *vb* **:** cause to believe — **con•vinc•ing•ly** *adv*

**con•viv•ial** *adj* **:** cheerful or festive — **con•viv•i•al•i•ty** *n*

**con•vo•lut•ed** *adj* **1 :** intricately folded **2 :** intricate

**con•vo•lu•tion** *n* **:** convoluted structure

**con•voy** *vb* **:** accompany for protection ~ *n* **:** group of vehicles or ships moving together

**con•vul•sion** *n* **:** violent involuntary muscle contraction — **con•vulse** *vb* — **con•vul•sive** *adj*

**coo** *n* **:** sound of a pigeon — **coo** *vb*

**cook** *n* **:** one who prepares food ~ *vb* **:** prepare food — **cook•book** *n* — **cook•er** *n* — **cook•ery** *n* — **cook•ware** *n*

**cook•ie, cooky** *n* **:** small sweet flat cake

**cool** *adj* **1 :** moderately cold **2 :** not excited **3 :** unfriendly ~ *vb* **:** make or become cool ~ *n* **1 :** cool time or place **2 :** composure — **cool•ant** *n* — **cool•er** *n* — **cool•ly** *adv* — **cool•ness** *n*

**coop** *n* **:** enclosure usu. for poultry ~ *vb* **:** confine in or as if in a coop

**co–op** *n* **:** cooperative

**co•op•er•ate** *vb* **:** act jointly — **co•op•er•a•tion** *n* — **co•op•er•a•tive** *adj or n*

**co•or•di•nate** *adj* **:** equal esp. in rank ~ *n* **:** any of a set of numbers used in specifying the location of a point on a surface or in space ~ *vb* **1 :** make or become coordinate **2 :** work or act together harmoniously — **co•or•di•nate•ly** *adv* — **co•or•di•na•tion** *n* — **co•or•di•na•tor** *n*

**cop** *n* **:** police officer

**cope** *vb* **:** deal with difficulties

**co•pi•lot** *n* **:** assistant airplane pilot

**cop•ing** *n* **:** top layer of a wall

**co•pi•ous** *adj* **:** very abundant — **co•pi•ous•ly** *adv* — **co•pi•ous•ness** *n*

**cop•per** *n* **1 :** malleable reddish metallic chemical element **2 :** penny — **cop•pery** *adj*

**copy** *n* **1 :** imitation or reproduction of an original **2 :** writing to be set for printing ~ *vb* **1 :** make a copy of **2 :** imitate — **copi•er** *n* — **copy•ist** *n*

**copy•right** *n* **:** sole right to a literary or artistic work ~ *vb* **:** get a copyright on

**cor•al** *n* **1 :** skeletal material of colonies of tiny sea polyps **2 :** deep pink — **coral** *adj*

**cord** *n* **1 :** usu. heavy string **2 :** long slender anatomical structure **3 :** measure of firewood equal to 128 cu. ft. **4 :** small electrical cable ~ *vb* **1 :** tie or furnish with a cord **2 :** pile (wood) in cords

**cor•dial** *adj* **:** warmly welcoming — **cor•di•al•i•ty** *n* — **cor•dial•ly** *adv*

**cor•du•roy** *n* **1 :** heavy ribbed fabric **2** *pl* **:** trousers of corduroy

**core** *n* **1 :** central part of some fruits **2 :** inmost part ~ *vb* **:** take out the core of — **cor•er** *n*

**cork** *n* **1 :** tough elastic bark of a European oak (**cork oak**) **2 :** stopper of cork ~ *vb* **:** stop up with a cork — **corky** *adj*

**[1]corn** *n* **:** cereal grass (as Indian corn) or its seeds ~ *vb* **:** cure or preserve in brine — **corn•cob** *n* — **corn•meal** *n* — **corn•stalk** *n* — **corn•starch** *n*

**[2]corn** *n* **:** local hardening and thickening of skin

**cor•nea** *n* **:** transparent part of the coat of the eyeball — **cor•ne•al** *adj*

**cor•ner** *n* **1 :** point or angle formed by the meeting of lines or sides **2 :** place where two streets meet **3 :** inescapable position **4 :** control of the supply of something ~ *vb* **1 :** drive into a corner **2 :** get a corner on **3 :** turn a corner

**cor•ner•stone** *n* **1 :** stone at a corner of a wall **2 :** something basic

**cor•net** *n* **:** trumpetlike instrument

**cor•o•nary** *adj* **:** relating to the heart or its blood vessels ~ *n* **1 :** thrombosis of an artery supplying the heart **2 :** heart attack

**cor•o•na•tion** *n* **:** crowning of a monarch

**cor•o•ner** *n* **:** public official who investigates causes of suspicious deaths

**[1]cor•po•ral** *adj* **:** bodily

**[2]corporal** *n* **:** noncommissioned officer ranking below a sergeant

**cor•po•ra•tion** *n* **:** legal creation with the rights and liabilities of a person — **cor•po•rate** *adj*

**cor•po•re•al** *adj* **:** physical or material — **cor•po•re•al•ly** *adv*

**corps** *n* **1 :** subdivision of a military force **2 :** working group

**corpse** *n* **:** dead body

**cor•pus•cle** *n* **:** blood cell

**cor•ral** *n* **:** enclosure for animals — **corral** *vb*

**cor•rect** *vb* **1 :** make right **2 :** chastise ~ *adj* **1 :** true or factual **2 :** conforming to a standard — **cor•rec•tion** *n* — **cor•rec•tive** *adj* — **cor•rect•ly** *adv* — **cor•rect•ness** *n*

**cor•re•late** *vb* **:** show a connection between — **cor•re•late** *n* — **cor•re•la•tion** *n* — **cor•rel•a•tive** *n or adj*

**cor•re•spond** *vb* **1 :** match **2 :** communicate by letter — **cor•re•spon•dence** *n* — **cor•re•spond•ing•ly** *adv*

**cor•re•spon•dent** *n* **1 :** person one writes to **2 :** reporter

**cor•ri•dor** *n* **:** passageway connecting rooms

**cor•rode** *vb* **:** wear away by chemical action — **cor•ro•sion** *n* — **cor•ro•sive** *adj or n*

**cor•rupt** *vb* **1 :** change from good to bad **2 :** bribe ~ *adj* **:** morally debased — **cor•rupt•ible** *adj* — **cor•rup•tion** *n*

**cor•sage** *n* **:** bouquet worn by a woman

**cos•met•ic** *n* **:** beautifying preparation ~ *adj* **:** relating to beautifying

**cos•mic** *adj* **1 :** relating to the universe **2 :** vast or grand

**cos•mo•naut** *n* **:** Soviet or Russian astronaut

**cos•mo•pol•i•tan** *adj* **:** belonging to all the world — **cos•mo•pol•i•tan** *n*

**cos•mos** *n* **:** universe

**cost** *n* **1 :** amount paid for something **2 :** loss or penalty ~ *vb* **cost; cost 1 :** require so much in payment **2 :** cause to pay, suffer, or lose — **cost•li•ness** *n* — **cost•ly** *adj*

**cos•tume** *n* **:** clothing

**co•sy** *var of* COZY

**cot** *n* **:** small bed

**cote** *n* **:** small shed or coop

**cot•tage** *n* **:** small house

**cot•ton** *n* **:** soft fibrous plant substance or thread or cloth made of it — **cot•ton•seed** *n* — **cot•tony** *adj*

**cot•ton•mouth** *n* **:** poisonous snake

**couch** *vb* **1 :** lie or place on a couch **2 :** phrase ~ *n* **:** bed or sofa

**couch potato** *n* **:** one who spends a great deal of time watching television

**cou•gar** *n* **:** large tawny wild American cat

**cough** *vb* **:** force air from the lungs with short sharp noises — **cough** *n*

**could** *past of* CAN

**couldn't :** could not

**coun•cil** *n* **1 :** assembly or meeting **2 :** body of lawmakers — **coun•cil•lor, coun•cil•or** *n* — **coun•cil•man** *n* — **coun•cil•wom•an** *n*

**coun•sel** *n* **1 :** advice **2 :** deliberation together **3** *pl* **coun•sel :** lawyer ~ *vb* **1 :** advise **2 :** consult together — **coun•sel•or, coun•sel•lor** *n*

**[1]count** *vb* **1 :** name or indicate one by one to find the total number **2 :** recite numbers in order **3 :** rely **4 :** be of value or account ~ *n* **1 :** act of counting or the total obtained by counting **2 :** charge in an indictment — **count•able** *adj* — **count•less** *adj*

**[2]count** *n* **:** European nobleman

**coun•te•nance** *n* **:** face or facial expression ~ *vb* **:** allow or encourage

**[1]count•er** *n* **1 :** piece for reckoning or games **2 :** surface over which business is transacted

**[2]count•er** *n* **:** one that counts

**[3]coun•ter** *vb* **:** oppose ~ *adv* **:** in an opposite direction ~ *n* **:** offsetting force or move ~ *adj* **:** contrary

**coun•ter•act** *vb* **:** lessen the force of — **coun•ter•ac•tive** *adj*

**coun•ter•bal•ance** *n* **:** balancing influence or weight ~ *vb* **:** oppose or balance

**coun•ter•clock•wise** *adv or adj* **:** opposite to the way a clock's hands move

**coun•ter•feit** *vb* **1 :** copy in order to deceive **2 :** pretend ~ *adj* **:** not genuine ~ *n* **:** fraudulent copy — **coun•ter•feit•er** *n*

**coun•ter•part** *n* **:** one that is similar or corresponds

**coun•ter•sign** *n* **:** secret signal ~ *vb* **:** add a confirming signature to

**count•ess** *n* **:** wife or widow of a count or an earl or a woman holding that rank in her own right

**coun•try** *n* **1 :** nation **2 :** rural area ~ *adj* **:** rural — **coun•try•man** *n*

**coun•try•side** *n* **:** rural area or its people

**coun•ty** *n* **:** local government division esp. of a state

**coup** *n* **1 :** brilliant sudden action or plan **2 :** sudden overthrow of a government
**coupe** *n* **:** 2-door automobile with an enclosed body
**cou•ple** *vb* **:** link together ~ *n* **1 :** pair **2 :** two persons closely associated or married
**cou•pling** *n* **:** connecting device
**cou•pon** *n* **:** certificate redeemable for goods or a cash discount
**cour•age** *n* **:** ability to conquer fear or despair — **cou•ra•geous** *adj*
**course** *n* **1 :** progress **2 :** ground over which something moves **3 :** part of a meal served at one time **4 :** method of procedure **5 :** subject taught in a series of classes ~ *vb* **1 :** hunt with dogs **2 :** run speedily — **of course :** as might be expected
**court** *n* **1 :** residence of a sovereign **2 :** sovereign and his or her officials and advisers **3 :** area enclosed by a building **4 :** space marked for playing a game **5 :** place where justice is administered ~ *vb* **:** seek to win the affections of — **court•house** *n* — **court•room** *n* — **court•ship** *n*
**cour•te•ous** *adj* **:** showing politeness and respect for others — **cour•te•ous•ly** *adv*
**cour•te•sy** *n* **:** courteous behavior
**court–mar•tial** *n* **courts–mar•tial :** military trial court — **court–martial** *vb*
**court•yard** *n* **:** enclosure open to the sky that is attached to a house
**cous•in** *n* **:** child of one's uncle or aunt
**cove** *n* **:** sheltered inlet or bay
**cov•e•nant** *n* **:** binding agreement — **cov•e•nant** *vb*
**cov•er** *vb* **1 :** place something over or upon **2 :** protect or hide **3 :** include or deal with ~ *n* **:** something that covers — **cov•er•age** *n*
**co•vert** *adj* **:** secret ~ *n* **:** thicket that shelters animals
**cov•et** *vb* **:** desire enviously — **cov•et•ous** *adj*
[1]**cow** *n* **:** large adult female animal (as of cattle) — **cow•hide** *n*
[2]**cow** *vb* **:** intimidate
**cow•ard** *n* **:** one who lacks courage — **cow•ard•ice** *n* — **cow•ard•ly** *adv or adj*
**cow•boy** *n* **:** a mounted ranch hand who tends cattle
**cow•er** *vb* **:** shrink from fear or cold
**cow•girl** *n* **:** woman ranch hand who tends cattle
**coy** *adj* **:** shy or pretending shyness
**coy•ote** *n* **:** small No. American wolf
**co•zy** *adj* **:** snug
**crab** *n* **:** short broad shellfish with pincers
**crab•by** *adj* **:** cross
[1]**crack** *vb* **1 :** break with a sharp sound **2 :** fail in tone **3 :** break without completely separating ~ *n* **1 :** sudden sharp noise **2 :** witty remark **3 :** narrow break **4 :** sharp blow **5 :** try
[2]**crack** *adj* **:** extremely proficient
**crack•down** *n* **:** disciplinary action — **crack down** *vb*
**crack•er** *n* **:** thin crisp bakery product
**crack•le** *vb* **1 :** make snapping noises **2 :** develop fine cracks in a surface — **crack•le** *n*
**crack–up** *n* **:** crash
**cra•dle** *n* **:** baby's bed ~ *vb* **1 :** place in a cradle **2 :** hold securely
**craft** *n* **1 :** occupation requiring special skill **2 :** craftiness **3** *pl usu* **craft :** structure designed to provide transportation **4** *pl usu* **craft :** small boat — **crafts•man** *n* — **crafts•man•ship** *n*
**crafty** *adj* **:** sly — **craft•i•ness** *n*
**crag** *n* **:** steep cliff — **crag•gy** *adj*
**cram** *vb* **1 :** eat greedily **2 :** pack in tight **3 :** study intensely for a test
**cramp** *n* **1 :** sudden painful contraction of muscle **2** *pl* **:** sharp abdominal pains ~ *vb* **1 :** affect with cramp **2 :** restrain
**cran•ber•ry** *n* **:** red acid berry of a trailing plant
**crane** *n* **1 :** tall wading bird **2 :** machine for lifting heavy objects ~ *vb* **:** stretch one's neck to see
**crank** *n* **1 :** bent lever turned to operate a machine **2 :** eccentric ~ *vb* **:** start or operate by turning a crank
**cranky** *adj* **:** irritable
**crash** *vb* **1 :** break noisily **2 :** fall and hit something with noise and damage ~ *n* **1 :** loud sound **2 :** action of crashing **3 :** failure
**crate** *n* **:** wooden shipping container — **crate** *vb*
**cra•ter** *n* **:** volcanic depression
**crave** *vb* **:** long for — **crav•ing** *n*
**crawl** *vb* **1 :** move slowly (as by drawing the body along the ground) **2 :** swarm with creeping things ~ *n* **:** very slow pace
**cray•on** *n* **:** stick of chalk or wax used for drawing or coloring — **crayon** *vb*
**craze** *vb* **:** make or become insane ~ *n* **:** fad
**cra•zy** *adj* **1 :** mentally disordered **2 :** wildly impractical — **cra•zi•ly** *adv* — **cra•zi•ness** *n*
**creak** *vb or n* **:** squeak — **creaky** *adj*
**cream** *n* **1 :** yellowish fat-rich part of milk **2 :** thick smooth sauce, confection, or cosmetic **3 :** choicest part ~ *vb* **:** beat into creamy consistency — **creamy** *adj*
**cream•ery** *n* **:** place where butter and cheese are made
**crease** *n* **:** line made by folding — **crease** *vb*
**cre•ate** *vb* **:** bring into being — **cre•ation** *n* — **cre•ative** *adj* — **cre•ativ•i•ty** *n* — **cre•a•tor** *n*
**crea•ture** *n* **:** lower animal or human being
**cre•den•tials** *n pl* **:** evidence of qualifications or authority
**cred•i•ble** *adj* **:** believable — **cred•i•bil•i•ty** *n*
**cred•it** *n* **1 :** balance in a person's favor **2 :** time given to pay for goods **3 :** belief **4 :** esteem **5 :** source of honor ~ *vb* **1 :** believe **2 :** give credit to — **cred•it•able** *adj* — **cred•it•ably** *adv*
**credit card** *n* **:** a card authorizing purchases on credit
**cred•i•tor** *n* **:** person to whom money is owed
**creed** *n* **:** statement of essential beliefs
**creek** *n* **:** small stream
**creep** *vb* **(crept; crept) 1 :** crawl **2 :** grow over a surface like ivy — **creep** *n* — **creep•er** *n*
**cre•mate** *vb* **:** burn up (a corpse) — **cre•ma•tion** *n* — **cre•ma•to•ry** *n*
**cre•scen•do** *adv or adj* **:** growing louder — **crescendo** *n*
**cres•cent** *n* **:** shape of the moon between new moon and first quarter
**crest** *n* **1 :** tuft on a bird's head **2 :** top of a hill or wave **3 :** part of a coat of arms ~ *vb* **:** rise to a crest — **crest•ed** *adj*
**cre•vasse** *n* **:** deep fissure esp. in a glacier
**crev•ice** *n* **:** narrow fissure
**crew** *n* **:** body of workers (as on a ship) — **crew•man** *n*
**crib** *n* **1 :** grain storage bin **2 :** baby's bed ~ *vb* **:** put in a crib
**crick•et** *n* **:** insect noted for the chirping of the male
**crime** *n* **:** serious violation of law — **crim•i•nal** *n or adj*
**crin•kle** *vb* **:** wrinkle — **crinkle** *n* — **crin•kly** *adj*
**crip•ple** *n* **:** disabled person ~ *vb* **:** disable
**cri•sis** *n* **:** decisive or critical moment
**crisp** *adj* **1 :** easily crumbled **2 :** firm and fresh **3 :** lively **4 :** invigorating — **crisp** *vb* — **crisp•ly** *adv* — **crisp•ness** *n* — **crispy** *adj*
**criss•cross** *n* **:** pattern of crossed lines ~ *vb* **:** mark with or follow a crisscross
**cri•te•ri•on** *n* **:** standard
**crit•ic** *n* **1:** judge of literary or artistic works **2:** one who criticizes — **crit•i•cal** *adj* — **crit•i•cal•ly** *adv*
**crit•i•cize** *vb* **1 :** judge as a critic **2 :** find fault — **crit•i•cism** *n*
**croak** *n* **:** hoarse cry (as of a frog) — **croak** *vb*
**crock** *n* **:** thick earthenware pot or jar — **crock•ery** *n*
**croc•o•dile** *n* **:** large reptile of tropical waters
**cro•cus** *n* **:** herb with spring flowers
**crook** *n* **1 :** bent or curved tool or part **2 :** thief ~ *vb* **:** curve sharply
**crook•ed** *adj* **1 :** bent **2 :** dishonest — **crook•ed•ness** *n*
**crop** *n* **1 :** pouch in the throat of a bird or insect **2 :** short riding whip **3 :** something that can be harvested ~ *vb* **1 :** trim **2 :** appear unexpectedly — used with *up*
**cro•quet** *n* **:** lawn game of driving balls through wickets
**cross** *n* **1 :** figure or structure consisting of an upright and a cross piece **2 :** interbreeding of unlike strains ~ *vb* **1 :** intersect **2 :** cancel **3 :** go or extend across **4 :** interbreed ~ *adj* **1 :** going across **2 :** contrary **3 :** marked by bad temper — **cross•ing** *n* — **cross•ly** *adv*
**cross–ex•am•ine** *vb* **:** question about earlier testimony — **cross–ex•am•i•na•tion** *n*
**cross–eyed** *adj* **:** having the eye turned toward the nose
**cross–re•fer** *vb* **:** refer to another place (as in a book) — **cross–ref•er•ence** *n*
**cross•roads** *n* **:** place where two roads cross
**cross section** *n* **:** representative portion
**cross•walk** *n* **:** path for pedestrians crossing a street
**crotch** *n* **:** angle formed by the parting of 2 legs or branches
**crouch** *vb* **:** stoop over — **crouch** *n*
[1]**crow** *n* **:** large glossy black bird
[2]**crow** *vb* **1 :** make the loud sound of the cock **2 :** gloat ~ *n* **:** cry of the cock
**crowd** *vb* **:** collect or cram together ~ *n* **:** large number of people
**crown** *n* **1 :** wreath of honor or victory **2 :** royal headdress **3 :** top or highest part ~ *vb* **1 :** place a crown on **2 :** honor — **crowned** *adj*
**cru•cial** *adj* **:** vitally important
**cru•ci•fix** *n* **:** representation of Christ on the cross
**cru•ci•fix•ion** *n* **:** act of crucifying
**cru•ci•fy** *vb* **1 :** put to death on a cross **2 :** persecute
**crude** *adj* **1 :** not refined **2 :** lacking grace or elegance ~ *n* **:** unrefined petroleum — **crude•ly** *adv* — **cru•di•ty** *n*
**cru•el** *adj* **:** causing suffering to others — **cru•el•ly** *adv* — **cru•el•ty** *n*
**cruise** *vb* **1 :** sail to several ports **2 :** travel at the most efficient speed — **cruise** *n*
**cruis•er** *n* **1 :** ship of war **2 :** police car
**crumb** *n* **:** small fragment
**crum•ble** *vb* **:** break into small pieces — **crum•bly** *adj*
**crum•ple** *vb* **1 :** crush together **2 :** collapse
**crunch** *vb* **:** chew or press with a crushing noise ~ *n* **:** crunching sound — **crunchy** *adj*
**cru•sade** *n* **1** *cap* **:** medieval Christian expedition to the Holy Land **2 :** reform movement — **crusade** *vb* — **cru•sad•er** *n*
**crush** *vb* **1 :** squeeze out of shape **2 :** grind or pound to bits **3 :** suppress ~ *n* **1 :** severe crowding **2 :** infatuation
**crust** *n* **1 :** hard outer part of bread or a pie **2 :** hard surface layer — **crust•al** *adj* — **crusty** *adj*
**crutch** *n* **:** support for use by the disabled in walking
**cry** *vb* **1 :** call out **2 :** weep ~ *n* **1 :** shout **2 :** fit of weeping **3 :** characteristic sound of an animal
**cryp•tic** *adj* **:** enigmatic
**cryp•tog•ra•phy** *n* **:** coding and decoding of messages — **cryp•tog•ra•pher** *n*
**crys•tal** *n* **1 :** transparent quartz **2 :** something (as glass) like crystal **3 :** body formed by solidification that has a regular repeating atomic arrangement — **crys•tal•line** *adj*
**crys•tal•lize** *vb* **:** form crystals or a definite shape — **crys•tal•li•za•tion** *n*
**cub** *n* **:** young animal
**cube** *n* **1 :** solid having 6 equal square sides **2 :** product obtained by taking a number 3 times as a factor ~ *vb* **1 :** raise to the 3d power **2 :** form into a cube **3 :** cut into cubes — **cu•bic** *adj*
**cu•bi•cle** *n* **:** small room
**cuck•oo** *n* **:** brown European bird ~ *adj* **:** silly
**cu•cum•ber** *n* **:** fleshy fruit related to the gourds
**cud•dle** *vb* **:** lie close
[1]**cue** *n* **:** signal — **cue** *vb*
[2]**cue** *n* **:** stick used in pool
[1]**cuff** *n* **1 :** part of a sleeve encircling the wrist **2 :** folded trouser hem
[2]**cuff** *vb or n* **:** slap
**cu•li•nary** *adj* **:** of or relating to cookery
**cull** *vb* **:** select
**cul•pa•ble** *adj* **:** deserving blame
**cul•prit** *n* **:** guilty person
**cult** *n* **1 :** religious system **2 :** faddish devotion — **cult•ist** *n*
**cul•ti•vate** *vb* **1 :** prepare for crops **2 :** foster the growth of **3 :** refine — **cul•ti•va•tion** *n*
**cul•ture** *n* **1 :** cultivation **2 :** refinement of intellectual and artistic taste **3 :** particular form or stage of civilization — **cul•tur•al** *adj* — **cul•tured** *adj*
**cum•ber•some** *adj* **:** awkward to handle due to bulk
**cun•ning** *adj* **1 :** crafty **2 :** clever **3 :** appealing ~ *n* **1 :** skill **2 :** craftiness
**cup** *n* **1 :** small drinking vessel **2 :** contents of a cup **3 :** a half pint ~ *vb* **:** shape like a cup — **cup•ful** *n*
**cup•board** *n* **:** small storage closet
**cup•cake** *n* **:** small cake
**cu•ra•tor** *n* **:** one in charge of a museum or zoo
**curb** *n* **1 :** restraint **2 :** raised edging along a street ~ *vb* **:** hold back
**curd** *n* **:** coagulated milk
**cur•dle** *vb* **1 :** form curds **2 :** sour
**cure** *n* **1 :** recovery from disease **2 :** remedy ~ *vb* **1 :** restore to health **2 :** process for storage or use — **cur•able** *adj*
**cur•few** *n* **:** requirement to be off the streets at a set hour
**cu•ri•ous** *adj* **1 :** eager to learn **2 :** strange — **cu•ri•os•i•ty** *n* — **cu•ri•ous•ly** *adv* — **cu•ri•ous•ness** *n*
**curl** *vb* **1 :** form into ringlets **2 :** curve ~ *n* **1 :** ringlet of hair **2 :** something with a spiral form — **curl•er** *n* — **curly** *adj*
**cur•ren•cy** *n* **1 :** general use or acceptance **2 :** money
**cur•rent** *adj* **:** occurring in or belonging to the present ~ *n* **1 :** swiftest part of a stream **2 :** flow of electricity
**cur•ric•u•lum** *n* **:** course of study
**curse** *n* **1 :** a calling down of evil or harm upon one **2 :** affliction ~ *vb* **1 :** call down injury upon **2 :** swear at **3 :** afflict
**cur•sor** *n* **:** indicator on a computer screen
**curt** *adj* **:** rudely abrupt — **curt•ly** *adv* — **curt•ness** *n*
**cur•tail** *vb* **:** shorten — **cur•tail•ment** *n*
**cur•tain** *n* **:** hanging screen that can be drawn back or raised — **cur•tain** *vb*
**curt•sy, curt•sey** *n* **:** courteous bow made by bending the knees — **curt•sy, curt•sey** *vb*
**cur•va•ture** *n* **:** amount or state of curving
**curve** *vb* **:** bend from a straight line or course ~ *n* **1 :** a bending without angles **2 :** something curved
**cush•ion** *n* **1 :** soft pillow **2 :** something that eases or protects ~ *vb* **1 :** provide with a cushion **2 :** soften the force of

**cus·tard** *n* : sweetened cooked mixture of milk and eggs

**cus·to·dy** *n* : immediate care or charge — **cus·to·di·al** *adj* — **cus·to·di·an** *n*

**cus·tom** *n* **1** : habitual course of action **2** *pl* : import taxes ～ *adj* : made to personal order — **cus·tom·ar·i·ly** *adv* — **cus·tom·ary** *adj* — **custom–built** *adj* — **cus·tom–made** *adj*

**cus·tom·er** *n* : buyer

**cut** *vb* (**cut; cut**) **1** : penetrate or divide with a sharp edge **2** : experience the growth of (a tooth) through the gum **3** : shorten **4** : remove by severing **5** : intersect ～ *n* **1** : something separated by cutting **2** : reduction — **cut·ter** *n* — **cut in** *vb* : thrust oneself between others

**cute** *adj* : pretty

**cut·lery** *n* : cutting utensils

**cut·let** *n* : slice of meat

**cut·throat** *n* : murderer ～ *adj* : ruthless

**cy·ber·space** *n* : online world of the Internet

**cy·cle** *n* **1** : period of time for a series of repeated events **2** : recurring round of events **3** : long period of time **4** : bicycle or motorcycle ～ *vb* : ride a cycle — **cy·clic, cy·cli·cal** *adj* — **cy·clist** *n*

**cy·clone** *n* : tornado — **cy·clon·ic** *adj*

**cyl·in·der** *n* **1** : long round body or figure **2** : rotating chamber in a revolver **3** : piston chamber in an engine — **cy·lin·dri·cal** *adj*

**cyn·ic** *n* : one who attributes all actions to selfish motives — **cyn·i·cal** *adj* — **cyn·i·cism** *n*

**cyst** *n* : abnormal bodily sac — **cys·tic** *adj*

**czar** *n* : ruler of Russia until 1917 — **czar·ist** *n or adj*

# D

**d** *n* : 4th letter of the alphabet

**¹dab** *n* : gentle touch or stroke ～ *vb* : touch or apply lightly

**²dab** *n* : small amount

**dab·ble** *vb* **1** : splash **2** : work without serious effort — **dab·bler** *n*

**dad** *n* : father

**dad·dy** *n* : father

**daf·fo·dil** *n* : narcissus with trumpetlike flowers

**dag·ger** *n* : knife for stabbing

**dai·ly** *adj* **1** : occurring, done, or used every day or every weekday **2** : computed in terms of one day ～ *n* : daily newspaper — **daily** *adv*

**dain·ty** *n* : something delicious ～ *adj* : delicately pretty — **dain·ti·ly** *adv* — **dain·ti·ness** *n*

**dairy** *n* : farm that produces or company that processes milk — **dairy·maid** *n* — **dairy·man** *n*

**dai·sy** *n* : tall leafy-stemmed plant bearing showy flowers

**dal·ly** *vb* **1** : flirt **2** : dawdle — **dal·li·ance** *n*

**¹dam** *n* : female parent of a domestic animal

**²dam** *n* : barrier to hold back water — **dam** *vb*

**dam·age** *n* **1** : loss or harm due to injury **2** *pl* : compensation for loss or injury ～ *vb* : do damage to

**dame** *n* : woman of rank or authority

**damn** *vb* **1** : condemn to hell **2** : curse — **dam·na·ble** *adj* — **dam·na·tion** *n* — **damned** *adj*

**damp** *n* : moisture ～ *vb* **1** : reduce the draft in **2** : restrain **3** : moisten ～ *adj* : moist — **damp·en** *vb* — **damp·ness** *n*

**damp·er** *n* : movable plate to regulate a flue draft

**dam·sel** *n* : young woman

**dance** *vb* : move rhythmically to music ～ *n* : act of dancing or a gathering for dancing — **danc·er** *n*

**dan·de·li·on** *n* : common yellow-flowered herb

**dan·druff** *n* : whitish thin dry scales of skin on the scalp

**dan·dy** *n* **1** : man too concerned with clothes **2** : something excellent ～ *adj* : very good

**dan·ger** *n* **1** : exposure to injury or evil **2** : something that may cause injury — **dan·ger·ous** *adj*

**dan·gle** *vb* **1** : hang and swing freely **2** : be left without support or connection **3** : allow or cause to hang **4** : offer as an inducement

**dap·per** *adj* : neat and stylishly dressed

**dap·ple** *vb* : mark with colored spots

**dare** *vb* **1** : have sufficient courage **2** : urge or provoke to contend — **dare** *n* — **dar·ing** *n or adj*

**dare·dev·il** *n* : recklessly bold person

**dark** *adj* **1** : having little or no light **2** : not light in color **3** : gloomy ～ *n* : absence of light — **dark·en** *vb* — **dark·ly** *adv* — **dark·ness** *n*

**dar·ling** *n* **1** : beloved **2** : favorite ～ *adj* **1** : dearly loved **2** : very pleasing

**dart** *n* **1** : small pointed missile **2** *pl* : game of throwing darts at a target **3** : tapering fold in a garment **4** : quick movement ～ *vb* : move suddenly or rapidly

**dash** *vb* **1** : smash **2** : knock or hurl violently **3** : ruin **4** : perform or finish hastily **5** : move quickly ～ *n* **1** : sudden burst, splash, or stroke **2** : punctuation mark — **3** : tiny amount **4** : showiness or liveliness **5** : sudden rush **6** : short race **7** : dashboard

**dash·board** *n* : instrument panel

**da·ta** *n sing or pl* : factual information

**da·ta·base** *n* : data organized for computer search

**¹date** *n* : edible fruit of a palm

**²date** *n* **1** : day, month, or year when something is done or made **2** : historical time period **3** : social engagement or the person one goes out with ～ *vb* **1** : determine or record the date of **2** : have a date with **3** : originate — **to date** : up to now

**dat·ed** *adj* : old-fashioned

**daub** *vb* : smear ～ *n* : something daubed on — **daub·er** *n*

**daugh·ter** *n* : human female offspring

**daugh·ter–in–law** *n* (**daughters–in–law**) : wife of one's son

**daw·dle** *vb* **1** : waste time **2** : loiter

**dawn** *vb* **1** : grow light as the sun rises **2** : begin to appear, develop, or be understood ～ *n* : first appearance (as of daylight)

**day** *n* **1** : period of light between one night and the next **2** : 24 hours **3** : specified date **4** : particular time or age **5** : period of work for a day — **day·break** *n* — **day·light** *n* — **day·time** *n*

**day·dream** *n* : fantasy of wish fulfillment — **daydream** *vb*

**daze** *vb* **1** : stun by a blow **2** : dazzle — **daze** *n*

**daz·zle** *vb* **1** : overpower with light **2** : impress greatly — **dazzle** *n*

**dead** *adj* **1** : lifeless **2** : unresponsive or inactive **3** : exhausted **4** : obsolete **5** : precise ～ *n* **dead 1** : one that is dead — usu. with *the* **2** : most lifeless time ～ *adv* **1** : completely **2** : directly — **dead·en** *vb*

**dead·beat** *n* : one who will not pay debts

**dead heat** *n* : tie in a contest

**dead·line** *n* : time by which something must be finished

**dead·lock** *n* : struggle that neither side can win — **deadlock** *vb*

**dead·ly** *adj* **1** : capable of causing death **2** : very accurate **3** : fatal to spiritual progress **4** : suggestive of death **5** : very great ～ *adv* : extremely — **dead·li·ness** *n*

**dead·pan** *adj* : showing no expression — **dead·pan** *n or vb or adv*

**deaf** *adj* : unable or unwilling to hear — **deaf·en** *vb* — **deaf·ness** *n*

**deaf–mute** *n* : deaf person unable to speak

**deal** *n* **1** : indefinite quantity **2** : distribution of playing cards **3** : negotiation or agreement **4** : treatment received **5** : bargain ～ *vb* **dealt; dealt 1** : distribute playing cards **2** : be concerned with **3** : administer or deliver **4** : take action **5** : sell **6** : reach a state of acceptance — **deal·er** *n* — **deal·ing** *n*

**dean** *n* **1** : head of a group of clergy members **2** : university or school administrator **3** : senior member

**dear** *adj* **1** : highly valued or loved **2** : expensive ～ *n* : loved one — **dear·ly** *adv* — **dear·ness** *n*

**death** *n* **1** : end of life **2** : cause of loss of life **3** : state of being dead **4** : destruction or extinction — **death·less** *adj* — **death·ly** *adj or adv*

**de·base** *vb* : hurt the value or dignity of

**de·bate** *vb* : discuss a question by argument — **de·bat·able** *adj* — **debate** *n* — **de·bat·er** *n*

**de·bil·i·tate** *vb* : make ill or weak — **de·bil·i·ty** *n*

**deb·it** *n* : account entry of a payment or debt ～ *vb* : record as a debit

**de·bris** *n* : remains of something destroyed

**debt** *n* **1** : sin **2** : something owed **3** : state of owing — **debt·or** *n*

**de·but** *n* **1** : first public appearance **2** : formal entrance into society — **debut** *vb* — **deb·u·tante** *n*

**de·cade** *n* : 10 years

**dec·a·dence** *n* : deterioration — **dec·a·dent** *adj or n*

**de·cal** *n* : picture or design for transfer from prepared paper

**de·cap·i·tate** *vb* : behead — **de·cap·i·ta·tion** *n*

**de·cay** *vb* **1** : decline in condition **2** : decompose — **decay** *n*

**de·cease** *n* : death — **decease** *vb*

**de·ceit** *n* **1** : deception **2** : dishonesty — **de·ceit·ful** *adj* — **de·ceit·ful·ly** *adv* — **de·ceit·ful·ness** *n*

**de·ceive** *vb* : trick or mislead — **de·ceiv·er** *n*

**de·cel·er·ate** *vb* : slow down

**De·cem·ber** *n* : 12th month of the year having 31 days

**de·cent** *adj* **1** : good, right, or just **2** : wearing clothes **3** : not obscene **4** : fairly good — **de·cen·cy** *n* — **de·cent·ly** *adv*

**de·cep·tion** *n* **1** : act or fact of deceiving **2** : fraud — **de·cep·tive** *adj* — **de·cep·tive·ly** *adv* — **de·cep·tive·ness** *n*

**de·cide** *vb* **1** : make a choice or judgment **2** : bring to a conclusion **3** : cause to decide

**de·cid·ed** *adj* **1** : beyond doubt or question **2** : resolute — **de·cid·ed·ly** *adv*

**dec·i·mal** *n* : fraction in which the denominator is a power of 10 expressed by a point (**decimal point**) placed at the left — **decimal** *adj*

**de·ci·pher** *vb* : make out the meaning of — **de·ci·pher·able** *adj*

**de·ci·sion** *n* **1** : act or result of deciding **2** : determination

**de·ci·sive** *adj* **1** : having the power to decide **2** : conclusive **3** : showing determination — **de·ci·sive·ly** *adv* — **de·ci·sive·ness** *n*

**deck** *n* **1** : floor of a ship **2** : pack of playing cards ～ *vb* **1** : array or dress up **2** : knock down

**de·clare** *vb* **1** : make known formally **2** : state emphatically — **dec·la·ra·tion** *n* — **de·clar·a·tive** *adj* — **de·clar·a·to·ry** *adj* — **de·clar·er** *n*

**de·cline** *vb* **1** : turn or slope downward **2** : wane **3** : refuse to accept ～ *n* **1** : gradual wasting away **2** : change to a lower state or level **3** : a descending slope — **dec·li·na·tion** *n*

**de·code** *vb* : decipher (a coded message) — **de·cod·er** *n*

**de·com·pose** *vb* **1** : separate into parts **2** : decay — **de·com·po·si·tion** *n*

**de·con·ges·tant** *n* : agent that relieves congestion

**de·cor, dé·cor** *n* : room design or decoration

**dec·o·rate** *vb* **1** : add something attractive to **2** : honor with a medal — **dec·o·ra·tion** *n* — **dec·o·ra·tive** *adj* — **dec·o·ra·tor** *n*

**de·coy** *n* : something that tempts or draws attention from another ～ *vb* : tempt

**de·crease** *vb* : grow or cause to grow less — **decrease** *n*

**de·cree** *n* : official order — **de·cree** *vb*

**de·cre·scen·do** *adv or adj* : with a decrease in volume

**ded·i·cate** *vb* **1** : set apart for a purpose (as honor or worship) **2** : address to someone as a compliment — **ded·i·ca·tion** *n* — **ded·i·ca·to·ry** *adj*

**de·duce** *vb* : derive by reasoning — **de·duc·ible** *adj*

**de·duct** *vb* : subtract — **de·duct·ible** *adj* — **de·duc·tion** *n* — **de·duc·tive** *adj*

**deed** *n* **1** : exploit **2** : document showing ownership ～ *vb* : convey by deed

**deep** *adj* **1** : extending far or a specified distance down, back, within, or outward **2** : occupied **3** : dark and rich in color **4** : low in tone ～ *adv* **1** : deeply **2** : far along in time ～ *n* : deep place — **deep·en** *vb* — **deep·ly** *adv*

**deep–seat·ed** *adj* : firmly established

**deer** *n* (**deer**) : ruminant mammal with antlers in the male — **deer·skin** *n*

**de·fault** *n* : failure in a duty — **default** *vb* — **de·fault·er** *n*

**de·feat** *vb* **1** : frustrate **2** : win victory over ～ *n* : loss of a battle or contest

**def·e·cate** *vb* : discharge feces from the bowels — **def·e·ca·tion** *n*

**de·fect** *n* : imperfection ～ *vb* : desert — **de·fec·tion** *n* — **de·fec·tive** *adj* — **de·fec·tor** *n*

**de·fend** *vb* **1** : protect from danger or harm **2** : take the side of — **de·fend·er** *n*

**de·fen·dant** *n* : person charged or sued in a court

**de·fense** *n* **1** : act of defending **2** : something that defends **3** : party, group, or team that opposes another — **de·fense·less** *adj* — **de·fen·si·ble** *adj* — **de·fen·sive** *adj or n*

**de·fer** *vb* : postpone — **de·fer·ment** *n* — **de·fer·ra·ble** *adj*

**de·fi·ance** *n* : disposition to resist — **de·fi·ant** *adj*

**de·fi·cient** *adj* **1** : lacking something necessary **2** : not up to standard — **de·fi·cien·cy** *n*

**def·i·cit** *n* : shortage esp. in money

**de·fine** *vb* **1** : fix or mark the limits of **2** : clarify in outline **3** : set forth the meaning of — **de·fin·able** *adj* — **de·fin·ably** *adv* — **de·fin·er** *n* — **def·i·ni·tion** *n*

**def·i·nite** *adj* **1** : having distinct limits **2** : clear in meaning, intent, or identity **3** : typically designating an identified or immediately identifiable person or thing — **def·i·nite·ly** *adv*

**de·fin·i·tive** *adj* **1** : conclusive **2** : authoritative

**de·flate** *vb* **1** : release air or gas from **2** : reduce — **de·fla·tion** *n*

**de·flect** *vb* : turn aside — **de·flec·tion** *n*

**de·form** *vb* **1** : distort **2** : disfigure — **de·for·ma·tion** *n* — **de·for·mi·ty** *n*

**de·fraud** *vb* : cheat

**de·frost** *vb* **1** : thaw out **2** : free from ice — **de·frost·er** *n*

**de·funct** *adj* : dead

**de·fy** *vb* **1** : challenge **2** : boldly refuse to obey

**de·gen·er·ate** *adj* : degraded or corrupt ~ *n* : degenerate person ~ *vb* : become degenerate — **de·gen·er·a·cy** *n* — **de·gen·er·a·tion** *n* — **de·gen·er·a·tive** *adj*

**de·grade** *vb* **1** : reduce from a higher to a lower rank or degree **2** : debase **3** : decompose — **de·grad·able** *adj* — **deg·ra·da·tion** *n*

**de·gree** *n* **1** : step in a series **2** : extent, intensity, or scope **3** : title given to a college graduate **4** : a 360th part of the circumference of a circle **5** : unit for measuring temperature

**de·hy·drate** *vb* **1** : remove water from **2** : lose liquid — **de·hy·dra·tion** *n*

**de·i·fy** *vb* : make a god of — **de·i·fi·ca·tion** *n*

**de·i·ty** *n* **1** *cap* : God **2** : a god or goddess

**de·ject·ed** *adj* : sad — **de·jec·tion** *n*

**de·lay** *n* : a putting off of something ~ *vb* **1** : postpone **2** : stop or hinder for a time

**de·lec·ta·ble** *adj* : delicious

**del·e·gate** *n* : representative ~ *vb* **1** : entrust to another **2** : appoint as one's delegate — **del·e·ga·tion** *n*

**de·lete** *vb* : eliminate something written — **de·le·tion** *n*

**deli** *n* : a delicatessen

**de·lib·er·ate** *adj* **1** : determined after careful thought **2** : intentional **3** : not hurried ~ *vb* : consider carefully — **de·lib·er·ate·ly** *adv* — **de·lib·er·ate·ness** *n* — **de·lib·er·a·tion** *n* — **de·lib·er·a·tive** *adj*

**del·i·ca·cy** *n* **1** : something special and pleasing to eat **2** : fineness **3** : frailty

**del·i·cate** *adj* **1** : subtly pleasing to the senses **2** : dainty and charming **3** : sensitive or fragile **4** : requiring fine skill or tact — **del·i·cate·ly** *adv*

**del·i·ca·tes·sen** *n* : store that sells ready-to-eat food

**de·li·cious** *adj* : very pleasing esp. in taste or aroma — **de·li·cious·ly** *adv* — **de·li·cious·ness** *n*

**de·light** *n* **1** : great pleasure **2** : source of great pleasure ~ *vb* **1** : take great pleasure **2** : satisfy greatly — **de·light·ful** *adj* — **de·light·ful·ly** *adv*

**de·lin·quent** *n* : delinquent person ~ *adj* **1** : violating duty or law **2** : overdue in payment — **de·lin·quen·cy** *n*

**de·liv·er** *vb* **1** : set free **2** : hand over **3** : assist in birth **4** : say or speak **5** : send to an intended destination — **de·liv·er·ance** *n* — **de·liv·er·er** *n* — **de·liv·ery** *n*

**del·ta** *n* : triangle of land at the mouth of a river

**de·lude** *vb* : mislead or deceive — **de·lu·sion** *n*

**de·luxe** *adj* : very luxurious or elegant

**de·mand** *n* **1** : act of demanding **2** : something claimed as due **3** : ability and desire to buy **4** : urgent need ~ *vb* **1** : ask for with authority **2** : require

**de·mean** *vb* : degrade

**de·mean·or** *n* : behavior

**de·ment·ed** *adj* : crazy

**de·mer·it** *n* : mark given an offender

**de·mise** *n* **1** : death **2** : loss of status

**de·moc·ra·cy** *n* **1** : government in which the supreme power is held by the people **2** : political unit with democratic government — **dem·o·crat** *n* — **dem·o·crat·ic** *adj* — **dem·o·crat·i·cal·ly** *adv* — **de·moc·ra·tize** *vb*

**de·mol·ish** *vb* **1** : tear down or smash **2** : put an end to — **de·mo·li·tion** *n*

**de·mon** *n* : evil spirit — **de·mon·ic** *adj*

**dem·on·strate** *vb* **1** : show clearly or publicly **2** : prove **3** : explain — **dem·on·stra·ble** *adj* — **de·mon·stra·bly** *adv* — **dem·on·stra·tion** *n* — **de·mon·stra·tive** *adj or n* — **dem·on·stra·tor** *n*

**de·mote** *vb* : reduce to a lower rank — **de·mo·tion** *n*

**den** *n* **1** : animal's shelter **2** : hiding place **3** : cozy private little room

**de·ni·al** *n* : rejection of a request or of the validity of a statement

**den·im** *n* **1** : durable twilled cotton fabric **2** *pl* : pants of denim

**de·nom·i·na·tion** *n* **1** : religious body **2** : value or size in a series — **de·nom·i·na·tion·al** *adj*

**de·nom·i·na·tor** *n* : part of a fraction below the line

**de·nounce** *vb* **1** : pronounce blameworthy or evil **2** : inform against — **de·nun·ci·a·tion** *n*

**dense** *adj* **1** : thick, compact, or crowded **2** : stupid — **dense·ly** *adv* — **dense·ness** *n* — **den·si·ty** *n*

**dent** *n* : small depression — **dent** *vb*

**den·tal** *adj* : relating to teeth or dentistry

**den·tist** *n* : one who cares for and replaces teeth — **den·tist·ry** *n*

**den·ture** *n* : artificial teeth

**de·ny** *vb* **1** : declare untrue **2** : deny validity of **3** : refuse to grant

**de·odor·ant** *n* : preparation to prevent unpleasant odors — **de·odor·ize** *vb*

**de·part** *vb* **1** : go away or away from **2** : die — **de·par·ture** *n*

**de·part·ment** *n* **1** : area of responsibility or interest **2** : functional division — **de·part·men·tal** *adj*

**de·pend** *vb* **1** : rely for support **2** : be determined by or based on something else — **de·pend·abil·i·ty** *n* — **de·pend·able** *adj* — **de·pen·dence** *n* — **de·pen·den·cy** *n* — **de·pen·dent** *adj or n*

**de·pict** *vb* : show by or as if by a picture — **de·pic·tion** *n*

**de·plete** *vb* : use up resources of — **de·ple·tion** *n*

**de·plore** *vb* : regret strongly — **de·plor·able** *adj*

**de·port** *vb* **1** : behave **2** : send out of the country — **de·por·ta·tion** *n* — **de·port·ment** *n*

**de·pos·it** *vb* : place esp. for safekeeping ~ *n* **1** : state of being deposited **2** : something deposited **3** : act of depositing **4** : natural accumulation — **de·pos·i·tor** *n*

**de·pos·i·to·ry** *n* : place for deposit

**de·pot** *n* **1** : place for storage **2** : bus or railroad station

**de·prave** *vb* : corrupt morally — **de·praved** *adj* — **de·prav·i·ty** *n*

**de·pre·ci·ate** *vb* **1** : lessen in value **2** : belittle — **de·pre·ci·a·tion** *n*

**de·press** *vb* **1** : press down **2** : lessen the activity or force of **3** : discourage **4** : decrease the market value of — **de·pres·sant** *n or adj* — **de·pressed** *adj* — **de·pres·sive** *adj or n* — **de·pres·sor** *n*

**de·pres·sion** *n* **1** : act of depressing or state of being depressed **2** : depressed place **3** : period of low economic activity

**de·prive** *vb* : take or keep something away from — **de·pri·va·tion** *n*

**depth** *n* **1** : something that is deep **2** : distance down from a surface **3** : distance from front to back **4** : quality of being deep

**dep·u·ty** *n* : person appointed to act for another — **dep·u·tize** *vb*

**de·rail** *vb* : leave the rails — **de·rail·ment** *n*

**de·range** *vb* **1** : upset an arrangement of **2** : make insane — **de·range·ment** *n*

**der·by** *n* **1** : horse race **2** : stiff felt hat with dome-shaped crown

**de·reg·u·late** *vb* : remove restrictions on — **de·reg·u·la·tion** *n*

**der·e·lict** *adj* **1** : abandoned **2** : negligent ~ *n* **1** : something abandoned **2** : bum — **der·e·lic·tion** *n*

**de·ride** *vb* : make fun of — **de·ri·sion** *n* — **de·ri·sive** *adj* — **de·ri·sive·ly** *adv* — **de·ri·sive·ness** *n*

**de·rive** *vb* **1** : obtain from a source or parent **2** : come from a certain source **3** : infer or deduce — **der·i·va·tion** *n* — **de·riv·a·tive** *adj or n*

**der·ma·tol·o·gy** *n* : study of the skin and its disorders — **der·ma·tol·o·gist** *n*

**de·rog·a·to·ry** *adj* : intended to lower the reputation

**de·scend** *vb* **1** : move or climb down **2** : derive **3** : extend downward **4** : appear suddenly (as in an attack) — **de·scen·dant, de·scen·dent** *adj or n* — **de·scent** *n*

**de·scribe** *vb* : represent in words — **de·scrib·able** *adj* — **de·scrip·tion** *n* — **de·scrip·tive** *adj*

**des·e·crate** *vb* : treat (something sacred) with disrespect — **des·e·cra·tion** *n*

**de·seg·re·gate** *vb* : eliminate esp. racial segregation in — **de·seg·re·ga·tion** *n*

¹**des·ert** *n* : dry barren region — **desert** *adj*

²**de·sert** *n* : what one deserves

³**de·sert** *vb* : abandon — **de·sert·er** *n* — **de·ser·tion** *n*

**de·serve** *vb* : be worthy of

**de·sign** *vb* **1** : create and work out the details of **2** : make a pattern or sketch of ~ *n* **1** : mental project or plan **2** : purpose **3** : preliminary sketch **4** : underlying arrangement of elements **5** : decorative pattern — **de·sign·er** *n*

**des·ig·nate** *vb* **1** : indicate, specify, or name **2** : appoint — **des·ig·na·tion** *n*

**de·sire** *vb* **1** : feel desire for **2** : request ~ *n* **1** : strong conscious impulse to have, be, or do something **2** : something desired — **de·sir·abil·i·ty** *n* — **de·sir·able** *adj* — **de·sir·able·ness** *n* — **de·sir·ous** *adj*

**de·sist** *vb* : stop

**desk** *n* : table esp. for writing and reading

**des·o·late** *adj* **1** : lifeless **2** : hopelessly sad ~ *vb* : lay waste — **des·o·la·tion** *n*

**de·spair** *vb* : lose all hope ~ *n* : loss of hope

**des·per·ate** *adj* **1** : hopeless **2** : rash **3** : extremely intense — **des·per·ate·ly** *adv* — **des·per·a·tion** *n*

**de·spise** *vb* : feel contempt for — **de·spi·ca·ble** *adj*

**de·spite** *prep* : in spite of

**de·spon·den·cy** *n* : dejection — **de·spon·dent** *adj*

**des·sert** *n* : sweet food, fruit, or cheese ending a meal

**des·ti·na·tion** *n* : place where something or someone is going

**des·tine** *vb* **1** : designate, assign, or determine in advance **2** : direct

**des·ti·ny** *n* : that which is to happen in the future

**des·ti·tute** *adj* **1** : lacking something **2** : very poor — **des·ti·tu·tion** *n*

**de·stroy** *vb* : kill or put an end to — **de·stroy·er** *n* — **de·struc·ti·bil·i·ty** *n* — **de·struc·ti·ble** *adj* — **de·struc·tive** *adj* — **de·struc·tion** *n*

**de·tach** *vb* : separate — **de·tached** *adj* — **de·tach·ment** *n*

**de·tail** *n* : small item or part ~ *vb* : give details of

**de·tain** *vb* **1** : hold in custody **2** : delay

**de·tect** *vb* : discover — **de·tect·able** *adj* — **de·tec·tion** *n* — **de·tec·tor** *n*

**de·tec·tive** *n* : one who investigates crime

**de·ten·tion** *n* : confinement

**de·ter** *vb* : discourage or prevent — **de·ter·rence** *n* — **de·ter·rent** *adj or n*

**de·ter·gent** *n* : cleansing agent

**de·te·ri·o·rate** *vb* : make or become worse — **de·te·ri·o·ra·tion** *n*

**de·ter·mine** *vb* **1** : decide on, establish, or settle **2** : find out **3** : bring about as a result — **de·ter·mi·na·tion** *n*

**de·test** *vb* : hate — **de·test·able** *adj* — **de·tes·ta·tion** *n*

**det·o·nate** *vb* : explode — **det·o·na·tion** *n* — **det·o·na·tor** *n*

**de·tour** *n* : temporary indirect route — **detour** *vb*

**de·tract** *vb* : take away — **de·trac·tion** *n* — **de·trac·tor** *n*

**det·ri·ment** *n* : damage — **det·ri·men·tal** *adj* — **det·ri·men·tal·ly** *adv*

**deuce** *n* **1** : 2 in cards or dice **2** : tie in tennis **3** : devil — used as an oath

**de·val·ue** *vb* : reduce the value of — **de·val·u·a·tion** *n*

**dev·as·tate** *vb* : ruin — **dev·as·ta·tion** *n*

**de·vel·op** *vb* **1** : grow, increase, or evolve gradually **2** : cause to grow, increase, or reach full potential — **de·vel·op·er** *n* — **de·vel·op·ment** *n* — **de·vel·op·men·tal** *adj*

**de·vi·ate** *vb* : change esp. from a course or standard — **de·vi·ant** *adj or n* — **de·vi·ate** *n* — **de·vi·a·tion** *n*

**de·vice** *n* **1** : specialized piece of equipment or tool **2** : design

**dev·il** *n* **1** : personified supreme spirit of evil **2** : demon **3** : wicked person ~ *vb* **1** : season highly **2** : pester — **dev·il·ish** *adj* — **dev·il·ry, dev·il·try** *n*

**de·vi·ous** *adj* : tricky

**de·vise** *vb* **1** : invent **2** : plot **3** : give by will

**de·vote** *vb* : set apart for a special purpose — **de·vot·ed** *adj*

**dev·o·tee** *n* : ardent follower

**de·vo·tion** *n* **1** : prayer — *usu. pl.* **2** : loyalty and dedication — **de·vo·tion·al** *adj*

**de·vour** *vb* : consume ravenously — **de·vour·er** *n*

**de·vout** *adj* **1** : devoted to religion **2** : serious — **de·vout·ly** *adv* — **de·vout·ness** *n*

**dew** *n* : moisture condensed at night — **dew·drop** *n* — **dewy** *adj*

**dex·ter·ous** *adj* : skillful with the hands — **dex·ter·i·ty** *n* — **dex·ter·ous·ly** *adv*

**di·a·be·tes** *n* : disorder in which the body has too little insulin and too much sugar — **di·a·bet·ic** *adj or n*

**di·ag·no·sis** *n* : identifying of a disease from its symptoms — **di·ag·nose** *vb* — **di·ag·nos·tic** *adj*

**di·ag·o·nal** *adj* : extending from one corner to the opposite corner ~ *n* : diagonal line, direction, or arrangement — **di·ag·o·nal·ly** *adv*

**di·a·gram** *n* : explanatory drawing or plan ~ *vb* : represent by a diagram — **di·a·gram·mat·ic** *adj*

**di·al** *n* **1** : face of a clock, meter, or gauge **2** : control knob or wheel ~ *vb* : turn a dial to call, operate, or select

**di·a·lect** *n* : variety of language confined to a region or group

**di·a·logue** *n* : conversation

**di·am·e·ter** *n* **1** : straight line through the center of a circle **2** : thickness

**di·a·mond** *n* **1** : hard brilliant mineral that consists of crystalline carbon **2** : flat figure having 4 equal sides, 2 acute angles, and 2 obtuse angles **3** : playing card of a suit marked with a red diamond **4** : baseball field

**di·a·per** *n* : baby's garment for receiving bodily wastes ~ *vb* : put a diaper on

**di·a·phragm** *n* **1** : sheet of muscle between the chest and abdominal cavity **2** : contraceptive device

**di·ar·rhea** *n* : abnormally watery discharge from bowels

**di·a·ry** *n* : daily record of personal experiences — **di·a·rist** *n*

**dice** *n dice* : die or a game played with dice ~ *vb* : cut into small cubes

**dic·tate** *vb* **1** : speak for a person or a

machine to record **2 :** command ~ *n* **:** order — **dic·ta·tion** *n*

**dic·ta·tor** *n* **:** person ruling absolutely and often brutally — **dic·ta·to·ri·al** *adj* — **dic·ta·tor·ship** *n*

**dic·tio·nary** *n* **:** reference book of words with information about their meanings

**did** *past of* DO

**didn't :** did not

[1]**die** *vb* **1 :** stop living **2 :** pass out of existence **3 :** stop or become less active **4 :** long

[2]**die** *n* **1** *pl* **dice :** small marked cube used in gambling **2** *pl* **dies :** form for stamping or cutting

**die·sel** *n* **:** engine in which high compression causes ignition of the fuel

**di·et** *n* **:** food and drink regularly consumed (as by a person) ~ *vb* **:** eat less or according to certain rules — **di·etary** *adj or n* — **di·et·er** *n*

**dif·fer** *vb* **1 :** be unlike **2 :** vary **3 :** disagree — **dif·fer·ence** *n* — **dif·fer·ent** *adj* — **dif·fer·ent·ly** *adv*

**dif·fer·en·ti·ate** *vb* **1 :** make or become different **2 :** attain a specialized adult form during development **3 :** distinguish — **dif·fer·en·ti·a·tion** *n*

**dif·fi·cul·ty** *n* **1 :** difficult nature **2 :** great effort **3 :** something hard to do, understand, or deal with — **dif·fi·cult** *adj*

**dif·fuse** *adj* **1 :** wordy **2 :** not concentrated ~ *vb* **:** pour out or spread widely — **dif·fu·sion** *n*

**dig** *vb* **1 :** turn up soil **2 :** hollow out or form by removing earth **3 :** uncover by turning up earth ~ *n* **1 :** thrust **2 :** cutting remark — **dig in** *vb* **1 :** establish a defensive position **2 :** begin working or eating — **dig up** *vb* **:** discover

[1]**di·gest** *n* **:** body of information in shortened form

[2]**di·gest** *vb* **1 :** think over **2 :** convert (food) into a form that can be absorbed **3 :** summarize — **di·gest·ible** *adj* — **di·ges·tion** *n* — **di·ges·tive** *adj*

**dig·it** *n* **1 :** any of the figures 1 to 9 inclusive and usu. the symbol 0 **2 :** finger or toe

**dig·i·tal** *adj* **:** providing information in numerical digits — **dig·i·tal·ly** *adv*

**digital camera** *n* **:** camera that records images as digital data instead of on film

**dig·ni·fy** *vb* **:** give dignity or attention to

**dig·ni·tary** *n* **:** person of high position

**dig·ni·ty** *n* **1 :** quality or state of being worthy or honored **2 :** formal reserve (as of manner)

**dike** *n* **:** earth bank or dam

**di·lap·i·dat·ed** *adj* **:** fallen into partial ruin — **di·lap·i·da·tion** *n*

**di·late** *vb* **:** swell or expand — **dil·a·ta·tion** *n* — **di·la·tion** *n*

**di·lem·ma** *n* **1 :** undesirable choice **2 :** predicament

**dil·i·gent** *adj* **:** attentive and busy — **dil·i·gence** *n* — **dil·i·gent·ly** *adv*

**dill** *n* **:** herb with aromatic leaves and seeds

**dil·ly·dal·ly** *vb* **:** waste time by delay

**di·lute** *vb* **:** lessen the consistency or strength of by mixing with something else ~ *adj* **:** weak — **di·lu·tion** *n*

**dim** *adj* **1 :** not bright or distinct **2 :** having no luster **3 :** not seeing or understanding clearly — **dim** *vb* — **dim·ly** *adv* — **dim·mer** *n* — **dim·ness** *n*

**dime** *n* **:** U.S. coin worth ten cents

**di·men·sion** *n* **1 :** measurement of extension (as in length, height, or breadth) **2 :** extent — **di·men·sion·al** *adj*

**di·min·ish** *vb* **1 :** make less or cause to appear less **2 :** dwindle

**dim·ple** *n* **:** small depression esp. in the cheek or chin

**dine** *vb* **:** eat dinner

**din·er** *n* **1 :** person eating dinner **2 :** railroad dining car or restaurant resembling one

**din·ghy** *n* **:** small boat

**din·gy** *adj* **1 :** dirty **2 :** shabby — **din·gi·ness** *n*

**din·ner** *n* **:** main daily meal

**di·no·saur** *n* **:** extinct often huge reptile

**di·o·cese** *n* **:** territorial jurisdiction of a bishop — **di·oc·e·san** *adj or n*

**dip** *vb* **1 :** plunge into a liquid **2 :** take out with a ladle **3 :** lower and quickly raise again **4 :** sink or slope downward suddenly ~ *n* **1 :** plunge into water for sport **2 :** sudden downward movement or incline — **dip·per** *n*

**di·plo·ma** *n* **:** record of graduation from a school

**di·plo·ma·cy** *n* **1 :** business of conducting negotiations between nations **2 :** tact — **dip·lo·mat** *n* — **dip·lo·mat·ic** *adj*

**dire** *adj* **1 :** very horrible **2 :** extreme

**di·rect** *vb* **1 :** address **2 :** cause to move or to follow a certain course **3 :** show (someone) the way **4 :** regulate the activities or course of **5 :** request with authority ~ *adj* **1 :** leading to or coming from a point without deviation or interruption **2 :** frank — **direct** *adv* — **di·rect·ly** *adv* — **di·rect·ness** *n* — **di·rec·tor** *n*

**direct current** *n* **:** electric current flowing in one direction only

**di·rec·tion** *n* **1 :** supervision **2 :** order **3 :** course along which something moves — **di·rec·tion·al** *adj*

**di·rec·tive** *n* **:** order

**di·rec·to·ry** *n* **:** alphabetical list of names and addresses

**dirt** *n* **1 :** mud, dust, or grime that makes something unclean **2 :** soil

**dirty** *adj* **1 :** not clean **2 :** unfair **3 :** extremely improper or offensive ~ *vb* **:** make or become dirty — **dirt·i·ness** *n*

**dis·able** *vb* **:** make unable to function — **dis·abil·i·ty** *n*

**dis·ad·van·tage** *n* **:** something that hinders success — **dis·ad·van·ta·geous** *adj*

**dis·agree** *vb* **1 :** fail to agree **2 :** differ in opinion — **dis·agree·ment** *n*

**dis·agree·able** *adj* **:** unpleasant

**dis·al·low** *vb* **:** refuse to admit or recognize

**dis·ap·pear** *vb* **1 :** pass out of sight **2 :** cease to be — **dis·ap·pear·ance** *n*

**dis·ap·point** *vb* **:** fail to fulfill the expectation or hope of — **dis·ap·point·ment** *n*

**dis·ap·prove** *vb* **1 :** condemn or reject **2 :** feel or express dislike or rejection — **dis·ap·prov·al** *n* — **dis·ap·prov·ing·ly** *adv*

**dis·arm** *vb* **1 :** take weapons from **2 :** reduce armed forces **3 :** make harmless or friendly — **dis·ar·ma·ment** *n*

**di·sas·ter** *n* **:** sudden great misfortune — **di·sas·trous** *adj*

**dis·be·lieve** *vb* **:** hold not worthy of belief — **dis·be·lief** *n*

**disc** *var of* DISK

**dis·card** *vb* **:** get rid of as unwanted — **dis·card** *n*

**dis·cern** *vb* **:** discover with the eyes or the mind — **dis·cern·ible** *adj* — **dis·cern·ment** *n*

**dis·charge** *vb* **1 :** unload **2 :** shoot **3 :** set free **4 :** dismiss from service **5 :** let go or let off **6 :** give forth fluid ~ *n* **1 :** act of discharging **2 :** a flowing out (as of blood) **3 :** dismissal

**dis·ci·ple** *n* **:** one who helps spread another's teachings

**dis·ci·pline** *n* **1 :** field of study **2 :** training that corrects, molds, or perfects **3 :** punishment **4 :** control gained by obedience or training ~ *vb* **1 :** punish **2 :** train in self-control — **dis·ci·pli·nar·i·an** *n* — **dis·ci·plin·ary** *adj*

**dis·close** *vb* **:** reveal — **dis·clo·sure** *n*

**dis·col·or** *vb* **:** change the color of esp. for the worse — **dis·col·or·ation** *n*

**dis·com·fort** *n* **:** uneasiness

**dis·con·nect** *vb* **:** undo the connection of

**dis·con·tent** *n* **:** uneasiness of mind — **dis·con·tent·ed** *adj*

**dis·con·tin·ue** *vb* **:** end — **dis·con·tin·u·ance** *n* — **dis·con·ti·nu·i·ty** *n* — **dis·con·tin·u·ous** *adj*

**dis·cord** *n* **:** lack of harmony — **dis·cor·dant** *adj* — **dis·cor·dant·ly** *adv*

**dis·count** *n* **:** reduction from a regular price ~ *vb* **1 :** reduce the amount of **2 :** disregard — **discount** *adj* — **dis·count·er** *n*

**dis·cour·age** *vb* **1 :** deprive of courage, confidence, or enthusiasm **2 :** dissuade — **dis·cour·age·ment** *n*

**dis·cour·te·ous** *adj* **:** lacking courtesy — **dis·cour·te·ous·ly** *adv* — **dis·cour·te·sy** *n*

**dis·cov·er** *vb* **1 :** make known **2 :** obtain the first sight or knowledge of **3 :** find out — **dis·cov·er·er** *n* — **dis·cov·ery** *n*

**dis·cred·it** *vb* **1 :** disbelieve **2 :** destroy confidence in ~ *n* **1 :** loss of reputation **2 :** disbelief — **dis·cred·it·able** *adj*

**dis·creet** *adj* **:** capable of keeping a secret — **dis·creet·ly** *adv*

**dis·crep·an·cy** *n* **:** difference or disagreement

**dis·crete** *adj* **:** individually distinct

**dis·cre·tion** *n* **1 :** discreet quality **2 :** power of decision or choice — **dis·cre·tion·ary** *adj*

**dis·crim·i·nate** *vb* **1 :** distinguish **2 :** show favor or disfavor unjustly — **dis·crim·i·na·tion** *n* — **dis·crim·i·na·to·ry** *adj*

**dis·cus** *n* **:** disk hurled for distance in a contest

**dis·cuss** *vb* **:** talk about or present — **dis·cus·sion** *n*

**dis·dain** *n* **:** feeling of contempt ~ *vb* **:** look upon or reject with disdain — **dis·dain·ful** *adj* — **dis·dain·ful·ly** *adv*

**dis·ease** *n* **:** condition of a body that impairs its functioning — **dis·eased** *adj*

**dis·en·chant** *vb* **:** to free from illusion — **dis·en·chant·ment** *n*

**dis·en·chant·ed** *adj* **:** disappointed

**dis·en·gage** *vb* **:** release — **dis·en·gage·ment** *n*

**dis·en·tan·gle** *vb* **:** free from entanglement

**dis·fa·vor** *n* **:** disapproval

**dis·fig·ure** *vb* **:** spoil the appearance of — **dis·fig·ure·ment** *n*

**dis·grace** *vb* **:** bring disgrace to ~ *n* **1 :** shame **2 :** cause of shame — **dis·grace·ful** *adj* — **dis·grace·ful·ly** *adv*

**dis·guise** *vb* **:** hide the true identity or nature of ~ *n* **:** something that conceals

**dis·gust** *n* **:** strong aversion ~ *vb* **:** provoke disgust in — **dis·gust·ed·ly** *adv* — **dis·gust·ing·ly** *adv*

**dish** *n* **1 :** vessel for serving food or the food it holds **2 :** food prepared in a particular way ~ *vb* **:** put in a dish — **dish·cloth** *n* — **dish·rag** *n* — **dish·wash·er** *n* — **dish·wa·ter** *n*

**dis·har·mo·ny** *n* **:** lack of harmony — **dis·har·mo·ni·ous** *adj*

**dis·heart·en** *vb* **:** discourage

**di·shev·el** *vb* **:** throw into disorder — **di·shev·eled, di·shev·elled** *adj*

**dis·hon·est** *adj* **:** not honest — **dis·hon·est·ly** *adv* — **dis·hon·es·ty** *n*

**dis·hon·or** *n or vb* **:** disgrace — **dis·hon·or·able** *adj* — **dis·hon·or·ably** *adv*

**dis·il·lu·sion** *vb* **:** to free from illusion — **dis·il·lu·sion·ment** *n*

**dis·in·fect** *vb* **:** destroy disease germs in or on — **dis·in·fec·tant** *adj or n* — **dis·in·fec·tion** *n*

**dis·in·te·grate** *vb* **:** break into parts or small bits — **dis·in·te·gra·tion** *n*

**dis·in·ter·est·ed** *adj* **1 :** not interested **2 :** not prejudiced — **dis·in·ter·est·ed·ness** *n*

**disk** *n* **:** something round and flat

**dis·like** *n* **:** feeling that something is unpleasant and to be avoided ~ *vb* **:** regard with dislike

**dis·lo·cate** *vb* **:** move out of the usual or proper place — **dis·lo·ca·tion** *n*

**dis·lodge** *vb* **:** force out of a place

**dis·loy·al** *adj* **:** not loyal — **dis·loy·al·ty** *n*

**dis·mal** *adj* **:** showing or causing gloom — **dis·mal·ly** *adv*

**dis·man·tle** *vb* **:** take apart

**dis·may** *vb* **:** discourage — **dismay** *n*

**dis·mem·ber** *vb* **:** cut into pieces — **dis·mem·ber·ment** *n*

**dis·miss** *vb* **1 :** send away **2 :** remove from service **3 :** put aside or out of mind — **dis·miss·al** *n*

**dis·mount** *vb* **1 :** get down from something **2 :** take apart

**dis·obey** *vb* **:** refuse to obey — **dis·obe·di·ence** *n* — **dis·obe·di·ent** *adj*

**dis·or·der** *n* **1 :** lack of order **2 :** breach of public order **3 :** abnormal state of body or mind — **disorder** *vb* — **dis·or·der·li·ness** *n* — **dis·or·der·ly** *adj*

**dis·or·ga·nize** *vb* **:** throw into disorder — **dis·or·ga·ni·za·tion** *n*

**dis·own** *vb* **:** reject as not valid or not one's own

**dis·par·age** *vb* **:** say bad things about — **dis·par·age·ment** *n*

**dis·patch** *vb* **1 :** send **2 :** kill **3 :** attend to rapidly **4 :** defeat ~ *n* **1 :** message **2 :** news item from a correspondent **3 :** promptness and efficiency — **dis·patch·er** *n*

**dis·pense** *vb* **1 :** portion out **2 :** make up and give out (remedies) — **dis·pen·sa·tion** *n* — **dis·pens·er** *n* — **dis·pense with :** do without

**dis·perse** *vb* **:** scatter — **dis·per·sal** *n* — **dis·per·sion** *n*

**dis·place** *vb* **1 :** expel or force to flee from home or native land **2 :** take the place of — **dis·place·ment** *n*

**dis·play** *vb* **:** present to view — **display** *n*

**dis·please** *vb* **:** arouse the dislike of — **dis·plea·sure** *n*

**dis·pose** *vb* **1 :** give a tendency to **2 :** settle — **dis·pos·able** *adj* — **dis·pos·al** *n* — **dis·pos·er** *n* — **dispose of 1 :** determine the fate, condition, or use of **2 :** get rid of

**dis·po·si·tion** *n* **1 :** act or power of disposing of **2 :** arrangement **3 :** natural attitude

**dis·pro·por·tion** *n* **:** lack of proportion — **dis·pro·por·tion·ate** *adj*

**dis·prove** *vb* **:** prove false

**dis·pute** *vb* **1 :** argue **2 :** deny the truth or rightness of **3 :** struggle against or over ~ *n* **:** debate or quarrel — **dis·put·able** *adj* — **dis·pu·ta·tion** *n*

**dis·qual·i·fy** *vb* **:** make ineligible — **dis·qual·i·fi·ca·tion** *n*

**dis·re·gard** *vb* **:** pay no attention to ~ *n* **:** neglect

**dis·rep·u·ta·ble** *adj* **:** having a bad reputation — **dis·re·pute** *n*

**dis·re·spect** *n* **:** lack of respect — **dis·re·spect·ful** *adj*

**dis·rupt** *vb* **:** throw into disorder — **dis·rup·tion** *n* — **dis·rup·tive** *adj*

**dis·sat·is·fac·tion** *n* **:** lack of satisfaction

**dis·sat·is·fy** *vb* **:** fail to satisfy

**dis·sect** *vb* **:** cut into parts esp. to examine — **dis·sec·tion** *n*

**dis·sen·sion** *n* **:** discord

**dis·sent** *vb* **:** object or disagree ~ *n* **:** difference of opinion — **dis·sent·er** *n*

**dis·ser·vice** *n* **:** injury

**dis·sim·i·lar** *adj* **:** different — **dis·sim·i·lar·i·ty** *n*

**dis·si·pate** *vb* **1 :** break up and drive off **2 :** waste or lose through neglect — **dis·si·pa·tion** *n*

**dis·solve** *vb* **1 :** break up or bring to an end **2 :** pass or cause to pass into solution — **dis·so·lu·tion** *n*

**dis·so·nance** *n* **:** discord — **dis·so·nant** *adj*

**dis·suade** *vb* **:** persuade not to do something — **dis·sua·sion** *n*

**dis·tance** *n* **1 :** measure of separation in space or time **2 :** reserve

**dis·tant** *adj* **1 :** separate in space **2 :** remote in time, space, or relationship **3 :** reserved — **dis·tant·ly** *adv*

**dis•taste** *n* : dislike — **dis•taste•ful** *adj*
**dis•till** *vb* : obtain by distillation — **dis•til•late** *n* — **dis•till•er** *n* — **dis•till•ery** *n*
**dis•til•la•tion** *n* : purification of liquid by evaporating then condensing
**dis•tinct** *adj* **1** : distinguishable from others **2** : readily discerned — **dis•tinc•tion** *n* — **dis•tinc•tive** *adj* — **dis•tinc•tive•ly** *adv* — **dis•tinc•tive•ness** *n* — **dis•tinct•ly** *adv* — **dis•tinct•ness** *n*
**dis•tin•guish** *vb* **1** : perceive as different **2** : set apart **3** : discern **4** : make outstanding — **dis•tin•guish•able** *adj* — **dis•tin•guished** *adj*
**dis•tort** *vb* : twist out of shape, condition, or true meaning — **dis•tor•tion** *n*
**dis•tract** *vb* : divert the mind or attention of — **dis•trac•tion** *n*
**dis•tress** *n* **1** : suffering **2** : misfortune **3** : state of danger or great need ~ *vb* : subject to strain or distress — **dis•tress•ful** *adj*
**dis•trib•ute** *vb* **1** : divide among many **2** : spread or hand out — **dis•tri•bu•tion** *n* — **dis•trib•u•tive** *adj* — **dis•trib•u•tor** *n*
**dis•trict** *n* : territorial division
**dis•trust** *vb* : show lack of trust — **dis•trust** *n* — **dis•trust•ful** *adj*
**dis•turb** *vb* **1** : interfere with **2** : destroy the peace, composure, or order of — **dis•tur•bance** *n* — **dis•turb•er** *n*
**ditch** *n* : trench ~ *vb* **1** : dig a ditch in **2** : get rid of
**dit•to** *n* : more of the same
**dive** *vb* **1** : plunge into water headfirst **2** : go or put underwater **3** : descend quickly ~ *n* **1** : act of diving **2** : sharp decline — **div•er** *n*
**di•verge** *vb* **1** : move in different directions **2** : differ — **di•ver•gence** *n* — **di•ver•gent** *adj*
**di•verse** *adj* : involving different forms — **di•ver•si•fi•ca•tion** *n* — **di•ver•si•fy** *vb* — **di•ver•si•ty** *n*
**di•vert** *vb* **1** : turn from a course or purpose **2** : distract **3** : amuse — **di•ver•sion** *n*
**di•vide** *vb* **1** : separate **2** : distribute **3** : share **4** : subject to mathematical division — **di•vid•er** *n*
**div•i•dend** *n* **1** : individual share **2** : bonus **3** : number to be divided
**di•vine** *adj* **1** : relating to or being God or a god **2** : supremely good ~ *n* : clergy member ~ *vb* **1** : infer **2** : predict — **di•vine•ly** *adv* — **di•vin•er** *n* — **di•vin•i•ty** *n*
**di•vis•i•ble** *adj* : capable of being divided — **di•vis•i•bil•i•ty** *n*
**di•vi•sion** *n* **1** : distribution **2** : part of a whole **3** : disagreement **4** : process of finding out how many times one number is contained in another
**di•vi•sor** *n* : number by which a dividend is divided
**di•vorce** *n* : legal breaking up of a marriage — **di•vorce** *vb*
**di•vor•cée** *n* : divorced woman
**di•vulge** *vb* : reveal
**diz•zy** *adj* **1** : having a sensation of whirling **2** : causing or caused by giddiness — **diz•zi•ly** *adv* — **diz•zi•ness** *n*
**DNA** *n* : compound in cell nuclei that is the basis of heredity
**do** *vb* **did; done 1** : work to accomplish (an action or task) **2** : behave **3** : prepare or fix up **4** : fare **5** : finish **6** : serve the needs or purpose of **7** — used as an auxiliary verb — **do•er** *n* — **do away with 1** : get rid of **2** : destroy — **do by** : deal with — **do in** *vb* **1** : ruin **2** : kill
**doc•ile** *adj* : easily managed — **do•cil•i•ty** *n*
[1]**dock** *vb* **1** : shorten **2** : reduce
[2]**dock** *n* **1** : berth between 2 piers to receive ships **2** : loading wharf or platform ~ *vb* : bring or come into dock — **dock•work•er** *n*
**doc•tor** *n* **1** : person holding one of the highest academic degrees **2** : one (as a surgeon) skilled in healing arts ~ *vb* **1** : give medical treatment to **2** : repair or alter — **doc•tor•al** *adj*
**doc•trine** *n* : something taught — **doc•tri•nal** *adj*
**doc•u•ment** *n* : paper that furnishes information or legal proof — **doc•u•ment** *vb* — **doc•u•men•ta•tion** *n* — **doc•u•ment•er** *n*
**doc•u•men•ta•ry** *adj* **1** : of or relating to documents **2** : giving a factual presentation — **doc•u•men•ta•ry** *n*
**dodge** *vb* **1** : move quickly aside or out of the way of **2** : evade — **dodge** *n*
**doe** *n* : adult female deer — **doe•skin** *n*
**does** *pres 3d sing of* DO
**doesn't** : does not
**dog** *n* : flesh-eating domestic mammal ~ *vb* **1** : hunt down or track like a hound **2** : harass — **dog•catch•er** *n* — **dog•gy** *n or adj* — **dog•house** *n*
**dog–ear** *n* : turned-down corner of a page — **dog–ear** *vb* — **dog–eared** *adj*
**dog•ma** *n* : tenet or code of tenets
**dog•ma•tism** *n* : unwarranted stubbornness of opinion — **dog•ma•tic** *adj*
**do•ings** *n pl* : events
**dol•drums** *n pl* : spell of listlessness, despondency, or stagnation
**dole** *n* : distribution esp. of money to the needy or unemployed — **dole out** *vb* : give out esp. in small portions
**dole•ful** *adj* : sad — **dole•ful•ly** *adv*
**doll** *n* : small figure of a person used esp. as a child's toy
**dol•lar** *n* : any of various basic monetary units (as in the U.S. and Canada)
**dol•ly** *n* : small cart or wheeled platform
**dol•phin** *n* **1** : sea mammal related to the whales **2** : saltwater food fish
**do•main** *n* **1** : territory over which someone reigns **2** : sphere of activity or knowledge
**dome** *n* **1** : large hemispherical roof **2** : roofed stadium
**do•mes•tic** *adj* **1** : relating to the household or family **2** : relating and limited to one's own country **3** : tame ~ *n* : household servant — **do•mes•ti•cal•ly** *adv*
**do•mes•ti•cate** *vb* : tame — **do•mes•ti•ca•tion** *n*
**dom•i•nance** *n* : control — **dom•i•nant** *adj*
**dom•i•nate** *vb* **1** : have control over **2** : rise high above — **dom•i•na•tion** *n*
**dom•i•neer** *vb* : exercise arbitrary control
**do•min•ion** *n* **1** : supreme authority **2** : governed territory
**dom•i•no** *n* : flat rectangular block used as a piece in a game (**dominoes**)
**do•nate** *vb* : make a gift of — **do•na•tion** *n*
[1]**done** *past part of* DO
[2]**done** *adj* **1** : finished or ended **2** : cooked sufficiently
**don•key** *n* : sturdy domestic ass
**do•nor** *n* : one that gives
**don't:** do not
**doo•dle** *vb* : draw or scribble aimlessly — **doodle** *n*
**doom** *n* **1** : judgment **2** : fate **3** : ruin — **doom** *vb*
**door** *n* : passage for entrance or a movable barrier that can open or close such a passage — **door•jamb** *n* — **door•knob** *n* — **door•mat** *n* — **door•step** *n* — **door•way** *n*
**dope** *n* **1** : narcotic preparation **2** : stupid person **3** : information ~ *vb* : drug
**dor•mant** *adj* : not actively growing or functioning — **dor•man•cy** *n*
**dor•mi•to•ry** *n* : residence hall (as at a college)
**dose** *n* : quantity (as of medicine) taken at one time ~ *vb* : give medicine to — **dos•age** *n*
**dot** *n* **1** : small spot **2** : small round mark made with or as if with a pen ~ *vb* : mark with dots
**dote** *vb* **1** : act feebleminded **2** : be foolishly fond
**dou•ble** *adj* **1** : consisting of 2 members or parts **2** : being twice as great or as many **3** : folded in two ~ *n* **1** : something twice another **2** : one that resembles another ~ *adv* : doubly ~ *vb* **1** : make or become twice as great **2** : fold or bend **3** : clench
**dou•ble–cross** *vb* : deceive by trickery — **dou•ble–cross•er** *n*
**dou•bly** *adv* : to twice the degree
**doubt** *vb* **1** : be uncertain about **2** : show lack of trust **3** : consider unlikely ~ *n* **1** : uncertainty **2** : lack of trust **3** : inclination not to believe — **doubt•ful** *adj* — **doubt•ful•ly** *adv* — **doubt•less** *adv*
**dough** *n* : stiff mixture of flour and liquid — **doughy** *adj*
**dough•nut** *n* : small fried ring-shaped cake
**douse** *vb* **1** : plunge into or drench with water **2** : extinguish
[1]**dove** *n* : small wild pigeon
[2]**dove** *past of* DIVE
**dove•tail** *vb* : fit together neatly
**dow•el** *n* **1** : peg used for fastening two pieces **2** : wooden rod
[1]**down** *adv* **1** : toward or in a lower position or state **2** : to a lying or sitting position **3** : as a cash deposit **4** : on paper ~ *adj* **1** : lying on the ground **2** : directed or going downward **3** : being at a low level ~ *prep* : toward the bottom of ~ *vb* **1** : cause to go down **2** : defeat
[2]**down** *n* : fluffy feathers
**down•cast** *adj* **1** : sad **2** : directed down
**down•fall** *n* : ruin or cause of ruin
**down•grade** *n* : downward slope ~ *vb* : lower in grade or position
**down•heart•ed** *adj* : sad
**down•pour** *n* : heavy rain
**down•right** *adv* : thoroughly ~ *adj* : absolute or thorough
**down•size** *vb* : reduce in size
**down•stairs** *adv* : on or to a lower floor and esp. the main floor — **downstairs** *adj or n*
**down–to–earth** *adj* : practical
**down•town** *adv* : to, toward, or in the business center of a town — **down•town** *n or adj*
**down•ward, down•wards** *adv* : to a lower place or condition — **downward** *adj*
**down•wind** *adv or adj* : in the direction the wind is blowing
**downy** *adj* : resembling or covered with down
**dow•ry** *n* : property a woman gives her husband in marriage
**dox•ol•o•gy** *n* : hymn of praise to God
**doze** *vb* : sleep lightly — **doze** *n*
**doz•en** *n* : group of 12 — **doz•enth** *adj*
**drab** *adj* : dull — **drab•ly** *adv* — **drab•ness** *n*
**draft** *n* **1** : act of drawing or hauling **2** : act of drinking **3** : amount drunk at once **4** : preliminary outline or rough sketch **5** : selection from a pool or the selection process **6** : order for the payment of money **7** : air current ~ *vb* **1** : select usu. on a compulsory basis **2** : make a preliminary sketch, version, or plan of ~ *adj* : drawn from a container — **draft•ee** *n* — **drafty** *adj*
**drag** *n* **1** : something dragged over a surface or through water **2** : something that hinders progress or is boring **3** : act or an instance of dragging ~ *vb* **1** : haul **2** : move or work with difficulty **3** : pass slowly **4** : search or fish with a drag — **drag•ger** *n*
**dra•gon** *n* : fabled winged serpent
**drag•on•fly** *n* : large 4-winged insect
**drain** *vb* **1** : draw off or flow off gradually or completely **2** : exhaust ~ *n* : means or act of draining — **drain•age** *n* — **drain•er** *n* — **drain•pipe** *n*
**dra•ma** *n* **1** : composition for theatrical presentation esp. on a serious subject **2** : series of events involving conflicting forces — **dra•mat•ic** *adj* — **dra•mat•i•cal•ly** *adv* — **dram•a•tist** *n* — **dram•a•ti•za•tion** *n* — **dra•ma•tize** *vb*
**drank** *past of* DRINK
**drape** *vb* **1** : cover or adorn with folds of cloth **2** : cause to hang in flowing lines or folds ~ *n* : curtain
**drap•ery** *n* : decorative fabric hung esp. as a heavy curtain
**dras•tic** *adj* : extreme or harsh — **dras•ti•cal•ly** *adj*
**draw** *vb* **drew; drawn 1** : move or cause to move (as by pulling) **2** : attract or provoke **3** : extract **4** : take or receive (as money) **5** : bend a bow in preparation for shooting **6** : leave a contest undecided **7** : sketch **8** : write out **9** : deduce ~ *n* **1** : act, process, or result of drawing **2** : tie — **draw out** : cause to speak candidly — **draw up 1** : write out **2** : pull oneself erect **3** : bring or come to a stop
**draw•back** *n* : disadvantage
**draw•bridge** *n* : bridge that can be raised
**draw•er** *n* **1** : one that draws **2** : sliding boxlike compartment **3** *pl* : underpants
**draw•ing** *n* **1** : occasion of choosing by lot **2** : act or art of making a figure, plan, or sketch with lines **3** : something drawn
**drawl** *vb* : speak slowly — **drawl** *n*
**dread** *vb* : feel extreme fear or reluctance ~ *n* : great fear ~ *adj* : causing dread — **dread•ful** *adj* — **dread•ful•ly** *adv*
**dream** *n* **1** : series of thoughts or visions during sleep **2** : dreamlike vision **3** : something notable **4** : ideal ~ *vb* **1** : have a dream **2** : imagine — **dream•er** *n* — **dream•like** *adj* — **dreamy** *adj*
**drea•ry** *adj* : dismal — **drea•ri•ly** *adv*
**drench** *vb* : wet thoroughly
**dress** *vb* **1** : put clothes on **2** : decorate **3** : prepare (as a carcass) for use **4** : apply dressings, remedies, or fertilizer to ~ *n* **1** : apparel **2** : single garment of bodice and skirt ~ *adj* : suitable for a formal event — **dress•mak•er** *n* — **dress•mak•ing** *n*
**dress•er** *n* : bureau with a mirror
**dress•ing** *n* **1** : act or process of dressing **2** : sauce or a seasoned mixture **3** : material to cover an injury
**dressy** *adj* **1** : showy in dress **2** : stylish
**drew** *past of* DRAW
**drib•ble** *vb* **1** : fall or flow in drops **2** : drool — **dribble** *n*
**drier** *comparative of* DRY
**driest** *superlative of* DRY
**drift** *n* **1** : motion or course of something drifting **2** : mass piled up by wind **3** : general intention or meaning ~ *vb* **1** : float or be driven along (as by a current) **2** : wander without purpose **3** : pile up under force — **drift•er** *n* — **drift•wood** *n*
**drill** *vb* **1** : bore with a drill **2** : instruct by repetition ~ *n* **1** : tool for boring holes **2** : regularly practiced exercise — **drill•er** *n*
**drily** *var of* DRYLY
**drink** *vb* **drank; drunk 1** : swallow liquid **2** : absorb **3** : drink alcoholic beverages esp. to excess ~ *n* **1** : beverage **2** : alcoholic liquor — **drink•able** *adj* — **drink•er** *n*
**drip** *vb* : fall or let fall in drops ~ *n* **1** : a dripping **2** : sound of falling drops
**drive** *vb* **drove; driv•en 1** : urge or force onward **2** : direct the movement or course of **3** : compel **4** : cause to become **5** : propel forcefully ~ *n* **1** : trip in a vehicle **2** : intensive campaign **3** : aggressive or dynamic quality **4** : basic need — **driv•er** *n*
**drive–in** *adj* : accommodating patrons in cars — **drive–in** *n*
**driv•el** *vb* **1** : drool **2** : talk stupidly ~ *n* : nonsense
**drive•way** *n* : usu. short private road from the street to a house
**driz•zle** *n* : fine misty rain — **drizzle** *vb*
**drone** *n* **1** : male honeybee **2** : deep hum or buzz ~ *vb* : make a dull monotonous sound

**drool** *vb* : let liquid run from the mouth

**droop** *vb* **1** : hang or incline downward **2** : lose strength or spirit — **droop** *n* — **droopy** *adj*

**drop** *n* **1** : quantity of fluid in one spherical mass **2** *pl* : medicine used by drops **3** : decline or fall **4** : distance something drops ∼ *vb* **1** : fall in drops **2** : let fall **3** : convey **4** : go lower or become less strong or less active — **droplet** *n* — **drop•per** *n* — **drop back** *vb* : move toward the rear — **drop behind** : fail to keep up — **drop in** *vb* : pay an unexpected visit

**drought** *n* : long dry spell

**drove** *past of* DRIVE

**drown** *vb* **1** : suffocate in water **2** : overpower or become overpowered

**drowsy** *adj* : sleepy — **drows•i•ly** *adv* — **drows•i•ness** *n*

**drug** *n* **1** : substance used as or in medicine **2** : narcotic ∼ *vb* : affect with drugs — **drug•gist** *n* — **drug•store** *n*

**drum** *n* **1** : musical instrument that is a skin-covered cylinder beaten usu. with sticks **2** : drum-shaped object (as a container) ∼ *vb* **1** : beat a drum **2** : drive, force, or bring about by steady effort — **drum•beat** *n* — **drum•mer** *n*

**drum•stick** *n* **1** : stick for beating a drum **2** : lower part of a fowl's leg

**drunk** *adj* : having the faculties impaired by alcohol ∼ *n* : one who is drunk — **drunk•ard** *n* — **drunk•en** *adj* — **drunk•en•ly** *adv* — **drunk•en•ness** *n*

**dry** *adj* **1** : lacking water or moisture **2** : thirsty **3** : marked by the absence of alcoholic beverages **4** : uninteresting **5** : not sweet ∼ *vb* : make or become dry — **dry•ly** *adv* — **dry•ness** *n*

**dry–clean** *vb* : clean (fabrics) chiefly with solvents other than water — **dry cleaning** *n*

**dry•er** *n* : device for drying

**du•al** *adj* : twofold — **du•al•ism** *n* — **du•al•i•ty** *n*

**dub** *vb* : name

**du•bi•ous** *adj* **1** : uncertain **2** : questionable — **du•bi•ous•ly** *adv* — **du•bi•ous•ness** *n*

**duch•ess** *n* **1** : wife of a duke **2** : woman holding a ducal title

**¹duck** *n* : swimming bird related to the goose and swan ∼ *vb* **1** : thrust or plunge under water **2** : lower the head or body suddenly **3** : evade — **duck•ling** *n*

**²duck** *n* : cotton fabric

**duct** *n* : canal for conveying a fluid — **duct•less** *adj*

**dude** *n* **1** : dandy **2** : guy

**due** *adj* **1** : owed **2** : appropriate **3** : attributable **4** : scheduled ∼ *n* **1** : something due **2** *pl* : fee ∼ *adv* : directly

**du•el** *n* : combat between 2 persons — **du•el** *vb* — **du•el•ist** *n*

**du•et** *n* : musical composition for 2 performers

**dug** *past of* DIG

**dug•out** *n* **1** : boat made by hollowing out a log **2** : shelter made by digging

**duke** *n* : nobleman of the highest rank — **duke•dom** *n*

**dull** *adj* **1** : mentally slow **2** : blunt **3** : not brilliant or interesting — **dull** *vb* — **dul•lard** *n* — **dull•ness** *n* — **dul•ly** *adv*

**du•ly** *adv* : in a due manner or time

**dumb** *adj* **1** : mute **2** : stupid — **dumb•ly** *adv*

**dumb•bell** *n* **1** : short bar with weights on the ends used for exercise **2** : stupid person

**dumb•found, dum•found** *vb* : amaze

**dum•my** *n* **1** : stupid person **2** : imitative substitute

**dump** *vb* : let fall in a pile ∼ *n* : place for dumping something (as refuse) — **in the dumps** : sad

**dump•ling** *n* : small mass of boiled or steamed dough

**dumpy** *adj* : short and thick in build

**¹dun** *adj* : brownish gray

**²dun** *vb* : hound for payment of a debt

**dunce** *n* : stupid person

**dune** *n* : hill of sand

**dung** *n* : manure

**dun•ga•ree** *n* **1** : blue denim **2** *pl* : work clothes made of dungaree

**dun•geon** *n* : underground prison

**dunk** *vb* : dip temporarily into liquid

**duo** *n* : pair

**dupe** *n* : one easily deceived or cheated — **dupe** *vb*

**du•plex** *adj* : double ∼ *n* : 2-family house

**du•pli•cate** *adj* **1** : consisting of 2 identical items **2** : being just like another ∼ *n* : exact copy ∼ *vb* **1** : make an exact copy of **2** : repeat or equal — **du•pli•ca•tion** *n* — **du•pli•ca•tor** *n*

**du•ra•ble** *adj* : lasting a long time — **du•ra•bil•i•ty** *n*

**du•ra•tion** *n* : length of time something lasts

**du•ress** *n* : coercion

**dur•ing** *prep* **1** : throughout **2** : at some point in

**dusk** *n* : twilight — **dusky** *adj*

**dust** *n* : powdered matter ∼ *vb* **1** : remove dust from **2** : sprinkle with fine particles — **dust•er** *n* — **dust•pan** *n* — **dusty** *adj*

**du•ty** *n* **1** : action required by one's occupation or position **2** : moral or legal obligation **3** : tax — **du•te•ous** *adj* — **du•ti•able** *adj* — **du•ti•ful** *adj*

**DVD** *n* : digital video disk

**dwarf** *n* : one that is much below normal size ∼ *vb* **1** : stunt **2** : cause to seem smaller — **dwarf•ish** *adj*

**dwell** *vb* **1** : reside **2** : keep the attention directed — **dwell•er** *n* — **dwell•ing** *n*

**dwin•dle** *vb* : become steadily less

**dye** *n* : coloring material ∼ *vb* : give a new color to

**dying** *pres part of* DIE

**dyke** *var of* DIKE

**dy•nam•ic** *adj* **1** : relating to physical force producing motion **2** : energetic or forceful

**dy•na•mite** *n* : explosive made of nitroglycerin — **dynamite** *vb*

**dy•na•mo** *n* : electrical generator

**dy•nas•ty** *n* : succession of rulers of the same family — **dy•nas•tic** *adj*

**dys•lex•ia** *n* : disturbance of the ability to read — **dys•lex•ic** *adj*

**dys•tro•phy** *n* : disorder involving nervous and muscular tissue

# E

**e** *n* : 5th letter of the alphabet

**each** *adj* : being one of the class named ∼ *pron* : every individual one ∼ *adv* : apiece

**ea•ger** *adj* : enthusiastic or anxious — **ea•ger•ly** *adv* — **ea•ger•ness** *n*

**ea•gle** *n* : large bird of prey

**¹ear** *n* : organ of hearing or the outer part of this — **ear•ache** *n* — **ear•drum** *n* — **eared** *adj* — **ear•lobe** *n* — **ear•phone** *n* — **ear•ring** *n*

**²ear** *n* : fruiting head of a cereal

**earl** *n* : British nobleman — **earl•dom** *n*

**ear•ly** *adj* **1** : relating to or occurring near the beginning or before the usual time **2** : ancient — **early** *adv*

**earn** *vb* **1** : receive as a return for service **2** : deserve

**ear•nest** *n* : serious state of mind — **earnest** *adj* — **ear•nest•ly** *adv* — **ear•nest•ness** *n*

**earn•ings** *n pl* : something earned

**ear•shot** *n* : range of hearing

**earth** *n* **1** : soil or land **2** : planet inhabited by man — **earth•li•ness** *n* — **earth•ly** *adj* — **earth•ward** *adv*

**earth•quake** *n* : shaking or trembling of the earth

**earth•worm** *n* : long segmented worm

**earthy** *adj* **1** : relating to or consisting of earth **2** : practical **3** : coarse — **earth•i•ness** *n*

**ease** *n* **1** : comfort **2** : naturalness of manner **3** : freedom from difficulty ∼ *vb* **1** : relieve from distress **2** : lessen the tension of **3** : make easier

**ea•sel** *n* : frame to hold a painter's canvas

**east** *adv* : to or toward the east ∼ *adj* : situated toward or at or coming from the east ∼ *n* **1** : direction of sunrise **2** *cap* : regions to the east — **east•er•ly** *adv or adj* — **east•ward** *adv or adj* — **east•wards** *adv*

**East•er** *n* : church feast celebrating Christ's resurrection

**east•ern** *adj* **1** *cap* : relating to a region designated East **2** : lying toward or coming from the east — **East•ern•er** *n*

**easy** *adj* **1** : marked by ease **2** : lenient — **eas•i•ly** *adv* — **eas•i•ness** *n*

**easy–go•ing** *adj* : relaxed and casual

**eat** *vb* (**ate; eat•en**) **1** : take in as food **2** : use up or corrode — **eat•able** *adj or n* — **eat•er** *n*

**eaves•drop** *vb* : listen secretly — **eaves•drop•per** *n*

**ebb** *n* **1** : outward flow of the tide **2** : decline ∼ *vb* **1** : recede from the flood state **2** : wane

**ec•cen•tric** *adj* **1** : odd in behavior **2** : being off center — **eccentric** *n* — **ec•cen•tri•cal•ly** *adv* — **ec•cen•tric•i•ty** *n*

**ec•cle•si•as•ti•cal, ecclesiastic** *adj* : relating to a church — **ec•cle•si•as•ti•cal•ly** *adv*

**echo** *n* : repetition of a sound caused by a reflection of the sound waves — **echo** *vb*

**éclair** *n* : custard-filled pastry

**eclec•tic** *adj* : drawing or drawn from varied sources

**eclipse** *n* : total or partial obscuring of one celestial body by another — **eclipse** *vb*

**ecol•o•gy** *n* : science concerned with the interaction of organisms and their environment — **eco•log•i•cal** *adj* — **eco•log•i•cal•ly** *adv* — **ecol•o•gist** *n*

**eco•nom•ics** *n* : branch of knowledge dealing with goods and services — **econ•o•mist** *n*

**econ•o•my** *n* **1** : thrifty use of resources **2** : economic system — **eco•nom•ic** *adj* — **eco•nom•i•cal** *adj* — **eco•nom•i•cal•ly** *adv* — **econ•o•mize** *vb* — **econ•o•miz•er** *n* — **econ•o•my** *adj*

**ec•sta•sy** *n* : extreme emotional excitement — **ec•stat•ic** *adj* — **ec•stat•i•cal•ly** *adv*

**ec•u•men•i•cal** *adj* : promoting worldwide Christian unity

**ed•dy** *n* : whirlpool — **eddy** *vb*

**Eden** *n* : paradise

**edge** *n* **1** : cutting side of a blade **2** : line where something begins or ends ∼ *vb* **1** : give or form an edge **2** : move gradually **3** : narrowly defeat — **edg•er** *n*

**edge•wise** *adv* : sideways

**edgy** *adj* : nervous — **edg•i•ness** *n*

**ed•i•ble** *adj* : fit or safe to be eaten — **ed•i•bil•i•ty** *n* — **edible** *n*

**ed•it** *vb* **1** : revise and prepare for publication **2** : delete — **ed•i•tor** *n* — **ed•i•tor•ship** *n*

**edi•tion** *n* **1** : form in which a text is published **2** : total number published at one time

**ed•i•to•ri•al** *adj* **1** : relating to an editor or editing **2** : expressing opinion ∼ *n* : article (as in a newspaper) expressing the views of an editor — **ed•i•to•ri•al•ize** *vb* — **ed•i•to•ri•al•ly** *adv*

**ed•u•cate** *vb* **1** : give instruction to **2** : develop mentally and morally **3** : provide with information — **ed•u•ca•ble** *adj* — **ed•u•ca•tion** *n* — **ed•u•ca•tion•al** *adj* — **ed•u•ca•tor** *n*

**eel** *n* : snakelike fish

**ee•rie** *adj* : weird — **ee•ri•ly** *adv*

**ef•fect** *n* **1** : result **2** : meaning **3** : influence **4** *pl* : goods or possessions ∼ *vb* : cause to happen — **in effect** : in substance

**ef•fec•tive** *adj* **1** : producing a strong or desired effect **2** : being in operation — **ef•fec•tive•ly** *adv* — **ef•fec•tive•ness** *n*

**ef•fec•tu•al** *adj* : producing an intended effect — **ef•fec•tu•al•ly** *adv* — **ef•fec•tu•al•ness** *n*

**ef•fem•i•nate** *adj* : having qualities more typical of women than men — **ef•fem•i•na•cy** *n*

**ef•fer•vesce** *vb* **1** : bubble and hiss as gas escapes **2** : show exhilaration — **ef•fer•ves•cence** *n* — **ef•fer•ves•cent** *adj* — **ef•fer•ves•cent•ly** *adv*

**ef•fi•cient** *adj* : working well with little waste — **ef•fi•cien•cy** *n* — **ef•fi•cient•ly** *adv*

**ef•fort** *n* **1** : a putting forth of strength **2** : use of resources toward a goal **3** : product of effort — **ef•fort•less** *adj* — **ef•fort•less•ly** *adv*

**¹egg** *vb* : urge to action

**²egg** *n* **1** : rounded usu. hard-shelled reproductive body esp. of birds and reptiles from which the young hatches **2** : a female reproductive cell — **egg•shell** *n*

**egg•plant** *n* : edible purplish fruit of a plant related to the potato

**ego** *n* : self-esteem

**ego•cen•tric** *adj* : concerned only with one's own desires or interests

**ego•tism** *n* : exaggerated sense of self-importance — **ego•tist** *n* — **ego•tis•tic, ego•tis•ti•cal** *adj* — **ego•tis•ti•cal•ly** *adv*

**egre•gious** *adj* : notably bad — **egre•gious•ly** *adv*

**ei•der•down** *n* : soft down obtained from a northern sea duck (**eider**)

**eight** *n* **1** : one more than 7 **2** : 8th in a set or series **3** : something having 8 units — **eight** *adj or pron* — **eighth** *adj or adv or n*

**eigh•teen** *n* : one more than 17 — **eigh•teen** *adj or pron* — **eigh•teenth** *adj or n*

**eighty** *n* : 8 times 10 — **eight•i•eth** *adj or n* — **eighty** *adj or pron*

**ei•ther** *adj* **1** : both **2** : being the one or the other of two ∼ *pron* : one of two or more ∼ *conj* : one or the other

**ejac•u•late** *vb* **1** : say suddenly **2** : eject a fluid (as semen) — **ejac•u•la•tion** *n*

**eject** *vb* : drive or throw out — **ejec•tion** *n*

**eke** *vb* : barely gain with effort — usu. with *out*

**elab•o•rate** *adj* **1** : planned in detail **2** : complex and ornate ∼ *vb* : work out in detail — **elab•o•rate•ly** *adv* — **elab•o•rate•ness** *n* — **elab•o•ra•tion** *n*

**elapse** *vb* : slip by

**elas•tic** *adj* **1** : springy **2** : flexible ∼ *n* **1** : elastic material **2** : rubber band — **elas•tic•i•ty** *n*

**elate** *vb* : fill with joy — **ela•tion** *n*

**el•bow** *n* **1** : joint of the arm **2** : elbow-shaped bend or joint ∼ *vb* : push aside with the elbow

**el•der** *adj* : older ∼ *n* **1** : one who is older **2** : church officer

**el·der·ly** *adj* : past middle age

**el·dest** *adj* : oldest

**elect** *vb* : choose esp. by vote ~ *adj* : elected but not yet in office ~ *n* **elect** *pl* : exclusive group — **elec·tion** *n* — **elec·tive** *n or adj* — **elec·tor** *n* — **elec·tor·al** *adj*

**elec·tric** *adj* 1 *or* **elec·tri·cal** : relating to or run by electricity 2 : thrilling — **elec·tri·cal·ly** *adv*

**elec·tri·cian** *n* : person who installs or repairs electrical equipment

**elec·tric·i·ty** *n* 1 : fundamental form of energy occurring naturally (as in lightning) or produced artificially 2 : electric current

**elec·tri·fy** *vb* 1 : charge with electricity 2 : equip for use of electric power 3 : thrill — **elec·tri·fi·ca·tion** *n*

**elec·tro·cute** *vb* : kill by an electric shock — **elec·tro·cu·tion** *n*

**elec·tro·mag·net** *n* : magnet made using electric current

**elec·tro·mag·ne·tism** *n* : natural force responsible for interactions between charged particles — **elec·tro·mag·net·ic** *adj* — **elec·tro·mag·net·i·cal·ly** *adv*

**elec·tron** *n* : negatively charged particle within the atom

**elec·tron·ic** *adj* : relating to electrons or electronics — **elec·tron·i·cal·ly** *adv*

**elec·tron·ics** *n* : physics of electrons and their use esp. in devices

**el·e·gance** *n* : refined gracefulness — **el·e·gant** *adj* — **el·e·gant·ly** *adv*

**el·e·ment** *n* 1 *pl* : weather conditions 2 : natural environment 3 : constituent part 4 *pl* : simplest principles 5 : substance that has atoms of only one kind — **el·e·men·tal** *adj*

**el·e·men·ta·ry** *adj* 1 : simple 2 : relating to the basic subjects of education

**el·e·phant** *n* : huge mammal with a trunk and 2 ivory tusks

**el·e·vate** *vb* 1 : lift up 2 : exalt

**el·e·va·tion** *n* : height or a high place

**el·e·va·tor** *n* 1 : cage or platform for raising or lowering something 2 : grain storehouse

**elev·en** *n* 1 : one more than 10 2 : 11th in a set or series 3 : something having 11 units — **eleven** *adj or pron* — **elev·enth** *adj or n*

**elf** *n* **elves** : mischievous fairy — **elf·in** *adj* — **elf·ish** *adj*

**elic·it** *vb* : draw forth

**el·i·gi·ble** *adj* : qualified to participate or to be chosen — **el·i·gi·bil·i·ty** *n*

**elim·i·nate** *vb* : get rid of — **elim·i·na·tion** *n*

**elite** *n* : choice or select group

**elk** *n* : large deer

**el·lipse** *n* : oval

**el·lip·sis** *n* 1 : omission of a word 2 : marks (as . . .) to show omission

**el·lip·ti·cal, el·lip·tic** *adj* 1 : relating to or shaped like an ellipse 2 : relating to or marked by ellipsis

**elm** *n* : tall shade tree

**elon·gate** *vb* : make or grow longer — **elon·ga·tion** *n*

**elope** *vb* : run away esp. to be married — **elope·ment** *n* — **elop·er** *n*

**else** *adv* 1 : in a different way, time, or place 2 : otherwise ~ *adj* 1 : other 2 : more

**else·where** *adv* : in or to another place

**elude** *vb* : evade — **elu·sive** *adj* — **elu·sive·ly** *adv* — **elu·sive·ness** *n*

**elves** *pl of* ELF

**e–mail** *n* : message sent or received via computers

**em·bank·ment** *n* : protective barrier of earth

**em·bar·go** *n* : ban on trade — **em·bargo** *vb*

**em·bark** *vb* 1 : go on board a ship or airplane 2 : make a start — **em·bar·ka·tion** *n*

**em·bar·rass** *vb* : cause distress and self-consciousness — **em·bar·rass·ment** *n*

**em·bas·sy** *n* : residence and offices of an ambassador

**em·bel·lish** *vb* : decorate — **em·bel·lish·ment** *n*

**em·bez·zle** *vb* : steal (money) by falsifying records — **em·bez·zle·ment** *n* — **em·bez·zler** *n*

**em·blem** *n* : symbol — **em·blem·at·ic** *adj*

**em·body** *vb* : give definite form or expression to — **em·bod·i·ment** *n*

**em·brace** *vb* 1 : clasp in the arms 2 : welcome 3 : include — **embrace** *n*

**em·broi·der** *vb* : ornament with or do needlework — **em·broi·dery** *n*

**em·bryo** *n* : living being in its earliest stages of development — **em·bry·on·ic** *adj*

**em·er·ald** *n* : green gem ~ *adj* : bright green

**emerge** *vb* : rise, come forth, or appear — **emer·gence** *n* — **emer·gent** *adj*

**emer·gen·cy** *n* : condition requiring prompt action

**em·i·grate** *vb* : leave a country to settle elsewhere — **em·i·grant** *n* — **em·i·gra·tion** *n*

**em·i·nence** *n* 1 : prominence or superiority 2 : person of high rank

**em·i·nent** *adj* : prominent — **em·i·nent·ly** *adv*

**emis·sion** *n* : substance discharged into the air

**emit** *vb* : give off or out

**emo·tion** *n* : intense feeling — **emo·tion·al** *adj* — **emo·tion·al·ly** *adv*

**em·per·or** *n* : ruler of an empire

**em·pha·sis** *n* : stress

**em·pha·size** *vb* : stress

**em·phat·ic** *adj* : uttered with emphasis — **em·phat·i·cal·ly** *adv*

**em·pire** *n* : large state or a group of states

**em·ploy** *vb* 1 : use 2 : occupy ~ *n* : paid occupation — **em·ploy·ee, em·ploye** *n* — **em·ploy·er** *n* — **em·ploy·ment** *n*

**em·pow·er** *vb* : give power to — **em·pow·er·ment** *n*

**em·press** *n* 1 : wife of an emperor 2 : woman emperor

**emp·ty** *adj* 1 : containing nothing 2 : not occupied 3 : lacking value, sense, or purpose ~ *vb* : make or become empty — **emp·ti·ness** *n*

**em·u·late** *vb* : try to equal or excel — **em·u·la·tion** *n*

**emul·sion** *n* 1 : mixture of mutually insoluble liquids 2 : light-sensitive coating on photographic film

**en·able** *vb* : give power, capacity, or ability to

**en·act** *vb* 1 : make into law 2 : act out — **en·act·ment** *n*

**enam·el** *n* 1 : glasslike substance used to coat metal or pottery 2 : hard outer layer of a tooth 3 : glossy paint — **enamel** *vb*

**en·chant** *vb* 1 : bewitch 2 : fascinate — **en·chant·er** *n* — **en·chant·ment** *n* — **en·chant·ress** *n*

**en·cir·cle** *vb* : surround

**en·close** *vb* 1 : shut up or surround 2 : include — **en·clo·sure** *n*

**en·com·pass** *vb* : surround or include

**en·core** *n* : further performance

**en·coun·ter** *vb* 1 : fight 2 : meet unexpectedly — **encounter** *n*

**en·cour·age** *vb* 1 : inspire with courage and hope 2 : foster — **en·cour·age·ment** *n*

**en·crust** *vb* : coat or cover with or as if with a crust

**en·cy·clo·pe·dia** *n* : reference work on many subjects — **en·cy·clo·pe·dic** *adj*

**end** *n* 1 : point at which something stops or no longer exists 2 : process or act of stopping 3 : purpose ~ *vb* 1 : stop or finish 2 : be at the end of — **end·less** *adj* — **end·less·ly** *adv*

**en·dan·ger** *vb* : bring into danger

**en·dear** *vb* : make dear — **en·dear·ment** *n*

**en·deav·or** *vb or n* : attempt

**end·ing** *n* : end

**en·do·crine** *adj* : producing secretions distributed by the bloodstream

**en·dorse** *vb* 1 : sign one's name to 2 : approve — **en·dorse·ment** *n*

**en·dow** *vb* 1 : furnish with funds 2 : furnish naturally — **en·dow·ment** *n*

**en·dure** *vb* 1 : last 2 : suffer patiently 3 : tolerate — **en·dur·able** *adj* — **en·dur·ance** *n*

**en·e·my** *n* : one that attacks or tries to harm another

**en·er·get·ic** *adj* : full of energy or activity — **en·er·get·i·cal·ly** *adv*

**en·er·gize** *vb* : give energy to

**en·er·gy** *n* 1 : capacity for action 2 : vigorous action 3 : capacity for doing work

**en·er·vate** *vb* : make weak or listless — **en·er·va·tion** *n*

**en·force** *vb* 1 : compel 2 : carry out — **en·force·able** *adj* — **en·force·ment** *n*

**en·fran·chise** *vb* : grant voting rights to — **en·fran·chise·ment** *n*

**en·gage** *vb* 1 : participate or cause to participate 2 : bring or come into working contact 3 : bind by a pledge to marry 4 : hire 5 : bring or enter into conflict — **en·gage·ment** *n*

**en·gag·ing** *adj* : attractive

**en·gine** *n* 1 : machine that converts energy into mechanical motion 2 : locomotive

**en·gi·neer** *n* 1 : one trained in engineering 2 : engine operator ~ *vb* : lay out or manage as an engineer

**en·gi·neer·ing** *n* : practical application of science and mathematics

**en·grave** *vb* : cut into a surface — **en·grav·er** *n* — **en·grav·ing** *n*

**en·gross** *vb* : occupy fully

**en·gulf** *vb* : swallow up

**en·hance** *vb* : improve in value — **en·hance·ment** *n*

**enig·ma** *n* : puzzle or mystery — **enig·mat·ic** *adj* — **enig·mat·i·cal·ly** *adv*

**en·joy** *vb* : take pleasure in — **en·joy·able** *adj* — **en·joy·ment** *n*

**en·large** *vb* : make or grow larger — **en·large·ment** *n* — **en·larg·er** *n*

**en·light·en** *vb* : give knowledge or spiritual insight to — **en·light·en·ment** *n*

**en·list** *vb* 1 : join the armed forces 2 : get the aid of — **en·list·ee** *n* — **en·list·ment** *n*

**en·liv·en** *vb* : give life or spirit to

**enor·mi·ty** *n* 1 : great wickedness 2 : huge size

**enor·mous** *adj* : great in size, number, or degree — **enor·mous·ly** *adv* — **enor·mous·ness** *n*

**enough** *adj* : adequate ~ *adv* 1 : in an adequate manner 2 : in a tolerable degree ~ *pron* : adequate number, quantity, or amount

**en·quire, en·qui·ry** *var of* INQUIRE, INQUIRY

**en·rage** *vb* : fill with rage

**en·rich** *vb* : make rich — **en·rich·ment** *n*

**en·roll, en·rol** *vb* 1 : enter on a list 2 : become enrolled — **en·roll·ment** *n*

**en route** *adv or adj* : on or along the way

**en·sem·ble** *n* 1 : small group 2 : complete costume

**en·shrine** *vb* 1 : put in a shrine 2 : cherish

**en·sign** *n* 1 : flag 2 : lowest ranking commissioned officer in the navy

**en·slave** *vb* : make a slave of — **en·slave·ment** *n*

**en·sure** *vb* : guarantee

**en·tail** *vb* : involve as a necessary result

**en·tan·gle** *vb* : tangle — **en·tan·gle·ment** *n*

**en·ter** *vb* 1 : go or come in or into 2 : start 3 : set down (as in a list)

**en·ter·prise** *n* 1 : an undertaking 2 : business organization 3 : initiative

**en·ter·pris·ing** *adj* : showing initiative

**en·ter·tain** *vb* 1 : treat or receive as a guest 2 : hold in mind 3 : amuse — **en·ter·tain·er** *n* — **en·ter·tain·ment** *n*

**en·thrall, en·thral** *vb* : hold spellbound

**en·thu·si·asm** *n* : strong excitement of feeling or its cause — **en·thu·si·ast** *n* — **en·thu·si·as·tic** *adj* — **en·thu·si·as·ti·cal·ly** *adv*

**en·tice** *vb* : tempt — **en·tice·ment** *n*

**en·tire** *adj* : complete or whole — **en·tire·ly** *adv* — **en·tire·ty** *n*

**en·ti·tle** *vb* 1 : name 2 : give a right to

**en·ti·ty** *n* : something with separate existence

**en·tou·rage** *n* : group of attendants

**en·trails** *n pl* : intestines

¹**en·trance** *n* 1 : act of entering 2 : means or place of entering — **en·trant** *n*

²**en·trance** *vb* : fascinate or delight

**en·trap** *vb* : trap — **en·trap·ment** *n*

**en·treat** *vb* : ask urgently — **en·treaty** *n*

**en·trée, en·tree** *n* : principal dish of the meal

**en·tre·pre·neur** *n* : organizer or promoter of an enterprise

**en·trust** *vb* : commit to another with confidence

**en·try** *n* 1 : entrance 2 : an entering in a record or an item so entered

**enu·mer·ate** *vb* 1 : count 2 : list — **enu·mer·a·tion** *n*

**en·vel·op** *vb* : surround — **en·vel·op·ment** *n*

**en·ve·lope** *n* : paper container for a letter

**en·vi·ron·ment** *n* : surroundings — **en·vi·ron·men·tal** *adj*

**en·vi·ron·men·tal·ist** *n* : person concerned about the environment

**en·vi·rons** *n pl* : vicinity

**en·vi·sion** *vb* : picture to oneself

**en·vy** *n* 1 : resentful awareness of another's advantage 2 : object of envy ~ *vb* : feel envy toward or on account of — **en·vi·able** *adj* — **en·vi·ous** *adj* — **en·vi·ous·ly** *adv*

**en·zyme** *n* : biological catalyst

**eon** *n* : indefinitely long time

**ep·ic** *n* : long poem about a hero — **epic** *adj*

**ep·i·dem·ic** *adj* : affecting many persons at one time — **epidemic** *n*

**epi·der·mis** *n* : outer layer of skin

**epi·lep·sy** *n* : nervous disorder marked by convulsive attacks — **ep·i·lep·tic** *adj or n*

**epis·co·pal** *adj* : governed by bishops

**ep·i·sode** *n* : occurrence — **ep·i·sod·ic** *adj*

**ep·i·taph** *n* : inscription in memory of a dead person

**ep·i·thet** *n* : characterizing often abusive word or phrase

**epit·o·me** *n* 1 : summary 2 : ideal example — **epit·o·mize** *vb*

**ep·och** *n* : extended period — **ep·och·al** *adj*

**ep·oxy** *n* : synthetic resin used esp. in adhesives ~ *vb* : glue with epoxy

**equal** *adj* : of the same quantity, value, quality, number, or status as another ~ *n* : one that is equal ~ *vb* : be or become equal to — **equal·i·ty** *n* — **equal·ize** *vb* — **equal·ly** *adv*

**equate** *vb* : treat or regard as equal

**equa·tion** *n* : mathematical statement that two things are equal

**equa·tor** *n* : imaginary circle that separates the northern and southern hemispheres — **equa·to·ri·al** *adj*

**equi·lib·ri·um** *n* : state of balance

**equi·nox** *n* : time when day and night are everywhere of equal length

**equip** *vb* : furnish with needed resources — **equip·ment** *n*

**eq·ui·ta·ble** *adj* : fair

**eq·ui·ty** *n* 1 : justice 2 : value of a property less debt

**equiv·a·lent** *adj* : equal — **equiv·a·lence** *n* — **equivalent** *n*

**equiv·o·cate** *vb* 1 : use misleading language 2 : avoid answering definitely — **equiv·o·cal** *adj* — **equiv·o·ca·tion** *n*

**era** *n* : period of time associated with something

**erad·i·cate** *vb* : do away with

**erase** *vb* **:** rub or scratch out — **eras•er** *n* — **era•sure** *n*

**erect** *adj* **:** not leaning or lying down ∼ *vb* **1 :** build **2 :** bring to an upright position — **erec•tion** *n*

**erode** *vb* **:** wear away gradually

**ero•sion** *n* **:** process of eroding

**erot•ic** *adj* **:** sexually arousing — **erot•i•cal•ly** *adv* — **erot•i•cism** *n*

**err** *vb* **:** be or do wrong

**er•rand** *n* **:** short trip taken to do something often for another

**er•rat•ic** *adj* **1 :** eccentric **2 :** not consistent — **er•rat•i•cal•ly** *adv*

**er•ro•ne•ous** *adj* **:** wrong — **er•ro•ne•ous•ly** *adv*

**er•ror** *n* **1 :** something that is not accurate **2 :** state of being wrong

**erupt** *vb* **:** burst forth esp. suddenly and violently — **erup•tion** *n* — **erup•tive** *adj*

**es•ca•late** *vb* **:** become quickly larger or greater — **es•ca•la•tion** *n*

**es•ca•la•tor** *n* **:** moving stairs

**es•ca•pade** *n* **:** mischievous adventure

**es•cape** *vb* **:** get away or get away from ∼ *n* **1 :** flight from or avoidance of something unpleasant **2 :** leakage **3 :** means of escape ∼ *adj* **:** providing means of escape — **es•cap•ee** *n*

**es•cort** *n* **:** one accompanying another — **es•cort** *vb*

**esoph•a•gus** *n* **:** muscular tube connecting the mouth and stomach

**es•pe•cial•ly** *adv* **:** particularly or notably

**es•pi•o•nage** *n* **:** practice of spying

**espres•so** *n* **:** strong steam-brewed coffee

**es•quire** *n* — used as a title of courtesy

**es•say** *n* **:** literary composition ∼ *vb* **:** attempt — **es•say•ist** *n*

**es•sence** *n* **1 :** fundamental nature or quality **2 :** extract **3 :** perfume

**es•sen•tial** *adj* **:** basic or necessary — **essential** *n* — **es•sen•tial•ly** *adv*

**es•tab•lish** *vb* **1 :** bring into existence **2 :** put on a firm basis **3 :** cause to be recognized — **es•tab•lish•ment** *n*

**es•tate** *n* **1 :** one's possessions **2 :** large piece of land with a house

**es•teem** *n or vb* **:** regard

**es•ti•mate** *vb* **:** judge the approximate value, size, or cost ∼ *n* **1 :** rough or approximate calculation **2 :** statement of the cost of a job — **es•ti•ma•tion** *n* — **es•ti•ma•tor** *n*

**es•trange** *vb* **:** make hostile — **es•trange•ment** *n*

**et cet•era :** and others esp. of the same kind

**etch** *vb* **:** produce by corroding parts of a surface with acid — **etch•er** *n* — **etch•ing** *n*

**eter•nal** *adj* **:** lasting forever — **eter•nal•ly** *adv*

**eter•ni•ty** *n* **:** infinite duration

**eth•a•nol** *n* **:** alcohol

**eth•i•cal** *adj* **1 :** relating to ethics **2 :** honorable — **eth•i•cal•ly** *adv*

**eth•ics** *n sing or pl* **1 :** study of good and evil and moral duty **2 :** moral principles or practice

**eth•nic** *adj* **:** relating to races or groups of people with common customs ∼ *n* **:** member of a minority ethnic group

**et•i•quette** *n* **:** good manners

**Eu•cha•rist** *n* **:** Communion — **eu•cha•ris•tic** *adj*

**eu•lo•gy** *n* **:** speech in praise — **eu•lo•gis•tic** *adj* — **eu•lo•gize** *vb*

**eu•phe•mism** *n* **:** substitution of a pleasant expression for an unpleasant or offensive one — **eu•phe•mis•tic** *adj*

**eu•pho•ria** *n* **:** elation — **eu•phor•ic** *adj*

**eu•ro** *n* **:** common monetary unit of most of the European Union

**eu•tha•na•sia** *n* **:** mercy killing

**evac•u•ate** *vb* **1 :** discharge wastes from the body **2 :** remove or withdraw from — **evac•u•a•tion** *n*

**evade** *vb* **:** manage to avoid — **eva•sion** *n* — **eva•sive** *adj* — **eva•sive•ness** *n*

**eval•u•ate** *vb* **:** appraise — **eval•u•a•tion** *n*

**evan•ge•lism** *n* **:** the winning or revival of personal commitments to Christ — **evan•gel•i•cal** *adj* — **evan•ge•list** *n* — **evan•ge•lis•tic** *adj*

**evap•o•rate** *vb* **1 :** pass off in or convert into vapor **2 :** disappear quickly — **evap•o•ra•tion** *n* — **evap•ora•tor** *n*

**even** *adj* **1 :** smooth **2 :** equal or fair **3 :** fully revenged **4 :** divisible by 2 ∼ *adv* **1 :** already **2** — used for emphasis ∼ *vb* **:** make or become even — **even•ly** *adv* — **even•ness** *n*

**eve•ning** *n* **:** early part of the night

**event** *n* **1 :** occurrence **2 :** noteworthy happening **3 :** eventuality — **event•ful** *adj*

**even•tu•al** *adj* **:** later — **even•tu•al•ly** *adv*

**even•tu•al•i•ty** *n* **:** possible occurrence or outcome

**ev•er** *adv* **1 :** always **2 :** at any time **3 :** in any case

**ev•er•green** *adj* **:** having foliage that remains green — **evergreen** *n*

**ev•er•last•ing** *adj* **:** lasting forever

**ev•ery** *adj* **1 :** being each one of a group **2 :** all possible

**ev•ery•body** *pron* **:** every person

**ev•ery•day** *adj* **:** ordinary

**ev•ery•one** *pron* **:** every person

**ev•ery•thing** *pron* **:** all that exists

**ev•ery•where** *adv* **:** in every place or part

**evict** *vb* **:** force (a person) to move from a property — **evic•tion** *n*

**ev•i•dence** *n* **1 :** outward sign **2 :** proof or testimony

**ev•i•dent** *adj* **:** clear or obvious — **ev•i•dent•ly** *adv*

**evil** *adj* **:** wicked ∼ *n* **1 :** sin **2 :** source of sorrow or distress — **evil•do•er** *n* — **evil•ly** *adv*

**evoke** *vb* **:** call forth or up — **evo•ca•tion** *n* — **evoc•a•tive** *adj*

**evo•lu•tion** *n* **:** process of change by degrees — **evo•lu•tion•ary** *adj*

**evolve** *vb* **:** develop or change by degrees

**ewe** *n* **:** female sheep

**ex•act** *vb* **:** compel to furnish ∼ *adj* **:** precisely correct — **ex•act•ing** *adj* — **ex•ac•ti•tude** *n* — **ex•act•ly** *adv* — **ex•act•ness** *n*

**ex•ag•ger•ate** *vb* **:** say more than is true — **ex•ag•ger•at•ed•ly** *adv* — **ex•ag•ger•a•tion** *n* — **ex•ag•ger•a•tor** *n*

**ex•alt** *vb* **:** glorify — **ex•al•ta•tion** *n*

**ex•am** *n* **:** examination

**ex•am•ine** *vb* **1 :** inspect closely **2 :** test by questioning — **ex•am•i•na•tion** *n*

**ex•am•ple** *n* **1 :** representative sample **2 :** model **3 :** problem to be solved for teaching purposes

**ex•as•per•ate** *vb* **:** thoroughly annoy — **ex•as•per•a•tion** *n*

**ex•ca•vate** *vb* **:** dig or hollow out — **ex•ca•va•tion** *n* — **ex•ca•va•tor** *n*

**ex•ceed** *vb* **1 :** go or be beyond the limit of **2 :** do better than

**ex•ceed•ing•ly** *adv* **:** extremely

**ex•cel** *vb* **:** do extremely well or far better than

**ex•cel•len•cy** *n* — used as a title of honor

**ex•cel•lent** *adj* **:** very good — **ex•cel•lence** *n* — **ex•cel•lent•ly** *adv*

**ex•cept** *vb* **:** omit ∼ *prep* **:** excluding ∼ *conj* **:** but — **ex•cep•tion** *n*

**ex•cep•tion•al** *adj* **:** superior — **ex•cep•tion•al•ly** *adv*

**ex•cerpt** *n* **:** brief passage ∼ *vb* **:** select an excerpt

**ex•cess** *n* **:** amount left over — **excess** *adj* — **ex•ces•sive** *adj* — **ex•ces•sive•ly** *adv*

**ex•change** *n* **1 :** the giving or taking of one thing in return for another **2 :** marketplace esp. for securities ∼ *vb* **:** transfer in return for some equivalent — **ex•change•able** *adj*

**ex•cise** *n* **:** tax

**ex•cite** *vb* **1 :** stir up **2 :** kindle the emotions of — **ex•cit•abil•i•ty** *n* — **ex•cit•able** *adj* — **ex•ci•ta•tion** *n* — **ex•cit•ed•ly** *adv* — **ex•cite•ment** *n*

**ex•claim** *vb* **:** cry out esp. in delight — **ex•cla•ma•tion** *n* — **ex•clam•a•to•ry** *adj*

**exclamation point** *n* **:** punctuation mark ! used esp. after an interjection or exclamation

**ex•clude** *vb* **:** leave out — **ex•clu•sion** *n*

**ex•clu•sive** *adj* **1 :** reserved for particular persons **2 :** stylish **3 :** sole — **exclusive** *n* — **ex•clu•sive•ly** *adv* — **ex•clu•sive•ness** *n*

**ex•crete** *vb* **:** eliminate wastes from the body — **ex•cre•ment** *n* — **ex•cre•tion** *n* — **ex•cre•to•ry** *adj*

**ex•cru•ci•at•ing** *adj* **:** intensely painful — **ex•cru•ci•at•ing•ly** *adv*

**ex•cur•sion** *n* **:** pleasure trip

**ex•cuse** *vb* **1 :** pardon **2 :** release from an obligation **3 :** justify ∼ *n* **1 :** justification **2 :** apology

**ex•e•cute** *vb* **1 :** carry out fully **2 :** enforce **3 :** put to death — **ex•e•cu•tion** *n* — **ex•e•cu•tion•er** *n*

**ex•ec•u•tive** *adj* **:** relating to the carrying out of decisions, plans, or laws ∼ *n* **1 :** branch of government with executive duties **2 :** administrator

**ex•ec•u•tor** *n* **:** person named in a will to execute it

**ex•ec•u•trix** *n* **:** woman executor

**ex•em•pla•ry** *adj* **:** so commendable as to serve as a model

**ex•em•pli•fy** *vb* **:** serve as an example of — **ex•em•pli•fi•ca•tion** *n*

**ex•empt** *adj* **:** being free from some liability ∼ *vb* **:** make exempt — **ex•emp•tion** *n*

**ex•er•cise** *n* **1 :** a putting into action **2 :** exertion to develop endurance or a skill **3** *pl* **:** public ceremony ∼ *vb* **1 :** exert **2 :** engage in exercise — **ex•er•cis•er** *n*

**ex•ert** *vb* **:** put into action — **ex•er•tion** *n*

**ex•hale** *vb* **:** breathe out — **ex•ha•la•tion** *n*

**ex•haust** *vb* **1 :** draw out or develop completely **2 :** use up **3 :** tire or wear out ∼ *n* **:** waste steam or gas from an engine or a system for removing it — **ex•haus•tion** *n* — **ex•haus•tive** *adj*

**ex•hib•it** *vb* **:** display esp. publicly ∼ *n* **1 :** act of exhibiting **2 :** something exhibited — **ex•hi•bi•tion** *n* — **ex•hib•i•tor** *n*

**ex•hil•a•rate** *vb* **:** thrill — **ex•hil•a•ra•tion** *n*

**ex•ile** *n* **1 :** banishment **2 :** person banished from his or her country — **exile** *vb*

**ex•ist** *vb* **1 :** have real or actual being **2 :** live — **ex•is•tence** *n* — **ex•is•tent** *adj*

**ex•it** *n* **1 :** departure **2 :** way out of an enclosed space **3 :** way off an expressway — **exit** *vb*

**ex•o•dus** *n* **:** mass departure

**ex•on•er•ate** *vb* **:** free from blame — **ex•on•er•a•tion** *n*

**ex•or•bi•tant** *adj* **:** exceeding what is usual or proper

**ex•or•cise** *vb* **:** drive out (as an evil spirit) — **ex•or•cism** *n* — **ex•or•cist** *n*

**ex•ot•ic** *adj* **:** foreign or strange — **exotic** *n* — **ex•ot•i•cal•ly** *adv*

**ex•pand** *vb* **:** enlarge — **ex•pan•sion** *n* — **ex•pan•sive** *adj* — **ex•pan•sive•ly** *adv* — **ex•pan•sive•ness** *n*

**ex•panse** *n* **:** very large area

**ex•pa•tri•ate** *n* **:** exile — **ex•pa•tri•ate** *adj or vb*

**ex•pect** *vb* **1 :** look forward to **2 :** consider probable or one's due — **ex•pec•tan•cy** *n* — **ex•pec•tant** *adj* — **ex•pec•tant•ly** *adv* — **ex•pec•ta•tion** *n*

**ex•pe•di•ent** *adj* **:** convenient or advantageous rather than right or just ∼ *n* **:** convenient often makeshift means to an end

**ex•pe•dite** *vb* **:** carry out or handle promptly — **ex•pe•dit•er** *n* — **ex•pe•di•tious** *adj*

**ex•pe•di•tion** *n* **:** long journey for work or research or the people making this

**ex•pel** *vb* **:** force out

**ex•pend** *vb* **1 :** pay out **2 :** use up — **ex•pend•able** *adj* — **ex•pen•di•ture** *n*

**ex•pense** *n* **:** cost — **ex•pen•sive** *adj* — **ex•pen•sive•ly** *adv*

**ex•pe•ri•ence** *n* **1 :** a participating in or living through an event **2 :** an event that affects one **3 :** knowledge from doing ∼ *vb* **:** undergo

**ex•per•i•ment** *n* **:** test to discover something ∼ *vb* **:** make experiments — **ex•per•i•men•tal** *adj* — **ex•per•i•men•ta•tion** *n* — **ex•per•i•men•ter** *n*

**ex•pert** *adj* **:** thoroughly skilled ∼ *n* **:** person with special skill — **ex•pert•ly** *adv* — **ex•pert•ness** *n*

**ex•per•tise** *n* **:** skill

**ex•pire** *vb* **1 :** breathe out **2 :** die **3 :** end — **ex•pi•ra•tion** *n*

**ex•plain** *vb* **1 :** make clear **2 :** give the reason for — **ex•plain•able** *adj* — **ex•pla•na•tion** *n* — **ex•plan•a•to•ry** *adj*

**ex•ple•tive** *n* **:** usu. profane exclamation

**ex•plic•it** *adj* **:** absolutely clear or precise — **ex•plic•it•ly** *adv* — **ex•plic•it•ness** *n*

**ex•plode** *vb* **1 :** discredit **2 :** burst or cause to burst violently **3 :** increase rapidly — **ex•plo•sion** *n* — **ex•plo•sive** *adj* — **ex•plo•sive•ly** *adv*

**ex•ploit** *n* **:** heroic act ∼ *vb* **1 :** utilize **2 :** use unfairly — **ex•ploi•ta•tion** *n*

**ex•plore** *vb* **:** examine or range over thoroughly — **ex•plo•ra•tion** *n* — **ex•plor•ato•ry** *adj* — **ex•plor•er** *n*

**ex•po•nent** *n* **1 :** mathematical symbol showing how many times a number is to be repeated as a factor **2 :** advocate — **ex•po•nen•tial** *adj* — **ex•po•nen•tial•ly** *adv*

**ex•port** *vb* **:** send to foreign countries — **export** *n* — **ex•por•ta•tion** *n* — **ex•port•er** *n*

**ex•pose** *vb* **1 :** deprive of shelter or protection **2 :** subject (film) to light **3 :** make known — **ex•po•sure** *n*

**ex•po•sé, ex•po•se** *n* **:** exposure of something discreditable

**ex•po•si•tion** *n* **:** public exhibition

**[1]ex•press** *adj* **1 :** clear **2 :** specific **3 :** traveling at high speed with few stops — **express** *adv or n* — **ex•press•ly** *adv*

**[2]express** *vb* **1 :** make known in words or appearance **2 :** press out (as juice)

**ex•pres•sion** *n* **1 :** utterance **2 :** mathematical symbol **3 :** significant word or phrase **4 :** look on one's face — **ex•pres•sive** *adj* — **ex•pres•sive•ness** *n*

**ex•press•way** *n* **:** high-speed divided highway with limited access

**ex•pul•sion** *n* **:** an expelling or being expelled

**ex•qui•site** *adj* **1 :** flawlessly beautiful and delicate **2 :** keenly discriminating

**ex•tend** *vb* **1 :** stretch forth or out **2 :** prolong **3 :** enlarge — **ex•tend•able** *adj* — **ex•ten•sion** *n* — **ex•ten•sive** *adj* — **ex•ten•sive•ly** *adv*

**ex•tent** *n* **:** range, space, or degree to which something extends

**ex•ten•u•ate** *vb* **:** lessen the seriousness of — **ex•ten•u•a•tion** *n*

**ex•te•ri•or** *adj* **:** external ∼ *n* **:** external part or surface

**ex•ter•mi•nate** *vb* **:** destroy utterly — **ex•ter•mi•na•tion** *n* — **ex•ter•mi•na•tor** *n*

**ex•ter•nal** *adj* **:** relating to or on the outside — **ex•ter•nal•ly** *adv*

**ex•tinct** *adj* **:** no longer existing — **ex•tinc•tion** *n*

**ex•tin•guish** *vb* **:** cause to stop burning — **ex•tin•guish•able** *adj* — **ex•tin•guish•er** *n*

**ex•tort** *vb* **:** obtain by force or improper pressure — **ex•tor•tion** *n* — **ex•tor•tion•er** *n* — **ex•tor•tion•ist** *n*

**ex•tra** *adj* **1 :** additional **2 :** superior — **extra** *n or adv*

**ex•tract** *vb* **1 :** pull out forcibly **2 :** withdraw (as a juice) ∼ *n* **1 :** excerpt **2 :** product (as a juice) obtained by extracting — **ex•tract•able** *adj* — **ex•trac•tion** *n* — **ex•trac•tor** *n*

**ex·tra·cur·ric·u·lar** *adj* : lying outside the regular curriculum

**ex·tra·dite** *vb* : bring or deliver a suspect to a different jurisdiction for trial — **ex·tra·di·tion** *n*

**ex·tra·mar·i·tal** *adj* : relating to sexual relations of a married person outside of the marriage

**ex·tra·ne·ous** *adj* : not essential or relevant — **ex·tra·ne·ous·ly** *adv*

**ex·traor·di·nary** *adj* : notably unusual or exceptional — **ex·traor·di·nari·ly** *adv*

**ex·tra·sen·so·ry** *adj* : outside the ordinary senses

**ex·tra·ter·res·tri·al** *n* : one existing or coming from outside the earth ∼ *adj* : relating to an extraterrestrial

**ex·trav·a·gant** *adj* : wildly excessive, lavish, or costly — **ex·trav·a·gance** *n* — **ex·trav·a·gant·ly** *adv*

**ex·trav·a·gan·za** *n* : spectacular event

**ex·treme** *adj* **1** : very great or intense **2** : very severe **3** : not moderate **4** : most remote ∼ *n* **1** : extreme state **2** : something located at one end or the other of a range — **ex·treme·ly** *adv*

**ex·trem·i·ty** *n* **1** : most remote part **2** : human hand or foot **3** : extreme degree or state (as of need)

**ex·tro·vert** *n* : gregarious person — **ex·tro·ver·sion** *n* — **ex·tro·vert·ed** *adj*

**ex·u·ber·ant** *adj* : joyously free from restraint — **ex·u·ber·ance** *n* — **ex·u·ber·ant·ly** *adv*

**ex·ult** *vb* : rejoice — **ex·ul·tant** *adj* — **ex·ul·tant·ly** *adv* — **ex·ul·ta·tion** *n*

**eye** *n* **1** : organ of sight consisting of a globular structure (**eye·ball**) in a socket of the skull with thin movable covers (**eye·lids**) bordered with hairs (**eye·lash·es**) **2** : vision **3** : judgment **4** : something suggesting an eye ∼ *vb* : look at — **eye·brow** *n* — **eyed** *adj* — **eye·drop·per** *n* — **eye·glass·es** *n pl* — **eye·sight** *n* — **eye·strain** *n*

**eye·let** *n* : hole (as in cloth) for a lacing or rope

**eye–open·er** *n* : something startling — **eye–open·ing** *adj*

**eye·piece** *n* : lens at the eye end of an optical instrument

**eye·sore** *n* : unpleasant sight

**eye·tooth** *n* : upper canine tooth

**eye·wit·ness** *n* : person who actually sees something happen

# F

**f** *n* : 6th letter of the alphabet

**fa·ble** *n* **1** : legendary story **2** : story that teaches a lesson — **fa·bled** *adj*

**fab·ric** *n* **1** : structure **2** : material made usu. by weaving or knitting fibers

**fab·ri·cate** *vb* **1** : construct **2** : invent — **fab·ri·ca·tion** *n*

**fab·u·lous** *adj* **1** : like, told in, or based on fable **2** : incredible or marvelous — **fab·u·lous·ly** *adv*

**fa·cade** *n* **1** : principal face of a building **2** : false or superficial appearance

**face** *n* **1** : front or principal surface (as of the head) **2** : presence **3** : facial expression **4** : grimace **5** : outward appearance ∼ *vb* **1** : challenge or resist firmly or brazenly **2** : cover with different material **3** : sit or stand with the face toward **4** : have the front oriented toward — **faced** *adj* — **face·less** *adj* — **fa·cial** *adj or n*

**face–lift** *n* **1** : cosmetic surgery on the face **2** : modernization

**fa·ce·tious** *adj* : seeking to produce laughter — **fa·ce·tious·ly** *adv* — **fa·ce·tious·ness** *n*

**fa·cil·i·tate** *vb* : make easier

**fa·cil·i·ty** *n* **1** : ease in doing or using **2** : something built or installed to serve a purpose or facilitate an activity

**fac·ing** *n* : lining or covering or material for this

**fac·sim·i·le** *n* : exact copy

**fact** *n* **1** : act or action **2** : something that exists or is real **3** : piece of information — **fac·tu·al** *adj* — **fac·tu·al·ly** *adv*

**fac·tion** *n* : part of a larger group — **fac·tion·al·ism** *n*

**fac·tor** *n* **1** : something that has an effect **2** : gene **3** : number used in multiplying

**fac·to·ry** *n* : place for manufacturing

**fac·ul·ty** *n* **1** : ability to act **2** : power of the mind or body **3** : body of teachers or department of instruction

**fad** *n* : briefly popular practice or interest — **fad·dish** *adj* — **fad·dist** *n*

**fade** *vb* **1** : wither **2** : lose or cause to lose freshness or brilliance **3** : grow dim **4** : vanish

**Fahr·en·heit** *adj* : relating to a thermometer scale with the boiling point at 212 degrees and the freezing point at 32 degrees

**fail** *vb* **1** : decline in health **2** : die away **3** : stop functioning **4** : fail to be successful **5** : become bankrupt **6** : disappoint **7** : neglect ∼ *n* : act of failing

**fail·ing** *n* : slight defect in character or conduct ∼ *prep* : in the absence or lack of

**fail·ure** *n* **1** : absence of expected action or performance **2** : bankruptcy **3** : deficiency **4** : one that has failed

**faint** *adj* **1** : cowardly or spiritless **2** : weak and dizzy **3** : lacking vigor **4** : indistinct ∼ *vb* : lose consciousness ∼ *n* : act or condition of fainting — **faint·heart·ed** *adj* — **faint·ly** *adv* — **faint·ness** *n*

[1]**fair** *adj* **1** : pleasing in appearance **2** : not stormy or cloudy **3** : just or honest **4** : conforming with the rules **5** : open to legitimate pursuit or attack **6** : light in color **7** : adequate — **fair·ness** *n*

[2]**fair** *n* : exhibition for judging or selling — **fair·ground** *n*

**fair·ly** *adv* **1** : in a manner of speaking **2** : without bias **3** : somewhat

**fairy** *n* : usu. small imaginary being — **fairy tale** *n*

**fairy·land** *n* **1** : land of fairies **2** : beautiful or charming place

**faith** *n* **1** : allegiance **2** : belief and trust in God **3** : confidence **4** : system of religious beliefs — **faith·ful** *adj* — **faith·ful·ly** *adv* — **faith·ful·ness** *n* — **faith·less** *adj* — **faith·less·ly** *adv* — **faith·less·ness** *n*

**fake** *vb* **1** : falsify **2** : counterfeit ∼ *n* : copy, fraud, or impostor ∼ *adj* : not genuine — **fak·er** *n*

**fal·con** *n* : small long-winged hawk used esp. for hunting — **fal·con·ry** *n*

**fall** *vb* **fell; fall·en** **1** : go down by gravity **2** : hang freely **3** : go lower **4** : be defeated or ruined **5** : commit a sin **6** : happen at a certain time ∼ *n* **1** : act of falling **2** : autumn **3** : downfall **4** *pl* : waterfall **5** : distance something falls

**fal·la·cy** *n* **1** : false idea **2** : false reasoning — **fal·la·cious** *adj*

**fal·li·ble** *adj* : capable of making a mistake — **fal·li·bly** *adv*

**fall·out** *n* **1** : radioactive particles from a nuclear explosion **2** : secondary effects

**false** *adj* **1** : not genuine, true, faithful, or permanent **2** : misleading — **false·ly** *adv* — **false·ness** *n* — **fal·si·fi·ca·tion** *n* — **fal·si·fy** *vb* — **fal·si·ty** *n*

**false·hood** *n* : lie

**fal·ter** *vb* **1** : move unsteadily **2** : hesitate — **fal·ter·ing·ly** *adv*

**fame** *n* : public reputation — **famed** *adj*

[1]**fa·mil·iar** *n* **1** : companion **2** : guardian spirit

[2]**fa·mil·iar** *adj* **1** : closely acquainted **2** : forward **3** : frequently seen or experienced — **fa·mil·iar·i·ty** *n* — **fa·mil·iar·ize** *vb* — **fa·mil·iar·ly** *adv*

**fam·i·ly** *n* **1** : persons of common ancestry **2** : group living together **3** : parents and children **4** : group of related individuals

**fam·ine** *n* : extreme scarcity of food

**fa·mous** *adj* : widely known or celebrated

**fa·mous·ly** *adv* : very well

[1]**fan** *n* : device for producing a current of air ∼ *vb* **1** : move air with a fan **2** : direct a current of air upon **3** : stir to activity

[2]**fan** *n* : enthusiastic follower or admirer

**fa·nat·ic, fa·nat·i·cal** *adj* : excessively enthusiastic or devoted — **fanatic** *n* — **fa·nat·i·cism** *n*

**fan·ci·er** *n* : one devoted to raising a particular plant or animal

**fan·cy** *n* **1** : liking **2** : whim **3** : imagination ∼ *vb* **1** : like **2** : imagine ∼ *adj* **1** : not plain **2** : of superior quality — **fan·ci·ful** *adj* — **fan·ci·ful·ly** *adv* — **fan·ci·ly** *adv*

**fan·fare** *n* **1** : a sounding of trumpets **2** : showy display

**fan·tas·tic** *adj* **1** : imaginary or unrealistic **2** : exceedingly or unbelievably great — **fan·tas·ti·cal·ly** *adv*

**fan·ta·sy** *n* **1** : imagination **2** : product of the imagination — **fan·ta·size** *vb*

**FAQ** *abbr* frequently asked questions

**far** *adv* **1** : at or to a distance **2** : much **3** : to a degree **4** : to an advanced point or extent ∼ *adj* **1** : remote **2** : long **3** : being more distant

**farce** *n* **1** : satirical comedy with an improbable plot **2** : ridiculous display — **far·ci·cal** *adj*

[1]**fare** *vb* : get along

[2]**fare** *n* **1** : price of transportation **2** : range of food

**fare·well** *n* **1** : wish of welfare at parting **2** : departure — **fare·well** *adj*

**far–fetched** *adj* : improbable

**farm** *n* : place where something is raised for food ∼ *vb* **1** : use (land) as a farm **2** : raise plants or animals for food — **farm·er** *n* — **farm·hand** *n* — **farm·house** *n* — **farm·ing** *n* — **farm·land** *n* — **farm·yard** *n*

**far·sight·ed** *adj* **1** : better able to see distant things than near **2** : judicious or shrewd — **far·sight·ed·ness** *n*

**far·ther** *adv* **1** : at or to a greater distance or more advanced point **2** : to a greater degree or extent ∼ *adj* : more distant

**far·thest** *adj* : most distant ∼ *adv* **1** : to or at the greatest distance **2** : to the most advanced point **3** : by the greatest extent

**fas·ci·nate** *vb* : transfix and hold spellbound — **fas·ci·na·tion** *n*

**fash·ion** *n* **1** : manner **2** : prevailing custom or style ∼ *vb* : form or construct — **fash·ion·able** *adj* — **fash·ion·ably** *adv*

[1]**fast** *adj* **1** : firmly fixed, bound, or shut **2** : faithful **3** : moving or acting quickly **4** : indicating ahead of the correct time **5** : deep and undisturbed **6** : permanently dyed **7** : wild or promiscuous ∼ *adv* **1** : so as to be secure or bound **2** : soundly or deeply **3** : swiftly

[2]**fast** *vb* : abstain from food or eat sparingly ∼ *n* : act or time of fasting

**fas·ten** *vb* : attach esp. by pinning or tying — **fas·ten·er** *n* — **fas·ten·ing** *n*

**fat** *adj* **1** : having much fat **2** : thick ∼ *n* : animal tissue rich in greasy or oily matter — **fat·ness** *n* — **fat·ten** *vb* — **fat·ty** *adj or n*

**fa·tal** *adj* : causing death or ruin — **fa·tal·ism** *n* — **fa·tal·ist** *n* — **fa·tal·is·tic** *adj* — **fa·tal·is·ti·cal·ly** *adv* — **fa·tal·i·ty** *n* — **fa·tal·ly** *adv*

**fate** *n* **1** : principle, cause, or will held to determine events **2** : end or outcome — **fat·ed** *adj* — **fate·ful** *adj* — **fate·ful·ly** *adv*

**fa·ther** *n* **1** : male parent **2** *cap* : God **3** : originator — **father** *vb* — **fa·ther·hood** *n* — **fa·ther·land** *n* — **fa·ther·less** *adj* — **fa·ther·ly** *adj*

**father–in–law** *n* (**fa·thers–in–law**) : father of one's spouse

**fa·tigue** *n* **1** : weariness from labor or use **2** : tendency to break under repeated stress ∼ *vb* : tire out

**fau·cet** *n* : fixture for drawing off a liquid

**fault** *n* **1** : weakness in character **2** : something wrong or imperfect **3** : responsibility for something wrong **4** : fracture in the earth's crust ∼ *vb* : find fault in or with — **fault·find·er** *n* — **fault·find·ing** *n* — **fault·i·ly** *adv* — **fault·less** *adj* — **fault·less·ly** *adv* — **faulty** *adj*

**fau·na** *n* : animals or animal life esp. of a region — **fau·nal** *adj*

**fa·vor** *n* **1** : approval **2** : partiality **3** : act of kindness ∼ *vb* : regard or treat with favor — **fa·vor·able** *adj* — **fa·vor·ably** *adv*

**fa·vor·ite** *n* : one favored — **favorite** *adj* — **fa·vor·it·ism** *n*

**fawn** *n* : young deer

**faze** *vb* : disturb the composure of

**fear** *n* : unpleasant emotion caused by expectation or awareness of danger ∼ *vb* : be afraid of — **fear·ful** *adj* — **fear·ful·ly** *adv* — **fear·less** *adj* — **fear·less·ly** *adv* — **fear·less·ness** *n* — **fear·some** *adj*

**fea·si·ble** *adj* : capable of being done — **fea·si·bil·i·ty** *n* — **fea·si·bly** *adv*

**feast** *n* **1** : large or fancy meal **2** : religious festival ∼ *vb* : eat plentifully

**feat** *n* : notable deed

**feath·er** *n* : one of the light horny outgrowths that form the external covering of a bird's body — **feather** *vb* — **feath·ered** *adj* — **feath·er·less** *adj* — **feath·ery** *adj*

**fea·ture** *n* **1** : shape or appearance of the face **2** : part of the face **3** : prominent characteristic **4** : special attraction ∼ *vb* : give prominence to — **fea·ture·less** *adj*

**Feb·ru·ary** *n* : 2d month of the year having 28 and in leap years 29 days

**fed·er·al** *adj* : of or constituting a government with power distributed between a central authority and constituent units — **fed·er·al·ism** *n* — **fed·er·al·ist** *n or adj* — **fed·er·al·ly** *adv*

**fed·er·ate** *vb* : join in a union of organizations — **fed·er·a·tion** *n*

**fee** *n* : fixed charge

**fee·ble** *adj* : weak or ineffective — **fee·ble·mind·ed** *adj* — **fee·ble·mind·ed·ness** *n* — **fee·ble·ness** *n* — **fee·bly** *adv*

**feed** *vb* **1** : give food to **2** : eat **3** : furnish ∼ *n* : food for livestock — **feed·er** *n*

**feel** *vb* **felt; felt** **1** : perceive or examine through physical contact **2** : think or believe **3** : be conscious of **4** : seem **5** : have sympathy ∼ *n* **1** : sense of touch **2** : quality of a thing imparted through touch — **feel·er** *n*

**feel·ing** *n* **1** : sense of touch **2** : state of mind **3** *pl* : sensibilities **4** : opinion

**feet** *pl of* FOOT

**feign** *vb* : pretend

**fe·lic·i·tate** *vb* : congratulate — **fe·lic·i·ta·tion** *n*

**fe•line** adj : relating to cats — **feline** n

**fell** past of FALL

**fel•low** n **1** : companion or associate **2** : man or boy — **fel•low•ship** n

**fel•low•man** n : kindred human being

**fel•on** n : one who has committed a felony

**fel•o•ny** n : serious crime — **fe•lo•ni•ous** adj

[1]**felt** n : cloth made of pressed wool and fur

[2]**felt** past of FEEL

**fe•male** adj : relating to or being the sex that bears young — **female** n

**fem•i•nine** adj : relating to the female sex — **fem•i•nin•i•ty** n — **fem•i•nism** n — **fem•i•nist** n or adj

**fence** n : enclosing barrier esp. of wood or wire ~ vb **1** : enclose with a fence **2** : practice fencing — **fenc•er** n

**fenc•ing** n **1** : combat with swords for sport **2** : material for building fences

**fend•er** n : guard over an automobile wheel

**fer•ment** vb : cause or undergo chemical decomposition ~ n : agitation — **fer•men•ta•tion** n

**fern** n : flowerless seedless green plant

**fe•ro•cious** adj : fierce or savage — **fe•ro•cious•ly** adv — **fe•ro•cious•ness** n — **fe•roc•i•ty** n

**fer•ry** vb : carry by boat over water ~ n : boat used in ferrying — **fer•ry•boat** n

**fer•tile** adj **1** : producing plentifully **2** : capable of developing or reproducing — **fer•til•i•ty** n

**fer•til•ize** vb : make fertile — **fer•til•iza•tion** n — **fer•til•iz•er** n

**fes•ti•val** n : time of celebration

**fes•tive** adj : joyous or happy — **fes•tive•ly** adv — **fes•tiv•i•ty** n

**fe•tal** adj : of, relating to, or being a fetus

**fetch** vb **1** : go or come after and bring or take back **2** : sell for

**fetch•ing** adj : attractive — **fetch•ing•ly** adv

**fête** n : lavish party ~ vb : honor or commemorate with a fête

**fe•tish** n **1** : object believed to have magical powers **2** : object of unreasoning devotion or concern

**fe•tus** n : vertebrate not yet born or hatched

**feud** n : prolonged quarrel — **feud** vb

**feu•dal•ism** n : medieval political order in which land is granted in return for service — **feu•dal** adj — **feu•dal•is•tic** adj

**fe•ver** n **1** : abnormal rise in body temperature **2** : state of heightened emotion — **fe•ver•ish** adj — **fe•ver•ish•ly** adv

**few** pron : not many ~ adj : some but not many — often with a ~ n : small number — often with a

**few•er** pron : smaller number of things

**fi•an•cé** n : man one is engaged to

**fi•an•cée** n : woman one is engaged to

**fi•as•co** n : ridiculous failure

**fib** n : trivial lie — **fib** vb — **fib•ber** n

**fi•ber, fi•bre** n **1** : threadlike substance or structure (as a muscle cell or fine root) **2** : indigestible material in food **3** : element that gives texture or substance — **fi•brous** adj

**fi•ber•glass** n : glass in fibrous form in various products (as insulation)

**fick•le** adj : unpredictably changeable — **fick•le•ness** n

**fic•tion** n : a made-up story or literature consisting of these — **fic•tion•al** adj

**fic•ti•tious** adj : made up or pretended

**fid•dle** n : violin ~ vb **1** : play on the fiddle **2** : move the hands restlessly — **fid•dler** n

**fi•del•i•ty** n **1** : quality or state of being faithful **2** : quality of reproduction

**fid•get** n **1** pl : restlessness **2** : one that fidgets ~ vb : move restlessly — **fid•gety** adj

**field** n **1** : open country **2** : cleared land **3** : land yielding some special product **4** : sphere of activity **5** : area for sports **6** : region or space in which a given effect (as magnetism) exists ~ vb : put into the field — **field** adj — **field•er** n

**fiend** n **1** : devil **2** : extremely wicked person — **fiend•ish** adj — **fiend•ish•ly** adv

**fierce** adj **1** : violently hostile or aggressive **2** : intense **3** : menacing looking — **fierce•ly** adv — **fierce•ness** n

**fi•ery** adj **1** : burning **2** : hot or passionate — **fi•eri•ness** n

**fi•es•ta** n : festival

**fif•teen** n : one more than 14 — **fifteen** adj or pron — **fif•teenth** adj or n

**fifth** n **1** : one that is number 5 in a countable series **2** : one of 5 equal parts of something — **fifth** adj or adv

**fif•ty** n : 5 times 10 — **fif•ti•eth** adj or n — **fifty** adj or pron

**fif•ty–fif•ty** adv or adj : shared equally

**fig** n : pear-shaped edible fruit

**fight** vb **fought; fought** **1** : contend against another in battle **2** : box **3** : struggle ~ n **1** : hostile encounter **2** : boxing match **3** : verbal disagreement — **fight•er** n

**fig•ment** n : something imagined or made up

**fig•u•ra•tive** adj : metaphorical — **fig•u•ra•tive•ly** adv

**fig•ure** n **1** : symbol representing a number **2** pl : arithmetical calculations **3** : price **4** : shape or outline **5** : illustration **6** : pattern or design **7** : prominent person ~ vb **1** : be important **2** : calculate — **fig•ured** adj

[1]**file** n : tool for smoothing or sharpening ~ vb : rub or smooth with a file

[2]**file** vb **1** : arrange in order **2** : enter or record officially ~ n : device for keeping papers in order

[3]**file** n : row of persons or things one behind the other ~ vb : march in file

**fil•i•bus•ter** n : long speeches to delay a legislative vote — **filibuster** vb — **fil•i•bus•ter•er** n

**fill** vb **1** : make or become full **2** : stop up **3** : feed **4** : satisfy **5** : occupy fully **6** : spread through ~ n **1** : full supply **2** : material for filling — **fill•er** n — **fill•ing** n — **fill in** vb **1** : provide information to or for **2** : substitute

**fil•let** n : piece of boneless meat or fish ~ vb : cut into fillets

**fil•ly** n : young female horse

**film** n **1** : thin skin or membrane **2** : thin coating or layer **3** : strip of material used in taking pictures **4** : movie ~ vb : make a movie of — **filmy** adj

**fil•ter** n **1** : device for separating matter from a fluid **2** : device (as on a camera lens) that absorbs light ~ vb **1** : pass through a filter **2** : remove by means of a filter — **fil•ter•able** adj — **fil•tra•tion** n

**filth** n : repulsive dirt or refuse — **filth•i•ness** n — **filthy** adj

**fin** n **1** : thin external process controlling movement in an aquatic animal **2** : fin-shaped part (as on an airplane) — **finned** adj

**fi•nal** adj **1** : not to be changed **2** : ultimate **3** : coming at the end — **final** n — **fi•nal•ist** n — **fi•nal•i•ty** n — **fi•nal•ize** vb — **fi•nal•ly** adv

**fi•na•le** n : last or climactic part

**fi•nance** n **1** pl : money resources **2** : management of money affairs ~ vb **1** : raise funds for **2** : give necessary funds to **3** : sell on credit — **fi•nan•cier** n

**fi•nan•cial** adj : relating to finance — **fi•nan•cial•ly** adv

**finch** n : songbird (as a sparrow or linnet) with a strong bill

**find** vb **1** : discover or encounter **2** : obtain by effort **3** : experience or feel **4** : gain or regain the use of **5** : decide on (a verdict) ~ n **1** : act or instance of finding **2** : something found — **find•er** n — **find•ing** n — **find out** vb : learn, discover, or verify something

**fine** n : money paid as a penalty ~ vb : impose a fine on ~ adj **1** : free from impurity **2** : small or thin **3** : not coarse **4** : superior in quality or appearance ~ adv : finely — **fine•ly** adv — **fine•ness** n

**fin•ery** n : showy clothing and jewels

**fi•nesse** n **1** : delicate skill **2** : craftiness — **finesse** vb

**fin•ger** n **1** : one of the 5 divisions at the end of the hand and esp. one other than the thumb **2** : something like a finger **3** : part of a glove for a finger ~ vb **1** : touch with the fingers **2** : identify as if by pointing — **fin•gered** adj — **fin•ger•nail** n — **fin•ger•print** n or vb — **fin•ger•tip** n

**fin•icky** adj : excessively particular in taste or standards

**fin•ish** vb **1** : come or bring to an end **2** : use or dispose of entirely **3** : put a final coat or surface on ~ n **1** : end **2** : final treatment given a surface — **fin•ish•er** n

**fi•nite** adj : having definite limits

**fiord** var of FJORD

**fir** n : evergreen tree or its wood

**fire** n **1** : light or heat and esp. the flame of something burning **2** : destructive burning (as of a house) **3** : enthusiasm **4** : the shooting of weapons ~ vb **1** : kindle **2** : stir up or enliven **3** : dismiss from employment **4** : shoot **5** : bake — **fire•bomb** n or vb — **fire•fight•er** n — **fire•less** adj — **fire•proof** adj or vb — **fire•wood** n

**fire•arm** n : weapon (as a rifle) that works by an explosion of gunpowder

**fire•ball** n **1** : ball of fire **2** : brilliant meteor

**fire•crack•er** n : small firework that makes noise

**fire•fight•er** n : a person who fights fires

**fire•fly** n : night-flying beetle that produces a soft light

**fire•place** n : opening made in a chimney to hold an open fire

**fire•side** n **1** : place near the fire or hearth **2** : home ~ adj : having an informal quality

**fire•trap** n : place apt to catch on fire

**fire•work** n : device that explodes to produce noise or a display of light

[1]**firm** adj **1** : securely fixed in place **2** : strong or vigorous **3** : not subject to change **4** : resolute ~ vb : make or become firm — **firm•ly** adv — **firm•ness** n

[2]**firm** n : business enterprise

**first** adj **1** : being number one **2** : foremost ~ adv **1** : before any other **2** : for the first time ~ n **1** : number one **2** : one that is first — **first class** n — **first–class** adj or adv — **first•ly** adv — **first–rate** adj or adv

**first aid** n : emergency care

**fis•cal** adj : relating to money — **fis•cal•ly** adv

**fish** n **fish** : water animal with fins, gills, and usu. scales ~ vb **1** : try to catch fish **2** : grope — **fish•er** n — **fish•er•man** n — **fish•hook** n — **fish•ing** n

**fish•ery** n : fishing business or a place for this

**fishy** adj **1** : relating to or like fish **2** : questionable

**fis•sion** n : splitting of an atomic nucleus — **fis•sion•able** adj

**fist** n : hand doubled up — **fist•ed** adj — **fist•ful** n

[1]**fit** n : sudden attack of illness or emotion

[2]**fit** adj **1** : suitable **2** : qualified **3** : sound in body ~ vb **1** : be suitable to **2** : insert or adjust correctly **3** : make room for **4** : supply or equip **5** : belong ~ n : state of fitting or being fitted — **fit•ly** adv — **fit•ness** n — **fit•ter** n

**fit•ful** adj : restless — **fit•ful•ly** adv

**fit•ting** adj : suitable ~ n : a small part

**five** n **1** : one more than 4 **2** : 5th in a set or series **3** : something having 5 units — **five** adj or pron

**fix** vb **1** : attach **2** : establish **3** : make right **4** : prepare **5** : improperly influence ~ n **1** : predicament **2** : determination of location — **fixed** adj — **fixed•ly** adv — **fixed•ness** n — **fix•er** n

**fix•a•tion** n : obsessive attachment — **fix•ate** vb

**fix•ture** n : permanent part of something

**fizz** vb : make a hissing sound ~ n : effervescence

**fiz•zle** vb **1** : fizz **2** : fail ~ n : failure

**fjord** n : inlet of the sea between cliffs

**flab** n : flabby flesh

**flab•by** adj : not firm — **flab•bi•ness** n

[1]**flag** n **1** : fabric that is a symbol (as of a country) **2** : something used to signal ~ vb : signal with a flag — **flag•pole** n — **flag•staff** n

[2]**flag** vb : lose strength or spirit

**flag•el•late** vb : whip — **flag•el•la•tion** n

**flag•on** n : container for liquids

**fla•grant** adj : conspicuously bad — **fla•grant•ly** adv

**flair** n : natural aptitude

**flake** n : small flat piece ~ vb : separate or form into flakes

**flam•boy•ant** adj : showy — **flam•boy•ance** n — **flam•boy•ant•ly** adv

**flame** n **1** : glowing part of a fire **2** : state of combustion **3** : burning passion — **flame** vb — **flam•ing** adj

**flam•ma•ble** adj : easily ignited

**flank** n : side of something ~ vb **1** : attack or go around the side of **2** : be at the side of

**flan•nel** n : soft napped fabric

**flap** n **1** : slap **2** : something flat that hangs loose ~ vb **1** : move (wings) up and down **2** : swing back and forth noisily

**flap•jack** n : pancake

**flare** vb : become suddenly bright or excited ~ n : blaze of light

**flash** vb **1** : give off a sudden flame or burst of light **2** : appear or pass suddenly ~ n **1** : sudden burst of light or inspiration **2** : instant ~ adj : coming suddenly

**flash•light** n : small battery-operated light

**flashy** adj : showy — **flash•i•ly** adv — **flash•i•ness** n

**flat** adj **1** : smooth **2** : broad and thin **3** : definite **4** : uninteresting **5** : deflated **6** : below the true pitch ~ n **1** : level surface of land **2** : flat note in music **3** : apartment **4** : having lost air ~ adv **1** : exactly **2** : below the true pitch ~ vb : make flat — **flat•ly** adv — **flat•ness** n — **flat•ten** vb

**flat•foot** n **flat•feet** : foot condition in which the arch is flattened — **flat•foot•ed** adj

**flat–out** adj **1** : being maximum effort or speed **2** : downright

**flat•ter** vb **1** : praise insincerely **2** : judge or represent too favorably — **flat•ter•er** n — **flat•tery** n

**flat•u•lent** adj : full of gas — **flat•u•lence** n

**flaunt** vb : display ostentatiously — **flaunt** n

**fla•vor** n **1** : quality that affects the sense of taste **2** : something that adds flavor ~ vb : give flavor to — **fla•vor•ful** adj — **fla•vor•ing** n — **fla•vor•less** adj

**flaw** n : fault — **flaw•less** adj — **flaw•less•ly** adv — **flaw•less•ness** n

**flea** n : leaping bloodsucking insect

**fleck** vb or n : streak or spot

**flee** vb : run away

**fleece** n : sheep's wool ~ vb **1** : shear **2** : get money from dishonestly — **fleecy** adj

[1]**fleet** vb : pass rapidly ~ adj : swift — **fleet•ing** adj — **fleet•ness** n

[2]**fleet** n : group of ships

**flesh** n **1** : soft parts of an animal's body **2** : soft plant tissue (as fruit pulp) — **fleshed** adj — **fleshy** adj — **flesh out** vb : make fuller

**flew** past of FLY

**flex** vb : bend

**flex•i•ble** adj **1** : capable of being flexed **2** : adaptable — **flex•i•bil•i•ty** n — **flex•i•bly** adv

**flick** n : light jerky stroke ~ vb **1** : strike lightly **2** : flutter

**flick•er** *vb* **1 :** waver **2 :** burn unsteadily ~ *n* **1 :** sudden movement **2 :** wavering light

**fli•er** *n* **1 :** aviator **2 :** advertising circular

**[1]flight** *n* **1 :** act or instance of flying **2 :** ability to fly **3 :** a passing through air or space **4 :** series of stairs — **flight•less** *adj*

**[2]flight** *n* **:** act or instance of running away

**flighty** *adj* **:** capricious or silly — **flight•i•ness** *n*

**flim•sy** *adj* **1 :** not strong or well made **2 :** not believable — **flim•si•ly** *adv* — **flim•si•ness** *n*

**flinch** *vb* **:** shrink from pain

**fling** *vb* **1 :** move brusquely **2 :** throw ~ *n* **1 :** act or instance of flinging **2 :** attempt **3 :** period of self-indulgence

**flip** *vb* **1 :** cause to turn over quickly or many times **2 :** move with a quick push ~ *adj* **:** insolent — **flip** *n*

**flip•pant** *adj* **:** not serious enough — **flip•pan•cy** *n*

**flirt** *vb* **1 :** be playfully romantic **2 :** show casual interest ~ *n* **:** one who flirts — **flir•ta•tion** *n* — **flir•ta•tious** *adj*

**flit** *vb* **:** dart

**float** *n* **1 :** something that floats **2 :** vehicle carrying an exhibit ~ *vb* **1 :** rest on or in a fluid without sinking **2 :** wander **3 :** finance by issuing stock or bonds — **float•er** *n*

**flock** *n* **:** group of animals (as birds) or people ~ *vb* **:** gather or move as a group

**flood** *n* **1 :** great flow of water over the land **2 :** overwhelming volume ~ *vb* **:** cover or fill esp. with water — **flood•wa•ter** *n*

**floor** *n* **1 :** bottom of a room on which one stands **2 :** story of a building **3 :** lower limit ~ *vb* **1 :** furnish with a floor **2 :** knock down **3 :** amaze — **floor•board** *n* — **floor•ing** *n*

**flop** *vb* **1 :** flap **2 :** slump heavily **3 :** fail — **flop** *n*

**flop•py** *adj* **:** soft and flexible

**flo•ra** *n* **:** plants or plant life of a region

**flo•ral** *adj* **:** relating to flowers

**flo•rist** *n* **:** flower dealer

**floss** *n* **1 :** soft thread for embroidery **2 :** thread used to clean between teeth — **floss** *vb*

**flo•ta•tion** *n* **:** process or instance of floating

**[1]floun•der** *n* **flounder :** a flattened fish with both eyes on the upper side

**[2]flounder** *vb* **1 :** struggle for footing **2 :** proceed clumsily

**flour** *n* **:** finely ground meal ~ *vb* **:** coat with flour — **floury** *adj*

**flour•ish** *vb* **1 :** thrive **2 :** wave threateningly ~ *n* **1 :** embellishment **2 :** fanfare **3 :** wave **4 :** showiness of action

**flout** *vb* **:** treat with disdain

**flow** *vb* **1 :** move in a stream **2 :** proceed smoothly and readily ~ *n* **:** uninterrupted stream

**flow•er** *n* **1 :** showy plant shoot that bears seeds **2 :** state of flourishing ~ *vb* **1 :** produce flowers **2 :** flourish — **flow•ered** *adj* — **flow•er•less** *adj* — **flow•er•pot** *n* — **flow•ery** *adj*

**flown** *past part of* FLY

**flu** *n* **:** acute very contagious virus disease

**flub** *vb* **:** bungle — **flub** *n*

**fluc•tu•ate** *vb* **:** change rapidly esp. up and down — **fluc•tu•a•tion** *n*

**flue** *n* **:** smoke duct

**flu•ent** *adj* **:** speaking with ease — **flu•en•cy** *n* — **flu•ent•ly** *adv*

**fluff** *n* **1 :** something soft and light **2 :** blunder ~ *vb* **1 :** make fluffy **2 :** make a mistake — **fluffy** *adj*

**flu•id** *adj* **:** flowing ~ *n* **:** substance that can flow — **flu•id•i•ty** *n* — **flu•id•ly** *adv*

**fluke** *n* **:** stroke of luck

**flung** *past of* FLING

**flunk** *vb* **:** fail in school work

**flu•o•res•cence** *n* **:** emission of light after initial absorption — **flu•o•resce** *vb* — **flu•o•res•cent** *adj*

**flur•ry** *n* **1 :** light snowfall **2 :** bustle **3 :** brief burst of activity — **flurry** *vb*

**[1]flush** *vb* **:** cause (a bird) to fly from cover

**[2]flush** *n* **1 :** sudden flow (as of water) **2 :** sudden increase of emotion **3 :** blush ~ *vb* **1 :** blush **2 :** wash out with a rush of liquid ~ *adj* **1 :** filled to overflowing **2 :** of a reddish healthy color **3 :** smooth or level **4 :** abutting — **flush** *adv*

**flus•ter** *vb* **:** upset — **fluster** *n*

**flute** *n* **1 :** pipelike musical instrument **2 :** groove — **flut•ed** *adj* — **flut•ing** *n* — **flut•ist** *n*

**flut•ter** *vb* **1 :** flap the wings rapidly **2 :** move with quick wavering or flapping motions **3 :** behave in an agitated manner ~ *n* **1 :** a fluttering **2 :** state of confusion — **flut•tery** *adj*

**flux** *n* **:** state of continuous change

**[1]fly** *vb* **(flew; flown) 1 :** move through the air with wings **2 :** float or soar **3 :** flee **4 :** move or pass swiftly **5 :** operate an airplane

**[2]fly** *n* **:** garment closure

**[3]fly** *n* **:** winged insect

**fly•er** *var of* FLIER

**foam** *n* **1 :** mass of bubbles on top of a liquid **2 :** material of cellular form ~ *vb* **:** form foam — **foamy** *adj*

**fo•cus** *n* **1 :** point at which reflected or refracted rays meet **2 :** adjustment (as of eyeglasses) for clear vision **3 :** central point ~ *vb* **:** bring to a focus — **fo•cal** *adj* — **fo•cal•ly** *adv*

**foe** *n* **:** enemy

**fog** *n* **1 :** fine particles of water suspended near the ground **2 :** mental confusion ~ *vb* **:** obscure or be obscured with fog — **fog•gy** *adj* — **fog•horn** *n*

**foil** *n* **1 :** thin sheet of metal **2 :** one that sets off another by contrast

**[1]fold** *n* **1 :** enclosure for sheep **2 :** group with a common interest

**[2]fold** *vb* **1 :** lay one part over another **2 :** embrace ~ *n* **:** part folded

**fold•er** *n* **1 :** one that folds **2 :** circular **3 :** folded cover or envelope for papers

**fo•liage** *n* **:** plant leaves

**folk** *n* **1 :** people in general **2** *pl* **:** one's family ~ *adj* **:** relating to the common people

**folk•lore** *n* **:** customs and traditions of a people — **folk•lor•ist** *n*

**folksy** *adj* **:** friendly and informal

**fol•low** *vb* **1 :** go or come after **2 :** pursue **3 :** obey **4 :** proceed along **5 :** keep one's attention fixed on **6 :** result from — **fol•low•er** *n* — **fol•low•ing** *adj or prep*

**fol•ly** *n* **:** foolishness

**fond** *adj* **1 :** strongly attracted **2 :** affectionate **3 :** dear — **fond•ly** *adv* — **fond•ness** *n*

**fon•dle** *vb* **:** touch lovingly

**food** *n* **:** material eaten to sustain life

**fool** *n* **1 :** stupid person **2 :** jester ~ *vb* **1 :** waste time **2 :** meddle **3 :** deceive — **fool•ery** *n* — **fool•ish** *adj* — **fool•ish•ly** *adv* — **fool•ish•ness** *n* — **fool•proof** *adj*

**fool•har•dy** *adj* **:** rash — **fool•har•di•ness** *n*

**foot** *n* **(feet) 1 :** end part of a leg **2 :** unit of length equal to ⅓ yard **3 :** unit of verse meter **4 :** bottom — **foot•ed** *adj* — **foot•path** *n* — **foot•print** *n* — **foot•race** *n* — **foot•rest** *n* — **foot•step** *n* — **foot•wear** *n*

**foot•age** *n* **:** size expressed in feet

**foot•ball** *n* **:** ball game played by 2 teams on a rectangular field

**foot•hill** *n* **:** hill at the foot of higher hills

**foot•hold** *n* **:** support for the feet

**foot•ing** *n* **1 :** foothold **2 :** basis

**foot•lock•er** *n* **:** small trunk

**foot•loose** *adj* **:** having no ties

**foot•note** *n* **:** note at the bottom of a page

**foot•stool** *n* **:** stool to support the feet

**for** *prep* **1** — used to show preparation or purpose **2 :** because of **3** — used to show a recipient **4 :** in support of **5 :** so as to support or help cure **6 :** so as to be equal to **7 :** concerning **8 :** through the period of ~ *conj* **:** because

**for•bear** *vb* **1 :** refrain from **2 :** be patient — **for•bear•ance** *n*

**for•bid** *vb* **1 :** prohibit **2 :** order not to do something

**for•bid•ding** *adj* **:** tending to discourage

**force** *n* **1 :** exceptional strength or energy **2 :** military strength **3 :** body (as of persons) available for a purpose **4 :** violence **5 :** influence (as a push or pull) that causes motion ~ *vb* **1 :** compel **2 :** gain against resistance **3 :** break open — **force•ful** *adj* — **force•ful•ly** *adv* — **in force 1 :** in great numbers **2 :** valid

**forc•ible** *adj* **1 :** done by force **2 :** showing force — **forc•i•bly** *adv*

**ford** *n* **:** place to wade across a stream ~ *vb* **:** wade across

**fore** *adv* **:** in or toward the front ~ *adj* **:** being or coming before in time, place, or order ~ *n* **:** front

**fore•arm** *n* **:** part of the arm between the elbow and the wrist

**fore•bear** *n* **:** ancestor

**fore•bod•ing** *n* **:** premonition of disaster — **fore•bod•ing** *adj*

**fore•cast** *vb* **:** predict — **forecast** *n* — **fore•cast•er** *n*

**fore•close** *vb* **:** take legal measures to terminate a mortgage — **fore•clo•sure** *n*

**fore•fa•ther** *n* **:** ancestor

**fore•fin•ger** *n* **:** finger next to the thumb

**fore•foot** *n* **:** front foot of a quadruped

**fore•go** *vb* **:** precede — **fore•go•ing** *n*

**fore•gone** *adj* **:** determined in advance

**fore•ground** *n* **:** part of a scene nearest the viewer

**fore•hand** *n* **:** stroke (as in tennis) made with the palm of the hand turned forward — **fore•hand** *adj*

**fore•head** *n* **:** part of the face above the eyes

**for•eign** *adj* **1 :** situated outside a place or country and esp. one's own country **2 :** belonging to a different place or country **3 :** not pertinent **4 :** related to or dealing with other nations — **for•eign•er** *n*

**fore•leg** *n* **:** front leg

**fore•man** *n* **1 :** person who speaks for a jury **2 :** workman in charge

**fore•most** *adj* **:** first in time, place, or order — **foremost** *adv*

**fo•ren•sics** *n pl* **:** art or study of speaking or debating — **fo•ren•sic** *adj*

**fore•run•ner** *n* **:** one that goes before

**fore•see** *vb* **:** see or realize beforehand — **fore•see•able** *adj*

**fore•shad•ow** *vb* **:** hint or suggest beforehand

**fore•sight** *n* **:** care or provision for the future — **fore•sight•ed** *adj* — **fore•sight•ed•ness** *n*

**for•est** *n* **:** large thick growth of trees and underbrush — **for•est•ed** *adj* — **for•est•er** *n* — **for•est•land** *n* — **for•est•ry** *n*

**fore•stall** *vb* **:** prevent by acting in advance

**fore•taste** *n* **:** advance indication or notion ~ *vb* **:** anticipate

**fore•tell** *vb* **:** predict

**for•ev•er** *adv* **1 :** for a limitless time **2 :** always

**for•ev•er•more** *adv* **:** forever

**fore•warn** *vb* **:** warn beforehand

**for•feit** *vb* **:** lose or lose the right to by an error or crime ~ *n* **:** something forfeited — **for•fei•ture** *n*

**[1]forge** *vb* **:** workshop for shaping metal ~ *vb* **1 :** form (metal) by heating and hammering **2 :** imitate falsely esp. to defraud — **forg•er** *n* — **forg•ery** *n*

**[2]forge** *vb* **:** move ahead steadily

**for•get** *vb* **1 :** be unable to think of or recall **2 :** fail to think of at the proper time — **for•get•ta•ble** *adj* — **for•get•ful** *adj* — **for•get•ful•ly** *adv*

**for•give** *vb* **:** pardon — **for•giv•able** *adj* — **for•give•ness** *n*

**for•giv•ing** *adj* **1 :** able to forgive **2 :** allowing room for error or weakness

**for•go, fore•go** *vb* **:** do without

**fork** *n* **1 :** implement with prongs for lifting, holding, or digging **2 :** forked part **3 :** a dividing into branches or a place where something branches ~ *vb* **1 :** divide into branches **2 :** move with a fork — **forked** *adj*

**for•lorn** *adj* **1 :** deserted **2 :** wretched — **for•lorn•ly** *adv*

**form** *n* **1 :** shape **2 :** set way of doing or saying something **3 :** document with blanks to be filled in **4 :** manner of performing with respect to what is expected **5 :** mold **6 :** kind or variety **7 :** one of the ways in which a word is changed to show difference in use ~ *vb* **1 :** give form or shape to **2 :** train **3 :** develop **4 :** constitute — **for•ma•tive** *adj* — **form•less** *adj*

**for•mal** *adj* **:** following established custom ~ *n* **:** formal social event — **for•mal•i•ty** *n* — **for•mal•ize** *vb* — **for•mal•ly** *adv*

**for•mat** *n* **:** general style or arrangement of something — **format** *vb*

**for•ma•tion** *n* **1 :** a giving form to something **2 :** something formed **3 :** arrangement

**for•mer** *adj* **:** coming before in time — **for•mer•ly** *adv*

**for•mi•da•ble** *adj* **1 :** causing fear or dread **2 :** very difficult — **for•mi•da•bly** *adv*

**for•mu•la** *n* **1 :** set form of words for ceremonial use **2 :** recipe **3 :** milk mixture for a baby **4 :** group of symbols or figures briefly expressing information **5 :** set form or method

**for•mu•late** *vb* **:** design, devise — **for•mu•la•tion** *n*

**for•sake** *vb* **:** renounce completely

**for•swear** *vb* **1 :** renounce under oath **2 :** perjure

**for•syth•ia** *n* **:** shrub grown for its yellow flowers

**fort** *n* **1 :** fortified place **2 :** permanent army post

**forte** *n* **:** something at which a person excels

**forth** *adv* **:** forward

**forth•com•ing** *adj* **1 :** coming or available soon **2 :** open and direct

**forth•right** *adj* **:** direct — **forth•right•ly** *adv* — **forth•right•ness** *n*

**for•ti•fy** *vb* **:** make strong — **for•ti•fi•ca•tion** *n*

**for•ti•tude** *n* **:** ability to endure

**fort•night** *n* **:** 2 weeks — **fort•night•ly** *adj or adv*

**for•tress** *n* **:** strong fort

**for•tu•nate** *adj* **1 :** coming by good luck **2 :** lucky — **for•tu•nate•ly** *adv*

**for•tune** *n* **1 :** prosperity attained partly through luck **2 :** good or bad luck **3 :** destiny **4 :** wealth

**for•tune–tel•ler** *n* **:** one who foretells a person's future — **for•tune–tell•ing** *n or adj*

**for•ty** *n* **:** 4 times 10 — **for•ti•eth** *adj or n* — **for•ty** *adj or pron*

**fo•rum** *n* **1 :** Roman marketplace **2 :** medium for open discussion

**for•ward** *adj* **1 :** being near or at or belonging to the front **2 :** brash ~ *adv* **:** toward what is in front ~ *n* **:** player near the front of his team ~ *vb* **1 :** help onward **2 :** send on — **for•ward•er** *n* — **for•ward•ness** *n*

**for•wards** *adv* **:** forward

**fos•sil** *n* **:** preserved trace of an ancient plant or animal ~ *adj* **:** being or originating from a fossil — **fos•sil•ize** *vb*

**fos•ter** *adj* **:** being, having, or relating to substitute parents ~ *vb* **:** help to grow or develop

**fought** *past of* FIGHT

**foul** *adj* **1 :** offensive **2 :** clogged with dirt **3 :** abusive **4 :** wet and stormy **5 :** unfair ~ *n* **:** a breaking of the rules in a game ~ *adv* **:** foully ~ *vb* **1 :** make or become foul or filthy **2 :** tangle — **foul•ly** *adv* — **foul•mouthed** *adj* — **foul•ness** *n*

**foul–up** *n* : error or state of confusion — **foul up** *vb* : bungle

**found** *vb* : establish — **found•er** *n*

**foun•da•tion** *n* **1** : act of founding **2** : basis for something **3** : endowed institution **4** : supporting structure — **foun•da•tion•al** *adj*

**foun•der** *vb* : sink

**found•ry** *n* : place where metal is cast

**foun•tain** *n* **1** : spring of water **2** : source **3** : artificial jet of water

**four** *n* **1** : one more than 3 **2** : 4th in a set or series **3** : something having 4 units — **four** *adj or pron*

**four•score** *adj* : eighty

**four•some** *n* : group of 4

**four•teen** *n* : one more than 13 — **four•teen** *adj or pron* — **four•teenth** *adj or n*

**fourth** *n* **1** : one that is 4th **2** : one of 4 equal parts of something — **fourth** *adj or adv*

**fowl** *n* (**fowl**) **1** : bird **2** : chicken

**fox** *n* **1** : small mammal related to wolves **2** : clever person ~ *vb* : trick — **foxy** *adj*

**foy•er** *n* : entrance hallway

**frac•tion** *n* **1** : number indicating one or more equal parts of a whole **2** : portion — **frac•tion•al** *adj* — **frac•tion•al•ly** *adv*

**frac•ture** *n* : a breaking of something — **fracture** *vb*

**frag•ile** *adj* : easily broken — **fra•gil•i•ty** *n*

**frag•ment** *n* : part broken off ~ *vb* : break into parts — **frag•men•tary** *adj* — **frag•men•ta•tion** *n*

**fra•grant** *adj* : having a sweet smell — **fra•grance** *n* — **fra•grant•ly** *adv*

**frail** *adj* : weak or delicate — **frail•ty** *n*

**frame** *vb* **1** : plan **2** : formulate **3** : construct or arrange **4** : enclose in a frame **5** : make appear guilty ~ *n* **1** : makeup of the body **2** : supporting or enclosing structure **3** : state or disposition (as of mind) — **frame•work** *n*

**fran•chise** *n* **1** : special privilege **2** : the right to vote — **fran•chi•see** *n*

**frank** *adj* : direct and sincere — **frank•ly** *adv* — **frank•ness** *n*

**frank•furt•er, frank•furt** *n* : cooked sausage

**frank•in•cense** *n* : incense resin

**fran•tic** *adj* : wildly excited — **fran•ti•cal•ly** *adv*

**fra•ter•nal** *adj* **1** : brotherly **2** : of a fraternity — **fra•ter•nal•ly** *adv*

**fra•ter•ni•ty** *n* : men's student social group

**frat•er•nize** *vb* **1** : mingle as friends **2** : associate with members of a hostile group — **frat•er•ni•za•tion** *n*

**fraud** *n* : trickery — **fraud•u•lent** *adj* — **fraud•u•lent•ly** *adv*

**fray** *vb* **1** : wear by rubbing **2** : separate the threads of **3** : irritate

**fraz•zle** *vb* : wear out ~ *n* : exhaustion

**freak** *n* **1** : something abnormal or unusual **2** : enthusiast — **freak•ish** *adj* — **freak out** *vb* **1** : experience nightmarish hallucinations from drugs **2** : distress or become distressed

**freck•le** *n* : brown spot on the skin — **freckle** *vb*

**free** *adj* **1** : having liberty or independence **2** : not taxed **3** : given without charge **4** : voluntary **5** : not in use **6** : not fastened ~ *adv* : without charge ~ *vb* : set free — **free** *adv* — **free•born** *adj* — **free•dom** *n* — **free•ly** *adv*

**free•boo•ter** *n* : pirate

**free•load** *vb* : live off another's generosity — **free•load•er** *n*

**free•way** *n* : expressway

**freeze** *vb* **froze; fro•zen 1** : harden into ice **2** : become chilled **3** : damage by frost **4** : stick fast **5** : become motionless **6** : fix at one stage or level ~ *n* **1** : very cold weather **2** : state of being frozen — **freez•er** *n*

**freeze–dry** *vb* : preserve by freezing then drying — **freeze–dried** *adj*

**freight** *n* **1** : carrying of goods or payment for this **2** : shipped goods ~ *vb* : load or ship goods — **freigh•ter** *n*

**french fry** *vb* : fry in deep fat — **french fry** *n*

**fre•net•ic** *adj* : frantic — **fre•net•i•cal•ly** *adv*

**fren•zy** *n* : violent agitation — **fren•zied** *adj*

**fre•quen•cy** *n* **1** : frequent or regular occurrence **2** : number of cycles or sound waves per second

**fre•quent** *adj* : happening often ~ *vb* : go to habitually — **fre•quent•er** *n* — **fre•quent•ly** *adv*

**fresh** *adj* **1** : not salt **2** : pure **3** : not preserved **4** : not stale **5** : like new **6** : insolent — **fres•hen** *vb* — **fresh•ly** *adv* — **fresh•ness** *n*

**fresh•man** *n* : first-year student

**fret** *vb* **1** : worry or become irritated **2** : fray **3** : agitate ~ *n* **1** : worn spot **2** : irritation — **fret•ful** *adj* — **fret•ful•ly** *adv*

**fric•tion** *n* **1** : a rubbing between 2 surfaces **2** : clash of opinions — **fric•tion•al** *adj*

**Fri•day** *n* : 6th day of the week

**friend** *n* : person one likes — **friend•less** *adj* — **friend•li•ness** *n* — **friend•ly** *adj* — **friend•ship** *n*

**fright** *n* : sudden fear — **frigh•ten** *vb* — **fright•ful** *adj* — **fright•ful•ly** *adv* — **fright•ful•ness** *n*

**frig•id** *adj* : intensely cold — **fri•gid•i•ty** *n*

**frill** *n* **1** : ruffle **2** : pleasing but nonessential addition — **frilly** *adj*

**fringe** *n* **1** : ornamental border of short hanging threads or strips **2** : edge — **fringe** *vb*

**frisk** *vb* **1** : leap about **2** : search (a person) esp. for weapons

**frisky** *adj* : playful — **frisk•i•ly** *adv* — **frisk•i•ness** *n*

**friv•o•lous** *adj* : not important or serious — **fri•vol•i•ty** *n* — **friv•o•lous•ly** *adv*

**frizz** *vb* : curl tightly — **frizz** *n* — **frizzy** *adj*

**frock** *n* **1** : loose outer garment **2** : dress

**frog** *n* **1** : leaping amphibian **2** : hoarseness **3** : ornamental braid fastener **4** : small holder for flowers

**frol•ic** *vb* : romp ~ *n* : fun — **frol•ic•some** *adj*

**from** *prep* — used to show a starting point

**front** *n* **1** : face **2** : behavior **3** : main side of a building **4** : forward part **5** : boundary between air masses ~ *vb* **1** : have the main side adjacent to something **2** : serve as a front — **fron•tal** *adj*

**front•age** *n* : length of boundary line on a street

**fron•tier** *n* : outer edge of settled territory — **fron•tiers•man** *n*

**frost** *n* **1** : freezing temperature **2** : ice crystals on a surface ~ *vb* **1** : cover with frost **2** : put icing on (a cake) — **frosty** *adj*

**frost•bite** *n* : partial freezing of part of the body — **frost•bit•ten** *adj*

**frost•ing** *n* : icing

**froth** *n* : bubbles on a liquid — **frothy** *adj*

**frown** *vb or n* : scowl

**frow•sy, frow•zy** *adj* : untidy

**froze** *past of* FREEZE

**frozen** *past part of* FREEZE

**fru•gal** *adj* : thrifty — **fru•gal•i•ty** *n* — **fru•gal•ly** *adv*

**fruit** *n* **1** : usu. edible and sweet part of a seed plant **2** : result ~ *vb* : bear fruit — **fruit•cake** *n* — **fruit•ed** *adj* — **fruit•ful** *adj* — **fruit•ful•ness** *n* — **fruit•less** *adj* — **fruit•less•ly** *adv* — **fruity** *adj*

**fru•ition** *n* : completion

**frus•trate** *vb* **1** : block **2** : cause to fail — **frus•trat•ing•ly** *adv* — **frus•tra•tion** *n*

**[1]fry** *vb* **1** : cook esp. with fat or oil **2** : be cooked by frying ~ *n* **1** : something fried **2** : social gathering with fried food

**[2]fry** *n* **fry** : recently hatched fish

**fud•dy–dud•dy** *n* : one who is old-fashioned or unimaginative

**fudge** *vb* : cheat or exaggerate ~ *n* : creamy candy

**fu•el** *n* : material burned to produce heat or power ~ *vb* : provide with or take in fuel

**fu•gi•tive** *adj* **1** : running away or trying to escape **2** : not lasting — **fu•gi•tive** *n*

**ful•fill, ful•fil** *vb* **1** : perform **2** : satisfy — **ful•fill•ment** *n*

**full** *adj* **1** : filled **2** : complete **3** : rounded **4** : having an abundance of something ~ *adv* : entirely ~ *n* : utmost degree — **full•ness** *n* — **ful•ly** *adv*

**full–fledged** *adj* : fully developed

**fum•ble** *vb* : fail to hold something properly — **fumble** *n*

**fume** *n* : irritating gas ~ *vb* **1** : give off fumes **2** : show annoyance

**fu•mi•gate** *vb* : treat with pest-killing fumes — **fu•mi•gant** *n* — **fu•mi•ga•tion** *n*

**fun** *n* **1** : something providing amusement or enjoyment **2** : enjoyment ~ *adj* : full of fun

**func•tion** *n* **1** : special purpose **2** : formal ceremony or social affair ~ *vb* : have or carry on a function — **func•tion•al** *adj* — **func•tion•al•ly** *adv*

**func•tion•ary** *n* : official

**fund** *n* **1** : store **2** : sum of money intended for a special purpose **3** *pl* : available money ~ *vb* : provide funds for

**fun•da•men•tal** *adj* **1** : basic **2** : of central importance or necessity — **fun•da•men•tal** *n* — **fun•da•men•tal•ly** *adv*

**fu•ner•al** *n* : ceremony for a dead person — **fu•ner•al** *adj* — **fu•ne•re•al** *adj*

**fun•gus** *n* **fun•gi** : lower plant that lacks chlorophyll — **fun•gal** *adj* — **fun•gous** *adj*

**funk** *n* : state of depression

**funky** *adj* : unconventional and unsophisticated

**fun•nel** *n* **1** : cone-shaped utensil with a tube for directing the flow of a liquid **2** : ship's smokestack ~ *vb* : move to a central point or into a central channel

**fun•nies** *n pl* : section of comic strips

**fun•ny** *adj* **1** : amusing **2** : strange

**fur** *n* **1** : hairy coat of a mammal **2** : article of clothing made with fur — **fur** *adj* — **furred** *adj* — **fur•ry** *adj*

**fu•ri•ous** *adj* : fierce or angry — **fu•ri•ous•ly** *adv*

**fur•nace** *n* : enclosed structure in which heat is produced

**fur•nish** *vb* **1** : provide with what is needed **2** : make available for use

**fur•nish•ings** *n pl* **1** : articles or accessories of dress **2** : furniture

**fur•ni•ture** *n* : movable articles for a room

**fur•row** *n* **1** : trench made by a plow **2** : wrinkle or groove — **fur•row** *vb*

**fur•ther** *adv* **1** : at or to a more advanced point **2** : more ~ *adj* : additional ~ *vb* : promote — **fur•ther•ance** *n*

**fur•ther•more** *adv* : in addition

**fur•thest** *adv or adj* : farthest

**fur•tive** *adj* : slyly or secretly done — **fur•tive•ly** *adv* — **fur•tive•ness** *n*

**fu•ry** *n* **1** : intense rage **2** : violence

**[1]fuse** *n* **1** : cord lighted to transmit fire to an explosive **2** *usu* **fuze** : device for exploding a charge ~ *or* **fuze** *vb* : equip with a fuse

**[2]fuse** *vb* **1** : melt and run together **2** : unite ~ *n* : electrical safety device — **fus•ible** *adj*

**fu•sion** *n* **1** : process of merging by melting **2** : union of atomic nuclei

**fuss** *n* **1** : needless bustle or excitement **2** : show of attention **3** : objection or protest ~ *vb* : make a fuss

**fuss•bud•get** *n* : one who fusses or is fussy about trifles

**fussy** *adj* **1** : irritable **2** : paying very close attention to details — **fuss•i•ly** *adv* — **fuss•i•ness** *n*

**fu•tile** *adj* : useless or vain — **fu•til•i•ty** *n*

**fu•ton** *n* : a cotton-filled mattress

**fu•ture** *adj* : coming after the present ~ *n* **1** : time yet to come **2** : what will happen — **fu•tur•is•tic** *adj*

**fuze** *var of* FUSE

**fuzz** *n* : fine particles or fluff

**fuzzy** *adj* **1** : covered with or like fuzz **2** : indistinct — **fuzz•i•ness** *n*

# G

**g** *n* **1** : 7th letter of the alphabet **2** : unit of gravitational force

**gab** *vb* : chatter — **gab** *n* — **gab•by** *adj*

**ga•ble** *n* : triangular part of the end of a building — **ga•bled** *adj*

**gad•get** *n* : device — **gad•get•ry** *n*

**gaff** *n* : metal hook for lifting fish — **gaff** *vb*

**gaffe** *n* : social blunder

**gag** *vb* **1** : prevent from speaking or crying out by stopping up the mouth **2** : retch or cause to retch ~ *n* **1** : something that stops up the mouth **2** : laugh-provoking remark or act

**gag•gle** *n* : flock of geese

**gai•ety** *n* : high spirits

**gai•ly** *adv* : in a gay manner

**gain** *n* **1** : profit **2** : obtaining of profit or possessions **3** : increase ~ *vb* **1** : get possession of **2** : win **3** : arrive at **4** : increase or increase in **5** : profit — **gain•er** *n* — **gain•ful** *adj* — **gain•ful•ly** *adv*

**gait** *n* : manner of walking or running — **gait•ed** *adj*

**gal** *n* : girl

**ga•la** *n* : festive celebration — **gala** *adj*

**gal•axy** *n* : very large group of stars — **ga•lac•tic** *adj*

**gale** *n* **1** : strong wind **2** : outburst

**[1]gall** *n* **1** : bile **2** : insolence

**[2]gall** *n* **1** : skin sore caused by chafing **2** : swelling of plant tissue caused by parasites ~ *vb* **1** : chafe **2** : irritate or vex

**gal•lant** *n* : man very attentive to women ~ *adj* **1** : splendid **2** : brave **3** : polite and attentive to women — **gal•lant•ly** *adv* — **gal•lant•ry** *n*

**gall•blad•der** *n* : pouch attached to the liver in which bile is stored

**gal•lery** *n* **1** : outdoor balcony **2** : long narrow passage or hall **3** : room or building for exhibiting art **4** : spectators — **gal•ler•ied** *adj*

**gal•ley** *n* **1** : old ship propelled esp. by oars **2** : kitchen of a ship or airplane

**gal•lon** *n* : unit of liquid measure equal to 4 quarts

**gal•lop** *n* : fast 3-beat gait of a horse — **gallop** *vb* — **gal•lop•er** *n*

**gall•stone** *n* : abnormal concretion in the gallbladder or bile passages

**ga•lore** *adj* : in abundance

**ga•losh** *n* : overshoe — usu. pl.

**gal•va•nize** *vb* **1** : shock into action **2**

: coat (iron or steel) with zinc — **gal·va·ni·za·tion** n — **gal·va·niz·er** n

**gam·ble** vb **1** : play a game for stakes **2** : bet **3** : take a chance ∼ n : risky undertaking — **gam·bler** n

**game** n **1** : playing activity **2** : competition according to rules **3** : animals hunted for sport or food ∼ vb : gamble — adj **1** : plucky **2** : lame — **game·ly** adv — **game·ness** n

**game·keep·er** n : person in charge of game animals or birds

**gamy** or **gam·ey** adj : having the flavor of game esp. when slightly tainted — **gam·i·ness** n

¹**gan·der** n : male goose

²**gander** n : glance

**gang** n **1** : group of persons working together **2** : group of criminals ∼ vb : attack in a gang — with **up**

**gan·gling** adj : lanky

**gang·ster** n : member of criminal gang

**gap** n **1** : break in a barrier **2** : mountain pass **3** : empty space

**gape** vb **1** : open widely **2** : stare with mouth open — **gape** n

**ga·rage** n : shelter or repair shop for automobiles ∼ vb : put or keep in a garage

**garb** n : clothing ∼ vb : dress

**gar·bage** n **1** : food waste **2** : trash — **gar·bage·man** n

**gar·ble** vb : distort the meaning of

**gar·den** n **1** : plot for growing fruits, flowers, or vegetables **2** : public recreation area ∼ vb : work in a garden — **gar·den·er** n

**gar·de·nia** n : tree or shrub with fragrant white or yellow flowers or the flower

**gar·gan·tuan** adj : having tremendous size or volume

**gar·gle** vb : rinse the throat with liquid — **gargle** n

**gar·ish** adj : offensively bright or gaudy

**gar·lic** n : herb with pungent bulbs used in cooking — **gar·licky** adj

**gar·ment** n : article of clothing

**gar·nish** vb : add decoration to (as food) — **gar·nish** n

**gar·ru·lous** adj : talkative — **gar·ru·li·ty** n — **gar·ru·lous·ly** adv — **gar·ru·lous·ness** n

**gar·ter** n : band to hold up a stocking or sock

**gas** n **1** : fluid (as hydrogen or air) that tends to expand indefinitely **2** : gasoline ∼ vb **1** : treat with gas **2** : fill with gasoline — used with **up** — **gas·eous** adj

**gash** n : deep long cut — **gash** vb

**gas·ket** n : material or a part used to seal a joint

**gas·light** n : light of burning illuminating gas

**gas·o·line** n : flammable liquid from petroleum

**gasp** vb **1** : catch the breath audibly **2** : breathe laboriously — **gasp** n

**gas·tric** adj : relating to or located near the stomach

**gate** n : an opening for passage in a wall or fence — **gate·keep·er** n — **gate·post** n

**gath·er** vb **1** : bring or come together **2** : harvest **3** : pick up little by little **4** : deduce — **gath·er·er** n — **gath·er·ing** n

**gaudy** adj : tastelessly showy — **gaud·i·ly** adv — **gaud·i·ness** n

**gauge** n : instrument for measuring ∼ vb : measure

**gauze** n : thin often transparent fabric — **gauzy** adj

**gave** past of GIVE

**gav·el** n : mallet of a presiding officer, auctioneer, or judge

**gawk** vb : stare stupidly

**gay** adj **1** : merry **2** : bright and lively **3** : oriented toward one's own sex — **gay** n

**gaze** vb : fix the eyes in a steady intent look — **gaze** n — **gaz·er** n

**ga·zette** n : newspaper

**gaz·et·teer** n : geographical dictionary

**gear** n **1** : clothing **2** : equipment **3** : toothed wheel — **gear** vb — **gear·shift** n

**geek** n : socially inept person

**geese** pl of GOOSE

**gei·sha** n : Japanese girl or woman trained to entertain men

**gel·a·tin** n : sticky substance obtained from animal tissues by boiling — **ge·lat·i·nous** adj

**gem** n : cut and polished valuable stone — **gem·stone** n

**gen·der** n **1** : sex **2** : division of a class of words (as nouns) that determines agreement of other words

**gene** n : segment of DNA that controls inheritance of a trait

**ge·ne·al·o·gy** n : study of family pedigrees — **ge·ne·a·log·i·cal** adj — **ge·ne·a·log·i·cal·ly** adv — **ge·ne·al·o·gist** n

**gen·er·al** adj **1** : relating to the whole **2** : applicable to all of a group **3** : common or widespread ∼ n **1** : something that involves or is applicable to the whole **2** : commissioned officer of the highest rank in the army, air force, or marine corps — **gen·er·al·ly** adv — **in general** : for the most part

**gen·er·al·i·ty** n : general statement

**gen·er·al·ize** vb : reach a general conclusion esp. on the basis of particular instances — **gen·er·al·iza·tion** n

**gen·er·ate** vb : create or produce

**gen·er·a·tion** n **1** : living beings constituting a single step in a line of descent **2** : production — **gen·er·a·tive** adj

**gen·er·a·tor** n **1** : one that generates **2** : machine that turns mechanical into electrical energy

**ge·ner·ic** adj **1** : general **2** : not protected by a trademark **3** : relating to a genus — **generic** n

**gen·er·ous** adj : freely giving or sharing — **gen·er·os·i·ty** n — **gen·er·ous·ly** adv — **gen·er·ous·ness** n

**ge·net·ics** n : biology dealing with heredity and variation — **ge·net·ic** adj — **ge·net·i·cal·ly** adv — **ge·net·i·cist** n

**ge·nial** adj : cheerful — **ge·nial·i·ty** n — **ge·nial·ly** adv

**gen·i·tal** adj : concerned with reproduction — **gen·i·ta·lia** n pl — **gen·i·tal·ly** adv — **gen·i·tals** n pl

**ge·nius** n **1** : single strongly marked capacity **2** : extraordinary intellectual power or a person having such power

**geno·cide** n : systematic destruction of a racial or cultural group

**gen·teel** adj : polite or refined

**gen·tile** n : person who is not Jewish — **gentile** adj

**gen·til·i·ty** n **1** : good birth and family **2** : good manners

**gen·tle** adj **1** : of a family of high social station **2** : not harsh, stern, or violent **3** : soft or delicate ∼ vb : make gentle — **gen·tle·ness** n — **gen·tly** adv

**gen·tle·man** n : man of good family or manners — **gen·tle·man·ly** adv

**gen·try** n **1** : people of good birth or breeding **2** : people of a certain class

**gen·u·flect** vb : bend the knee in worship — **gen·u·flec·tion** n

**gen·u·ine** adj : being the same in fact as in appearance — **gen·u·ine·ly** adv — **gen·u·ine·ness** n

**ge·nus** n (**gen·era**) : category of biological classification

**ge·og·ra·phy** n **1** : study of the earth and its climate, products, and inhabitants **2** : natural features of a region — **ge·og·ra·pher** n — **geo·graph·ic**, **geo·graph·i·cal** adj — **geo·graph·i·cal·ly** adv

**ge·ol·o·gy** n : study of the history of the earth and its life esp. as recorded in rocks — **geo·log·ic**, **geo·log·i·cal** adj — **geo·log·i·cal·ly** adv — **ge·ol·o·gist** n

**ge·om·e·try** n : mathematics of the relations, properties, and measurements of solids, surfaces, lines, and angles — **geo·met·ric**, **geo·met·ri·cal** adj

**ge·ra·ni·um** n : garden plant with clusters of white, pink, or scarlet flowers

**ger·bil** n : a small Old World burrowing desert rodent

**ge·ri·at·ric** adj **1** : relating to aging or the aged **2** : old

**germ** n **1** : microorganism **2** : source or rudiment

**ger·mi·cide** n : agent that destroys germs — **ger·mi·cid·al** adj

**ger·mi·nate** vb : begin to develop — **ger·mi·na·tion** n

**ger·und** n : word having the characteristics of both verb and noun

**ges·ture** n **1** : movement of the body or limbs that expresses something **2** : something said or done for its effect on the attitudes of others — **ges·tur·al** adj — **gesture** vb

**ge·sund·heit** interj — used to wish good health to one who has just sneezed

**get** vb (**got**; **got/got·ten**) **1** : gain or be in possession of **2** : succeed in coming or going **3** : cause to come or go or to be in a certain condition or position **4** : become **5** : be subjected to **6** : understand **7** : be obliged — **get along** vb **1** : get by **2** : be on friendly terms — **get by** vb : meet one's needs

**get·away** n **1** : escape **2** : a starting or getting under way

**gey·ser** n : spring that intermittently shoots up hot water and steam

**ghast·ly** adj : horrible or shocking

**gher·kin** n : small pickle

**ghet·to** n : part of a city in which members of a minority group live

**ghost** n : disembodied soul — **ghost·ly** adv

**ghoul** n : legendary evil being that feeds on corpses — **ghoul·ish** adj

**GI** n : member of the U.S. armed forces

**gi·ant** n **1** : huge legendary being **2** : something very large or very powerful — **giant** adj

**gib·ber·ish** n : unintelligible speech or language

**gibe** vb : jeer at — **gibe** n

**gib·lets** n pl : edible fowl viscera

**gid·dy** adj **1** : silly **2** : dizzy — **gid·di·ness** n

**gift** n **1** : something given **2** : talent — **gift·ed** adj

**gi·gan·tic** adj : very big

**gig·gle** vb : laugh in a silly manner — **giggle** n — **gig·gly** adj

**gild** vb : cover with or as if with gold

**gill** n : organ of a fish for obtaining oxygen from water

**gilt** adj : gold in color ∼ n : gold or goldlike substance on the surface of an object

**gim·mick** n : new and ingenious scheme, feature, or device — **gim·mick·ry** n — **gim·micky** adj

**gin·ger** n : pungent aromatic spice from a tropical plant — **gin·ger·bread** n

**gin·ger·ly** adv : very cautiously

**gin·seng** n : aromatic root of a Chinese herb

**gi·raffe** n : African mammal with a very long neck

**gird·er** n : horizontal supporting beam

**gir·dle** n : woman's supporting undergarment ∼ vb : surround

**girl** n **1** : female child **2** : young woman **3** : sweetheart — **girl·hood** n — **girl·ish** adj

**girl·friend** n : frequent or regular female companion of a boy or man

**gist** n : main point or part

**give** vb (**gave**; **giv·en**) **1** : put into the possession or keeping of another **2** : pay **3** : perform **4** : contribute or donate **5** : produce **6** : utter **7** : yield to force, strain, or pressure ∼ n : capacity or tendency to yield to force or strain — **give in** vb : surrender — **give out** vb : become used up or exhausted — **give up** vb **1** : let out of one's control **2** : cease from trying, doing, or hoping

**give·away** n **1** : unintentional betrayal **2** : something given free

**giv·en** adj **1** : prone or disposed **2** : having been specified

**gla·cial** adj **1** : relating to glaciers **2** : very slow — **gla·cial·ly** adv

**gla·cier** n : large body of ice moving slowly

**glad** adj **1** : experiencing or causing pleasure, joy, or delight **2** : very willing — **glad·den** vb — **glad·ly** adv — **glad·ness** n

**glad·i·a·tor** n : one who fought to the death for the entertainment of ancient Romans — **glad·i·a·to·ri·al** adj

**glad·i·o·lus** n : plant related to the irises

**glam·our**, **glam·or** n : romantic or exciting attractiveness — **glam·or·ize** vb — **glam·or·ous** adj

**glance** vb **1** : strike and fly off to one side **2** : give a quick look ∼ n : quick look

**gland** n : group of cells that secretes a substance — **glan·du·lar** adj

**glare** vb **1** : shine with a harsh dazzling light **2** : stare angrily ∼ n **1** : harsh dazzling light **2** : angry stare

**glar·ing** adj : painfully obvious — **glar·ing·ly** adv

**glass** n **1** : hard usu. transparent material made by melting sand and other materials **2** : something made of glass **3** pl : lenses used to correct defects of vision — **glass** adj — **glass·blow·er** n — **glass·blow·ing** n — **glass·ful** n — **glass·ware** n — **glassy** adj

**glau·co·ma** n : state of increased pressure within the eyeball

**glaze** vb **1** : furnish with glass **2** : apply glaze to ∼ n : glassy surface or coating

**gleam** n **1** : transient or partly obscured light **2** : faint trace ∼ vb : send out gleams

**glean** vb : collect little by little — **glean·able** adj — **glean·er** n

**glee** n : joy — **glee·ful** adj

**glen** n : narrow hidden valley

**glib** adj : speaking or spoken with ease — **glib·ly** adv

**glide** vb : move or descend smoothly and effortlessly — **glide** n

**glid·er** n **1** : winged aircraft having no engine **2** : swinging porch seat

**glim·mer** vb : shine faintly or unsteadily ∼ n **1** : faint light **2** : small amount

**glimpse** vb : take a brief look at — **glimpse** n

**glint** vb : gleam or sparkle — **glint** n

**glis·ten** vb : shine or sparkle by reflection — **glisten** n

**glit·ter** vb : shine with brilliant or metallic luster ∼ n : small glittering ornaments — **glit·tery** adj

**glitz** n : extravagant showiness — **glitzy** adj

**gloat** vb : think of something with triumphant delight

**glob** n : large rounded lump

**glob·al** adj : worldwide — **glob·al·ly** adv

**globe** n **1** : sphere **2** : the earth or a model of it

**glob·u·lar** adj **1** : round **2** : made up of globules

**gloom** n **1** : darkness **2** : sadness — **gloom·i·ly** adv — **gloom·i·ness** n — **gloomy** adj

**glo·ry** n **1** : praise or honor offered in worship **2** : cause for praise or renown **3** : magnificence **4** : heavenly bliss ∼ vb : rejoice proudly — **glo·ri·fi·ca·tion** n — **glo·ri·fy** vb — **glo·ri·ous** adj — **glo·ri·ous·ly** adv

**gloss** n : luster — **gloss·i·ly** adv — **gloss·i·ness** n — **glossy** adj

**gloss over** vb **1** : mask the true nature of **2** : deal with only superficially

**glos·sa·ry** n : dictionary — **glos·sar·i·al** adj

**glove** n : hand covering with sections for each finger

**glow** vb **1** : shine with or as if with intense heat **2** : show exuberance ∼ n : brightness or warmth of color or feeling

**glow·er** vb : stare angrily — **glower** n

**glue** n : substance used for sticking things together — **glue** vb — **glu·ey** adj

**glum** *adj* **1** : sullen **2** : dismal

**glut** *vb* : fill to excess — **glut** *n*

**glu•ten** *n* : gluey protein substance in flour

**glut•ton** *n* : one who eats to excess — **glut•ton•ous** *adj* — **glut•tony** *n*

**gnarled** *adj* **1** : knotty **2** : gloomy or sullen

**gnat** *n* : small biting fly

**gnaw** *vb* : bite or chew on

**go** *vb* (**went; gone**) **1** : move, proceed, run, or pass **2** : leave **3** : extend or lead **4** : sell or amount — with *for* **5** : happen **6** — used in present participle to show intent or imminent action **7** : become **8** : fit or harmonize **9** : belong ~ *n* **1** : act or manner of going **2** : vigor **3** : attempt — **go back on** : betray — **go by the board** : be discarded — **go for** : favor — **go off** : explode — **go one better** : outdo — **go over 1** : examine **2** : study — **go to town** : be very successful — **on the go** : constantly active

**goad** *n* : something that urges — **goad** *vb*

**goal** *n* **1** : mark to reach in a race **2** : purpose **3** : object in a game through which a ball is propelled

**goal•ie** *n* : player who defends the goal

**goal•keep•er** *n* : goalie

**goat** *n* : horned ruminant mammal related to the sheep — **goat•skin** *n*

**¹gob•ble** *vb* : eat greedily

**²gob•ble** *vb* : make the noise of a turkey (**gob•bler**)

**gob•lin** *n* : ugly mischievous sprite

**god** *n* **1** *cap* : supreme being **2** : being with supernatural powers — **god•less** *adj* — **god•less•ness** *n* — **god•like** *adj* — **god•ly** *adj*

**god•child** *n* : person one sponsors at baptism — **god•daugh•ter** *n* — **god•son** *n*

**god•dess** *n* : female god

**god•par•ent** *n* : sponsor at baptism — **god•fa•ther** *n* — **god•moth•er** *n*

**goes** *pres 3d sing of* GO

**gog•gle** *vb* : stare wide-eyed

**gog•gles** *n pl* : protective glasses

**gold** *n* : malleable yellow metallic chemical element — **gold•smith** *n*

**gold•en** *adj* **1** : made of, containing, or relating to gold **2** : having the color of gold **3** : precious or favorable

**gold•fish** *n* : small usu. orange or golden carp

**golf** *n* : game played by hitting a small ball (**golf ball**) with clubs (**golf clubs**) into holes placed in a field (**golf course**) — **golf** *vb* — **golf•er** *n*

**gon•do•la** *n* **1** : long narrow boat used on the canals of Venice **2** : car suspended from a cable

**gon•do•lier** *n* : person who propels a gondola

**gone** *adj* **1** : past **2** : involved

**gon•er** *n* : hopeless case

**gong** *n* : metallic disk that makes a deep sound when struck

**goo** *n* : thick or sticky substance — **goo•ey** *adj*

**good** *adj* (**bet•ter; best**) **1** : satisfactory **2** : producing a beneficial effect **3** : considerable **4** : desirable **5** : well-behaved, kind, or virtuous ~ *n* **1** : something good **2** : benefit **3** *pl* : personal property **4** *pl* : wares ~ *adv* : well — **good–heart•ed** *adj* — **good–look•ing** *adj* — **good–na•tured** *adj* — **good•ness** *n* — **for good** : forever

**good–bye, good–by** *n* : parting remark

**Good Friday** *n* : Friday before Easter observed as the anniversary of the crucifixion of Christ

**good•ly** *adj* : considerable

**good•will** *n* **1** : good intention **2** : kindly feeling

**goody** *n* : something that is good esp. to eat

**goody–goody** *adj* : affectedly or annoyingly sweet or self-righteous — **goody–goody** *n*

**goof** *vb* **1** : blunder **2** : waste time — usu. with *off* or *around* — **goof** *n* — **goof–off** *n*

**goofy** *adj* : crazy — **goof•i•ness** *n*

**goose** *n* (**geese**) : large bird with webbed feet

**goose bumps** *n pl* : roughening of the skin caused by fear, excitement, or cold

**goose•flesh** *n* : goose bumps

**goose pimples** *n pl* : goose bumps

**go•pher** *n* : burrowing rodent

**¹gore** *n* : blood — **gory** *adj*

**²gore** *vb* : pierce or wound with a horn or tusk

**¹gorge** *n* : narrow ravine

**²gorge** *vb* : eat greedily

**gor•geous** *adj* : supremely beautiful

**go•ril•la** *n* : African manlike ape

**gos•pel** *n* **1** : teachings of Christ and the apostles **2** : something accepted as infallible truth — **gos•pel** *adj*

**gos•sip** *n* **1** : person who reveals personal information **2** : rumor or report of an intimate nature ~ *vb* : spread gossip — **gos•sipy** *adj*

**got** *past of* GET

**gotten** *past part of* GET

**gouge** *n* **1** : rounded chisel **2** : cavity or groove scooped out ~ *vb* **1** : cut or scratch a groove in **2** : to charge too much

**gourd** *n* **1** : any of a group of vines including the cucumber, squash, and melon **2** : inedible hard-shelled fruit of a gourd

**gour•met** *n* : connoisseur of food and drink

**gov•ern** *vb* **1** : control and direct policy in **2** : guide or influence strongly **3** : restrain — **gov•ern•ment** *n* — **gov•ern•men•tal** *adj*

**gov•ern•ess** *n* : female teacher in a private home

**gov•er•nor** *n* **1** : head of a political unit **2** : automatic speed-control device — **gov•er•nor•ship** *n*

**gown** *n* **1** : loose flowing outer garment **2** : woman's formal evening dress — **gown** *vb*

**grab** *vb* : take by sudden grasp — **grab** *n*

**grace** *n* **1** : unmerited divine assistance **2** : short prayer before or after a meal **3** : temporary relief **4** : ease of movement or bearing ~ *vb* **1** : honor **2** : adorn — **graceful** *adj* — **grace•ful•ly** *adv* — **grace•ful•ness** *n* — **grace•less** *adj*

**gra•cious** *adj* : marked by kindness and courtesy or charm and taste — **gra•cious•ly** *adv* — **gra•cious•ness** *n*

**grack•le** *n* : American blackbird

**grade** *n* **1** : stage in a series, order, or ranking **2** : division of school representing one year's work **3** : mark of accomplishment in school **4** : degree of slope ~ *vb* **1** : arrange in grades **2** : make level or evenly sloping **3** : give a grade to — **grad•er** *n* — **gra•da•tion** *n*

**grade school** *n* : school including the first six or the first eight grades

**gra•di•ent** *n* : slope

**grad•u•al** *adj* : going by steps or degrees — **grad•u•al•ly** *adv*

**grad•u•ate** *n* : holder of a diploma ~ *adj* : of or relating to studies beyond the bachelor's degree ~ *vb* **1** : grant or receive a diploma **2** : mark with degrees of measurement — **grad•u•a•tion** *n*

**graf•fi•ti** *n pl* : inscriptions on a wall

**graft** *vb* : join one thing to another so that they grow together ~ *n* **1** : grafted plant **2** : the getting of money dishonestly or the money so gained — **graft•er** *n*

**grain** *n* **1** : seeds or fruits of cereal grasses **2** : small hard particle **3** : arrangement of fibers in wood — **grained** *adj* — **grainy** *adj*

**gram** *n* : metric unit of weight equal to ¹⁄₁₀₀₀ kilogram

**gram•mar** *n* : study of words and their functions and relations in the sentence — **gram•mar•i•an** *n* — **gram•mat•i•cal** *adj* — **gram•mat•i•cal•ly** *adv*

**grammar school** *n* : grade school

**grand** *adj* **1** : large or striking in size or scope **2** : fine and imposing **3** : very good — **grand•ly** *adv* — **grand•ness** *n*

**grand•child** *n* : child of one's son or daughter — **grand•daugh•ter** *n* — **grand•son** *n*

**grand•par•ent** *n* : parent of one's father or mother — **grand•fa•ther** *n* — **grand•moth•er** *n*

**grand•stand** *n* : usu. roofed stand for spectators

**grant** *vb* **1** : consent to **2** : give **3** : admit as true ~ *n* **1** : act of granting **2** : something granted — **grant•ee** *n* — **grant•er** *n* — **grant•or** *n*

**gran•u•late** *vb* : form into grains or crystals — **gran•u•la•tion** *n*

**gran•ule** *n* : small particle — **gran•u•lar** *adj* — **gran•u•lar•i•ty** *n*

**grape** *n* : smooth juicy edible berry of a woody vine (**grape•vine**)

**grape•fruit** *n* : large edible yellow-skinned citrus fruit

**graph** *n* : diagram that shows relationships between things — **graph** *vb*

**graph•ic** *adj* **1** : vividly described **2** : relating to the arts (**graphic arts**) of representation and printing on flat surfaces ~ *n* **1** : picture used for illustration **2** *pl* : computer screen display — **graph•i•cal•ly** *adv*

**graph•ite** *n* : soft carbon used for lead pencils and lubricants

**grasp** *vb* **1** : take or seize firmly **2** : understand ~ *n* **1** : one's hold or control **2** : one's reach **3** : comprehension

**grass** *n* : plant with jointed stem and narrow leaves — **grass•land** *n* — **grassy** *adj*

**grass•hop•per** *n* : leaping plant-eating insect

**¹grate** *n* **1** : grating **2** : frame of iron bars to hold burning fuel

**²grate** *vb* **1** : pulverize by rubbing against something rough **2** : irritate — **grat•er** *n* — **grat•ing•ly** *adv*

**grate•ful** *adj* : thankful or appreciative — **grate•ful•ly** *adv* — **grate•ful•ness** *n*

**grat•i•fy** *vb* : give pleasure to — **grat•i•fi•ca•tion** *n*

**grat•ing** *n* : framework with bars across it

**grat•i•tude** *n* : state of being grateful

**gra•tu•ity** *n* : tip

**¹grave** *n* : place of burial — **grave•stone** *n* — **grave•yard** *n*

**²grave** *adj* **1** : threatening great harm or danger **2** : solemn — **grave•ly** *adv* — **grave•ness** *n*

**grav•el** *n* : loose rounded fragments of rock — **grav•el•ly** *adj*

**grav•i•ta•tion** *n* : natural force of attraction that tends to draw bodies together — **grav•i•ta•tion•al** *adj*

**grav•i•ty** *n* **1** : serious importance **2** : gravitation

**gra•vy** *n* : sauce made from thickened juices of cooked meat

**gray** *adj* **1** : of the color gray **2** : having gray hair ~ *n* : neutral color between black and white ~ *vb* : make or become gray — **gray•ish** *adj* — **gray•ness** *n*

**¹graze** *vb* : feed on herbage or pasture — **graz•er** *n*

**²graze** *vb* : touch lightly in passing

**grease** *n* : thick oily material or fat ~ *vb* : smear or lubricate with grease — **greasy** *adj*

**great** *adj* **1** : large in size or number **2** : larger than usual — **great•ly** *adv* — **great•ness** *n*

**greed** *n* : selfish desire beyond reason — **greed•i•ly** *adv* — **greed•i•ness** *n* — **greedy** *adj*

**green** *adj* **1** : of the color green **2** : not yet ripe **3** : not having experience ~ *vb* : become green ~ *n* **1** : color between blue and yellow **2** *pl* : leafy parts of plants — **green•ish** *adj* — **green•ness** *n*

**green•ery** *n* : green foliage or plants

**green•house** *n* : glass structure for the growing of plants

**greet** *vb* **1** : address with expressions of kind wishes **2** : react to — **greet•er** *n*

**greet•ing** *n* **1** : friendly address on meeting **2** *pl* : best wishes

**gre•gar•i•ous** *adj* : social or companionable — **gre•gar•i•ous•ly** *adv* — **gre•gar•i•ous•ness** *n*

**gre•nade** *n* : small missile filled with explosive or chemicals

**grew** *past of* GROW

**grey** *var of* GRAY

**grey•hound** *n* : tall slender dog noted for speed

**grid** *n* **1** : grating **2** : evenly spaced horizontal and vertical lines (as on a map)

**grid•dle** *n* : flat metal surface for cooking

**grid•iron** *n* **1** : grate for broiling **2** : football field

**grief** *n* **1** : emotional suffering caused by or as if by bereavement **2** : disaster

**griev•ance** *n* : complaint

**grieve** *vb* : feel or cause to feel grief or sorrow

**griev•ous** *adj* **1** : oppressive **2** : causing grief or sorrow — **griev•ous•ly** *adv*

**grill** *vb* **1** : cook on a grill **2** : question intensely ~ *n* **1** : griddle **2** : informal restaurant

**grille, grill** *n* : grating forming a barrier or screen — **grill•work** *n*

**grim** *adj* **1** : harsh and forbidding in appearance **2** : relentless — **grim•ly** *adv* — **grim•ness** *n*

**gri•mace** *n* : facial expression of disgust — **grimace** *vb*

**grime** *n* : embedded or accumulated dirt — **grimy** *adj*

**grin** *vb* : smile so as to show the teeth — **grin** *n*

**grind** *vb* (**ground; ground**) **1** : reduce to powder **2** : wear down or sharpen by friction **3** : operate or produce by turning a crank ~ *n* : monotonous labor or routine — **grind•er** *n* — **grind•stone** *n*

**grip** *vb* : seize or hold firmly ~ *n* **1** : grasp **2** : control **3** : device for holding

**gripe** *vb* **1** : cause pains in the bowels **2** : complain — **gripe** *n*

**gris•ly** *adj* : horrible or gruesome

**grist** *n* : grain to be ground or already ground — **grist•mill** *n*

**gris•tle** *n* : cartilage — **gris•tly** *adj*

**grit** *n* **1** : hard sharp granule **2** : material composed of granules **3** : steadfast courage ~ *vb* : press with a grating noise — **grit•ty** *adj*

**groan** *vb* **1** : moan **2** : creak under a strain — **groan** *n*

**gro•cery** *n* **1** : food store **2** *pl* : food and commodities sold in a grocery — **gro•cer** *n*

**grog•gy** *adj* : dazed and unsteady on the feet — **grog•gi•ly** *adv* — **grog•gi•ness** *n*

**groin** *n* : juncture of the lower abdomen and inner thigh

**groom** *n* **1** : one who cares for horses **2** : bridegroom ~ *vb* **1** : clean and care for (as a horse) **2** : make neat or attractive **3** : prepare

**groove** *n* **1** : long narrow channel **2** : fixed routine — **groove** *vb*

**grope** *vb* : search for by feeling

**¹gross** *adj* **1** : glaringly noticeable **2** : bulky **3** : consisting of an overall total exclusive of deductions **4** : vulgar ~ *n* : the whole before any deductions ~ *vb* : earn as a total — **gross•ly** *adv* — **gross•ness** *n*

**²gross** *n* : 12 dozen

**grouch** *n* : complaining person — **grouch** *vb* — **grouchy** *adj*

**¹ground** *n* **1** : bottom of a body of water **2** *pl* : sediment **3** : basis for something **4** : surface of the earth **5** : conductor that makes electrical connection with the earth or a framework ~ *vb* **1** : force or bring down to the ground **2** : give basic knowledge to **3** : connect with an electrical ground — **ground•less** *adj*

**²ground** *past of* GRIND

**ground·hog** *n* : thick-bodied short-legged burrowing rodent

**group** *n* : number of associated individuals ~ *vb* : gather or collect into groups

**grove** *n* : small group of trees

**grow** *vb* (**grew; grown**) **1** : come into existence and develop to maturity **2** : be able to grow **3** : advance or increase **4** : become **5** : cultivate — **grow·er** *n*

**growl** *vb* : utter a deep threatening sound — **growl** *n*

**grown–up** *n* : adult — **grown–up** *adj*

**growth** *n* **1** : stage in growing **2** : process of growing **3** : result of something growing

**grub** *vb* **1** : root out by digging **2** : search about ~ *n* **1** : thick wormlike larva **2** : food

**grub·by** *adj* : dirty — **grub·bi·ness** *n*

**grudge** *vb* : be reluctant to give ~ *n* : feeling of ill will

**gru·el·ing, gru·el·ling** *adj* : requiring extreme effort

**grue·some** *adj* : horribly repulsive

**gruff** *adj* : rough in speech or manner — **gruff·ly** *adv*

**grum·ble** *vb* : mutter in discontent — **grum·bler** *n*

**grumpy** *adj* : cross — **grump·i·ly** *adv* — **grump·i·ness** *n*

**grunge** *n* **1** : something shabby, tattered, or dirty **2** : rock music expressing alienation and discontent — **grun·gy** *adj*

**grunt** *n* : deep guttural sound — **grunt** *vb*

**guar·an·tee** *n* **1** : assurance of the fulfillment of a condition **2** : something given or held as a security ~ *vb* **1** : promise to be responsible for **2** : state with certainty — **guar·an·tor** *n*

**guar·an·ty** *n* **1** : promise to answer for another's failure to pay a debt **2** : guarantee **3** : pledge ~ *vb* : guarantee

**guard** *n* **1** : defensive position **2** : act of protecting **3** : an individual or group that guards against danger **4** : protective or safety device ~ *vb* **1** : protect or watch over **2** : take precautions — **guard·house** *n* — **guard·room** *n*

**guard·ian** *n* : one who has responsibility for the care of the person or property of another — **guard·ian·ship** *n*

**guer·ril·la, gue·ril·la** *n* : soldier engaged in small-scale harassing tactics

**guess** *vb* **1** : form an opinion from little evidence **2** : state correctly solely by chance **3** : think or believe — **guess** *n*

**guest** *n* **1** : person to whom hospitality (as of a house) is extended **2** : patron of a commercial establishment (as a hotel) **3** : person not a regular cast member who appears on a program

**guide** *n* **1** : one that leads or gives direction to another **2** : device on a machine to direct motion ~ *vb* **1** : show the way to **2** : direct — **guid·able** *adj* — **guid·ance** *n* — **guide·book** *n*

**guide·line** *n* : summary of procedures regarding policy or conduct

**guild** *n* : association

**guile** *n* : craftiness — **guile·ful** *adj* — **guile·less** *adj* — **guile·less·ness** *n*

**guilt** *n* **1** : fact of having committed an offense **2** : feeling of responsibility for offenses — **guilt·i·ly** *adv* — **guilt·i·ness** *n* — **guilty** *adj*

**guinea pig** *n* : small So. American rodent

**guise** *n* : external appearance

**gui·tar** *n* : 6-stringed musical instrument played by plucking

**gulf** *n* **1** : extension of an ocean or a sea into the land **2** : wide gap

**¹gull** *n* : seabird with webbed feet

**²gull** *vb* : make a dupe of ~ *n* : dupe — **gull·ible** *adj*

**gul·ly** *n* : trench worn by running water

**gulp** *vb* : swallow hurriedly or greedily — **gulp** *n*

**¹gum** *n* : tissue along the jaw at the base of the teeth

**²gum** *n* **1** : sticky plant substance **2** : gum usu. of sweetened chicle prepared for chewing — **gum·my** *adj*

**gum·drop** *n* : gumlike candy

**gun** *n* **1** : cannon **2** : portable firearm **3** : discharge of a gun **4** : something like a gun ~ *vb* : hunt with a gun — **gun·ner** *n* — **gun·fight** *n* — **gun·fight·er** *n* — **gun·fire** *n* — **gunman** *n* — **gun·pow·der** *n* — **gun·shot** *n* — **gun·smith** *n*

**gun·wale** *n* : upper edge of a boat's side

**gup·py** *n* : tiny tropical fish

**gur·gle** *vb* : make a sound like that of a flowing and gently splashing liquid — **gur·gle** *n*

**gu·ru** *n* **1** : personal religious teacher in Hinduism **2** : expert

**gush** *vb* : pour forth violently or enthusiastically — **gush·er** *n*

**gust** *n* **1** : sudden brief rush of wind **2** : sudden outburst — **gust** *vb* — **gusty** *adj*

**gus·to** *n* : zest

**gut** *n* **1** *pl* : intestines **2** : digestive canal **3** *pl* : courage ~ *vb* : remove the intestines of

**gut·ter** *n* : channel for carrying off rainwater

**¹guy** *n* : rope, chain, or rod attached to something to steady it — **guy** *vb*

**²guy** *n* : person

**guz·zle** *vb* : drink greedily

**gym** *n* : gymnasium

**gym·na·si·um** *n* : place for indoor sports

**gym·nas·tics** *n* : physical exercises performed in a gymnasium — **gym·nast** *n* — **gym·nas·tic** *adj*

**gyp** *n* **1** : cheat **2** : trickery — **gyp** *vb*

**gy·rate** *vb* : revolve around a center — **gy·ra·tion** *n*

**gy·ro·scope** *n* : wheel mounted to spin rapidly about an axis that is free to turn in various directions

# H

**h** *n* : 8th letter of the alphabet

**hab·it** *n* **1** : monk's or nun's clothing **2** : usual behavior **3** : addiction — **hab·it–form·ing** *adj* — **ha·bit·u·al** *adj* — **ha·bit·u·al·ly** *adv*

**hab·i·tat** *n* : place where a plant or animal naturally occurs

**hab·i·ta·tion** *n* **1** : occupancy **2** : dwelling place

**hab·it·able** *adj* : capable of being lived in

**¹hack** *vb* **1** : cut with repeated irregular blows **2** : cough in a short dry manner **3** : manage successfully — **hack** *n* — **hack·er** *n*

**²hack** *n* **1** : horse or vehicle for hire **2** : saddle horse **3** : writer for hire — **hack** *adj* — **hack·man** *n*

**hack·saw** *n* : saw for metal

**had** *past of* HAVE

**hag** *n* **1** : witch **2** : ugly old woman

**hag·gard** *adj* : worn or emaciated — **hag·gard·ly** *adv*

**hag·gle** *vb* : argue in bargaining — **hag·gler** *n*

**¹hail** *n* **1** : precipitation in small lumps of ice **2** : something like a rain of hail ~ *vb* : rain hail — **hail·stone** *n* — **hail·storm** *n*

**²hail** *vb* **1** : greet or salute **2** : summon ~ *n* : expression of greeting or praise — often used as an interjection

**hair** *n* : threadlike growth from the skin — **hair·brush** *n* — **hair·cut** *n* — **hair·dress·er** *n* — **haired** *adj* — **hair·i·ness** *n* — **hair·less** *adj* — **hair·line** *n* — **hair·pin** *n* — **hair·style** *n* — **hair·styl·ing** *n* — **hair·styl·ist** *n* — **hairy** *adj*

**hair·breadth, hairs·breadth** *n* : tiny distance or margin

**hair·do** *n* : style of wearing hair

**hair–rais·ing** *adj* : causing terror or astonishment

**hale** *adj* : healthy or robust

**half** *n* (**halves**) : either of 2 equal parts ~ *adj* **1** : being a half or nearly a half **2** : partial — **half** *adv*

**half brother** *n* : brother related through one parent only

**half·heart·ed** *adj* : without enthusiasm — **half·heart·ed·ly** *adv*

**half–life** *n* : time for half of something to undergo a process

**half sister** *n* : sister related through one parent only

**half·way** *adj* : midway between 2 points — **half·way** *adv*

**half–wit** *n* : foolish person — **half–wit·ted** *adj*

**hal·i·but** *n* (**halibut**) : large flattened fish with both eyes on the upper side

**hall** *n* **1** : large public or college or university building **2** : lobby **3** : auditorium

**hal·le·lu·jah** *interj* — used to express praise, joy, or thanks

**hall·mark** *n* : distinguishing characteristic

**hal·low** *vb* : consecrate — **hal·lowed** *adj*

**Hal·low·een** *n* : evening of October 31 observed esp. by children in merrymaking and masquerading

**hal·lu·ci·na·tion** *n* : perception of objects that are not real — **hal·lu·ci·nate** *vb* — **hal·lu·ci·na·to·ry** *adj*

**ha·lo** *n* : circle of light appearing to surround a shining body

**halt** *vb* : stop or cause to stop — **halt** *n*

**hal·ter** *n* **1** : rope or strap for leading or tying an animal **2** : brief blouse held up by straps ~ *vb* : catch (an animal) with a halter

**halve** *vb* **1** : divide into halves **2** : reduce to half

**halves** *pl of* HALF

**ham** *n* **1** : thigh — usu. pl. **2** : cut esp. of pork from the thigh **3** : showy actor **4** : amateur radio operator ~ *vb* : overplay a part — **ham** *adj*

**ham·burg·er, ham·burg** *n* : ground beef or a sandwich made with this

**ham·mer** *n* **1** : hand tool for pounding **2** : gun part whose striking explodes the charge ~ *vb* : beat, drive, or shape with a hammer — **hammer out** *vb* : produce with effort

**ham·mock** *n* : swinging bed hung by cords at each end

**¹ham·per** *vb* : impede

**²hamper** *n* : large covered basket

**ham·ster** *n* : thickly built shorttailed rodent

**ham·string** *vb* **1** : cripple by cutting the leg tendons **2** : make ineffective or powerless

**hand** *n* **1** : end of a front limb adapted for grasping **2** : side **3** : promise of marriage **4** : handwriting **5** : assistance or participation **6** : applause **7** : cards held by a player **8** : worker ~ *vb* : lead, assist, give, or pass with the hand — **hand·clasp** *n* — **hand·craft** *vb* — **hand·ful** *n* — **hand·gun** *n* — **hand·less** *adj* — **hand·made** *adj* — **hand·rail** *n* — **hand·saw** *n* — **hand·shake** *n* — **hand·wo·ven** *adj* — **hand·writ·ing** *n* — **hand·writ·ten** *adj*

**hand·bag** *n* : woman's purse

**hand·book** *n* : concise reference book

**hand·cuffs** *n pl* : locking bracelets that bind the wrists together — **handcuff** *vb*

**hand·i·cap** *n* **1** : advantage given or disadvantage imposed to equalize a competition **2** : disadvantage — **hand·icap** *vb* — **hand·i·capped** *adj* — **hand·i·cap·per** *n*

**hand·i·craft** *n* **1** : manual skill **2** : article made by hand — **hand·i·craft·er** *n*

**hand·ker·chief** *n* : small piece of cloth carried for personal use

**han·dle** *n* : part to be grasped ~ *vb* **1** : touch, hold, or manage with the hands **2** : deal with **3** : deal or trade in — **han·dle·bar** *n* — **han·dled** *adj* — **han·dler** *n*

**hand·some** *adj* **1** : sizable **2** : generous **3** : having a pleasing appearance — **hand·some·ly** *adv* — **hand·some·ness** *n*

**hand·spring** *n* : somersault on the hands

**handy** *adj* **1** : conveniently near **2** : easily used **3** : dexterous — **hand·i·ly** *adv* — **hand·i·ness** *n*

**handy·man** *n* : one who does odd jobs

**hang** *vb* **1** : fasten or remain fastened to an elevated point without support from below **2** : suspend by the neck until dead — past tense often *hanged* **3** : droop ~ *n* **1** : way a thing hangs **2** : an understanding of something — **hang·er** *n* — **hang·ing** *n*

**han·gar** *n* : airplane shelter

**hang·nail** *n* : loose skin near a fingernail

**hang·out** *n* : place where one likes to spend time

**han·ker** *vb* : desire strongly — **han·ker·ing** *n*

**han·ky–pan·ky** *n* : questionable or underhanded activity

**Ha·nuk·kah** *n* : 8-day Jewish holiday commemorating the rededication of the Temple of Jerusalem after its defilement by Antiochus of Syria

**hap·haz·ard** *adj* : having no plan or order — **hap·haz·ard·ly** *adv*

**hap·pen** *vb* **1** : take place **2** : be fortunate to encounter something unexpectedly — often used with infinitive

**hap·pen·ing** *n* : occurrence

**hap·py** *adj* **1** : fortunate **2** : content, pleased, or joyous — **hap·pi·ly** *adv* — **hap·pi·ness** *n*

**ha·rass** *vb* **1** : disturb and impede by repeated raids **2** : annoy continually — **ha·rass·ment** *n*

**har·bor** *n* : protected body of water suitable for anchorage ~ *vb* **1** : give refuge to **2** : hold as a thought or feeling

**hard** *adj* **1** : not easily penetrated **2** : firm or definite **3** : close or searching **4** : severe or without apparent feelings **5** : strenuous or difficult **6** : physically strong or intense — **hard** *adv* — **hard·ness** *n*

**hard·en** *vb* : make or become hard or harder — **hard·en·er** *n*

**hard·head·ed** *adj* **1** : stubborn **2** : realistic — **hard·head·ed·ly** *adv* — **hard·head·ed·ness** *n*

**hard–heart·ed** *adj* : lacking sympathy — **hard–heart·ed·ly** *adv* — **hard–heart·ed·ness** *n*

**hard·ly** *adv* **1** : only just **2** : certainly not

**hard·ship** *n* : suffering or privation

**hard·ware** *n* **1** : cutlery or tools made of metal **2** : physical components of a vehicle or apparatus

**har·dy** *adj* : able to withstand adverse conditions — **har·di·ly** *adv* — **har·di·ness** *n*

**hark** *vb* : listen

**harm** *n* **1** : physical or mental damage **2** : mischief ~ *vb* : cause harm — **harm·ful** *adj* — **harm·ful·ly** *adv* — **harm·ful·ness** *n* — **harm·less** *adj* — **harm·less·ly** *adv* — **harm·less·ness** *n*

**har·mon·i·ca** *n* : small wind instrument with metallic reeds

**har·mo·ny** *n* **1** : musical combination

of sounds **2 :** pleasing arrangement of parts **3 :** lack of conflict **4 :** internal calm — **har•mon•ic** *adj* — **har•mon•i•cal•ly** *adv* — **har•mo•ni•ous** *adj* — **har•mo•ni•ous•ly** *adv* — **har•mo•ni•ous•ness** *n* — **har•mo•ni•za•tion** *n* — **har•mo•nize** *vb*

**har•ness** *n* **:** gear of a draft animal ~ *vb* **1 :** put a harness on **2 :** put to use

**harp** *n* **:** musical instrument with many strings plucked by the fingers ~ *vb* **1 :** play on a harp **2 :** dwell on a subject tiresomely — **harp•er** *n* — **harp•ist** *n*

**har•row** *n* **:** implement used to break up soil ~ *vb* **1 :** cultivate with a harrow **2 :** distress

**harsh** *adj* **1 :** disagreeably rough **2 :** severe — **harsh•ly** *adv* — **harsh•ness** *n*

**har•vest** *n* **1 :** act or time of gathering in a crop **2 :** mature crop — **harvest** *vb* — **har•vest•er** *n*

**has** *pres 3d sing of* HAVE

**hash** *vb* **:** chop into small pieces ~ *n* **:** chopped meat mixed with potatoes and browned

**has•sle** *n* **1 :** quarrel **2 :** struggle **3 :** cause of annoyance — **hassle** *vb*

**haste** *n* **1 :** rapidity of motion **2 :** rash action **3 :** excessive eagerness — **hast•i•ly** *adv* — **hast•i•ness** *n* — **hasty** *adj*

**has•ten** *vb* **:** hurry

**hat** *n* **:** covering for the head

**[1]hatch** *n* **:** small door or opening — **hatch•way** *n*

**[2]hatch** *vb* **:** emerge from an egg — **hatch•ery** *n*

**hatch•et** *n* **:** short-handled ax

**hate** *n* **:** intense hostility and aversion ~ *vb* **1 :** express or feel hate **2 :** dislike — **hate•ful** *adj* — **hate•ful•ly** *adv* — **hate•ful•ness** *n* — **hat•er** *n*

**ha•tred** *n* **:** hate

**haugh•ty** *adj* **:** disdainfully proud — **haugh•ti•ly** *adv* — **haugh•ti•ness** *n*

**haul** *vb* **1 :** draw or pull **2 :** transport or carry ~ *n* **1 :** amount collected **2 :** load or the distance it is transported — **haul•er** *n*

**haunt** *vb* **1 :** visit often **2 :** visit or inhabit as a ghost ~ *n* **:** place frequented — **haunt•er** *n* — **haunt•ing•ly** *adv*

**have** *vb* (**had; had**) **1 :** hold in possession, service, or affection **2 :** be compelled or forced — used with *to* **3 —** used as an auxiliary with the past participle to form the present perfect, past perfect, or future perfect **4 :** obtain or receive **5 :** undergo **6 :** cause to **7 :** bear — **have to do with :** have in the way of connection or relation with or effect on

**hav•oc** *n* **1 :** wide destruction **2 :** great confusion

**[1]hawk** *n* **:** bird of prey with a strong hooked bill and sharp talons

**[2]hawk** *vb* **:** offer for sale by calling out in the street — **hawk•er** *n*

**hay** *n* **:** herbs (as grass) cut and dried for use as fodder — **hay** *vb* — **hay•loft** *n* — **hay•mow** *n* — **hay•stack** *n*

**hay•wire** *adj* **:** being out of order

**haz•ard** *n* **1 :** source of danger **2 :** chance ~ *vb* **:** venture or risk — **haz•ard•ous** *adj*

**[1]haze** *n* **:** fine dust, smoke, or light vapor in the air that reduces visibility

**[2]haze** *vb* **:** harass by abusive and humiliating tricks

**ha•zel** *n* **1 :** shrub or small tree bearing edible nuts (**ha•zel•nuts**) **2 :** light brown color

**hazy** *adj* **1 :** obscured by haze **2 :** vague or indefinite — **haz•i•ly** *adv* — **haz•i•ness** *n*

**he** *pron* **1 :** that male one **2 :** a or the person

**head** *n* **1 :** front or upper part of the body **2 :** mind **3 :** upper or higher end **4 :** director or leader **5 :** place of leadership or honor ~ *adj* **:** principal or chief ~ *vb* **1 :** provide with or form a head **2 :** put, stand, or be at the head **3 :** point or proceed in a certain direction — **head•ache** *n* — **head•band** *n* — **head•dress** *n* — **head•ed** *adj* — **head•first** *adv or adj* — **head•gear** *n* — **head•less** *adj* — **head•rest** *n* — **head•ship** *n* — **head•wait•er** *n*

**head•ing** *n* **1 :** direction in which a plane or ship heads **2 :** something (as a title) standing at the top or beginning

**head•light** *n* **:** light on the front of a vehicle

**head•line** *n* **:** introductory line of a newspaper story printed in large type

**head–on** *adj* **:** having the front facing in the direction of initial contact — **head–on** *adv*

**head•phone** *n* **:** an earphone held on by a band over the head — usu. pl.

**head•quar•ters** *n sing or pl* **:** command or administrative center

**head•strong** *adj* **:** stubborn or willful

**heady** *adj* **1 :** tending to make one giddy or elated **2 :** shrewd

**heal** *vb* **:** make or become sound or whole — **heal•er** *n*

**health** *n* **:** sound physical or mental condition

**health•ful** *adj* **:** beneficial to health — **health•ful•ly** *adv* — **health•ful•ness** *n*

**healthy** *adj* **:** enjoying or typical of good health — **health•i•ly** *adv* — **health•i•ness** *n*

**heap** *n* **:** pile ~ *vb* **:** throw or lay in a heap

**hear** *vb* **1 :** perceive by the ear **2 :** heed **3 :** learn

**hear•ing** *n* **1 :** process or power of perceiving sound **2 :** earshot **3 :** session in which witnesses are heard

**hear•say** *n* **:** rumor

**hearse** *n* **:** vehicle for carrying the dead to the grave

**heart** *n* **1 :** hollow muscular organ that keeps up the circulation of the blood **2 :** playing card of a suit marked with a red heart **3 :** whole personality or the emotional or moral part of it **4 :** courage **5 :** essential part — **heart•beat** *n* — **heart•ed** *adj*

**heart•ache** *n* **:** anguish of mind

**heart•break** *n* **:** crushing grief — **heart•break•er** *n* — **heart•break•ing** *adj* — **heart•bro•ken** *adj*

**heart•burn** *n* **:** burning distress in the heart area after eating

**heart•en** *vb* **:** encourage

**hearth** *n* **1 :** area in front of a fireplace **2 :** home — **hearth•stone** *n*

**heart•less** *adj* **:** cruel

**heart•warm•ing** *adj* **:** inspiring sympathetic feeling

**hearty** *adj* **1 :** vigorously healthy **2 :** nourishing — **heart•i•ly** *adv* — **heart•i•ness** *n*

**heat** *vb* **:** make or become warm or hot ~ *n* **1 :** condition of being hot **2 :** form of energy that causes a body to rise in temperature **3 :** intensity of feeling — **heat•ed•ly** *adv* — **heat•er** *n*

**hea•then** *n* **:** person who is godless or not civilized — **heathen** *adj*

**heave** *vb* **1 :** rise or lift upward **2 :** throw **3 :** rise and fall ~ *n* **1 :** an effort to lift or raise **2 :** throw

**heav•en** *n* **1** *pl* **:** sky **2 :** abode of the Deity and of the blessed dead **3 :** place of supreme happiness — **heav•en•ly** *adj* — **heav•en•ward** *adv or adj*

**heavy** *adj* **1 :** having great weight **2 :** hard to bear **3 :** greater than the average — **heav•i•ly** *adv* — **heavi•ness** *n* — **heavy•weight** *n*

**heck•le** *vb* **:** harass with gibes — **heck•ler** *n*

**hec•tic** *adj* **:** filled with excitement, activity, or confusion — **hec•ti•cal•ly** *adv*

**hedge** *n* **1 :** fence or boundary of shrubs or small trees **2 :** means of protection ~ *vb* **1 :** protect oneself against loss **2 :** evade the risk of commitment — **hedg•er** *n*

**heed** *vb* **:** pay attention ~ *n* **:** attention — **heed•ful** *adj* — **heed•ful•ly** *adv* — **heed•ful•ness** *n* — **heed•less** *adj* — **heed•less•ly** *adv* — **heed•less•ness** *n*

**heel** *n* **1 :** back of the foot **2 :** crusty end of a loaf of bread **3 :** solid piece forming the back of the sole of a shoe — **heel•less** *adj*

**hefty** *adj* **:** big and bulky

**height** *n* **1 :** highest part or point **2 :** distance from bottom to top **3 :** altitude

**height•en** *vb* **:** increase in amount or degree

**heir** *n* **:** one who inherits or is entitled to inherit property

**heir•ess** *n* **:** female heir esp. to great wealth

**held** *past of* HOLD

**he•li•cop•ter** *n* **:** aircraft supported in the air by rotors

**he•li•um** *n* **:** very light nonflammable gaseous chemical element

**hell** *n* **1 :** nether world in which the dead continue to exist **2 :** realm of the devil **3 :** place or state of torment or destruction — **hell•ish** *adj*

**hel•lo** *n* **:** expression of greeting

**helm** *n* **:** lever or wheel for steering a ship — **helms•man** *n*

**hel•met** *n* **:** protective covering for the head

**help** *vb* **1 :** supply what is needed **2 :** be of use **3 :** refrain from or prevent ~ *n* **1 :** something that helps or is a source of help **2 :** one who helps another — **help•er** *n* — **help•ful** *adj* — **help•ful•ly** *adv* — **help•ful•ness** *n* — **help•less** *adj* — **help•less•ly** *adv* — **help•less•ness** *n*

**help•ing** *n* **:** portion of food

**hem** *n* **:** border of an article of cloth doubled back and stitched down ~ *vb* **1 :** sew a hem **2 :** surround restrictively — **hem•line** *n*

**hemi•sphere** *n* **:** one of the halves of the earth divided by the equator into northern and southern parts (**northern hemisphere, southern hemisphere**) or by a meridian into eastern and western parts (**eastern hemisphere, western hemisphere**) — **hemi•spher•ic, hemi•spher•i•cal** *adj*

**hem•or•rhage** *n* **:** large discharge of blood — **hemorrhage** *vb* — **hem•or•rhag•ic** *adj*

**hen** *n* **:** female domestic fowl

**hence** *adv* **1 :** away **2 :** therefore **3 :** from this source or origin

**hence•forth** *adv* **:** from this point on

**her** *adj* **:** of or relating to her or herself ~ *pron objective case of* SHE

**herb** *n* **1 :** seed plant that lacks woody tissue **2 :** plant or plant part valued for medicinal or savory qualities — **her•ba•ceous** *adj* — **herb•age** *n* — **herb•al** *n or adj* — **herb•al•ist** *n*

**her•bi•cide** *n* **:** agent that destroys plants — **her•bi•cid•al** *adj*

**herd** *n* **:** group of animals of one kind ~ *vb* **:** assemble or move in a herd — **herd•er** *n* — **herds•man** *n*

**here** *adv* **1 :** in, at, or to this place **2 :** now **3 :** at or in this point or particular **4 :** in the present life or state ~ *n* **:** this place — **here•abouts, here•about** *adv*

**here•af•ter** *adv* **:** in some future time or state ~ *n* **:** existence beyond earthly life

**he•red•i•tary** *adj* **1 :** genetically passed or passable from parent to offspring **2 :** passing by inheritance — **he•red•i•ty** *n*

**her•e•sy** *n* **:** opinion or doctrine contrary to church dogma — **her•e•tic** *n* — **he•re•ti•cal** *adj*

**here•to•fore** *adv* **:** up to this time

**her•i•tage** *n* **1 :** inheritance **2 :** birthright

**her•mit** *n* **:** one who lives in solitude

**he•ro** *n* **:** one that is much admired or shows great courage — **he•ro•ic** *adj* — **he•ro•i•cal•ly** *adv* — **he•ro•ics** *n pl* — **her•o•ism** *n*

**her•o•in** *n* **:** strongly addictive narcotic

**her•o•ine** *n* **:** woman of heroic achievements or qualities

**her•on** *n* **:** long-legged long-billed wading bird

**hers** *pron* **:** one or the ones belonging to her

**her•self** *pron* **:** she, her — used reflexively or for emphasis

**hertz** *n* **hertz :** unit of frequency equal to one cycle per second

**hes•i•tant** *adj* **:** tending to hesitate — **hes•i•tance** *n* — **hes•i•tan•cy** *n* — **hes•i•tant•ly** *adv*

**hes•i•tate** *vb* **1 :** hold back esp. in doubt **2 :** pause — **hes•i•ta•tion** *n*

**hew** *vb* **1 :** cut or shape with or as if with an ax **2 :** conform strictly — **hew•er** *n*

**hex** *vb* **:** put an evil spell on — **hex** *n*

**hexa•gon** *n* **:** 6-sided polygon — **hex•ag•o•nal** *adj*

**hi•ber•nate** *vb* **:** pass the winter in a torpid or resting state — **hi•ber•na•tion** *n* — **hi•ber•na•tor** *n*

**hic•cup** *vb* **:** to inhale spasmodically and make a peculiar sound ~ *n pl* **:** attack of hiccuping

**[1]hide** *vb* **hid; hid•den/hid :** put or remain out of sight — **hid•er** *n*

**[2]hide** *n* **:** animal skin

**hid•eous** *adj* **:** very ugly — **hid•eous•ly** *adv* — **hid•eous•ness** *n*

**hi•er•ar•chy** *n* **:** persons or things arranged in a graded series — **hi•er•ar•chi•cal** *adj*

**high** *adj* **1 :** having large extension upward **2 :** elevated in pitch **3 :** exalted in character **4 :** of greater degree or amount than average **5 :** expensive **6 :** excited or stupefied by alcohol or a drug ~ *adv* **:** at or to a high place or degree ~ *n* **1 :** elevated point or level **2 :** automobile gear giving the highest speed — **high•ly** *adv* — **high•ness** *n*

**high–definition** *adj* **:** being or relating to a television system with twice as many scan lines per frame as a conventional system

**high•light** *n* **:** event or detail of major importance ~ *vb* **1 :** emphasize **2 :** be a highlight of

**high school** *n* **:** school usu. including grades 9 to 12 or 10 to 12

**high–strung** *adj* **:** very nervous or sensitive

**high•way** *n* **:** public road

**hi•jack** *vb* **:** steal esp. by commandeering a vehicle — **hijack** *n* — **hi•jack•er** *n*

**hike** *vb* **1 :** raise quickly **2 :** take a long walk ~ *n* **1 :** long walk **2 :** increase — **hik•er** *n*

**hi•lar•i•ous** *adj* **:** extremely funny — **hi•lar•i•ous•ly** *adv* — **hi•lar•i•ty** *n*

**hill** *n* **:** place where the land rises — **hill•side** *n* — **hill•top** *n* — **hilly** *adj*

**him** *pron, objective case of* HE

**him•self** *pron* **:** he, him — used reflexively or for emphasis

**hind** *adj* **:** back — **hind•most** *adj*

**hin•der** *vb* **:** obstruct or hold back

**hin•drance** *n* **:** something that hinders

**hind•sight** *n* **:** understanding of an event after it has happened

**Hin•du•ism** *n* **:** body of religious beliefs and practices native to India — **Hin•du** *n or adj*

**hinge** *n* **:** jointed piece on which a swinging part (as a door) turns ~ *vb* **1 :** attach by or furnish with hinges **2 :** depend

**hint** *n* **1 :** indirect suggestion **2 :** clue **3 :** very small amount — **hint** *vb*

**hip** *n* **:** part of the body on either side just below the waist — **hip•bone** *n*

**hip•po•pot•a•mus** *n* **:** large thick-skinned African river animal

**hire** *n* **1 :** payment for labor **2 :** employment **3 :** one who is hired ~ *vb* **:** employ for pay

**his** *adj* **:** of or belonging to him ~ *pron* **:** ones belonging to him

**hiss** *vb* **1 :** make a sibilant sound **2 :** show dislike by hissing — **hiss** *n*

**his•to•ry** *n* **1 :** chronological record of significant events **2 :** study of past events **3 :** an established record —

**his·to·ri·an** *n* — **his·tor·ic, his·tor·i·cal** *adj* — **his·tor·i·cal·ly** *adv*

**hit** *vb* **hit; hit 1** : reach with a blow **2** : come or cause to come in contact **3** : affect detrimentally — *n* **1** : blow **2** : great success — **hit·ter** *n*

**hitch** *vb* **1** : move by jerks **2** : catch by a hook **3** : hitchhike — *n* **1** : jerk **2** : sudden halt

**hitch·hike** *vb* : travel by securing free rides from passing vehicles — **hitch·hik·er** *n*

**hive** *n* **1** : container housing honeybees **2** : colony of bees — **hive** *vb*

**HMO** *n* : comprehensive health-care organization financed by clients

**hoard** *n* : hidden accumulation — **hoard** *vb* — **hoard·er** *n*

**hoarse** *adj* **1** : harsh in sound **2** : speaking in a harsh strained voice — **hoarse·ly** *adv* — **hoarse·ness** *n*

**hoax** *n* : act intended to trick or dupe — **hoax** *vb* — **hoax·er** *n*

**hob·ble** *vb* : limp along — *n* : hobbling movement

**hob·by** *n* : interest engaged in for relaxation — **hob·by·ist** *n*

**hob·nail** *n* : short nail for studding shoe soles — **hob·nailed** *adj*

**hock·ey** *n* : game played on ice or a field by 2 teams

**hodge·podge** *n* : heterogeneous mixture

**hoe** *n* : long-handled tool for cultivating or weeding — **hoe** *vb*

**hog** *n* **1** : domestic adult swine **2** : glutton — *vb* : take selfishly — **hog·gish** *adj*

**hoist** *vb* : lift — *n* **1** : lift **2** : apparatus for hoisting

**hold** *vb* (**held; held**) **1** : possess **2** : restrain **3** : have a grasp on **4** : remain or keep in a particular situation or position **5** : contain **6** : regard **7** : cause to occur **8** : occupy esp. by appointment or election — *n* **1** : act or manner of holding **2** : restraining or controlling influence — **hold·er** *n* — **hold forth** : speak at length — **hold to** : adhere to — **hold with** : agree with

**hold·up** *n* **1** : robbery at the point of a gun **2** : delay

**hole** *n* **1** : opening into or through something **2** : hollow place (as a pit) **3** : den — **hole** *vb*

**hol·i·day** *n* **1** : day of freedom from work **2** : vacation — **holiday** *vb*

**ho·lis·tic** *adj* : relating to a whole (as the body)

**hol·ler** *vb* : cry out — **hol·ler** *n*

**hol·low** *adj* **1** : somewhat depressed **2** : having a cavity within **3** : sounding like a noise made in an empty place **4** : empty of value or meaning — *vb* : make or become hollow — *n* **1** : surface depression **2** : cavity — **hol·low·ness** *n*

**hol·ly** *n* : evergreen tree or shrub with glossy leaves

**ho·lo·caust** *n* : thorough destruction esp. by fire

**ho·ly** *adj* **1** : sacred **2** : spiritually pure — **ho·li·ness** *n*

**hom·age** *n* : reverent regard

**home** *n* **1** : residence **2** : congenial environment **3** : place of origin or refuge — *vb* : go or return home — **home·bred** *adj* — **home·com·ing** *n* — **hom·ey** *adj* — **home·grown** *adj* — **home·land** *n* — **home·less** *adj* — **home·made** *adj*

**home·ly** *adj* : plain or unattractive — **home·li·ness** *n*

**home·sick** *adj* : longing for home — **home·sick·ness** *n*

**home·stead** *n* : home and land occupied and worked by a family — **home·stead·er** *n*

**home·work** *n* : school lessons to be done outside the classroom

**ho·mo·ge·neous** *adj* : of the same or a similar kind — **ho·mo·ge·ne·i·ty** *n* — **ho·mo·ge·neous·ly** *adv*

**ho·mog·e·nize** *vb* : make the particles in (as milk) of uniform size and even distribution — **ho·mog·e·ni·za·tion** *n* — **ho·mog·e·niz·er** *n*

**Ho·mo sa·pi·ens** *n* : humankind

**hon·est** *adj* **1** : free from deception **2** : trustworthy **3** : frank — **hon·est·ly** *adv* — **hon·es·ty** *n*

**hon·ey** *n* : sweet sticky substance made by bees (**hon·ey·bees**) from the nectar of flowers — **hon·ey·comb** *n*

**hon·ey·moon** *n* : holiday taken by a newly married couple — **honeymoon** *vb*

**honk** *n* : cry of a goose or a similar sound — **honk** *vb* — **honk·er** *n*

**hon·or** *n* **1** : good name **2** : outward respect or symbol of this **3** : privilege **4** : person of superior rank or position — used esp. as a title **5** : something or someone worthy of respect **6** : integrity — *vb* **1** : regard with honor **2** : confer honor on **3** : fulfill the terms of — **hon·or·able** *adj* — **hon·or·ably** *adv* — **hon·or·ari·ly** *adv* — **hon·or·ary** *adj* — **hon·or·ee** *n*

**hood** *n* **1** : part of a garment that covers the head **2** : covering over an automobile engine compartment — **hood·ed** *adj*

**hood·wink** *vb* : deceive

**hoof** *n* : horny covering of the toes of some mammals (as horses or cattle) — **hoofed** *adj*

**hook** *n* : curved or bent device for catching, holding, or pulling — *vb* : seize or make fast with a hook — **hook·er** *n*

**hoop** *n* : circular strip, figure, or object

**hoot** *vb* **1** : shout in contempt **2** : make the cry of an owl — **hoot** *n* — **hoot·er** *n*

**hop** *vb* : move by quick springy leaps — **hop** *n*

**hope** *vb* : desire with expectation of fulfillment — *n* **1** : act of hoping **2** : something hoped for — **hope·ful** *adj* — **hope·ful·ly** *adv* — **hope·ful·ness** *n* — **hope·less** *adj* — **hope·less·ly** *adv* — **hope·less·ness** *n*

**ho·ri·zon** *n* : apparent junction of earth and sky — **hor·i·zon·tal** *adj* — **hor·i·zon·tal·ly** *adv*

**hor·mone** *n* : cell product in body fluids that has a specific effect on other cells — **hor·mon·al** *adj*

**horn** *n* **1** : hard bony projection on the head of a hoofed animal **2** : brass wind instrument — **horned** *adj* — **horn·less** *adj* — **horny** *adj*

**hor·net** *n* : large social wasp

**hor·ren·dous** *adj* : horrible

**hor·ri·ble** *adj* **1** : having or causing horror **2** : highly disagreeable — **hor·ri·ble·ness** *n* — **hor·ri·bly** *adv*

**hor·ri·fy** *vb* : cause to feel horror

**hor·ror** *n* **1** : intense fear, dread, or dismay **2** : intense repugnance **3** : something horrible

**horse** *n* : large solid-hoofed domesticated mammal — **horse·back** *n or adv* — **horse·hair** *n* — **horse·hide** *n* — **horse·less** *adj* — **horse·man** *n* — **horse·man·ship** *n* — **horse·wom·an** *n* — **hors·ey, horsy** *adj*

**horse·play** *n* : rough boisterous play

**horse·pow·er** *n* : unit of mechanical power

**horse·shoe** *n* : U-shaped protective metal plate fitted to the rim of a horse's hoof

**hor·ti·cul·ture** *n* : science of growing fruits, vegetables, and flowers — **hor·ti·cul·tur·al** *adj* — **hor·ti·cul·tur·ist** *n*

**hose** *n* **1** *pl* **hose** : stocking or sock **2** *pl* **hos·es** : flexible tube for conveying fluids — *vb* : spray, water, or wash with a hose

**hos·pi·ta·ble** *adj* : given to generous and cordial reception of guests — **hos·pi·ta·bly** *adv*

**hos·pi·tal** *n* : institution where the sick or injured receive medical care — **hos·pi·tal·i·za·tion** *n* — **hos·pi·tal·ize** *vb*

**hos·pi·tal·i·ty** *n* : hospitable treatment, reception, or disposition

**¹host** *n* **1** : army **2** : multitude

**²host** *n* : one who receives or entertains guests — **host** *vb*

**³host** *n* : eucharistic bread

**hos·tage** *n* : person held to guarantee that promises be kept or demands met

**host·ess** *n* : woman who is host

**hos·tile** *adj* : openly or actively unfriendly or opposed to someone or something — **hostile** *n* — **hos·tile·ly** *adv* — **hos·til·i·ty** *n*

**hot** *adj* **1** : having a high temperature **2** : giving a sensation of heat or burning **3** : ardent **4** : pungent — **hot** *adv* — **hot·ly** *adv* — **hot·ness** *n*

**hot dog** *n* : frankfurter

**ho·tel** *n* : building where lodging and personal services are provided

**hound** *n* : long-eared hunting dog — *vb* : pursue relentlessly

**hour** *n* **1** : 24th part of a day **2** : time of day — **hour·ly** *adv or adj*

**hour·glass** *n* : glass vessel for measuring time

**house** *n* **1** : building to live in **2** : household **3** : legislative body **4** : business firm — *vb* : provide with or take shelter — **house·boat** *n* — **house·clean** *vb* — **house·clean·ing** *n* — **house·ful** *n* — **house·keep·er** *n* — **house·keep·ing** *n* — **house·maid** *n* — **house·wares** *n pl* — **house·work** *n*

**house·bro·ken** *adj* : trained in excretory habits acceptable in indoor living

**house·fly** *n* : two-winged fly common about human habitations

**house·hold** *n* : those who dwell as a family under the same roof — *adj* **1** : domestic **2** : common or familiar — **house·hold·er** *n*

**house·wife** *n* (**house·wives**) : married woman in charge of a household — **house·wife·ly** *adj* — **house·wif·ery** *n*

**hov·er** *vb* **1** : remain suspended in the air **2** : move about in the vicinity

**how** *adv* **1** : in what way or condition **2** : for what reason **3** : to what extent — *conj* : the way or manner in which

**how·ev·er** *conj* : in whatever manner — *adv* **1** : to whatever degree or in whatever manner **2** : in spite of that

**howl** *vb* : emit a loud long doleful sound like a dog — **howl** *n* — **howl·er** *n*

**hub** *n* : central part of a circular object (as of a wheel) — **hub·cap** *n*

**hud·dle** *vb* **1** : crowd together **2** : confer — **hud·dle** *n*

**hue** *n* : color or gradation of color — **hued** *adj*

**hug** *vb* **1** : press tightly in the arms **2** : stay close to — **hug** *n*

**huge** *adj* : very large or extensive — **huge·ly** *adv* — **huge·ness** *n*

**hulk** *n* **1** : bulky or unwieldy person or thing **2** : old ship unfit for service — **hulk·ing** *adj*

**hull** *n* **1** : outer covering of a fruit or seed **2** : frame or body of a ship or boat — *vb* : remove the hulls of — **hull·er** *n*

**hum** *vb* **1** : make a prolonged sound like that of the speech sound /m/ **2** : be busily active **3** : run smoothly **4** : sing with closed lips — **hum** *n* — **hum·mer** *n*

**hu·man** *adj* **1** : of or relating to the species people belong to **2** : by, for, or like people — **human** *n* — **hu·man·kind** *n* — **hu·man·ly** *adv* — **hu·man·ness** *n*

**hu·mane** *adj* : showing compassion or consideration for others — **hu·mane·ly** *adv* — **hu·mane·ness** *n*

**hu·man·ism** *n* : doctrine or way of life centered on human interests or values — **hu·man·ist** *n or adj* — **hu·man·is·tic** *adj*

**hu·man·i·tar·i·an** *n* : person promoting human welfare — **hu·man·i·tar·i·an** *adj* — **hu·man·i·tar·i·an·ism** *n*

**hu·man·i·ty** *n* **1** : human or humane quality or state **2** : the human race

**hum·ble** *adj* **1** : not proud or haughty **2** : not pretentious — *vb* : make humble — **hum·ble·ness** *n* — **hum·bler** *n* — **hum·bly** *adv*

**hu·mid** *adj* : containing or characterized by moisture — **hu·mid·i·fi·ca·tion** *n* — **hu·mid·i·fi·er** *n* — **hu·mid·i·fy** *vb* — **hu·mid·ly** *adv*

**hu·mid·i·ty** *n* : atmospheric moisture

**hu·mil·i·ate** *vb* : injure the self-respect of — **hu·mil·i·at·ing·ly** *adv* — **hu·mil·i·ation** *n*

**hu·mil·i·ty** *n* : humble quality or state

**hu·mor** *n* **1** : mood **2** : quality of being laughably ludicrous or incongruous **3** : appreciation of what is ludicrous or incongruous **4** : something intended to be funny — *vb* : comply with the wishes or mood of — **hu·mor·ist** *n* — **hu·mor·less** *adj* — **hu·mor·less·ly** *adv* — **hu·mor·less·ness** *n* — **hu·mor·ous** *adj* — **hu·mor·ous·ly** *adv* — **hu·mor·ous·ness** *n*

**hump** *n* : rounded protuberance — **humped** *adj*

**hunch** *vb* : assume or cause to assume a bent or crooked posture — *n* : strong intuitive feeling

**hun·dred** *n* : 10 times 10 — **hundred** *adj* — **hun·dredth** *adj or n*

**hun·ger** *n* **1** : craving or urgent need for food **2** : strong desire — **hunger** *vb* — **hun·gri·ly** *adv* — **hun·gry** *adj*

**hunk** *n* : large piece

**hunt** *vb* **1** : pursue for food or sport **2** : try to find — *n* : act or instance of hunting — **hunt·er** *n*

**hur·dle** *n* **1** : barrier to leap over in a race **2** : obstacle — **hur·dle** *vb* — **hur·dler** *n*

**hurl** *vb* : throw with violence — **hurl** *n* — **hurl·er** *n*

**hur·rah** *interj* — used to express joy or approval

**hur·ri·cane** *n* : tropical storm with winds of 74 miles per hour or greater

**hur·ry** *vb* : go or cause to go with haste — *n* : extreme haste — **hur·ried·ly** *adv* — **hur·ried·ness** *n*

**hurt** *vb* **hurt; hurt 1** : feel or cause pain **2** : do harm to — *n* **1** : bodily injury **2** : harm — **hurt·ful** *adj* — **hurt·ful·ness** *n*

**hur·tle** *vb* : move rapidly or forcefully

**hus·band** *n* : married man — *vb* : manage prudently

**hus·band·ry** *n* **1** : careful use **2** : agriculture

**hush** *vb* : make or become quiet — *n* : silence

**husk** *n* : outer covering of a seed or fruit — *vb* : strip the husk from — **husk·er** *n*

**¹hus·ky** *adj* : hoarse — **hus·ki·ly** *adv* — **hus·ki·ness** *n*

**²husky** *adj* : burly — **husk·i·ness** *n*

**hus·tle** *vb* **1** : hurry **2** : work energetically — **hustle** *n* — **hus·tler** *n*

**hut** *n* : small often temporary dwelling

**hy·brid** *n* : offspring of genetically differing parents — **hybrid** *adj* — **hy·brid·iza·tion** *n* — **hy·brid·ize** *vb* — **hy·brid·iz·er** *n*

**hy·drant** *n* : pipe from which water may be drawn to fight fires

**hy·dro·elec·tric** *adj* : producing electricity by waterpower — **hy·dro·elec·tric·i·ty** *n*

**hy·dro·gen** *n* : very light gaseous colorless odorless flammable chemical element

**hy·giene** *n* : conditions or practices conducive to health — **hy·gien·ic** *adj* — **hy·gien·i·cal·ly** *adv* — **hy·gien·ist** *n*

**hying** *pres part of* HIE

**hymn** *n* : song of praise esp. to God — **hymn** *vb*

**hym·nal** *n* : book of hymns

**hype** *vb* : publicize extravagantly — **hype** *n*

**hy·phen** *n* : punctuation mark - used to divide or compound words — **hyphen** *vb*

**hy·phen·ate** *vb* : connect or divide with a hyphen — **hy·phen·ation** *n*

**hyp•no•sis** *n* : induced state like sleep in which the subject is responsive to suggestions of the inducer (**hyp•no•tist**) — **hyp•no•tism** *n* — **hyp•no•tiz•able** *adj* — **hyp•no•tize** *vb*

**hy•poc•ri•sy** *n* : a feigning to be what one is not — **hyp•o•crite** *n* — **hyp•o•crit•i•cal** *adj* — **hyp•o•crit•i•cal•ly** *adv*

**hy•pot•e•nuse** *n* : side of a right-angled triangle opposite the right angle

**hy•poth•e•sis** *n* : assumption made in order to test its consequences — **hy•poth•e•size** *vb* — **hy•po•thet•i•cal** *adj* — **hy•po•thet•i•cal•ly** *adv*

**hys•te•ria** *n* : uncontrollable fear or outburst of emotion — **hys•ter•i•cal** *adj* — **hys•ter•i•cal•ly** *adv*

**hys•ter•ics** *n pl* : uncontrollable laughter or crying

# I

**i** *n* : 9th letter of the alphabet

**I** *pron* : the speaker

**ice** *n* **1** : frozen water **2** : flavored frozen dessert ∼ *vb* **1** : freeze **2** : chill **3** : cover with icing

**ice•berg** *n* : large floating mass of ice

**ice cream** *n* : sweet frozen food

**ice–skate** *vb* : skate on ice — **ice skater** *n*

**ici•cle** *n* : hanging mass of ice

**ic•ing** *n* : sweet usu. creamy coating for baked goods

**icon** *n* **1** : religious image **2** : small picture on a computer screen identified with an available function

**icy** *adj* **1** : covered with or consisting of ice **2** : very cold — **ic•i•ly** *adv* — **ic•i•ness** *n*

**idea** *n* **1** : something imagined in the mind **2** : purpose or plan

**ide•al** *adj* **1** : imaginary **2** : perfect ∼ *n* **1** : standard of excellence **2** : model **3** : aim — **ide•al•ly** *adv*

**ide•al•ize** *vb* : think of or represent as ideal — **ide•al•ism** *n* — **ide•al•ist** *n* — **ide•al•is•tic** *adj* — **ide•al•is•ti•cal•ly** *adv* — **ide•al•i•za•tion** *n*

**iden•ti•cal** *adj* **1** : being the same **2** : exactly or essentially alike

**iden•ti•fy** *vb* **1** : associate **2** : establish the identity of — **iden•ti•fi•able** *adj* — **iden•ti•fi•ca•tion** *n* — **iden•ti•fi•er** *n*

**iden•ti•ty** *n* **1** : sameness of essential character **2** : individuality **3** : fact of being what is supposed

**id•i•om** *n* **1** : language peculiar to a person or group **2** : expression with a special meaning — **id•i•om•at•ic** *adj* — **id•i•om•at•i•cal•ly** *adv*

**id•i•ot** *n* : mentally retarded or foolish person — **id•i•o•cy** *n* — **id•i•ot•ic** *adj* — **id•i•ot•i•cal•ly** *adv*

**idle** *adj* **1** : worthless **2** : inactive **3** : lazy ∼ *vb* : spend time doing nothing — **idle•ness** *n* — **idler** *n* — **idly** *adv*

**idol** *n* **1** : image of a god **2** : object of devotion — **idol•iza•tion** *n* — **idol•ize** *vb*

**idyll** *n* : period of peace and contentment — **idyl•lic** *adj*

**if** *conj* **1** : in the event that **2** : whether **3** : even though

**ig•loo** *n* : hut made of snow blocks

**ig•nite** *vb* : set afire or catch fire — **ig•nit•able** *adj* — **ig•ni•tion** *n*

**ig•no•rant** *adj* **1** : lacking knowledge **2** : showing a lack of knowledge or intelligence **3** : unaware — **ig•no•rance** *n* — **ig•no•rant•ly** *adv*

**ig•nore** *vb* : refuse to notice

**ill** *adj* **worse; worst** **1** : sick **2** : bad **3** : rude or unacceptable **4** : hostile ∼ *adv* **1** : with displeasure **2** : harshly **3** : scarcely **4** : badly ∼ *n* **1** : evil **2** : misfortune **3** : sickness — **ill•ness** *n*

**il•le•gal** *adj* : not lawful — **il•le•gal•i•ty** *n* — **il•le•gal•ly** *adv*

**il•leg•i•ble** *adj* : not legible — **il•leg•i•bil•i•ty** *n* — **il•leg•i•bly** *adv*

**il•le•git•i•mate** *adj* **1** : born of unmarried parents **2** : illegal — **il•le•git•i•ma•cy** *n* — **il•le•git•i•mate•ly** *adv*

**il•lic•it** *adj* : not lawful — **il•lic•it•ly** *adv*

**il•lit•er•ate** *adj* : unable to read or write — **il•lit•er•a•cy** *n* — **il•lit•er•ate** *n*

**il•log•i•cal** *adj* : contrary to sound reasoning — **il•log•i•cal•ly** *adv*

**il•lu•mi•nate** *vb* **1** : light up **2** : make clear — **il•lu•mi•nat•ing•ly** *adv* — **il•lu•mi•na•tion** *n*

**il•lu•sion** *n* **1** : mistaken idea **2** : misleading visual image — **il•lu•so•ry** *adj*

**il•lus•trate** *vb* **1** : explain by example **2** : provide with pictures or figures — **il•lus•tra•tion** *n* — **il•lus•tra•tive** *adj* — **il•lus•tra•tive•ly** *adv* — **il•lus•tra•tor** *n*

**il•lus•tri•ous** *adj* : notably or brilliantly outstanding — **il•lus•tri•ous•ness** *n*

**im•age** *n* **1** : likeness **2** : visual counterpart of an object formed by a lens or mirror **3** : mental picture ∼ *vb* : create a representation of — **im•ag•ery** *n*

**imag•i•nary** *adj* : existing only in the imagination

**imag•i•na•tion** *n* **1** : act or power of forming a mental image **2** : creative ability

**imag•ine** *vb* : form a mental picture of something not present — **imag•in•able** *adj* — **imag•in•ably** *adv* — **imag•i•na•tive** *adj* — **imag•i•na•tive•ly** *adv*

**im•be•cile** *n* : idiot — **imbecile, im•be•cil•ic** *adj* — **im•be•cil•i•ty** *n*

**im•i•tate** *vb* **1** : follow as a model **2** : mimic — **im•i•ta•tion** *n or adj* — **im•i•ta•tive** *adj* — **im•i•ta•tor** *n*

**im•mac•u•late** *adj* : without stain or blemish — **im•mac•u•late•ly** *adv*

**im•ma•te•ri•al** *adj* **1** : spiritual **2** : not relevant — **im•ma•te•ri•al•i•ty** *n*

**im•ma•ture** *adj* : not yet mature — **im•ma•tu•ri•ty** *n*

**im•me•di•a•cy** *n* : quality or state of being urgent

**im•me•di•ate** *adj* **1** : direct **2** : being next in line **3** : made or done at once **4** : not distant — **im•me•di•ate•ly** *adv*

**im•mense** *adj* : vast — **im•mense•ly** *adv* — **im•men•si•ty** *n*

**im•merse** *vb* **1** : plunge or dip esp. into liquid **2** : engross — **im•mer•sion** *n*

**im•mi•grate** *vb* : come into a place and take up residence — **im•mi•grant** *n* — **im•mi•gra•tion** *n*

**im•mo•late** *vb* : offer in sacrifice — **im•mo•la•tion** *n*

**im•mor•al** *adj* : not moral — **im•mo•ral•i•ty** *n* — **im•mor•al•ly** *adv*

**im•mor•tal** *adj* **1** : not mortal **2** : having lasting fame ∼ *n* : one exempt from death or oblivion — **im•mor•tal•i•ty** *n* — **im•mor•tal•ize** *vb*

**im•mune** *adj* : not liable esp. to disease — **im•mu•ni•ty** *n* — **im•mu•ni•za•tion** *n* — **im•mu•nize** *vb*

**im•mu•nol•o•gy** *n* : science of immunity to disease — **im•mu•no•log•ic, im•mu•no•log•i•cal** *adj* — **im•mu•nol•o•gist** *n*

**im•pact** *vb* **1** : press close **2** : have an effect on ∼ *n* **1** : forceful contact **2** : influence

**im•pair** *vb* : diminish in quantity, value, or ability — **im•pair•ment** *n*

**im•pale** *vb* : pierce with something pointed

**im•par•tial** *adj* : not partial — **im•par•tial•i•ty** *n* — **im•par•tial•ly** *adv*

**im•passe** *n* : inescapable predicament

**im•pas•sive** *adj* : showing no feeling or interest — **im•pas•sive•ly** *adv* — **im•pas•siv•i•ty** *n*

**im•pa•tient** *adj* : not patient — **im•pa•tience** *n* — **im•pa•tient•ly** *adv*

**im•peach** *vb* **1** : charge (an official) with misconduct **2** : cast doubt on **3** : remove from office for misconduct — **im•peach•ment** *n*

**im•pec•ca•ble** *adj* : faultless — **im•pec•ca•bly** *adv*

**im•pede** *vb* : interfere with

**im•ped•i•ment** *n* **1** : hindrance **2** : speech defect

**im•per•a•tive** *adj* **1** : expressing a command **2** : urgent ∼ *n* **1** : imperative mood or verb form **2** : unavoidable fact, need, or obligation — **im•per•a•tive•ly** *adv*

**im•per•cep•ti•ble** *adj* : not perceptible — **im•per•cep•ti•bly** *adv*

**im•per•fect** *adj* : not perfect — **im•per•fec•tion** *n* — **im•per•fect•ly** *adv*

**im•pe•ri•al** *adj* **1** : relating to an empire or an emperor **2** : royal

**im•pe•ri•al•ism** *n* : policy of controlling other nations — **im•pe•ri•al•ist** *n or adj* — **im•pe•ri•al•is•tic** *adj* — **im•pe•ri•al•is•ti•cal•ly** *adv*

**im•per•ma•nent** *adj* : not permanent — **im•per•ma•nent•ly** *adv*

**im•per•son•al** *adj* : not involving human personality or emotion — **im•per•son•al•i•ty** *n* — **im•per•son•al•ly** *adv*

**im•per•son•ate** *vb* : assume the character of — **im•per•son•ation** *n* — **im•per•son•a•tor** *n*

**im•per•ti•nent** *adj* **1** : irrelevant **2** : insolent — **im•per•ti•nence** *n* — **im•per•ti•nent•ly** *adv*

**im•per•vi•ous** *adj* : incapable of being penetrated or affected

**im•pe•tus** *n* : driving force

**im•plant** *vb* **1** : set firmly or deeply **2** : fix in the mind or spirit ∼ *n* : something implanted in tissue — **im•plan•ta•tion** *n*

**im•plau•si•ble** *adj* : not plausible — **im•plau•si•bil•i•ty** *n*

**im•ple•ment** *n* : tool, utensil ∼ *vb* : put into practice — **im•ple•men•ta•tion** *n*

**im•pli•cate** *vb* : involve

**im•pli•ca•tion** *n* **1** : an implying **2** : something implied

**im•plic•it** *adj* **1** : understood though only implied **2** : complete and unquestioning — **im•plic•it•ly** *adv*

**im•plode** *vb* : burst inward — **im•plo•sion** *n* — **im•plo•sive** *adj*

**im•ply** *vb* : express indirectly

**im•po•lite** *adj* : not polite

**im•pon•der•able** *adj* : incapable of being precisely evaluated — **im•pon•der•able** *n*

**im•port** *vb* **1** : mean **2** : bring in from an external source ∼ *n* **1** : meaning **2** : importance **3** : something imported — **im•por•ta•tion** *n* — **im•port•er** *n*

**im•por•tant** *adj* : having great worth, significance, or influence — **im•por•tance** *n* — **im•por•tant•ly** *adv*

**im•pose** *vb* **1** : establish as compulsory **2** : take unwarranted advantage of — **im•po•si•tion** *n*

**im•pos•ing** *adj* : impressive — **im•pos•ing•ly** *adv*

**im•pos•si•ble** *adj* **1** : incapable of occurring **2** : enormously difficult — **im•pos•si•bil•i•ty** *n* — **im•pos•si•bly** *adv*

**im•pos•tor, im•pos•ter** *n* : one who assumes an identity or title to deceive — **im•pos•ture** *n*

**im•prac•ti•cal** *adj* : not practical

**im•pre•cise** *adj* : not precise — **im•pre•cise•ly** *adv* — **im•pre•cise•ness** *n* — **im•pre•ci•sion** *n*

**im•preg•nate** *vb* **1** : make pregnant **2** : cause to be filled, permeated, or saturated — **im•preg•na•tion** *n*

**im•press** *vb* **1** : apply with or produce by pressure **2** : press, stamp, or print in or upon **3** : produce a vivid impression of **4** : affect (as the mind) forcibly — **im•pres•sive** *adj* — **im•pres•sive•ly** *adv* — **im•pres•sive•ness** *n* — **im•pres•sion** *n* — **im•pres•sion•able** *adj*

**im•pris•on** *vb* : put in prison — **im•pris•on•ment** *n*

**im•prob•able** *adj* : unlikely to be true or to occur — **im•prob•a•bil•i•ty** *n* — **im•prob•a•bly** *adv*

**im•prop•er** *adj* : not proper — **im•prop•er•ly** *adv*

**im•prove** *vb* : grow or make better — **im•prov•able** *adj* — **im•prove•ment** *n*

**im•pro•vise** *vb* : make, invent, or arrange without prior planning — **im•pro•vi•sa•tion** *n* — **im•pro•vis•er, im•pro•vi•sor** *n*

**im•pu•dent** *adj* : insolent — **im•pu•dence** *n* — **im•pu•dent•ly** *adv*

**im•pugn** *vb* : attack as false

**im•pulse** *n* **1** : moving force **2** : sudden inclination — **im•pul•sive** *adj* — **im•pul•sive•ly** *adv* — **im•pul•sive•ness** *n*

**im•pure** *adj* : not pure — **im•pu•ri•ty** *n*

**in** *prep* **1** : used to indicate location, inclusion, situation, or manner **2** : into **3** : during ∼ *adv* : to or toward the inside ∼ *adj* : located inside

**in•ac•tive** *adj* : not active or in use

**in•an•i•mate** *adj* : not animate or animated — **in•an•i•mate•ly** *adv* — **in•an•i•mate•ness** *n*

**in•au•gu•rate** *vb* **1** : install in office **2** : start — **in•au•gu•ral** *adj* — **in•au•gu•ra•tion** *n*

**in•cal•cu•la•ble** *adj* : too large to be calculated — **in•cal•cu•la•bly** *adv*

**in•can•ta•tion** *n* : use of spoken or sung charms or spells as a magic ritual

**in•ca•pac•i•tate** *vb* : disable

**in•car•cer•ate** *vb* : imprison — **in•car•cer•a•tion** *n*

**in•cen•tive** *n* : inducement to do something

**in•cep•tion** *n* : beginning

**in•ces•sant** *adj* : continuing without interruption — **in•ces•sant•ly** *adv*

**inch** *n* : unit of length equal to ¹⁄₁₂ foot ∼ *vb* : move by small degrees

**in•ci•dent** *n* : occurrence — **in•ci•dence** *n* — **in•ci•dent** *adj*

**in•ci•den•tal** *adj* **1** : subordinate, nonessential, or attendant **2** : met by chance ∼ *n* **1** : something incidental **2** *pl* : minor expenses that are not itemized — **in•ci•den•tal•ly** *adv*

**in•cite** *vb* : arouse to action — **in•cite•ment** *n*

**in•cline** *vb* **1** : bow **2** : tend toward an opinion **3** : slope ∼ *n* : slope — **in•cli•na•tion** *n* — **in•clin•er** *n*

**in•clude** *vb* : take in or comprise — **in•clu•sion** *n* — **in•clu•sive** *adj*

**in•come** *n* : money gained (as from work or investment)

**in•com•pa•ra•ble** *adj* : eminent beyond comparison

**in•com•pe•tent** *adj* : lacking sufficient knowledge or skill — **in•com•pe•tence** *n* — **in•com•pe•ten•cy** *n* — **in•com•pe•tent** *n*

**in•con•ceiv•able** *adj* **1** : impossible to comprehend **2** : unbelievable — **in•con•ceiv•ably** *adv*

**in•con•se•quen•tial** *adj* : not important — **in•con•se•quence** *n* — **in•con•se•quen•tial•ly** *adv*

**in•con•ve•nience** *n* **1** : discomfort **2** : something that causes trouble or annoyance ∼ *vb* : cause inconvenience to

— in·con·ve·nient *adj* — in·con·ve·nient·ly *adv*

**in·cor·po·rate** *vb* **1** : blend **2** : form into a legal body — in·cor·po·rat·ed *adj* — in·cor·po·ra·tion *n*

**in·cor·rect** *adj* : not correct or proper — in·cor·rect·ly *adv*

**in·crease** *vb* : make or become greater ~ *n* **1** : enlargement in size **2** : something added — in·creas·ing·ly *adv*

**in·cred·i·ble** *adj* : too extraordinary to be believed — in·cred·ibil·i·ty *n* — in·cred·i·bly *adv*

**in·crim·i·nate** *vb* : show to be guilty of a crime — in·crim·i·na·tion *n* — in·crim·i·na·to·ry *adj*

**in·cur** *vb* : become liable or subject to

**in·deed** *adv* : without question

**in·def·i·nite** *adj* **1** : not defining or identifying **2** : not precise **3** : having no fixed limit — in·def·i·nite·ly *adv*

**in·den·ta·tion** *n* **1** : notch, recess, or dent **2** : action of indenting **3** : space at the beginning of a paragraph — in·dent *vb*

**Independence Day** *n* : July 4 observed as a legal holiday in commemoration of the adoption of the Declaration of Independence in 1776

**in·de·pen·dent** *adj* **1** : not governed by another **2** : not requiring or relying on something or somebody else **3** : not easily influenced — in·de·pen·dence *n* — in·de·pen·dent *n* — in·de·pen·dent·ly *adv*

**in·dex** *n* **1** : alphabetical list of items (as topics in a book) **2** : a number that serves as a measure or indicator of something ~ *vb* **1** : provide with an index **2** : serve as an index of

**in·di·cate** *vb* **1** : point out or to **2** : show indirectly **3** : state briefly — in·di·ca·tion *n* — in·dic·a·tive *adj* — in·di·ca·tor *n*

**in·dict** *vb* : charge with a crime — in·dict·able *adj* — in·dict·ment *n*

**in·dif·fer·ent** *adj* **1** : having no preference **2** : showing neither interest nor dislike **3** : mediocre — in·dif·fer·ence *n* — in·dif·fer·ent·ly *adv*

**in·dig·e·nous** *adj* : native to a particular region

**in·di·ges·tion** *n* : discomfort from inability to digest food

**in·dig·na·tion** *n* : anger aroused by something unjust or unworthy — in·dig·nant *adj* — in·dig·nant·ly *adv* — in·dig·ni·ty *n*

**in·di·rect** *adj* : not straight or straightforward — in·di·rec·tion *n* — in·di·rect·ly *adv* — in·di·rect·ness *n*

**in·dis·crim·i·nate** *adj* **1** : not careful or discriminating **2** : haphazard — in·dis·crim·i·nate·ly *adv*

**in·dis·tinct** *adj* : not clearly recognizable or understandable — in·dis·tinct·ly *adv*

**in·di·vid·u·al** *n* **1** : single member of a category **2** : person — in·di·vid·u·al *adj* — in·di·vid·u·al·i·ty *n* — in·di·vid·u·al·ly *adv*

**in·di·vid·u·al·ize** *vb* **1** : make individual **2** : treat individually

**in·doc·tri·nate** *vb* : instruct in fundamentals (as of a doctrine) — in·doc·tri·na·tion *n*

**in·doors** *adv* : in or into a building

**in·duce** *vb* **1** : persuade **2** : bring about — in·duce·ment *n* — in·duc·er *n*

**in·duct** *vb* **1** : put in office **2** : admit as a member **3** : enroll (as for military service) — in·duct·ee *n* — in·duc·tion *n*

**in·dulge** *vb* : yield to the desire of or for — in·dul·gence *n* — in·dul·gent *adj* — in·dul·gent·ly *adv*

**in·dus·tri·ous** *adj* : diligent or busy — in·dus·tri·ous·ly *adv* — in·dus·tri·ous·ness *n*

**in·dus·try** *n* **1** : diligence **2** : manufacturing enterprises or activity — in·dus·tri·al *adj* — in·dus·tri·al·ist *n* — in·dus·tri·al·iza·tion *n* — in·dus·tri·al·ize *vb* — in·dus·tri·al·ly *adv*

**in·ept** *adj* **1** : inappropriate or foolish **2** : generally incompetent — in·ep·ti·tude *n* — in·ept·ly *adv* — in·ept·ness *n*

**in·equal·i·ty** *n* : quality of being unequal or uneven

**in·ert** *adj* **1** : powerless to move or act **2** : sluggish — in·ert·ly *adv* — in·ert·ness *n*

**in·ev·i·ta·ble** *adj* : incapable of being avoided or escaped — in·ev·i·ta·bil·i·ty *n* — in·ev·i·ta·bly *adv*

**in·ex·cus·able** *adj* : being without excuse or justification — in·ex·cus·ably *adv*

**in·fa·mous** *adj* : having the worst kind of reputation — in·fa·mous·ly *adv* — in·fa·my *n*

**in·fant** *n* : baby — in·fan·cy *n* — in·fan·tile *adj*

**in·fat·u·ate** *vb* : inspire with foolish love or admiration — in·fat·u·a·tion *n*

**in·fect** *vb* : contaminate with disease-producing matter — in·fec·tion *n* — in·fec·tious *adj* — in·fec·tive *adj*

**in·fer** *vb* : deduce — in·fer·ence *n* — in·fer·en·tial *adj*

**in·fe·ri·or** *adj* **1** : being lower in position, degree, rank, or merit **2** : of lesser quality — inferior *n* — in·fe·ri·or·i·ty *n*

**in·fest** *vb* : swarm or grow in or over — in·fes·ta·tion *n*

**in·fi·del·i·ty** *n* : lack of faithfulness

**in·fil·trate** *vb* : enter or become established in without being noticed — in·fil·tra·tion *n*

**in·fi·nite** *adj* **1** : having no limit or extending indefinitely **2** : vast — in·fi·nite *n* — in·fi·nite·ly *adv* — in·fin·i·tude *n*

**in·fin·i·tive** *n* : verb form in English usu. used with *to*

**in·fin·i·ty** *n* **1** : quality or state of being infinite **2** : indefinitely great number or amount

**in·flame** *vb* **1** : excite to intense action or feeling **2** : affect or become affected with red and painful response to injury — in·flam·ma·tion *n* — in·flam·ma·to·ry *adj*

**in·flam·ma·ble** *adj* : flammable

**in·flate** *vb* **1** : swell or puff up (as with gas) **2** : expand or increase abnormally — in·flat·able *adj*

**in·fla·tion** *n* **1** : act of inflating **2** : continual rise in prices — in·fla·tion·ary *adj*

**in·flec·tion** *n* **1** : change in pitch or loudness of the voice **2** : change in form of a word — in·flect *vb* — in·flec·tion·al *adj*

**in·flu·ence** *n* **1** : power or capacity of causing an effect in indirect or intangible ways **2** : one that exerts influence ~ *vb* : affect or alter by influence — in·flu·en·tial *adj*

**in·flux** *n* : a flowing in

**in·form** *vb* : give information or knowledge to — in·for·mant *n* — in·for·ma·tion *n* — in·for·ma·tion·al *adj* — in·for·ma·tive *adj* — in·form·er *n*

**in·for·mal** *adj* **1** : without formality or ceremony **2** : for ordinary or familiar use — in·for·mal·i·ty *n* — in·for·mal·ly *adv*

**in·fringe** *vb* : violate another's right or privilege — in·fringe·ment *n*

**in·fu·ri·ate** *vb* : make furious — in·fu·ri·at·ing·ly *adv*

**in·ge·nious** *adj* : very clever — in·ge·nious·ly *adv* — in·ge·nious·ness *n*

**in·ge·nu·ity** *n* : skill or cleverness in planning or inventing

**in·gen·u·ous** *adj* : innocent and candid — in·gen·u·ous·ly *adv* — in·gen·u·ous·ness *n*

**in·gre·di·ent** *n* : one of the substances that make up a mixture

**in·hab·it** *vb* : live or dwell in — in·hab·it·able *adj* — in·hab·it·ant *n*

**in·hale** *vb* : breathe in — in·hal·ant *n* — in·ha·la·tion *n* — in·hal·er *n*

**in·her·ent** *adj* : being an essential part of something — in·her·ent·ly *adv*

**in·her·it** *vb* : receive from one's ancestors — in·her·it·able *adj* — in·her·i·tance *n* — in·her·i·tor *n*

**in·hib·it** *vb* : hold in check — in·hi·bi·tion *n*

**in·hu·man** *adj* : cruel or impersonal — in·hu·man·i·ty *n* — in·hu·man·ly *adv* — in·hu·man·ness *n*

**ini·tial** *adj* **1** : of or relating to the beginning **2** : first ~ *n* : 1st letter of a word or name ~ *vb* : put initials on — ini·tial·ly *adv*

**ini·ti·ate** *vb* **1** : start **2** : induct into membership **3** : instruct in the rudiments of something — ini·ti·ate *n* — ini·ti·a·tion *n* — ini·tia·to·ry *adj*

**ini·tia·tive** *n* **1** : first step **2** : readiness to undertake something on one's own

**in·ject** *vb* : force or introduce into something — in·jec·tion *n*

**in·junc·tion** *n* : court writ requiring one to do or to refrain from doing a specified act

**in·jure** *vb* : do damage, hurt, or a wrong to

**in·ju·ry** *n* **1** : act that injures **2** : hurt, damage, or loss sustained — in·ju·ri·ous *adj*

**in·jus·tice** *n* : unjust act

**ink** *n* : usu. liquid and colored material for writing and printing ~ *vb* : put ink on — ink·well *n* — inky *adj*

**in–law** *n* : relative by marriage

**in·lay** *vb* : set into a surface for decoration ~ *n* **1** : inlaid work **2** : shaped filling cemented into a tooth

**inn** *n* : hotel — inn·keep·er *n*

**in·ner** *adj* : being on the inside

**in·no·cent** *adj* **1** : free from guilt **2** : harmless **3** : not sophisticated — in·no·cence *n* — in·no·cent *n* — in·no·cent·ly *adv*

**in·no·va·tion** *n* : new idea or method — in·no·vate *vb* — in·no·va·tive *adj* — in·no·va·tor *n*

**in·or·di·nate** *adj* : unusual or excessive — in·or·di·nate·ly *adv*

**in·or·gan·ic** *adj* : made of mineral matter

**in·put** *n* : something put in — in·put *vb*

**in·quire** *vb* **1** : ask **2** : investigate — in·quir·er *n* — in·quir·ing·ly *adv* — in·qui·ry *n*

**in·quis·i·tive** *adj* : curious — in·quis·i·tive·ly *adv* — in·quis·i·tive·ness *n*

**in·sane** *adj* **1** : not sane **2** : absurd — in·sane·ly *adv* — in·san·i·ty *n*

**in·scribe** *vb* **1** : write **2** : engrave **3** : dedicate (a book) to someone — in·scrip·tion *n*

**in·sect** *n* : small usu. winged animal with 6 legs

**in·sec·ti·cide** *n* : insect poison — in·sec·ti·cid·al *adj*

**in·se·cure** *adj* **1** : not certain **2** : not safe **3** : fearful — in·se·cure·ly *adv* — in·se·cu·ri·ty *n*

**in·sen·si·ble** *adj* **1** : unconscious **2** : unable to feel **3** : unaware — in·sen·si·bil·i·ty *n* — in·sen·si·bly *adv*

**in·sert** *vb* : put in — in·sert *n* — in·ser·tion *n*

**in·side** *n* **1** : inner side **2** *pl* : internal organs ~ *prep* **1** : in or into the inside of **2** : within ~ *adv* **1** : on the inner side **2** : into the interior — in·side *adj* — in·sid·er *n*

**in·sight** *n* : understanding — in·sight·ful *adj*

**in·sin·u·ate** *vb* **1** : imply **2** : bring in artfully — in·sin·u·a·tion *n*

**in·sist** *vb* : be firmly demanding — in·sis·tence *n* — in·sis·tent *adj* — in·sis·tent·ly *adv*

**in·so·lent** *adj* : bold and contemptuous — in·so·lence *n*

**in·sol·vent** *adj* : unable or insufficient to pay debts — in·sol·ven·cy *n*

**in·som·nia** *n* : inability to sleep — in·som·ni·ac *n*

**in·spect** *vb* : view closely and critically — in·spec·tion *n* — in·spec·tor *n*

**in·spire** *vb* **1** : inhale **2** : influence by example **3** : bring about **4** : stir to action — in·spi·ra·tion *n* — in·spi·ra·tion·al *adj* — in·spir·er *n*

**in·stall, in·stal** *vb* **1** : induct into office **2** : set up for use — in·stal·la·tion *n*

**in·stall·ment** *n* : partial payment

**in·stance** *n* **1** : request or instigation **2** : example

**in·stant** *n* : moment ~ *adj* **1** : immediate **2** : ready to mix — in·stan·ta·neous *adj* — in·stan·ta·neous·ly *adv* — in·stant·ly *adv*

**in·stead** *adv* : as a substitute or alternative

**instead of** *prep* : as a substitute for or alternative to

**in·stinct** *n* **1** : natural talent **2** : natural inherited or subconsciously motivated behavior — in·stinc·tive *adj* — in·stinc·tive·ly *adv* — in·stinc·tu·al *adj*

**in·sti·tute** *vb* : establish, start, or organize ~ *n* **1** : organization promoting a cause **2** : school

**in·sti·tu·tion** *n* **1** : act of instituting **2** : custom **3** : corporation or society of a public character — in·sti·tu·tion·al *adj* — in·sti·tu·tion·al·ize *vb* — in·sti·tu·tion·al·ly *adv*

**in·struct** *vb* **1** : teach **2** : give an order to — in·struc·tion *n* — in·struc·tion·al *adj* — in·struc·tive *adj* — in·struc·tor *n* — in·struc·tor·ship *n*

**in·stru·ment** *n* **1** : something that produces music **2** : means **3** : device for doing work and esp. precision work **4** : legal document — in·stru·men·tal *adj* — in·stru·men·tal·ist *n* — in·stru·men·tal·i·ty *n* — in·stru·men·ta·tion *n*

**in·su·late** *vb* : protect from heat loss or electricity — in·su·la·tion *n* — in·su·la·tor *n*

**in·sult** *vb* : treat with contempt ~ *n* : insulting act or remark — in·sult·ing·ly *adv*

**in·sure** *vb* **1** : guarantee against loss **2** : make certain — in·sur·able *adj* — in·sur·ance *n* — in·sured *n* — in·sur·er *n*

**in·tact** *adj* : not damaged

**in·take** *n* **1** : opening through which something enters **2** : act of taking in **3** : amount taken in

**in·te·ger** *n* : number that is not a fraction and does not include a fraction

**in·te·grate** *vb* **1** : unite **2** : end segregation of or at — in·te·gra·tion *n*

**in·teg·ri·ty** *n* **1** : soundness **2** : adherence to a code of values **3** : completeness

**in·tel·lect** *n* : power of knowing or thinking — in·tel·lec·tu·al *adj or n* — in·tel·lec·tu·al·ism *n* — in·tel·lec·tu·al·ly *adv*

**in·tel·li·gence** *n* **1** : ability to learn and understand **2** : mental acuteness **3** : information — in·tel·li·gent *adj* — in·tel·li·gent·ly *adv*

**in·tend** *vb* : have as a purpose — in·tend·ed *n or adj*

**in·tense** *adj* **1** : extreme **2** : deeply felt — in·tense·ly *adv* — in·ten·si·fi·ca·tion *n* — in·ten·si·fy *vb* — in·ten·si·ty *n* — in·ten·sive *adj* — in·ten·sive·ly *adv*

**¹in·tent** *n* : purpose — in·ten·tion *n* — in·ten·tion·al *adj* — in·ten·tion·al·ly *adv*

**²in·tent** *adj* : concentrated — in·tent·ly *adv* — in·tent·ness *n*

**in·ter·ac·tion** *n* : mutual influence — in·ter·act *vb* — in·ter·ac·tive *adj*

**in·ter·breed** *vb* : breed together

**in·ter·cede** *vb* : act to reconcile — in·ter·ces·sion *n* — in·ter·ces·sor *n*

**in·ter·cept** *vb* : interrupt the progress of — in·ter·cept *n* — in·ter·cep·tion *n* — in·ter·cep·tor *n*

**in·ter·change** *vb* **1** : exchange **2** : change places ~ *n* **1** : exchange **2** : junction of highways — in·ter·change·able *adj*

**in·ter·est** *n* **1** : right **2** : benefit **3** : charge for borrowed money **4** : readiness to pay special attention **5** : quality that causes interest ~ *vb* **1** : concern **2** : get the attention of — in·ter·est·ing *adj* — in·ter·est·ing·ly *adv*

**in·ter·fere** vb 1 : collide or be in opposition 2 : try to run the affairs of others — **in·ter·fer·ence** n

**in·te·ri·or** adj : being on the inside ∼ n 1 : inside 2 : inland area

**in·ter·jec·tion** n : an exclamatory word — **in·ter·jec·tion·al·ly** adv

**in·ter·lock** vb 1 : unite by or as by lacing together 2 : connect for mutual effect — **in·ter·lock** n

**in·ter·me·di·ary** n : agent between individuals or groups — **intermediary** adj

**in·ter·me·di·ate** adj : between extremes — **in·ter·me·di·ate** n

**in·ter·mis·sion** n : break in a performance

**in·ter·mix** vb : mix together — **in·ter·mix·ture** n

**in·tern** n : advanced student (as in medicine) gaining supervised experience ∼ vb : act as an intern — **in·tern·ship** n

**in·ter·nal** adj 1 : inward 2 : inside of the body 3 : relating to or existing in the mind — **in·ter·nal·ly** adv

**in·ter·na·tion·al** adj : affecting 2 or more nations ∼ n : something having international scope — **in·ter·na·tion·al·ism** n — **in·ter·na·tion·al·ize** vb — **in·ter·na·tion·al·ly** adv

**In·ter·net** n : network that connects computer networks worldwide

**in·ter·pret** vb : explain the meaning of — **in·ter·pre·ta·tion** n — **in·ter·pre·ta·tive** adj — **in·ter·pret·er** n — **in·ter·pre·tive** adj

**in·ter·ro·gate** vb : question — **in·ter·ro·ga·tion** n — **in·ter·rog·a·tive** adj or n — **in·ter·ro·ga·tor** n — **in·ter·rog·a·to·ry** adj

**in·ter·rupt** vb : intrude so as to hinder or end continuity — **in·ter·rupt·er** n — **in·ter·rup·tion** n — **in·ter·rup·tive** adv

**in·ter·sect** vb 1 : cut across or divide 2 : cross — **in·ter·sec·tion** n

**in·ter·twine** vb : twist together — **in·ter·twine·ment** n

**in·ter·val** n 1 : time between 2 : space between

**in·ter·vene** vb 1 : happen between events 2 : intercede — **in·ter·ven·tion** n

**in·ter·view** n : a meeting to get information — **in·ter·view** vb — **in·ter·view·er** n

**in·tes·tine** n : tubular part of the digestive system after the stomach including a long narrow upper part (**small intestine**) followed by a broader shorter

lower part (**large intestine**) — **in·tes·ti·nal** adj

**in·ti·mate** vb : hint ∼ adj 1 : very friendly 2 : suggesting privacy 3 : very personal ∼ n : close friend — **in·ti·ma·cy** n — **in·ti·mate·ly** adv — **in·ti·ma·tion** n

**in·tim·i·date** vb : make fearful — **in·tim·i·da·tion** n

**in·to** prep 1 : to the inside of 2 : to the condition of 3 : against

**in·to·na·tion** n : way of singing or speaking

**in·tox·i·cate** vb : make drunk — **in·tox·i·cant** n or adj — **in·tox·i·ca·tion** n

**in·tri·cate** adj : very complex and delicate — **in·tri·ca·cy** n — **in·tri·cate·ly** adv

**in·trigue** vb 1 : scheme 2 : arouse curiosity of ∼ n : secret scheme — **in·trigu·ing·ly** adv

**in·tro·duce** vb 1 : bring in esp. for the 1st time 2 : cause to be acquainted 3 : bring to notice 4 : put in — **in·tro·duc·tion** n — **in·tro·duc·to·ry** adj

**in·tro·vert** n : shy or reserved person — **in·tro·ver·sion** n — **in·tro·vert** adj — **in·tro·vert·ed** adj

**in·trude** vb 1 : thrust in 2 : go beyond usual or proper limits — **in·trud·er** n — **in·tru·sion** n — **in·tru·sive** adj — **in·tru·sive·ness** n

**in·tu·i·tion** n : quick and ready insight — **in·tu·it** vb — **in·tu·i·tive** adj — **in·tu·i·tive·ly** adv

**in·vade** vb : enter for conquest — **in·vad·er** n — **in·va·sion** n

¹**in·val·id** adj : not true or legal — **in·va·lid·i·ty** n — **in·val·id·ly** adv

²**in·va·lid** adj : sickly ∼ n : one chronically ill

**in·val·i·date** vb : make invalid — **in·val·i·da·tion** n

**in·valu·able** adj : extremely valuable

**in·vent** vb 1 : think up 2 : create for the 1st time — **in·ven·tion** n — **in·ven·tive** adj — **in·ven·tive·ness** n — **in·ven·tor** n

**in·ven·to·ry** n 1 : list of goods 2 : stock — **in·ven·to·ry** vb

**in·vert** vb 1 : turn upside down or inside out 2 : reverse — **in·ver·sion** n

**in·ver·te·brate** adj : lacking a backbone ∼ n : invertebrate animal

**in·vest** vb 1 : give power or authority to 2 : endow with a quality 3 : commit money to someone else's use in hope of profit — **in·vest·ment** n — **in·ves·tor** n

**in·ves·ti·gate** vb : study closely and systematically — **in·ves·ti·ga·tion** n — **in·ves·ti·ga·tive** adj — **in·ves·ti·ga·tor** n

**in·vig·o·rate** vb : give life and energy to — **in·vig·o·ra·tion** n

**in·vis·i·ble** adj : not visible

**in·vite** vb 1 : entice 2 : increase the likelihood of 3 : request the presence or participation of 4 : encourage — **in·vi·ta·tion** n — **in·vit·ing** adj

**in·vo·ca·tion** n 1 : prayer 2 : incantation

**in·voice** n : itemized bill for goods shipped ∼ vb : bill

**in·vol·un·tary** adj : done without control or choice — **in·vol·un·tari·ly** adv

**in·volve** vb 1 : draw in as a participant 2 : relate closely 3 : require as a necessary part 4 : occupy fully — **in·volve·ment** n

**in·volved** adj : intricate

**inward, in·wards** adv : toward the inside, center, or inner being — **in·ward·ly** adv

**io·dine** n 1 : nonmetallic chemical element 2 : solution of iodine used as an antiseptic

**ion** n : electrically charged particle — **ion·ic** adj — **ion·iz·able** adj — **ion·i·za·tion** n — **ion·ize** vb — **ion·iz·er** n

**IOU** n : acknowledgment of a debt

**irate** adj : aroused to intense anger — **irate·ly** adv

**ire** n : anger

**iris** n 1 : colored part around the pupil of the eye 2 : plant with long leaves and large showy flowers

**irk** vb : annoy — **irk·some** adj — **irk·some·ly** adv

**iron** n 1 : heavy metallic chemical element 2 : something made of iron 3 : heated device for pressing clothes 4 : hardness, determination ∼ vb : press or smooth out with an iron — **iron·ware** n — **iron·work** n — **iron·work·er** n — **iron·works** n pl

**iro·ny** n 1 : use of words to express the opposite of the literal meaning 2 : incongruity between the actual and expected result of events — **iron·ic, iron·i·cal** adj — **iron·i·cal·ly** adv

**ir·ra·tio·nal** adj 1 : incapable of reasoning 2 : not based on reason — **ir·ra·tio·nal·i·ty** n — **ir·ra·tio·nal·ly** adv

**ir·reg·u·lar** adj : not regular or normal — **ir·reg·u·lar** n — **ir·reg·u·lar·i·ty** n — **ir·reg·u·lar·ly** adv

**ir·rel·e·vant** adj : not relevant — **ir·rel·e·vance** n

**ir·re·place·able** adj : not replaceable

**ir·re·sist·ible** adj : impossible to successfully resist — **ir·re·sist·ibly** adv

**ir·re·spon·si·ble** adj : not responsible — **ir·re·spon·si·bil·i·ty** n — **ir·re·spon·si·bly** adv

**ir·rev·er·ence** n 1 : lack of reverence 2 : irreverent act or utterance — **ir·rev·er·ent** adj

**ir·re·vers·ible** adj : incapable of being reversed

**ir·ri·gate** vb : supply with water by artificial means — **ir·ri·ga·tion** n

**ir·ri·tate** vb 1 : excite to anger 2 : make sore or inflamed — **ir·ri·ta·bil·i·ty** n — **ir·ri·ta·ble** adj — **ir·ri·ta·bly** adv — **ir·ri·tant** adj or n — **ir·ri·tat·ing·ly** adv — **ir·ri·ta·tion** n

**is** pres 3d sing of BE

**Is·lam** n : religious faith of Muslims — **Is·lam·ic** adj

**is·land** n : body of land surrounded by water — **is·land·er** n

**isle** n : small island

**iso·late** vb : place or keep by itself — **iso·la·tion** n

**isos·ce·les** adj : having 2 equal sides

**is·sue** vb 1 : go, come, or flow out 2 : descend from a specified ancestor 3 : emanate or result 4 : put forth or distribute officially ∼ n 1 : action of issuing 2 : offspring 3 : result 4 : point of controversy 5 : act of giving out or printing 6 : quantity given out or printed — **is·su·ance** n — **is·su·er** n

**it** pron 1 : that one — used of a lifeless thing or an abstract entity 2 — used as an anticipatory subject or object ∼ n : player who tries to catch others (as in a game of tag)

**itch** n 1 : uneasy irritating skin sensation 2 : skin disorder 3 : persistent desire — **itch** vb — **itchy** adj

**item** n 1 : particular in a list, account, or series 2 : piece of news — **item·iza·tion** n — **item·ize** vb

**itin·er·ary** n : route or outline of a journey

**its** adj : relating to it

**it·self** pron : it — used reflexively or for emphasis

**ivo·ry** n 1 : hard creamy-white material of elephants' tusks 2 : pale yellow color

**ivy** n : trailing woody vine with evergreen leaves

# J

**j** n : 10th letter of the alphabet

**jab** vb : thrust quickly or abruptly ∼ n : short straight punch

**jab·ber** vb : talk rapidly or unintelligibly — **jabber** n

**jack** n 1 : mechanical device to raise a heavy body 2 : small flag 3 : small 6-pointed metal object used in a game (**jacks**) 4 : electrical socket ∼ vb 1 : raise with a jack 2 : increase

**jack·ass** n 1 : male ass 2 : stupid person

**jack·et** n : garment for the upper body

**jack·ham·mer** n : pneumatic tool for drilling

**jack·knife** n jack·knives : pocketknife ∼ vb : fold like a jackknife

**jack-o'-lan·tern** n : lantern made of a carved pumpkin

**jack·pot** n : sum of money won

**jade** n : usu. green gemstone

**jad·ed** adj : dulled or bored by having too much

**jag·ged** adj : sharply notched

**jail** n : prison — **jail** vb — **jail·break** n — **jail·er, jail·or** n

**ja·la·pe·ño** n : Mexican hot pepper

**jam** vb 1 : press into a tight position 2 : cause to become wedged and unworkable ∼ n 1 : crowded mass that

blocks or impedes 2 : difficult situation 3 : thick sweet food made of cooked fruit

**jan·gle** vb : make a harsh ringing sound — **jangle** n

**jan·i·tor** n : person who has the care of a building — **jan·i·to·ri·al** adj

**Jan·u·ary** n : 1st month of the year having 31 days

¹**jar** vb 1 : have a harsh or disagreeable effect 2 : vibrate or shake ∼ n 1 : jolt 2 : painful effect

²**jar** n : wide-mouthed container

**jar·gon** n : special vocabulary of a group

**jaw** n 1 : either of the bony or cartilaginous structures that support the mouth 2 : one of 2 movable parts for holding or crushing ∼ vb : talk indignantly or at length — **jaw·bone** n — **jawed** adj

**jay** n : noisy brightly colored bird

**jay·walk** vb : cross a street carelessly — **jay·walk·er** n

**jazz** vb : enliven ∼ n 1 : kind of American music involving improvisation 2 : empty talk — **jazzy** adj

**jeal·ous** adj : suspicious of a rival or of one believed to enjoy an advantage — **jeal·ous·ly** adv — **jeal·ou·sy** n

**jeans** n pl : pants made of durable twilled cotton cloth

**jeep** n : 4-wheel army vehicle

**jeer** vb 1 : speak or cry out in derision 2 : ridicule ∼ n : taunt

**Je·ho·vah** n : God

**jell** vb 1 : come to the consistency of jelly 2 : take shape

**jel·ly** n : a substance (as food) with a soft somewhat elastic consistency — **jelly** vb

**jel·ly·fish** n : sea animal with a saucer-shaped jellylike body

**jeop·ar·dize** vb : exposure to death, loss, or injury — **jeop·ar·dy** n

**jerk** vb 1 : give a sharp quick push, pull, or twist 2 : move in short abrupt motions ∼ n 1 : short quick pull or twist 2 : stupid or foolish person — **jerk·i·ly** adv — **jerky** adj

**jest** n : witty remark — **jest** vb

**jest·er** n : one employed to entertain a court

**jet** vb 1 : spout or emit in a stream 2 : travel by jet ∼ n 1 : forceful rush of fluid through a narrow opening 2 : jet-propelled airplane

**jet–pro·pelled** adj : driven by an engine (**jet engine**) that produces propulsion

(**jet propulsion**) by the rearward discharge of a jet of fluid

**Jew** n : one whose religion is Judaism — **Jew·ish** adj

**jew·el** n 1 : ornament of precious metal 2 : gem ∼ vb : adorn with jewels — **jew·el·er, jew·el·ler** n — **jew·el·ry** n

**jibe** vb : be in agreement

**jif·fy** n : short time

**jig·gle** vb : move with quick little jerks — **jiggle** n

**jilt** vb : drop (a lover) without apparent feelings

**jim·my** n : small crowbar ∼ vb : pry open

**jin·gle** vb : make a light tinkling sound ∼ n 1 : light tinkling sound 2 : short verse or song

**jinx** n : one that brings bad luck — **jinx** vb

**jit·ters** n pl : extreme nervousness — **jit·tery** adj

**job** n 1 : something that has to be done 2 : regular employment — **job·hold·er** n — **job·less** adj

**jock·ey** n : one who rides a horse in a race ∼ vb : manipulate or maneuver adroitly

**jog** vb 1 : give a slight shake or push to 2 : run or ride at a slow pace ∼ n 1 : slight shake 2 : slow pace — **jog·ger** n

**join** *vb* **1** : come or bring together **2** : become a member of — **join•er** *n*

**joint** *n* **1** : point of contact between bones **2** : place where 2 parts connect **3** : often disreputable place ~ *adj* : common to 2 or more — **joint•ed** *adj* — **joint•ly** *adv*

**joke** *n* : something said or done to provoke laughter ~ *vb* : make jokes — **jok•er** *n* — **jok•ing•ly** *adv*

**jol•ly** *adj* : full of high spirits — **jol•li•ty** *n*

**jolt** *vb* **1** : move with a sudden jerky motion **2** : give a jolt to ~ *n* **1** : abrupt jerky blow or movement **2** : sudden shock — **jolt•er** *n*

**jos•tle** *vb* : push or shove

**jot** *n* : least bit ~ *vb* : write briefly and hurriedly

**jour•nal** *n* **1** : brief account of daily events **2** : periodical (as a newspaper) — **jour•nal•ism** *n* — **jour•nal•ist** *n* — **jour•nal•is•tic** *adj*

**jour•ney** *n* : a going from one place to another ~ *vb* : make a journey

**joy** *n* **1** : feeling of happiness **2** : source of happiness — **joy** *vb* — **joy•ful** *adj* — **joy•ful•ly** *adv* — **joy•less** *adj*

**joy•ous** *adj* — **joy•ous•ly** *adv* — **joy•ous•ness** *n*

**joy•ride** *n* : reckless ride for pleasure — **joy•rid•er** *n* — **joy•rid•ing** *n*

**ju•bi•lant** *adj* : expressing great joy — **ju•bi•lant•ly** *adv* — **ju•bi•la•tion** *n*

**Ju•da•ism** *n* : religion developed among the ancient Hebrews — **Ju•da•ic** *adj*

**judge** *vb* **1** : form an opinion **2** : decide as a judge ~ *n* **1** : public official authorized to decide questions brought before a court **2** : one who gives an authoritative opinion — **judg•ment, judge•ment** *n* — **judg•men•tal** *adj* — **judg•men•tal•ly** *adv* — **judge•ship** *n*

**ju•di•cial** *adj* : relating to the judiciary — **ju•di•cial•ly** *adv*

**ju•di•cia•ry** *n* : system of courts of law or the judges of them — **ju•di•cial** *adj* — **ju•di•cial•ly** *adv* — **ju•di•cia•ry** *n*

**ju•di•cious** *adj* : having or characterized by sound judgment — **ju•di•cious•ly** *adv*

**ju•do** *n* : form of wrestling — **ju•do•ist** *n*

**jug** *n* : large deep container with a narrow mouth and a handle

**jug•gle** *vb* **1** : keep several objects in motion in the air at the same time **2** : manipulate for an often tricky purpose — **jug•gler** *n*

**juice** *n* **1** : extractable fluid contents of cells or tissues **2** : electricity — **juic•er** *n* — **juic•i•ly** *adv* — **juic•i•ness** *n* — **juicy** *adj*

**ju•jube** *n* : gummy candy

**juke•box** *n* : coin-operated machine for playing music recordings

**Ju•ly** *n* : 7th month of the year having 31 days

**jum•ble** *vb* : mix in a confused mass — **jumble** *n*

**jum•bo** *n* : very large version — **jum•bo** *adj*

**jump** *vb* **1** : rise into or through the air esp. by muscular effort **2** : pass over **3** : give a start **4** : rise or increase sharply ~ *n* **1** : a jumping **2** : sharp sudden increase **3** : initial advantage

**¹jump•er** *n* : one that jumps

**²jumper** *n* : sleeveless one-piece dress

**jumpy** *adj* : nervous or jittery

**junc•tion** *n* **1** : a joining **2** : place or point of meeting

**June** *n* : 6th month of the year having 30 days

**jun•gle** *n* : thick tangled mass of tropical vegetation

**ju•nior** *n* **1** : person who is younger or of lower rank than another **2** : student in the next-to-last year ~ *adj* : younger or lower in rank

**junk** *n* **1** : discarded articles **2** : shoddy product ~ *vb* : discard or scrap — **junky** *adj*

**ju•ris•dic•tion** *n* **1** : right or authority to interpret and apply the law **2** : limits within which authority may be exercised — **ju•ris•dic•tion•al** *adj*

**ju•ry** *n* : body of persons sworn to give a verdict on a matter — **ju•ror** *n*

**just** *adj* **1** : reasonable **2** : correct or proper **3** : morally or legally right **4** : deserved ~ *adv* **1** : exactly **2** : very recently **3** : barely **4** : only **5** : quite **6** : possibly — **just•ly** *adv* — **just•ness** *n*

**jus•tice** *n* **1** : administration of what is just **2** : judge **3** : administration of law **4** : fairness

**jus•ti•fy** *vb* : prove to be just, right, or reasonable — **jus•ti•fi•able** *adj* — **jus•ti•fi•ca•tion** *n*

**ju•ve•nile** *adj* : relating to children or young people ~ *n* : young person

# K

**k** *n* : 11th letter of the alphabet

**ka•lei•do•scope** *n* : device containing loose bits of colored material reflecting in many patterns — **ka•lei•do•scop•ic** *adj* — **ka•lei•do•scop•i•cal•ly** *adv*

**kan•ga•roo** *n* : large leaping Australian mammal

**kar•a•o•ke** *n* : device that plays accompaniments for singers

**kar•at** *n* : unit of gold content

**ka•ra•te** *n* : art of self-defense by crippling kicks and punches

**keen** *adj* **1** : sharp **2** : severe **3** : enthusiastic **4** : mentally alert — **keen•ly** *adv* — **keen•ness** *n*

**keep** *vb* (**kept; kept**) **1** : perform **2** : guard **3** : maintain **4** : retain in one's possession **5** : detain **6** : continue in good condition **7** : refrain ~ *n* **1** : fortress **2** : means by which one is kept — **keep•er** *n*

**keep•sake** *n* : souvenir

**keg** *n* : small cask or barrel

**ken•nel** *n* : dog shelter — **ken•nel** *vb*

**ker•nel** *n* **1** : inner softer part of a seed or nut **2** : whole seed of a cereal **3** : central part

**ketch•up** *n* : spicy tomato sauce

**ket•tle** *n* : vessel for boiling liquids

**key** *n* **1** : usu. metal piece to open a lock **2** : explanation **3** : lever pressed by a finger in playing an instrument or operating a machine **4** : leading individual or principle **5** : system of musical tones or pitch ~ *vb* : cause to be in tune ~

*adj* : basic — **key•hole** *n* — **key up** *vb* : make nervous

**key•board** *n* : arrangement of keys

**kha•ki** *n* : light yellowish brown color

**kick** *vb* **1** : strike out or hit with the foot **2** : object strongly ~ *n* : thrust with the foot **2** : stimulating effect — **kick•er** *n*

**kid** *n* **1** : young goat **2** : child ~ *vb* **1** : deceive as a joke **2** : tease — **kid•der** *n* — **kid•ding•ly** *adv*

**kid•nap** *vb* : carry a person away by illegal force — **kid•nap•per, kid•nap•er** *n*

**kid•ney** *n* : either of a pair of organs that excrete urine

**kill** *vb* **1** : deprive of life **2** : finish **3** : use up (time) ~ *n* : act of killing — **kill•er** *n*

**ki•lo** *n* : kilogram

**ki•lo•gram** *n* : metric unit of weight equal to 2.2 pounds

**ki•lo•hertz** *n* : 1000 hertz

**ki•lo•me•ter** *n* : 1000 meters

**kilo•watt** *n* : 1000 watts

**kin** *n* **1** : one's relatives **2** : kinsman

**kind** *n* **1** : essential quality **2** : group with common traits **3** : variety ~ *adj* **1** : of a sympathetic nature **2** : arising from sympathy — **kind•heart•ed** *adj* — **kind•ness** *n*

**kin•der•gar•ten** *n* : class for young children — **kin•der•gart•ner** *n*

**kin•dle** *vb* **1** : set on fire or start burning **2** : stir up — **kin•dling** *n*

**kind•ly** *adj* : of a sympathetic nature ~

*adv* **1** : sympathetically **2** : courteously — **kind•li•ness** *n*

**kin•folk, kinfolks** *n pl* : kin — **kins•man** *n* — **kins•wom•an** *n*

**king** *n* : male sovereign — **king•dom** *n* — **king•less** *adj* — **king•ly** *adj* — **king•ship** *n*

**kink** *n* **1** : short tight twist or curl **2** : cramp — **kinky** *adj*

**kin•ship** *n* : relationship

**kiss** *vb* : touch with the lips as a mark of affection — **kiss** *n*

**kit** *n* : set of articles (as tools or parts)

**kitch•en** *n* : room with cooking facilities

**kite** *n* **1** : small hawk **2** : covered framework flown at the end of a string

**kit•ten** *n* : young cat — **kit•ten•ish** *adj*

**¹kit•ty** *n* : kitten

**²kitty** *n* : fund or pool (as in a card game)

**kit•ty-cor•ner, kit•ty-cor•nered** *var of* CATERCORNER

**klep•to•ma•nia** *n* : neurotic impulse to steal — **klep•to•ma•ni•ac** *n*

**knack** *n* **1** : clever way of doing something **2** : natural aptitude

**knead** *vb* **1** : work and press with the hands **2** : massage — **knead•er** *n*

**knee** *n* : joint in the middle part of the leg — **knee•cap** *n* — **kneed** *adj*

**kneel** *vb* (**knelt; knelt**) : rest on one's knees

**knew** *past of* KNOW

**knick•knack** *n* : small decorative object

**knife** *n* **knives** : sharp blade with a handle ~ *vb* : stab or cut with a knife

**knight** *n* **1** : mounted warrior of feudal

times **2** : man honored by a sovereign ~ *vb* : make a knight of — **knight•hood** *n* — **knight•ly** *adv*

**knit** *vb* **1** : link firmly or closely **2** : form a fabric by interlacing yarn or thread ~ *n* : knitted garment — **knit•ter** *n*

**knob** *n* : rounded protuberance or handle — **knobbed** *adj* — **knob•by** *adj*

**knock** *vb* **1** : strike with a sharp blow **2** : collide **3** : find fault with ~ *n* : sharp blow — **knock•er** *n* — **knock out** *vb* : make unconscious

**knot** *n* **1** : interlacing (as of string) that forms a lump **2** : base of a woody branch in the stem **3** : group **4** : one nautical mile per hour ~ *vb* : tie in or with a knot — **knot•ty** *adj*

**know** *vb* **knew; known** **1** : perceive directly or understand **2** : be familiar with — **know•able** *adj* — **know•er** *n*

**know•ing** *adj* : shrewdly and keenly alert — **know•ing•ly** *adv*

**knowl•edge** *n* **1** : understanding gained by experience **2** : range of information — **knowl•edge•able** *adj*

**knuck•le** *n* : rounded knob at a finger joint

**Ko•ran** *n* : book of Islam containing revelations made to Muhammad by Allah

**ko•sher** *adj* : ritually fit for use according to Jewish law

**Kwan•zaa, Kwan•za** *n* : African-American festival held from December 26 to January 1

# L

**l** *n* : 12th letter of the alphabet

**lab** *n* : laboratory

**la•bel** *n* **1** : identification slip **2** : identifying word or phrase ~ *vb* : put a label on

**la•bor** *n* **1** : physical or mental effort **2** : physical efforts of childbirth **3** : task **4** : people who work manually ~ *vb* : work esp. with great effort — **la•bor•er** *n* — **la•bo•ri•ous** *adj* — **la•bo•ri•ous•ly** *adv*

**lab•o•ra•to•ry** *n* : place for experimental testing

**Labor Day** *n* : 1st Monday in September

observed as a legal holiday in recognition of working people

**lab•y•rinth** *n* : maze — **lab•y•rin•thine** *adj*

**lace** *n* **1** : cord or string for tying **2** : fine net usu. figured fabric ~ *vb* **1** : tie **2** : adorn with lace — **lacy** *adj*

**lac•er•ate** *vb* : tear roughly — **lac•er•a•tion** *n*

**lack** *vb* : be missing or deficient in ~ *n* : deficiency

**lack•lus•ter** *adj* : dull

**lac•tate** *vb* : secrete milk — **lac•ta•tion** *n*

**lad** *n* : boy

**lad•der** *n* : device with steps or rungs for climbing

**la•dle** *n* : spoon with a deep bowl — **ladle** *vb*

**la•dy** *n* **1** : woman of rank or authority **2** : woman

**lag** *vb* : fail to keep up ~ *n* **1** : a falling behind **2** : interval — **lag•gard** *n* — **lag•gard•ly** *adv or adj*

**la•goon** *n* : shallow sound, channel, or pond near or connecting with a larger body of water

**laid** *past of* LAY

**lain** *past part of* LIE

**lair** *n* : den

**la•ity** *n* : people of a religious faith who are not clergy members

**lake** *n* : inland body of water

**la•ma** *n* : Buddhist monk

**lamb** *n* : young sheep or its flesh used as food

**lam•baste, lam•bast** *vb* **1** : beat **2** : censure

**lame** *adj* **1** : having a limb disabled **2** : weak ~ *vb* : make lame — **lame•ly** *adv* — **lame•ness** *n*

**la•ment** *vb* **1** : mourn **2** : express sorrow for ~ *n* **1** : mourning **2** : complaint — **lam·en·ta·ble** *adj* — **lam·en·ta·bly** *adv* — **lam·en·ta·tion** *n*

**lam·i·nat·ed** *adj* : made of thin layers of material — **lam·i·nate** *vb* — **lam·i·nate** *n or adj* — **lam·i·na·tion** *n*

**lamp** *n* : device for producing light or heat

**lam·poon** *n* : satire — **lam·poon** *vb*

**lance** *n* : spear ∼ *vb* : pierce or open with a lancet

**land** *n* **1** : solid part of the surface of the earth **2** : country ∼ *vb* **1** : go ashore **2** : catch or gain **3** : touch the ground or a surface — **land·less** *adj* — **land·own·er** *n*

**land·fill** *n* : dump

**land·ing** *n* **1** : action of one that lands **2** : place for loading passengers and cargo **3** : level part of a staircase

**land·lord** *n* : owner of property

**land·mark** *n* **1** : object that marks a boundary or serves as a guide **2** : event that marks a turning point

**land·scape** *n* : view of natural scenery ∼ *vb* : beautify a piece of land (as by decorative planting)

**land·slide** *n* **1** : slipping down of a mass of earth **2** : overwhelming victory

**lane** *n* : narrow way

**lan·guage** *n* : words and the methods of combining them for communication

**lanky** *adj* : tall and thin

**lan·tern** *n* : enclosed portable light

**¹lap** *n* **1** : front part of the lower trunk and thighs of a seated person **2** : overlapping part **3** : one complete circuit completing a course (as around a track or pool) ∼ *vb* : fold over

**²lap** *vb* **1** : scoop up with the tongue **2** : splash gently

**la·pel** *n* : fold of the front of a coat

**lapse** *n* **1** : slight error **2** : termination of a right or privilege **3** : interval ∼ *vb* **1** : slip **2** : become less **3** : cease

**lap·top** *adj* : of a size that may be used on one's lap

**lar·ce·ny** *n* : theft — **lar·ce·nous** *adj*

**large** *adj* : greater than average — **large·ly** *adv* — **large·ness** *n*

**lar·i·at** *n* : lasso

**lar·va** *n* : wormlike form of an insect — **lar·val** *adj*

**lar·yn·gi·tis** *n* : inflammation of the upper part of the throat

**la·sa·gna** *n* : flat noodles baked usu. with tomato sauce, meat, and cheese

**la·ser** *n* : device that produces an intense light beam

**lash** *vb* : whip ∼ *n* **1** : stroke esp. of a whip **2** : eyelash

**lass** *n* : girl

**lass·ie** *n* : girl

**las·so** *n* : rope with a noose for catching livestock — **las·so** *vb*

**¹last** *vb* : continue in existence or operation

**²last** *adj* **1** : final **2** : previous **3** : least likely ∼ *adv* **1** : at the end **2** : most recently **3** : in conclusion ∼ *n* : something that is last — **last·ly** *adv* — **at last** : finally

**latch** *vb* : catch or get hold ∼ *n* : catch that holds a door closed

**late** *adj* **1** : coming or staying after the proper time **2** : advanced toward the end **3** : recently deceased **4** : recent — **late** *adv* — **late·com·er** *n* — **late·ly** *adv* — **late·ness** *n*

**la·tent** *adj* : present but not visible or expressed — **la·ten·cy** *n*

**lat·er** *adv* : at some time after the present time

**lat·er·al** *adj* : on or toward the side — **lat·er·al·ly** *adv*

**la·tex** *n* : emulsion of synthetic rubber or plastic

**lath·er** *n* : foam ∼ *vb* : form or spread lather

**lat·i·tude** *n* **1** : distance north or south from the earth's equator **2** : freedom of action

**lat·ter** *adj* **1** : more recent **2** : being the second of 2 — **lat·ter·ly** *adv*

**lat·tice** *n* : framework of crossed strips

**laud** *vb or n* : praise — **laud·able** *adj* — **laud·ably** *adv*

**laugh** *vb* : show mirth, joy, or scorn with a smile and explosive sound — **laugh** *n* — **laugh·able** *adj* — **laugh·ing·ly** *adv* — **laugh·ter** *n*

**laugh·ing·stock** *n* : object of ridicule

**launch** *vb* **1** : hurl or send off **2** : set afloat **3** : start — **launch** *n* — **launch·er** *n*

**laun·der** *vb* : wash or iron fabrics — **laun·der·er** *n* — **laun·dress** *n* — **laun·dry** *n*

**lau·rel** *n* **1** : small evergreen tree **2** : honor

**la·va** *n* : volcanic molten rock

**lav·a·to·ry** *n* : bathroom

**lav·ish** *adj* : expended profusely ∼ *vb* : expend or give freely — **lav·ish·ly** *adv* — **lav·ish·ness** *n*

**law** *n* **1** : established rule of conduct **2** : body of such rules **3** : principle of construction or procedure **4** : rule stating uniform behavior under uniform conditions **5** : lawyer's profession — **law·break·er** *n* — **law·ful** *adj* — **law·ful·ly** *adv* — **law·giv·er** *n* — **law·less** *adj* — **law·less·ly** *adv* — **law·less·ness** *n* — **law·mak·er** *n* — **law·man** *n* — **law·suit** *n*

**lawn** *n* : grass-covered yard

**law·yer** *n* : legal practitioner

**lax** *adj* : not strict or tense — **lax·i·ty** *n* — **lax·ly** *adv*

**¹lay** *vb* **laid; laid** **1** : put or set down **2** : produce eggs **3** : bet **4** : impose as a duty or burden **5** : put forward ∼ *n* : way something lies or is laid

**²lay** *past of* LIE

**³lay** *adj* : of the laity — **lay·man** *n* — **lay·wom·an** *n*

**lay·er** *n* **1** : one that lays **2** : one thickness over or under another

**lay·off** *n* : temporary dismissal of a worker

**lay·out** *n* : arrangement

**la·zy** *adj* : disliking activity or exertion — **la·zi·ly** *adv* — **la·zi·ness** *n*

**lead** *vb* **led; led** **1** : guide on a way **2** : direct the activity of **3** : go at the head of **4** : tend to a definite result ∼ *n* : position in front — **lead·er** *n* — **lead·er·less** *adj* — **lead·er·ship** *n*

**leaf** *n* (**leaves**) **1** : green outgrowth of a plant stem **2** : leaflike thing ∼ *vb* **1** : produce leaves **2** : turn book pages — **leaf·age** *n* — **leafed** *adj* — **leaf·less** *adj* — **leafy** *adj* — **leaved** *adj*

**leaf·let** *n* : pamphlet

**league** *n* : association for a common purpose — **league** *vb* — **leagu·er** *n*

**leak** *vb* **1** : enter or escape through a leak **2** : become or make known ∼ *n* : opening that accidentally admits or lets out a substance — **leak·age** *n* — **leaky** *adj*

**¹lean** *vb* **1** : bend from a vertical position **2** : rely on for support **3** : incline in opinion — **lean** *n*

**²lean** *adj* **1** : lacking in flesh **2** : lacking richness — **lean·ness** *n*

**leap** *vb* : jump — **leap** *n*

**leap year** *n* : 366-day year

**learn** *vb* **1** : gain understanding or skill by study or experience **2** : memorize **3** : find out — **learn·er** *n*

**learn·ed** *adj* : having great learning — **learn·ed·ness** *n*

**learn·ing** *n* : knowledge

**lease** *n* : contract transferring real estate for a term and usu. for rent ∼ *vb* : grant by or hold under a lease

**leash** *n* : line to hold an animal — **leash** *vb*

**least** *adj* **1** : lowest in importance or position **2** : smallest **3** : scantiest ∼ *n* : one that is least ∼ *adv* : in the smallest or lowest degree

**leath·er** *n* : dressed animal skin — **leath·ern** *adj* — **leath·ery** *adj*

**¹leave** *vb* **left; left** **1** : bequeath **2** : allow or cause to remain **3** : have as a remainder **4** : go away ∼ *n* **1** : permission **2** : authorized absence **3** : departure

**²leave** *vb* : produce leaves

**leaves** *pl of* LEAF

**lech·ery** *n* : inordinate indulgence in sex — **lech·er** *n* — **lech·er·ous** *adj* — **lech·er·ous·ly** *adv* — **lech·er·ous·ness** *n*

**lec·ture** *n* **1** : instructive talk **2** : reprimand — **lec·ture** *vb* — **lec·tur·er** *n* — **lec·ture·ship** *n*

**led** *past of* LEAD

**ledge** *n* : shelflike projection

**leery** *adj* : suspicious or wary

**lee·ward** *adj* : situated away from the wind ∼ *n* : the lee side

**lee·way** *n* : allowable margin

**¹left** *adj* : on the same side of the body as the heart ∼ *n* : left hand — **left** *adv*

**²left** *past of* LEAVE

**leg** *n* **1** : limb of an animal that supports the body **2** : something like a leg **3** : clothing to cover the leg ∼ *vb* : walk or run — **leg·ged** *adj* — **leg·less** *adj*

**leg·a·cy** *n* : inheritance

**le·gal** *adj* **1** : relating to law or lawyers **2** : lawful — **le·gal·is·tic** *adj* — **le·gal·i·ty** *n* — **le·gal·ize** *vb* — **le·gal·ly** *adv*

**leg·end** *n* **1** : story handed down from the past **2** : inscription **3** : explanation of map symbols — **leg·end·ary** *adj*

**leg·i·ble** *adj* : capable of being read — **leg·i·bil·i·ty** *n* — **leg·i·bly** *adv*

**le·gion** *n* **1** : large army unit **2** : multitude **3** : association of former servicemen — **le·gion·ary** *n* — **le·gion·naire** *n*

**leg·is·late** *vb* : enact or bring about with laws — **leg·is·la·tion** *n* — **leg·is·la·tive** *adj* — **leg·is·la·tor** *n* — **leg·is·la·ture** *n*

**le·git·i·mate** *adj* **1** : lawfully begotten **2** : genuine **3** : conforming with law or accepted standards — **le·git·i·ma·cy** *n* — **le·git·i·mate·ly** *adv* — **le·git·i·mize** *vb*

**lei·sure** *n* **1** : free time **2** : ease **3** : convenience — **lei·sure·ly** *adj or adv*

**lem·on** *n* : yellow citrus fruit — **lem·on·ade** *n* — **lem·ony** *adj*

**lend** *vb* (**lent; lent**) **1** : give for temporary use **2** : furnish — **lend·er** *n*

**length** *n* **1** : longest dimension **2** : duration in time **3** : piece to be joined to others — **length·en** *vb* — **length·wise** *adv or adj* — **lengthy** *adj*

**le·nient** *adj* : of mild and tolerant disposition or effect — **le·ni·en·cy** *n* — **le·ni·ent·ly** *adv*

**lens** *n* **1** : curved piece for forming an image in an optical instrument **2** : transparent body in the eye that focuses light rays

**lent** *past of* LEND

**Lent** *n* : 40-day period of penitence and fasting from Ash Wednesday to Easter — **Lent·en** *adj*

**leop·ard** *n* : large tawny black-spotted cat

**less** *adj* **1** : fewer **2** : of lower rank, degree, or importance **3** : smaller ∼ *adv* : to a lesser degree ∼ *n, pl* **less** : smaller portion ∼ *prep* : minus — **less·en** *vb*

**less·er** *adj* : of less size, quality, or significance

**les·son** *n* **1** : reading or exercise to be studied by a pupil **2** : something learned

**let** *vb* **let; let** **1** : cause to **2** : rent **3** : permit

**le·thal** *adj* : deadly — **le·thal·ly** *adv*

**let·ter** *n* **1** : unit of an alphabet **2** : written or printed communication **3** *pl* : literature or learning **4** : literal meaning ∼ *vb* : mark with letters — **let·ter·er** *n*

**let·tuce** *n* : garden plant with crisp leaves

**lev·ee** *n* : embankment to prevent flooding

**lev·el** *n* **1** : device for establishing a flat surface **2** : horizontal surface **3** : position in a scale ∼ *vb* **1** : make flat or level **2** : aim **3** : tear down ∼ *adj* **1** : having an even surface **2** : of the same

height or rank — **lev·el·er** *n* — **lev·el·ly** *adv* — **lev·el·ness** *n*

**le·ver** *n* : bar for prying or dislodging something — **le·ver·age** *n*

**li·a·ble** *adj* **1** : legally obligated **2** : probable **3** : likely to be affected — **li·a·bil·i·ty** *n*

**li·ar** *n* : one who lies

**li·bel** *n* : action, crime, or an instance of injuring a person's reputation esp. by something written ∼ *vb* : make or publish a libel — **li·bel·er** *n* — **li·bel·ist** *n* — **li·bel·ous, li·bel·lous** *adj*

**lib·er·al** *adj* : not stingy, narrow, or conservative — **liberal** *n* — **lib·er·al·ism** *n* — **lib·er·al·i·ty** *n* — **lib·er·al·ize** *vb* — **lib·er·al·ly** *adv*

**lib·er·ate** *vb* : set free — **lib·er·a·tion** *n* — **lib·er·a·tor** *n*

**lib·er·ty** *n* **1** : quality or state of being free **2** : action going beyond normal limits

**li·brary** *n* **1** : place where books are kept for use **2** : collection of books — **li·brar·i·an** *n*

**lice** *pl of* LOUSE

**li·cense, li·cence** *n* **1** : legal permission to engage in some activity **2** : document or tag providing proof of a license **3** : irresponsible use of freedom — **license** *vb* — **li·cens·ee** *n*

**lick** *vb* **1** : draw the tongue over **2** : beat ∼ *n* **1** : stroke of the tongue **2** : small amount

**lic·o·rice** *n* : dried root of a European legume or candy flavored by it

**lid** *n* **1** : movable cover **2** : eyelid

**¹lie** *vb* **lay; lain** **1** : be in, rest in, or assume a horizontal position **2** : occupy a certain relative position ∼ *n* : position in which something lies

**²lie** *vb* : tell a lie ∼ *n* : untrue statement

**life** *n* (**lives**) **1** : quality that distinguishes a vital and functional being from a dead body or inanimate matter **2** : physical and mental experiences of an individual **3** : biography **4** : period of existence **5** : way of living **6** : liveliness — **life·guard** *n or vb* — **life·less** *adj* — **life·like** *adj* — **life·time** *n*

**life·blood** *n* : basic source of strength and vitality

**life·sav·ing** *n* : art or practice of saving lives — **life·sav·er** *n*

**lift** *vb* **1** : move upward or cause to move upward **2** : put an end to — **lift** *n* — **lift·er** *n*

**lift·off** *n* : vertical takeoff by a rocket

**¹light** *n* **1** : radiation that makes vision possible **2** : daylight **3** : source of light **4** : public knowledge **5** : aspect **6** : celebrity **7** : flame for lighting ∼ *adj* **1** : bright **2** : weak in color ∼ *vb* **1** : make or become light **2** : cause to burn — **light·en** *vb* — **light·er** *n* — **light·ness** *n* — **light·proof** *adj*

**²light** *adj* : not heavy, serious, or abundant — **light** *adv* — **light·en** *vb* — **light·ly** *adv* — **light·ness** *n* — **light·weight** *adj*

**light·heart·ed** *adj* : free from worry — **light·heart·ed·ly** *adv* — **light·heart·ed·ness** *n*

**light·ning** *n* : flashing discharge of atmospheric electricity

**¹like** *vb* **1** : enjoy **2** : desire ∼ *n* : preference — **lik·able, like·able** *adj*

**²like** *adj* : similar ∼ *prep* **1** : similar or similarly to **2** : typical of **3** : such as ∼ *n* : counterpart ∼ *conj* : as or as if — **like·ness** *n* — **like·wise** *adv*

**like·ly** *adj* **1** : probable **2** : believable ∼ *adv* : in all probability — **like·li·hood** *n*

**lik·en** *vb* : compare

**lily** *n* : tall bulbous herb with funnel-shaped flowers

**limb** *n* **1** : projecting appendage used in moving or grasping **2** : tree branch — **limb·less** *adj*

**lim·ber** *adj* : supple or agile ∼ *vb* : make or become limber

**lime** *n* : small green lemonlike citrus fruit — **lime·ade** *n*

**lim·er·ick** *n* : light poem of 5 lines

**lim·it** *n* **1** : boundary **2** : something that restrains or confines ∼ *vb* : set limits on — **lim·i·ta·tion** *n* — **lim·it·less** *adj*

**lim·ou·sine** *n* : large luxurious sedan

**limp** *vb* : walk lamely ∼ *n* : limping movement or gait — *adj* : lacking firmness and body — **limp·ly** *adv* — **limp·ness** *n*

¹**line** *vb* : cover the inner surface of — **lin·ing** *n*

²**line** *n* **1** : cord, rope, or wire **2** : row or something like a row **3** : note **4** : course of action or thought **5** : state of agreement **6** : occupation **7** : limit **8** : transportation system **9** : long narrow mark ∼ *vb* **1** : mark with a line **2** : place in a line **3** : form a line — **lin·er** *n*

**lin·e·ar** *adj* **1** : straight **2** : long and narrow

**lin·en** *n* **1** : cloth or thread made of flax **2** : household articles made of linen cloth

**lin·ger** *vb* : be slow to leave or act — **lin·ger·er** *n*

**lin·guist** *n* **1** : person skilled in speech or languages **2** : student of language — **lin·guis·tic** *adj* — **lin·guis·tics** *n pl*

**link** *n* **1** : connecting structure (as a ring of a chain) **2** : bond — **link** *vb* — **link·age** *n* — **link·er** *n*

**lint** *n* : fine fluff or loose short fibers from fabric

**li·on** *n* : large cat of Africa and Asia — **li·on·ess** *n*

**lip** *n* **1** : either of the 2 fleshy folds surrounding the mouth **2** : edge of something hollow — **lipped** *adj* — **lip-read·ing** *n*

**lip·stick** *n* : stick of cosmetic to color lips

**liq·ue·fy** *vb* : make or become liquid — **liq·ue·fi·er** *n*

**liq·uid** *adj* **1** : flowing freely like water **2** : neither solid nor gaseous **3** : of or convertible to cash — **liquid** *n* — **li·quid·i·ty** *n*

**liq·ui·date** *vb* **1** : pay off **2** : dispose of — **liq·ui·da·tion** *n*

**li·quor** *n* : usu. distilled liquid containing alcohol

**lisp** *vb* : pronounce *s* and *z* imperfectly — **lisp** *n*

**list** *n* **1** : series of names or items ∼ *vb* **1** : make a list of **2** : put on a list

**lis·ten** *vb* **1** : pay attention in order to hear **2** : heed — **lis·ten·er** *n*

**list·less** *adj* : having no desire to act — **list·less·ly** *adv* — **list·less·ness** *n*

**lit** *past of* LIGHT

**li·ter** *n* : unit of liquid measure equal to about 1.06 quarts

**lit·er·al** *adj* : being exactly as stated — **lit·er·al·ly** *adv*

**lit·er·ary** *adj* : relating to literature

**lit·er·ate** *adj* : able to read and write — **lit·er·a·cy** *n*

**lit·er·a·ture** *n* : writings of enduring interest

**lit·i·gate** *vb* : carry on a lawsuit — **lit·i·gant** *n* — **lit·i·ga·tion** *n* — **li·ti·gious** *adj* — **li·ti·gious·ness** *n*

**lit·ter** *n* **1** : animal offspring of one birth **2** : stretcher **3** : rubbish **4** : material to absorb animal waste ∼ *vb* **1** : give birth to young **2** : strew with litter

**lit·tle** *adj* **lit·tler/less/less·er; lit·tlest/least 1** : not big **2** : not much **3** : not important ∼ *adv* **1** : slightly **2** : not often ∼ *n* : small amount — **lit·tle·ness** *n*

¹**live** *vb* **1** : be alive **2** : conduct one's life **3** : nourish oneself **4** : reside — **liv·able** *adj* — **liv·a·bil·i·ty** *n*

²**live** *adj* **1** : having life **2** : burning **3** : connected to electric power **4** : not exploded **5** : of continuing interest **6** : involving the actual presence of real people

**live·li·hood** *n* : means of supporting one's life

**live·ly** *adj* : full of life and vigor — **live·li·ness** *n*

**liv·er** *n* : organ that secretes bile

**lives** *pl of* LIFE

**liv·ing** *adj* : having life ∼ *n* : livelihood

**load** *n* **1** : cargo **2** : supported weight **3** : burden **4** : a large quantity — usu. pl. ∼ *vb* **1** : put a load on **2** : burden **3** : put ammunition in

¹**loaf** *n* : mass of bread

²**loaf** *vb* : waste time — **loaf·er** *n*

**loan** *n* **1** : money borrowed at interest **2** : something lent temporarily **3** : grant of use ∼ *vb* : lend

**loath·ing** *n* : extreme disgust

**lob** *vb* : throw or hit in a high arc — **lob** *n*

**lob·by** *n* **1** : public waiting room at the entrance of a building **2** : persons lobbying ∼ *vb* : try to influence legislators — **lob·by·ist** *n*

**lob·ster** *n* : marine crustacean with 2 large pincerlike claws

**lo·cal** *adj* : confined to or serving a limited area — **local** *n* — **lo·cal·i·za·tion** *n* — **lo·cal·ize** *vb* — **lo·cal·ly** *adv*

**lo·cale** *n* : setting for an event — **lo·cal·i·ty** *n*

**lo·cate** *vb* **1** : settle **2** : find a site for **3** : discover the place of — **lo·ca·tion** *n*

**lock** *n* **1** : fastener using a bolt **2** : enclosure in a canal to raise or lower boats ∼ *vb* **1** : make fast with a lock **2** : confine **3** : interlock

**lock·er** *n* : storage compartment

**lo·co·mo·tion** *n* : power of moving — **lo·co·mo·tive** *adj*

**lodge** *vb* **1** : provide quarters for **2** : come to rest **3** : file ∼ *n* **1** : special house (as for hunters) **2** : animal's den **3** : branch of a fraternal organization — **lodg·er** *n* — **lodg·ing** *n* — **lodg·ment, lodge·ment** *n*

**loft** *n* **1** : attic **2** : upper floor (as of a warehouse)

**lofty** *adj* **1** : noble **2** : proud **3** : tall or high — **loft·i·ly** *adv* — **loft·i·ness** *n*

**log** *n* **1** : unshaped timber **2** : daily record of a ship's or plane's progress ∼ *vb* **1** : cut (trees) for lumber **2** : enter in a log — **log·ger** *n*

**log·ic** *n* **1** : science of reasoning **2** : sound reasoning — **log·i·cal** *adj* — **log·i·cal·ly** *adv* — **lo·gi·cian** *n*

**lo·gis·tics** *n sing or pl* : procurement and movement of people and supplies — **lo·gis·tic** *adj*

**loin** *n* **1** : part of the body on each side of the spine between the hip and lower ribs **2** *pl* : pubic regions

**loi·ter** *vb* : remain around a place idly — **loi·ter·er** *n*

**lol·li·pop, lol·ly·pop** *n* : hard candy on a stick

**lone** *adj* **1** : alone or isolated **2** : only — **lone·li·ness** *n* — **lone·ly** *adj* — **lon·er** *n*

**lone·some** *adj* : sad from lack of company — **lone·some·ly** *adv* — **lone·some·ness** *n*

**long** *adj* **1** : extending far or for a considerable time **2** : having a specified length **3** : tedious **4** : well supplied — used with *on* ∼ *adv* : for a long time ∼ *n* : long period ∼ *vb* : feel a strong desire — **long·ing** *n* — **long·ing·ly** *adv*

**lon·gev·i·ty** *n* : long life

**lon·gi·tude** *n* : angular distance east or west from a meridian

**look** *vb* **1** : see **2** : seem **3** : direct one's attention **4** : face ∼ *n* **1** : action of looking **2** : appearance of the face **3** : aspect — **look after** : take care of

**look for 1** : expect **2** : search for

**look·out** *n* **1** : one who watches **2** : careful watch

¹**loom** *n* : frame or machine for weaving

²**loom** *vb* : appear large and indistinct or impressive

**loop** *n* **1** : doubling of a line that leaves an opening **2** : something like a loop — **loop** *vb*

**loop·hole** *n* : means of evading

**loose** *adj* **1** : not fixed tight **2** : not restrained **3** : not dense **4** : slack **5** : not exact ∼ *vb* **1** : release **2** : untie or relax — **loose** *adv* — **loose·ly** *adv* — **loos·en** *vb* — **loose·ness** *n*

**loot** *n or vb* : plunder — **loot·er** *n*

**lop·sid·ed** *adj* **1** : leaning to one side **2** : not symmetrical — **lop·sid·ed·ly** *adv* — **lop·sid·ed·ness** *n*

**lord** *n* **1** : one with authority over others **2** : British nobleman — **lord·ship** *n*

**lord·ly** *adj* : haughty

**lore** *n* : traditional knowledge

**lose** *vb* **lost; lost 1** : have pass from one's possession **2** : be deprived of **3** : waste **4** : be defeated in **5** : fail to keep to or hold **6** : get rid of — **los·er** *n*

**loss** *n* **1** : something lost **2** *pl* : killed, wounded, or captured soldiers **3** : failure to win

**lost** *adj* **1** : not used, won, or claimed **2** : unable to find the way

**lot** *n* **1** : object used in deciding something by chance **2** : share **3** : fate **4** : plot of land **5** : much

**lo·tion** *n* : liquid to rub on the skin

**lot·tery** *n* : drawing of lots with prizes going to winners

**loud** *adj* **1** : high in volume of sound **2** : noisy **3** : obtrusive in color or pattern — **loud** *adv* — **loud·ly** *adv* — **loud·ness** *n* — **loud·speak·er** *n*

**lounge** *vb* : act or move lazily ∼ *n* : room with comfortable furniture

**louse** *n* **lice** : parasitic wingless usu. flat insect

**lousy** *adj* **1** : infested with lice **2** : not good — **lous·i·ly** *adv* — **lous·i·ness** *n*

**love** *n* **1** : strong affection **2** : warm attachment **3** : beloved person ∼ *vb* **1** : feel affection for **2** : enjoy greatly — **lov·able** *adj* — **love·less** *adj* — **lov·er** *n* — **lov·ing·ly** *adv*

**love·ly** *adj* : beautiful — **love·li·ness** *n* — **lovely** *adv*

**low** *adj* **1** : not high or tall **2** : below normal level **3** : not loud **4** : humble **5** : sad **6** : less than usual **7** : falling short of a standard **8** : unfavorable ∼ *n* **1** : something low **2** : automobile gear giving the slowest speed — **low** *adv* — **low·ness** *n*

**low·er** *vb* **1** : drop **2** : let descend **3** : reduce in amount

**low·ly** *adj* **1** : humble **2** : low in rank — **low·li·ness** *n*

**loy·al** *adj* : faithful to a country, cause, or friend — **loy·al·ist** *n* — **loy·al·ly** *adv* — **loy·al·ty** *n*

**lu·bri·cate** *vb* : apply a lubricant to — **lu·bri·cant** *n* — **lu·bri·ca·tion** *n* — **lu·bri·ca·tor** *n*

**lu·cid** *adj* **1** : mentally sound **2** : easily understood — **lu·cid·i·ty** *n* — **lu·cid·ly** *adv* — **lu·cid·ness** *n*

**luck** *n* **1** : chance **2** : good fortune — **luck·i·ly** *adv* — **luck·i·ness** *n* — **luck·less** *adj* — **lucky** *adj*

**lu·cra·tive** *adj* : profitable — **lu·cra·tive·ly** *adv* — **lu·cra·tive·ness** *n*

**lu·di·crous** *adj* : comically ridiculous — **lu·di·crous·ly** *adv* — **lu·di·crous·ness** *n*

**lug** *vb* : drag or carry laboriously

**lug·gage** *n* : baggage

**lull** *vb* : make or become quiet or relaxed ∼ *n* : temporary calm

**lul·la·by** *n* : song to lull children to sleep

**lum·ber** *n* : timber dressed for use ∼ *vb* : cut logs — **lum·ber·man** *n* — **lum·ber·yard** *n*

**lu·mi·nous** *adj* : emitting light — **lu·mi·nance** *n* — **lu·mi·nos·i·ty** *n* — **lu·mi·nous·ly** *adv*

**lump** *n* **1** : mass of irregular shape **2** : abnormal swelling ∼ *vb* : heap together — **lump·ish** *adj* — **lumpy** *adj*

**lu·na·cy** *n* : state of insanity

**lu·nar** *adj* : of the moon

**lu·na·tic** *adj* : insane — **lu·na·tic** *n*

**lunch** *n* : noon meal ∼ *vb* : eat lunch

**lung** *n* : breathing organ in the chest — **lunged** *adj*

**lunge** *n* **1** : sudden thrust **2** : sudden move forward — **lunge** *vb*

**lurch** *n* : sudden swaying — **lurch** *vb*

**lure** *n* **1** : something that attracts **2** : artificial fish bait ∼ *vb* : attract

**lu·rid** *adj* **1** : gruesome **2** : sensational — **lu·rid·ly** *adv*

**lurk** *vb* : lie in wait

**lus·cious** *adj* **1** : pleasingly sweet in taste or smell **2** : sensually appealing — **lus·cious·ly** *adv* — **lus·cious·ness** *n*

**lush** *adj* : covered with abundant growth

**lust** *n* **1** : intense sexual desire **2** : intense longing — **lust** *vb* — **lust·ful** *adj*

**lus·ter, lus·tre** *n* **1** : brightness from reflected light **2** : magnificence — **lus·ter·less** *adj* — **lus·trous** *adj*

**lusty** *adj* : full of vitality — **lust·i·ly** *adv* — **lust·i·ness** *n*

**lux·u·ri·ant** *adj* **1** : growing plentifully **2** : rich and varied — **lux·u·ri·ance** *n* — **lux·u·ri·ant·ly** *adv* — **lux·u·ri·ate** *vb*

**lux·u·ry** *n* **1** : great comfort **2** : something adding to pleasure or comfort — **lux·u·ri·ous** *adj* — **lux·u·ri·ous·ly** *adv*

**lye** *n* : caustic alkaline substance

**lying** *pres part of* LIE

**lynch** *vb* : put to death by mob action — **lynch·er** *n*

**lyr·ic** *adj* **1** : suitable for singing **2** : expressing direct personal emotion ∼ *n* **1** : lyric poem **2** *pl* : words of a song — **lyr·i·cal** *adj*

# M

**m** *n* : 13th letter of the alphabet

**ma'am** *n* : madam

**ma·ca·bre** *adj* : gruesome

**mac·a·ro·ni** *n* : tube-shaped pasta

**mac·a·roon** *n* : cookie of ground almonds or coconut

**mace** *n* : spice from the fibrous coating of the nutmeg

**ma·chete** *n* : large heavy knife

**ma·chine** *n* : combination of mechanical or electrical parts ∼ *vb* : modify by machine-operated tools — **ma·chin·able** *adj* — **ma·chin·ery** *n* — **ma·chin·ist** *n*

**mac·ra·mé** *n* : coarse lace or fringe made by knotting

**mad** *adj* **1** : insane or rabid **2** : rash and foolish **3** : angry **4** : carried away by enthusiasm — **mad·den** *vb* — **mad·den·ing·ly** *adv* — **mad·ly** *adv* — **mad·ness** *n*

**mad·am** *n* — used in polite address to a woman

**made** *past of* MAKE

**ma·de·moi·selle** *n* : an unmarried girl or woman — used as a title for a woman esp. of French nationality

**mad·house** *n* **1** : insane asylum **2** : place of great uproar or confusion

**Ma·fia** *n* : secret criminal organization

**mag·a·zine** *n* **1** : storehouse **2** : publication issued at regular intervals **3** : cartridge container in a gun

**mag·ic** *n* **1** : art of using supernatural powers **2** : extraordinary power or influence **3** : sleight of hand — **magic, mag·i·cal** *adj* — **mag·i·cal·ly** *adv* — **ma·gi·cian** *n*

**mag·is·trate** *n* : judge — **mag·is·te·ri·al** *adj* — **mag·is·tra·cy** *n*

**mag·net** *n* **1** : body that attracts iron **2** : something that attracts — **mag·net·ic** *adj* — **mag·net·i·cal·ly** *adv* — **mag·ne·tism** *n*

**mag·ne·tize** *vb* **1** : attract like a magnet **2** : give magnetic properties to — **mag·ne·tiz·able** *adj* — **mag·ne·ti·za·tion** *n* — **mag·ne·tiz·er** *n*

**mag·nif·i·cent** *adj* : splendid — **mag·nif·i·cence** *n* — **mag·nif·i·cent·ly** *adv*

**mag·ni·fy** *vb* **1** : intensify **2** : enlarge — **mag·ni·fi·ca·tion** *n* — **mag·ni·fi·er** *n*

**mag·ni·tude** *n* **1** : greatness of size or extent **2** : quantity

**ma·hog·a·ny** *n* : tropical evergreen tree or its reddish brown wood

**maid** *n* **1** : unmarried young woman **2** : female servant

**mail** *n* **1** : something sent or carried in the postal system **2** : postal system ~ *vb* : send by mail — **mail·box** *n* — **mail·man** *n*

**main** *n* **1** : force **2** : ocean **3** : principal pipe, duct, or circuit of a utility system ~ *adj* : chief — **main·ly** *adv*

**main·land** *n* : part of a country on a continent

**main·stream** *n* : prevailing current or direction of activity or influence — **mainstream** *adj*

**main·tain** *vb* **1** : keep in an existing state (as of repair) **2** : sustain **3** : declare — **main·tain·abil·i·ty** *n* — **main·tain·able** *adj* — **main·te·nance** *n*

**maj·es·ty** *n* **1** : sovereign power or dignity — used as a title **2** : grandeur or splendor — **ma·jes·tic** *adj* — **ma·jes·ti·cal·ly** *adv*

**ma·jor** *adj* **1** : larger or greater **2** : noteworthy or conspicuous ~ *n* **1** : commissioned officer (as in the army) ranking next below a lieutenant colonel **2** : main field of study ~ *vb* : pursue an academic major

**ma·jor·i·ty** *n* **1** : age of full civil rights **2** : quantity more than half

**make** *vb* (**made; made**) **1** : cause to exist, occur, or appear **2** : fashion or manufacture **3** : formulate in the mind **4** : constitute **5** : prepare **6** : cause to be or become **7** : carry out or perform **8** : compel **9** : gain **10** : have an effect — used with *for* ~ *n* : brand — **mak·er** *n* — **make do** *vb* : get along with what is available — **make good** *vb* **1** : repay **2** : succeed — **make out** *vb* **1** : draw up or write **2** : discern or understand **3** : fare — **make up** *vb* **1** : invent **2** : become reconciled **3** : compensate for

**make–be·lieve** *n* : a pretending to believe ~ *adj* : imagined or pretended

**make·shift** *n* : temporary substitute — **makeshift** *adj*

**make·up** *n* **1** : way in which something is constituted **2** : cosmetics

**mal·a·dy** *n* : disease or disorder

**male** *adj* **1** : relating to the sex that performs a fertilizing function **2** : masculine ~ *n* : male individual — **male·ness** *n*

**ma·lev·o·lent** *adj* : malicious or spiteful — **ma·lev·o·lence** *n*

**mal·for·ma·tion** *n* : distortion or faulty formation — **mal·formed** *adj*

**mal·func·tion** *vb* : fail to operate properly — **mal·func·tion** *n*

**mal·ice** *n* : desire to cause pain or injury to another — **ma·li·cious** *adj* — **ma·li·cious·ly** *adv*

**ma·lig·nant** *adj* **1** : harmful **2** : likely to cause death — **ma·lig·nan·cy** *n* — **ma·lig·nant·ly** *adv* — **ma·lig·ni·ty** *n*

**mall** *n* **1** : shaded promenade **2** : concourse providing access to rows of shops

**mal·let** *n* : hammerlike tool

**mal·nu·tri·tion** *n* : inadequate nutrition — **mal·nour·ished** *adj*

**mal·prac·tice** *n* : failure of professional duty

**ma·ma, mam·ma** *n* : mother

**mam·mal** *n* : warm-blooded vertebrate animal that nourishes its young with milk — **mam·ma·li·an** *adj or n*

**mam·mo·gram** *n* : X-ray photograph of the breasts

**man** *n* (**men**) **1** : human being **2** : adult male **3** : mankind ~ *vb* : supply with people for working — **man·hood** *n* — **man·hunt** *n* — **man·like** *adj* — **man·li·ness** *n* — **man·ly** *adj or adv* — **man–made** *adj* — **man·nish** *adj* — **man·nish·ly** *adv* — **man·nish·ness** *n* — **man–size, man–sized** *adj*

**man·age** *vb* **1** : control **2** : direct or carry on business or affairs **3** : cope — **man·age·abil·i·ty** *n* — **man·age·able** *adj* — **man·age·able·ness** *n* — **man·age·ably** *adv* — **man·age·ment** *n* — **man·ag·er** *n* — **man·a·ge·ri·al** *adj*

**man·date** *n* : authoritative command

**man·da·to·ry** *adj* : obligatory

**mane** *n* : animal's neck hair — **maned** *adj*

**ma·neu·ver** *n* **1** : planned movement of troops or ships **2** : military training exercise **3** : clever or skillful move or action — **maneuver** *vb* — **ma·neu·ver·abil·i·ty** *n*

**man·gle** *vb* **1** : mutilate **2** : bungle — **man·gler** *n*

**man·hole** *n* : entry to a sewer

**ma·nia** *n* **1** : insanity marked by uncontrollable emotion or excitement **2** : excessive enthusiasm — **ma·ni·ac** *n* — **ma·ni·a·cal** *adj* — **man·ic** *adj or n*

**man·i·cure** *n* : treatment for the fingernails ~ *vb* **1** : do manicure work on **2** : trim precisely — **man·i·cur·ist** *n*

**man·i·fest** *adj* : clear to the senses or to the mind ~ *vb* : make evident — **man·i·fes·ta·tion** *n* — **man·i·fest·ly** *adv*

**ma·nip·u·late** *vb* **1** : treat or operate manually or mechanically **2** : influence esp. by cunning — **ma·nip·u·la·tion** *n* — **ma·nip·u·la·tive** *adj* — **ma·nip·u·la·tor** *n*

**man·kind** *n* : human race

**man·ne·quin** *n* : dummy used to display clothes

**man·ner** *n* **1** : kind **2** : usual way of acting **3** : artistic method **4** *pl* : social conduct

**man·ner·ism** *n* : individual peculiarity of action

**man·ner·ly** *adj* : polite — **man·ner·li·ness** *n* — **mannerly** *adv*

**man·or** *n* : country estate — **ma·no·ri·al** *adj*

**man·pow·er** *n* : supply of people available for service

**man·sion** *n* : very big house

**man·slaugh·ter** *n* : unintentional killing of a person

**man·tle** *n* **1** : sleeveless cloak **2** : something that covers, enfolds, or envelops — **man·tle** *vb*

**man·u·al** *adj* : involving the hands or physical force ~ *n* : handbook — **man·u·al·ly** *adv*

**man·u·fac·ture** *n* : process of making atricles by hand or by machinery ~ *vb* : make from raw materials — **man·u·fac·tur·er** *n*

**ma·nure** *n* : animal excrement used as fertilizer

**manu·script** *n* **1** : something written or typed **2** : document submitted for publication

**many** *adj* **more; most** : consisting of a large number — **many** *n or pron*

**map** *n* : representation of a geographical area ~ *vb* **1** : make a map of **2** : plan in detail — **map·pa·ble** *adj* — **map·per** *n*

**ma·ple** *n* : tree with hard light-colored wood

**mar** *vb* : damage

**mar·a·thon** *n* **1** : long-distance race **2** : test of endurance — **mar·a·thon·er** *n*

**mar·ble** *n* **1** : crystallized limestone **2** : small glass ball used in a children's game (**marbles**)

**march** *vb* : move with regular steps or in a purposeful manner ~ *n* **1** : distance covered in a march **2** : measured stride **3** : forward movement **4** : music for marching — **march·er** *n*

**March** *n* : 3d month of the year having 31 days

**mar·ga·rine** *n* : butter substitute made usu. from vegetable oils

**mar·gin** *n* **1** : edge **2** : spare amount, measure, or degree — **mar·gin·al** *adj* — **mar·gin·al·ly** *adv*

**ma·ri·na** *n* : place for mooring pleasure boats

**ma·rine** *adj* **1** : relating to the sea **2** : relating to marines ~ *n* : infantry soldier associated with a navy

**mar·i·tal** *adj* : relating to marriage

**mar·i·time** *adj* : relating to the sea or commerce on the sea

**mark** *n* **1** : something aimed at **2** : something (as a line) designed to record position **3** : visible sign **4** : written symbol **5** : grade **6** : lasting impression **7** : blemish ~ *vb* **1** : designate or set apart by a mark or make a mark on **2** : characterize **3** : remark — **mark·er** *n*

**mar·ket** *n* **1** : buying and selling of goods or the place this happens **2** : demand for commodities **3** : store ~ *vb* : sell — **mar·ket·able** *adj* — **mar·ket·place** *n*

**ma·roon** *vb* : isolate without hope of escape

**mar·riage** *n* **1** : state of being married **2** : wedding ceremony — **mar·riage·able** *adj*

**mar·ry** *vb* **1** : join as husband and wife **2** : take or give in marriage — **mar·ried** *adj or n*

**marsh** *n* : soft wet land — **marshy** *adj*

**mar·shal** *n* **1** : leader of ceremony **2** : usu. high military or administrative officer ~ *vb* **1** : arrange in order, rank, or position **2** : lead with ceremony

**marsh·mal·low** *n* : spongy candy

**mart** *n* : market

**mar·tial** *adj* **1** : relating to war or an army **2** : warlike

**mar·tyr** *n* : one who dies or makes a great sacrifice for a cause ~ *vb* : make a martyr of — **mar·tyr·dom** *n*

**mar·vel** *vb* : feel surprise or wonder ~ *n* : something amazing — **mar·vel·ous, mar·vel·lous** *adj* — **mar·vel·ous·ly** *adv* — **mar·vel·ous·ness** *n*

**mas·cara** *n* : eye cosmetic

**mas·cot** *n* : one believed to bring good luck

**mas·cu·line** *adj* : relating to the male sex — **mas·cu·lin·i·ty** *n*

**mash** *n* **1** : crushed steeped grain for fermenting **2** : soft pulpy mass ~ *vb* **1** : reduce to a pulpy mass **2** : smash — **mash·er** *n*

**mask** *n* : disguise for the face ~ *vb* **1** : disguise **2** : cover to protect — **mask·er** *n*

**mas·quer·ade** *n* **1** : costume party **2** : disguise ~ *vb* **1** : disguise oneself **2** : take part in a costume party — **mas·quer·ad·er** *n*

**mass** *n* **1** : large amount of matter or number of things **2** : expanse or magnitude **3** : great body of people — usu. pl. ~ *vb* : form into a mass — **mass·less** *adj* — **massy** *adj*

**Mass** *n* : worship service of the Roman Catholic Church

**mas·sa·cre** *n* : wholesale slaughter — **mas·sa·cre** *vb*

**mas·sage** *n* : a rubbing of the body — **mas·sage** *vb*

**mas·sive** *adj* **1** : being a large mass **2** : large in scope — **mas·sive·ly** *adv* — **mas·sive·ness** *n*

**mast** *n* : tall pole esp. for supporting sails — **mast·ed** *adj*

**mas·ter** *n* **1** : male teacher **2** : holder of an academic degree between a bachelor's and a doctor's **3** : one highly skilled **4** : one in authority ~ *vb* **1** : subdue **2** : become proficient in — **mas·ter·ful** *adj* — **mas·ter·ful·ly** *adv* — **mas·ter·ly** *adj* — **mas·tery** *n*

**mas·ter·piece** *n* : great piece of work

**mat** *n* **1** : coarse woven or plaited fabric **2** : mass of tangled strands **3** : thick pad ~ *vb* : form into a mat

[1]**match** *n* **1** : one equal to another **2** : one able to cope with another **3** : suitable pairing **4** : game **5** : marriage ~ *vb* **1** : set in competition **2** : marry **3** : be or provide the equal of **4** : fit or go together — **match·less** *adj* — **match·mak·er** *n*

[2]**match** *n* : piece of wood or paper material with a combustible tip

**mate** *n* **1** : companion **2** : subordinate officer on a ship **3** : one of a pair ~ *vb* **1** : fit together **2** : come together as a pair esp. for reproduction

**ma·te·ri·al** *adj* **1** : natural **2** : relating to matter **3** : important **4** : of a physical or worldly nature ~ *n* : stuff something is made of — **ma·te·ri·al·ism** *n* — **ma·te·ri·al·ist** *n or adj* — **ma·te·ri·al·is·tic** *adj* — **ma·te·ri·al·ize** *vb* — **ma·te·ri·al·i·za·tion** *n* — **ma·te·ri·al·ly** *adv*

**ma·ter·nal** *adj* : motherly — **ma·ter·nal·ly** *adv*

**ma·ter·ni·ty** *n* **1** : state of being a mother **2** : hospital's childbirth facility ~ *adj* **1** : worn during pregnancy **2** : relating to the period close to childbirth

**math** *n* : mathematics

**math·e·mat·ics** *n pl* : science of numbers and of shapes in space — **math·e·mat·i·cal** *adj* — **math·e·mat·i·cal·ly** *adv* — **math·e·ma·ti·cian** *n*

**mat·i·nee, mat·i·née** *n* : afternoon performance

**mat·ri·mo·ny** *n* : marriage — **mat·ri·mo·ni·al** *adj* — **mat·ri·mo·ni·al·ly** *adv*

**ma·trix** *n* : something (as a mold) that gives form, foundation, or origin to something else enclosed in it

**mat·ter** *n* **1** : subject of interest **2** *pl* : circumstances **3** : trouble **4** : physical substance ~ *vb* : be important

**mat·tress** *n* : pad to sleep on

**ma·ture** *adj* **1** : carefully considered **2** : fully grown or developed **3** : due for payment ~ *vb* : become mature — **mat·u·ra·tion** *n* — **ma·ture·ly** *adv* — **ma·tu·ri·ty** *n*

**maul** *n* : heavy hammer ~ *vb* **1** : beat **2** : handle roughly

**mau·so·le·um** *n* : large above-ground tomb

**max·i·mum** *n* **1** : greatest quantity **2** : upper limit **3** : largest number — **maximum** *adj* — **max·i·mize** *vb*

**may** *verbal auxiliary, past* **might 1** : have permission **2** : be likely to **3** — used to express desire, purpose, or contingency

**May** *n* : 5th month of the year having 31 days

**may·be** *adv* : perhaps

**may·on·naise** *n* : creamy white sandwich spread

**may·or** *n* : chief city official — **may·or·al** *adj* — **may·or·al·ty** *n*

**maze** *n* : confusing network of passages — **mazy** *adj*

**me** *pron, objective case of* I
**mead•ow** *n* **:** low-lying usu. level grassland — **mead•ow•land** *n*
**mea•ger, mea•gre** *adj* **1 :** thin **2 :** lacking richness or strength — **mea•ger•ly** *adv* — **mea•ger•ness** *n*
[1]**meal** *n* **1 :** food to be eaten at one time **2 :** act of eating — **meal•time** *n*
[2]**meal** *n* **:** ground grain — **mealy** *adj*
[1]**mean** *adj* **1 :** humble **2 :** worthy of or showing little regard **3 :** stingy **4 :** malicious — **mean•ly** *adv* — **mean•ness** *n*
[2]**mean** *vb* **meant; meant 1 :** intend **2 :** serve to convey, show, or indicate **3 :** be important — **mean•ing** *n* — **mean•ing•ful** *adj* — **mean•ing•ful•ly** *adv* — **mean•ing•less** *adj*
[3]**mean** *n* **1 :** middle point **2** *pl* **:** something that helps gain an end **3** *pl* **:** material resources **4 :** sum of several quantities divided by the number of quantities ~ *adj* **:** being a mean
**mean•time** *n* **:** intervening time — **meantime** *adv*
**mean•while** *n* **:** meantime ~ *adv* **1 :** meantime **2 :** at the same time
**mea•sles** *n pl* **:** disease that is marked by red spots on the skin
**mea•sure** *n* **1 :** moderate amount **2 :** dimensions or amount **3 :** something to show amount **4 :** unit or system of measurement **5 :** act of measuring **6 :** means to an end ~ *vb* **1 :** find out or mark off size or amount of **2 :** have a specified measurement — **mea•sur•able** *adj* — **mea•sur•ably** *adv* — **mea•sure•less** *adj* — **mea•sure•ment** *n* — **mea•sur•er** *n*
**meat** *n* **1 :** food **2 :** animal flesh used as food — **meat•ball** *n* — **meaty** *adj*
**me•chan•ic** *n* **:** worker who repairs machinery
**me•chan•i•cal** *adj* **1 :** relating to machines or mechanics **2 :** involuntary — **me•chan•i•cal•ly** *adv*
**me•chan•ics** *n sing or pl* **1 :** branch of physics dealing with energy and forces in relation to bodies **2 :** mechanical details
**mech•a•nism** *n* **1 :** piece of machinery **2 :** technique for gaining a result **3 :** basic processes producing a phenomenon — **mech•a•nis•tic** *adj* — **mech•a•ni•za•tion** *n* — **mech•a•nize** *vb* — **mech•a•niz•er** *n*
**med•al** *n* **1 :** religious pin or pendant **2 :** coinlike commemorative metal piece
**med•dle** *vb* **:** interfere — **med•dler** *n* — **med•dle•some** *adj*
**me•dia** *n pl* **:** communications organizations
**me•di•an** *n* **:** middle value in a range — **me•di•an** *adj*
**me•di•ate** *vb* **:** help settle a dispute — **me•di•a•tion** *n* — **me•di•a•tor** *n*
**med•i•cal** *adj* **:** relating to medicine — **med•i•cal•ly** *adv*
**med•i•ca•tion** *n* **1 :** act of medicating **2 :** medicine — **med•i•cate** *vb*
**med•i•cine** *n* **1 :** preparation used to treat disease **2 :** science dealing with the cure of disease — **me•dic•i•nal** *adj* — **me•dic•i•nal•ly** *adv*
**me•di•eval, me•di•ae•val** *adj* **:** of or relating to the Middle Ages — **me•di•e•val•ist** *n*
**me•di•o•cre** *adj* **:** not very good — **me•di•oc•ri•ty** *n*
**med•i•tate** *vb* **:** contemplate — **med•i•ta•tion** *n* — **med•i•ta•tive** *adj* — **med•i•ta•tive•ly** *adv*
**me•di•um** *n* **1 :** middle position or degree **2 :** means of effecting or conveying something **3 :** surrounding substance **4 :** means of communication **5 :** mode of artistic expression — **me•di•um** *adj*
**meek** *adj* **1 :** having a mild manner or personality **2 :** lacking spirit — **meek•ly** *adv* — **meek•ness** *n*
**meet** *vb* **met; met 1 :** run into **2 :** join **3 :** oppose **4 :** assemble **5 :** satisfy **6 :** be introduced to ~ *n* **:** sports team competition
**meet•ing** *n* **:** a getting together — **meet•ing•house** *n*
**mega•byte** *n* **:** unit of computer storage capacity
**mega•hertz** *n* **:** one million hertz
**mel•an•choly** *n* **:** depression — **mel•an•chol•ic** *adj* — **melancholy** *adj*
**mel•low** *adj* **1 :** grown gentle or mild **2 :** rich and full — **mel•low** *vb* — **mel•low•ness** *n*
**mel•o•dy** *n* **1 :** agreeable sound **2 :** succession of musical notes — **me•lod•ic** *adj* — **me•lod•i•cal•ly** *adv* — **me•lo•di•ous** *adj* — **me•lo•di•ous•ly** *adv* — **me•lo•di•ous•ness** *n*
**mel•on** *n* **:** gourdlike fruit
**melt** *vb* **1 :** change from solid to liquid usu. by heat **2 :** dissolve or disappear gradually **3 :** move or be moved emotionally
**mem•ber** *n* **1 :** part of a person, animal, or plant **2 :** one of a group **3 :** part of a whole — **mem•ber•ship** *n*
**memo** *n* **:** memorandum
**mem•o•ra•bil•ia** *n pl* **1 :** memorable things **2 :** souvenirs
**mem•o•ra•ble** *adj* **:** worth remembering — **mem•o•ra•bil•i•ty** *n* — **mem•o•ra•ble•ness** *n* — **mem•o•ra•bly** *adv*
**mem•o•ran•dum** *n* **:** informal note
**me•mo•ri•al** *n* **:** something (as a monument) meant to keep remembrance alive — **memorial** *adj* — **me•mo•ri•al•ize** *vb*
**Memorial Day** *n* **:** last Monday in May or formerly May 30 observed as a legal holiday in commemoration of dead servicemen
**mem•o•ry** *n* **1 :** power of remembering **2 :** something remembered **3 :** commemoration **4 :** time within which past events are remembered — **mem•o•ri•za•tion** *n* — **mem•o•rize** *vb* — **mem•o•riz•er** *n*
**men** *pl of* MAN
**men•ace** *n* **:** threat of danger ~ *vb* **1 :** threaten **2 :** endanger — **men•ac•ing•ly** *adv*
**mend** *vb* **1 :** improve **2 :** repair **3 :** heal — **mend** *n* — **mend•er** *n*
**me•nial** *adj* **1 :** relating to servants **2 :** humble ~ *n* **:** domestic servant — **me•ni•al•ly** *adv*
**meno•pause** *n* **:** time when menstruation ends — **meno•paus•al** *adj*
**me•no•rah** *n* **:** candelabrum used in Jewish worship
**men•stru•a•tion** *n* **:** monthly discharge of blood from the uterus — **men•stru•al** *adj* — **men•stru•ate** *vb*
**men•tal** *adj* **:** relating to the mind or its disorders — **men•tal•i•ty** *n* — **men•tal•ly** *adv*
**men•tion** *vb* **:** refer to — **men•tion** *n*
**men•tor** *n* **:** instructor
**menu** *n* **1 :** restaurant's list of food **2 :** list of offerings
**me•ow** *n* **:** characteristic cry of a cat — **meow** *vb*
**mer•chan•dise** *n* **:** goods bought and sold ~ *vb* **:** buy and sell — **mer•chan•dis•er** *n*
**mer•chant** *n* **:** one who buys and sells
**mer•cu•ry** *n* **:** heavy liquid metallic chemical element
**mer•cy** *n* **1 :** show of pity or leniency **2 :** divine blessing — **mer•ci•ful** *adj* — **mer•ci•ful•ly** *adv* — **mer•ci•less** *adj* — **mer•ci•less•ly** *adv* — **mercy** *adj*
**mere** *adj, superlative* **mer•est :** nothing more than — **mere•ly** *adv*
**merge** *vb* **1 :** unite **2 :** blend — **merg•er** *n*
**me•rid•i•an** *n* **:** imaginary circle on the earth's surface passing through the poles — **me•rid•i•an** *adj*
**mer•it** *n* **1 :** praiseworthy quality **2** *pl* **:** rights and wrongs of a legal case ~ *vb* **:** deserve — **mer•i•to•ri•ous** *adj* — **mer•i•to•ri•ous•ly** *adv* — **mer•i•to•ri•ous•ness** *n*
**mer•ry** *adj* **:** full of high spirits — **mer•ri•ly** *adv* — **mer•ri•ment** *n* — **mer•ry•mak•er** *n* — **mer•ry•mak•ing** *n*
**merry–go–round** *n* **:** revolving amusement ride
**mesdames** *pl of* MADAM *or of* MADAME *or of* MRS.
**mesdemoiselles** *pl of* MADEMOISELLE
**mesh** *n* **1 :** one of the openings in a net **2 :** net fabric **3 :** working contact ~ *vb* **:** fit together properly — **meshed** *adj*
**mes•mer•ize** *vb* **:** hypnotize
**mess** *n* **1 :** meal eaten by a group **2 :** confused, dirty, or offensive state ~ *vb* **1 :** make dirty or untidy **2 :** work at something in a casual manner **3 :** interfere — **messy** *adj*
**mes•sage** *n* **:** news, information, or a command sent by one person to another
**mes•sen•ger** *n* **:** one who carries a message or does an errand
**messieurs** *pl of* MONSIEUR
**Messrs.** *pl of* MR.
**met** *past of* MEET
**me•tab•o•lism** *n* **:** biochemical processes necessary to life — **met•a•bol•ic** *adj* — **me•tab•o•lize** *vb*
**met•al** *n* **:** shiny substance that can be melted and shaped and conducts heat and electricity — **me•tal•lic** *adj* — **met•al•ware** *n* — **met•al•work** *n* — **met•al•work•er** *n* — **met•al•work•ing** *n*
**met•a•phor** *n* **:** use of a word denoting one kind of object or idea in place of another to suggest a likeness between them — **met•a•phor•i•cal** *adj*
**me•te•or** *n* **:** small body that produces a streak of light as it burns up in the atmosphere
**me•te•or•ic** *adj* **1 :** relating to a meteor **2 :** sudden and spectacular — **me•te•or•i•cal•ly** *adv*
**me•te•o•rol•o•gy** *n* **:** science of weather — **me•te•o•ro•log•ic, me•te•o•ro•log•i•cal** *adj* — **me•te•o•rol•o•gist** *n*
[1]**me•ter** *n* **:** unit of length equal to 39.37 inches
[2]**me•ter** *n* **:** measuring instrument
**meth•od** *n* **1 :** procedure for achieving an end **2 :** orderly arrangement or plan — **me•thod•i•cal** *adj* — **me•thod•i•cal•ly** *adv* — **me•thod•i•cal•ness** *n*
**met•ric, met•ri•cal** *adj* **:** relating to meter or the metric system — **met•ri•cal•ly** *adv*
**metric system** *n* **:** system of weights and measures using the meter and kilogram
**me•trop•o•lis** *n* **:** major city — **met•ro•pol•i•tan** *adj*
**mice** *pl of* MOUSE
**mi•cro•or•gan•ism** *n* **:** very tiny living thing
**mi•cro•phone** *n* **:** instrument for changing sound waves into variations of an electric current
**mi•cro•scope** *n* **:** optical device for magnifying tiny objects — **mi•cro•scop•ic** *adj* — **mi•cro•scop•i•cal•ly** *adv* — **mi•cros•copy** *n*
**mi•cro•wave** *n* **1 :** short radio wave **2 :** oven that cooks food using microwaves ~ *vb* **:** heat or cook in a microwave oven — **mi•cro•wav•able, mi•cro•wave•able** *adj*
**mid** *adj* **:** middle — **mid•point** *n* — **mid•stream** *n* — **mid•sum•mer** *n* — **mid•town** *n or adj* — **mid•week** *n* — **mid•win•ter** *n* — **mid•year** *n*
**mid•air** *n* **:** a point in the air well above the ground
**mid•day** *n* **:** noon
**mid•dle** *adj* **1 :** equally distant from the extremes **2 :** being at neither extreme ~ *n* **:** middle part or point
**Middle Ages** *n pl* **:** period from about A.D. 500 to about 1500
**midg•et** *n* **:** very small person or thing
**mid•night** *n* **:** 12 o'clock at night
**midst** *n* **:** position close to or surrounded by others — **midst** *prep*
[1]**might** *past of* MAY — used to express permission or possibility or as a polite alternative to *may*
[2]**might** *n* **:** power or resources
**mighty** *adj* **1 :** very strong **2 :** great — **might•i•ly** *adv* — **might•i•ness** *n* — **mighty** *adv*
**mi•graine** *n* **:** severe headache often with nausea
**mi•grate** *vb* **1 :** move from one place to another **2 :** pass periodically from one region or climate to another — **mi•grant** *n* — **mi•gra•tion** *n* — **mi•gra•to•ry** *adj*
**mild** *adj* **1 :** gentle in nature or behavior **2 :** moderate in action or effect — **mild•ly** *adv* — **mild•ness** *n*
**mil•dew** *n* **:** whitish fungal growth — **mil•dew** *vb*
**mile** *n* **:** unit of length equal to 5280 feet
**mile•age** *n* **1 :** allowance per mile for traveling expenses **2 :** amount or rate of use expressed in miles
**mile•stone** *n* **:** significant point in development
**mil•i•tant** *adj* **:** aggressively active or hostile — **mil•i•tan•cy** *n* — **militant** *n* — **mil•i•tant•ly** *adv*
**mil•i•tary** *adj* **1 :** relating to soldiers, arms, or war **2 :** relating to or performed by armed forces ~ *n* **:** armed forces or the people in them — **mil•i•tar•i•ly** *adv* — **mil•i•tar•ism** *n* — **mil•i•ta•rist** *n* — **mil•i•tar•is•tic** *adj*
**mi•li•tia** *n* **:** civilian soldiers — **mi•li•tia•man** *n*
**milk** *n* **:** white nutritive fluid secreted by female mammals for feeding their young ~ *vb* **1 :** draw off the milk of **2 :** draw something from as if by milking — **milk•er** *n* — **milk•i•ness** *n* — **milky** *adj*
**mill** *n* **1 :** building in which grain is ground into flour **2 :** manufacturing plant **3 :** machine used esp. for forming or processing ~ *vb* **1 :** subject to a process in a mill **2 :** move in a circle — **mill•er** *n*
**mil•len•ni•um** *n* **:** a period of 1000 years
**mil•li•gram** *n* **:** 1/1000 gram
**mil•li•li•ter** *n* **:** 1/1000 liter
**mil•li•me•ter :** 1/1000 meter
**mil•lion** *n* **:** 1000 thousands — **mil•lion** *adj* — **mil•lionth** *adj or n*
**mil•lion•aire** *n* **:** person worth a million or more (as of dollars)
**mime** *n* **1 :** mimic **2 :** pantomime — **mime** *vb*
**mim•ic** *n* **:** one that mimics ~ *vb* **1 :** imitate closely **2 :** ridicule by imitation — **mim•ic•ry** *n*
**mince** *vb* **1 :** cut into small pieces **2 :** choose (one's words) carefully **3 :** walk in a prim affected manner
**mind** *n* **1 :** memory **2 :** the part of an individual that feels, perceives, and esp. reasons **3 :** intention **4 :** normal mental condition **5 :** opinion **6 :** intellectual ability ~ *vb* **1 :** attend to **2 :** obey **3 :** be concerned about **4 :** be careful — **mind•ed** *adj* — **mind•less** *adj* — **mind•less•ly** *adv* — **mind•less•ness** *n*
**mind•ful** *adj* **:** aware or attentive — **mind•ful•ly** *adv* — **mind•ful•ness** *n*
[1]**mine** *pron* **:** that which belongs to me
[2]**mine** *n* **1 :** excavation from which minerals are taken **2 :** explosive device placed in the ground or water for destroying enemy vehicles or vessels that later pass ~ *vb* **1 :** get ore from **2 :** place military mines in — **mine•field** *n* — **min•er** *n*
**min•er•al** *n* **1 :** crystalline substance not of organic origin **2 :** useful natural substance (as coal) obtained from the ground — **min•er•al** *adj* — **min•er•al•o•gy** *n* — **min•er•al•o•gist** *n*
**min•gle** *vb* **:** bring together or mix
**min•ia•ture** *n* **:** tiny copy or very small version — **miniature** *adj* — **min•ia•tur•ist** *n* — **min•ia•tur•ize** *vb*
**min•i•mal** *adj* **:** relating to or being a minimum — **min•i•mal•ly** *adv*
**min•i•mize** *vb* **1 :** reduce to a minimum **2 :** underestimate intentionally
**min•i•mum** *n* **:** lowest quantity or amount — **min•i•mum** *adj*

**mini•skirt** *n* : very short skirt

**min•is•ter** *n* **1** : Protestant member of the clergy **2** : high officer of state **3** : diplomatic representative ~ *vb* : give aid or service — **min•is•te•ri•al** *adj* — **min•is•tra•tion** *n*

**min•is•try** *n* **1** : office or duties of a minister **2** : body of ministers **3** : government department headed by a minister

**mini•van** *n* : small van

**mi•nor** *adj* **1** : less in size, importance, or value **2** : not serious ~ *n* **1** : person not yet of legal age **2** : secondary field of academic specialization

**mi•nor•i•ty** *n* **1** : time or state of being a minor **2** : smaller number (as of votes) **3** : part of a population differing from others (as in race or religion)

**[1]mint** *n* **1** : fragrant herb that yields a flavoring oil **2** : mint-flavored piece of candy — **minty** *adj*

**[2]mint** *n* **1** : place where coins are made **2** : vast sum ~ *adj* : unused — **mint** *vb* — **mint•er** *n*

**mi•nus** *prep* **1** : diminished by **2** : lacking ~ *n* : negative quantity or quality

**mi•nus•cule, min•is•cule** *adj* : very small

**[1]min•ute** *n* **1** : 60th part of an hour or of a degree **2** : short time **3** *pl* : official record of a meeting

**[2]mi•nute** *adj* **1** : very small **2** : marked by close attention to details — **mi•nute•ly** *adv* — **mi•nute•ness** *n*

**mir•a•cle** *n* **1** : extraordinary event taken as a sign of divine intervention in human affairs **2** : marvel — **mi•rac•u•lous** *adj* — **mi•rac•u•lous•ly** *adv*

**mir•ror** *n* : smooth surface (as of glass) that reflects images ~ *vb* : reflect in or as if in a mirror

**mirth** *n* : gladness and laughter — **mirth•ful** *adj* — **mirth•ful•ly** *adv* — **mirth•ful•ness** *n* — **mirth•less** *adj*

**mis•be•have** *vb* : behave improperly — **mis•be•hav•er** *n* — **mis•be•hav•ior** *n*

**mis•cel•la•neous** *adj* : consisting of many things of different kinds — **mis•cel•la•ny** *n* — **mis•cel•la•neous•ly** *adv* — **mis•cel•la•neous•ness** *n*

**mis•chief** *n* : conduct esp. of a child that annoys or causes minor damage

**mis•chie•vous** *adj* **1** : causing annoyance or minor injury **2** : irresponsibly playful — **mis•chie•vous•ly** *adv* — **mis•chie•vous•ness** *n*

**mis•de•mean•or** *n* : crime less serious than a felony

**mi•ser** *n* : person who hoards and is stingy with money — **mi•ser•li•ness** *n* — **mi•ser•ly** *adj*

**mis•er•a•ble** *adj* **1** : wretchedly deficient **2** : causing extreme discomfort **3** : shameful — **mis•er•a•ble•ness** *n* — **mis•er•a•bly** *adv*

**mis•ery** *n* : suffering and want caused by distress or poverty

**mis•fit** *n* : person poorly adjusted to his environment

**mis•for•tune** *n* **1** : bad luck **2** : unfortunate condition or event

**mis•giv•ing** *n* : doubt or concern

**mis•in•ter•pret** *vb* : understand or explain wrongly — **mis•in•ter•pre•ta•tion** *n*

**mis•lay** *vb* : misplace

**mis•lead** *vb* : lead in a wrong direction or into error — **mis•lead•ing** *adj* — **mis•lead•ing•ly** *adv*

**mis•place** *vb* : put in a wrong or unremembered place

**mis•pro•nounce** *vb* : pronounce incorrectly — **mis•pro•nun•ci•a•tion** *n*

**mis•quote** *vb* : quote incorrectly — **mis•quo•ta•tion** *n*

**mis•rep•re•sent** *vb* : represent falsely or unfairly — **mis•rep•re•sen•ta•tion** *n*

**[1]miss** *vb* **1** : fail to hit, reach, or contact **2** : notice the absence of **3** : fail to obtain **4** : avoid **5** : omit — **miss** *n*

**[2]miss** *n* : young unmarried woman or girl — often used as a title

**mis•sile** *n* : object (as a stone or rocket) thrown or shot

**miss•ing** *adj* : absent or lost

**mis•sion** *n* **1** : ministry sent by a church to spread its teaching **2** : group of diplomats sent to a foreign country **3** : task

**mis•sion•ary** *adj* : relating to religious missions ~ *n* : person sent to spread religious faith

**mis•spell** *vb* : spell incorrectly — **mis•spell•ing** *n*

**mis•step** *n* **1** : wrong step **2** : mistake

**mist** *n* : particles of water falling as fine rain

**mis•take** *n* **1** : misunderstanding or wrong belief **2** : wrong action or statement — **mis•take** *vb* — **mis•tak•en** *adj* — **mis•tak•en•ly** *adv*

**mis•ter** *n* : sir — used without a name in addressing a man

**mis•treat** *vb* : treat badly — **mis•treat•ment** *n*

**mis•tress** *n* **1** : woman in control **2** : a woman not his wife with whom a married man has recurrent sexual relations

**misty** *adj* **1** : obscured by mist **2** : tearful — **mist•i•ly** *adv* — **mist•i•ness** *n*

**mis•un•der•stand** *vb* **1** : fail to understand **2** : interpret incorrectly — **mis•un•der•stand•ing** *n*

**mis•use** *vb* **1** : use incorrectly **2** : mistreat — **mis•use** *n*

**mitt** *n* : mittenlike baseball glove

**mit•ten** *n* : hand covering without finger sections

**mix** *vb* : combine or join into one mass or group ~ *n* : commercially prepared food mixture — **mix•able** *adj* — **mix•er** *n* — **mix up** *vb* : confuse

**mix•ture** *n* : act or product of mixing

**mix–up** *n* : instance of confusion

**moan** *n* : low prolonged sound of pain or grief — **moan** *vb*

**mob** *n* **1** : large disorderly crowd **2** : criminal gang ~ *vb* : crowd around and attack or annoy

**mo•bile** *adj* : capable of moving or being moved ~ *n* : suspended art construction with freely moving parts — **mo•bil•i•ty** *n*

**mo•bi•lize** *vb* : assemble and make ready for war duty — **mo•bi•li•za•tion** *n*

**moc•ca•sin** *n* **1** : heelless shoe **2** : venomous U.S. snake

**mock** *vb* **1** : ridicule **2** : mimic in derision ~ *adj* **1** : simulated **2** : phony — **mock•er** *n* — **mock•ery** *n* — **mock•ing•ly** *adv*

**mode** *n* **1** : particular form or variety **2** : style — **mod•al** *adj* — **mod•ish** *adj*

**mod•el** *n* **1** : structural design **2** : miniature representation **3** : something worthy of copying **4** : one who poses for an artist or displays clothes **5** : type or design ~ *vb* **1** : shape **2** : work as a model ~ *adj* **1** : serving as a pattern **2** : being a miniature representation of

**mo•dem** *n* : device by which a computer communicates with another computer over telephone lines

**mod•er•ate** *adj* : avoiding extremes ~ *vb* **1** : lessen the intensity of **2** : act as one who presides — **mod•er•ate** *n* — **mod•er•ate•ly** *adv* — **mod•er•ate•ness** *n* — **mod•er•a•tor** *n* — **mod•er•a•tion** *n*

**mod•ern** *adj* : relating to or characteristic of the present — **modern** *n* — **mo•der•ni•ty** *n* — **mod•ern•i•za•tion** *n* — **mod•ern•ize** *vb* — **mod•ern•iz•er** *n* — **mod•ern•ly** *adv* — **mod•ern•ness** *n*

**mod•est** *adj* **1** : having a moderate estimate of oneself **2** : reserved or decent in thoughts or actions **3** : limited in size, amount, or aim — **mod•est•ly** *adv* — **mod•es•ty** *n*

**mod•i•fy** *vb* **1** : limit the meaning of **2** : change — **mod•i•fi•ca•tion** *n* — **mod•i•fi•er** *n*

**mod•u•late** *vb* **1** : keep in proper measure or proportion **2** : vary a radio wave — **mod•u•la•tion** *n* — **mod•u•la•tor** *n* — **mod•u•la•to•ry** *adj*

**moist** *adj* : slightly or moderately wet — **moist•en** *vb* — **moist•en•er** *n* — **moist•ly** *adv* — **moist•ness** *n*

**mois•ture** *n* : small amount of liquid that causes dampness — **mois•tur•ize** *vb* — **mois•tur•iz•er** *n*

**mo•lar** *n* : grinding tooth — **mo•lar** *adj*

**mo•las•ses** *n* : thick brown syrup from raw sugar

**[1]mold** *n* : frame or cavity for forming ~ *vb* : shape in or as if in a mold — **mold•er** *n*

**[2]mold** *n* : surface growth of fungus ~ *vb* : become moldy — **mold•i•ness** *n* — **moldy** *adj*

**[1]mole** *n* : spot on the skin

**[2]mole** *n* : small burrowing mammal — **mole•hill** *n*

**mo•lest** *vb* **1** : annoy or disturb **2** : force physical and usu. sexual contact on — **mo•les•ta•tion** *n* — **mo•lest•er** *n*

**mol•li•fy** *vb* : soothe in temper — **mol•li•fi•ca•tion** *n*

**mom** *n* : mother

**mo•ment** *n* **1** : tiny portion of time **2** : time of excellence **3** : importance

**mo•men•tary** *adj* : continuing only a moment — **mo•men•tar•i•ly** *adv* — **mo•men•tar•i•ness** *n*

**mo•men•tous** *adj* : very important — **mo•men•tous•ly** *adv* — **mo•men•tous•ness** *n*

**mo•men•tum** *n* : force of a moving body

**mon•arch** *n* : ruler of a kingdom or empire — **mo•nar•chi•cal** *adj* — **mon•ar•chy** *n*

**mon•as•tery** *n* : house for monks — **mo•nas•tic** *adj or n* — **mo•nas•ti•cal•ly** *adv* — **mo•nas•ti•cism** *n*

**Mon•day** *n* : 2d day of the week

**mon•ey** *n* **1** : something (as coins or paper currency) used in buying **2** : wealth — **mon•e•tary** *adj* — **mon•eyed** *adj* — **mon•ey•lend•er** *n*

**mon•i•tor** *n* **1** : student assistant **2** : television screen ~ *vb* : watch or observe esp. for quality

**monk** *n* : member of a religious order living in a monastery — **monk•ish** *adj*

**mon•key** *n* : small long-tailed arboreal primate

**mono•logue** *n* : long speech — **mono•logu•ist, mo•no•lo•gist** *n*

**mo•nop•o•ly** *n* **1** : exclusive ownership or control of a commodity **2** : one controlling a monopoly — **mo•nop•o•list** *n* — **mo•nop•o•lis•tic** *adj* — **mo•nop•o•li•za•tion** *n* — **mo•nop•o•lize** *vb*

**mo•not•o•nous** *adj* **1** : sounded in one unvarying tone **2** : tediously uniform — **mo•not•o•nous•ly** *adv* — **mo•not•o•nous•ness** *n* — **mo•not•o•ny** *n*

**mon•ster** *n* **1** : abnormal or terrifying animal **2** : ugly, wicked, or cruel person — **mon•stros•i•ty** *n* — **mon•strous** *adj* — **mon•strous•ly** *adv*

**month** *n* : 12th part of a year — **month•ly** *adv or adj or n*

**mon•u•ment** *n* : structure erected in remembrance

**mon•u•men•tal** *adj* **1** : serving as a monument **2** : outstanding **3** : very great — **mon•u•men•tal•ly** *adv*

**moo** *vb* : make the noise of a cow — **moo** *n*

**mood** *n* : state of mind or emotion

**moody** *adj* **1** : sad **2** : subject to changing moods and esp. to bad moods — **mood•i•ly** *adv* — **mood•i•ness** *n*

**moon** *n* : natural satellite (as of earth) — **moon•beam** *n* — **moon•light** *n* — **moon•lit** *adj*

**moor** *vb* : fasten with line or anchor

**moor•ing** *n* : place where boat can be moored

**moose** *n* (**moose**) : large heavy-antlered deer

**moot** *adj* : open to question

**mop** *n* : floor-cleaning implement ~ *vb* : use a mop on

**mope** *vb* : be sad or listless

**mor•al** *adj* **1** : relating to principles of right and wrong **2** : conforming to a standard of right behavior **3** : relating to or acting on the mind, character, or will ~ *n* **1** : point of a story **2** *pl* : moral practices or teachings — **mor•al•ist** *n* — **mor•al•is•tic** *adj* — **mor•al•i•ty** *n* — **mor•al•ize** *vb* — **mor•al•ly** *adv*

**mo•rale** *n* : emotional attitude

**mor•a•to•ri•um** *n* : suspension of activity

**mor•bid** *adj* **1** : relating to disease **2** : gruesome — **mor•bid•i•ty** *n* — **mor•bid•ly** *adv* — **mor•bid•ness** *n*

**more** *adj* **1** : greater **2** : additional ~ *adv* **1** : in addition **2** : to a greater degree ~ *n* **1** : greater quantity **2** : additional amount ~ *pron* : additional ones

**morgue** *n* : temporary holding place for dead bodies

**morn** *n* : morning

**morn•ing** *n* : time from sunrise to noon

**mo•ron** *n* **1** : mentally retarded person **2** : very stupid person — **mo•ron•ic** *adj* — **mo•ron•i•cal•ly** *adv*

**mor•sel** *n* : small piece or quantity

**mor•tal** *adj* **1** : causing or subject to death **2** : extreme — **mortal** *n* — **mor•tal•i•ty** *n* — **mor•tal•ly** *adv*

**mort•gage** *n* : transfer of property rights as security for a loan — **mortgage** *vb* — **mort•gag•ee** *n* — **mort•ga•gor** *n*

**mo•sa•ic** *n* : inlaid stone decoration — **mosaic** *adj*

**Mos•lem** *var of* MUSLIM

**mosque** *n* : building where Muslims worship

**mos•qui•to** *n* : biting bloodsucking insect

**moss** *n* : green seedless plant — **mossy** *adj*

**most** *adj* **1** : majority of **2** : greatest ~ *adv* : to the greatest or a very great degree ~ *n* : greatest amount ~ *pron* : greatest number or part

**most•ly** *adv* : mainly

**mo•tel** *n* : hotel with rooms accessible from the parking lot

**moth** *n* : small pale insect related to the butterflies

**moth•er** *n* **1** : female parent **2** : source ~ *vb* **1** : give birth to **2** : cherish or protect — **moth•er•hood** *n* — **moth•er•land** *n* — **moth•er•less** *adj* — **moth•er•ly** *adj*

**moth•er–in–law** *n* **mothers–in–law** : spouse's mother

**mo•tif** *n* : dominant theme

**mo•tion** *n* **1** : act or instance of moving **2** : proposal for action ~ *vb* : direct by a movement — **mo•tion•less** *adj* — **mo•tion•less•ly** *adv* — **mo•tion•less•ness** *n*

**motion picture** *n* : movie

**mo•ti•vate** *vb* : provide with a motive — **mo•ti•va•tion** *n* — **mo•ti•va•tor** *n*

**mo•tive** *n* : cause of a person's action ~ *adj* **1** : moving to action **2** : relating to motion — **mo•tive•less** *adj*

**mo•tor** *n* : unit that supplies power or motion ~ *vb* : travel by automobile — **mo•tor•bike** *n* — **mo•tor•boat** *n* — **mo•tor•cy•cle** *n* — **mo•tor•ist** *n* — **mo•tor•ize** *vb*

**mot•to** *n* : brief guiding rule

**mould** *var of* MOLD

**mound** *n* : pile (as of earth)

**mount** *vb* **1** : increase in amount **2** : get up on **3** : put in position ~ *n* **1** : frame or support **2** : horse to ride — **mount•able** *adj* — **mount•er** *n*

**moun•tain** *n* : elevated land higher than a hill — **moun•tain•ous** *adj* — **moun•tain•top** *n*

**mourn** *vb* : feel or express grief — **mourn•er** *n* — **mourn•ful** *adj* — **mourn•ful•ly** *adv* — **mourn•ful•ness** *n* — **mourn•ing** *n*

**mouse** *n* (**mice**) **1** : small rodent **2** : device for controlling cursor movement on a computer display — **mouse•trap** *n or vb* — **mousy, mous•ey** *adj*

**mousse** *n* **1** : light chilled dessert **2** : foamy hair-styling preparation

**mous•tache** *var of* MUSTACHE

**mouth** *n* : opening through which an animal takes in food ~ *vb* **1** : speak **2** : repeat without comprehension or sincerity **3** : form soundlessly with the lips — **mouthed** adj — **mouth·ful** n

**mouth·piece** n **1** : part (as of a musical instrument) held in or to the mouth **2** : person who speaks for another

**move** vb **1** : go or cause to go to another point **2** : change residence **3** : change or cause to change position **4** : take or cause to take action **5** : make a formal request **6** : stir the emotions ~ n **1** : act or instance of moving **2** : step taken to achieve a goal — **mov·able**, **move·able** adj — **move·ment** n — **mov·er** n

**mov·ie** n : projected picture in which persons and objects seem to move

**mow** vb : cut with a machine — **mow·er** n

**Mr.** n (**Messrs.**) — conventional title for a man

**Mrs.** n (**Mes·dames**) — conventional title for a married woman

**Ms.** n — conventional title for a woman

**much** adj **more; most** : great in quantity, extent, or degree ~ adv **more; most** : to a great degree or extent ~ n : great quantity, extent, or degree

**muck** n : manure, dirt, or mud — **mucky** adj

**mu·cus** n : slippery protective secretion of membranes (**mucous membranes**) lining body cavities — **mu·cous** adj

**mud** n : soft wet earth — **mud·di·ly** adv — **mud·di·ness** n — **mud·dy** adj or vb

**mud·dle** vb **1** : make, be, or act confused **2** : make a mess of — **muddle** n — **mud·dle·head·ed** adj

**muf·fin** n : soft cake baked in a cup-shaped container

**muf·fle** vb **1** : wrap up **2** : dull the sound of — **muf·fler** n

---

¹**mug** n : drinking cup ~ vb : make faces

²**mug** vb : assault with intent to rob — **mug·ger** n

**mug·gy** adj : hot and humid — **mug·gi·ness** n

¹**mule** n **1** : offspring of a male ass and a female horse **2** : stubborn person — **mul·ish** adj — **mul·ish·ly** adv — **mul·ish·ness** n

²**mule** n : backless shoe

**mull** vb : ponder

**mul·ti·ple** adj **1** : several or many **2** : various ~ n : product of one number by another

**mul·ti·pli·ca·tion** n **1** : increase **2** : short method of repeated addition

**mul·ti·ply** vb **1** : increase in number **2** : perform multiplication — **mul·ti·pli·er** n

**mul·ti·tude** n : great number — **mul·ti·tu·di·nous** adj

**mum·ble** vb : speak indistinctly — **mum·ble** n — **mum·bler** n

**mum·my** n : embalmed body — **mum·mi·fi·ca·tion** n — **mum·mi·fy** vb

**mumps** n sing or pl : virus disease with swelling esp. of the salivary glands

**munch** vb : chew

**mun·dane** adj **1** : relating to the world **2** : lacking concern for the ideal or spiritual — **mun·dane·ly** adv

**mu·nic·i·pal** adj : of or relating to a town or city — **mu·nic·i·pal·i·ty** n

**mur·der** n : unlawful killing of a person ~ vb : commit a murder — **mur·der·er** n — **mur·der·ess** n — **mur·der·ous** adj — **mur·der·ous·ly** adv

**mur·mur** n **1** : muttered complaint **2** : low indistinct sound — **murmur** vb — **mur·mur·er** n — **mur·mur·ous** adj

**mus·cle** n **1** : body tissue capable of contracting to produce motion **2** :

---

strength ~ vb : force one's way — **mus·cled** adj — **mus·cu·lar** adj — **mus·cu·lar·i·ty** n

¹**muse** vb : ponder — **mus·ing·ly** adv

²**muse** n : source of inspiration

**mu·se·um** n : institution displaying objects of interest

**mush** n **1** : corn meal boiled in water or something of similar consistency **2** : sentimental nonsense — **mushy** adj

**mush·room** n : caplike organ of a fungus ~ vb : grow rapidly

**mu·sic** n : vocal or instrumental sounds — **mu·si·cal** adj or n — **mu·si·cal·ly** adv

**mu·si·cian** n : composer or performer of music — **mu·si·cian·ly** adj — **mu·si·cian·ship** n

**musk** n : strong-smelling substance from an Asiatic deer used in perfume — **musk·i·ness** n — **musky** adj

**Mus·lim** n : adherent of Islam — **Muslim** adj

**mus·lin** n : cotton fabric

**muss** n : untidy state ~ vb : mess up the arrangement of — **muss·i·ly** adv — **muss·i·ness** n — **mussy** adj

**must** vb : used as an auxiliary esp. to express a command, obligation, or necessity ~ n : something necessary

**mus·tache** n : hair of the human upper lip

**mus·tard** n : pungent yellow seasoning

**mus·ter** vb **1** : assemble **2** : arouse ~ n : assembled group

**musty** adj : stale — **must·i·ly** adv — **must·i·ness** n

**mu·tate** vb : undergo change in a hereditary character — **mu·tant** adj or n — **mu·ta·tion** n — **mu·ta·tive** adj

**mute** adj **1** : unable to speak **2** : silent ~ n **1** : one who is mute **2** : muffling

---

device ~ vb : muffle — **mute·ly** adv — **mute·ness** n

**mu·ti·late** vb : damage seriously (as by cutting off or altering an essential part) — **mu·ti·la·tion** n — **mu·ti·la·tor** n

**mu·ti·ny** n : rebellion — **mu·ti·neer** n — **mu·ti·nous** adj — **mu·ti·nous·ly** adv — **mutiny** vb

**mutt** n : dog that is of mixed breed

**mut·ter** vb **1** : speak indistinctly or softly **2** : grumble — **mutter** n

**mu·tu·al** adj **1** : given or felt by one another in equal amount **2** : common — **mu·tu·al·ly** adv

**muz·zle** n **1** : nose and jaws of an animal **2** : muzzle covering to immobilize an animal's jaws **3** : discharge end of a gun ~ vb : restrain with or as if with a muzzle

**my** adj **1** : relating to me or myself **2** : used interjectionally esp. to express surprise

**myr·i·ad** n : indefinitely large number — **myriad** adj

**my·self** pron : I, me — used reflexively or for emphasis

**mys·tery** n **1** : religious truth **2** : something not understood **3** : puzzling or secret quality or state — **mys·te·ri·ous** adj — **mys·te·ri·ous·ly** adv — **mys·te·ri·ous·ness** n

**mys·tic** adj : spiritual or mysterious ~ n : one who has spiritual experiences — **mys·ti·cal** adj — **mys·ti·cal·ly** adj — **mys·ti·cism** n

**mys·ti·fy** vb : perplex — **mys·ti·fi·ca·tion** n

**myth** n **1** : legendary narrative explaining a belief or phenomenon **2** : imaginary person or thing — **myth·i·cal** adj

**my·thol·o·gy** n : body of myths — **myth·o·log·i·cal** adj — **my·thol·o·gist** n

---

# N

**n** n : 14th letter of the alphabet

**nab** vb : seize or arrest

**na·cho** n : tortilla chip topped with a savory mixture and cheese and broiled

**nag** vb **1** : complain **2** : scold or urge continually **3** : be persistently annoying ~ n : one who nags habitually

**nail** n **1** : horny sheath at the end of each finger and toe **2** : pointed metal fastener ~ vb : fasten with a nail — **nail·er** n

**na·ive, na·ïve** adj **1** : innocent and unsophisticated **2** : easily deceived — **na·ive·ly** adv — **na·ive·ness** n — **na·ïve·té** n

**na·ked** adj **1** : having no clothes on **2** : not covered **3** : plain or obvious **4** : without aid — **na·ked·ly** adv — **na·ked·ness** n

**name** n **1** : word by which a person or thing is known **2** : disparaging word for someone **3** : distinguished reputation ~ vb **1** : give a name to **2** : mention or identify by name **3** : nominate or appoint ~ adj **1** : relating to a name **2** : prominent — **name·able** adj — **name·less** adj — **name·less·ly** adv

**name·ly** adv : that is to say

**nap** vb **1** : sleep briefly **2** : be off guard ~ n : short sleep

**nape** n : back of the neck

**nap·kin** n : small cloth for use at the table

**nar·cot·ic** n : painkilling addictive drug — **nar·cot·ic** adj

**nar·rate** vb : tell (a story) — **nar·ra·tion** n — **nar·ra·tive** n or adj — **nar·ra·tor** n

**nar·row** adj **1** : of less than standard width **2** : limited **3** : not liberal **4** : barely successful ~ vb : make narrow — **nar·row·ly** adv — **nar·row·ness** n

**nar·row–mind·ed** adj : shallow, provincial, or bigoted

---

**nasal** adj : relating to or uttered through the nose — **na·sal·ly** adv

**nas·ty** adj **1** : filthy **2** : extremely improper or offensive **3** : malicious or spiteful **4** : difficult or disagreeable **5** : unfair — **nas·ti·ly** adv — **nas·ti·ness** n

**na·tion** n **1** : people of similar characteristics **2** : community with its own territory and government — **na·tion·al** adj or n — **na·tion·al·ly** adv — **na·tion·hood** n — **na·tion·wide** adj

**na·tion·al·ism** n : devotion to national interests, unity, and independence — **na·tion·al·ist** n or adj — **na·tion·al·is·tic** adj

**na·tion·al·i·ty** n **1** : national character **2** : membership in a nation **3** : political independence **4** : ethnic group

**na·tion·al·ize** vb **1** : make national **2** : place under government control — **na·tion·al·i·za·tion** n

**na·tive** adj **1** : belonging to a person at or by way of birth **2** : born or produced in a particular place ~ n : one who belongs to a country by birth

**Na·tiv·i·ty** n **1** : birth of Christ **2** not cap : birth

**nat·u·ral** adj **1** : relating to or determined by nature **2** : not artificial **3** : simple and sincere **4** : lifelike ~ n : one having an innate talent — **nat·u·ral·ness** n

**nat·u·ral·ism** n : realism in art and literature — **nat·u·ral·ist** n — **nat·u·ral·is·tic** adj

**nat·u·ral·ize** vb **1** : become or cause to become established **2** : confer citizenship on — **nat·u·ral·i·za·tion** n

**nat·u·ral·ly** adv **1** : in a natural way **2** : as might be expected

**na·ture** n **1** : basic quality of something **2** : kind **3** : disposition **4** : physical universe **5** : natural environment

---

**naugh·ty** adj **1** : disobedient or misbehaving **2** : improper — **naught·i·ly** adv — **naught·i·ness** n

**nau·sea** n **1** : sickness of the stomach with a desire to vomit **2** : extreme disgust — **nau·se·ate** vb — **nau·seous** adj

**nau·ti·cal** adj : relating to ships and sailing — **nau·ti·cal·ly** adv

**na·val** adj : relating to a navy

**na·vel** n : depression in the abdomen

**nav·i·gate** vb **1** : sail on or through **2** : direct the course of — **nav·i·ga·ble** adj — **nav·i·ga·bil·i·ty** n — **nav·i·ga·tion** n — **nav·i·ga·tor** n

**na·vy** n **1** : fleet **2** : nation's organization for sea warfare

**near** adv : at or close to ~ prep : close to ~ adj **1** : not far away **2** : very much like ~ vb : approach — **near·ly** adv — **near·ness** n

**near·by** adv or adj : near

**near·sight·ed** adj : seeing well at short distances only — **near·sight·ed·ly** adv — **near·sight·ed·ness** n

**neat** adj **1** : not diluted **2** : tastefully simple **3** : orderly and clean — **neat** adv — **neat·ly** adv — **neat·ness** n

**nec·es·sary** n : indispensable item ~ adj **1** : inevitable **2** : compulsory **3** : positively needed — **nec·es·sar·i·ly** adv — **ne·ces·si·tate** vb — **ne·ces·si·ty** n

**neck** n **1** : body part connecting the head and trunk **2** : part of a garment at the neck **3** : narrow part ~ vb : kiss and caress — **necked** adj

**neck·lace** n : ornament worn around the neck

**neck·tie** n : ornamental cloth tied under a collar

**nec·tar·ine** n : smooth-skinned peach

**need** n **1** : obligation **2** : lack of something or what is lacking **3** : poverty ~

---

vb **1** : be in want **2** : have cause for **3** : be under obligation — **need·ful** adj — **need·less** adj — **need·less·ly** adv — **needy** adj

**nee·dle** n **1** : pointed sewing implement or something like it **2** : movable bar in a compass **3** : hollow instrument for injecting or withdrawing material ~ vb : incite to action by repeated gibes — **nee·dle·work** n

**ne·gate** vb **1** : deny **2** : nullify — **ne·ga·tion** n

**neg·a·tive** adj **1** : marked by denial or refusal **2** : showing a lack of something suspected or desirable **3** : less than zero **4** : having more electrons than protons **5** : having light and shadow images reversed ~ n **1** : negative word or vote **2** : a negative number **3** : negative photographic image — **neg·a·tive·ly** adv — **neg·a·tive·ness** n — **neg·a·tiv·i·ty** n

**ne·glect** vb **1** : disregard **2** : leave unattended to ~ n **1** : act of neglecting **2** : condition of being neglected — **ne·glect·ful** adj

**neg·li·gent** adj : marked by neglect — **neg·li·gence** n — **neg·li·gent·ly** adv

**ne·go·ti·ate** vb **1** : confer with another to settle a matter **2** : obtain cash for **3** : get through successfully — **ne·go·tia·ble** adj — **ne·go·ti·a·tion** n — **ne·go·ti·a·tor** n

**neigh·bor** n **1** : one living nearby **2** : fellowman ~ vb : be near or next to — **neigh·bor·hood** n — **neigh·bor·li·ness** n — **neigh·bor·ly** adv

**nei·ther** pron or adj : not the one or the other ~ conj **1** : not either **2** : nor

**neph·ew** n : a son of one's brother, sister, brother-in-law, or sister-in-law

**nerd** n : one who is not stylish or socially at ease — **nerdy** adj

**nerve** n **1** : strand of body tissue that

**connects** the brain with other parts of the body **2** : self-control **3** : daring **4** *pl* : nervousness — **nerved** *adj* — **nerve·less** *adj* — **nervy** *adj*

**ner·vous** *adj* **1** : relating to or made up of nerves **2** : easily excited **3** : timid or fearful — **ner·vous·ly** *adv* — **ner·vous·ness** *n*

**nest** *n* **1** : shelter prepared by a bird for its eggs **2** : place where eggs (as of insects or fish) are laid and hatched **3** : snug retreat **4** : set of objects fitting one inside or under another ~ *vb* : build or occupy a nest

**nes·tle** *vb* : settle snugly (as in a nest)

**net** *n* : fabric with spaces between strands or something made of this ~ *vb* : cover with or catch in a net

**net·work** *n* : system of crossing or connected elements

**neu·rot·ic** *adj* : relating to neurosis ~ *n* : unstable person — **neu·rot·i·cal·ly** *adv*

**neu·tral** *adj* **1** : not favoring either side **2** : being neither one thing nor the other **3** : not decided in color **4** : not electrically charged ~ *n* **1** : one that is neutral **2** : position of gears that are not engaged — **neu·tral·i·za·tion** *n* — **neu·tral·ize** *vb*

**nev·er** *adv* **1** : not ever **2** : not in any degree, way, or condition

**nev·er·the·less** *adv* : in spite of that

**new** *adj* **1** : not old or familiar **2** : different from the former **3** : recently discovered or learned **4** : not accustomed **5** : refreshed or regenerated **6** : being such for the first time ~ *adv* : newly — **new·ish** *adj* — **new·ly** *adv* — **new·ness** *n*

**news** *n* : report of recent events — **news·cast** *n* — **news·cast·er** *n* — **news·let·ter** *n* — **news·mag·a·zine** *n* — **news·man** *n* — **news·pa·per** *n* — **news·pa·per·man** *n* — **news·stand** *n* — **news·wom·an** *n* — **news·wor·thy** *adj*

**New Year's Day** *n* : January 1 observed as a legal holiday

**next** *adj* : immediately preceding or following ~ *adv* **1** : in the time or place nearest **2** : at the first time yet to come ~ *prep* : nearest to

**nib·ble** *vb* : bite gently or bit by bit ~ *n* : small bite

**nice** *adj* **1** : exhibiting or requiring excessive care **2** : very precise or delicate **3** : pleasing **4** : respectable — **nice·ly** *adv* — **nice·ness** *n* — **nice·ty** *n*

**niche** *n* **1** : recess in a wall **2** : fitting place, work, or use

**nick** *n* **1** : small broken area or chip **2** : critical moment — *vb* : make a nick in

**nick·el** *n* **1** : hard silver-white metallic chemical element used in alloys **2** : U.S. 5-cent piece

**nick·name** *n* : informal substitute name — **nick·name** *vb*

**niece** *n* : a daughter of one's brother, sister, brother-in-law, or sister-in-law

**night** *n* **1** : period between dusk and dawn **2** : the coming of night — **night** *adj* — **night·ly** *adj or adv* — **night·time** *n*

**night·club** *n* : place for drinking and entertainment open at night

**night·mare** *n* : frightening dream — **night·mare** *adj* — **night·mar·ish** *adj*

**nil** *n* : nothing

**nim·ble** *adj* **1** : agile **2** : clever — **nim·ble·ness** *n* — **nim·bly** *adv*

**nine** *n* **1** : one more than 8 **2** : 9th in a set or series — **nine** *adj or pron* — **ninth** *adj or adv or n*

**nine·teen** *n* : one more than 18 — **nineteen** *adj or pron* — **nine·teenth** *adj or n*

**nine·ty** *n* : 9 times 10 — **nine·ti·eth** *adj or n* — **nine·ty** *adj or pron*

**nip** *vb* **1** : catch hold of and squeeze tightly **2** : pinch or bite off **3** : destroy the growth or fulfillment of ~ *n* **1** : biting cold **2** : pungent flavor **3** : pinch or bite

**nip·per** *n* **1** : one that nips **2** *pl* : pincers **3** : small boy

**nip·py** *adj* **1** : pungent **2** : chilly

**ni·tro·gen** *n* : tasteless odorless gaseous chemical element

**nit·wit** *n* : stupid person

**no** *adv* **1** — used to express the negative **2** : in no respect or degree **3** : not so **4** — used as an interjection of surprise or doubt ~ *adj* **1** : not any **2** : not a ~ *n* **1** : refusal **2** : negative vote

**no·ble** *adj* **1** : illustrious **2** : aristocratic **3** : marked by much dignity **4** : of outstanding character ~ *n* : nobleman — **no·ble·ness** *n* — **no·bly** *adv*

**no·ble·man** *n* : a person of aristocratic rank

**no·body** *pron* : no person ~ *n* : person of no influence or importance

**no-brain·er** : something that requires a minimum of thought

**nod** *vb* **1** : bend the head downward or forward (as in bowing or going to sleep or as a sign of assent) **2** : move up and down **3** : show by a nod of the head — **nod** *n*

**no·el** *n* **1** : Christmas carol **2** *cap* : Christmas season

**noes** *pl of* NO

**noise** *n* : loud or unpleasant sound ~ *vb* : spread by rumor — **noise·less** *adj* — **noise·less·ly** *adv* — **noise·mak·er** *n* — **nois·i·ly** *adv* — **nois·i·ness** *n* — **noisy** *adj*

**no·mad** *n* : one who has no permanent home — **no·mad** *adj* — **no·mad·ic** *adj*

**nom·i·nate** *vb* : propose or choose as a candidate — **nom·i·na·tion** *n* — **nom·i·nee** *n*

**non·cha·lant** *adj* : showing indifference — **non·cha·lance** *n* — **non·cha·lant·ly** *adv*

**non·con·form·ist** *n* : one who does not conform to an established belief or mode of behavior — **non·con·for·mi·ty** *n*

**none** *pron* : not any ~ *adv* : not at all

**non·per·son** *n* : person without social or legal status

**non·sense** *n* : foolish or meaningless words or actions — **non·sen·si·cal** *adj* — **non·sen·si·cal·ly** *adv*

**noo·dle** *n* : ribbon-shaped food paste

**nook** *n* **1** : inside corner **2** : private place

**noon** *n* : middle of the day — **noon** *adj* — **noon·time** *n*

**noose** *n* : rope loop that slips down tight

**nor** *conj* : and not — used esp. after *neither* to introduce and negate the 2d member of a series

**norm** *n* **1** : standard usu. derived from an average **2** : typical widespread practice or custom

**nor·mal** *adj* : average, regular, or standard — **nor·mal·cy** *n* — **nor·mal·i·ty** *n* — **nor·mal·i·za·tion** *n* — **nor·mal·ize** *vb* — **nor·mal·ly** *adv*

**north** *adv* : to or toward the north ~ *adj* : situated toward, at, or coming from the north ~ *n* **1** : direction to the left of one facing east **2** *cap* : regions to the north — **north·er·ly** *adv or adj* — **north·ern** *adj* — **North·ern·er** *n* — **north·ern·most** *adj* — **north·ward** *adv or adj* — **north·wards** *adv*

**north·east** *n* **1** : direction between north and east **2** *cap* : regions to the northeast — **northeast** *adj or adv* — **north·east·er·ly** *adv or adj* — **north·east·ern** *adj*

**north pole** *n* : northernmost point of the earth

**north·west** *n* **1** : direction between north and west **2** *cap* : regions to the northwest — **northwest** *adj or adv* — **north·west·er·ly** *adv or adj* — **north·west·ern** *adj*

**nose** *n* **1** : part of the face containing the nostrils **2** : sense of smell **3** : front part ~ *vb* **1** : detect by smell **2** : push aside with the nose **3** : pry **4** : inch ahead — **nose·bleed** *n* — **nosed** *adj* — **nose out** *vb* : narrowly defeat

**nos·tal·gia** *n* : wistful yearning for something past — **nos·tal·gic** *adj*

**nos·tril** *n* : opening of the nose

**nosy, nos·ey** *adj* : tending to pry

**not** *adv* — used to make a statement negative

**no·ta·ble** *adj* **1** : noteworthy **2** : distinguished ~ *n* : notable person — **no·ta·bil·i·ty** *n* — **no·ta·bly** *adv*

**no·ta·ry public** *n* : public official who attests writings to make them legally authentic

**notch** *n* : V-shaped hollow — **notch** *vb*

**note** *vb* **1** : notice **2** : write down ~ *n* **1** : musical tone **2** : written comment or record **3** : short informal letter **4** : notice or heed — **note·book** *n*

**note·wor·thy** *adj* : worthy of special mention

**noth·ing** *pron* **1** : no thing **2** : no part **3** : one of no value or importance ~ *adv* : not at all ~ *n* **1** : something that does not exist **2** : zero **3** : one of little or no importance — **noth·ing·ness** *n*

**no·tice** *n* **1** : warning or announcement **2** : attention ~ *vb* : take notice of — **no·tice·able** *adj* — **no·tice·ably** *adv*

**no·ti·fy** *vb* : give notice of or to — **no·ti·fi·ca·tion** *n*

**no·tion** *n* **1** : idea or opinion **2** : whim

**no·to·ri·ous** *adj* : widely and unfavorably known — **no·to·ri·e·ty** *n* — **no·to·ri·ous·ly** *adv*

**not·with·stand·ing** *prep* : in spite of ~ *adv* : nevertheless ~ *conj* : although

**noun** *n* : word that is the name of a person, place, or thing

**nour·ish** *vb* : promote the growth of — **nour·ish·ing** *adj* — **nour·ish·ment** *n*

**nov·el** *adj* : new or strange ~ *n* : long invented prose story — **nov·el·ist** *n*

**nov·el·ty** *n* **1** : something new or unusual **2** : newness **3** : small manufactured article — usu. pl.

**No·vem·ber** *n* : 11th month of the year having 30 days

**nov·ice** *n* **1** : one preparing to take vows in a religious order **2** : one who does not have experience or training

**now** *adv* **1** : at the present time or moment **2** : immediately **3** : under these circumstances ~ *conj* : in view of the fact ~ *n* : present time

**no·where** *adv* : not anywhere — **no·where** *n*

**nu·cle·ar** *adj* **1** : relating to the atomic nucleus or atomic energy **2** : relating to a weapon whose power is from a nuclear reaction

**nu·cle·us** *n* : central mass or part (as of a cell or an atom)

**nude** *adj* : naked ~ *n* : nude human figure — **nu·di·ty** *n*

**nudge** *vb* : touch or push gently — **nudge** *n*

**nui·sance** *n* : something annoying

**null** *adj* : having no legal or binding force — **nul·li·ty** *n*

**nul·li·fy** *vb* : make valueless or of no legal force — **nul·li·fi·ca·tion** *n*

**numb** *adj* : lacking feeling — **numb** *vb* — **numb·ly** *adv* — **numbness** *n*

**num·ber** *n* **1** : total of individuals taken together **2** : indefinite total **3** : unit of a mathematical system **4** : numeral **5** : one in a sequence ~ *vb* **1** : count **2** : assign a number to **3** : comprise in number — **num·ber·less** *adj* — **nu·mer·i·cal** *adj* — **nu·mer·i·cal·ly** *adv*

**nu·mer·al** *n* : conventional symbol representing a number

**nu·mer·a·tor** *n* : part of a fraction above the line

**nu·mer·ous** *adj* : consisting of a great number

**nun** *n* : woman belonging to a religious order — **nun·nery** *n*

**nurse** *n* **1** : one hired to care for children **2** : person trained to care for sick people ~ *vb* **1** : provide with milk from the breast **2** : care for

**nurs·ery** *n* **1** : place where children are cared for **2** : place where young plants are grown

**nur·ture** *n* **1** : training or upbringing **2** : food or nourishment ~ *vb* **1** : care for or feed **2** : educate

**nut** *n* **1** : dry hard-shelled fruit or seed with a firm inner kernel **2** : metal block with a screw hole through it **3** : foolish, eccentric, or crazy person **4** : enthusiast — **nut·crack·er** *n* — **nut·shell** *n* — **nut·ty** *adj*

**nu·tri·tion** *n* : act or process of nourishing esp. with food — **nu·tri·tion·al** *adj* — **nu·tri·tious** *adj* — **nu·tri·tive** *adj*

**nuts** *adj* **1** : enthusiastic **2** : crazy

**nuz·zle** *vb* **1** : touch with or as if with the nose **2** : snuggle

**ny·lon** *n* **1** : tough synthetic material used esp. in textiles **2** *pl* : stockings made of nylon

# O

**o** *n* **1** : 15th letter of the alphabet **2** : zero

**oaf** *n* : stupid or awkward person — **oaf·ish** *adj*

**oak** *n* : tree bearing a thin-shelled nut or its wood — **oak·en** *adj*

**oar** *n* : pole with a blade at the end used to propel a boat

**oa·sis** *n* : fertile area in a desert

**oat** *n* : cereal grass or its edible seed — **oat·cake** *n* — **oat·en** *adj* — **oat·meal** *n*

**oath** *n* **1** : solemn appeal to God as a pledge of sincerity **2** : profane utterance

**obe·di·ent** *adj* : willing to obey — **obe·di·ence** *n* — **obe·di·ent·ly** *adv*

**obese** *adj* : extremely fat — **obe·si·ty** *n*

**obey** *vb* **1** : follow the commands or guidance of **2** : behave in accordance with

**obit·u·ary** *n* : death notice

**¹ob·ject** *n* **1** : something that may be seen or felt **2** : purpose **3** : noun or equivalent toward which the action of a verb is directed or which follows a preposition

**²object** *vb* : offer opposition or disapproval — **ob·jec·tion** *n* — **ob·jec·tion·able** *adj* — **ob·jec·tion·ably** *adv* — **ob·jec·tor** *n*

**ob·jec·tive** *adj* **1** : relating to an object or end **2** : existing outside an individual's thoughts or feelings **3** : treating facts without distortion **4** : relating to or being a grammatical case marking objects ~ *n* : aim or end of action — **ob·jec·tive·ly** *adv* — **ob·jec·tive·ness** *n* — **ob·jec·tiv·i·ty** *n*

**ob·li·gate** *vb* : bind legally or morally — **ob·li·ga·tion** *n* — **oblig·a·to·ry** *adj*

**oblige** *vb* **1** : compel **2** : do a favor for — **oblig·ing** *adj* — **oblig·ing·ly** *adv*

**oblit·er·ate** *vb* : completely remove or destroy — **oblit·er·a·tion** *n*

**obliv·i·on** *n* **1** : state of having lost conscious awareness **2** : state of being forgotten

**obliv·i·ous** *adj* : not aware or mindful

— used with *to* or *of* — **obliv•i•ous•ly** *adv* — **obliv•i•ous•ness** *n*

**ob•long** *adj* **:** longer in one direction than in the other with opposite sides parallel — **oblong** *n*

**ob•nox•ious** *adj* **:** repugnant — **ob•nox•ious•ly** *adv* — **ob•nox•ious•ness** *n*

**ob•scene** *adj* **:** repugnantly improper or offensive — **ob•scene•ly** *adv* — **ob•scen•i•ty** *n*

**ob•scure** *adj* **1 :** dim or hazy **2 :** not well known **3 :** vague ~ *vb* **:** make indistinct or unclear — **ob•scure•ly** *adv* — **ob•scu•ri•ty** *n*

**ob•ser•va•to•ry** *n* **:** place for observing astronomical phenomena

**ob•serve** *vb* **1 :** conform to **2 :** celebrate **3 :** see, watch, or notice **4 :** remark — **ob•serv•able** *adj* — **ob•ser•vance** *n* — **ob•ser•vant** *adj* — **ob•ser•va•tion** *n*

**ob•sess** *vb* **:** preoccupy intensely or abnormally — **ob•ses•sion** *n* — **ob•ses•sive** *adj* — **ob•ses•sive•ly** *adv*

**ob•so•lete** *adj* **:** no longer in use

**ob•sta•cle** *n* **:** something that stands in the way or opposes

**ob•sti•nate** *adj* **:** stubborn — **ob•sti•na•cy** *n* — **ob•sti•nate•ly** *adv*

**ob•struct** *vb* **:** block or impede — **ob•struc•tion** *n* — **ob•struc•tive** *adj* — **ob•struc•tor** *n*

**ob•tain** *vb* **1 :** gain by effort **2 :** be generally recognized — **ob•tain•able** *adj*

**ob•vi•ous** *adj* **:** plain or unmistakable — **ob•vi•ous•ly** *adv* — **ob•vi•ous•ness** *n*

**oc•ca•sion** *n* **1 :** favorable opportunity **2 :** cause **3 :** time of an event **4 :** special event ~ *vb* **:** cause — **oc•ca•sion•al** *adj* — **oc•ca•sion•al•ly** *adv*

**oc•cu•pa•tion** *n* **1 :** vocation **2 :** action or state of occupying — **oc•cu•pa•tion•al** *adj* — **oc•cu•pa•tion•al•ly** *adv*

**oc•cu•py** *vb* **1 :** engage the attention of **2 :** fill up **3 :** take or hold possession of **4 :** reside in — **oc•cu•pan•cy** *n* — **oc•cu•pant** *n* — **oc•cu•pi•er** *n*

**oc•cur** *vb* **1 :** be found or met with **2 :** take place **3 :** come to mind

**oc•cur•rence** *n* **:** something that takes place

**ocean** *n* **1 :** whole body of salt water **2 :** very large body of water — **ocean•front** *n* — **ocean•go•ing** *adj* — **oce•an•ic** *adj*

**o'•clock** *adv* **:** according to the clock

**oc•ta•gon** *n* **:** 8-sided polygon — **oc•tag•o•nal** *adj*

**Oc•to•ber** *n* **:** 10th month of the year having 31 days

**oc•to•pus** *n* **:** sea mollusk with 8 arms

**odd** *adj* **1 :** being only one of a pair or set **2 :** not divisible by two without a remainder **3 :** additional to what is usual or to the number mentioned **4 :** queer — **odd•i•ty** *n* — **odd•ly** *adv* — **odd•ness** *n*

**odds** *n pl* **1 :** difference by which one thing is favored **2 :** disagreement **3 :** ratio between winnings and the amount of the bet

**odor** *n* **:** quality that affects the sense of smell — **odor•less** *adj* — **odor•ous** *adj*

**of** *prep* **1 :** from **2 :** distinguished by **3 :** because of **4 :** made or written by **5 :** made with, being, or containing **6 :** belonging to or connected with **7 :** about **8 :** that is **9 :** concerning **10 :** before

**off** *adv* **1 :** from a place **2 :** unattached or removed **3 :** to a state of being no longer in use **4 :** away from work **5 :** at a distance in time or space ~ *prep* **1 :** away from **2 :** at the expense of **3 :** not engaged in or abstaining from **4 :** below the usual level of ~ *adj* **1 :** not operating, up to standard, or correct **2 :** remote **3 :** provided for

**of•fend** *vb* **1 :** sin or act in violation **2 :** hurt, annoy, or insult — **of•fend•er** *n*

**of•fense, of•fence** *n* **:** attack, misdeed, or insult — **of•fen•sive** *adj* — **of•fen•sive•ly** *adv* — **of•fen•sive•ness** *n*

**of•fer** *vb* **1 :** present for acceptance **2 :** propose **3 :** put up (an effort) ~ *n* **1 :** proposal **2 :** bid — **of•fer•ing** *n*

**of•fice** *n* **1 :** position of authority (as in government) **2 :** rite **3 :** place where a business is transacted — **of•fice•hold•er** *n*

**of•fi•cer** *n* **1 :** one charged with law enforcement **2 :** one who holds an office of trust or authority **3 :** one who holds a commission in the armed forces

**of•fi•cial** *n* **:** one in office ~ *adj* **:** authorized or authoritative — **of•fi•cial•dom** *n* — **of•fi•cial•ly** *adv*

**of•fi•ci•ate** *vb* **:** perform a ceremony or function

**off•spring** *n* **offspring :** one coming into being through animal or plant reproduction

**of•ten** *adv* **:** many times — **of•ten•times, oft•times** *adv*

**oh** *interj* **1 —** used to express an emotion **2 —** used in direct address

**oil** *n* **1 :** greasy liquid substance **2 :** petroleum ~ *vb* **:** put oil in or on — **oil•er** *n* — **oil•i•ness** *n* — **oily** *adj*

**oint•ment** *n* **:** oily medicinal preparation

**OK** *or* **okay** *adv or adj* **:** all right ~ *vb* **:** approve ~ *n* **:** approval

**old** *adj* **1 :** of long standing **2 :** of a specified age **3 :** relating to a past era **4 :** having existed a long time — **old•ish** *adj*

**old–fash•ioned** *adj* **1 :** out-of-date **2 :** conservative

**ol•fac•to•ry** *adj* **:** relating to the sense of smell

**ol•ive** *n* **1 :** evergreen tree bearing small edible fruit or the fruit **2 :** dull yellowish green color

**om•e•let, om•e•lette** *n* **:** beaten eggs lightly fried and folded

**omen** *n* **:** sign or warning of the future

**om•i•nous** *adj* **:** presaging evil — **om•i•nous•ly** *adv* — **om•i•nous•ness** *n*

**omit** *vb* **1 :** leave out **2 :** fail to perform — **omis•si•ble** *adj* — **omis•sion** *n*

**om•nip•o•tent** *adj* **:** almighty — **om•nip•o•tence** *n* — **om•nip•o•tent•ly** *adv*

**on** *prep* **1 :** in or to a position over and in contact with **2 :** at or to **3 :** about **4 :** from **5 :** with regard to **6 :** in a state or process **7 :** during the time of ~ *adv* **1 :** in or into contact with **2 :** forward **3 :** into operation

**once** *adv* **1 :** one time only **2 :** at any one time **3 :** formerly ~ *n* **:** one time ~ *conj* **:** as soon as ~ *adj* **:** former — **at once 1 :** simultaneously **2 :** immediately

**one** *adj* **1 :** being a single thing **2 :** being one in particular **3 :** being the same in kind ~ *pron* **1 :** certain indefinitely indicated person or thing **2 :** a person in general ~ *n* **1 :** 1st in a series **2 :** single person or thing — **one•ness** *n*

**oner•ous** *adj* **:** imposing a burden

**one•self** *pron* **:** one's own self — usu. used reflexively or for emphasis

**one•time** *adj* **:** former

**one–way** *adj* **:** made or for use in only one direction

**on•ion** *n* **:** plant grown for its pungent edible bulb or this bulb

**on•ly** *adj* **:** alone in its class ~ *adv* **1 :** merely or exactly **2 :** solely **3 :** at the very least **4 :** as a result ~ *conj* **:** but

**on•set** *n* **:** start

**on•to** *prep* **:** to a position or point on

**on•ward** *adv or adj* **:** forward

**ooze** *n* **:** soft mud ~ *vb* **:** flow or leak out slowly — **oozy** *adj*

**opaque** *adj* **1 :** blocking light **2 :** not easily understood — **opaque•ly** *adv*

**open** *adj* **1 :** not shut or shut up **2 :** not secret or hidden **3 :** frank or generous **4 :** extended **5 :** free from controls **6 :** not decided ~ *vb* **1 :** make or become open **2 :** make or become functional **3 :** start ~ *n* **:** outdoors — **open•er** *n* — **open•ly** *adv* — **open•ness** *n*

**open•hand•ed** *adj* **:** generous — **open•hand•ed•ly** *adv*

**open•ing** *n* **1 :** act or instance of making open **2 :** something that is open **3 :** opportunity

**op•era** *n* **:** drama set to music — **op•er•at•ic** *adj*

**op•er•ate** *vb* **1 :** perform work **2 :** perform an operation **3 :** manage — **op•er•a•ble** *adj* — **op•er•a•tive** *adj* — **op•er•a•tor** *n*

**op•er•a•tion** *n* **1 :** act or process of operating **2 :** surgical work on a living body **3 :** military action or mission — **op•er•a•tion•al** *adj*

**opin•ion** *n* **1 :** belief **2 :** judgment **3 :** formal statement by an expert

**opin•ion•at•ed** *adj* **:** stubborn in one's opinions

**op•po•nent** *n* **:** one that opposes

**op•por•tune** *adj* **:** suitable or timely — **op•por•tune•ly** *adv*

**op•por•tun•ism** *n* **:** a taking advantage of opportunities — **op•por•tun•ist** *n* — **op•por•tu•nis•tic** *adj*

**op•por•tu•ni•ty** *n* **:** favorable time

**op•pose** *vb* **1 :** place opposite or against something **2 :** resist — **op•po•si•tion** *n*

**op•po•site** *n* **:** one that is opposed ~ *adj* **1 :** set facing something that is at the other side or end **2 :** opposed or contrary ~ *adv* **:** on opposite sides ~ *prep* **:** across from — **op•po•site•ly** *adv*

**op•press** *vb* **1 :** persecute **2 :** weigh down — **op•pres•sion** *n* — **op•pres•sive** *adj* — **op•pres•sive•ly** *adv* — **op•pres•sor** *n*

**op•ti•cal** *adj* **:** relating to optics, vision, or the eye

**op•ti•mism** *n* **:** tendency to hope for the best — **op•ti•mist** *n* — **op•ti•mis•tic** *adj* — **op•ti•mis•ti•cal•ly** *adv*

**op•tion** *n* **1 :** ability to choose **2 :** right to buy or sell a stock **3 :** alternative — **op•tion•al** *adj*

**or** *conj* — used to indicate an alternative

**oral** *adj* **1 :** spoken **2 :** relating to the mouth — **oral•ly** *adv*

**or•ange** *n* **1 :** reddish yellow citrus fruit **2 :** color between red and yellow — **or•ange•ade** *n*

**ora•tion** *n* **:** elaborate formal speech — **or•a•tor** *n*

**or•bit** *n* **:** path made by one body revolving around another ~ *vb* **:** revolve around — **or•bit•al** *adj* — **or•bit•er** *n*

**or•chard** *n* **:** place where fruit or nut trees are grown — **or•chard•ist** *n*

**or•ches•tra** *n* **1 :** group of musicians **2 :** front seats of a theater's main floor — **or•ches•tral** *adj* — **or•ches•tral•ly** *adv*

**or•deal** *n* **:** severely trying experience

**or•der** *n* **1 :** rank, class, or special group **2 :** arrangement **3 :** rule of law **4 :** authoritative regulation or instruction **5 :** working condition **6 :** special request for a purchase or what is purchased ~ *vb* **1 :** arrange **2 :** give an order to **3 :** place an order for

**or•der•ly** *adj* **1 :** being in order or tidy **2 :** well behaved ~ *n* **1 :** officer's attendant **2 :** hospital attendant — **or•der•li•ness** *n*

**or•di•nal** *n* **:** number indicating order in a series

**or•di•nance** *n* **:** municipal law

**or•di•nary** *adj* **:** of common occurrence, quality, or ability — **or•di•nar•i•ly** *adv*

**ore** *n* **:** mineral containing a valuable constituent

**or•gan** *n* **1 :** air-powered or electronic keyboard instrument **2 :** animal or plant structure with special function **3 :** periodical

**or•gan•ic** *adj* **1 :** relating to a bodily organ **2 :** relating to living things **3 :** relating to or containing carbon or its compounds **4 :** relating to foods produced without the use of laboratory-made products — **or•gan•i•cal•ly** *adv*

**or•gan•ism** *n* **:** a living thing

**or•ga•nize** *vb* **:** form parts into a functioning whole — **or•ga•ni•za•tion** *n* — **or•ga•ni•za•tion•al** *adj* — **or•ga•niz•er** *n*

**ori•ent** *vb* **1 :** set in a definite position **2 :** acquaint with a situation — **ori•en•ta•tion** *n*

**or•i•fice** *n* **:** opening

**or•i•gin** *n* **1 :** ancestry **2 :** rise, beginning, or derivation from a source — **orig•i•nate** *vb* — **orig•i•na•tor** *n*

**orig•i•nal** *n* **:** something from which a copy is made ~ *adj* **1 :** first **2 :** not copied from something else **3 :** inventive — **orig•i•nal•i•ty** *n* — **orig•i•nal•ly** *adv*

**or•na•ment** *n* **:** something that adorns ~ *vb* **:** provide with ornament — **or•na•men•tal** *adj* — **or•na•men•ta•tion** *n*

**or•nate** *adj* **:** elaborately decorated — **or•nate•ly** *adv* — **or•nate•ness** *n*

**or•phan** *n* **:** child whose parents are dead — **orphan** *vb* — **or•phan•age** *n*

**or•tho•dox** *adj* **1 :** conforming to established doctrine **2** *cap* **:** of or relating to a Christian church originating in the Eastern Roman Empire — **or•tho•doxy** *n*

**os•mo•sis** *n* **:** diffusion esp. of water through a membrane — **os•mot•ic** *adj*

**os•ten•ta•tion** *n* **:** pretentious display — **os•ten•ta•tious** *adj* — **os•ten•ta•tious•ly** *adv*

**os•tra•cize** *vb* **:** exclude by common consent — **os•tra•cism** *n*

**oth•er** *adj* **1 :** being the one left **2 :** alternate **3 :** additional ~ *pron* **1 :** remaining one **2 :** different one

**oth•er•wise** *adv* **1 :** in a different way **2 :** in different circumstances **3 :** in other respects — **oth•er•wise** *adj*

**ought** *verbal auxiliary* — used to express obligation, advisability, or expectation

**ounce** *n* **1 :** unit of weight equal to about 28.3 grams **2 :** unit of capacity equal to about 29.6 milliliters

**our** *adj* **:** of or relating to us

**ours** *pron* **:** that which belongs to us

**our•selves** *pron* **:** we, us — used reflexively or for emphasis

**out** *adv* **1 :** away from the inside or center **2 :** beyond control **3 :** to extinction, exhaustion, or completion **4 :** in or into the open ~ *vb* **:** become known ~ *adj* **1 :** situated outside **2 :** absent ~ *prep* **1 :** out through **2 :** outward on or along — **out•bound** *adj* — **out•build•ing** *n*

**out•break** *n* **:** sudden occurrence

**out•burst** *n* **:** violent expression of feeling

**out•cast** *n* **:** person cast out by society

**out•come** *n* **:** result

**out•dat•ed** *adj* **:** out-of-date

**out•do** *vb* **:** do better than

**out•doors** *adv* **:** in or into the open air ~ *n* **:** open air — **out•door** *adj*

**out•er** *adj* **1 :** external **2 :** farther out — **out•er•most** *adj*

**out•fit** *n* **1 :** equipment for a special purpose **2 :** group ~ *vb* **:** equip — **out•fit•ter** *n*

**out•ing** *n* **:** excursion

**outlast** *vb* **:** last longer than

**out•law** *n* **:** lawless person ~ *vb* **:** make illegal

**out•lay** *n* **:** expenditure

**out•let** *n* **1 :** exit **2 :** means of release **3 :** market for goods **4 :** electrical device that gives access to wiring

**out•line** *n* **1 :** line marking the outer limits **2 :** summary ~ *vb* **1 :** draw the outline of **2 :** indicate the chief parts of

**out·look** n 1 : viewpoint 2 : prospect for the future

**out of** prep 1 : out from within 2 : beyond the limits of 3 : among 4 — used to indicate absence or loss 5 : because of 6 : from or with

**out—of—date** adj : no longer current or useful

**out·put** n : amount produced ~ vb : produce

**out·rage** n 1 : violent or shameful act 2 : injury or insult 3 : extreme anger ~ vb 1 : subject to violent injury 2 : make very angry

**out·ra·geous** adj : extremely offensive or shameful — **out·ra·geous·ly** adv — **out·ra·geous·ness** n

**out·right** adv 1 : completely 2 : instantly ~ adj 1 : complete 2 : given without reservation

**out·side** n 1 : place beyond a boundary 2 : exterior 3 : utmost limit ~ adj 1 : outer 2 : coming from without 3 : remote ~ adv : on or to the outside ~ prep 1 : on or to the outside of 2 : beyond the limits of

**out·sid·er** n : one who does not belong to a group

**out·smart** vb : outwit

**out·spo·ken** adj : direct and open in speech — **out·spo·ken·ness** n

**out·stand·ing** adj 1 : not yet paid 2 : very good — **out·stand·ing·ly** adv

**out·strip** vb 1 : go faster than 2 : surpass

**out·ward** adj 1 : being toward the outside 2 : showing outwardly — **out·ward** adv — **out·ward·ly** adv

**out·wit** vb : get the better of by superior cleverness

**oval** adj : having the shape of an egg — **oval** n

**ova·tion** n : enthusiastic applause

**ov·en** n : chamber (as in a stove) for baking

**over** adv 1 : across 2 : upside down 3 : in excess or addition 4 : above 5 : at an end 6 : again ~ prep 1 : above in position or authority 2 : more than 3 : along, through, or across 4 : because of ~ adj 1 : upper 2 : remaining 3 : ended

**over·age** n : surplus

**over·all** adj : including everything

**over·alls** n pl : pants with an extra piece covering the chest

**over·bear·ing** adj : arrogant

**over·blown** adj : pretentious

**over·cast** adj : clouded over ~ n : cloud covering

**over·coat** n : outer coat

**over·come** vb 1 : defeat 2 : make helpless or exhausted

**over·do** vb : do too much

**over·flow** vb 1 : flood 2 : flow over — **overflow** n

**over·hang** vb : jut out over ~ n : something that overhangs

**over·haul** vb 1 : repair 2 : overtake

**over·head** adv : aloft ~ adj : situated above ~ n : general business expenses

**over·hear** vb : hear without the speaker's knowledge

**over·joyed** adj : filled with joy

**over·lap** vb : lap over — **overlap** n

**over·look** vb 1 : look down on 2 : fail to see 3 : ignore 4 : pardon 5 : supervise ~ n : observation point

**over·ly** adv : excessively

**over·night** adv 1 : through the night 2 : suddenly — **overnight** adj

**over·pass** n : bridge over a road

**over·pow·er** vb : conquer

**over·rule** vb : rule against or set aside

**over·run** vb 1 : swarm or flow over 2 : go beyond ~ n : an exceeding of estimated costs

**over·see** vb : supervise — **over·seer** n

**over·sight** n : inadvertent omission or error

**over·take** vb : catch up with

**over·throw** vb 1 : upset 2 : defeat — **overthrow** n

**over·time** n : extra working time — **overtime** adv

**over·turn** vb 1 : turn over 2 : nullify

**over·view** n : brief survey

**over·whelm** vb : overcome completely — **over·whelm·ing·ly** adv

**owe** vb 1 : have an obligation to pay 2 : be indebted to or for

**owl** n : nocturnal bird of prey — **owl·ish** adj — **owl·ish·ly** adv

**own** adj : belonging to oneself ~ vb 1 : have as property 2 : acknowledge ~ pron : one or ones belonging to oneself — **own·er** n — **own·er·ship** n

**ox** n (**ox·en**) : bovine mammal and esp. a castrated bull

**ox·y·gen** n : gaseous chemical element essential for life

**ozone** n : very reactive bluish form of oxygen

# P

**p** n : 16th letter of the alphabet

**pace** n 1 : walking step 2 : rate of progress ~ vb 1 : go at a pace 2 : cover with slow steps 3 : set the pace of

**pace·mak·er** n : electrical device to regulate heartbeat

**pa·cif·ic** adj : calm or peaceful

**pac·i·fy** vb : make calm — **pac·i·fi·ca·tion** n — **pac·i·fi·er** n — **pac·i·fism** n — **pac·i·fist** n or adj — **pac·i·fis·tic** adj

**pack** n 1 : compact bundle 2 : group of animals ~ vb 1 : put into a container 2 : fill tightly or completely 3 : send without ceremony — **pack·er** n

**pack·age** n : items bundled together ~ vb : enclose in a package

**pack·et** n : small package

**pact** n : agreement

**pad** n 1 : cushioning part or thing 2 : floating leaf of a water plant 3 : tablet of paper ~ vb 1 : furnish with a pad 2 : expand with needless matter — **pad·ding** n

**pad·dle** n : implement with a flat blade ~ vb : move, beat, or stir with a paddle

**pad·lock** n : lock with a U-shaped catch — **padlock** vb

**pa·gan** n or adj : heathen — **pa·gan·ism** n

¹**page** n : messenger ~ vb : summon by repeated calls — **pag·er** n

²**page** n 1 : single leaf (as of a book) or one side of the leaf 2 : information at a single World Wide Web address

**pag·eant** n : elaborate spectacle or procession — **pag·eant·ry** n

**pa·go·da** n : tower with roofs curving upward

**paid** past of PAY

**pail** n : cylindrical container with a handle — **pail·ful** n

**pain** n 1 : punishment or penalty 2 : suffering of body or mind 3 pl : great care ~ vb : cause or experience pain — **pain·ful** adj — **pain·ful·ly** adv — **pain·kill·er** n — **pain·kill·ing** adj — **pain·less** adj — **pain·less·ly** adv

**pains·tak·ing** adj : taking great care — **pains·tak·ing** n — **pains·tak·ing·ly** adv

**paint** vb 1 : apply color or paint to 2 : portray esp. in color ~ n : mixture of pigment and liquid — **paint·brush** n — **paint·er** n — **paint·ing** n

**pair** n : a set of two ~ vb : put or go together as a pair

**pa·ja·mas** n pl : loose suit for sleeping

**pal** n : close friend

**pal·ace** n 1 : residence of a chief of state 2 : mansion — **pa·la·tial** adj

**pal·ate** n 1 : roof of the mouth 2 : taste — **pal·at·able** adj — **pal·a·tal** adj

**pale** adj 1 : lacking in color or brightness 2 : light in color or shade ~ vb : make or become pale — **pale·ness** n

**pal·ette** n : board on which paints are laid and mixed

**pall** n 1 : cloth draped over a coffin 2 : something that produces gloom

**pall·bear·er** n : one who attends the coffin at a funeral

**pal·let** n 1 : makeshift bed 2 : portable storage platform

**pal·lor** n : paleness

¹**palm** n 1 : tall tropical tree crowned with large leaves 2 : symbol of victory

²**palm** n : underside of the hand ~ vb 1 : conceal in the hand 2 : impose by fraud

**pal·pa·ble** adj 1 : capable of being touched 2 : obvious — **pal·pa·bly** adv

**pal·pi·tate** vb : beat rapidly — **pal·pi·ta·tion** n

**pam·per** vb : spoil or indulge

**pam·phlet** n : unbound publication — **pam·phle·teer** n

**pan** n : broad, shallow, and open container ~ vb 1 : wash gravel in a pan to search for gold 2 : criticize severely

**pan·cake** n : fried flat cake

**pan·cre·as** n : gland that produces insulin — **pan·cre·at·ic** adj

**pan·da** n : black-and-white bearlike animal

**pan·de·mo·ni·um** n : wild uproar

**pan·der** n : one who caters to others' desires or weaknesses ~ vb : act as a pander

**pane** n : sheet of glass

**pan·el** n 1 : list of persons (as jurors) 2 : discussion group 3 : flat piece of construction material 4 : board with instruments or controls ~ vb : decorate with panels — **pan·el·ing** n — **pan·el·ist** n

**pan·han·dle** vb : ask for money on the street — **pan·han·dler** n

**pan·ic** n : sudden overpowering fright ~ vb : affect or be affected with panic — **pan·icky** adj

**pan·o·ra·ma** n : view in every direction — **pan·o·ram·ic** adj

**pant** vb 1 : breathe with great effort 2 : yearn ~ n : panting sound

**pant·ies** n pl : woman's or child's short underpants

**pan·to·mime** n 1 : play without words 2 : expression by bodily or facial movements ~ vb : represent by pantomime

**pan·try** n : storage room for food and dishes

**pants** n pl 1 : 2-legged outer garment 2 : panties

**pa·pal** adj : relating to the pope

**pa·per** n 1 : pliable substance used to write or print on, to wrap things in, or to cover walls 2 : printed or written document 3 : newspaper — **paper** adj or vb — **pa·per·hang·er** n — **pa·per·weight** n — **pa·pery** adj

**pa·pier–mâ·ché** n : molding material of waste paper

**par** n 1 : stated value 2 : common level 3 : accepted standard or normal condition — **par** adj

**para·chute** n : large umbrella-shaped device for making a descent through air — **parachute** vb — **para·chut·ist** n

**pa·rade** n 1 : pompous display 2 : ceremonial formation and march ~ vb 1 : march in a parade 2 : show off

**par·a·dise** n : place of bliss

**par·a·dox** n : statement that seems contrary to common sense yet is perhaps true — **par·a·dox·i·cal** adj — **par·a·dox·i·cal·ly** adv

**para·graph** n : unified division of a piece of writing ~ vb : divide into paragraphs

**par·al·lel** adj 1 : lying or moving in the same direction but always the same distance apart 2 : similar ~ n 1 : parallel line, curve, or surface 2 : line of latitude 3 : similarity ~ vb 1 : compare 2 : correspond to — **par·al·lel·ism** n

**par·al·lel·o·gram** n : 4-sided polygon with opposite sides equal and parallel

**pa·ral·y·sis** n : loss of function and esp. of voluntary motion — **par·a·lyt·ic** adj or n

**par·a·lyze** vb : affect with paralysis — **par·a·lyz·ing·ly** adv

**para·med·ic** n : person trained to provide initial emergency medical treatment

**para·noia** n : mental disorder marked by irrational suspicion — **para·noid** adj or n

**par·a·pher·na·lia** n sing or pl : equipment

**para·phrase** n : restatement of a text giving the meaning in different words — **paraphrase** vb

**par·a·site** n : organism living on another — **par·a·sit·ic** adj — **par·a·sit·ism** n

**par·cel** n 1 : lot 2 : package ~ vb : divide into portions

**parch** vb : toast or shrivel with dry heat

**par·don** n : excusing of an offense ~ vb : free from penalty — **par·don·able** adj — **par·don·er** n

**pare** vb 1 : trim off an outside part 2 : reduce as if by paring — **par·er** n

**par·ent** n : one that begets or brings up offspring — **par·ent·age** n — **pa·ren·tal** adj — **par·ent·hood** n

**pa·ren·the·sis** n 1 : word or phrase inserted in a passage 2 : one of a pair of punctuation marks ( ) — **par·en·thet·ic**, **par·en·thet·i·cal** adj — **par·en·thet·i·cal·ly** adv

**par·ish** n : local church community

**pa·rish·io·ner** n : member of a parish

**park** n : land set aside for recreation or for its beauty ~ vb : leave a vehicle standing

**par·ka** n : usu. hooded heavy jacket

**park·way** n : broad landscaped thoroughfare

**par·lay** n : the risking of a stake plus its winnings — **par·lay** vb

**par·ley** n : conference about a dispute — **par·ley** vb

**par·lia·ment** n : legislative assembly — **par·lia·men·tar·i·an** n — **par·lia·men·ta·ry** adj

**par·lor** n 1 : reception room 2 : place of business

**par·o·dy** n : humorous or satirical imitation — **par·o·dy** vb

**pa·role** n : conditional release of a prisoner — **pa·role** vb — **pa·rol·ee** n

**par·ra·keet** var of PARAKEET

**par·rot** n : bright-colored tropical bird

**pars·ley** n : garden plant used as a seasoning or garnish

**par·son** n : minister

**par·son·age** n : parson's house

**part** n 1 : one of the units into which a larger whole is divided 2 : function or role ~ vb 1 : take leave 2 : separate 3 : go away 4 : give up

**par•take** *vb* : have or take a share — **par•tak•er** *n*
**par•tial** *adj* **1** : favoring one over another **2** : affecting a part only — **par•tial•i•ty** *n* — **par•tial•ly** *adv*
**par•tic•i•pate** *vb* : take part in something — **par•tic•i•pant** *adj or n* — **par•tic•i•pa•tion** *n* — **par•tic•i•pa•to•ry** *adj*
**par•ti•cle** *n* : small bit
**par•tic•u•lar** *adj* **1** : relating to a specific person or thing **2** : individual **3** : hard to please ~ *n* : detail — **par•tic•u•lar•ly** *adv*
**par•ti•san** *n* **1** : adherent **2** : guerrilla — **par•ti•san** *adj* — **par•ti•san•ship** *n*
**par•ti•tion** *n* **1** : distribution **2** : something that divides — **partition** *vb*
**part•ly** *adv* : in some degree
**part•ner** *n* **1** : associate **2** : companion **3** : business associate — **part•ner•ship** *n*
**part of speech** : class of words distinguished esp. according to function
**par•ty** *n* **1** : political organization **2** : participant **3** : company of persons esp. with a purpose **4** : social gathering
**pass** *vb* **1** : move past, over, or through **2** : go away or die **3** : allow to elapse **4** : go unchallenged **5** : transfer or undergo transfer **6** : render a judgment **7** : occur **8** : enact **9** : undergo testing successfully **10** : be regarded **11** : decline ~ *n* **1** : low place in a mountain range **2** : act of passing **3** : accomplishment **4** : permission to leave, enter, or move about — **pass•able** *adj* — **pass•ably** *adv* — **pass•er** *n* — **pass•er•by** *n*
**pas•sage** *n* **1** : process of passing **2** : means of passing **3** : voyage **4** : right to pass **5** : literary selection — **pas•sage•way** *n*
**pas•sé** *adj* : out-of-date
**pas•sen•ger** *n* : traveler in a conveyance
**pas•sion** *n* **1** : strong feeling esp. of anger, love, or desire **2** : object of affection or enthusiasm — **pas•sion•ate** *adj* — **pas•sion•ate•ly** *adv* — **pas•sion•less** *adj*
**pas•sive** *adj* **1** : not active but acted upon **2** : submissive — **pas•sive** *n* — **pas•sive•ly** *adv* — **pas•siv•i•ty** *n*
**Pass•over** *n* : Jewish holiday celebrated in March or April in commemoration of the Hebrews' liberation from slavery in Egypt
**pass•port** *n* : government document needed for travel abroad
**pass•word** *n* **1** : word or phrase spoken to pass a guard **2** : sequence of characters needed to get into a computer system
**past** *adj* **1** : ago **2** : just gone by **3** : having existed before the present **4** : expressing past time ~ *prep or adv* : beyond ~ *n* **1** : time gone by **2** : verb tense expressing time gone by **3** : past life
**pas•ta** *n* : fresh or dried shaped dough
**paste** *n* **1** : smooth ground food **2** : moist adhesive ~ *vb* : attach with paste — **pasty** *adj*
**pas•tel** *n* : light color — **pas•tel** *adj*
**pas•teur•ize** *vb* : heat (as milk) so as to kill germs — **pas•teur•i•za•tion** *n*
**pas•time** *n* : amusement
**pas•tor** *n* : priest or minister serving a church or parish — **pas•tor•ate** *n*
**past•ry** *n* : sweet baked goods
**pas•ture** *n* : land used for grazing ~ *vb* : graze
**pat** *n* **1** : light tap **2** : small mass ~ *vb* : tap gently ~ *adj or adv* **1** : apt or glib **2** : not yielding
**patch** *n* **1** : piece used for mending **2** : small area distinct from surrounding area ~ *vb* **1** : mend with a patch **2** : make of fragments **3** : repair hastily — **patchy** *adj*
**pa•tent** *adj* **1** : obvious **2** : protected by a patent ~ *n* : document conferring or securing a right ~ *vb* : secure by patent — **pat•ent•ly** *adv*
**pa•ter•nal** *adj* **1** : fatherly **2** : related through or inherited from a father — **pa•ter•nal•ly** *adv*
**pa•ter•ni•ty** *n* : fatherhood
**path** *n* **1** : trodden way **2** : route or course — **path•find•er** *n* — **path•way** *n* — **path•less** *adj*
**pa•thet•ic** *adj* : pitiful — **pa•thet•i•cal•ly** *adv*
**pa•tience** *n* : habit or fact of being patient
**pa•tient** *adj* : bearing pain or trials without complaint ~ *n* : one under medical care — **pa•tient•ly** *adv*
**pa•tio** *n* **1** : courtyard **2** : paved recreation area near a house
**pa•tri•arch** *n* **1** : man revered as father or founder **2** : venerable old man — **pa•tri•ar•chal** *adj* — **pa•tri•ar•chy** *n*
**pa•tri•ot** *n* : one who loves his or her country — **pa•tri•ot•ic** *adj* — **pa•tri•ot•i•cal•ly** *adv* — **pa•tri•o•tism** *n*
**pa•trol** *n* **1** : a going around for observation or security **2** : group on patrol ~ *vb* : carry out a patrol
**pa•tron** *n* **1** : special protector **2** : wealthy supporter **3** : customer — **pa•tron•age** *n*
**pa•tron•ize** *vb* **1** : be a customer of **2** : treat with condescension
**pat•tern** *n* **1** : model for imitation or for making things **2** : artistic design **3** : noticeable formation or set of characteristics ~ *vb* : form according to a pattern
**pat•ty** *n* : small flat cake
**paunch** *n* : large belly — **paunchy** *adj*
**pau•per** *n* : poor person — **pau•per•ism** *n* — **pau•per•ize** *vb*
**pause** *n* : temporary stop ~ *vb* : stop briefly
**pave** *vb* : cover to smooth or firm the surface — **pave•ment** *n* — **pav•ing** *n*
**pa•vil•ion** *n* **1** : large tent **2** : light structure used for entertainment or shelter
**paw** *n* : foot of a 4-legged clawed animal ~ *vb* **1** : handle clumsily or rudely **2** : touch or strike with a paw
**pawn** *n* **1** : goods deposited as security for a loan **2** : state of being pledged ~ *vb* : deposit as a pledge — **pawn•bro•ker** *n* — **pawn•shop** *n*
**pay** *vb* **(paid; paid) 1** : make due return for goods or services **2** : discharge indebtedness for **3** : retaliate for **4** : give freely or as fitting **5** : be profitable ~ *n* **1** : status of being paid **2** : something paid — **pay•able** *adj* — **pay•check** *n* — **pay•ee** *n* — **pay•er** *n* — **pay•ment** *n*
**PC** *n* : small personal computer
**pea** *n* : round edible seed of a leguminous vine
**peace** *n* **1** : state of calm and quiet **2** : absence of war or strife — **peace•able** *adj* — **peace•ably** *adv* — **peace•ful** *adj* — **peace•ful•ly** *adv* — **peace•keep•er** *n* — **peace•keep•ing** *n* — **peace•mak•er** *n* — **peace•time** *n*
**peach** *n* : sweet juicy fruit of a flowering tree or this tree
**peak** *n* **1** : pointed or projecting part **2** : top of a hill **3** : highest level ~ *vb* : reach a maximum — **peak** *adj*
**pea•nut** *n* : annual herb that bears underground pods or the pod or the edible seed inside
**pear** *n* : fleshy fruit of a tree related to the apple
**pearl** *n* : gem formed within an oyster — **pearly** *adj*
**peas•ant** *n* : tiller of the soil — **peas•ant•ry** *n*
**peat** *n* : decayed organic deposit often dried for fuel — **peaty** *adj*
**peb•ble** *n* : small stone — **peb•bly** *adj*
**pe•can** *n* : hickory tree bearing a smooth-shelled nut or the nut
**1peck** *n* : unit of dry measure equal to 8 quarts
**2peck** *vb* : strike or pick up with the bill ~ *n* : quick sharp stroke
**pe•cu•liar** *adj* **1** : characteristic of only one **2** : strange — **pe•cu•liar•i•ty** *n* — **pe•cu•liar•ly** *adv*
**ped•al** *n* : lever worked by the foot ~ *adj* : relating to the foot ~ *vb* : use a pedal
**ped•dle** *vb* : offer for sale — **ped•dler** *n*
**ped•es•tal** *n* : support or foot of something upright
**pe•des•tri•an** *adj* **1** : ordinary **2** : walking ~ *n* : person who walks
**peek** *vb* **1** : look furtively **2** : glance — **peek** *n*
**peel** *vb* **1** : strip the skin or rind from **2** : lose the outer layer ~ *n* : skin or rind — **peel•ing** *n*
**1peep** *vb* : utter faint shrill sounds — **cheep** *n*
**2peep** *vb* **1** : look slyly **2** : begin to emerge ~ *n* : brief look — **peep•er** *n* — **peep•hole** *n*
**1peer** *n* **1** : one's equal **2** : nobleman — **peer•age** *n*
**2peer** *vb* : look intently or curiously
**peer•less** *adj* : having no equal
**peeve** *vb* : make resentful ~ *n* : complaint — **peev•ish** *adj* — **peev•ish•ly** *adv* — **peev•ish•ness** *n*
**peg** *n* : small pinlike piece ~ *vb* **1** : put a peg into **2** : fix or mark with or as if with pegs
**pel•let** *n* : little ball — **pel•let•al** *adj* — **pel•let•ize** *vb*
**1pelt** *n* : skin of a fur-bearing animal
**2pelt** *vb* : strike with blows or missiles
**pel•vis** *n* : cavity formed by the hip bones — **pel•vic** *adj*
**1pen** *n* : enclosure for animals ~ *vb* : shut in a pen
**2pen** *n* : tool for writing with ink ~ *vb* : write
**pe•nal** *adj* : relating to punishment — **pe•nal•ize** *vb* — **pen•al•ty** *n*
**pen•cil** *n* : writing or drawing tool with a solid marking substance (as graphite) as its core ~ *vb* : draw or write with a pencil
**pen•dant** *n* : hanging ornament
**pen•dent, pen•dant** *adj* : hanging
**pend•ing** *prep* : while awaiting ~ *adj* : not yet decided
**pen•du•lum** *n* : a hanging weight that is free to swing
**pen•e•trate** *vb* **1** : enter into **2** : permeate **3** : see into — **pen•e•tra•ble** *adj* — **pen•e•tra•tion** *n* — **pen•e•tra•tive** *adj*
**pen•guin** *n* : short-legged flightless seabird
**pen•in•su•la** *n* : land extending out into the water — **pen•in•su•lar** *adj*
**pen•i•ten•tia•ry** *n* : state or federal prison
**pen•nant** *n* : nautical or championship flag
**pen•ny** *n* **1** : monetary unit equal to 1/100 pound **2** : cent — **pen•ni•less** *adj*
**pen•sion** *n* : retirement income ~ *vb* : pay a pension to — **pen•sion•er** *n*
**pen•sive** *adj* : thoughtful — **pen•sive•ly** *adv*
**pent•a•gon** *n* : 5-sided polygon — **pen•tag•o•nal** *adj*
**peo•ple** *n* **1 people** *pl* : human beings in general **2 people** *pl* : human beings in a certain group (as a family) or community **3** *pl* **peoples** : tribe, nation, or race ~ *vb* : constitute the population of
**pep** *n* : brisk energy ~ *vb* : put pep into — **pep•py** *adj*
**pep•per** *n* **1** : pungent seasoning from the berry (**peppercorn**) of a shrub **2** : vegetable grown for its hot or sweet fruit ~ *vb* : season with pepper — **pep•pery** *adj*
**pep•per•mint** *n* : pungent aromatic mint
**per** *prep* **1** : by means of **2** : for each **3** : according to
**per•ceive** *vb* **1** : realize **2** : become aware of through the senses — **per•ceiv•able** *adj* — **per•cep•ti•ble** *adj* — **per•cep•ti•bly** *adv* — **per•cep•tion** *n* — **per•cep•tive** *n* — **per•cep•tive•ly** *adv*
**per•cent** *adv* : in each hundred ~ *n* **per•cent 1** : one part in a hundred **2** : percentage
**per•cent•age** *n* : part expressed in hundredths
**per•cen•tile** *n* : a standing on a scale of 0–100
**perch** *n* : resting place for birds ~ *vb* : settle on a resting place
**per•co•late** *vb* : trickle or filter down through a substance — **per•co•la•tor** *n*
**per•cus•sion** *n* **1** : sharp blow **2** : musical instrument sounded by striking
**pe•ren•ni•al** *adj* **1** : present at all seasons **2** : continuing from year to year **3** : recurring regularly ~ *n* : perennial plant — **pe•ren•ni•al•ly** *adv*
**per•fect** *adj* **1** : being without fault or defect **2** : exact **3** : complete ~ *vb* : make perfect — **per•fect•ibil•i•ty** *n* — **per•fect•ible** *adj* — **per•fect•ly** *adv* — **per•fect•ness** *n*
**per•fec•tion** *n* **1** : quality or state of being perfect **2** : highest degree of excellence — **per•fec•tion•ist** *n*
**per•fo•rate** *vb* : make a hole in — **per•fo•ra•tion** *n*
**per•form** *vb* **1** : carry out **2** : do in a set manner **3** : give a public presentation — **per•for•mance** *n* — **per•form•er** *n*
**per•fume** *n* **1** : pleasant odor **2** : something that gives a scent ~ *vb* : add scent to
**per•haps** *adv* : possibly but not certainly
**per•il** *n* : danger — **per•il•ous** *adj* — **per•il•ous•ly** *adv*
**pe•rim•e•ter** *n* : outer boundary of a body or figure
**pe•ri•od** *n* **1** : punctuation mark . used esp. to mark the end of a declarative sentence or an abbreviation **2** : division of time **3** : stage in a process or development
**pe•ri•od•ic** *adj* : occurring at regular intervals — **pe•ri•od•i•cal** *n* — **pe•ri•od•i•cal•ly** *adv*
**pe•riph•ery** *n* : outer boundary — **pe•riph•er•al** *adj*
**per•ish** *vb* : die or spoil — **per•ish•able** *adj or n*
**per•ju•ry** *n* : lying under oath — **per•jure** *vb* — **per•jur•er** *n*
**perk** *vb* **1** : thrust (as the head) up jauntily **2** : freshen **3** : gain vigor or spirit — **perky** *adj*
**per•ma•nent** *adj* : lasting ~ *n* : hair wave — **per•ma•nence** *n* — **per•ma•nent•ly** *adv*
**per•me•ate** *vb* **1** : seep through **2** : become spread throughout — **per•me•able** *adj* — **per•me•a•bil•i•ty** *n* — **per•me•ation** *n*
**per•mit** *vb* **1** : approve **2** : make possible ~ *n* : license — **per•mis•si•ble** *adj* — **per•mis•sion** *n* — **per•mis•sive** *adj* — **per•miss•ive•ly** *adv* — **per•mis•sive•ness** *n*
**per•pen•dic•u•lar** *adj* **1** : vertical **2** : meeting at a right angle — **perpendicular** *n* — **per•pen•dic•u•lar•i•ty** *n* — **per•pen•dic•u•lar•ly** *adv*
**per•pe•trate** *vb* : be guilty of doing — **per•pe•tra•tion** *n* — **per•pe•tra•tor** *n*
**per•pet•u•al** *adj* **1** : continuing forever **2** : occurring continually — **per•pet•u•al•ly** *adv* — **per•pet•u•ate** *vb* — **per•pe•tu•ity** *n*
**per•plex** *vb* : confuse — **per•plex•i•ty** *n*
**per•se•cute** *vb* : harass, afflict — **per•se•cu•tion** *n* — **per•se•cu•tor** *n*
**per•se•vere** *vb* : persist — **per•se•ver•ance** *n*
**per•sist** *vb* **1** : go on resolutely in spite of difficulties **2** : continue to exist — **per•sis•tence** *n* — **per•sis•ten•cy** *n* — **per•sis•tent** *adj* — **per•sis•tent•ly** *adv*
**per•son** *n* **1** : human being **2** : human being's body or individuality **3** : reference to the speaker, one spoken to, or one spoken of
**per•son•able** *adj* : having a pleasing personality
**per•son•al** *adj* **1** : relating to a particular person **2** : done in person **3** : affecting one's body **4** : offensive to a certain individual — **per•son•al•ize** *vb* — **per•son•al•ly** *adv*
**per•son•al•i•ty** *n* **1** : manner and disposition of an individual **2** : distinctive or well-known person

**per•son•i•fy** *vb* **1 :** represent as a human being **2 :** be the embodiment of — **per•son•i•fi•ca•tion** *n*
**per•son•nel** *n* **:** body of persons employed
**per•spec•tive** *n* **1 :** apparent depth and distance in painting **2 :** view of things in their true relationship or importance
**per•spire** *vb* **:** sweat — **per•spi•ra•tion** *n*
**per•suade** *vb* **:** win over to a belief or course of action by argument or entreaty — **per•sua•sion** *n* — **per•sua•sive** *adj* — **per•sua•sive•ly** *adv* — **per•sua•sive•ness** *n*
**per•tain** *vb* **1 :** belong **2 :** relate
**per•ti•nent** *adj* **:** relevant — **per•ti•nence** *n*
**per•verse** *adj* **1 :** corrupt **2 :** unreasonably contrary — **per•verse•ly** *adv* — **per•verse•ness** *n* — **per•ver•sion** *n* — **per•ver•si•ty** *n*
**per•vert** *vb* **:** corrupt or distort ∼ *n* **:** one that is perverted
**pes•si•mism** *n* **:** inclination to expect the worst — **pes•si•mist** *n* — **pes•si•mis•tic** *adj*
**pest** *n* **1 :** nuisance **2 :** plant or animal detrimental to humans or their crops — **pes•ti•cide** *n*
**pes•ter** *vb* **:** harass with petty matters
**pet** *n* **1 :** domesticated animal kept for pleasure **2 :** favorite ∼ *vb* **:** stroke gently or lovingly
**pet•al** *n* **:** modified leaf of a flower head
**pe•ti•tion** *n* **:** formal written request ∼ *vb* **:** make a request — **pe•ti•tion•er** *n*
**pet•ri•fy** *vb* **1 :** change into stony material **2 :** make rigid or inactive (as from fear) — **pet•ri•fac•tion** *n*
**pe•tro•leum** *n* **:** raw oil obtained from the ground
**pet•ty** *adj* **1 :** minor **2 :** of no importance **3 :** narrow-minded or mean — **pet•ti•ly** *adv* — **pet•ti•ness** *n*
**pew** *n* **:** bench with a back used in a church
**pH** *n* **:** number expressing relative acidity and alkalinity
**phantasy** *var of* FANTASY
**phan•tom** *n* **:** something that only appears to be real — **phan•tom** *adj*
**phar•ma•ceu•ti•cal** *adj* **:** relating to pharmacy or the making and selling of medicinal drugs — **phar•ma•ceu•ti•cal** *n*
**phar•ma•cy** *n* **1 :** art or practice of preparing and dispensing medical drugs **2 :** drugstore — **phar•ma•cist** *n*
**phar•ynx** *n* **:** space behind the mouth into which the nostrils, esophagus, and windpipe open — **pha•ryn•ge•al** *adj*
**phase** *n* **1 :** particular appearance or stage in a recurring series of changes **2 :** stage in a process — **phase in** *vb* **:** introduce in stages — **phase out** *vb* **:** discontinue gradually
**phe•nom•e•non** *n* **1** *pl* **phe•nom•e•na :** observable fact or event **2** *pl* **phe•nom•e•nons :** prodigy — **phe•nom•e•nal** *adj*
**phi•los•o•phy** *n* **1 :** critical study of fundamental beliefs **2 :** sciences and liberal arts exclusive of medicine, law, and theology **3 :** system of ideas **4 :** sum of personal convictions — **phil•o•soph•ic, phil•o•soph•i•cal** *adj* — **phil•o•soph•i•cal•ly** *adv* — **phi•los•o•phize** *vb* — **phi•los•o•pher** *n*
**pho•bia** *n* **:** irrational persistent fear
**phone** *n* **:** telephone ∼ *vb* **:** call on a telephone
**pho•no•graph** *n* **:** instrument that reproduces sounds from a grooved disc
**pho•ny, pho•ney** *adj* **:** not sincere or genuine — **phony** *n*
**pho•to** *n* **:** photograph — **pho•to** *vb or adj*
**pho•to•copy** *n* **:** photographic copy (as of a printed page) — **pho•to•copy** *vb*
**pho•to•graph** *n* **:** picture taken by photography — **pho•to•graph** *vb* — **pho•tog•ra•pher** *n* — **pho•to•graph•ic** *adj* — **pho•to•graph•i•cal•ly** *adv* — **pho•tog•ra•phy** *n*
**phrase** *n* **1 :** brief expression **2 :** group of related words that express a thought ∼ *vb* **:** express in a particular manner
**phys•i•cal** *adj* **1 :** relating to nature **2 :** material as opposed to mental or spiritual **3 :** relating to the body ∼ *n* **:** medical examination — **phys•i•cal•ly** *adv*
**phy•si•cian** *n* **:** doctor of medicine
**phys•i•cist** *n* **:** specialist in physics
**phys•ics** *n* **:** science that deals with matter and motion
**phy•sique** *n* **:** build of a person's body
**pi•ano** *n* **:** musical instrument with strings sounded by hammers operated from a keyboard — **pi•a•nist** *n*
[1]**pick** *vb* **1 :** break up with a pointed instrument **2 :** remove bit by bit **3 :** gather by plucking **4 :** select **5 :** rob **6 :** provoke **7 :** unlock with a wire **8 :** eat sparingly ∼ *n* **1 :** act of choosing **2 :** choicest one — **pick•er** *n* — **pick up** *vb* **1 :** improve **2 :** put in order
[2]**pick** *n* **:** pointed digging tool
**pick•le** *n* **1 :** brine or vinegar solution for preserving foods or a food preserved in a pickle **2 :** bad state — **pickle** *vb*
**pick•up** *n* **1 :** revival or acceleration **2 :** light truck with an open body
**pic•nic** *n* **:** outing with food usu. eaten in the open ∼ *vb* **:** go on a picnic
**pic•ture** *n* **1 :** representation by painting, drawing, or photography **2 :** vivid description **3 :** copy **4 :** movie ∼ *vb* **:** form a mental image of — **pic•to•ri•al** *adj* — **pic•tur•esque** *adj*
**pie** *n* **:** pastry crust and a filling
**piece** *n* **1 :** part of a whole **2 :** one of a group or set **3 :** single item **4 :** product of creative work ∼ *vb* **:** join into a whole
**pier** *n* **1 :** support for a bridge span **2 :** deck or wharf built out over water **3 :** pillar
**pierce** *vb* **1 :** enter or thrust into or through **2 :** penetrate **3 :** see through
**pig** *n* **1 :** young swine **2 :** dirty or greedy individual **3 :** iron casting — **pig•gish** *adj* — **pig•let** *n* — **pig•pen** *n* — **pig•sty** *n*
**pi•geon** *n* **:** stout-bodied short-legged bird
**pig•gy•back** *adv or adj* **:** up on the back and shoulders
**pig•ment** *n* **:** coloring matter — **pig•men•ta•tion** *n*
**pig•tail** *n* **:** tight braid of hair
**pike** *n* **:** turnpike
**pile** *n* **:** quantity of things thrown on one another ∼ *vb* **:** heap up, accumulate
**pil•grim** *n* **1 :** one who travels to a shrine or holy place in devotion **2** *cap* **:** one of the English settlers in America in 1620
**pil•grim•age** *n* **:** pilgrim's journey
**pill** *n* **:** small rounded mass of medicine — **pill•box** *n*
**pil•lar** *n* **:** upright usu. supporting column — **pil•lared** *adj*
**pil•low** *n* **:** soft cushion for the head — **pil•low•case** *n*
**pi•lot** *n* **1 :** helmsman **2 :** person licensed to take ships into and out of a port **3 :** guide **4 :** one that flies an aircraft or spacecraft ∼ *vb* **:** act as pilot of — **pi•lot•less** *adj*
**pim•ple** *n* **:** small inflamed swelling on the skin — **pim•ply** *adj*
**pin** *n* **1 :** fastener made of a small pointed piece of wire **2 :** ornament or emblem fastened to clothing with a pin **3 :** wooden object used as a target in bowling ∼ *vb* **1 :** fasten with a pin **2 :** hold fast or immobile — **pin•hole** *n*
**pin•a•fore** *n* **:** sleeveless dress or apron fastened at the back
**pin•cer** *n* **1** *pl* **:** gripping tool with 2 jaws **2 :** pincerlike claw
**pinch** *vb* **1 :** squeeze between the finger and thumb or between the jaws of a tool **2 :** compress painfully **3 :** restrict **4 :** steal ∼ *n* **1 :** emergency **2 :** painful effect **3 :** act of pinching **4 :** very small quantity
**pin•cush•ion** *n* **:** cushion for storing pins
[1]**pine** *n* **:** evergreen cone-bearing tree or its wood
[2]**pine** *vb* **1 :** lose health through distress **2 :** yearn for intensely
**pine•ap•ple** *n* **:** tropical plant bearing an edible juicy fruit
**pink** *n* **:** light red color — **pink** *adj* — **pink•ish** *adj*
**pin•point** *vb* **:** locate, hit, or aim with great precision
**pint** *n* **:** one-half quart
**pi•o•neer** *n* **1 :** one that originates or helps open up a new line of thought or activity **2 :** early settler ∼ *vb* **:** act as a pioneer
**pi•ous** *adj* **1 :** conscientious in religious practices **2 :** affectedly religious — **pi•ous•ly** *adv*
**pipe** *n* **1 :** tube that produces music when air is forced through **2 :** bagpipe **3 :** long tube for conducting a fluid **4 :** smoking tool ∼ *vb* **1 :** play on a pipe **2 :** speak in a high voice **3 :** convey by pipes — **pip•er** *n*
**pipe•line** *n* **1 :** line of pipe **2 :** channel for information
**pi•ra•cy** *n* **1 :** robbery on the seas **2 :** unauthorized use of another's production or invention
**pi•rate** *n* **:** one who commits piracy — **pi•rate** *vb* — **pi•rat•i•cal** *adj*
**pis** *pl of* PI
**pis•tol** *n* **:** firearm held with one hand
**pis•ton** *n* **:** sliding piece that receives and transmits motion usu. inside a cylinder
[1]**pit** *n* **1 :** hole or shaft in the ground **2 :** depressed or enclosed place for a special purpose **3 :** hell **4 :** hollow or indentation ∼ *vb* **1 :** form pits in **2 :** become marred with pits
[2]**pit** *n* **:** stony seed of some fruits ∼ *vb* **:** remove the pit from
**pitch** *vb* **1 :** erect and fix firmly in place **2 :** throw **3 :** set at a particular tone level **4 :** fall headlong ∼ *n* **1 :** action or manner of pitching **2 :** degree of slope **3 :** relative highness of a tone **4 :** sales talk — **pitched** *adj*
[1]**pitch•er** *n* **:** container for liquids
[2]**pitcher** *n* **:** one that pitches (as in baseball)
**pitch•fork** *n* **:** long-handled fork for pitching hay
**pit•tance** *n* **:** small portion or amount
**pity** *n* **1 :** sympathetic sorrow **2 :** something to be regretted ∼ *vb* **:** feel pity for — **piti•able** *adj* — **piti•ful** *adj* — **piti•ful•ly** *adv* — **piti•less** *adj* — **piti•less•ly** *adv*
**piv•ot** *n* **:** fixed pin on which something turns ∼ *vb* **:** turn on or as if on a pivot — **piv•ot•al** *adj*
**piz•za** *n* **:** thin pie of bread dough spread with a spiced mixture (as of tomatoes, cheese, and meat)
**piz•zazz, pi•zazz** *n* **:** glamour
**piz•ze•ria** *n* **:** pizza restaurant
**pla•cate** *vb* **:** appease — **pla•ca•ble** *adj*
**place** *n* **1 :** space or room **2 :** indefinite area **3 :** a particular building, locality, area, or part **4 :** relative position in a scale or sequence **5 :** seat **6 :** job ∼ *vb* **1 :** put in a place **2 :** identify — **place•ment** *n*
**plac•id** *adj* **:** undisturbed or peaceful — **pla•cid•i•ty** *n* — **plac•id•ly** *adv*
**pla•gia•rize** *vb* **:** use (words or ideas) of another as if your own — **pla•gia•rism** *n* — **pla•gia•rist** *n*
**plague** *n* **1 :** disastrous evil **2 :** destructive contagious bacterial disease ∼ *vb* **1 :** afflict with disease or disaster **2 :** harass
**plaid** *n* **:** woolen fabric with a pattern of crossing stripes or the pattern itself — **plaid** *adj*
**plain** *n* **:** expanse of relatively level treeless country ∼ *adj* **1 :** lacking ornament **2 :** not concealed or disguised **3 :** easily understood **4 :** frank **5 :** not fancy or pretty — **plain•ly** *adv* — **plain•ness** *n*
**plain•tiff** *n* **:** complaining party in a lawsuit
**plait** *n* **1 :** pleat **2 :** braid of hair or straw — **plait** *vb*
**plan** *n* **1 :** drawing or diagram **2 :** method for accomplishing something ∼ *vb* **1 :** form a plan of **2 :** intend — **plan•less** *adj* — **plan•ner** *n*
**plane** *n* **1 :** level surface **2 :** level of existence, consciousness, or development **3 :** airplane ∼ *adj* **1 :** flat **2 :** dealing with flat surfaces or figures
**plan•et** *n* **:** celestial body that revolves around the sun — **plan•e•tary** *adj*
**plank** *n* **1 :** heavy thick board **2 :** article in the platform of a political party — **plank•ing** *n*
**plant** *vb* **1 :** set in the ground to grow **2 :** place firmly or forcibly ∼ *n* **1 :** living thing without sense organs that cannot move about **2 :** land, buildings, and machinery used esp. in manufacture
**plan•tain** *n* **:** banana plant with starchy greenish fruit
**plan•ta•tion** *n* **:** agricultural estate usu. worked by resident laborers
**plant•er** *n* **1 :** plantation owner **2 :** plant container
**plasma TV** *n* **:** television screen in which cells of ionized gas emit light upon receiving an electric current
**plas•ter** *n* **1 :** medicated dressing **2 :** hardening paste for coating walls and ceilings ∼ *vb* **:** cover with plaster — **plas•ter•er** *n*
**plas•tic** *adj* **:** capable of being molded ∼ *n* **:** material that can be formed into rigid objects, films, or filaments — **plas•tic•i•ty** *n*
**plate** *n* **1 :** flat thin piece **2 :** plated metalware **3 :** shallow usu. circular dish **4 :** denture or the part of it that fits to the mouth **5 :** something printed from an engraving ∼ *vb* **:** overlay with metal — **plat•ing** *n*
**pla•teau** *n* **:** large level area of high land
**plat•form** *n* **1 :** raised flooring or stage **2 :** declaration of principles for a political party
**plat•i•num** *n* **:** heavy grayish-white metallic chemical element
**plat•ter** *n* **:** large serving plate
**plau•si•ble** *adj* **:** reasonable or believable — **plau•si•bil•i•ty** *n* — **plau•si•bly** *adv*
**play** *n* **1 :** action in a game **2 :** recreational activity **3 :** light or fitful movement **4 :** free movement **5 :** stage representation of a drama ∼ *vb* **1 :** engage in recreation **2 :** move or toy with aimlessly **3 :** perform music **4 :** act in a drama — **play•act•ing** *n* — **play•er** *n* — **play•ful** *adj* — **play•ful•ly** *adv* — **play•ful•ness** *n* — **play•ground** *n* — **play•mate** *n* — **play•pen** *n* — **play•suit** *n* — **play•thing** *n*
**play•house** *n* **1 :** theater **2 :** small house for children to play in
**play•wright** *n* **:** writer of plays
**pla•za** *n* **1 :** public square **2 :** shopping mall
**plea** *n* **1 :** defendant's answer to charges **2 :** urgent request
**plead** *vb* **1 :** argue for or against in court **2 :** answer to a charge or indictment **3 :** appeal earnestly — **plead•er** *n*
**pleas•ant** *adj* **1 :** giving pleasure **2 :** marked by pleasing behavior or appearance — **pleas•ant•ly** *adv* — **pleas•ant•ness** *n* — **pleas•ant•ry** *n*
**please** *vb* **1 :** give pleasure or satisfaction to **2 :** desire or intend
**pleas•ing** *adj* **:** giving pleasure — **pleas•ing•ly** *adv*
**plea•sure** *n* **1 :** desire or inclination **2 :** enjoyment **3 :** source of delight — **plea•sur•able** *adj* — **plea•sur•ably** *adv*
**pleat** *vb* **:** arrange in pleats ∼ *n* **:** fold in cloth
**pledge** *n* **1 :** something given as security **2 :** promise or vow ∼ *vb* **1 :** offer as or bind by a pledge **2 :** promise
**plen•ty** *n* **:** more than adequate number

or amount — **plen•ti•ful** *adj* — **plen•ti•ful•ly** *adv*
**pli•able** *adj* : flexible
**pli•ant** *adj* : flexible — **pli•an•cy** *n*
**pli•ers** *n pl* : pinching or gripping tool
**plight** *n* : bad state
**plod** *vb* **1** : walk heavily or slowly **2** : work laboriously and monotonously — **plod•der** *n* — **plod•ding•ly** *adv*
**plot** *n* **1** : small area of ground **2** : ground plan **3** : main story development (as of a book or movie) **4** : secret plan for doing something ~ *vb* **1** : make a plot or plan of **2** : plan or contrive — **plot•ter** *n*
**plow, plough** *n* **1** : tool used to turn soil **2** : device for pushing material aside ~ *vb* **1** : break up with a plow **2** : cleave or move through like a plow — **plow•man** *n*
**ploy** *n* : clever maneuver
**pluck** *vb* **1** : pull off or out **2** : tug or twitch ~ *n* **1** : act or instance of plucking **2** : spirit or courage
**plucky** *adj* : courageous or spirited
**plug** *n* **1** : something for sealing an opening **2** : electrical connector at the end of a cord **3** : piece of favorable publicity ~ *vb* **1** : stop or make tight or secure by inserting a plug **2** : publicize
**plum** *n* **1** : smooth-skinned juicy fruit **2** : fine reward
**plumb** *n* : weight on the end of a line (**plumb line**) to show vertical direction ~ *adv* **1** : vertically **2** : completely ~ *vb* : sound or test with a plumb ~ *adj* : vertical
**plumb•er** *n* : one who repairs usu. water pipes and fixtures
**plumb•ing** *n* : system of water pipes in a building
**plume** *n* : large, conspicuous, or showy feather ~ *vb* **1** : provide or deck with feathers **2** : indulge in pride — **plumed** *adj*
**plum•met** *vb* : drop straight down
**plump** *adj* : having a full rounded form — **plump•ness** *n*
**plun•der** *vb* : rob or take goods by force (as in war) ~ *n* : something taken in plundering — **plun•der•er** *n*
**plunge** *vb* **1** : thrust or drive with force **2** : leap or dive into water **3** : begin an action suddenly **4** : dip or move suddenly forward or down ~ *n* : act or instance of plunging — **plung•er** *n*
**plu•ral** *adj* : relating to a word form denoting more than one — **plu•ral** *n* — **plu•ral•i•za•tion** *n* — **plu•ral•ize** *vb*
**plu•ral•i•ty** *n* : greatest number of votes cast when not a majority
**plus** *prep* : with the addition of ~ *n* **1** : sign + (**plus sign**) in mathematics to indicate addition **2** : added or positive quantity **3** : advantage ~ *adj* : being more or in addition ~ *conj* : and
**plush** *n* : fabric with a long pile ~ *adj* : luxurious — **plush•ly** *adv* — **plushy** *adj* — **plush•ness** *n*
[1]**ply** *n* : fold, thickness, or strand of which something is made — **ply•wood** *n*
[2]**ply** *vb* **1** : use or work at **2** : keep supplying something to **3** : travel regularly usu. by sea
**pneu•mat•ic** *adj* **1** : moved by air pressure **2** : filled with compressed air — **pneu•mat•i•cal•ly** *adv*
**pneu•mo•nia** *n* : inflammatory lung disease
**pock•et** *n* **1** : small open bag sewn into a garment **2** : container or receptacle **3** : isolated area or group ~ *vb* : put in a pocket — **pock•et•ful** *n* — **pock•et•knife** *n*
**pock•et•book** *n* **1** : purse **2** : financial resources
**pod** *n* **1** : dry fruit that splits open when ripe **2** : compartment on a ship or craft
**po•et•ry** *n* **1** : metrical writing **2** : poems — **po•em** *n* — **po•et** *n* — **po•et•ic, po•et•i•cal** *adj*
**point** *n* **1** : individual often essential detail **2** : purpose **3** : particular place, time, or stage **4** : sharp end **5** : projecting piece of land **6** : dot or period **7** : division of the compass **8** : unit of counting ~ *vb* **1** : sharpen **2** : indicate direction by extending a finger **3** : direct attention to **4** : aim — **point•ed•ly** *adv* — **point•less** *adj*
**point•er** *n* **1** : one that points out **2** : large short-haired hunting dog **3** : hint or tip
**poise** *vb* : balance ~ *n* : self-possessed calmness
**poi•son** *n* : chemical that can injure or kill ~ *vb* **1** : injure or kill with poison **2** : apply poison to **3** : affect destructively — **poi•son•er** *n* — **poi•son•ous** *adj*
**poke** *vb* **1** : prod **2** : dawdle ~ *n* : quick thrust
[1]**pok•er** *n* : rod for stirring a fire
[2]**poker** *n* : card game for gambling
**po•lar** *adj* : relating to a geographical or magnetic pole
**po•lar•ize** *vb* **1** : cause to have magnetic poles **2** : break up into opposing groups — **po•lar•i•za•tion** *n*
[1]**pole** *n* : long slender piece of wood or metal
[2]**pole** *n* **1** : either end of the earth's axis **2** : battery terminal **3** : either end of a magnet
**po•lice** *n* (**police**) **1** : department of government that keeps public order and enforces the laws **2** : members of the police ~ *vb* : regulate and keep in order — **po•lice•man** *n* — **po•lice•wom•an** *n*
[1]**pol•i•cy** *n* : course of action selected to guide decisions
[2]**policy** *n* : insurance contract — **pol•i•cy•hold•er** *n*
**pol•ish** *vb* **1** : make smooth and glossy **2** : develop or refine ~ *n* **1** : shiny surface **2** : refinement
**po•lite** *adj* : marked by courteous social conduct — **po•lite•ly** *adv* — **po•lite•ness** *n*
**pol•i•tics** *n sing or pl* : practice of government and managing of public affairs — **po•lit•i•cal** *adj* — **po•lit•i•cal•ly** *adv* — **pol•i•ti•cian** *n*
**pol•ka dot** *n* : one of a series of regular dots in a pattern
**poll** *n* **1** : head **2** : place where votes are cast — usu. pl. **3** : a sampling of opinion ~ *vb* **1** : cut off **2** : receive or record votes **3** : question in a poll — **poll•ster** *n*
**pol•len** *n* : spores of a seed plant
**pol•li•na•tion** *n* : the carrying of pollen to fertilize the seed — **pol•li•nate** *vb* — **pol•li•na•tor** *n*
**pol•lute** *vb* : contaminating with waste products — **pol•lut•ant** *n* — **pol•lut•er** *n* — **pol•lu•tion** *n*
**poly•es•ter** *n* : synthetic fiber
**poly•gon** *n* : closed plane figure with straight sides
**pom•mel** *n* **1** : knob on the hilt of a sword **2** : knob at the front of a saddle ~ *vb* : pummel
**pomp•ous** *adj* : pretentiously dignified — **pom•pos•i•ty** *n* — **pomp•ous•ly** *adv*
**pon•cho** *n* : blanketlike cloak
**pond** *n* : small body of water
**pon•der** *vb* : consider
**pon•der•ous** *adj* **1** : very heavy **2** : clumsy **3** : oppressively dull
**pon•tiff** *n* : pope — **pon•tif•i•cal** *adj*
**pon•tif•i•cate** *vb* : talk pompously
**po•ny** *n* : small horse
**po•ny•tail** *n* : hair arrangement like the tail of a pony
**poo•dle** *n* : dog with a curly coat
**pool** *n* **1** : small body of water **2** : puddle
**poor** *adj* **1** : lacking material possessions **2** : less than adequate **3** : arousing pity **4** : unfavorable — **poor•ly** *adv*
[1]**pop** *vb* **1** : move suddenly **2** : burst with or make a sharp sound **3** : protrude ~ *n* **1** : sharp explosive sound **2** : flavored soft drink
[2]**pop** *adj* : popular
**pop•corn** *n* : corn whose kernels burst open into a light mass when heated
**pope** *n, often cap* : head of the Roman Catholic Church
**pop•u•lar** *adj* **1** : relating to the general public **2** : widely accepted **3** : commonly liked — **pop•u•lar•i•ty** *n* — **pop•u•lar•ize** *vb* — **pop•u•lar•ly** *adv*
**pop•u•la•tion** *n* : people or number of people in an area
**porch** *n* : covered entrance
**pore** *n* : tiny hole (as in the skin) — **pored** *adj*
**pork** *n* : pig meat
**po•rous** *adj* : permeable to fluids — **po•ros•i•ty** *n*
**port** *n* **1** : harbor **2** : city with a harbor
**por•ta•ble** *adj* : capable of being carried — **por•ta•ble** *n*
**por•tent** *n* : something that foreshadows a coming event — **por•ten•tous** *adj*
**por•ter** *n* : baggage carrier
**port•fo•lio** *n* **1** : portable case for papers **2** : office or function of a diplomat **3** : investor's securities
**por•tion** *n* : part or share of a whole ~ *vb* : divide into or allot portions
**por•trait** *n* : picture of a person — **por•trait•ist** *n* — **por•trai•ture** *n*
**por•tray** *vb* **1** : make a picture of **2** : describe in words **3** : play the role of — **por•tray•al** *n*
**pose** *vb* **1** : assume a posture or attitude **2** : propose **3** : pretend to be what one is not ~ *n* **1** : sustained posture **2** : pretense — **pos•er** *n*
**po•si•tion** *n* **1** : stand taken on a question **2** : place or location **3** : status **4** : job — **position** *vb*
**pos•i•tive** *adj* **1** : definite **2** : confident **3** : relating to or being an adjective or adverb form that denotes no increase **4** : greater than zero **5** : having a deficiency of electrons **6** : affirmative — **pos•i•tive•ly** *adv* — **pos•i•tive•ness** *n*
**pos•sess** *vb* **1** : have as property or as a quality **2** : control — **pos•ses•sion** *n* — **pos•ses•sor** *n*
**pos•ses•sive** *adj* **1** : relating to a grammatical case denoting ownership **2** : jealous — **pos•ses•sive** *n* — **pos•ses•sive•ness** *n*
**pos•si•ble** *adj* **1** : that can be done **2** : potential — **pos•si•bil•i•ty** *n* — **pos•si•bly** *adv*
[1]**post** *n* : upright stake serving to support or mark ~ *vb* : put up or announce by a notice
[2]**post** *vb* **1** : mail **2** : inform
[3]**post** *n* **1** : sentry's station **2** : assigned task **3** : army camp ~ *vb* : station
**post•age** *n* : fee for mail
**post•al** *adj* : relating to the mail
**post•er** *n* : large usu. printed notice
**post•hu•mous** *adj* : occurring after one's death — **post•hu•mous•ly** *adv*
**post•mark** *n* : official mark on mail — **post•mark** *vb*
**post office** *n* : agency or building for mail service
**post•pone** *vb* : put off to a later time — **post•pone•ment** *n*
**pos•tu•late** *vb* : assume as true ~ *n* : assumption
**pos•ture** *n* : bearing of the body ~ *vb* : strike a pose
**pot** *n* : rounded container ~ *vb* : place in a pot — **pot•ful** *n*
**po•ta•to** *n* : edible plant tuber
**po•tent** *adj* : powerful or effective — **po•ten•cy** *n*
**po•ten•tial** *adj* : capable of becoming actual ~ *n* **1** : something that can become actual **2** : degree of electrification with reference to a standard — **po•ten•ti•al•i•ty** *n* — **po•ten•tial•ly** *adv*
**pot•hole** *n* : large hole in a road surface
**pot•luck** *n* : whatever food is available
**pot•pour•ri** *n* **1** : mix of flowers, herbs, and spices used for scent **2** : miscellaneous collection
**pot•shot** *n* **1** : casual or easy shot **2** : random critical remark
**pot•tery** *n* : objects (as dishes) made from clay — **pot•ter** *n*
**pouch** *n* **1** : small bag **2** : bodily sac
**poul•try** *n* : domesticated fowl
**pounce** *vb* : spring or swoop upon and seize
[1]**pound** *n* **1** : unit of weight equal to 16 ounces **2** : monetary unit (as of the United Kingdom) — **pound•age** *n*
[2]**pound** *vb* **1** : crush by beating **2** : strike heavily **3** : drill **4** : move along heavily
**pour** *vb* **1** : flow or supply esp. copiously **2** : rain hard
**pout** *vb* : look sullen — **pout** *n*
**pov•er•ty** *n* **1** : lack of money or possessions **2** : poor quality
**pow•der** *n* : dry material of fine particles ~ *vb* : sprinkle or cover with powder — **pow•dery** *adj*
**pow•er** *n* **1** : position of authority **2** : ability to act **3** : one that has power **4** : physical might **5** : force or energy used to do work ~ *vb* : supply with power — **pow•er•ful** *adj* — **pow•er•ful•ly** *adv* — **pow•er•less** *adj*
**prac•ti•cal** *adj* **1** : relating to practice **2** : virtual **3** : capable of being put to use **4** : inclined to action as opposed to speculation — **prac•ti•cal•i•ty** *n* — **prac•ti•cal•ly** *adv*
**prac•tice, prac•tise** *vb* **1** : perform repeatedly to become proficient **2** : do or perform customarily **3** : be professionally engaged in ~ *n* **1** : actual performance **2** : habit **3** : exercise for proficiency **4** : exercise of a profession
**prag•ma•tism** *n* : practical approach to problems — **prag•mat•ic** *adj* — **prag•mat•i•cal•ly** *adv* — **prag•ma•tist** *n*
**prai•rie** *n* : broad grassy rolling tract of land
**praise** *vb* **1** : express approval of **2** : glorify — **praise** *n* — **praise•wor•thy** *adj*
**prance** *vb* **1** : spring from the hind legs **2** : swagger — **prance** *n* — **pranc•er** *n*
**prank** *n* : playful or mischievous act — **prank•ster** *n*
**pray** *vb* **1** : entreat **2** : ask earnestly for something **3** : address God or a god
**prayer** *n* **1** : earnest request **2** : an addressing of God or a god **3** : words used in praying — **prayer•ful** *adj* — **prayer•ful•ly** *adv*
**preach** *vb* **1** : deliver a sermon **2** : advocate earnestly — **preach•er** *n* — **preach•ment** *n*
**pre•car•i•ous** *adj* : dangerously insecure — **pre•car•i•ous•ly** *adv* — **pre•car•i•ous•ness** *n*
**pre•cau•tion** *n* : care taken beforehand — **pre•cau•tion•ary** *adj*
**pre•cede** *vb* : be, go, or come ahead of — **pre•ce•dence** *n* — **prec•e•dent** *n*
**pre•cinct** *n* **1** : district of a city **2** *pl* : vicinity
**pre•cious** *adj* **1** : of great value **2** : greatly cherished **3** : affected
**pre•cip•i•tate** *vb* **1** : cause to happen quickly or abruptly **2** : cause to separate out of a liquid **3** : fall as rain, snow, or hail ~ *n* : solid matter precipitated from a liquid ~ *adj* : unduly hasty — **pre•cip•i•tate•ly** *adv* — **pre•cip•i•tate•ness** *n* — **pre•cip•i•tous** *adj* — **pre•cip•i•tous•ly** *adv*
**pre•cip•i•ta•tion** *n* **1** : rash haste **2** : rain, snow, or hail
**pre•cise** *adj* **1** : definite **2** : highly accurate — **pre•cise•ly** *adv* — **pre•cise•ness** *n*
**pre•ci•sion** *n* : quality or state of being precise
**pre•clude** *vb* : make impossible
**pre•co•cious** *adj* : exceptionally advanced — **pre•co•cious•ly** *adv* — **pre•coc•i•ty** *n*
**pred•a•to•ry** *adj* : preying upon others — **pred•a•tor** *n*

**pre•de•ces•sor** *n* : a previous holder of a position

**pre•des•tine** *vb* : settle beforehand — **pre•des•ti•na•tion** *n*

**pre•dic•a•ment** *n* : difficult situation

**pred•i•cate** *n* : part of a sentence that states something about the subject ~ *vb* 1 : affirm 2 : establish — **pred•i•ca•tion** *n*

**pre•dict** *vb* : declare in advance — **pre•dict•abil•i•ty** *n* — **pre•dict•able** *adj* — **pre•dict•ably** *adv* — **pre•dic•tion** *n*

**pre•dis•pose** *vb* : cause to be favorable or likely to respond to something beforehand — **pre•dis•po•si•tion** *n*

**pre•dom•i•nate** *vb* : be superior — **pre•dom•i•nance** *n* — **pre•dom•i•nant** *adj* — **pre•dom•i•nant•ly** *adv*

**pre•em•i•nent** *adj* : having highest rank — **pre•em•i•nence** *n* — **pre•em•i•nent•ly** *adv*

**pre•empt** *vb* 1 : seize for oneself 2 : take the place of — **pre•emp•tion** *n* — **pre•emp•tive** *adj*

**pre•fab•ri•cat•ed** *adj* : manufactured for rapid assembly elsewhere — **pre•fab•ri•ca•tion** *n*

**pref•ace** *n* : introductory comments ~ *vb* : introduce with a preface — **pref•a•to•ry** *adj*

**pre•fer** *vb* 1 : like better 2 : bring (as a charge) against a person — **pref•er•a•ble** *adj* — **pref•er•a•bly** *adv* — **pref•er•ence** *n* — **pref•er•en•tial** *adj*

[1]**pre•fix** *vb* : place before

[2]**pre•fix** *n* : affix at the beginning of a word

**preg•nant** *adj* 1 : containing unborn young 2 : meaningful — **preg•nan•cy** *n*

**pre•his•tor•ic, pre•his•tor•i•cal** *adj* : relating to the period before written history

**prej•u•dice** *n* 1 : damage esp. to one's rights 2 : unreasonable attitude for or against something ~ *vb* 1 : damage 2 : cause to have prejudice — **prej•u•di•cial** *adj*

**pre•lim•i•nary** *n* : something that precedes or introduces — **pre•lim•i•nary** *adj*

**pre•lude** *n* : introductory performance, event, or musical piece

**pre•ma•ture** *adj* : coming before the usual or proper time — **pre•ma•ture•ly** *adv*

**pre•mier** *adj* : first in rank or importance ~ *n* : prime minister — **pre•mier•ship** *n*

**pre•miere** *n* : 1st performance ~ *vb* : give a 1st performance of

**prem•ise** *n* 1 : statement made or implied as a basis of argument 2 *pl* : piece of land with the structures on it

**pre•mi•um** *n* 1 : bonus 2 : sum over the stated value 3 : sum paid for insurance 4 : high value

**pre•mo•ni•tion** *n* : feeling that something is about to happen — **pre•mon•i•to•ry** *adj*

**pre•oc•cu•py** *vb* : occupy the attention of — **pre•oc•cu•pa•tion** *n* — **pre•oc•cu•pied** *adj*

**pre•pare** *vb* 1 : make or get ready often beforehand 2 : put together or compound — **prep•a•ra•tion** *n* — **pre•pa•ra•to•ry** *adj* — **pre•pared•ness** *n*

**prep•o•si•tion** *n* : word that combines with a noun or pronoun to form a phrase — **prep•o•si•tion•al** *adj*

**pre•req•ui•site** *n* : something required beforehand — **prerequisite** *adj*

**pre•rog•a•tive** *n* : special right or power

**pre•scribe** *vb* 1 : lay down as a guide 2 : direct the use of as a remedy

**pre•scrip•tion** *n* : written direction for the preparation and use of a medicine or the medicine prescribed

**pres•ence** *n* 1 : fact or condition of being present 2 : appearance or bearing

[1]**pres•ent** *n* : gift

[2]**pre•sent** *vb* 1 : introduce 2 : bring before the public 3 : make a gift to or of 4 : bring before a court for inquiry — **pre•sent•able** *adj* — **pre•sen•ta•tion** *n* — **pre•sent•ment** *n*

[3]**pres•ent** *adj* : now existing, in progress, or attending ~ *n* : the time or moment now existing — **pres•ent•ly** *adv*

**present participle** *n* : participle that typically expresses present action

**pre•serve** *vb* 1 : keep safe from danger or spoilage 2 : maintain ~ *n* 1 : preserved fruit — often in pl. 2 : area for protection of natural resources — **pres•er•va•tion** *n* — **pre•ser•va•tive** *adj or n* — **pre•serv•er** *n*

**pre•side** *vb* 1 : act as chairman 2 : exercise control

**pres•i•dent** *n* 1 : one chosen to preside 2 : chief official (as of a company or nation) — **pres•i•den•cy** *n* — **pres•i•den•tial** *adj*

**press** *n* 1 : crowded condition 2 : machine or device for exerting pressure and esp. for printing 3 : pressure 4 : printing or publishing establishment 5 : news media and esp. newspapers ~ *vb* 1 : lie against and exert pressure on 2 : smooth with an iron or squeeze with something heavy 3 : urge 4 : crowd 5 : force one's way — **press•er** *n*

**press•ing** *adj* : urgent

**pres•sure** *n* 1 : burden of distress or urgent business 2 : direct application of force — **pres•sure** *vb* — **pres•sur•i•za•tion** *n* — **pres•sur•ize** *vb*

**pres•tige** *n* : estimation in the eyes of people — **pres•ti•gious** *adj*

**pres•to** *adv or adj* : quickly

**pre•sume** *vb* 1 : assume authority without right to do so 2 : take for granted — **pre•sum•able** *adj* — **pre•sum•ably** *adv* — **pre•sump•tion** *n* — **pre•sump•tive** *adj*

**pre•sump•tu•ous** *adj* : too bold or forward — **pre•sump•tu•ous•ly** *adv*

**pre•sup•pose** *vb* : take for granted — **pre•sup•po•si•tion** *n*

**pre•tend** *vb* 1 : act as if something is real or true when it is not 2 : act in a way that is false 3 : lay claim — **pre•tend•er** *n*

**pre•tense, pre•tence** *n* 1 : insincere effort 2 : deception — **pre•ten•sion** *n*

**pre•ten•tious** *adj* : overly showy or self-important — **pre•ten•tious•ly** *adv* — **pre•ten•tious•ness** *n*

**pre•text** *n* : falsely stated purpose

**pret•ty** *adj* : pleasing by delicacy or attractiveness ~ *adv* : in some degree ~ *vb* : make pretty — **pret•ti•ly** *adv* — **pret•ti•ness** *n*

**pre•vail** *vb* 1 : triumph 2 : urge successfully 3 : be frequent, widespread, or dominant

**prev•a•lent** *adj* : widespread — **prev•a•lence** *n*

**pre•vent** *vb* : keep from happening or acting — **pre•vent•able** *adj* — **pre•ven•tion** *n* — **pre•ven•tive** *adj or n* — **pre•ven•ta•tive** *adj or n*

**pre•view** *vb* : view or show beforehand — **preview** *n*

**pre•vi•ous** *adj* : having gone, happened, or existed before — **pre•vi•ous•ly** *adv*

**prey** *n* 1 : animal taken for food by another 2 : victim ~ *vb* 1 : seize and devour animals as prey 2 : have a harmful effect on

**price** *n* : cost ~ *vb* : set a price on — **pric•ey** *adj* — **price•less** *adj*

**prick** *n* 1 : tear or small wound made by a point 2 : something sharp or pointed ~ *vb* : pierce slightly with a sharp point — **prick•er** *n*

**pride** *n* : quality or state of being proud ~ *vb* : indulge in pride — **pride•ful** *adj*

**priest** *n* : person having authority to perform the sacred rites of a religion — **priest•ess** *n* — **priest•hood** *n* — **priest•li•ness** *n* — **priest•ly** *adj*

**pri•ma•ry** *adj* : first in order of time, rank, or importance ~ *n* : preliminary election — **pri•mar•i•ly** *adv*

**pri•mate** *n* 1 : highest-ranking bishop 2 : mammal of the group that includes humans and monkeys

**prime** *n* : earliest or best part or period ~ *adj* : standing first (as in significance or quality) ~ *vb* 1 : fill or load 2 : lay a preparatory coating on

**prime minister** *n* : chief executive of a parliamentary government

[1]**prim•er** *n* : small introductory book

[2]**prim•er** *n* 1 : device for igniting an explosive 2 : material for priming a surface

**prim•i•tive** *adj* 1 : relating to or characteristic of an early stage of development 2 : of or relating to a tribal people or culture ~ *n* : one that is primitive — **prim•i•tive•ly** *adv* — **prim•i•tive•ness** *n*

**prince** *n* 1 : ruler 2 : son of a king or queen — **prince•ly** *adj*

**prin•cess** *n* 1 : daughter of a king or queen 2 : wife of a prince

**prin•ci•pal** *adj* : most important ~ *n* 1 : leading person 2 : head of a school 3 : sum lent at interest — **prin•ci•pal•ly** *adv*

**prin•ci•pal•i•ty** *n* : territory of a prince

**prin•ci•ple** *n* 1 : general or fundamental law 2 : rule or code of conduct or devotion to such a code

**print** *n* 1 : mark or impression made by pressure 2 : printed state or form 3 : printed matter 4 : copy made by printing 5 : cloth with a figure stamped on it ~ *vb* 1 : produce impressions of (as from type) 2 : write in letters like those of printer's type — **print•able** *adj* — **print•er** *n* — **print•out** *n* — **print out** *vb*

**pri•or** *adj* : coming before in time, order, or importance — **pri•or•i•ty** *n*

**prism** *n* : transparent 3-sided object that separates light into colors — **pris•mat•ic** *adj*

**pris•on** *n* : place where criminals are confined — **pris•on•er** *n*

**pris•sy** *adj* : overly prim — **pris•si•ness** *n*

**pris•tine** *adj* : pure

**pri•va•cy** *n* : quality or state of being apart from others

**pri•vate** *adj* 1 : belonging to a particular individual or group 2 : carried on independently 3 : withdrawn from company or observation ~ *n* : enlisted person of the lowest rank in the marine corps or of one of the two lowest ranks in the army — **pri•vate•ly** *adv*

**priv•i•lege** *n* : right granted as an advantage or favor — **priv•i•leged** *adj*

[1]**prize** *n* 1 : something offered or striven for in competition or in contests of chance 2 : something very desirable — **prize** *adj* — **prize•win•ner** *n* — **prize•win•ning** *adj*

[2]**prize** *vb* : value highly

[1]**pro** *n* : favorable argument or person ~ *adv* : in favor

[2]**pro** *n or adj* : professional

**prob•a•ble** *adj* : seeming true or real or to have a good chance of happening — **prob•a•bil•i•ty** *n* — **prob•a•bly** *adv*

**pro•bate** *n* : judicial determination of the validity of a will ~ *vb* : establish by probate

**pro•ba•tion** *n* 1 : period of testing and trial 2 : freedom for a convict during good behavior under supervision — **pro•ba•tion•ary** *adj* — **pro•ba•tion•er** *n*

**probe** *n* 1 : slender instrument for examining a cavity 2 : investigation ~ *vb* 1 : examine with a probe 2 : investigate

**prob•lem** *n* 1 : question to be solved 2 : source of perplexity or vexation — **prob•lem** *adj* — **prob•lem•at•ic** *adj* — **prob•lem•at•i•cal** *adj*

**pro•ce•dure** *n* 1 : way of doing something 2 : series of steps in regular order — **pro•ce•dur•al** *adj*

**pro•ceed** *vb* 1 : come forth 2 : go on in an orderly way 3 : begin and carry on an action 4 : advance

**pro•ceeds** *n pl* : total money taken in

**pro•cess** *n* 1 : something going on 2 : natural phenomenon marked by gradual changes 3 : series of actions or operations directed toward a result 4 : summons 5 : projecting part ~ *vb* : subject to a process — **pro•ces•sor** *n*

**pro•ces•sion** *n* : group moving along in an orderly way

**pro•claim** *vb* : announce publicly or with conviction — **proc•la•ma•tion** *n*

**pro•cras•ti•nate** *vb* : put something off until later — **pro•cras•ti•na•tion** *n* — **pro•cras•ti•na•tor** *n*

**pro•cure** *vb* : get possession of — **pro•cur•able** *adj* — **pro•cure•ment** *n* — **pro•cur•er** *n*

**prod** *vb* : push with or as if with a pointed instrument — **prod** *n*

**prod•i•gal** *adj* : recklessly extravagant or wasteful — **prodigal** *n* — **prod•i•gal•i•ty** *n*

**prod•i•gy** *n* : extraordinary person or thing

**pro•duce** *vb* 1 : present to view 2 : give birth to 3 : bring into existence ~ *n* 1 : product 2 : agricultural products — **pro•duc•er** *n*

**prod•uct** *n* 1 : number resulting from multiplication 2 : something produced

**pro•duc•tion** *n* : act, process, or result of producing — **pro•duc•tive** *adj* — **pro•duc•tive•ness** *n* — **pro•duc•tiv•i•ty** *n*

**pro•fane** *vb* : treat with irreverence ~ *adj* 1 : not concerned with religion 2 : serving to debase what is holy — **pro•fane•ly** *adv* — **pro•fane•ness** *n* — **pro•fan•i•ty** *n*

**pro•fes•sion** *n* 1 : open declaration of belief 2 : occupation requiring specialized knowledge and academic training

**pro•fes•sion•al** *adj* 1 : of, relating to, or engaged in a profession 2 : playing sport for pay — **pro•fes•sion•al** *n* — **pro•fes•sion•al•ism** *n* — **pro•fes•sion•al•ize** *vb* — **pro•fes•sion•al•ly** *adv*

**pro•fes•sor** *n* : university or college teacher — **pro•fes•so•ri•al** *adj* — **pro•fes•sor•ship** *n*

**pro•fi•cient** *adj* : very good at something — **pro•fi•cien•cy** *n* — **proficient** *n* — **pro•fi•cient•ly** *adv*

**pro•file** *n* : picture in outline — **profile** *vb*

**prof•it** *n* 1 : valuable return 2 : excess of the selling price of goods over cost ~ *vb* : gain a profit — **prof•it•able** *adj* — **prof•it•ably** *adv* — **prof•it•less** *adj*

**pro•found** *adj* 1 : marked by intellectual depth or insight 2 : deeply felt — **pro•found•ly** *adv* — **pro•fun•di•ty** *n*

**prog•no•sis** *n* : prospect of recovery from disease

**pro•gram** *n* 1 : outline of the order to be pursued or the subjects included (as in a performance) 2 : plan of procedure 3 : coded instructions for a computer ~ *vb* 1 : enter in a program 2 : provide a computer with a program — **pro•gram•ma•bil•i•ty** *n* — **pro•gram•ma•ble** *adj* — **pro•gram•mer** *n*

**prog•ress** *n* : movement forward or to a better condition ~ *vb* 1 : move forward 2 : improve — **pro•gres•sion** *n* — **pro•gres•sive** *adj* — **pro•gres•sive•ly** *adv*

**pro•hib•it** *vb* : prevent by authority — **pro•hi•bi•tion** *n* — **pro•hi•bi•tion•ist** *n* — **pro•hib•i•tive** *adj* — **pro•hib•i•tive•ly** *adv* — **pro•hib•i•to•ry** *adj*

**proj•ect** *n* : planned undertaking ~ *vb* 1 : design or plan 2 : protrude 3 : throw forward — **pro•jec•tion** *n*

**pro•jec•tor** *n* : device for projecting pictures on a screen

**pro•le•tar•i•at** *n* : laboring class

**pro•lif•er•ate** *vb* : grow or increase in number rapidly — **pro•lif•er•a•tion** *n*

**pro•lif•ic** *adj* : producing abundantly — **pro•lif•i•cal•ly** *adv*

**pro•logue** *n* : preface

**pro•long** *vb* : lengthen in time or extent — **pro•lon•ga•tion** *n*

**prom** *n* : formal school dance

**prom•e•nade** *n* **1** : leisurely walk **2** : place for strolling — **promenade** *vb*

**prom•i•nence** *n* **1** : quality, state, or fact of being readily noticeable or distinguished **2** : something that stands out — **prom•i•nent** *adj* — **prom•i•nent•ly** *adv*

**prom•ise** *n* **1** : statement that one will do or not do something **2** : basis for expectation — **prom•ise** *vb* — **prom•is•so•ry** *adj*

**prom•is•ing** *adj* : likely to succeed — **prom•is•ing•ly** *adv*

**pro•mote** *vb* **1** : advance in rank **2** : contribute to the growth, development, or prosperity of — **pro•mot•er** *n* — **pro•mo•tion** *n* — **pro•mo•tion•al** *adj*

**[1]prompt** *vb* **1** : incite **2** : give a cue to (an actor or singer) — **prompt•er** *n*

**[2]prompt** *adj* : ready and quick — **prompt•ly** *adv* — **prompt•ness** *n*

**prone** *adj* **1** : having a tendency **2** : lying face downward — **prone•ness** *n*

**pro•noun** *n* : word used as a substitute for a noun

**pro•nounce** *vb* **1** : utter officially or as an opinion **2** : say or speak esp. correctly — **pro•nounce•able** *adj* — **pro•nounce•ment** *n* — **pro•nun•ci•a•tion** *n*

**proof** *n* **1** : evidence of a truth or fact **2** : trial impression or print

**prop** *vb* **1** : support **2** : sustain — **prop** *n*

**pro•pa•gan•da** *n* : the spreading of ideas or information to further or damage a cause — **pro•pa•gan•dist** *n* — **pro•pa•gan•dize** *vb*

**prop•a•gate** *vb* **1** : reproduce biologically **2** : cause to spread — **prop•a•ga•tion** *n*

**pro•pel** *vb* : drive forward — **pro•pel•lant, pro•pel•lent** *n or adj*

**pro•pel•ler** *n* : hub with revolving blades that propels a craft

**prop•er** *adj* **1** : suitable or right **2** : limited to a specified thing **3** : correct **4** : strictly adhering to standards of social manners, dignity, or good taste — **prop•er•ly** *adv*

**prop•er•ty** *n* **1** : quality peculiar to an individual **2** : something owned **3** : piece of real estate **4** : ownership

**proph•et** *n* : one who utters revelations or predicts events — **proph•e•cy** *n* — **proph•et•ess** *n* — **pro•phet•ic** *adj* — **pro•phet•i•cal•ly** *adv*

**pro•por•tion** *n* **1** : relation of one part to another or to the whole with respect to magnitude, quantity, or degree **2** : symmetry **3** : share ~ *vb* : adjust in size in relation to others — **pro•por•tion•al** *adj* — **pro•por•tion•al•ly** *adv* — **pro•por•tion•ate** *adj* — **pro•por•tion•ate•ly** *adv*

**pro•pose** *vb* **1** : plan or intend **2** : make an offer of marriage **3** : present for consideration — **pro•pos•al** *n* — **prop•o•si•tion** *n*

**pro•pri•etor** *n* : owner — **pro•pri•etary** *adj* — **pro•pri•etor•ship** *n* — **pro•pri•etress** *n* — **pro•pri•ety** *n*

**pro•pul•sion** *n* **1** : action of propelling **2** : driving power — **pro•pul•sive** *adj*

**pro•scribe** *vb* : prohibit — **pro•scrip•tion** *n*

**prose** *n* : ordinary language

**pros•e•cute** *vb* **1** : follow to the end **2** : seek legal punishment of — **pros•e•cu•tion** *n* — **pros•e•cu•tor** *n*

**pros•pect** *n* **1** : extensive view **2** : something awaited **3** : potential buyer ~ *vb* : look for mineral deposits — **pro•spec•tive** *adj* — **pro•spec•tive•ly** *adv* — **pros•pec•tor** *n*

**pros•per** *vb* : thrive or succeed — **pros•per•ous** *adj*

**pros•per•i•ty** *n* : economic well-being

**pros•trate** *adj* : stretched out with face on the ground ~ *vb* **1** : fall or throw (oneself) into a prostrate position **2** : reduce to helplessness — **pros•tra•tion** *n*

**pro•tect** *vb* : shield from injury — **pro•tec•tion** *n* — **pro•tec•tive** *adj* — **pro•tec•tor** *n*

**pro•tein** *n* : complex combination of amino acids present in living matter

**pro•test** *n* **1** : organized public demonstration of disapproval **2** : strong objection ~ *vb* **1** : assert positively **2** : object strongly — **pro•tes•ta•tion** *n* — **pro•test•er, pro•tes•tor** *n*

**Prot•es•tant** *n* : Christian not of a Catholic or Orthodox church — **Prot•es•tant•ism** *n*

**pro•to•type** *n* : original model

**pro•trac•tor** *n* : instrument for drawing and measuring angles

**pro•trude** *vb* : stick out or cause to stick out — **pro•tru•sion** *n*

**pro•tu•ber•ance** *n* : something that protrudes — **pro•tu•ber•ant** *adj*

**proud** *adj* **1** : having or showing excessive self-esteem **2** : highly pleased **3** : having proper self-respect **4** : glorious — **proud•ly** *adv*

**prove** *vb* (**proved; proved/prov•en**) **1** : test by experiment or by a standard **2** : establish the truth of by argument or evidence **3** : turn out esp. after trial or test — **prov•able** *adj*

**prov•erb** *n* : short meaningful popular saying — **pro•ver•bi•al** *adj*

**pro•vide** *vb* **1** : take measures beforehand **2** : make a stipulation **3** : supply what is needed — **pro•vid•er** *n*

**prov•i•dence** *n* **1** *often cap* : divine guidance **2** *cap* : God **3** : quality of being provident

**prov•i•dent** *adj* **1** : making provision for the future **2** : thrifty — **prov•i•dent•ly** *adv*

**prov•ince** *n* **1** : administrative district **2** *pl* : all of a country outside the metropolis **3** : sphere

**pro•vin•cial** *adj* **1** : relating to a province **2** : limited in outlook — **pro•vin•cial•ism** *n*

**pro•vi•sion** *n* **1** : act of providing **2** : stock of food — usu. in pl. **3** : stipulation ~ *vb* : supply with provisions

**pro•vi•sion•al** *adj* : provided for a temporary need — **pro•vi•sion•al•ly** *adv*

**pro•voke** *vb* **1** : incite to anger **2** : stir up on purpose — **prov•o•ca•tion** *n* — **pro•voc•a•tive** *adj*

**prowl** *vb* : roam about stealthily — **prowl** *n* — **prowl•er** *n*

**prox•im•i•ty** *n* : nearness

**proxy** *n* : authority to act for another — **proxy** *adj*

**prude** *n* : one who shows extreme modesty — **prud•ery** *n* — **prud•ish** *adj*

**pru•dent** *adj* **1** : shrewd **2** : cautious **3** : thrifty — **pru•dence** *n* — **pru•den•tial** *adj* — **pru•dent•ly** *adv*

**[1]prune** *n* : dried plum

**[2]prune** *vb* : cut off unwanted parts

**[1]pry** *vb* : look closely or inquisitively

**[2]pry** *vb* : raise, move, or pull apart with a lever

**psalm** *n* : sacred song or poem — **psalm•ist** *n*

**psy•che** *n* : soul or mind

**psy•chi•a•try** *n* : branch of medicine dealing with mental, emotional, and behavioral disorders — **psy•chi•at•ric** *adj* — **psy•chi•a•trist** *n*

**psy•chic** *adj* **1** : relating to the psyche **2** : sensitive to supernatural forces ~ *n* : person sensitive to supernatural forces — **psy•chi•cal•ly** *adv*

**psy•chol•o•gy** *n* **1** : science of mind and behavior **2** : mental and behavioral aspect (as of an individual) — **psy•cho•log•i•cal** *adj* — **psy•cho•log•i•cal•ly** *adv* — **psy•chol•o•gist** *n*

**pub•lic** *adj* **1** : relating to the people as a whole **2** : civic **3** : not private **4** : open to all **5** : well-known ~ *n* : people as a whole — **pub•lic•ly** *adv*

**pub•lic•i•ty** *n* **1** : news information given out to gain public attention **2** : public attention

**pub•li•cize** *vb* : bring to public attention — **pub•li•cist** *n*

**pub•lish** *vb* **1** : announce publicly **2** : reproduce for sale esp. by printing — **pub•li•ca•tion** *n* — **pub•lish•er** *n*

**pud•ding** *n* : creamy dessert

**pud•dle** *n* : very small pool of water

**puff** *vb* **1** : blow in short gusts **2** : pant **3** : enlarge ~ *n* **1** : short discharge (as of air) **2** : slight swelling **3** : something light and fluffy — **puffy** *adj*

**puke** *vb* : vomit — **puke** *n*

**pull** *vb* **1** : exert force so as to draw (something) toward or out **2** : move **3** : stretch or tear ~ *n* **1** : act of pulling **2** : influence **3** : device for pulling something — **pull•er** *n*

**pul•ley** *n* : wheel with a grooved rim

**pulp** *n* **1** : soft part of a fruit or vegetable **2** : soft moist mass (as of mashed wood) — **pulpy** *adj*

**pul•pit** *n* : raised desk used in preaching

**pul•sate** *vb* : expand and contract rhythmically — **pul•sa•tion** *n*

**pulse** *n* : arterial throbbing caused by heart contractions — **pulse** *vb*

**pul•ver•ize** *vb* : beat or grind into a powder

**pum•mel** *vb* : beat

**[1]pump** *n* : device for moving or compressing fluids ~ *vb* **1** : raise (as water) with a pump **2** : fill by means of a pump — with *up* **3** : move like a pump — **pump•er** *n*

**[2]pump** *n* : woman's low shoe

**pump•kin** *n* : large usu. orange fruit of a vine related to the gourd

**pun** *n* : humorous use of a word in a way that suggests two or more interpretations — **pun** *vb*

**[1]punch** *vb* **1** : strike with the fist **2** : perforate with a punch ~ *n* : quick blow with the fist — **punch•er** *n*

**[2]punch** *n* : mixed beverage often including fruit juice

**punc•tu•al** *adj* : prompt — **punc•tu•al•i•ty** *n* — **punc•tu•al•ly** *adv*

**punc•tu•ate** *vb* : mark with symbols to clarify meaning — **punc•tu•a•tion** *n*

**punc•ture** *n* : act or result of puncturing ~ *vb* : make a hole in

**pun•gent** *adj* : having a sharp or stinging odor or taste — **pun•gen•cy** *n* — **pun•gent•ly** *adv*

**pun•ish** *vb* : impose a penalty on or for — **pun•ish•able** *adj* — **pun•ish•ment** *n*

**punt** *vb* : kick a ball dropped from the hands ~ *n* : act of punting a ball

**pu•ny** *adj* : slight in power or size

**pup** *n* : young dog

**[1]pu•pil** *n* : young person in school

**[2]pu•pil** *n* : dark central opening of the iris of the eye

**pup•pet** *n* : small doll moved by hand or by strings — **pup•pe•teer** *n*

**pup•py** *n* : young dog

**pur•chase** *vb* : obtain in exchange for money ~ *n* **1** : act of purchasing **2** : something purchased **3** : secure grasp — **pur•chas•er** *n*

**pure** *adj* : free of foreign matter, contamination, or corruption — **pure•ly** *adv*

**purge** *vb* **1** : purify esp. from sin **2** : have or cause emptying of the bowels **3** : get rid of ~ *n* **1** : act or result of purging **2** : something that purges — **pur•ga•tive** *adj or n*

**pu•ri•fy** *vb* : make or become pure — **pu•ri•fi•ca•tion** *n* — **pu•ri•fi•er** *n*

**Pu•rim** *n* : Jewish holiday celebrated in February or March in commemoration of the deliverance of the Jews from the massacre plotted by Haman

**pu•ri•ty** *n* : quality or state of being pure

**pur•ple** *n* : bluish red color — **pur•plish** *adj*

**pur•pose** *n* **1** : something (as a result) aimed at **2** : resolution ~ *vb* : intend — **pur•pose•ful** *adj* — **pur•pose•ful•ly** *adv* — **pur•pose•less** *adj* — **pur•pose•ly** *adv*

**purse** *n* **1** : bag or pouch for money and small objects **2** : financial resource **3** : prize money

**pur•su•ant to** *prep* : according to

**pur•sue** *vb* **1** : follow in order to overtake **2** : seek to accomplish **3** : proceed along **4** : engage in — **pur•su•er** *n*

**pur•suit** *n* **1** : act of pursuing **2** : occupation

**pur•vey** *vb* : supply (as provisions) usu. as a business — **pur•vey•or** *n*

**push** *vb* **1** : press against to move forward **2** : urge on or provoke ~ *n* **1** : vigorous effort **2** : act of pushing — **push•cart** *n* — **push•er** *n*

**pushy** *adj* : objectionably aggressive

**put** *vb* (**put; put**) **1** : bring to a specified position or condition **2** : subject to pain, suffering, or death **3** : impose or cause to exist **4** : express **5** : cause to be used or employed — **put off** *vb* : postpone or delay — **put out** *vb* : bother or inconvenience — **put up** *vb* **1** : prepare for storage **2** : lodge **3** : contribute or pay — **put up with** : endure

**pu•tre•fy** *vb* : make or become rotten — **pu•tre•fac•tion** *n* — **pu•trid** *adj* — **pu•trid•i•ty** *n*

**puz•zle** *vb* **1** : confuse **2** : attempt to solve — used with *out* or *over* ~ *n* : something that confuses or tests ingenuity — **puz•zle•ment** *n* — **puz•zler** *n*

**pyg•my** *n* : dwarf — **pyg•my** *adj*

**py•lon** *n* : tower or tall post

**pyr•a•mid** *n* : structure with a square base and 4 triangular sides meeting at a point

**py•ro•ma•nia** *n* : irresistible impulse to start fires — **py•ro•ma•ni•ac** *n*

**py•ro•tech•nics** *n pl* : spectacular display (as of fireworks) — **py•ro•tech•nic** *adj*

# Q

**q** *n* : 17th letter of the alphabet

**[1]quack** *vb* : make a cry like that of a duck — **quack** *n*

**[2]quack** *n* : one who pretends to have medical or healing skill — **quack** *adj* — **quack•ery** *n*

**quad•ran•gle** *n* : rectangular courtyard

**quad•ri•lat•er•al** *n* : 4-sided polygon

**quad•ru•ped** *n* : animal having 4 feet

**qua•dru•ple** *vb* : multiply by 4 ~ *adj* : being 4 times as great or as many

**qua•dru•plet** *n* : one of 4 offspring born at one birth

**quail** *n* (**quail**) : short-winged plump game bird

**quaint** *adj* : pleasingly old-fashioned or odd — **quaint•ly** *adv* — **quaint•ness** *n*

**quake** *vb* : shake or tremble ~ *n* : earthquake

**qual•i•fy** *vb* **1** : modify or limit **2** : fit by skill or training for some purpose **3** : become eligible — **qual•i•fi•ca•tion** *n* — **qual•i•fied** *adj* — **qual•i•fi•er** *n*

**qual·i·ty** *n* **1 :** peculiar and essential character, nature, or feature **2 :** excellence or distinction

**quan·ti·ty** *n* **1 :** something that can be measured or numbered **2 :** considerable amount

**quar·an·tine** *n* **1 :** restraint on the movements of persons or goods to prevent the spread of pests or disease **2 :** place or period of quarantine — **quarantine** *vb*

**quar·rel** *n* **:** basis of conflict — **quarrel** *vb* — **quar·rel·some** *adj*

[1]**quar·ry** *n* **:** prey

[2]**quar·ry** *n* **:** excavation for obtaining stone — **quar·ry** *vb*

**quart** *n* **:** unit of liquid measure equal to .95 liter or of dry measure equal to 1.10 liters

**quar·ter** *n* **1 :** ¼ part **2 :** ¼ of a dollar **3 :** city district **4** *pl* **:** place to live esp. for a time **5 :** mercy ~ *vb* **:** divide into 4 equal parts

**quar·ter·ly** *adv or adj* **:** at 3-month intervals ~ *n* **:** periodical published 4 times a year

**quar·tet** *n* **1 :** music for 4 performers **2 :** group of 4

**quay** *n* **:** wharf

**quea·sy** *adj* **:** nauseated — **quea·si·ly** *adv* — **quea·si·ness** *n*

**queen** *n* **1 :** wife or widow of a king **2 :** female monarch **3 :** woman of rank, power, or attractiveness **4 :** fertile female of a social insect — **queen·ly** *adj*

**queer** *adj* **:** differing from the usual or normal — **queer·ly** *adv* — **queer·ness** *n*

**quench** *vb* **1 :** put out **2 :** satisfy (a thirst) — **quench·able** *adj* — **quench·er** *n*

**que·ry** *n* **:** question — **que·ry** *vb*

**quest** *n or vb* **:** search

**ques·tion** *n* **1 :** something asked **2 :** subject for debate **3 :** dispute ~ *vb* **1 :** ask questions **2 :** doubt or dispute **3 :** subject to analysis — **ques·tion·er** *n*

**ques·tion·able** *adj* **1 :** not certain **2 :** of doubtful truth or morality — **ques·tion·ably** *adv*

**ques·tion·naire** *n* **:** set of questions

**queue** *n* **1 :** braid of hair **2 :** a waiting line ~ *vb* **:** line up

**quib·ble** *n* **:** minor objection — **quibble** *vb* — **quib·bler** *n*

**quick** *adj* **1 :** rapid **2 :** alert or perceptive ~ *n* **:** sensitive area of living flesh — **quick** *adv* — **quick·ly** *adv* — **quick·ness** *n*

**quick·en** *vb* **1 :** come to life **2 :** increase in speed

**qui·et** *adj* **1 :** marked by little motion or activity **2 :** gentle **3 :** free from noise **4 :** not showy **5 :** isolated ~ *vb* **:** pacify — **quiet** *adv or n* — **qui·et·ly** *adv* — **qui·et·ness** *n*

**quilt** *n* **:** padded bedspread ~ *vb* **:** stitch or sew in layers with padding in between

**quin·tet** *n* **1 :** music for 5 performers **2 :** group of 5

**quin·tu·ple** *adj* **1 :** having 5 units or members **2 :** being 5 times as great or as many — **quintuple** *n or vb*

**quip** *vb* **:** make a clever remark — **quip** *n*

**quirk** *n* **:** peculiarity of action or behavior — **quirky** *adj*

**quit** *vb* **quit; quit 1 :** stop **2 :** leave — **quit·ter** *n*

**quite** *adv* **1 :** completely **2 :** to a considerable extent

**quiv·er** *vb* **:** shake or tremble — **quiv·er** *n*

**quiz** *n* **:** short test ~ *vb* **:** question closely

**quiz·zi·cal** *adj* **1 :** teasing **2 :** curious

**quo·rum** *n* **:** required number of members present

**quo·ta** *n* **:** proportional part or share

**quote** *vb* **1 :** repeat (another's words) exactly **2 :** state (a price) — **quot·able** *adj* — **quo·ta·tion** *n* — **quote** *n*

**quo·tient** *n* **:** number obtained from division

# R

**r** *n* **:** 18th letter of the alphabet

**rab·bet** *n* **:** groove in a board

**rab·bi** *n* **:** Jewish religious leader — **rab·bin·ate** *n* — **rab·bin·ic, rab·bin·i·cal** *adj*

**rab·bit** *n* **:** long-eared burrowing mammal

**ra·bid** *adj* **1 :** violent **2 :** fanatical **3 :** affected with rabies — **ra·bid·ly** *adv*

**ra·bies** *n* **:** acute deadly virus disease

**rac·coon** *n* **:** tree-dwelling mammal with a black mask and a bushy ringed tail

[1]**race** *n* **1 :** strong current of water **2 :** contest of speed **3 :** election campaign ~ *vb* **1 :** run in a race **2 :** rush — **race·course** *n* — **race·horse** *n* — **rac·er** *n* — **race·track** *n*

[2]**race** *n* **1 :** family, tribe, people, or nation of the same stock **2 :** division of mankind based on hereditary traits — **ra·cial** *adj* — **ra·cial·ly** *adv*

**rac·ism** *n* **:** discrimination based on the belief that some races are by nature superior — **rac·ist** *n*

**rack** *n* **1 :** framework for display or storage **2 :** instrument that stretches the body for torture ~ *vb* **:** torture with or as if with a rack

[1]**rack·et** *n* **:** bat with a tight netting across an open frame

[2]**racket** *n* **1 :** confused noise **2 :** fraudulent scheme — **rack·e·teer** *n* — **rack·e·teer·ing** *n*

**racy** *adj* **:** being or bordering on being highly improper or offensive — **rac·i·ly** *adv* — **rac·i·ness** *n*

**ra·dar** *n* **:** radio device for determining distance and direction of distant objects

**ra·di·ant** *adj* **1 :** glowing **2 :** beaming with happiness **3 :** transmitted by radiation — **ra·di·ance** *n* — **ra·di·ant·ly** *adv*

**ra·di·ate** *vb* **1 :** issue rays or in rays **2 :** spread from a center — **ra·di·a·tion** *n*

**ra·di·a·tor** *n* **:** cooling or heating device

**rad·i·cal** *adj* **1 :** fundamental **2 :** extreme ~ *n* **:** person favoring extreme changes — **rad·i·cal·ism** *n* — **rad·i·cal·ly** *adv*

**radii** *pl of* RADIUS

**ra·dio** *n* **1 :** wireless transmission or reception of sound by means of electric waves **2 :** radio receiving set ~ *vb* **:** send a message to by radio — **radio** *adj*

**ra·dio·ac·tiv·i·ty** *n* **:** property of an element that emits energy through nuclear disintegration — **ra·dio·ac·tive** *adj*

**rad·ish** *n* **:** pungent fleshy root usu. eaten raw

**ra·di·us (ra·dii)** *n* **1 :** line from the center of a circle or sphere to the circumference or surface **2 :** area defined by a radius

[1]**raft** *n* **:** flat floating platform ~ *vb* **:** travel or transport by raft

[2]**raft** *n* **:** large amount or number

**raf·ter** *n* **:** beam supporting a roof

**rag** *n* **:** waste piece of cloth

**rage** *n* **1 :** violent anger **2 :** state of being currently widely popular ~ *vb* **1 :** be extremely angry or violent **2 :** be out of control

**rag·ged** *adj* **:** torn — **rag·ged·ly** *adv* — **rag·ged·ness** *n*

**raid** *n* **:** sudden usu. surprise attack — **raid** *vb* — **raid·er** *n*

**rail** *n* **1 :** bar serving as a guard or barrier **2 :** bar forming a track for wheeled vehicles **3 :** railroad

**rail·ing** *n* **:** rail or a barrier of rails

**rail·road** *n* **:** road for a train laid with iron rails and wooden ties ~ *vb* **:** force something hastily — **rail·road·er** *n* — **rail·road·ing** *n*

**rain 1 :** water falling in drops from the clouds **2 :** shower of objects ~ *vb* **:** fall as or like rain — **rain·bow** *n* — **rain·coat** *n* — **rain·drop** *n* — **rain·fall** *n* — **rain·mak·er** *n* — **rain·mak·ing** *n* — **rain·storm** *n* — **rain·water** *n* — **rainy** *adj*

**raise** *vb* **1 :** lift **2 :** arouse **3 :** erect **4 :** collect **5 :** breed, grow, or bring up **6 :** increase **7 :** make light ~ *n* **:** increase esp. in pay — **rais·er** *n*

**rai·sin** *n* **:** dried grape

**rake** *n* **:** garden tool for smoothing or sweeping ~ *vb* **1 :** gather, loosen, or smooth with or as if with a rake **2 :** sweep with gunfire

**ral·ly** *vb* **1 :** bring or come together **2 :** revive or recover **3 :** make a comeback ~ *n* **1 :** act of rallying **2 :** mass meeting

**ram** *n* **1 :** male sheep **2 :** beam used in battering down walls or doors ~ *vb* **1 :** force or drive in or through **2 :** strike against violently

**RAM** *n* **:** main internal storage area in a computer

**ram·ble** *vb* **:** wander — **ram·ble** *n* — **ram·bler** *n*

**ramp** *n* **:** sloping passage or connecting roadway

**ram·page** *vb* **:** rush about wildly ~ *n* **:** violent or riotous action or behavior

**ran** *past of* RUN

**ranch** *n* **1 :** establishment for the raising of cattle, sheep, or horses **2 :** specialized farm ~ *vb* **:** operate a ranch — **ranch·er** *n*

**ran·cid** *adj* **:** smelling or tasting as if spoiled — **ran·cid·i·ty** *n*

**ran·dom** *adj* **:** occurring by chance — **ran·dom·ize** *vb* — **ran·dom·ly** *adv* — **ran·dom·ness** *n* — **at random :** without definite aim or method

**rang** *past of* RING

**range** *n* **1 :** series of things in a row **2 :** open land for grazing **3 :** cooking stove **4 :** variation within limits **5 :** place for target practice **6 :** extent ~ *vb* **1 :** arrange **2 :** roam at large, freely, or over **3 :** vary within limits

**rang·er** *n* **:** officer who manages and protects public lands

**rank** *n* **1 :** line of soldiers **2 :** orderly arrangement **3 :** grade of official standing **4 :** position within a group ~ *vb* **1 :** arrange in formation or according to class **2 :** take or have a relative position

**ran·sack** *vb* **:** search through and rob

**ran·som** *n* **:** something demanded for the freedom of a captive ~ *vb* **:** gain the freedom of by paying a price — **ran·som·er** *n*

**rant** *vb* **:** talk or scold violently — **rant·er** *n* — **rant·ing·ly** *adv*

[1]**rap** *n* **:** sharp blow or rebuke ~ *vb* **:** strike or criticize sharply

[2]**rap** *vb* **:** talk freely

**rape** *vb* **:** force to have sexual intercourse — **rape** *n* — **rap·er** *n* — **rap·ist** *n*

**rap·id** *adj* **:** very fast — **ra·pid·i·ty** *n* — **rap·id·ly** *adv*

**rap·ture** *n* **:** spiritual or emotional ecstasy — **rap·tur·ous** *adj* — **rap·tur·ous·ly** *adv*

[1]**rare** *adj* **:** having a portion relatively uncooked

[2]**rare** *adj* **1 :** not dense **2 :** unusually fine **3 :** seldom met with — **rare·ly** *adv* — **rare·ness** *n* — **rar·i·ty** *n*

**ras·cal** *n* **:** mean, dishonest, or mischievous person — **ras·cal·i·ty** *n* — **ras·cal·ly** *adj*

[1]**rash** *adj* **:** too hasty in decision or action — **rash·ly** *adv* — **rash·ness** *n*

[2]**rash** *n* **:** a breaking out of the skin with red spots

**rasp** *vb* **1 :** rub with or as if with a rough file **2 :** speak in a grating tone ~ *n* **:** coarse file

**rasp·ber·ry** *n* **:** edible red or black berry

**rat** *n* **:** destructive rodent larger than the mouse ~ *vb* **:** betray or inform on

**rate** *n* **1 :** quantity, amount, or degree measured in relation to some other quantity **2 :** rank ~ *vb* **1 :** estimate or determine the rank or quality of **2 :** deserve — **rat·ing** *n*

**rath·er** *adv* **1 :** preferably **2 :** on the other hand **3 :** more properly **4 :** somewhat

**rat·i·fy** *vb* **:** approve and accept formally — **rat·i·fi·ca·tion** *n*

**ra·tio** *n* **:** relation in number, quantity, or degree between things

**ra·tion** *n* **:** share or allotment (as of food) ~ *vb* **:** use or allot sparingly

**ra·tio·nal** *adj* **1 :** having reason or sanity **2 :** relating to reason — **ra·tio·nal·ly** *adv*

**ra·tio·nale** *n* **1 :** explanation of principles of belief or practice **2 :** underlying reason

**ra·tio·nal·ize** *vb* **:** justify (as one's behavior or weaknesses) esp. to oneself — **ra·tio·nal·i·za·tion** *n*

**rat·tle** *vb* **1 :** make a series of clattering sounds **2 :** say briskly **3 :** confuse or upset ~ *n* **1 :** series of clattering sounds **2 :** something (as a toy) that rattles

**rat·ty** *adj* **:** shabby

**rave** *vb* **1 :** talk wildly in or as if in delirium **2 :** talk with extreme enthusiasm ~ *n* **1 :** act of raving **2 :** enthusiastic praise

**rav·el** *vb* **1 :** have threads become separated **2 :** tangle ~ *n* **1 :** something tangled **2 :** loose thread

**raw** *adj* **1 :** not cooked **2 :** not processed **3 :** not trained **4 :** having the surface rubbed off **5 :** cold and damp **6 :** vulgar — **raw·ness** *n*

**ray** *n* **1 :** thin beam of radiant energy (as light) **2 :** tiny bit

**ray·on** *n* **:** fabric made from cellulose fiber

**ra·zor** *n* **:** sharp cutting instrument used to shave off hair

**reach** *vb* **1 :** stretch out **2 :** touch or try to touch or grasp **3 :** extend to or arrive at **4 :** communicate with ~ *n* **1 :** act of reaching **2 :** distance one can reach **3 :** ability to reach — **reach·able** *adj* — **reach·er** *n*

**re·act** *vb* **1 :** act in response to some influence or stimulus **2 :** undergo chemical change — **re·ac·tion** *n* — **re·ac·tion·ary** *adj or n* — **re·ac·tive** *adj* — **re·ac·tor** *n*

**read** *vb* **1 :** understand written language **2 :** utter aloud printed words **3 :** interpret **4 :** study **5 :** indicate ~ *adj* **:** informed by reading — **read·a·bil·i·ty** *n* — **read·able** *adj* — **read·ably** *adv* — **read·er** *n* — **read·er·ship** *n* — **read·ing** *n*

**ready** *adj* **1 :** prepared or available for use or action **2 :** willing to do something ~ *vb* **:** make ready ~ *n* **:** state of being ready — **read·i·ly** *adv* — **read·i·ness** *n*

**re·al** *adj* **1 :** relating to fixed or immovable things (as land) **2 :** genuine **3 :** not imaginary ~ *adv* **:** very — **re·al·ness** *n* — **for real 1 :** in earnest **2**

: genuine — **re•al•i•ty** *n* — **re•al•ly** *adv*

**real estate** *n* : property in houses and land

**re•al•ism** *n* **1** : disposition to deal with facts practically **2** : faithful portrayal of reality — **re•al•ist** *adj or n* — **re•al•is•tic** *adj* — **re•al•is•ti•cal•ly** *adv*

**re•al•ize** *vb* **1** : make actual **2** : obtain **3** : be aware of — **re•al•iz•able** *adj* — **re•al•i•za•tion** *n*

**reap** *vb* : cut or clear (as a crop) with a scythe or machine — **reap•er** *n*

**[1]rear** *vb* **1** : raise upright **2** : breed or bring up **3** : rise on the hind legs

**[2]rear** *n* **1** : back **2** : position at the back of something ~ *adj* : being at the back — **rear•ward** *adj or adv*

**rea•son** *n* **1** : explanation or justification **2** : motive for action or belief **3** : power or process of thinking ~ *vb* **1** : use the faculty of reason **2** : try to persuade another — **rea•son•er** *n* — **rea•son•ing** *n*

**rea•son•able** *adj* **1** : being within the bounds of reason **2** : not expensive — **rea•son•able•ness** *n* — **rea•son•ably** *adv*

**re•bate** *n* : return of part of a payment — **rebate** *vb*

**reb•el** *n* : one that resists authority ~ *vb* **1** : resist authority **2** : feel or exhibit anger — **reb•el** *adj* — **re•bel•lion** *n* — **re•bel•lious** *adj* — **re•bel•lious•ly** *adv* — **re•bel•lious•ness** *n*

**re•bound** *vb* **1** : spring back on striking something **2** : recover from a reverse ~ *n* **1** : action of rebounding **2** : reaction to a reverse

**re•buke** *vb* : criticize sharply

**re•call** *vb* **1** : call back **2** : remember **3** : revoke ~ *n* **1** : a summons to return **2** : remembrance **3** : act of revoking

**re•cede** *vb* **1** : move back or away **2** : slant backward

**re•ceipt** *n* **1** : act of receiving **2** : something (as payment) received — usu. in pl. **3** : writing acknowledging something received

**re•ceive** *vb* **1** : take in or accept **2** : greet or entertain (visitors) **3** : pick up radio waves and convert into sounds or pictures — **re•ceiv•able** *adj* — **re•ceiv•er** *n*

**re•cent** *adj* **1** : having lately come into existence **2** : of the present time or time just past — **re•cent•ly** *adv* — **re•cent•ness** *n*

**re•cep•ta•cle** *n* : container

**re•cep•tion** *n* **1** : act of receiving **2** : social gathering at which guests are formally welcomed

**re•cep•tion•ist** *n* : person employed to greet callers

**re•cep•tive** *adj* : open and responsive to ideas, impressions, or suggestions — **re•cep•tive•ly** *adv* — **re•cep•tive•ness** *n* — **re•cep•tiv•i•ty** *n*

**re•cess** *n* **1** : indentation in a line or surface **2** : suspension of a session for rest ~ *vb* **1** : make a recess in or put into a recess **2** : interrupt a session for a recess

**re•ces•sion** *n* **1** : departing procession **2** : period of reduced economic activity

**rec•i•pe** *n* : instructions for making something

**re•cip•i•ent** *n* : one that receives

**re•cip•ro•cal** *adj* **1** : affecting each in the same way **2** : so related that one is equivalent to the other — **re•cip•ro•cal•ly** *adv* — **re•ci•proc•i•ty** *n*

**re•cip•ro•cate** *vb* : make a return for something done or given — **re•cip•ro•ca•tion** *n*

**re•cit•al** *n* **1** : public reading or recitation **2** : music or dance concert or exhibition by pupils — **re•cit•al•ist** *n*

**re•cite** *vb* **1** : repeat verbatim **2** : recount — **rec•i•ta•tion** *n* — **re•cit•er** *n*

**reck•less** *adj* : lacking caution — **reck•less•ly** *adv* — **reck•less•ness** *n*

**reck•on** *vb* **1** : count or calculate **2** : consider — **reck•on•ing** *n*

**re•claim** *vb* **1** : change to a desirable condition **2** : obtain from a waste product or by-product **3** : demand or obtain the return of — **re•claim•able** *adj* — **rec•la•ma•tion** *n*

**re•cline** *vb* : lean backward or lie down

**rec•og•nize** *vb* **1** : identify as previously known **2** : take notice of **3** : acknowledge esp. with appreciation — **rec•og•ni•tion** *n* — **rec•og•niz•able** *adj* — **rec•og•niz•ably** *adv*

**rec•ol•lect** *vb* : remember

**rec•ol•lec•tion** *n* **1** : act or power of recollecting **2** : something recollected

**rec•om•mend** *vb* **1** : present as deserving of acceptance or trial **2** : advise — **rec•om•mend•able** *adj* — **rec•om•men•da•tion** *n*

**rec•on•cile** *vb* **1** : cause to be friendly again **2** : adjust or settle **3** : bring to acceptance — **rec•on•cil•able** *adj* — **rec•on•cile•ment** *n* — **rec•on•cil•er** *n* — **rec•on•cil•i•a•tion** *n*

**re•con•di•tion** *vb* : restore to good condition

**re•cord** *vb* **1** : set down in writing **2** : register permanently **3** : indicate **4** : preserve (as sound or images) for later reproduction ~ *n* **1** : something recorded **2** : best performance — **re•cord•er** *n*

**[1]re•count** *vb* : relate in detail

**[2]re•count** *vb* : count again — **re•count** *n*

**re•cov•er** *vb* **1** : regain position, poise, or health **2** : gain compensation for a loss — **re•cov•er•able** *adj* — **re•cov•ery** *n*

**rec•re•a•tion** *n* : a refreshing of strength or spirits as a change from work or study — **rec•re•a•tion•al** *adj*

**re•cruit** *n* : newly enlisted member ~ *vb* : enlist the membership or services of — **re•cruit•er** *n* — **re•cruit•ment** *n*

**rect•an•gle** *n* : 4-sided figure with 4 right angles — **rect•an•gu•lar** *adj*

**rec•ti•fy** *vb* : make or set right — **rec•ti•fi•ca•tion** *n*

**rec•tor** *n* : pastor

**rec•to•ry** *n* : rector's residence

**re•cu•per•ate** *vb* : recover (as from illness) — **re•cu•per•a•tion** *n* — **re•cu•per•a•tive** *adj*

**re•cur** *vb* **1** : return in thought or talk **2** : occur again — **re•cur•rence** *n* — **re•cur•rent** *adj*

**re•cy•cle** *vb* : process (as glass or cans) in order to regain a material for human use — **re•cy•cla•ble** *adj*

**red** *n* **1** : color of blood or of the ruby **2** *cap* : communist — **red** *adj* — **red•dish** *adj* — **red•ness** *n*

**red•den** *vb* : make or become red or reddish

**re•deem** *vb* **1** : regain, free, or rescue by paying a price **2** : atone for **3** : free from sin **4** : convert into something of value — **re•deem•able** *adj* — **re•deem•er** *n*

**re•demp•tion** *n* : act of redeeming — **re•demp•tive** *adj* — **re•demp•to•ry** *adj*

**re•duce** *vb* **1** : lessen **2** : put in a lower rank **3** : lose weight — **re•duc•er** *n* — **re•duc•ible** *adj*

**re•duc•tion** *n* **1** : act of reducing **2** : amount lost in reducing **3** : something made by reducing

**re•dun•dant** *adj* : using more words than necessary — **re•dun•dan•cy** *n* — **re•dun•dant•ly** *adv*

**reed** *n* **1** : tall slender grass of wet areas **2** : thin springy strip that vibrates to produce tones in certain wind instruments — **reedy** *adj*

**reef** *n* : ridge of rocks or sand at or near the surface of the water

**reek** *n* : strong or disagreeable fume or odor ~ *vb* : give off a reek

**reel** *n* : revolvable device on which something flexible is wound or a quantity of something wound on it ~ *vb* **1** : wind on a reel **2** : pull in by reeling — **reel•able** *adj* — **reel•er** *n*

**re•fer** *vb* **1** : direct or send to some person or place **2** : submit for consideration or action **3** : have connection **4** : mention or allude to something — **re•fer•able** *adj* — **re•fer•ral** *n*

**ref•er•ee** *n* **1** : one to whom an issue is referred for settlement **2** : sports official ~ *vb* : act as referee

**ref•er•ence** *n* **1** : act of referring **2** : a bearing on a matter **3** : consultation for information **4** : person who can speak for one's character or ability or a recommendation given by such a person

**ref•er•en•dum** *n* : a submitting of legislative measures for voters' approval or rejection

**re•fill** *vb* : fill again — **re•fill** *n* — **re•fill•able** *adj*

**re•fine** *vb* **1** : free from impurities or waste matter **2** : improve or perfect **3** : free or become free of what is coarse or uncouth — **re•fine•ment** *n* — **re•fin•er** *n*

**re•flect** *vb* **1** : bend or cast back (as light or heat) **2** : bring as a result **3** : cast reproach or blame **4** : ponder — **re•flec•tion** *n* — **re•flec•tive** *adj* — **re•flec•tor** *n*

**re•flex** *n* : automatic response to a stimulus ~ *adj* **1** : bent back **2** : relating to a reflex — **re•flex•ly** *adv*

**re•flex•ive** *adj* : of or relating to an action directed back upon the doer or the grammatical subject — **reflexive** *n* — **re•flex•ive•ly** *adv* — **re•flex•ive•ness** *n*

**re•form** *vb* : make or become better esp. by correcting bad habits — **reform** *n* — **re•form•able** *adj* — **re•for•ma•tive** *adj* — **re•form•er** *n*

**re•frac•tion** *n* : the bending of a ray (as of light) when it passes from one medium into another — **re•frac•tive** *adj*

**re•frain** *vb* : hold oneself back ~ *n* : verse recurring regularly in a song — **re•frain•ment** *n*

**re•fresh** *vb* **1** : make or become fresh or fresher **2** : supply or take refreshment — **re•fresh•er** *n* — **re•fresh•ing•ly** *adv*

**re•fresh•ment** *n* **1** : act of refreshing **2** *pl* : light meal

**re•frig•er•ate** *vb* : chill or freeze (food) for preservation — **re•frig•er•ant** *adj or n* — **re•frig•er•a•tion** *n* — **re•frig•er•a•tor** *n*

**ref•uge** *n* **1** : protection from danger **2** : place that provides protection

**ref•u•gee** *n* : person who flees for safety

**re•fund** *vb* : give or put back (money) ~ *n* **1** : act of refunding **2** : sum refunded — **re•fund•able** *adj*

**[1]re•fuse** *vb* : decline to accept, do, or give — **re•fus•al** *n*

**[2]ref•use** *n* : worthless matter

**re•gal** *adj* **1** : befitting a king **2** : marked by much dignity — **re•gal•ly** *adv*

**re•gard** *n* **1** : consideration **2** : feeling of approval and liking **3** *pl* : friendly greetings **4** : relation ~ *vb* **1** : pay attention to **2** : show respect for **3** : have an opinion of **4** : look at **5** : relate to — **re•gard•ful** *adj* — **re•gard•less** *adj*

**re•gard•ing** *prep* : concerning

**re•gen•er•ate** *adj* **1** : formed or created again **2** : spiritually reborn ~ *vb* **1** : reform completely **2** : replace (a lost body part) by new tissue growth **3** : give new life to — **re•gen•er•a•tion** *n* — **re•gen•er•a•tive** *adj* — **re•gen•er•a•tor** *n*

**re•gent** *n* **1** : person who rules during the childhood, absence, or incapacity of the sovereign **2** : member of a governing board — **re•gen•cy** *n*

**re•gime** *n* : government in power

**reg•i•men** *n* : systematic course of treatment or training

**re•gion** *n* : indefinitely defined area — **re•gion•al** *adj* — **re•gion•al•ly** *adv*

**reg•is•ter** *n* **1** : record of items or details or a book for keeping such a record **2** : device to regulate ventilation **3** : counting or recording device **4** : range of a voice or instrument ~ *vb* **1** : enter in a register **2** : record automatically **3** : get special care for mail by paying more postage

**reg•is•tra•tion** *n* **1** : act of registering **2** : entry in a register

**reg•is•try** *n* **1** : enrollment **2** : place of registration **3** : official record book

**re•gret** *vb* **1** : mourn the loss or death of **2** : be very sorry for ~ *n* **1** : sorrow or the expression of sorrow **2** *pl* : message declining an invitation — **re•gret•ful** *adj* — **re•gret•ful•ly** *adv* — **re•gret•ta•ble** *adj* — **re•gret•ta•bly** *adv* — **re•gret•ter** *n*

**reg•u•lar** *adj* **1** : conforming to what is usual, normal, or average **2** : steady, uniform, or unvarying — **regular** *n* — **reg•u•lar•i•ty** *n* — **reg•u•lar•ize** *vb* — **reg•u•lar•ly** *adv*

**reg•u•late** *vb* **1** : govern according to rule **2** : adjust to a standard — **reg•u•la•tion** *n* — **reg•u•la•tive** *adj* — **reg•u•la•tor** *n* — **reg•u•la•to•ry** *adj*

**re•ha•bil•i•tate** *vb* **1** : restore to a previous state or position **2** : make good or usable again — **re•ha•bil•i•ta•tion** *n*

**re•hearse** *vb* **1** : repeat or recount **2** : engage in a practice performance of — **re•hears•al** *n* — **re•hears•er** *n*

**reign** *n* : sovereign's authority or rule ~ *vb* : rule as a sovereign

**re•im•burse** *vb* : repay — **re•im•burs•able** *adj* — **re•im•burse•ment** *n*

**rein** *n* **1** : strap fastened to a bit to control an animal **2** : restraining influence ~ *vb* : direct by reins

**rein•deer** *n* : large deer

**re•in•force** *vb* : strengthen or support — **re•in•force•ment** *n* — **re•in•forc•er** *n*

**re•ject** *vb* **1** : refuse to grant or consider **2** : refuse to admit, believe, or receive **3** : throw out as useless or unsatisfactory ~ *n* : rejected person or thing — **re•jec•tion** *n*

**re•joice** *vb* : feel joy — **re•joic•er** *n*

**re•join** *vb* **1** : join again **2** : say in answer

**re•ju•ve•nate** *vb* : make young again — **re•ju•ve•na•tion** *n*

**re•lapse** *n* : recurrence of illness after a period of improvement ~ *vb* : suffer a relapse

**re•late** *vb* **1** : give a report of **2** : show a connection between **3** : have a relationship — **re•lat•able** *adj* — **re•lat•er, re•la•tor** *n* — **re•la•tion** *n*

**re•la•tion•ship** *n* : state of being related or interrelated

**rel•a•tive** *n* : person connected with another by blood or marriage ~ *adj* : considered in comparison with something else — **rel•a•tive•ly** *adv* — **rel•a•tive•ness** *n*

**re•lax** *vb* **1** : make or become less tense or rigid **2** : make less severe **3** : seek rest or recreation — **re•lax•er** *n*

**re•lax•a•tion** *n* **1** : lessening of tension **2** : recreation

**re•lay** *n* : fresh supply (as of horses or people) arranged to relieve others ~ *vb* : pass along in stages

**re•lease** *vb* **1** : free from confinement or oppression **2** : give up claim to or control over **3** : permit publication, performance, exhibition, or sale ~ *n* **1** : relief from trouble **2** : discharge from an obligation **3** : act of releasing or what is released

**re•lent** *vb* : become less severe

**re•lent•less** *adj* : mercilessly severe or persistent — **re•lent•less•ly** *adv* — **re•lent•less•ness** *n*

**rel•e•vance** *n* : relation to the matter at hand — **rel•e•vant** *adj* — **rel•e•vant•ly** *adv*

**re•li•able** *adj* : fit to be trusted — **re•li•abil•i•ty** *n* — **re•li•able•ness** *n* — **re•li•ably** *adv*

**re•li•ant** *adj* : dependent — **re•li•ance** *n*

**re•lieve** *vb* **1** : free from a burden or distress **2** : release from a post or duty **3**

: break the monotony of — **re•lief** *n* — **re•liev•er** *n*

**re•li•gion** *n* **1 :** service and worship of God **2 :** set or system of religious beliefs — **re•li•gion•ist** *n*

**re•li•gious** *adj* **1 :** relating or devoted to an ultimate reality or deity **2 :** relating to religious beliefs or observances **3 :** marked by intense feelings — **re•li•gious•ly** *adv*

**rel•ish** *n* **1 :** keen enjoyment **2 :** highly seasoned sauce (as of pickles) ~ *vb* **:** enjoy — **rel•ish•able** *adj*

**re•luc•tant** *adj* **:** feeling or showing doubt or unwillingness — **re•luc•tance** *n* — **re•luc•tant•ly** *adv*

**re•ly** *vb* **:** place faith or confidence — often with *on*

**re•main** *vb* **1 :** be left after others have been removed **2 :** be something yet to be done **3 :** stay behind **4 :** continue unchanged — **re•mains** *n* — **re•main•der** *n*

**re•mark** *vb* **:** express as an observation ~ *n* **:** passing comment

**re•mark•able** *adj* **:** extraordinary — **re•mark•able•ness** *n* — **re•mark•ably** *adv*

**rem•e•dy** *n* **1 :** medicine that cures **2 :** something that corrects an evil or compensates for a loss ~ *vb* **:** provide or serve as a remedy for

**re•mem•ber** *vb* **1 :** think of again **2 :** keep from forgetting **3 :** convey greetings from

**re•mem•brance** *n* **1 :** act of remembering **2 :** something that serves to bring to mind

**re•mind** *vb* **:** cause to remember — **re•mind•er** *n*

**rem•nant** *n* **:** small part or trace remaining

**re•mod•el** *vb* **:** alter the structure of

**re•mon•strate** *vb* **:** speak in protest, reproof, or opposition — **re•mon•strance** *n* — **re•mon•stra•tion** *n*

**re•morse** *n* **:** distress arising from a sense of guilt — **re•morse•ful** *adj* — **re•morse•less** *adj*

**re•mote** *adj* **1 :** far off in place or time **2 :** hard to reach or find **3 :** acting, acted on, or controlled indirectly or from afar **4 :** slight **5 :** distant in manner — **re•mote•ly** *adv* — **re•mote•ness** *n*

**re•move** *vb* **1 :** move by lifting or taking off or away **2 :** get rid of — **re•mov•able** *adj* — **re•mov•al** *n* — **re•mov•er** *n*

**re•mu•ner•ate** *vb* **:** pay — **re•mu•ner•a•tion** *n* — **re•mu•ner•a•tor** *n*

**rend** *vb* **(rent; rent) :** tear apart forcibly

**ren•der** *vb* **1 :** extract by heating **2 :** hand over or give up **3 :** do (a service) for another **4 :** cause to be or become

**ren•dez•vous** *n* **1 :** place appointed for a meeting **2 :** meeting at an appointed place ~ *vb* **:** meet at a rendezvous

**ren•e•gade** *n* **:** deserter of one faith or cause for another

**re•new** *vb* **1 :** make or become new, fresh, or strong again **2 :** begin again **3 :** grant or obtain an extension of — **re•new•able** *adj* — **re•new•al** *n* — **re•new•er** *n*

**re•nounce** *vb* **:** give up, refuse, or resign — **re•nounce•ment** *n*

**ren•o•vate** *vb* **:** make like new again — **ren•o•va•tion** *n* — **ren•o•va•tor** *n*

**re•nown** *n* **:** state of being widely known and honored — **renowned** *adj*

**rent** *n* **:** money paid or due periodically for the use of another's property ~ *vb* **:** hold or give possession and use of for rent — **rent•al** *n or adj* — **rent•er** *n*

**repair** *vb* **:** restore to good condition ~ *n* **1 :** act or instance of repairing **2 :** condition — **re•pair•er** *n* — **re•pair•man** *n*

**re•pay** *vb* **:** pay back — **re•pay•able** *adj* — **re•pay•ment** *n*

**re•peal** *vb* **:** annul by legislative action — **repeal** *n* — **re•peal•er** *n*

**re•peat** *vb* **:** say or do again ~ *n* **1 :** act of repeating **2 :** something repeated — **re•peat•able** *adj* — **re•peat•ed•ly** *adv* — **re•peat•er** *n*

**re•pel** *vb* **1 :** drive away **2 :** disgust — **re•pel•lent** *adj or n*

**re•pent** *vb* **1 :** turn from sin **2 :** regret — **re•pen•tance** *n* — **re•pen•tant** *adj*

**rep•e•ti•tion** *n* **:** act or instance of repeating

**rep•e•ti•tious** *adj* **:** tediously repeating — **rep•e•ti•tious•ly** *adv* — **rep•e•ti•tious•ness** *n*

**re•pet•i•tive** *adj* **:** repetitious — **re•pet•i•tive•ly** *adv* — **re•pet•i•tive•ness** *n*

**re•place** *vb* **1 :** restore to a former position **2 :** take the place of **3 :** put something new in the place of — **re•place•able** *adj* — **re•place•ment** *n* — **re•plac•er** *n*

**re•plen•ish** *vb* **:** stock or supply anew — **re•plen•ish•ment** *n*

**rep•li•ca** *n* **:** exact copy

**rep•li•cate** *vb* **:** duplicate or repeat — **rep•li•cate** *n* — **rep•li•ca•tion** *n*

**re•ply** *vb* **:** say or do in answer ~ *n* **:** answer

**re•port** *n* **1 :** rumor **2 :** statement of information (as events or causes) **3 :** explosive noise ~ *vb* **1 :** give an account of **2 :** present an account of (an event) as news **3 :** present oneself **4 :** make known to authorities — **re•port•age** *n* — **re•port•ed•ly** *adv* — **re•port•er** *n* — **re•por•to•ri•al** *adj*

**re•pose** *vb* **:** lay or lie at rest ~ *n* **1 :** state of resting **2 :** calm or peace — **re•pose•ful** *adj*

**re•pos•sess** *vb* **:** regain possession and legal ownership of — **re•pos•ses•sion** *n*

**rep•re•sent** *vb* **1 :** serve as a sign or symbol of **2 :** act or speak for **3 :** describe as having a specified quality or character — **rep•re•sen•ta•tion** *n*

**rep•re•sen•ta•tive** *adj* **1 :** standing or acting for another **2 :** carried on by elected representatives ~ *n* **1 :** typical example **2 :** one that represents another **3 :** member of usu. the lower house of a legislature — **rep•re•sen•ta•tive•ly***adv* — **rep•re•sen•ta•tive•ness** *n*

**re•press** *vb* **:** restrain or suppress — **re•pres•sion** *n* — **re•pres•sive** *adj*

**rep•ri•mand** *n* **:** formal or severe criticism — **rep•ri•mand** *vb*

**re•proach** *n* **1 :** disgrace **2 :** rebuke ~ *vb* **:** express disapproval to — **re•proach•ful** *adj* — **re•proach•ful•ly** *adv* — **re•proach•ful•ness** *n*

**re•pro•duce** *vb* **1 :** produce again or anew **2 :** produce offspring — **re•pro•duc•ible** *adj* — **re•pro•duc•tion** *n* — **re•pro•duc•tive** *adj*

**rep•tile** *n* **:** air-breathing scaly vertebrate — **rep•til•ian** *adj or n*

**re•pub•lic** *n* **:** country with representative government

**re•pub•li•can** *adj* **1 :** relating to or resembling a republic **2 :** supporting a republic — **republican** *n* — **re•pub•li•can•ism** *n*

**re•pug•nant** *adj* **:** contrary to one's tastes or principles — **re•pug•nance** *n* — **re•pug•nant•ly** *adv*

**re•pulse** *vb* **1 :** drive or beat back **2 :** treat with contempt **3 :** be repugnant to — **repulse** *n* — **re•pul•sion** *n*

**re•pul•sive** *adj* **:** arousing aversion or disgust — **re•pul•sive•ly** *adv* — **re•pul•sive•ness** *n*

**rep•u•ta•ble** *adj* **:** having a good reputation — **rep•u•ta•bly** *adv*

**rep•u•ta•tion** *n* **:** one's character or public esteem

**re•quest** *n* **:** act or instance of asking for something or a thing asked for ~ *vb* **1 :** make a request of **2 :** ask for — **re•quest•er** *n*

**re•quire** *vb* **1 :** insist on **2 :** call for as essential — **re•quire•ment** *n*

**res•cue** *vb* **:** set free from danger or confinement — **rescue** *n* — **res•cu•er** *n*

**re•search** *n* **:** careful or diligent search esp. for new knowledge — **research** *vb* — **re•search•er** *n*

**re•sem•ble** *vb* **:** be like or similar to — **re•sem•blance** *n*

**re•sent** *vb* **:** feel or show annoyance at — **re•sent•ful** *adj* — **re•sent•ful•ly** *adv* — **re•sent•ment** *n*

**res•er•va•tion** *n* **1 :** act of reserving or something reserved **2 :** limiting condition

**re•serve** *vb* **1 :** store for future use **2 :** set aside for special use ~ *n* **1 :** something reserved **2 :** restraint in words or bearing **3 :** military forces withheld from action or not part of the regular services — **re•served** *adj*

**res•er•voir** *n* **:** place where something (as water) is kept in store

**re•side** *vb* **1 :** make one's home **2 :** be present

**res•i•dence** *n* **1 :** act or fact of residing in a place **2 :** place where one lives — **res•i•dent** *adj or n* — **res•i•den•tial** *adj*

**res•i•due** *n* **:** part remaining — **re•sid•u•al** *adj*

**re•sign** *vb* **1 :** give up deliberately **2 :** give (oneself) over without resistance — **res•ig•na•tion** *n* — **re•sign•ed•ly** *adv*

**res•in** *n* **:** substance from the gum or sap of trees — **res•in•ous** *adj*

**re•sist** *vb* **1 :** withstand the force or effect of **2 :** fight against — **re•sist•ible** *adj* — **re•sist•less** *adj*

**re•sis•tance** *n* **1 :** act of resisting **2 :** ability of an organism to resist disease **3 :** opposition to electric current

**re•sis•tant** *adj* **:** giving resistance

**res•o•lute** *adj* **:** having a fixed purpose — **res•o•lute•ly** *adv* — **res•o•lute•ness** *n*

**res•o•lu•tion** *n* **1 :** process of resolving **2 :** firmness of purpose **3 :** statement of the opinion, will, or intent of a body

**re•solve** *vb* **1 :** find an answer to **2 :** make a formal resolution ~ *n* **1 :** something resolved **2 :** steadfast purpose — **re•solv•able** *adj*

**res•o•nant** *adj* **1 :** continuing to sound **2 :** relating to intensification or prolongation of sound (as by a vibrating body) — **res•o•nance** *n* — **res•o•nant•ly** *adv*

**re•sort** *n* **1 :** source of help **2 :** place to go for vacation ~ *vb* **1 :** go often or habitually **2 :** have recourse

**re•source** *n* **1 :** new or reserve source **2** *pl* **:** available funds **3 :** ability to handle situations — **re•source•ful** *adj* — **re•source•ful•ness** *n*

**re•spect** *n* **1 :** relation to something **2 :** high or special regard **3 :** detail ~ *vb* **:** consider deserving of high regard — **re•spect•able** *adj* — **re•spect•abil•i•ty** *n* — **re•spect•ably** *adv* — **re•spect•er** *n* — **re•spect•ful** *adj* — **re•spect•ful•ly** *adv* — **re•spect•ful•ness** *n*

**re•spec•tive** *adj* **:** individual and specific — **re•spec•tive•ly** *adv*

**res•pi•ra•tion** *n* **:** act or process of breathing — **res•pi•ra•to•ry** *adj* — **re•spire** *vb*

**res•pi•ra•tor** *n* **:** device for artificial respiration

**re•spond** *vb* **1 :** answer **2 :** react — **re•spon•dent** *n or adj* — **re•spond•er** *n*

**re•sponse** *n* **1 :** act of responding **2 :** answer

**re•spon•si•ble** *adj* **1 :** answerable for acts or decisions **2 :** able to fulfill obligations **3 :** having important duties — **re•spon•si•bil•i•ty** *n* — **re•spon•si•ble•ness** *n* — **re•spon•si•bly** *adv*

**re•spon•sive** *adj* **:** quick to respond — **re•spon•sive•ly** *adv* — **re•spon•sive•ness** *n*

**¹rest** *n* **1 :** sleep **2 :** freedom from work or activity **3 :** state of inactivity **4 :** something used as a support ~ *vb* **1 :** get rest **2 :** cease action or motion **3 :** give rest to **4 :** sit or lie fixed or supported **5 :** depend — **rest•ful** *adj* — **rest•ful•ly** *adv*

**²rest** *n* **:** remainder

**res•tau•rant** *n* **:** public eating place

**rest•less** *adj* **1 :** lacking or giving no rest **2 :** always moving **3 :** uneasy — **rest•less•ly** *adv* — **rest•less•ness** *n*

**re•store** *vb* **1 :** give back **2 :** put back into use or into a former state — **re•stor•able** *adj* — **res•to•ra•tion** *n* — **re•stor•ative** *n or adj* — **re•stor•er** *n*

**re•strain** *vb* **:** limit or keep under control — **re•strain•able** *adj* — **re•strained** *adj* — **re•strain•ed•ly** *adv* — **re•strain•er** *n* — **re•straint** *n*

**re•strict** *vb* **1 :** confine within bounds **2 :** limit use of — **re•stric•tion** *n* — **re•stric•tive** *adj* — **re•stric•tive•ly** *adv*

**re•sult** *vb* **:** come about because of something else ~ *n* **1 :** thing that results **2 :** something obtained by calculation or investigation — **re•sul•tant** *adj or n*

**re•sume** *vb* **:** return to or take up again after interruption — **re•sump•tion** *n*

**ré•su•mé, re•su•me, re•su•mé** *n* **:** summary of one's career and qualifications

**res•ur•rect** *vb* **1 :** raise from the dead **2 :** bring to attention or use again — **res•ur•rec•tion** *n*

**re•sus•ci•tate** *vb* **:** bring back from apparent death — **re•sus•ci•ta•tion** *n* — **re•sus•ci•ta•tor** *n*

**re•tail** *vb* **:** sell in small quantities directly to the consumer ~ *n* **:** business of selling to consumers — **retail** *adj or adv* — **re•tail•er** *n*

**re•tain** *vb* **1 :** keep or hold onto **2 :** engage the services of

**re•tain•er** *n* **1 :** household servant **2 :** retaining fee

**re•tal•i•ate** *vb* **:** return (as an injury) in kind — **re•tal•i•a•tion** *n* — **re•tal•ia•to•ry** *adj*

**re•tard** *vb* **:** hold back — **re•tar•da•tion** *n*

**re•tard•ed** *adj* **:** slow or limited in intellectual development

**retch** *vb* **:** try to vomit

**re•ten•tion** *n* **1 :** state of being retained **2 :** ability to retain — **re•ten•tive** *adj*

**ret•i•na** *n* **:** sensory membrane lining the eye — **ret•i•nal** *adj*

**re•tire** *vb* **1 :** withdraw for privacy **2 :** end a career **3 :** go to bed — **re•tir•ee** *n* — **re•tire•ment** *n*

**re•tort** *vb* **:** say in reply ~ *n* **:** quick, witty, or cutting answer

**re•trace** *vb* **:** go over again or in reverse

**re•tract** *vb* **1 :** draw back or in **2 :** withdraw a charge or promise — **re•tract•able** *adj* — **re•trac•tion** *n*

**re•treat** *n* **1 :** act of withdrawing **2 :** place of privacy or safety or meditation and study ~ *vb* **:** make a retreat

**ret•ri•bu•tion** *n* **:** retaliation — **re•trib•u•tive** *adj* — **re•trib•u•to•ry** *adj*

**re•trieve** *vb* **1 :** search for and bring in game **2 :** recover — **re•triev•able** *adj* — **re•triev•al** *n*

**ret•ro•ac•tive** *adj* **:** made effective as of a prior date — **ret•ro•ac•tive•ly** *adv*

**ret•ro•spect** *n* **:** review of past events — **ret•ro•spec•tion** *n* — **ret•ro•spec•tive** *adj* — **ret•ro•spec•tive•ly** *adv*

**re•turn** *vb* **1 :** go or come back **2 :** pass, give, or send back to an earlier possessor **3 :** answer **4 :** bring in as a profit **5 :** give or do in return ~ *n* **1 :** act of returning or something returned **2** *pl* **:** report of balloting results **3 :** statement of taxable income **4 :** profit — **re•turn** *adj* — **re•turn•able** *adj or n* — **re•turn•er** *n*

**re•union** *n* **1 :** act of reuniting **2 :** a meeting of persons after a separation

**re•veal** *vb* **1 :** make known **2 :** show plainly

**rev•el** *vb* **1 :** take part in a revel **2 :** take great pleasure ~ *n* **:** wild party or celebration — **rev•el•er, rev•el•ler** *n* — **rev•el•ry** *n*

**rev•e•la•tion** *n* **1 :** act of revealing **2 :** something enlightening or astonishing

**re•venge** *vb* **:** avenge ~ *n* **1 :** desire for

retaliation **2 :** act of retaliation — **re•venge•ful** *adj* — **re•veng•er** *n*

**rev•e•nue** *n* **:** money collected by a government

**re•ver•ber•ate** *vb* **:** sound in a series of echoes — **re•ver•ber•a•tion** *n*

**re•vere** *vb* **:** show honor and devotion to — **rev•er•ence** *n* — **rev•er•ent** *adj* — **rev•er•ent•ly** *adv*

**rev•er•end** *adj* **:** worthy of reverence ~ *n* **:** clergy member

**rev•er•ie** *n* **:** daydream

**re•verse** *adj* **1 :** opposite to a previous or normal condition **2 :** acting in an opposite way ~ *vb* **1 :** turn upside down or completely around **2 :** change to the contrary or in the opposite direction ~ *n* **1 :** something contrary **2 :** change for the worse **3 :** back of something — **re•ver•sal** *n* — **re•verse•ly** *adv* — **re•vers•ible** *adj*

**re•view** *n* **1 :** formal inspection **2 :** general survey **3 :** critical evaluation **4 :** second or repeated study or examination ~ *vb* **1 :** examine or study again **2 :** reexamine judicially **3 :** look back over **4 :** examine critically **5 :** inspect — **re•view•er** *n*

**re•vise** *vb* **1 :** look over something written to correct or improve **2 :** make a new version of — **re•vis•able** *adj* — **revise** *n* — **re•vis•er, re•vi•sor** *n* — **re•vi•sion** *n*

**re•vive** *vb* **:** bring back to life or consciousness or into use — **re•viv•al** *n* — **re•viv•er** *n*

**re•voke** *vb* **:** annul by recalling — **re•vok•er** *n*

**re•volt** *vb* **1 :** throw off allegiance **2 :** cause or experience disgust or shock ~ *n* **:** rebellion or revolution — **re•volt•er** *n*

**re•volt•ing** *adj* **:** extremely offensive — **re•volt•ing•ly** *adv*

**rev•o•lu•tion** *n* **1 :** rotation **2 :** progress in an orbit **3 :** sudden, radical, or complete change (as overthrow of a government) — **rev•o•lu•tion•ary** *adj or n* — **rev•o•lu•tion•ize** *vb*

**re•volve** *vb* **1 :** ponder **2 :** move in an orbit **3 :** rotate — **re•volv•able** *adj*

**re•volv•er** *n* **:** pistol with a revolving cylinder

**re•vul•sion** *n* **:** complete dislike or repugnance

**re•ward** *vb* **:** give a reward to or for ~ *n* **:** something offered for service or achievement

**re•write** *vb* **:** revise — **rewrite** *n*

**rhap•so•dy** *n* **1 :** expression of extravagant praise **2 :** flowing free-form musical composition — **rhap•sod•ic** *adj* — **rhap•sod•i•cal•ly** *adv* — **rhap•so•dize** *vb*

**rho•do•den•dron** *n* **:** flowering evergreen shrub

**rhyme** *n* **1 :** correspondence in terminal sounds **2 :** verse that rhymes ~ *vb* **:** make or have rhymes

**rhythm** *n* **:** regular succession of sounds or motions — **rhyth•mic, rhyth•mi•cal** *adj* — **rhyth•mi•cal•ly** *adv*

**rib** *n* **1 :** curved bone joined to the spine **2 :** riblike thing ~ *vb* **1 :** furnish or mark with ribs **2 :** tease — **rib•ber** *n*

**rib•bon** *n* **1 :** narrow strip of fabric used esp. for decoration **2 :** strip of inked cloth (as in a typewriter)

**rice** *n* **:** starchy edible seeds of an annual cereal grass

**rich** *adj* **1 :** having a lot of money or possessions **2 :** valuable **3 :** containing much sugar, fat, or seasoning **4 :** abundant **5 :** deep and pleasing in color or tone **6 :** fertile — **rich•ly** *adv* — **rich•ness** *n*

**rich•es** *n pl* **:** wealth

**rid** *vb* **:** make free of something unwanted — **rid•dance** *n*

**rid•dle** *n* **:** puzzling question ~ *vb* **:** speak in riddles

**ride** *vb* (**rode; rid•den**) **1 :** be carried along **2 :** sit on and cause to move **3 :** travel over a surface **4 :** tease or nag ~ *n* **1 :** trip on an animal or in a vehicle **2 :** mechanical device ridden for amusement — **rid•er** *n* — **rid•er•less** *adj*

**ridge** *n* **1 :** range of hills **2 :** raised line or strip **3 :** line of intersection of 2 sloping surfaces — **ridgy** *adj*

**rid•i•cule** *vb* **:** laugh at or make fun of — **ridicule** *n*

**ri•dic•u•lous** *adj* **:** arousing ridicule — **ri•dic•u•lous•ly** *adv* — **ri•dic•u•lous•ness** *n*

**rifle** *n* **:** long shoulder weapon with spiral grooves in the bore — **ri•fle•man** *n* — **ri•fling** *n*

[1]**rig** *vb* **1 :** fit out with rigging **2 :** set up esp. as a makeshift ~ *n* **1 :** distinctive shape, number, and arrangement of sails and masts of a sailing ship **2 :** equipment **3 :** carriage with its horse

[2]**rig** *vb* **:** manipulate esp. by deceptive or dishonest means

**right** *adj* **1 :** meeting a standard of conduct **2 :** correct **3 :** genuine **4 :** normal **5 :** opposite of left ~ *n* **1 :** something that is correct, just, proper, or honorable **2 :** something to which one has a just claim **3 :** something that is on the right side ~ *adv* **1 :** according to what is right **2 :** immediately **3 :** completely **4 :** on or to the right ~ *vb* **1 :** restore to a proper state **2 :** bring or become upright again — **right•er** *n* — **right•ness** *n* — **right•ward** *adj*

**righ•teous** *adj* **:** acting or being in accordance with what is just or moral — **righ•teous•ly** *adv* — **righ•teous•ness** *n*

**rig•id** *adj* **:** lacking flexibility — **ri•gid•i•ty** *n* — **rig•id•ly** *adv*

**rig•or** *n* **:** severity — **rig•or•ous** *adj* — **rig•or•ous•ly** *adv*

**rim** *n* **:** edge esp. of something curved ~ *vb* **:** border

**rind** *n* **:** usu. hard or tough outer layer

[1]**ring** *n* **1 :** circular band used as an ornament or for holding or fastening **2 :** something circular **3 :** place for contest or display **4 :** group with a selfish or dishonest aim ~ *vb* **:** surround — **ringed** *adj* — **ring•like** *adj*

[2]**ring** *vb* **1 :** sound resonantly when struck **2 :** cause to make a metallic sound by striking **3 :** produce a strong echoing sound **4 :** call esp. by a bell ~ *n* **1 :** resonant sound or tone **2 :** act or instance of ringing — **ring•er** *n*

**ring•tone** *n* **:** sound of a cell phone to indicate an incoming call

**rink** *n* **:** enclosed place for skating

**rinse** *vb* **1 :** cleanse usu. with water only **2 :** treat (hair) with a rinse ~ *n* **:** liquid used for rinsing — **rins•er** *n*

**ri•ot** *n* **1 :** violent public disorder **2 :** random or disorderly lavish display — **riot** *vb* — **ri•ot•er** *n* — **ri•ot•ous** *adj*

**rip** *vb* **:** cut or tear open ~ *n* **:** rent made by ripping — **rip•per** *n*

**ripe** *adj* **:** fully grown, developed, or prepared — **ripe•ly** *adv* — **rip•en** *vb* — **ripe•ness** *n*

**rip•ple** *vb* **1 :** become lightly ruffled on the surface **2 :** sound like rippling water — **ripple** *n*

**rise** *vb* (**rose; ris•en**) **1 :** get up from sitting, kneeling, or lying **2 :** take arms **3 :** appear above the horizon **4 :** move upward **5 :** gain a higher position or rank **6 :** increase ~ *n* **1 :** act of rising **2 :** origin **3 :** elevation **4 :** increase **5 :** upward slope **6 :** area of high ground — **ris•er** *n*

**risk** *n* **:** exposure to loss or injury — **risk** *vb* — **risk•i•ness** *n* — **risky** *adj*

**rite** *n* **1 :** set form for conducting a ceremony **2 :** customary ceremonies of a church **3 :** ceremonial action

**rit•u•al** *n* **:** rite — **ritual** *adj* — **rit•u•al•ism** *n* — **rit•u•al•is•tic** *adj* — **rit•u•al•is•ti•cal•ly** *adv* — **rit•u•al•ly** *adv*

**ri•val** *n* **1 :** competitor **2 :** peer ~ *vb* **1 :** be in competition with **2 :** equal — **rival** *adj* — **ri•val•ry** *n*

**riv•er** *n* **:** large natural stream of water — **riv•er•bank** *n* — **riv•er•bed** *n* — **riv•er•boat** *n* — **riv•er•side** *n*

**road** *n* **:** open way for vehicles, persons, and animals — **road•bed** *n* — **road•block** *n* — **road•side** *n or adj* — **road•way** *n*

**roam** *vb* **:** wander

**roar** *vb* **:** utter a full loud prolonged sound — **roar** *n* — **roar•er** *n*

**roast** *vb* **1 :** cook by dry heat **2 :** criticize severely ~ *n* **:** piece of meat suitable for roasting — **roast** *adj* — **roast•er** *n*

**rob** *vb* **1 :** steal from **2 :** commit robbery — **rob•ber** *n*

**rob•bery** *n* **:** theft of something from a person by use of violence or threat

**robe** *n* **1 :** long flowing outer garment **2 :** covering for the lower body ~ *vb* **:** clothe with or as if with a robe

**rob•in** *n* **:** No. American thrush with a reddish breast

**ro•bot** *n* **1 :** machine that looks and acts like a human being **2 :** efficient but insensitive person — **ro•bot•ic** *adj*

[1]**rock** *vb* **:** sway or cause to sway back and forth ~ *n* **1 :** rocking movement **2 :** popular music marked by repetition and a strong beat

[2]**rock** *n* **:** mass of hard mineral material — **rock** *adj* — **rocky** *adj*

**rock•er** *n* **1 :** curved piece on which a chair rocks **2 :** chair that rocks

**rock•et** *n* **1 :** self-propelled firework or missile **2 :** jet engine that carries its own oxygen ~ *vb* **:** rise abruptly and rapidly — **rock•et•ry** *n*

**rod** *n* **1 :** straight slender stick **2 :** unit of length equal to 5 yards

**rode** *past of* RIDE

**ro•deo** *n* **:** contest of cowboy skills

**rogue** *n* **:** dishonest or mischievous person — **rogu•ery** *n* — **rogu•ish** *adj* — **rogu•ish•ly** *adv* — **rogu•ish•ness** *n*

**role** *n* **1 :** part to play **2 :** function

**roll** *n* **1 :** official record or list of names **2 :** something rolled up or rounded **3 :** bread baked in a small rounded mass **4 :** sound of rapid drum strokes **5 :** heavy reverberating sound **6 :** rolling movement ~ *vb* **1 :** move by turning over **2 :** move on wheels **3 :** flow in a continuous stream **4 :** swing from side to side **5 :** shape or be shaped in rounded form **6 :** press with a revolving cylinder — **roll•er** *n*

**Ro•man Cath•o•lic** *n* **:** member of a Christian church led by a pope — **Roman Cath•o•lic** *adj* — **Ro•man Ca•thol•i•cism** *n*

**ro•mance** *n* **1 :** medieval tale of knightly adventure **2 :** love story **3 :** love affair ~ *vb* **1 :** have romantic fancies **2 :** have a love affair with — **ro•manc•er** *n*

**ro•man•tic** *adj* **1 :** visionary or imaginative **2 :** appealing to one's emotions — **ro•man•ti•cal•ly** *adv*

**romp** *vb* **:** play actively and noisily — **romp** *n*

**roof** *n* **:** upper covering part of a building ~ *vb* **:** cover with a roof — **roofed** *adj* — **roof•ing** *n* — **roof•less** *adj* — **roof•top** *n*

**rook** *n* **:** crowlike bird

**rook•ie** *n* **:** novice

**room** *n* **1 :** sufficient space **2 :** partitioned part of a building ~ *vb* **:** occupy lodgings — **room•er** *n* — **room•ful** *n* — **roomy** *adj*

**roost•er** *n* **:** adult male domestic chicken

**root** *n* **1 :** leafless underground part of a seed plant **2 :** rootlike thing or part **3 :** source **4 :** essential core ~ *vb* **:** form, fix, or become fixed by roots — **root•less** *adj* — **root•let** *n* — **root•like** *adj*

[3]**root** *vb* **:** applaud or encourage noisily — **root•er** *n*

**rope** *n* **:** large strong cord of strands of fiber ~ *vb* **1 :** tie with a rope **2 :** lasso

**ro•sa•ry** *n* **1 :** string of beads used in praying **2 :** Roman Catholic devotion

[1]**rose** *past of* RISE

[2]**rose** *n* **1 :** prickly shrub with bright flowers **2 :** purplish red — **rose** *adj* — **rose•bud** *n* — **rose•bush** *n*

**Rosh Ha•sha•nah** *n* **:** Jewish New Year observed as a religious holiday in September or October

**rosy** *adj* **1 :** of the color rose **2 :** hopeful — **ros•i•ly** *adv* — **ros•i•ness** *n*

**rot** *vb* **:** undergo decomposition ~ *n* **1 :** decay **2 :** disease in which tissue breaks down

**ro•ta•ry** *adj* **1 :** turning on an axis **2 :** having a rotating part

**ro•tate** *vb* **1 :** turn about an axis or a center **2 :** alternate in a series — **ro•ta•tion** *n* — **ro•ta•tor** *n*

**ro•tor** *n* **1 :** part that rotates **2 :** system of rotating horizontal blades for supporting a helicopter

**rot•ten** *adj* **1 :** having rotted **2 :** corrupt **3 :** extremely unpleasant or inferior — **rot•ten•ness** *n*

**rough** *adj* **1 :** not smooth **2 :** not calm **3 :** harsh, violent, or rugged **4 :** crudely or hastily done ~ *n* **:** rough state or something in that state ~ *vb* **1 :** roughen **2 :** handle roughly **3 :** make roughly — **rough•en** *vb* — **rough•ly** *adv* — **rough•ness** *n*

**round** *adj* **1 :** having every part the same distance from the center **2 :** cylindrical **3 :** complete **4 :** approximate **5 :** blunt **6 :** moving in or forming a circle ~ *n* **1 :** round or curved thing **2 :** series of recurring actions or events **3 :** period of time or a unit of action **4 :** fired shot **5 :** cut of beef ~ *vb* **1 :** make or become round **2 :** go around **3 :** finish **4 :** express as an approximation — **round•ish** *adj* — **round•ly** *adv* — **round•ness** *n*

**rout** *n* **1 :** state of wild confusion **2 :** disastrous defeat ~ *vb* **:** defeat decisively

**route** *n* **:** line of travel ~ *vb* **:** send by a selected route

**rou•tine** *n* **1 :** regular course of procedure **2 :** an often repeated speech, formula, or part — **routine** *adj* — **rou•tine•ly** *adv*

**rove** *vb* **:** wander or roam — **rov•er** *n*

[1]**row** *vb* **1 :** propel a boat with oars **2 :** carry in a rowboat ~ *n* **:** act of rowing — **row•boat** *n* — **row•er** *n*

[2]**row** *n* **:** number of objects in a line

[3]**row** *n* **:** noisy quarrel — **row** *vb*

**row•dy** *adj* **:** coarse or boisterous in behavior — **row•di•ness** *n* — **rowdy** *n*

**roy•al** *adj* **:** relating to or befitting a king ~ *n* **:** person of royal blood — **roy•al•ly** *adv* — **roy•al•ty** *n*

**rub** *vb* **1 :** use pressure and friction on a body **2 :** scour, polish, erase, or smear by pressure and friction **3 :** chafe with friction ~ *n* **:** difficulty

**rub•ber** *n* **1 :** one that rubs **2 :** waterproof elastic substance or something made of it — **rub•ber** *adj* — **rub•ber•ize** *vb* — **rub•bery** *adj*

**rub•bish** *n* **:** waste or trash

**ru•by** *n* **:** precious red stone or its color — **ruby** *adj*

**rude** *adj* **1 :** roughly made **2 :** impolite — **rude•ly** *adv* — **rude•ness** *n*

**rue** *vb* **:** feel regret for ~ *n* **:** regret — **rue•ful** *adj* — **rue•ful•ly** *adv* — **rue•ful•ness** *n*

**ruf•fle** *vb* **1 :** draw into or provide with pleats **2 :** roughen the surface of **3 :** irritate ~ *n* **:** strip of fabric pleated on one edge — **ruf•fly** *adj*

**rug** *n* **:** piece of heavy fabric used as a floor covering

**rug•ged** *adj* **1 :** having a rough uneven surface **2 :** severe **3 :** strong — **rug•ged•ly** *adv* — **rug•ged•ness** *n*

**ru•in** *n* **1 :** complete collapse or destruction **2 :** remains of something destroyed — usu. in pl. **3 :** cause of destruction ~ *vb* **1 :** destroy **2 :** damage beyond repair **3 :** bankrupt

**ru•in•ous** *adj* **:** causing ruin — **ruin•ous•ly** *adv*

**rule** *n* **1 :** guide or principle for governing action **2 :** usual way of doing something **3** : government **4** : straight strip (as of wood or metal) marked off in units for measuring ～ *vb* **1** : govern **2** : give as a decision — **rul•er** *n*

**rum** *n* : liquor made from molasses or sugarcane

**rum•ble** *vb* : make a low heavy rolling sound — **rumble** *n*

**ru•mor** *n* **1** : common talk **2** : widespread statement not authenticated — **rumor** *vb*

**rump** *n* : rear part of an animal

**rum•ple** *vb* : tousle or wrinkle — **rumple** *n*

**run** *vb* **ran; run** **1** : go rapidly or hurriedly **2** : enter a race or election **3** : operate **4** : continue in force **5** : flow rapidly **6** : take a certain direction **7** : manage **8** : incur ～ *n* **1** : act of running **2** : brook **3** : continuous series **4** : usual kind **5** : freedom of movement **6** : lengthwise ravel

**run•away** *n* : fugitive ～ *adj* **1** : fugitive **2** : out of control

**¹rung** *past part of* RING

**²rung** *n* : horizontal piece of a chair or ladder

**run•ner** *n* **1** : one that runs **2** : thin piece or part on which something slides

**3** : slender creeping branch of a plant

**run•ning** *adj* **1** : flowing **2** : continuous

**runt** *n* : small person or animal — **runty** *adj*

**rup•ture** *n* **1** : breaking or tearing apart ～ *vb* : cause or undergo rupture

**ru•ral** *adj* : relating to the country or agriculture

**rush** *vb* **1** : move forward or act with too great haste **2** : perform in a short time ～ *n* : violent forward motion ～ *adj* : requiring speed — **rush•er** *n*

**rust** *n* **1** : reddish coating on exposed iron **2** : reddish brown color — **rust** *vb* — **rusty** *adj*

**rus•tic** *adj* : relating to or suitable for the country or country dwellers ～ *n* : rustic person — **rus•ti•cal•ly** *adv*

**rus•tle** *vb* **1** : make or cause a rustle **2** : forage food **3** : steal cattle from the range ～ *n* : series of small sounds — **rus•tler** *n*

**rut** *n* **1** : track worn by wheels or feet **2** : set routine — **rut•ted** *adj*

**ruth•less** *adj* : having no pity — **ruth•less•ly** *adv* — **ruth•less•ness** *n*

**RV** *n* recreational vehicle

**rye** *n* **1** : cereal grass grown for grain **2** : whiskey from rye

# S

**s** *n* : 19th letter of the alphabet

**Sab•bath** *n* **1** : Saturday observed as a day of worship by Jews and some Christians **2** : Sunday observed as a day of worship by Christians

**sab•o•tage** *n* : deliberate destruction or hampering ～ *vb* : wreck through sabotage

**sack** *n* : bag ～ *vb* : fire

**sac•ra•ment** *n* : formal religious act or rite — **sac•ra•men•tal** *adj*

**sa•cred** *adj* **1** : set apart for or worthy of worship **2** : worthy of reverence **3** : relating to religion — **sa•cred•ly** *adv* — **sa•cred•ness** *n*

**sac•ri•fice** *n* **1** : the offering of something precious to a deity or the thing offered **2** : loss or deprivation ～ *vb* : offer or give up as a sacrifice — **sac•ri•fi•cial** *adj*

**sac•ri•lege** *n* : violation of something sacred — **sac•ri•le•gious** *adj*

**sad** *adj* **1** : affected with grief or sorrow **2** : causing sorrow — **sad•den** *vb* — **sad•ly** *adv* — **sad•ness** *n*

**sad•dle** *n* : seat for riding on horseback ～ *vb* : put a saddle on

**sa•dism** *n* : delight in cruelty — **sa•dist** *n* — **sa•dis•tic** *adj* — **sa•dis•ti•cal•ly** *adv*

**sa•fa•ri** *n* : hunting expedition in Africa

**safe** *adj* **1** : free from harm **2** : providing safety ～ *n* : container to keep valuables safe — **safe•keep•ing** *n* — **safe•ly** *adv*

**safe•guard** *n* : measure or device for preventing accidents — **safe•guard** *vb*

**safe•ty** *n* **1** : freedom from danger **2** : protective device

**sag** *vb* : droop, sink, or settle — **sag** *n*

**sage** *adj* : wise or prudent ～ *n* : wise man — **sage•ly** *adv*

**said** *past of* SAY

**sail** *n* **1** : fabric used to catch the wind and move a boat or ship **2** : trip on a sailboat ～ *vb* **1** : travel on a ship or sailboat **2** : move with ease or grace — **sail•boat** *n* — **sail•or** *n*

**saint** *n* : holy or godly person — **saint•ed** *adj* — **saint•hood** *n* — **saint•li•ness** *n* — **saint•ly** *adj*

**sake** *n* **1** : purpose or reason **2** : one's good or benefit

**sal•ad** *n* : dish usu. of raw lettuce, vegetables, or fruit

**sa•la•mi** *n* : highly seasoned dried sausage

**sal•a•ry** *n* : regular payment for services

**sale** *n* **1** : transfer of ownership of property for money **2** : selling at bargain prices **3** *pl* : activities involved in selling — **sal•able, sale•able** *adj* — **sales•man** *n* — **sales•per•son** *n* — **sales•wom•an** *n*

**sa•li•va** *n* : liquid secreted into the mouth — **sal•i•vary** *adj* — **sal•i•vate** *vb* — **sal•i•va•tion** *n*

**salm•on** *n* (**salmon**) **1** : food fish with pink or red flesh **2** : deep yellowish pink color

**sa•lon** *n* : elegant room or shop

**sa•loon** *n* **1** : public cabin on a passenger ship **2** : barroom

**sal•sa** *n* : spicy sauce of tomatoes, onions, and hot peppers

**salt** *n* **1** : white crystalline substance that consists of sodium and chlorine **2** : compound formed usu. from acid and metal — **salt** *vb or adj* — **salt•i•ness** *n* — **salty** *adj*

**sa•lute** *vb* : honor by ceremony or formal movement — **salute** *n*

**sal•vage** *n* : something saved from destruction ～ *vb* : rescue or save

**sal•va•tion** *n* : saving of a person from sin or danger

**same** *adj* : being the one referred to ～ *pron* : the same one or ones ～ *adv* : in the same manner — **same•ness** *n*

**sam•ple** *n* : piece or part that shows the quality of a whole ～ *vb* : judge by a sample

**sanc•ti•mo•nious** *adj* : hypocritically pious — **sanc•ti•mo•nious•ly** *adv*

**sanc•tion** *n* **1** : authoritative approval **2** : coercive measure — usu. pl ～ *vb* : approve

**sanc•tu•ary** *n* **1** : consecrated place **2** : place of refuge

**sand** *n* : loose granular particles of rock ～ *vb* : smooth with an abrasive — **sand•bank** *n* — **sand•er** *n* — **sand•storm** *n* — **sandy** *adj*

**san•dal** *n* : shoe consisting of a sole strapped to the foot

**sand•wich** *n* : bread surrounding a filling ～ *vb* : squeeze or crowd in

**sane** *adj* **1** : mentally healthy **2** : sensible — **sane•ly** *adv*

**sang** *past of* SING

**san•i•tary** *adj* **1** : relating to health **2** : free from filth or infective matter

**san•i•ta•tion** *n* : protection of health by maintenance of sanitary conditions

**san•i•ty** *n* : soundness of mind

**sank** *past of* SINK

**¹sap** *n* **1** : fluid that circulates through a plant **2** : gullible person

**²sap** *vb* **1** : undermine **2** : weaken or exhaust gradually

**sap•py** *adj* **1** : full of sap **2** : overly sentimental

**sar•casm** *n* **1** : cutting remark **2** : ironical criticism or reproach — **sar•cas•tic** *adj* — **sar•cas•ti•cal•ly** *adv*

**¹sash** *n* : broad band worn around the waist or over the shoulder

**²sash** *n* **1** : frame for a pane of glass in a door or window **2** : movable part of a window

**sassy** *adj* : insolent

**sat** *past of* SIT

**Sa•tan** *n* : devil — **sa•tan•ic** *adj* — **sa•tan•i•cal•ly** *adv*

**satch•el** *n* : small bag

**sate** *vb* : satisfy fully

**sat•el•lite** *n* : body or object that revolves around a larger celestial body

**sat•in** *n* : glossy fabric — **sat•iny** *adj*

**sat•ire** *n* : literary ridicule done with humor — **sa•tir•ic, sa•tir•i•cal** *adj* — **sa•tir•i•cal•ly** *adv* — **sat•i•rist** *n* — **sat•i•rize** *vb*

**sat•is•fac•tion** *n* : state of being satisfied — **sat•is•fac•to•ri•ly** *adv* — **sat•is•fac•to•ry** *adj* — **sat•is•fy** *vb* — **sat•is•fy•ing•ly** *adv*

**sat•u•rate** *vb* : soak or charge thoroughly — **sat•u•ra•tion** *n*

**Sat•ur•day** *n* : 7th day of the week

**sauce** *n* : fluid dressing or topping for food — **sauce•pan** *n*

**sau•cer** *n* : small shallow dish under a cup

**sau•na** *n* : steam or dry heat bath or a room or cabinet used for such a bath

**sau•sage** *n* : minced and highly seasoned meat

**sau•té** *vb* : fry in a little fat — **sauté** *n*

**sav•age** *adj* **1** : wild **2** : cruel ～ *n* : person belonging to a primitive society — **sav•age•ly** *adv* — **sav•age•ness** *n* — **sav•age•ry** *n*

**save** *vb* **1** : rescue from danger **2** : guard from destruction **3** : redeem from sin **4** : put aside as a reserve — **sav•er** *n*

**sav•ior, sav•iour** *n* **1** : one who saves **2** *cap* : Jesus Christ

**¹saw** *past of* SEE

**²saw** *n* : cutting tool with teeth ～ *vb* : cut with a saw — **saw•dust** *n* — **saw•mill** *n* — **saw•yer** *n*

**say** *vb* **said; said** **1** : express in words **2** : state positively ～ *n* **1** : expression of opinion **2** : power of decision

**say•ing** *n* : commonly repeated statement

**scab** *n* **1** : protective crust over a sore or wound **2** : worker taking a striker's job ～ *vb* **1** : become covered with a scab **2** : work as a scab — **scab•by** *adj*

**scald** *vb* **1** : burn with hot liquid or steam **2** : heat to the boiling point

**¹scale** *n* : weighing device ～ *vb* : weigh

**²scale** *n* **1** : thin plate esp. on the body of a fish or reptile **2** : thin coating or layer ～ *vb* : strip of scales — **scaled** *adj* — **scale•less** *adj* — **scaly** *adj*

**³scale** *n* **1** : graduated series **2** : size of a sample (as a model) in proportion to the size of the actual thing **3** : standard of estimation or judgment **4** : series of musical tones ～ *vb* **1** : climb by a ladder **2** : arrange in a graded series

**scalp** *n* : skin and flesh of the head ～ *vb* **1** : remove the scalp from **2** : resell at a greatly increased price — **scalp•er** *n*

**scam•per** *vb* : run nimbly — **scam•per** *n*

**scan** *vb* **1** : read (verses) so as to show meter **2** : examine closely or hastily **3** : examine with a sensing device — **scan** *n* — **scan•ner** *n*

**scan•dal** *n* **1** : disgraceful situation **2** : malicious gossip — **scan•dal•ize** *vb* — **scan•dal•ous** *adj*

**scant** *adj* : barely sufficient ～ *vb* : hold back from being generous — **scant•i•ly** *adv* — **scanty** *adj*

**scar** *n* : mark where a wound has healed — **scar** *vb*

**scarce** *adj* : lacking in quantity or number — **scar•ci•ty** *n*

**scarce•ly** *adv* **1** : barely **2** : almost not

**scare** *vb* : frighten ～ *n* : fright — **scary** *adj*

**scarf** *n* : cloth worn about the shoulders or the neck

**scat•ter** *vb* **1** : spread about irregularly **2** : disperse

**scav•en•ger** *n* **1** : person that collects refuse or waste **2** : animal that feeds on decayed matter — **scav•enge** *vb*

**scene** *n* **1** : single situation in a play or movie **2** : stage setting **3** : view **4** : display of emotion — **sce•nic** *adj*

**scen•ery** *n* **1** : painted setting for a stage **2** : picturesque view

**scent** *vb* **1** : smell **2** : fill with odor ～ *n* **1** : odor **2** : sense of smell **3** : perfume — **scent•ed** *adj*

**sched•ule** *n* : list showing sequence of events ～ *vb* : make a schedule of

**scheme** *n* **1** : crafty plot **2** : systematic design ～ *vb* : form a plot — **sche•mat•ic** *adj* — **schem•er** *n*

**schol•ar** *n* : student or learned person — **schol•ar•ly** *adj*

**schol•ar•ship** *n* **1** : qualities or learning of a serious student **2** : money given to a student to pay for education

**scho•las•tic** *adj* : relating to schools, scholars, or scholarship

**¹school** *n* **1** : institution for learning **2** : pupils in a school **3** : group with shared beliefs ～ *vb* : teach — **school•boy** *n* — **school•girl** *n* — **school•house** *n* — **school•mate** *n* — **school•room** *n* — **school•teach•er** *n*

**²school** *n* : large number of fish swimming together

**sci•ence** *n* : branch of systematic study esp. of the physical world — **sci•en•tif•ic** *adj* — **sci•en•tif•i•cal•ly** *adv* — **sci•en•tist** *n*

**scis•sors** *n pl* : small shears

**scold** *n* : person who scolds ～ *vb* : criticize severely

**scoop** *n* : shovellike utensil ～ *vb* **1** : take out with a scoop **2** : dig out

**scoot•er** *n* : child's foot-propelled vehicle

**scope** *n* **1** : extent **2** : room for development

**scorch** *vb* : burn the surface of

**score** *n* **1** *pl* **score** : twenty **2** : cut **3** : record of points made (as in a game) **4** : debt **5** : music of a composition ～ *vb* **1** : record **2** : mark with lines **3** : gain in a game **4** : assign a grade to **5** : compose a score for — **score•less** *adj* — **scor•er** *n*

**scorn** *n* : emotion involving both anger and disgust ～ *vb* : hold in contempt — **scorn•er** *n* — **scorn•ful** *adj* — **scorn•ful•ly** *adv*

**scout** *vb* : inspect or observe to get information ～ *n* : person sent out to get information

**scowl** *vb* : make a frowning expression of displeasure — **scowl** *n*

**scram** *vb* : go away at once

**scram•ble** *vb* **1** : clamber clumsily around **2** : struggle for possession of something **3** : mix together **4** : cook (eggs) by stirring during frying — **scram•ble** *n*

**scrap** *n* **1 :** fragment **2 :** discarded material ~ *vb* **:** get rid of as useless

**scrape** *vb* **1 :** remove by drawing a knife over **2 :** clean or smooth by rubbing **3 :** draw across a surface with a grating sound **4 :** damage by contact with a rough surface **5 :** gather or proceed with difficulty ~ *n* **1 :** act of scraping **2 :** predicament — **scrap•er** *n*

**scratch** *vb* **1 :** scrape or dig with or as if with claws or nails **2 :** cause to move gratingly **3 :** delete by or as if by drawing a line through ~ *n* **:** mark or sound made in scratching — **scratchy** *adj*

**scrawl** *vb* **:** write hastily and carelessly — **scrawl** *n*

**scream** *vb* **:** cry out loudly and shrilly ~ *n* **:** loud shrill cry

**screen** *n* **1 :** device or partition used to protect or decorate **2 :** surface on which pictures appear (as in movies) ~ *vb* **:** shield or separate with or as if with a screen

**screw** *n* **1 :** grooved fastening device **2 :** propeller ~ *vb* **1 :** fasten by means of a screw **2 :** move spirally

**screw•driv•er** *n* **:** tool for turning screws

**scrib•ble** *vb* **:** write hastily or carelessly — **scrib•ble** *n* — **scrib•bler** *n*

**script** *n* **:** text (as of a play)

**scrip•ture** *n* **:** sacred writings of a religion — **scrip•tur•al** *adj*

**scroll** *n* **1 :** roll of paper for writing a document **2 :** spiral or coiled design

**scrub** *vb* **:** clean or wash by rubbing — **scrub** *n*

**scru•ple** *n* **:** reluctance due to ethical considerations — **scru•ple** *vb* — **scru•pu•lous** *adj* — **scru•pu•lous•ly** *adv*

**scru•ti•ny** *n* **:** careful inspection — **scru•ti•nize** *vb*

**scuff** *vb* **:** scratch, scrape, or wear away — **scuff** *n*

**scuf•fle** *vb* **1 :** struggle at close quarters **2 :** shuffle one's feet — **scuf•fle** *n*

**sculp•ture** *n* **:** work of art carved or molded ~ *vb* **:** form as sculpture — **sculp•tor** *n* — **sculp•tur•al** *adj*

**scum** *n* **:** slimy film on a liquid

**sea** *n* **1 :** large body of salt water **2 :** ocean **3 :** rough water — **sea** *adj* — **sea•bird** *n* — **sea•coast** *n* — **sea•food** *n* — **sea•port** *n* — **sea•shore** *n* — **sea•wa•ter** *n* — **sea•weed** *n*

[1]**seal** *n* **:** large sea mammal of cold regions — **seal•skin** *n*

[2]**seal** *n* **1 :** device for stamping a design **2 :** something that closes ~ *vb* **1 :** affix a seal to **2 :** close up securely **3 :** determine finally — **seal•ant** *n* — **seal•er** *n*

**seam** *n* **1 :** line of junction of 2 edges **2 :** layer of a mineral ~ *vb* **:** join by sewing — **seam•less** *adj*

**search** *vb* **1 :** look through **2 :** seek — **search** *n* — **search•er** *n* — **search•light** *n*

**search engine** *n* **:** computer software used to search for specified information on the World Wide Web

[1]**sea•son** *n* **1 :** division of the year **2 :** customary time for something — **sea•son•al** *adj* — **sea•son•al•ly** *adv*

[2]**season** *vb* **1 :** add spice to (food) **2 :** make strong or fit for use — **sea•son•ing** *n*

**seat** *n* **1 :** place to sit **2 :** chair, bench, or stool for sitting on **3 :** place that serves as a capital or center ~ *vb* **1 :** place in or on a seat **2 :** provide seats for

[1]**sec•ond** *adj* **:** next after the 1st ~ *n* **1 :** one that is second **2 :** one who assists (as in a duel) — **sec•ond, sec•ond•ly** *adv* — **sec•ond•ary** *adj*

[2]**sec•ond** *n* **1 :** 60th part of a minute **2 :** moment

**sec•ond•hand** *adj* **1 :** not original **2 :** used before

**se•cret** *adj* **1 :** hidden **2 :** kept from general knowledge — **se•cre•cy** *n* — **secret** *n* — **se•cre•tive** *adj* — **se•cret•ly** *adv*

**sec•re•tary** *n* **1 :** one hired to handle correspondence and other tasks for a superior **2 :** official in charge of correspondence or records **3 :** head of a government department — **sec•re•tari•al** *adj*

[1]**se•crete** *vb* **:** produce from or as if from a gland — **se•cre•tion** *n*

[2]**se•crete** *vb* **:** hide

**sect** *n* **:** religious group — **sec•tar•i•an** *adj*

**sec•tion** *n* **:** distinct part — **sec•tion•al** *adj*

**sec•u•lar** *adj* **1 :** not sacred **2 :** not monastic

**se•cure** *adj* **:** free from danger or loss ~ *vb* **1 :** fasten safely **2 :** get — **se•cure•ly** *adv* — **se•cu•ri•ty** *n*

**se•dan** *n* **1 :** chair carried by 2 men **2 :** enclosed automobile

[1]**se•date** *adj* **:** quiet and dignified — **se•date•ly** *adv*

[2]**sedate** *vb* **:** dose with sedatives — **se•da•tion** *n* — **sed•a•tive** *n*

**sed•i•ment** *n* **:** material that settles to the bottom of a liquid or is deposited by water or a glacier — **sed•i•men•ta•ry** *adj* — **sed•i•men•ta•tion** *n*

**se•duce** *vb* **1 :** lead astray **2 :** entice to sexual intercourse — **se•duc•er** *n* — **se•duc•tion** *n* — **se•duc•tive** *adj*

**see** *vb* **saw; seen 1 :** perceive by the eye **2 :** have experience of **3 :** understand **4 :** make sure **5 :** meet with or escort

**seed** *n* **1 :** part by which a plant is propagated **2 :** source ~ *vb* **1 :** sow **2 :** remove seeds from — **seed•less** *adj*

**seed•ling** *n* **:** young plant grown from seed

**seedy** *adj* **1 :** full of seeds **2 :** shabby

**seek** *vb* (**sought; sought**) **1 :** search for **2 :** try to reach or obtain — **seek•er** *n*

**seem** *vb* **:** give the impression of being — **seem•ing•ly** *adv*

**seem•ly** *adj* **:** proper or fit

**seep** *vb* **:** leak through fine pores or cracks — **seep•age** *n*

**see•saw** *n* **:** board balanced in the middle — **seesaw** *vb*

**seg•ment** *n* **:** division of a thing — **seg•ment•ed** *adj*

**seg•re•gate** *vb* **1 :** cut off from others **2 :** separate by races — **seg•re•ga•tion** *n*

**seize** *vb* **:** take by force — **sei•zure** *n*

**sel•dom** *adv* **:** not often

**se•lect** *adj* **1 :** favored **2 :** discriminating ~ *vb* **:** take by preference — **se•lec•tive** *adj* — **se•lec•tion** *n*

**self** *n* **selves :** essential person distinct from others

**self–con•fi•dent** *adj* **:** confident in oneself and in one's powers and abilities — **self–con•fi•dence** *n*

**self–con•scious** *adj* **:** uncomfortably aware of oneself as an object of observation — **self–con•scious•ly** *adv* — **self–con•scious•ness** *n*

**self–con•trol** *n* **:** restraint over one's own impulses, emotions, or desires

**self–es•teem** *n* **:** respect for and confidence in oneself

**self•ish** *adj* **:** excessively or exclusively concerned with one's own well-being — **self•ish•ly** *adv* — **self•ish•ness** *n*

**self•less** *adj* **:** unselfish — **self•less•ness** *n*

**sell** *vb* (**sold; sold**) **1 :** transfer (property) esp. for money **2 :** deal in as a business **3 :** be sold — **sell•er** *n*

**selves** *pl of* SELF

**se•man•tic** *adj* **:** relating to meaning in language — **se•man•tics** *n sing or pl*

**se•mes•ter** *n* **:** half a school year

**semi•co•lon** *n* **:** punctuation mark ;

**semi•fi•nal** *adj* **:** being next to the final — **semifinal** *n*

**sen•ate** *n* **:** upper branch of a legislature — **sen•a•tor** *n* — **sen•a•to•rial** *adj*

**send** *vb* (**sent; sent**) **1 :** cause to go **2 :** propel — **send•er** *n*

**se•nior** *adj* **:** older or higher ranking — **se•nior** *n* — **se•nior•i•ty** *n*

**sen•sa•tion** *n* **1 :** bodily feeling **2 :** condition of excitement or the cause of it — **sen•sa•tion•al** *adj*

**sense** *n* **1 :** meaning **2 :** faculty of perceiving something physical **3 :** sound mental capacity ~ *vb* **1 :** perceive by the senses **2 :** detect automatically — **sense•less** *adj* — **sense•less•ly** *adv*

**sen•si•bil•i•ty** *n* **:** delicacy of feeling

**sen•si•ble** *adj* **1 :** capable of sensing or being sensed **2 :** aware or conscious **3 :** reasonable — **sen•si•bly** *adv*

**sen•si•tive** *adj* **1 :** subject to excitation by or responsive to stimuli **2 :** having power of feeling **3 :** easily affected — **sen•si•tive•ness** *n* — **sen•si•tiv•i•ty** *n*

**sen•si•tize** *vb* **:** make or become sensitive

**sen•so•ry** *adj* **:** relating to sensation or the senses

**sen•su•al** *adj* **1 :** pleasing the senses **2 :** devoted to the pleasures of the senses — **sen•su•al•ist** *n* — **sen•su•al•i•ty** *n* — **sen•su•al•ly** *adv*

**sen•su•ous** *adj* **:** having strong appeal to the senses

**sent** *past of* SEND

**sen•tence** *n* **1 :** judgment of a court **2 :** grammatically self-contained speech unit ~ *vb* **:** impose a sentence on

**sen•ti•ment** *n* **1 :** belief **2 :** feeling

**sen•ti•men•tal** *adj* **:** influenced by tender feelings — **sen•ti•men•tal•ism** *n* — **sen•ti•men•tal•ist** *n* — **sen•ti•men•tal•i•ty** *n* — **sen•ti•men•tal•ize** *vb* — **sen•ti•men•tal•ly** *adv*

**sep•a•rate** *vb* **1 :** set or keep apart **2 :** become divided or detached ~ *adj* **1 :** not connected or shared **2 :** distinct from each other — **sep•a•ra•ble** *adj* — **sep•a•rate•ly** *adv* — **sep•a•ra•tion** *n* — **sep•a•ra•tor** *n*

**Sep•tem•ber** *n* **:** 9th month of the year having 30 days

**se•quel** *n* **1 :** consequence or result **2 :** continuation of a story

**se•quence** *n* **:** continuous or connected series — **se•quen•tial** *adj* — **se•quen•tial•ly** *adv*

**ser•e•nade** *n* **:** music sung or played esp. to a woman being courted — **serenade** *vb*

**se•rene** *adj* **:** tranquil — **se•rene•ly** *adv* — **se•ren•i•ty** *n*

**ser•geant** *n* **:** noncommissioned officer (as in the army)

**se•ri•al** *adj* **:** being or relating to a series or sequence ~ *n* **:** story appearing in parts — **se•ri•al•ly** *adv*

**se•ries** *n* **:** number of things in order

**se•ri•ous** *adj* **1 :** subdued in appearance or manner **2 :** sincere **3 :** of great importance — **se•ri•ous•ly** *adv* — **se•ri•ous•ness** *n*

**ser•mon** *n* **:** lecture on religion or behavior

**ser•pent** *n* **:** snake — **ser•pen•tine** *adj*

**ser•vant** *n* **:** person employed for domestic work

**serve** *vb* **1 :** work through or perform a term of service **2 :** be of use **3 :** prove adequate **4 :** hand out (food or drink) **5 :** be of service to — **serv•er** *n*

**ser•vice** *n* **1 :** act or means of serving **2 :** meeting for worship **3 :** branch of public employment or the persons in it **4 :** set of dishes or table utensils **5 :** benefit ~ *vb* **:** repair — **ser•vice•able** *adj* — **ser•vice•man** *n* — **ser•vice•wom•an** *n*

**ses•sion** *n* **:** meeting

**set** *vb* **set; set 1 :** cause to sit **2 :** place **3 :** settle, arrange, or adjust **4 :** cause to be or do **5 :** become fixed or solid **6 :** sink below the horizon ~ *adj* **:** settled ~ *n* **1 :** group classed together **2 :** setting for the scene of a play or film **3 :** electronic apparatus **4 :** collection of mathematical elements — **set forth :** begin a trip — **set off** *vb* **:** set forth — **set out** *vb* **:** begin a trip or undertaking — **set up** *vb* **1 :** assemble or erect **2 :** cause

**set•back** *n* **:** reverse

**set•ting** *n* **:** the time, place, and circumstances in which something occurs

**set•tle** *vb* **1 :** come to rest **2 :** sink gradually **3 :** establish in residence **4 :** adjust or arrange **5 :** calm **6 :** dispose of (as by paying) **7 :** decide or agree on — **set•tle•ment** *n* — **set•tler** *n*

**sev•en** *n* **:** one more than 6 — **seven** *adj or pron* — **sev•enth** *adj or adv or n*

**sev•en•teen** *n* **:** one more than 16 — **seventeen** *adj or pron* — **sev•en•teenth** *adj or n*

**sev•en•ty** *n* **:** 7 times 10 — **sev•en•ti•eth** *adj or n* — **sev•en•ty** *adj or pron*

**sev•er** *vb* **:** cut off or apart — **sev•er•ance** *n*

**sev•er•al** *adj* **1 :** distinct **2 :** consisting of an indefinite but not large number — **sev•er•al•ly** *adv*

**se•vere** *adj* **1 :** strict **2 :** restrained or unadorned **3 :** painful or distressing **4 :** hard to endure — **se•vere•ly** *adv* — **se•ver•i•ty** *n*

**sew** *vb* **:** join or fasten by stitches — **sew•ing** *n*

**sew•age** *n* **:** liquid household waste

[1]**sew•er** *n* **:** one that sews

[2]**sew•er** *n* **:** pipe or channel to carry off waste matter

**sex** *n* **:** either of 2 divisions into which organisms are grouped according to their reproductive roles — **sexed** *adj* — **sex•less** *adj* — **sex•u•al** *adj* — **sex•u•al•i•ty** *n* — **sex•u•al•ly** *adv* — **sexy** *adj*

**sex•ism** *n* **:** discrimination based on sex and esp. against women — **sex•ist** *adj or n*

**shab•by** *adj* **1 :** worn and faded **2 :** dressed in worn clothes **3 :** not generous or fair — **shab•bi•ly** *adv* — **shab•bi•ness** *n*

**shack** *n* **:** hut

**shade** *n* **1 :** space sheltered from the light esp. of the sun **2 :** gradation of color **3 :** small difference **4 :** something that shades ~ *vb* **1 :** shelter from light and heat **2 :** add shades of color to **3 :** show slight differences esp. in color or meaning

**shad•ow** *n* **1 :** shade cast upon a surface by something blocking light **2 :** trace **3 :** gloomy influence ~ *vb* **1 :** cast a shadow **2 :** follow closely — **shad•owy** *adj*

**shady** *adj* **1 :** giving shade **2 :** of dubious honesty

**shaft** *n* **1 :** long slender cylindrical part **2 :** deep vertical opening (as of a mine)

**shag•gy** *adj* **1 :** covered with long hair or wool **2 :** not neat and combed

**shake** *vb* **shook; shak•en 1 :** move or cause to move quickly back and forth **2 :** distress **3 :** clasp (hands) as friendly gesture — **shake** *n* — **shak•er** *n*

**shaky** *adj* **:** not sound, stable, or reliable — **shak•i•ly** *adv* — **shak•i•ness** *n*

**shall** *vb, past* **should** — used as an auxiliary to express a command, futurity, or determination

**shal•low** *adj* **1 :** not deep **2 :** not intellectually profound

**sham•bles** *n* **:** state of disorder

**shame** *n* **1 :** distress over guilt or disgrace **2 :** cause of shame or regret ~ *vb* **1 :** make ashamed **2 :** disgrace — **shame•ful** *adj* — **shame•ful•ly** *adv* — **shame•less** *adj* — **shame•less•ly** *adv*

**sham•poo** *vb* **:** wash one's hair ~ *n* **:** act of or preparation used in shampooing

**shape** *vb* **:** form esp. in a particular structure or appearance ~ *n* **1 :** distinctive appearance or arrangement of parts **2 :** condition — **shape•less** *adj* — **shape•li•ness** *n* — **shape•ly** *adj*

**share** *n* **1 :** portion belonging to one **2 :** interest in a company's stock ~ *vb* **:** divide or use with others — **share•hold•er** *n* — **shar•er** *n*

**shark** *n* **:** voracious sea fish

**sharp** *adj* **1 :** having a good point or cutting edge **2 :** alert, clever, or sarcastic **3 :** vigorous or fierce **4 :** having prominent angles or a sudden change in direction **5 :** distinct **6 :** higher than the true pitch ~ *adv* **:** exactly ~ *n* **:** sharp note — **shar•pen** *vb* — **sharp•en•er** *n* — **sharp•ly** *adv* — **sharp•ness** *n*

**shat•ter** *vb* **:** smash or burst into fragments — **shat•ter•proof** *adj*

**shave** *vb* **1 :** cut off with a razor **2 :** make bare by cutting the hair from **3 :** slice very thin ~ *n* **:** act or instance of shaving — **shav•er** *n*

**shawl** *n* **:** loose covering for the head or shoulders

**she** *pron* **:** that female one

**shear** *vb* **1 :** trim wool from **2 :** cut off with scissorlike action

**shears** *n pl* **:** cutting tool with 2 blades fastened so that the edges slide by each other

**shed** *vb* **1 :** give off (as tears or hair) **2 :** cause to flow or diffuse ~ *n* **:** small storage building

**sheen** *n* **:** subdued luster

**sheep** *n* (**sheep**) **:** domesticated mammal covered with wool — **sheep•skin** *n*

**sheep•ish** *adj* **:** embarrassed by awareness of a fault

**sheer** *adj* **1 :** pure **2 :** very steep **3 :** very thin or transparent

**sheet** *n* **:** broad flat piece (as of cloth or paper)

**shelf** *n* (**shelves**) **1 :** flat narrow structure used for storage or display **2 :** sandbank or rock ledge

**shell** *n* **1 :** hard or tough outer covering **2 :** case holding explosive powder and projectile for a weapon **3 :** light racing boat with oars ~ *vb* **1 :** remove the shell of **2 :** bombard — **shelled** *adj* — **shell•er** *n*

**shel•ter** *n* **:** something that gives protection ~ *vb* **:** give refuge to

**shep•herd** *n* **:** one that tends sheep ~ *vb* **:** act as a shepherd or guardian

**sher•bet, sher•bert** *n* **:** fruit-flavored frozen dessert

**sher•iff** *n* **:** county law officer

**shield** *n* **1 :** broad piece of armor carried on the arm **2 :** something that protects — **shield** *vb*

**shier** *comparative of* SHY

**shiest** *superlative of* SHY

**shift** *vb* **1 :** change place, position, or direction **2 :** get by ~ *n* **1 :** loose-fitting dress **2 :** an act or instance of shifting **3 :** scheduled work period

**shift•less** *adj* **:** lazy

**shifty** *adj* **:** tricky or untrustworthy

**shin** *n* **:** front part of the leg below the knee ~ *vb* **:** climb by sliding the body close along

**shine** *vb* **1 :** give off or cause to give off light **2 :** be outstanding **3 :** polish ~ *n* **:** brilliance

**shiny** *adj* **:** bright or polished

**ship** *n* **1 :** large oceangoing vessel **2 :** aircraft or spacecraft ~ *vb* **1 :** put on a ship **2 :** transport by carrier — **ship•board** *n* — **ship•build•er** *n* — **ship•per** *n* — **ship•wreck** *n or vb* — **ship•yard** *n*

**ship•ment** *n* **:** an act of shipping or the goods shipped

**shirk** *vb* **:** evade — **shirk•er** *n*

**shirt** *n* **:** garment for covering the torso — **shirt•less** *adj*

**shiv•er** *vb* **:** tremble — **shiv•er** *n* — **shiv•ery** *adj*

**shock** *n* **1 :** forceful impact **2 :** violent mental or emotional disturbance **3 :** effect of a charge of electricity **4 :** depression of the vital bodily processes ~ *vb* **1 :** strike with surprise, horror, or disgust **2 :** subject to an electrical shock — **shock•proof** *adj*

**shod•dy** *adj* **:** poorly made or done — **shod•di•ly** *adv* — **shod•di•ness** *n*

**shoe** *n* **1 :** covering for the human foot **2 :** horseshoe ~ *vb* **shod; shod:** put horseshoes on — **shoe•lace** *n* — **shoe•ma•ker** *n*

**shone** *past of* SHINE

**shook** *past of* SHAKE

**shoot** *vb* **shot; shot 1 :** propel (as an arrow or bullet) **2 :** wound or kill with a missile **3 :** discharge (a weapon) **4 :** drive (as a ball) at a goal **5 :** photograph **6 :** move swiftly ~ *n* **:** new plant growth — **shoot•er** *n*

**shop** *n* **:** place where things are made or sold ~ *vb* **:** visit stores — **shop•keep•er** *n* — **shop•per** *n*

**shop•lift** *vb* **:** steal goods from a store — **shop•lift•er** *n*

**[1]shore** *n* **:** land along the edge of water — **shore•bird** *n* — **shore•line** *n*

**[2]shore** *vb* **:** prop up ~ *n* **:** something that props

**short** *adj* **1 :** not long or tall or extending far **2 :** brief in time **3 :** curt **4 :** not having or being enough ~ *adv* **:** curtly ~ *n* **1** *pl* **:** short drawers or trousers **2 :** short circuit — **short•en** *vb* — **short•ly** *adv* — **short•ness** *n*

**short•age** *n* **:** deficiency

**short•cut** *n* **1 :** more direct route than that usu. taken **2 :** quicker way of doing something

**short•hand** *n* **:** method of speed writing

**shot** *n* **1 :** act of shooting **2 :** attempt (as at making a goal) **3 :** small pellets forming a charge **4 :** range or reach **5 :** photograph **6 :** injection of medicine **7 :** small serving of liquor — **shot•gun** *n*

**should** *past of* SHALL — used as an auxiliary to express condition, obligation, or probability

**shoul•der** *n* **1 :** part of the body where the arm joins the trunk **2 :** part that projects or lies to the side ~ *vb* **:** push with or bear on the shoulder

**shout** *vb* **:** give voice loudly — **shout** *n*

**shove** *vb* **:** push along or away — **shove** *n*

**shov•el** *n* **:** broad tool for digging or lifting ~ *vb* **:** take up or dig with a shovel

**show** *vb* **1 :** present to view **2 :** reveal or demonstrate **3 :** teach **4 :** prove **5 :** conduct or escort **6 :** appear or be noticeable ~ *n* **1 :** demonstrative display **2 :** spectacle **3 :** theatrical, radio, or television program — **show•case** *n* — **show off** *vb* **1 :** display proudly **2 :** act so as to attract attention — **show up** *vb* **:** arrive

**show•er** *n* **1 :** brief fall of rain **2 :** bath in which water sprinkles down on the person or a facility for such a bath **3 :** party at which someone gets gifts ~ *vb* **1 :** rain or fall in a shower **2 :** bathe in a shower — **show•ery** *adj*

**showy** *adj* **:** very noticeable or overly elaborate — **show•i•ly** *adv* — **show•i•ness** *n*

**shrank** *past of* SHRINK

**shred** *n* **:** narrow strip cut or torn off ~ *vb* **:** cut or tear into shreds

**shrewd** *adj* **:** clever — **shrewd•ly** *adv* — **shrewd•ness** *n*

**shriek** *n* **:** shrill cry — **shriek** *vb*

**shrill** *adj* **:** piercing and high-pitched — **shril•ly** *adv*

**shrimp** *n* **:** small sea crustacean

**shrine** *n* **1 :** tomb of a saint **2 :** hallowed place

**shrink** *vb* **shrank/shrunk; shrunk/shrunk•en 1 :** draw back or away **2 :** become smaller — **shrink•able** *adj*

**shriv•el** *vb* **:** shrink or wither into wrinkles

**shrub** *n* **:** low woody plant — **shrub•by** *adj*

**shrub•bery** *n* **:** growth of shrubs

**shrug** *vb* **:** hunch the shoulders up in doubt, indifference, or uncertainty — **shrug** *n*

**shrunk** *past part of* SHRINK

**shrunk•en** *past part of* SHRINK

**shud•der** *vb* **:** tremble — **shud•der** *n*

**shuf•fle** *vb* **1 :** mix together **2 :** walk with a sliding movement — **shuf•fle** *n*

**shun** *vb* **:** keep away from

**shut** *vb* (**shut; shut**) **1 :** bar passage into or through (as by moving a lid or door) **2 :** suspend activity — **shut out** *vb* **:** exclude — **shut up** *vb* **:** stop or cause to stop talking

**shut•ter** *n* **1 :** movable cover for a window **2 :** camera part that exposes film

**shut•tle** *n* **1 :** part of a weaving machine that carries thread back and forth **2 :** vehicle traveling back and forth over a short route ~ *vb* **:** move back and forth frequently

**shy** *adj* **1 :** sensitive and hesitant in dealing with others **2 :** wary **3 :** lacking ~ *vb* **:** draw back (as in fright) — **shy•ly** *adv* — **shy•ness** *n*

**sick** *adj* **1 :** not in good health **2 :** nauseated **3 :** relating to or meant for the sick — **sick•bed** *n* — **sick•en** *vb* — **sick•ly** *adj* — **sick•ness** *n*

**side** *n* **1 :** part to left or right of an object or the torso **2 :** edge or surface away from the center or at an angle to top and bottom or ends **3 :** contrasting or opposing position or group — **sid•ed** *adj*

**side•swipe** *vb* **:** strike with a glancing blow — **side•swipe** *n*

**side•track** *vb* **:** lead aside or astray

**side•walk** *n* **:** paved walk at the side of a road

**side•ways** *adv or adj* **1 :** to or from the side **2 :** with one side to the front

**sift** *vb* **1 :** pass through a sieve **2 :** examine carefully — **sift•er** *n*

**sigh** *n* **:** audible release of the breath (as to express weariness) — **sigh** *vb*

**sight** *n* **1 :** something seen or worth seeing **2 :** process, power, or range of seeing **3 :** device used in aiming **4 :** view or glimpse ~ *vb* **:** get sight of — **sight•ed** *adj* — **sight•less** *adj* — **sight–see•ing** *adj* — **sight•seer** *n*

**sign** *n* **1 :** symbol **2 :** gesture expressing a command or thought **3 :** public notice to advertise or warn **4 :** trace ~ *vb* **1 :** mark with or make a sign **2 :** write one's name on — **sign•er** *n*

**sig•nal** *n* **1 :** sign of command or warning **2 :** electronic transmission ~ *vb* **:** communicate or notify by signals ~ *adj* **:** distinguished

**sig•na•ture** *n* **:** one's name written by oneself

**sig•ni•fy** *vb* **1 :** show by a sign **2 :** mean — **sig•nif•i•cance** *n* — **sig•nif•i•cant** *adj* — **sig•nif•i•cant•ly** *adv* — **sig•ni•fi•ca•tion** *n*

**si•lence** *n* **:** state of being without sound ~ *vb* **:** keep from making noise or sound — **si•lenc•er** *n* — **si•lent** *adj* — **si•lent•ly** *adv*

**silk** *n* **1 :** fine strong lustrous protein fiber from moth larvae (**silkworms** ) **2 :** thread or cloth made from silk — **silk•en** *adj* — **silky** *adj*

**sil•ly** *adj* **:** foolish or stupid — **sil•li•ness** *n*

**sil•ver** *n* **1 :** white ductile metallic chemical element **2 :** table utensils ~ *adj* **:** having the color of silver — **sil•very** *adj*

**sim•i•lar** *adj* **:** resembling each other in some ways — **sim•i•lar•i•ty** *n* — **sim•i•lar•ly** *adv*

**sim•ple** *adj* **1 :** free from dishonesty, vanity, or pretense **2 :** of humble origin or modest position **3 :** not complex **4 :** lacking education, experience, or intelligence — **sim•ple•ness** *n* — **sim•ply** *adv*

**sim•plic•i•ty** *n* **:** state or fact of being simple

**sim•pli•fy** *vb* **:** make easier — **sim•pli•fi•ca•tion** *n*

**sim•u•late** *vb* **:** create the effect or appearance of — **sim•u•la•tion** *n* — **sim•u•la•tor** *n*

**si•mul•ta•ne•ous** *adj* **:** occurring or operating at the same time — **si•mul•ta•ne•ous•ly** *adv* — **simul•ta•ne•ous•ness** *n*

**sin** *n* **:** offense against God ~ *vb* **:** commit a sin — **sin•ful** *adj* — **sin•less** *adj* — **sin•ner** *n*

**since** *adv* **1 :** from a past time until now **2 :** backward in time ~ *prep* **1 :** in the period after **2 :** continuously from ~ *conj* **1 :** from the time when **2 :** because

**sin•cere** *adj* **:** genuine or honest — **sin•cere•ly** *adv* — **sin•cer•i•ty** *n*

**sing** *vb* **sang; sung :** produce musical tones with the voice — **sing•er** *n*

**sin•gle** *adj* **1 :** one only **2 :** unmarried ~ *n* **:** separate one — **sin•gle•ness** *n* — **sin•gly** *adv* — **single out** *vb* **:** select or set aside

**sin•gu•lar** *adj* **1 :** relating to a word form denoting one **2 :** outstanding or superior **3 :** queer — **sin•gu•lar** *n* — **sin•gu•lar•i•ty** *n* — **sin•gu•lar•ly** *adv*

**sink** *vb* (**sank; sunk**) **1 :** go or put underwater **2 :** grow worse **3 :** make by digging or boring **4 :** invest ~ *n* **:** basin with a drain

**sip** *vb* **:** drink in small quantities — **sip** *n*

**sir** *n* **1** — used before the first name of a knight or baronet **2** — used as a respectful form of address

**si•ren** *n* **1 :** seductive woman **2 :** wailing warning whistle

**sis•sy** *n* **:** timid or effeminate boy

**sis•ter** *n* **:** female sharing one or both parents with another person — **sis•ter•hood** *n* — **sis•ter•ly** *adj*

**sis•ter–in–law** *n* **sis•ters–in–law :** sister of one's spouse or wife of one's brother

**sit** *vb* **sat; sat 1 :** rest on the buttocks **2 :** settle on a resting place **3 :** hold a session **4 :** pose for a portrait **5 :** have a location **6 :** rest or fix in place — **sit•ter** *n*

**site** *n* **1 :** place **2 :** Web site

**sit•u•a•tion** *n* **1 :** location **2 :** condition **3 :** job

**six** *n* **:** one more than 5 — **six** *adj or pron* — **sixth** *adj or adv or n*

**six•teen** *n* **:** one more than 15 — **six•teen** *adj or pron* — **six•teenth** *adj or n*

**six•ty** *n* **:** 6 times 10 — **six•ti•eth** *adj or n* — **sixty** *adj or pron*

**size** *n* **:** measurement of the amount of space something takes up ~ *vb* **:** grade according to size — **siz•able** *adj* — **siz•ably** *adv*

**skate** *n* **1 :** metal runner on a shoe for gliding over ice **2 :** roller skate — **skate** *vb* — **skat•er** *n*

**skel•e•ton** *n* **:** bony framework — **skel•e•tal** *adj*

**skep•tic** *n* **:** one who is critical or doubting — **skep•ti•cal** *adj* — **skep•ti•cism** *n*

**sketch** *n* **1 :** rough drawing **2 :** short story or essay — **sketch** *vb* — **sketchy** *adj*

**ski** *n* **:** long strip for gliding over snow or water — **ski** *vb* — **ski•er** *n*

**skid** *n* **1 :** plank for supporting something or on which it slides **2 :** act of skidding ~ *vb* **:** slide sideways

**skill** *n* **:** developed or learned ability — **skilled** *adj* — **skill•ful** *adj* — **skill•ful•ly** *adv*

**skim** *vb* **1 :** take off from the top of a liquid **2 :** read or move over swiftly ~ *adj* **:** having the cream removed — **skim•mer** *n*

**skin** *n* **1 :** outer layer of an animal body **2 :** rind ~ *vb* **:** take the skin from — **skin•less** *adj* — **skinned** *adj* — **skin•tight** *adj*

**skin•ny** *adj* **:** very thin

**skip** *vb* **1 :** move with leaps **2 :** read past or ignore — **skip** *n*

**skirt** *n* **:** garment or part of a garment that hangs below the waist ~ *vb* **:** pass around the edge of

**skull** *n* **:** bony case that protects the brain

**sky** *n* **1 :** upper air **2 :** heaven — **sky•line** *n* — **sky•ward** *adv or adj*

**sky•scrap•er** *n* **:** very tall building

**slab** *n* **:** thick slice

**slack** *adj* **1 :** careless **2 :** not taut **3 :** not busy ~ *n* **1 :** part hanging loose **2** *pl* **:** casual trousers — **slack•en** *vb* — **slack•ly** *adv* — **slack•ness** *n*

**slain** *past part of* SLAY

**slam** *n* **:** heavy jarring impact ~ *vb* **:** shut, strike, or throw violently and loudly

**slang** *n* **:** informal nonstandard vocabulary — **slangy** *adj*

**slant** *vb* **1 :** slope **2 :** present with a special viewpoint ~ *n* **:** sloping direction, line, or plane

**slap** *vb* **:** strike sharply with the open hand — **slap** *n*

**slash** *vb* **1 :** cut with sweeping strokes **2 :** reduce sharply ~ *n* **:** gash

**slaugh•ter** *n* **1 :** butchering of livestock for market **2 :** great and cruel destruction of lives ~ *vb* **:** commit slaughter upon — **slaugh•ter•house** *n*

**slave** *n* **:** one owned and forced into service by another ~ *vb* **:** work as or like a slave — **slave** *adj* — **slav•ery** *n* — **slav•ish** *adj* — **slav•ish•ly** *adv*

**slay** *vb* **(slew/slayed; slain) 1** *past slew* **:** kill **2** *past slayed* **:** overwhelm with amusement — **slay•er** *n*

**sled** *n* **:** vehicle on runners — **sled** *vb*

**sleek** *adj* **:** smooth or glossy — **sleek** *vb*

**sleep** *n* **:** natural suspension of consciousness ~ *vb* **(slept; slept) :** rest in a state of sleep — **sleep•er** *n* — **sleep•i•ly** *adv* — **sleep•i•ness** *n* — **sleep•less** *adj* — **sleep•walk•er** *n* — **sleepy** *adj*

**sleeve** *n* **:** part of a garment for the arm — **sleeve•less** *adj*

**sleigh** *n* **:** horse-drawn sled with seats ~ *vb* **:** drive or ride in a sleigh

**slen•der** *adj* **1 :** thin esp. in physique **2 :** scanty

**slew** *past of* SLAY

**slice** *n* **:** thin flat piece ~ *vb* **:** cut a slice from

**slick** *adj* **1 :** very smooth **2 :** clever — **slick** *vb*

**slide** *vb* **:** move smoothly along a surface ~ *n* **1 :** act of sliding **2 :** surface on which something slides **3 :** transparent picture for projection

**slier** *comparative of* SLY

**sliest** *superlative of* SLY

**slight** *adj* **1 :** slender **2 :** frail **3 :** small in degree ~ *vb* **1 :** ignore or treat as not important — **slight** *n* — **slight•ly** *adv*

**slim** *adj* **1 :** slender **2 :** scanty ~ *vb* **:** make or become slender

**slime** *n* **:** dirty slippery film (as on water) — **slimy** *adj*

**sling** *vb* **(slung; slung) :** hurl with or as if with a sling ~ *n* **1 :** strap for swinging and hurling stones **2 :** looped strap or bandage to lift or support

**slink** *vb* **(slunk; slunk) :** move stealthily or sinuously — **slinky** *adj*

[1]**slip** *vb* **1 :** escape quietly or secretly **2 :** slide along smoothly **3 :** make a mistake **4 :** to pass without being noticed or done **5 :** fall off from a standard ~ *n* **1 :** ship's berth **2 :** sudden mishap **3 :** mistake **4 :** woman's undergarment

[2]**slip** *n* **1 :** plant shoot **2 :** small strip (as of paper)

**slip•per** *n* **:** shoe that slips on easily

**slip•pery** *adj* **1 :** slick enough to slide on **2 :** tricky — **slip•peri•ness** *n*

**slit** *vb* **(slit; slit) :** make a slit in ~ *n* **:** long narrow cut

**slob** *n* **:** untidy person

**slob•ber** *vb* **:** dribble saliva — **slob•ber** *n*

**slo•gan** *n* **:** word or phrase expressing the aim of a cause

**slop** *n* **:** food waste for animal feed ~ *vb* **:** spill

**slope** *vb* **:** deviate from the vertical or horizontal ~ *n* **:** upward or downward slant

**slop•py** *adj* **1 :** muddy **2 :** untidy

**slot** *n* **:** narrow opening

**slow** *adj* **1 :** sluggish or stupid **2 :** moving, working, or happening at less than the usual speed ~ *vb* **1 :** make slow **2 :** go slower — **slow** *adv* — **slow•ly** *adv* — **slow•ness** *n*

**slug•gish** *adj* **:** slow in movement or flow — **slug•gish•ly** *adv* — **slug•gish•ness** *n*

**slum** *n* **:** thickly populated area marked by poverty

**slum•ber** *vb or n* **:** sleep

**slump** *vb* **1 :** sink suddenly **2 :** assume an extremely relaxed or stooped posture — **slump** *n*

**slung** *past of* SLING

**slunk** *past of* SLINK

**slur** *vb* **:** run (words or notes) together — **slur** *n*

**sly** *adj* **:** given to or showing secrecy and deception — **sly•ly** *adv* — **sly•ness** *n*

**smack** *vb* **1 :** move (the lips) so as to make a sharp noise **2 :** kiss or slap with a loud noise ~ *n* **1 :** sharp noise made by the lips **2 :** noisy slap

**small** *adj* **1 :** little in size or amount **2 :** few in number **3 :** trivial — **small•ish** *adj* — **small•ness** *n*

**smart** *vb* **1 :** cause or feel stinging pain **2 :** endure distress ~ *adj* **1 :** intelligent or resourceful **2 :** stylish — **smart** *n* — **smart•ly** *adv* — **smart•ness** *n*

**smash** *vb* **:** break or be broken into pieces ~ *n* **1 :** smashing blow **2 :** act or sound of smashing

**smear** *n* **:** greasy stain ~ *vb* **1 :** spread (something sticky) **2 :** smudge **3 :** spread malicious gossip about someone

**smell** *vb* **1 :** perceive the odor of **2 :** have or give off an odor ~ *n* **1 :** sense by which one perceives odor **2 :** odor — **smelly** *adj*

**smelt** *vb* **:** melt or fuse (ore) in order to separate the metal — **smelt•er** *n*

**smile** *n* **:** facial expression with the mouth turned up usu. to show pleasure — **smile** *vb*

**smog** *n* **:** fog and smoke — **smog•gy** *adj*

**smoke** *n* **:** sooty gas from burning ~ *vb* **1 :** give off smoke **2 :** inhale the fumes of burning tobacco **3 :** cure (as meat) with smoke — **smoke•less** *adj* — **smok•er** *n* — **smoky** *adj*

**smooth** *adj* **1 :** having a surface without irregularities **2 :** not jarring or jolting ~ *vb* **:** make smooth — **smooth•ly** *adv* — **smooth•ness** *n*

**smoth•er** *vb* **1 :** kill by depriving of air **2 :** cover thickly

**smudge** *vb* **:** soil or blur by rubbing ~ *n* **1 :** thick smoke **2 :** dirty spot

**smug•gle** *vb* **:** import or export secretly or illegally — **smug•gler** *n*

**snack** *n* **:** light meal

**snag** *n* **:** unexpected difficulty ~ *vb* **:** become caught on something that sticks out

**snake** *n* **:** long-bodied limbless reptile — **snake•bite** *n*

**snap** *vb* **1 :** bite at something **2 :** utter angry words **3 :** break suddenly with a sharp sound ~ *n* **1 :** act or sound of snapping **2 :** fastening that closes with a click **3 :** something easy to do — **snap•per** *n* — **snap•pish** *adj* — **snap•py** *adj*

**snap•shot** *n* **:** casual photograph

**snare** *n* **:** trap for catching game ~ *vb* **:** capture or hold with or as if with a snare

[1]**snarl** *n* **:** tangle ~ *vb* **:** cause to become knotted

[2]**snarl** *vb or n* **:** growl

**snatch** *vb* **1 :** try to grab something suddenly **2 :** seize or take away suddenly ~ *n* **1 :** act of snatching **2 :** something brief or fragmentary

**sneak** *vb* **:** move or take in a furtive manner ~ *n* **:** one who acts in a furtive manner — **sneak•i•ly** *adv* — **sneak•ing•ly** *adv* — **sneaky** *adj*

**sneak•er** *n* **:** sports shoe

**sneer** *vb* **:** smile scornfully — **sneer** *n*

**sneeze** *vb* **:** force the breath out with sudden and involuntary violence — **sneeze** *n*

**snick•er** *n* **:** partly suppressed laugh — **snicker** *vb*

**sniff** *vb* **1 :** draw air audibly up the nose **2 :** detect by smelling — **sniff** *n*

**snob** *n* **:** one who acts superior to others — **snob•bery** *n* — **snob•bish** *adj* — **snob•bish•ly** *adv* — **snob•bish•ness** *n*

**snoop** *vb* **:** pry in a furtive way ~ *n* **:** prying person

**snooze** *vb* **:** take a nap — **snooze** *n*

**snore** *vb* **:** breathe with a hoarse noise while sleeping — **snore** *n*

**snort** *vb* **:** force air noisily through the nose — **snort** *n*

**snow** *n* **:** crystals formed from water vapor ~ *vb* **:** fall as snow — **snow•ball** *n* — **snow•bank** *n* — **snow•drift** *n* — **snow•fall** *n* — **snow•plow** *n* — **snow•storm** *n* — **snowy** *adj*

**snuff** *vb* **:** put out (a candle) — **snuff•er** *n*

**snug** *adj* **1 :** warm, secure, and comfortable **2 :** fitting closely — **snug•ly** *adv* — **snug•ness** *n*

**snug•gle** *vb* **:** curl up comfortably

**so** *adv* **1 :** in the manner or to the extent indicated **2 :** in the same way **3 :** therefore **4 :** finally **5 :** thus ~ *conj* **:** for that reason

**soak** *vb* **1 :** lie in a liquid **2 :** absorb ~ *n* **:** act of soaking

**soap** *n* **:** cleaning substance — **soap** *vb* — **soapy** *adj*

**soar** *vb* **:** fly upward on or as if on wings

**sob** *vb* **:** weep with convulsive heavings of the chest — **sob** *n*

**so•ber** *adj* **1 :** not drunk **2 :** serious or solemn — **so•ber•ly** *adv*

**soc•cer** *n* **:** game played by kicking a ball

**so•cia•ble** *adj* **:** friendly — **so•cia•bil•i•ty** *n* — **so•cia•bly** *adv*

**so•cial** *adj* **1 :** relating to pleasant companionship **2 :** naturally living or growing in groups **3 :** relating to human society ~ *n* **:** social gathering — **so•cial•ly** *adv*

**so•cial•ism** *n* **:** social system based on government control of the production and distribution of goods — **so•cial•ist** *n or adj* — **so•cial•is•tic** *adj*

**so•cial•ize** *vb* **1 :** regulate by socialism **2 :** adapt to social needs **3 :** participate in a social gathering — **so•cial•i•za•tion** *n*

**so•ci•ety** *n* **1 :** companionship **2 :** community life **3 :** rich or fashionable class **4 :** voluntary group

**so•ci•ol•o•gy** *n* **:** study of social relationships — **so•ci•o•log•i•cal** *adj* — **so•ci•ol•o•gist** *n*

[1]**sock** *n* **:** short stocking

[2]**sock** *vb or n* **:** punch

**sock•et** *n* **:** hollow part that holds something

**so•da** *n* **1 :** carbonated water or a soft drink **2 :** ice cream drink made with soda

**so•fa** *n* **:** wide padded chair

**soft** *adj* **1 :** not hard, rough, or harsh **2 :** containing no alcohol — **soft•en** *vb* — **soft•en•er** *n* — **soft•ly** *adv* — **soft•ness** *n*

**soft•ball** *n* **:** game like baseball

**soft•ware** *n* **:** computer programs

**sog•gy** *adj* **:** heavy with moisture — **sog•gi•ness** *n*

[1]**soil** *vb* **:** make or become dirty ~ *n* **:** embedded dirt

[2]**soil** *n* **:** loose surface material of the earth

**so•lar** *adj* **:** relating to the sun or the energy in sunlight

**sold** *past of* SELL

**sol•dier** *n* **:** person in military service ~ *vb* **:** serve as a soldier — **sol•dier•ly** *adj or adv*

[1]**sole** *n* **:** bottom of the foot or a shoe — **soled** *adj*

[2]**sole** *adj* **:** single or only — **sole•ly** *adv*

**sol•emn** *adj* **1 :** dignified and ceremonial **2 :** highly serious — **so•lem•ni•ty** *n* — **sol•emn•ly** *adv*

**so•lic•it** *vb* **:** ask for — **so•lic•i•ta•tion** *n*

**so•lic•i•tor** *n* **1 :** one that solicits **2 :** lawyer

**sol•id** *adj* **1 :** not hollow **2 :** having 3 dimensions **3 :** hard **4 :** of good quality **5 :** of one character ~ *n* **1 :** 3-dimensional figure **2 :** substance in solid form — **solid** *adv* — **so•lid•i•ty** *n* — **sol•id•ly** *adv* — **sol•id•ness** *n*

**sol•i•dar•i•ty** *n* **:** unity of purpose

**sol•i•tary** *adj* **1 :** alone **2 :** isolated **3 :** single

**so•lo** *n* **:** performance by only one person ~ *adv* **:** alone — **solo** *adj or vb* — **so•lo•ist** *n*

**so•lu•tion** *n* **1 :** answer to a problem **2 :** homogeneous liquid mixture

**solve** *vb* **:** find a solution for — **solv•able** *adj*

**sol•vent** *adj* **1 :** able to pay all debts **2 :** dissolving or able to dissolve ~ *n* **:** substance that dissolves or disperses another substance — **sol•ven•cy** *n*

**some** *adj* **1 :** one unspecified **2 :** unspecified or indefinite number of **3 :** at least a few or a little ~ *pron* **:** a certain number or amount

**som•er•sault** *n* **:** body flip — **som•er•sault** *vb*

**some•what** *adv* **:** in some degree

**son** *n* **:** male offspring

**song** *n* **:** music and words to be sung

**son–in–law** *n* **sons–in–law :** husband of one's daughter

**soon** *adv* **1 :** before long **2 :** promptly **3 :** early

**soot** *n* **:** fine black substance formed by combustion — **sooty** *adj*

**soothe** *vb* **:** calm or comfort — **sooth•er** *n*

**so•phis•ti•cat•ed** *adj* **1 :** complex **2 :** wise, cultured, or shrewd in human affairs — **so•phis•ti•ca•tion** *n*

**soph•o•more** *n* **:** 2d-year student

**so•pra•no** *n* **:** highest singing voice

**sore** *adj* **1 :** causing pain or distress **2 :** severe or intense **3 :** angry ~ *n* **:** sore usu. infected spot on the body — **sore•ly** *adv* — **sore•ness** *n*

**sor•row** *n* **:** deep distress, sadness, or regret or a cause of this — **sor•row•ful** *adj* — **sor•row•ful•ly** *adv*

**sor•ry** *adj* **1 :** feeling sorrow, regret, or penitence **2 :** dismal

**sort** *n* **1 :** kind **2 :** nature ~ *vb* **:** classify — **out of sorts :** grouchy

**SOS** *n* **:** call for help

**so–so** *adj or adv* **:** barely acceptable

**sought** *past of* SEEK

**soul** *n* **1 :** immaterial essence of an individual life **2 :** essential part **3 :** person

**soul•ful** *adj* **:** full of or expressing deep feeling — **soul•ful•ly** *adv*

[1]**sound** *adj* **1 :** free from fault, error, or illness **2 :** firm or hard **3 :** showing good judgment — **sound•ly** *adv* — **sound•ness** *n*

[2]**sound** *n* **1 :** sensation of hearing **2 :** energy of vibration sensed in hearing **3 :** something heard ~ *vb* **1 :** make or cause to make a sound **2 :** seem — **sound•less** *adj* — **sound•less•ly** *adv* — **sound•proof** *adj or vb*

**soup** *n* **:** broth usu. containing pieces of solid food — **soupy** *adj*

**sour** *adj* **1 :** having an acid or tart taste **2 :** disagreeable ~ *vb* **:** become or make sour — **sour•ish** *adj* — **sour•ly** *adv* — **sour•ness** *n*

**source** *n* **1 :** point of origin **2 :** one that provides something needed

**souse** *vb* **1 :** pickle **2 :** immerse **3 :** intoxicate ~ *n* **1 :** something pickled **2 :** drunkard

**south** *adv* **:** to or toward the south ~ *adj* **:** situated toward, at, or coming from the south ~ *n* **1 :** direction to the right of sunrise **2** *cap* **:** regions to the south — **south•er•ly** *adv or adj* — **south•ern** *adj* — **South•ern•er** *n* — **south•ern•most** *adj* — **southward** *adv or adj* — **south•wards** *adv*

**south•east** *n* **1 :** direction between south and east **2** *cap* **:** regions to the southeast — **south•east** *adj or adv* — **south•east•er•ly** *adv or adj* — **south•east•ern** *adj*

**south pole** *n* : the southernmost point of the earth
**south•west** *n* **1** : direction between south and west **2** *cap* : regions to the southwest — **south•west** *adj or adv* — **south•west•er•ly** *adv or adj* — **south•west•ern** *adj*
**sou•ve•nir** *n* : something that is a reminder of a place or event
**sow** *vb* **1** : plant or strew with seed **2** : scatter abroad — **sow•er** *n*
**sox** *pl of* SOCK
**space** *n* **1** : period of time **2** : area in, around, or between **3** : region beyond earth's atmosphere **4** : accommodations ~ *vb* : place at intervals — **space•craft** *n* — **space•flight** *n* — **space•man** *n* — **space•ship** *n*
**spa•cious** *adj* : large or roomy — **spa•cious•ly** *adv* — **spa•cious•ness** *n*
[1]**spade** *n or vb* : shovel — **spade•ful** *n*
[2]**spade** *n* : playing card marked with a black figure like an inverted heart
**spa•ghet•ti** *n* : pasta strings
**spam** *n* : unsolicited commercial e-mail
**span** *n* **1** : amount of time **2** : distance between supports ~ *vb* : extend across
**spank** *vb* : hit on the buttocks with an open hand
**spare** *adj* **1** : held in reserve **2** : thin or scanty ~ *vb* **1** : reserve or avoid using **2** : avoid punishing or killing — **spare** *n*
**spark** *n* **1** : tiny hot and glowing particle **2** : smallest beginning or germ **3** : visible electrical discharge ~ *vb* **1** : emit or produce sparks **2** : stir to activity
**spar•kle** *vb* **1** : flash **2** : effervesce ~ *n* : gleam — **spark•ler** *n*
**sparse** *adj* : thinly scattered — **sparse•ly** *adv*
**spasm** *n* **1** : involuntary muscular contraction **2** : sudden, violent, and temporary effort or feeling — **spas•mod•ic** *adj* — **spas•mod•i•cal•ly** *adv*
**spa•tial** *adj* : relating to space — **spa•tial•ly** *adv*
**spat•ter** *vb* : splash with drops of liquid — **spat•ter** *n*
**spawn** *vb* **1** : produce eggs or offspring **2** : bring forth ~ *n* : egg cluster — **spawn•er** *n*
**speak** *vb* (**spoke; spo•ken**) **1** : utter words **2** : express orally **3** : address an audience **4** : use (a language) in talking — **speak•er** *n*
**spear** *n* : long pointed weapon ~ *vb* : strike or pierce with a spear
**spe•cial** *adj* **1** : unusual or unique **2** : particularly favored **3** : set aside for a particular use — **special** *n* — **spe•cial•ly** *adv*
**spe•cial•ist** *n* **1** : person who specializes in a particular branch of learning or activity **2** : any of four enlisted ranks in the army corresponding to the grades of corporal through sergeant first class
**spe•cial•ize** *vb* : concentrate one's efforts — **spe•cial•i•za•tion** *n*
**spe•cial•ty** *n* : area or field in which one specializes
**spe•cies** *n* : biological grouping of closely related organisms
**spe•cif•ic** *adj* : definite or exact — **spe•cif•i•cal•ly** *adv*
**spec•i•fy** *vb* : mention precisely or by name — **spec•i•fi•ca•tion** *n*
**spec•i•men** *n* : typical example
**speck** *n* : tiny particle or blemish — **speck** *vb*
**spec•ta•cle** *n* **1** : impressive public display **2** *pl* : eyeglasses
**spec•tac•u•lar** *adj* : sensational or showy
**spec•ta•tor** *n* : person who looks on
**spec•u•late** *vb* **1** : think about things yet unknown **2** : risk money in a business deal in hope of high profit — **spec•u•la•tion** *n* — **spec•u•la•tive** *adj* — **spec•u•la•tor** *n*
**speech** *n* **1** : power, act, or manner of speaking **2** : talk given to an audience — **speech•less** *adj*
**speed** *n* **1** : quality of being fast **2** : rate of motion or performance ~ *vb* **sped; sped:** go at a great or excessive rate of speed — **speed•boat** *n* — **speed•er** *n* — **speed•i•ly** *adv* — **speed•up** *n* — **speedy** *adj*
[1]**spell** *n* : influence of or like magic
[2]**spell** *vb* **1** : name, write, or print the letters of **2** : mean — **spell•er** *n*
**spend** *vb* (**spent; spent**) **1** : pay out **2** : cause or allow to pass — **spend•er** *n*
**sperm** *n* : semen or a germ cell in it
**sphere** *n* **1** : figure with every point on its surface at an equal distance from the center **2** : round body **3** : range of action or influence — **spher•i•cal** *adj*
**spice** *n* **1** : aromatic plant product for seasoning food **2** : interesting quality — **spice** *vb* — **spicy** *adj*
**spi•der** *n* : small insectlike animal with 8 legs — **spi•dery** *adj*
**spike** *n* : very large nail ~ *vb* : fasten or pierce with a spike — **spiked** *adj*
**spill** *vb* **1** : fall, flow, or run out unintentionally **2** : divulge ~ *n* **1** : act of spilling **2** : something spilled — **spill•able** *adj*
**spin** *vb* (**spun; spun**) **1** : draw out fiber and twist into thread **2** : form thread from a sticky body fluid **3** : revolve or cause to revolve extremely fast ~ *n* : rapid rotating motion — **spin•ner** *n*
**spin•ach** *n* : garden herb with edible leaves
**spine** *n* **1** : backbone **2** : stiff sharp projection on a plant or animal — **spine•less** *adj* — **spiny** *adj*
**spi•ral** *adj* : circling or winding around a single point or line — **spiral** *n or vb* — **spi•ral•ly** *adv*
**spire** *n* : usu. tapering church tower — **spiry** *adj*
**spir•it** *n* **1** : life-giving force **2** *cap* : presence of God **3** : ghost **4** : mood **5** : vivacity or enthusiasm **6** *pl* : alcoholic liquor ~ *vb* : carry off secretly — **spir•it•ed** *adj* — **spir•it•less** *adj*
**spir•i•tu•al** *adj* **1** : relating to the spirit or sacred matters **2** : deeply religious ~ *n* : religious folk song — **spir•i•tu•al•i•ty** *n* — **spir•i•tu•al•ly** *adv*
**spit** *vb* (**spit/spat; spit/spat**) : eject saliva from the mouth ~ *n* **1** : saliva **2** : perfect likeness
**spite** *n* : petty ill will ~ *vb* : annoy or offend — **spite•ful** *adj* — **spite•ful•ly** *adv* — **in spite of** : in defiance or contempt of
**splash** *vb* : scatter a liquid on — **splash** *n*
**splat•ter** *vb* : spatter — **splat•ter** *n*
**splen•did** *adj* **1** : impressive in beauty or brilliance **2** : outstanding — **splen•did•ly** *adv*
**splen•dor** *n* **1** : brilliance **2** : magnificence
**splice** *vb* : join (2 things) end to end — **splice** *n*
**splint** *n* **1** : thin strip of wood **2** : something that keeps an injured body part in place
**splin•ter** *n* : thin needlelike piece ~ *vb* : break into splinters
**split** *vb* **split; split** : divide lengthwise or along a grain — **split** *n*
**spoil** *n* : plunder ~ *vb* **1** : ruin **2** : rot **3** : pamper excessively — **spoil•age** *n* — **spoil•er** *n*
**spoke** *past of* SPEAK
**spo•ken** *past part of* SPEAK
**sponge** *n* **1** : porous water-absorbing mass that forms the skeleton of some marine animals **2** : spongelike material used for wiping ~ *vb* **1** : wipe with a sponge **2** : live at another's expense — **spongy** *adj*
**spon•sor** *n* : one who assumes responsibility for another or who provides financial support — **spon•sor** *vb* — **spon•sor•ship** *n*
**spon•ta•ne•ous** *adj* : done, produced, or occurring naturally or without planning — **spon•ta•ne•i•ty** *n* — **spon•ta•ne•ous•ly** *adv*
**spook** *n* : ghost ~ *vb* : frighten — **spooky** *adj*
**spool** *n* : cylinder on which something is wound
**spoon** *n* : utensil consisting of a small shallow bowl with a handle — **spoon** *vb* — **spoon•ful** *n*
**sport** *vb* **1** : frolic **2** : show off ~ *n* **1** : physical activity engaged in for pleasure **2** : jest **3** : person who shows good sportsmanship — **sport•ive** *adj* — **sporty** *adj*
**sports•man•ship** *n* : ability to be gracious in winning or losing
**spot** *n* **1** : blemish **2** : distinctive small part **3** : location ~ *vb* **1** : mark with spots **2** : see or recognize ~ *adj* : made at random or in limited numbers — **spot•less** *adj* — **spot•less•ly** *adv*
**spouse** *n* : one's husband or wife
**spout** *vb* **1** : shoot forth in a stream **2** : say pompously ~ *n* **1** : opening through which liquid spouts **2** : jet of liquid
**sprain** *n* : twisting injury to a joint ~ *vb* : injure with a sprain
**sprawl** *vb* : lie or sit with limbs spread out — **sprawl** *n*
**spray** *n* **1** : mist **2** : device that discharges liquid as a mist — **spray** *vb* — **spray•er** *n*
**spread** *vb* **1** : open up or unfold **2** : scatter or smear over a surface **3** : cause to be known or to exist over a wide area ~ *n* **1** : extent to which something is spread **2** : cloth cover **3** : something intended to be spread — **spread•er** *n*
**spring** *vb* **1** : move or grow quickly or by elastic force **2** : come from by descent **3** : make known suddenly ~ *n* **1** : source **2** : flow of water from underground **3** : season between winter and summer **4** : elastic body or device (as a coil of wire) **5** : leap **6** : elastic power — **springy** *adj*
**sprin•kle** *vb* : scatter in small drops or particles ~ *n* : light rainfall — **sprin•kler** *n*
**sprite** *n* : elf or elfish person
**sprout** *vb* : send out new growth ~ *n* : plant shoot
**spruce** *adj* : neat and stylish in appearance ~ *vb* : make or become neat
**spun** *past of* SPIN
**spur** *n* **1** : pointed device used to urge on a horse **2** : something that urges to action **3** : projecting part ~ *vb* : urge on — **spurred** *adj*
[1]**spurt** *n* : burst of effort, speed, or activity ~ *vb* : make a spurt
[2]**spurt** *vb* : gush out ~ *n* : sudden gush
**sput•ter** *vb* **1** : talk hastily and indistinctly in excitement **2** : make popping sounds — **sput•ter** *n*
**spy** *vb* : watch or try to gather information secretly — **spy** *n*
**squab•ble** *n or vb* : dispute
**squad** *n* : small group
**square** *n* **1** : instrument for measuring right angles **2** : flat figure that has 4 equal sides and 4 right angles **3** : open area in a city **4** : product of number multiplied by itself ~ *adj* **1** : being a square in form **2** : having sides meet at right angles **3** : multiplied by itself **4** : being a square unit of area **5** : honest ~ *vb* **1** : form into a square **2** : multiply (a number) by itself **3** : conform **4** : settle — **square•ly** *adv*
[1]**squash** *vb* **1** : press flat **2** : suppress
[2]**squash** *n* : garden vegetable
**squat** *vb* **1** : stoop or sit on one's heels **2** : settle on land one does not own ~ *n* : act or posture of squatting ~ *adj* : short and thick — **squat•ter** *n*
**squeak** *vb* : make a thin high-pitched sound — **squeak** *n* — **squeaky** *adj*
**squeal** *vb* **1** : make a shrill sound or cry **2** : protest — **squeal** *n*
**squeeze** *vb* **1** : apply pressure to **2** : extract by pressure — **squeeze** *n* — **squeez•er** *n*
**squint** *vb* : look with the eyes partly closed — **squint** *n or adj*
**squirm** *vb* : wriggle
**squir•rel** *n* : rodent with a long bushy tail
**squirt** *vb* : eject liquid in a spurt — **squirt** *n*
**stab** *n* **1** : wound made by a pointed weapon **2** : quick thrust **3** : attempt ~ *vb* : pierce or wound with or as if with a pointed weapon
[1]**sta•ble** *n* : building for domestic animals ~ *vb* : keep in a stable
[2]**stable** *adj* **1** : firmly established **2** : mentally and emotionally healthy **3** : steady — **sta•bil•i•ty** *n* — **sta•bil•iza•tion** *n* — **sta•bi•lize** *vb* — **sta•bi•liz•er** *n*
**stack** *n* : large pile ~ *vb* : pile up
**sta•di•um** *n* : outdoor sports arena
**staff** *n* **1** : rod or supporting cane **2** : people assisting a leader **3** : 5 horizontal lines on which music is written ~ *vb* : supply with workers — **staff•er** *n*
**stag** *n* : male deer ~ *adj* : only for men ~ *adv* : without a date
**stage** *n* **1** : raised platform for a speaker or performers **2** : theater **3** : step in a process ~ *vb* : produce (a play)
**stag•ger** *vb* **1** : reel or cause to reel from side to side **2** : overlap or alternate — **stagger** *n* — **stag•ger•ing•ly** *adv*
**stag•nant** *adj* : not moving or active — **stag•nate** *vb* — **stag•na•tion** *n*
**staid** *past of* STAY
**stain** *vb* **1** : discolor **2** : dye (as wood) **3** : disgrace ~ *n* **1** : discolored area **2** : mark of guilt **3** : coloring preparation — **stain•less** *adj*
**stair** *n* **1** : step in a series for going from one level to another **2** *pl* : flight of steps — **stair•way** *n* — **stair•case** *n*
**stake** *n* **1** : usu. small post driven into the ground **2** : bet **3** : prize in a contest ~ *vb* **1** : mark or secure with a stake **2** : bet
**stale** *adj* **1** : having lost good taste and quality from age **2** : no longer new, strong, or effective — **stale•ness** *n*
**stale•mate** *n* : deadlock — **stale•mate** *vb*
[1]**stalk** *vb* **1** : walk stiffly or proudly **2** : pursue stealthily
[2]**stalk** *n* : plant stem — **stalked** *adj*
[1]**stall** *n* **1** : compartment in a stable **2** : booth where articles are sold
[2]**stall** *vb* : bring or come to a standstill unintentionally
[3]**stall** *vb* : delay, evade, or keep a situation going to gain advantage or time
**stam•i•na** *n* : endurance
**stam•mer** *vb* : hesitate in speaking — **stammer** *n*
**stamp** *vb* **1** : pound with the sole of the foot or a heavy implement **2** : impress or imprint **3** : cut out with a die **4** : attach a postage stamp to ~ *n* **1** : device for stamping **2** : act of stamping **3** : government seal showing a tax or fee has been paid
**stance** *n* : way of standing
**stand** *vb* (**stood; stood**) **1** : be at rest in or assume an upright position **2** : remain unchanged **3** : be steadfast **4** : maintain a relative position or rank **5** : set upright **6** : undergo or endure ~ *n* **1** : act or place of standing, staying, or resisting **2** : sales booth **3** : structure for holding something upright **4** : group of plants growing together **5** *pl* : tiered seats **6** : opinion or viewpoint
**stan•dard** *n* **1** : symbolic figure or flag **2** : model, rule, or guide **3** : upright support — **stan•dard** *adj* — **stan•dard•i•za•tion** *n* — **stan•dard•ize** *vb*
**stank** *past of* STINK
[1]**sta•ple** *n* : U-shaped wire fastener — **staple** *vb* — **sta•pler** *n*
[2]**sta•ple** *n* : chief commodity or item — **staple** *adj*
**star** *n* **1** : celestial body visible as a point of light **2** : 5- or 6-pointed figure

representing a star **3** : leading performer ~ *vb* **1** : mark with a star **2** : play the leading role — **stardom** *n* — **star·less** *adj* — **star·light** *n* — **starry** *adj*

**starch** *n* : nourishing carbohydrate from plants also used in adhesives and laundering ~ *vb* : stiffen with starch — **starchy** *adj*

**stare** *vb* : look intently with wide-open eyes — **stare** *n* — **star·er** *n*

**start** *vb* **1** : twitch or jerk (as from surprise) **2** : perform or show performance of the first part of an action or process ~ *n* **1** : sudden involuntary motion **2** : beginning — **start·er** *n*

**star·tle** *vb* : frighten or surprise suddenly

**starve** *vb* **1** : suffer or die from hunger **2** : kill with hunger — **star·va·tion** *n*

**stash** *vb* : store in a secret place for future use — **stash** *n*

**state** *n* **1** : condition of being **2** : condition of mind **3** : nation or a political unit within it ~ *vb* **1** : express in words **2** : establish — **state·hood** *n* — **state·ment** *n*

**stat·ic** *adj* **1** : relating to bodies at rest or forces in equilibrium **2** : not moving **3** : relating to stationary charges of electricity ~ *n* : noise on radio or television from electrical disturbances

**sta·tion** *n* **1** : place of duty **2** : regular stop on a bus or train route **3** : social standing **4** : place where radio or television programs originate ~ *vb* : assign to a station

**sta·tion·ary** *adj* **1** : not moving or not movable **2** : not changing

**sta·tio·nery** *n* : letter paper with envelopes

**sta·tis·tics** *n pl* : numerical facts collected for study — **sta·tis·ti·cal** *adj* — **sta·tis·ti·cal·ly** *adv* — **stat·is·ti·cian** *n*

**stat·ue** *n* : solid 3-dimensional likeness — **stat·u·ette** *n*

**stat·ure** *n* **1** : height **2** : status gained by achievement

**sta·tus** *n* : relative situation or condition

**sta·tus quo** *n* : existing state of affairs

**stat·ute** *n* : law — **stat·u·to·ry** *adj*

[1]**stay** *n* : support ~ *vb* : prop up

[2]**stay** *vb* **1** : pause **2** : remain **3** : reside **4** : stop or postpone **5** : satisfy for a time ~ *n* : a staying

**stead·fast** *adj* : faithful or determined — **stead·fast·ly** *adv*

**steady** *adj* **1** : firm in position or sure in movement **2** : calm or reliable **3** : constant **4** : regular ~ *vb* : make or become steady — **steadi·ly** *adv* — **steadi·ness** *n* — **steady** *adv*

**steak** *n* : thick slice of meat

**steal** *vb* (**stole; sto·len**) **1** : take and carry away wrongfully and with intent to keep **2** : move secretly or slowly

**steam** *n* : vapor of boiling water ~ *vb* : give off steam — **steam·boat** *n* — **steam·ship** *n* — **steamy** *adj*

**steel** *n* : tough carbon-containing iron ~ *vb* : fill with courage — **steel** *adj* — **steely** *adj*

**steep** *adj* : having a very sharp slope or great elevation — **steep·ly** *adv* — **steep·ness** *n*

**steer** *vb* **1** : direct the course of (as a ship or car) **2** : guide

**stem** *n* : main upright part of a plant ~ *vb* **1** : derive **2** : make progress against — **stem·less** *adj* — **stemmed** *adj*

**stem cell** *n* : undifferentiated cell that may give rise to many different types of cells

**step** *n* **1** : single action of a leg in walking or running **2** : rest for the foot in going up or down **3** : degree, rank, or stage **4** : way of walking ~ *vb* **1** : move by steps **2** : press with the foot

**ste·reo·phon·ic** *adj* : relating to a 3-dimensional effect of reproduced sound — **ste·reo** *adj or n*

**ste·reo·type** *n* : gross often mistaken generalization — **stereotype** *vb* — **ste·reo·typ·i·cal** *adj* — **ste·reo·typi·cal·ly** *adv*

**ster·ile** *adj* **1** : unable to bear fruit, crops, or offspring **2** : free from disease germs — **ste·ril·i·ty** *n* — **ster·il·i·za·tion** *n* — **ster·il·ize** *vb* — **ster·il·iz·er** *n*

**stern** *adj* : severe — **stern·ly** *adv* — **stern·ness** *n*

**stew** *n* **1** : dish of boiled meat and vegetables **2** : state of worry or agitation — **stew** *vb*

**stew·ard** *n* **1** : manager of an estate or an organization **2** : person on a ship or airliner who looks after passenger comfort — **stew·ard·ship** *n*

**stew·ard·ess** *n* : woman who is a steward (as on an airplane)

[1]**stick** *n* **1** : cut or broken branch **2** : long thin piece of wood or something resembling it

[2]**stick** *vb* **stuck; stuck 1** : stab **2** : thrust or project **3** : hold fast to something **4** : attach **5** : become jammed or fixed

**stick·er** *n* : adhesive label

**sticky** *adj* **1** : adhesive or gluey **2** : muggy **3** : difficult

**stiff** *adj* **1** : not bending easily **2** : tense **3** : formal **4** : strong **5** : severe — **stiff·en** *vb* — **stiff·en·er** *n* — **stiff·ly** *adv* — **stiff·ness** *n*

**still** *adj* **1** : motionless **2** : silent ~ *vb* : make or become still ~ *adv* **1** : without motion **2** : up to and during this time **3** : in spite of that ~ *n* : silence — **still·ness** *n*

**stim·u·late** *vb* : make active — **stim·u·lant** *n or adj* — **stim·u·la·tion** *n*

**stim·u·lus** *n* : something that stimulates

**sting** *vb* (**stung; stung**) **1** : prick painfully **2** : cause to suffer acutely ~ *n* : act of stinging or a resulting wound — **sting·er** *n*

**stin·gy** *adj* : not generous — **stin·gi·ness** *n*

**stink** *vb* (**stank/stunk; stunk**) : have a strong offensive odor — **stink** *n* — **stink·er** *n*

**stip·u·late** *vb* : demand as a condition — **stip·u·la·tion** *n*

**stir** *vb* **1** : move slightly **2** : prod or push into activity **3** : mix by continued circular movement ~ *n* : act or result of stirring

**stitch** *n* **1** : loop formed by a needle in sewing **2** : sudden sharp pain ~ *vb* **1** : fasten or decorate with stitches **2** : sew

**stock** *n* **1** : block or part of wood **2** : original from which others derive **3** : farm animals **4** : supply of goods **5** : money invested in a large business **6** *pl* : instrument of punishment like a pillory with holes for the feet or feet and hands ~ *vb* : provide with stock

**stock·ing** *n* : close-fitting covering for the foot and leg

**stock·pile** *n* : reserve supply — **stock·pile** *vb*

**stole** *past of* STEAL

**stolen** *past part of* STEAL

**stom·ach** *n* **1** : saclike digestive organ **2** : abdomen **3** : appetite or desire ~ *vb* : put up with — **stom·ach·ache** *n*

**stomp** *vb* : stamp

**stone** *n* **1** : hardened earth or mineral matter **2** : small piece of rock **3** : seed that is hard or has a hard covering ~ *vb* : pelt or kill with stones — **stony** *adj*

**stood** *past of* STAND

**stool** *n* **1** : seat usu. without back or arms **2** : footstool **3** : discharge of feces

**stoop** *vb* **1** : bend over **2** : lower oneself ~ *n* **1** : act of bending over **2** : bent position of shoulders

**stop** *vb* **1** : block an opening **2** : end or cause to end **3** : pause for rest or a visit in a journey ~ *n* **1** : plug **2** : act or place of stopping **3** : delay in a journey — **stop·light** *n* — **stop·page** *n* — **stop·per** *n*

**stor·age** *n* : safekeeping of goods (as in a warehouse)

**store** *vb* : put aside for future use ~ *n* **1** : something stored **2** : retail business establishment — **store·house** *n* — **store·keep·er** *n* — **store·room** *n*

**storm** *n* **1** : heavy fall of rain or snow **2** : violent outbreak ~ *vb* **1** : rain or snow heavily **2** : rage **3** : make an attack against — **stormy** *adj*

[1]**sto·ry** *n* **1** : narrative **2** : report — **sto·ry·tell·er** *n*

[2]**story** *n* : floor of a building

**stove** *n* : apparatus for providing heat (as for cooking or heating)

**strad·dle** *vb* : stand over or sit on with legs on opposite sides — **strad·dle** *n*

**strag·gle** *vb* : wander or become separated from others — **strag·gler** *n*

**straight** *adj* **1** : having no bends, turns, or twists **2** : just, proper, or honest **3** : neat and orderly ~ *adv* : in a straight manner — **straight·en** *vb*

**straight·for·ward** *adj* : frank or honest

[1]**strain** *n* **1** : line of descent from common ancestors **2** : trace

[2]**strain** *vb* **1** : exert to the utmost **2** : filter or remove by filtering **3** : injure by improper use ~ *n* **1** : excessive tension or exertion **2** : bodily injury from excessive effort — **strain·er** *n*

**strait** *n* **1** : narrow channel connecting 2 bodies of water **2** *pl* : distress

[1]**strand** *vb* **1** : drive or cast upon the shore **2** : leave helpless

[2]**strand** *n* **1** : twisted fiber of a rope **2** : length of something ropelike

**strange** *adj* **1** : unusual or queer **2** : new — **strang·er** *n* — **strange·ly** *adv* — **strange·ness** *n*

**stran·gle** *vb* : choke to death — **stran·gler** *n* — **stran·gu·la·tion** *n*

**strap** *n* : narrow strip of flexible material used esp. for fastening ~ *vb* **1** : secure with a strap **2** : beat with a strap — **strap·less** *n*

**strat·e·gy** *n* : carefully worked out plan of action — **stra·te·gic** *adj* — **strat·e·gist** *n*

**straw** *n* **1** : grass stems after grain is removed **2** : tube for drinking ~ *adj* : made of straw

**straw·ber·ry** *n* : juicy red pulpy fruit

**stray** *vb* : wander or deviate ~ *n* : person or animal that strays ~ *adj* : separated from or not related to anything close by

**streak** *n* **1** : mark of a different color **2** : narrow band of light **3** : trace **4** : run (as of luck) or series ~ *vb* **1** : form streaks in or on **2** : move fast

**stream** *n* **1** : flow of water on land **2** : steady flow (as of water or air) ~ *vb* **1** : flow in a stream **2** : pour out streams

**stream·lined** *adj* **1** : made with contours to reduce air or water resistance **2** : simplified **3** : modernized — **stream·line** *vb*

**street** *n* : thoroughfare esp. in a city or town

**strength** *n* **1** : quality of being strong **2** : toughness **3** : intensity

**strength·en** *vb* : make, grow, or become stronger — **strength·en·er** *n*

**stress** *n* **1** : pressure or strain that tends to distort a body **2** : relative prominence given to one thing among others **3** : state of physical or mental tension or something inducing it ~ *vb* : put stress on — **stress·ful** *adj*

**stretch** *vb* **1** : spread or reach out **2** : draw out in length or breadth **3** : make taut **4** : exaggerate **5** : become extended without breaking ~ *n* : act of extending beyond normal limits

**stretch·er** *n* : device for carrying a sick or injured person

**strew** *vb* **1** : scatter **2** : cover by scattering something over

**strict** *adj* **1** : allowing no escape or evasion **2** : precise — **strict·ly** *adv* — **strict·ness** *n*

**stride** *vb* (**strode; strid·den**) : walk or run with long steps ~ *n* **1** : long step **2** : manner of striding

**strike** *vb* (**struck; struck**) **1** : hit sharply **2** : delete **3** : produce by impressing **4** : cause to sound **5** : afflict **6** : occur to or impress **7** : cause (a match) to ignite by rubbing **8** : refrain from working **9** : find **10** : take on (as a pose) ~ *n* **1** : act or instance of striking **2** : work stoppage **3** : military attack — **strik·er** *n* — **strike out** *vb* : start out vigorously — **strike up** *vb* : start

**string** *n* **1** : line usu. of twisted threads **2** : series **3** *pl* : stringed instruments ~ *vb* **strung; strung 1** : thread on or with a string **2** : hang or fasten by a string

**strin·gent** *adj* : severe

**stringy** *adj* : tough or fibrous

[1]**strip** *vb* **1** : take the covering or clothing from **2** : undress — **strip·per** *n*

[2]**strip** *n* : long narrow flat piece

**stripe** *n* : distinctive line or long narrow section ~ *vb* : make stripes on — **striped** *adj*

**strive** *vb* (**strove; stri·ven/strived**) **1** : struggle **2** : try hard

**strode** *past of* STRIDE

**stroke** *vb* : rub gently ~ *n* **1** : act of swinging or striking **2** : sudden action

**stroll** *vb* : walk leisurely — **stroll** *n* — **stroll·er** *n*

**strong** *adj* **1** : capable of exerting great force or of withstanding stress or violence **2** : healthy **3** : having intense feelings for a cause — **strong·ly** *adv*

**struck** *past of* STRIKE

**struc·ture** *n* **1** : building **2** : arrangement of elements ~ *vb* : make into a structure — **struc·tur·al** *adj*

**strug·gle** *vb* **1** : make strenuous efforts to overcome an adversary **2** : proceed with great effort ~ *n* **1** : strenuous effort **2** : intense competition for superiority

**strung** *past of* STRING

**strut** *vb* : walk in a proud or showy manner ~ *n* **1** : proud walk **2** : supporting bar or rod

**stub·born** *adj* **1** : determined not to yield **2** : hard to control — **stub·born·ly** *adv* — **stub·born·ness** *n*

**stuck** *past of* STICK

**stuck–up** *adj* : conceited

[1]**stud** *n* : male horse kept for breeding

[2]**stud** *n* **1** : upright beam for holding wall material **2** : projecting nail, pin, or rod ~ *vb* : supply or dot with studs

**stu·dent** *n* : one who studies

**stu·dio** *n* **1** : artist's workroom **2** : place where movies are made or television or radio shows are broadcast

**stu·di·ous** *adj* : devoted to study — **stu·di·ous·ly** *adv*

**study** *n* **1** : act or process of learning about something **2** : branch of learning **3** : careful examination **4** : room for reading or studying ~ *vb* : apply the attention and mind to a subject

**stuff** *n* **1** : personal property **2** : raw or fundamental material **3** : unspecified material or things ~ *vb* : fill by packing things in — **stuff·ing** *n*

**stuffy** *adj* **1** : lacking fresh air **2** : unimaginative or pompous

**stum·ble** *vb* **1** : lose one's balance or fall in walking or running **2** : speak or act clumsily **3** : happen by chance — **stum·ble** *n*

**stump** *n* : part left when something is cut off ~ *vb* : confuse — **stumpy** *adj*

**stun** *vb* **1** : make senseless or dizzy by or as if by a blow **2** : bewilder

**stung** *past of* STING

**stunk** *past of* STINK

**stun·ning** *adj* **1** : astonishing or incredible **2** : strikingly beautiful — **stun·ning·ly** *adv*

[1]**stunt** *vb* : hinder the normal growth or progress of

[2]**stunt** *n* : spectacular feat

**stu·pid** *adj* : not sensible or intelligent — **stu·pid·i·ty** *n* — **stu·pid·ly** *adv*

**stur·dy** *adj* : strong — **stur·di·ly** *adv* — **stur·di·ness** *n*

**stut·ter** *vb or n* : stammer

**sty** *n* : pig pen

**style** *n* **1 :** distinctive way of speaking, writing, or acting **2 :** elegant or fashionable way of living ~ *vb* **1 :** name **2 :** give a particular design or style to — **styl·ish** *adj* — **styl·ish·ly** *adv* — **styl·ish·ness** *n* — **styl·ist** *n* — **styl·ize** *vb*

[1]**sub** *n or vb* **:** substitute

[2]**sub** *n* **:** submarine

**sub·con·scious** *adj* **:** existing without conscious awareness ~ *n* **:** part of the mind concerned with subconscious activities — **sub·con·scious·ly** *adv*

**sub·due** *vb* **1 :** bring under control **2 :** reduce the intensity of

**sub·ject** *n* **1 :** person under the authority of another **2 :** something being discussed or studied **3 :** word or word group about which something is said in a sentence ~ *adj* **1 :** being under one's authority **2 :** prone **3 :** dependent on some condition or act ~ *vb* **1 :** bring under control **2 :** cause to undergo — **sub·jec·tion** *n*

**sub·jec·tive** *adj* **:** deriving from an individual viewpoint or bias — **sub·jec·tive·ly** *adv* — **sub·jec·tiv·i·ty** *n*

**sub·ma·rine** *adj* **:** existing, acting, or growing under the sea ~ *n* **:** underwater boat

**sub·mit** *vb* **1 :** yield **2 :** give or offer — **sub·mis·sion** *n* — **sub·mis·sive** *adj*

**sub·or·di·nate** *adj* **:** lower in rank ~ *n* **:** one that is subordinate ~ *vb* **:** place in a lower rank or class — **sub·or·di·na·tion** *n*

**sub·scribe** *vb* **1 :** give consent or approval **2 :** agree to support or to receive and pay for — **sub·scrib·er** *n*

**sub·scrip·tion** *n* **:** order for regular receipt of a publication

**sub·se·quent** *adj* **:** following after — **sub·se·quent·ly** *adv*

**sub·sid·iary** *adj* **1 :** furnishing support **2 :** of secondary importance ~ *n* **:** company controlled by another company

**sub·si·dy** *n* **:** gift of supporting funds — **sub·si·dize** *vb*

**sub·stance** *n* **1 :** essence or essential part **2 :** physical material **3 :** wealth

**sub·stan·tial** *adj* **1 :** plentiful **2 :** considerable — **sub·stan·tial·ly** *adv*

**sub·stan·ti·ate** *vb* **:** verify — **sub·stan·ti·a·tion** *n*

**sub·sti·tute** *n* **:** replacement ~ *vb* **:** put or serve in place of another — **substitute** *adj* — **sub·sti·tu·tion** *n*

**sub·tle** *adj* **1 :** hardly noticeable **2 :** clever — **sub·tle·ty** *n* — **sub·tly** *adv*

**sub·tract** *vb* **:** take away (as one number from another) — **sub·trac·tion** *n*

**sub·urb** *n* **:** residential area adjacent to a city — **sub·ur·ban** *adj or n* — **sub·ur·ban·ite** *n*

**sub·way** *n* **:** underground electric railway

**suc·ceed** *vb* **1 :** follow (someone) in a job, role, or title **2 :** attain a desired object or end

**suc·cess** *n* **1 :** favorable outcome **2 :** gaining of wealth and fame **3 :** one that succeeds — **suc·cess·ful** *adj* — **suc·cess·ful·ly** *adv*

**suc·ces·sion** *n* **1 :** order, act, or right of succeeding **2 :** series

**such** *adj* **1 :** of this or that kind **2 :** having a specified quality — **such** *pron or adv*

**suck** *vb* **1 :** draw in liquid with the mouth **2 :** draw liquid from by or as if by mouth — **suck** *n* — **suc·tion** *n*

**sud·den** *adj* **1 :** happening unexpectedly **2 :** steep **3 :** hasty — **sud·den·ly** *adv* — **sud·den·ness** *n*

**suds** *n pl* **:** soapy water esp. when frothy — **sudsy** *adj*

**sue** *vb* **1 :** petition **2 :** bring legal action against

**suf·fer** *vb* **1 :** experience pain, loss, or hardship **2 :** permit — **suf·fer·er** *n*

**suf·fer·ing** *n* **:** pain or hardship

**suf·fi·cient** *adj* **:** adequate — **suf·fi·cien·cy** *n* — **suf·ficient·ly** *adv*

**suf·fix** *n* **:** letters added at the end of a word — **suffix** *vb* — **suf·fix·a·tion** *n*

**suf·fo·cate** *vb* **:** suffer or die or cause to die from lack of air — **suf·fo·cat·ing·ly** *adv* — **suf·fo·ca·tion** *n*

**sug·ar** *n* **:** sweet substance ~ *vb* **:** mix, cover, or sprinkle with sugar — **sug·ar·cane** *n* — **sug·ary** *adj*

**sug·gest** *vb* **1 :** put into someone's mind **2 :** remind one by association of ideas — **sug·gest·ible** *adj* — **sug·ges·tion** *n* — **sug·ges·tive** *adj* — **sug·ges·tive·ly** *adv* — **sug·ges·tive·ness** *n*

**sui·cide** *n* **1 :** act of killing oneself purposely **2 :** one who commits suicide — **sui·cid·al** *adj*

**suit** *n* **1 :** action in court to recover a right or claim **2 :** number of things used or worn together **3 :** one of the 4 sets of playing cards ~ *vb* **1 :** be appropriate or becoming to **2 :** meet the needs of — **suit·abil·i·ty** *n* — **suit·able** *adj* — **suit·ably** *adv*

**suite** *n* **1 :** group of rooms **2 :** set of matched furniture

**sul·len** *adj* **1 :** gloomily silent **2 :** dismal — **sul·len·ly** *adv* — **sul·len·ness** *n*

**sum** *n* **1 :** amount **2 :** gist **3 :** result of addition ~ *vb* **:** find the sum of

**sum·ma·ry** *adj* **1 :** concise **2 :** done without delay or formality ~ *n* **:** concise statement — **sum·mar·i·ly** *adv* — **sum·ma·rize** *vb* — **sum·ma·tion** *n*

**sum·mer** *n* **:** season in which the sun shines most directly — **sum·mery** *adj*

**sum·mon** *vb* **1 :** send for or call together **2 :** order to appear in court — **sum·mon·er** *n*

**sun** *n* **1 :** shining celestial body around which the planets revolve **2 :** light of the sun ~ *vb* **:** expose to the sun — **sun·beam** *n* — **sun·block** *n* — **sun·burn** *n or vb* — **sun·glass·es** *n pl* — **sun·light** *n* — **sun·ny** *adj* — **sun·rise** *n* — **sun·set** *n* — **sun·shine** *n* — **sun·tan** *n*

**Sun·day** *n* **:** 1st day of the week

**sung** *past of* SING

**sunk** *past of* SINK

**super** *adj* **:** very fine

**su·perb** *adj* **:** outstanding — **su·perb·ly** *adv*

**su·per·fi·cial** *adj* **:** relating to what is only apparent — **su·per·fi·ci·al·i·ty** *n* — **su·per·fi·cial·ly** *adv*

**su·per·in·tend** *vb* **:** have charge and oversight of — **su·per·in·ten·dence** *n* — **su·per·in·ten·den·cy** *n* — **su·per·in·ten·dent** *n*

**su·pe·ri·or** *adj* **1 :** higher, better, or more important **2 :** haughty — **superior** *n* — **su·pe·ri·or·i·ty** *n*

**su·per·la·tive** *adj* **1 :** relating to or being an adjective or adverb form that denotes an extreme level **2 :** surpassing others — **superlative** *n* — **su·per·la·tive·ly** *adv*

**su·per·nat·u·ral** *adj* **:** beyond the observable physical world — **su·per·nat·u·ral·ly** *adv*

**su·per·pow·er** *n* **:** politically and militarily dominant nation

**su·per·sede** *vb* **:** take the place of

**su·per·sti·tion** *n* **:** beliefs based on ignorance, fear of the unknown, or trust in magic — **su·per·sti·tious** *adj*

**su·per·vise** *vb* **:** have charge of — **su·per·vi·sion** *n* — **su·per·vi·sor** *n* — **su·per·vi·so·ry** *adj*

**sup·per** *n* **:** evening meal

**sup·ple·ment** *n* **:** something that adds to or makes up for a lack — **supplement** *vb* — **sup·ple·men·tal** *adj* — **sup·ple·men·ta·ry** *adj*

**sup·ply** *vb* **:** furnish ~ *n* **1 :** amount needed or available **2** *pl* **:** provisions — **sup·pli·er** *n*

**sup·port** *vb* **1 :** take sides with **2 :** provide with food, clothing, and shelter **3 :** hold up or serve as a foundation for — **support** *n* — **sup·port·able** *adj* — **sup·port·er** *n*

**sup·pose** *vb* **1 :** assume to be true **2 :** expect **3 :** think probable — **sup·po·si·tion** *n*

**sup·press** *vb* **1 :** put an end to by authority **2 :** keep from being known **3 :** hold back — **sup·pres·sant** *n* — **sup·pres·sion** *n*

**su·preme** *adj* **1 :** highest in rank or authority **2 :** greatest possible — **su·preme·ly** *adv*

**Supreme Being** *n* **:** God

**sur·charge** *n* **1 :** excessive load or burden **2 :** extra fee or cost

**sure** *adj* **1 :** confident **2 :** reliable **3 :** not to be disputed **4 :** bound to happen ~ *adv* **:** surely — **sure·ness** *n*

**sure·ly** *adv* **1 :** in a sure manner **2 :** without doubt **3 :** indeed

**surf** *n* **:** waves that break on the shore ~ *vb* **:** ride the surf — **surf·board** *n* — **surf·er** *n* — **surf·ing** *n*

**sur·face** *n* **1 :** the outside of an object **2 :** outward aspect ~ *vb* **:** rise to the surface

**sur·geon** *n* **:** physician who specializes in surgery

**sur·gery** *n* **:** medical treatment involving cutting open the body

**sur·gi·cal** *adj* **:** relating to surgeons or surgery — **sur·gi·cal·ly** *adv*

**sur·name** *n* **:** family name

**sur·pass** *vb* **:** go beyond or exceed — **sur·pass·ing·ly** *adv*

**sur·plus** *n* **:** quantity left over

**sur·prise** *vb* **1 :** come upon or affect unexpectedly **2 :** amaze — **surprise** *n* — **sur·pris·ing** *adj* — **sur·pris·ing·ly** *adv*

**sur·ren·der** *vb* **:** give up oneself or a possession to another ~ *n* **:** act of surrendering

**sur·round** *vb* **:** enclose on all sides

**sur·round·ings** *n pl* **:** objects, conditions, or area around something

**sur·veil·lance** *n* **:** careful watch

**sur·vey** *vb* **1 :** look over and examine closely **2 :** make a survey of (as a tract of land) ~ *n* **1 :** inspection **2 :** process of measuring (as land) — **sur·vey·or** *n*

**sur·vive** *vb* **1 :** remain alive or in existence **2 :** outlive or outlast — **sur·viv·al** *n* — **sur·vi·vor** *n*

**sus·pect** *adj* **1 :** regarded with suspicion **2 :** questionable ~ *n* **:** one who is suspected (as of a crime) ~ *vb* **1 :** have doubts of **2 :** believe guilty without proof **3 :** guess

**sus·pend** *vb* **1 :** temporarily stop or keep from a function or job **2 :** withhold (judgment) temporarily **3 :** hang

**sus·pense** *n* **:** excitement and uncertainty as to outcome — **sus·pense·ful** *adj*

**sus·pen·sion** *n* **:** act of suspending or the state or period of being suspended

**sus·pi·cion** *n* **1 :** act of suspecting something **2 :** trace

**sus·pi·cious** *adj* **1 :** arousing suspicion **2 :** inclined to suspect — **sus·pi·cious·ly** *adv*

**sus·tain** *vb* **1 :** provide with nourishment **2 :** keep going **3 :** hold up **4 :** suffer **5 :** support or prove

**swag·ger** *vb* **1 :** walk with a conceited swing **2 :** boast — **swag·ger** *n*

[1]**swal·low** *n* **:** small migratory bird

[2]**swal·low** *vb* **1 :** take into the stomach through the throat **2 :** envelop or take in **3 :** accept too easily — **swal·low** *n*

**swam** *past of* SWIM

**swamp** *n* **:** wet spongy land ~ *vb* **:** deluge (as with water) — **swampy** *adj*

**swan** *n* **:** white long-necked swimming bird

**swap** *vb* **:** trade — **swap** *n*

**swat** *vb* **:** hit sharply — **swat** *n* — **swat·ter** *n*

**sway** *vb* **1 :** swing gently from side to side **2 :** influence ~ *n* **1 :** gentle swinging from side to side **2 :** controlling power or influence

**swear** *vb* (**swore; sworn**) **1 :** make or cause to make a solemn statement under oath **2 :** use profane language — **swear·er** *n* — **swear·ing** *n*

**sweat** *vb* **1 :** excrete salty moisture from skin glands **2 :** form drops of moisture on the surface **3 :** work or cause to work hard — **sweat** *n* — **sweaty** *adj*

**sweat·er** *n* **:** knitted jacket or pullover

**sweat·shirt** *n* **:** loose collarless heavy cotton jersey pullover

**sweep** *vb* (**swept; swept**) **1 :** remove or clean by a brush or a single forceful wipe (as of the hand) **2 :** move over with speed and force (as of the hand) **3 :** move or extend in a wide curve ~ *n* **1 :** a clearing off or away **2 :** single forceful wipe or swinging movement **3 :** scope — **sweep·er** *n* — **sweep·ing** *adj*

**sweet** *adj* **1 :** being or causing the pleasing taste typical of sugar **2 :** not stale or spoiled **3 :** not salted **4 :** pleasant **5 :** much loved ~ *n* **:** something sweet — **sweet·en** *vb* — **sweet·ly** *adv* — **sweet·ness** *n* — **sweet·en·er** *n*

**sweet·heart** *n* **:** person one loves

**swell** *vb* (**swelled; swelled/swol·len**) **1 :** enlarge **2 :** bulge **3 :** fill or be filled with emotion ~ *n* **1 :** long rolling ocean wave **2 :** condition of bulging — **swell·ing** *n*

**swept** *past of* SWEEP

**swerve** *vb* **:** move abruptly aside from a course — **swerve** *n*

**swift** *adj* **1 :** moving with great speed **2 :** occurring suddenly — **swift·ly** *adv* — **swift·ness** *n*

**swim** *vb* (**swam; swum**) **1 :** propel oneself in water **2 :** float in or be surrounded with a liquid **3 :** be dizzy ~ *n* **:** act or period of swimming — **swim·mer** *n*

**swin·dle** *vb* **:** cheat (someone) of money or property — **swindle** *n* — **swin·dler** *n*

**swine** *n* (**swine**) **:** short-legged hoofed mammal with a snout — **swin·ish** *adj*

**swing** *vb* (**swung; swung**) **1 :** move or cause to move rapidly in an arc **2 :** sway or cause to sway back and forth **3 :** hang so as to sway or sag **4 :** turn on a hinge or pivot **5 :** manage or handle successfully ~ *n* **1 :** act or instance of swinging **2 :** swinging movement (as in trying to hit something) **3 :** suspended seat for swinging — **swing** *adj* — **swing·er** *n*

**swipe** *n* **:** strong sweeping blow ~ *vb* **1 :** strike or wipe with a sweeping motion **2 :** steal esp. with a quick movement

**swirl** *vb* **:** move or cause to move in a circle — **swirl** *n*

**switch** *n* **1 :** slender flexible whip or twig **2 :** blow with a switch **3 :** shift, change, or reversal **4 :** device that opens or closes an electrical circuit ~ *vb* **1 :** punish or urge on with a switch **2 :** change or reverse roles, positions, or subjects **3 :** operate a switch of

**switch·board** *n* **:** panel of switches to make and break telephone connections

**swiv·el** *vb* **:** swing or turn on a pivot — **swivel** *n*

**swollen** *past part of* SWELL

**swoop** *vb* **:** make a swift diving attack — **swoop** *n*

**sword** *n* **:** thrusting or cutting weapon with a long blade

**swore** *past of* SWEAR

**sworn** *past part of* SWEAR

**swum** *past part of* SWIM

**swung** *past of* SWING

**syl·la·ble** *n* **:** unit of a spoken word — **syl·lab·ic** *adj*

**sym·bol** *n* **:** something that represents or suggests another thing — **sym·bol·ic** *adj* — **sym·bol·i·cal·ly** *adv* — **sym·bol·ism** *n* — **sym·bol·ize** *vb*

**sym·me·try** *n* **:** regularity and balance in the arrangement of parts — **sym·met·ri·cal** *adj* — **sym·met·ri·cal·ly** *adv*

**sym·pa·thy** *n* **1 :** ability to understand or share the feelings of another **2 :** expression of sorrow for another's misfortune — **sym·pa·thet·ic** *adj* — **sym·pa·thet·i·cal·ly** *adv* — **sym·pa·thize** *vb*

**sym·pho·ny** *n* **:** composition for an

orchestra or the orchestra itself — sym•phon•ic *adj*

**symp•tom** *n* : unusual feeling or reaction that is a sign of disease — symp•tom•at•ic *adj*

**syn•a•gogue, syn•a•gog** *n* : Jewish house of worship

**syn•chro•nize** *vb* **1** : occur or cause to occur at the same instant **2** : cause to agree in time — syn•chro•ni•za•tion *n*

**syn•drome** *n* : particular group of symptoms

**syn•onym** *n* : word with the same meaning as another — syn•on•y•mous *adj* — syn•on•y•my *n*

**syn•the•sis** *n* : combination of parts or elements into a whole — syn•the•size *vb*

**syn•thet•ic** *adj* : artificially made — synthetic *n* — syn•thet•i•cal•ly *adv*

**syr•up** *n* : thick sticky sweet liquid — syr•upy *adj*

**sys•tem** *n* **1** : arrangement of units that function together **2** : regular order — sys•tem•at•ic *adj* — sys•tem•at•i•cal•ly *adv* — sys•tem•a•tize *vb* — sys•tem•ic *adj*

# T

**t** *n* : 20th letter of the alphabet

**tab•by** *n* : domestic cat

**ta•ble** *n* **1** : piece of furniture having a smooth slab fixed on legs **2** : supply of food **3** : arrangement of data in columns **4** : short list — ta•ble•cloth *n* — ta•ble•top *n* — ta•ble•ware *n* — tab•u•lar *adj*

**ta•ble•spoon** *n* **1** : large serving spoon **2** : measuring spoon holding ½ fluid ounce — ta•ble•spoon•ful *n*

**tab•let** *n* **1** : flat slab suited for an inscription **2** : collection of sheets of paper glued together at one edge **3** : disk-shaped pill

**tab•loid** *n* : newspaper of small page size

**tack** *n* **1** : small sharp nail **2** : course of action ~ *vb* **1** : fasten with tacks **2** : add on

**tack•le** *n* **1** : equipment **2** : arrangement of ropes and pulleys **3** : act of tackling ~ *vb* **1** : seize or throw down **2** : start dealing with

**tacky** *adj* : cheap or gaudy

**tact** *n* : sense of the proper thing to say or do — tact•ful *adj* — tact•ful•ly *adv* — tact•less *adj* — tact•less•ly *adv*

**tac•tic** *n* : action as part of a plan

**taf•fy** *n* : candy stretched until porous

**[1]tag** *n* : piece of hanging or attached material ~ *vb* **1** : provide or mark with a tag **2** : follow closely

**[2]tag** *n* : children's game of trying to catch one another ~ *vb* : touch a person in tag

**tail** *n* **1** : rear end or a growth extending from the rear end of an animal **2** : back or last part **3** : the reverse of a coin ~ *vb* : follow — tailed *adj* — tail•less *adj* — tail•light *n*

**tai•lor** *n* : one who makes or alters garments ~ *vb* **1** : fashion or alter (clothes) **2** : make or adapt for a special purpose

**take** *vb* (**took; tak•en**) **1** : get into one's possession **2** : become affected by **3** : receive into one's body (as by eating) **4** : pick out or remove **5** : use for transportation **6** : need or make use of **7** : lead, carry, or cause to go to another place **8** : undertake and do, make, or perform ~ *n* : amount taken — take•over *n* — tak•er *n* — take advantage of : profit by — take exception : object — take off *vb* **1** : remove **2** : go away **3** : mimic **4** : begin flight — take over *vb* : assume control or possession of or responsibility for — take place : happen

**tale** *n* **1** : story or anecdote **2** : falsehood

**tal•ent** *n* : natural mental or creative ability — tal•ent•ed *adj*

**talk** *vb* **1** : express one's thoughts in speech **2** : discuss **3** : influence to a position or course of action by talking ~ *n* **1** : act of talking **2** : formal discussion **3** : rumor **4** : informal lecture — talk•a•tive *adj* — talk•er *n*

**tall** *adj* : extending to a great or specified height — tall•ness *n*

**tame** *adj* **1** : changed from being wild to being controllable by man **2** : docile **3** : dull ~ *vb* : make or become tame — tam•able, tame•able *adj* — tame•ly *adv* — tam•er *n*

**tan** *vb* **1** : change (hide) into leather esp. by soaking in a liquid containing tannin **2** : make or become brown (as by exposure to the sun) ~ *n* **1** : brown skin color induced by the sun **2** : light yellowish brown — tan•ner *n* — tan•nery *n*

**tan•gi•ble** *adj* **1** : able to be touched **2** : substantially real — tan•gi•bly *adv*

**tan•gle** *vb* : unite in intricate confusion ~ *n* : tangled twisted mass

**tank** *n* **1** : large artificial receptacle for liquids **2** : armored military vehicle — tank•ful *n*

**tank•er** *n* : vehicle or vessel with tanks for transporting a liquid

**[1]tap** *n* **1** : faucet **2** : act of tapping ~ *vb* **1** : pierce so as to draw off fluid **2** : connect into — tap•per *n*

**[2]tap** *vb* : rap lightly ~ *n* : light stroke or its sound

**tape** *n* **1** : narrow flexible strip (as of cloth, plastic, or metal) **2** : tape measure ~ *vb* **1** : fasten with tape **2** : record on tape

**ta•per** *n* **1** : slender wax candle **2** : gradual lessening of width in a long object ~ *vb* **1** : make or become smaller toward one end **2** : diminish gradually

**tar** *n* : thick dark sticky liquid distilled (as from coal) ~ *vb* : treat or smear with tar

**tar•dy** *adj* : late — tar•di•ly *adv* — tar•di•ness *n*

**tar•get** *n* **1** : mark to shoot at **2** : goal to be achieved ~ *vb* **1** : make a target of **2** : establish as a goal

**tar•iff** *n* **1** : duty or rate of duty imposed on imported goods **2** : schedule of tariffs, rates, or charges

**[1]tart** *adj* **1** : pleasantly sharp to the taste **2** : caustic — tart•ly *adv* — tart•ness *n*

**[2]tart** *n* : small pie

**task** *n* : assigned work

**taste** *vb* **1** : test or determine the flavor of **2** : eat or drink in small quantities **3** : have a specific flavor ~ *n* **1** : small amount tasted **2** : bit **3** : special sense that identifies sweet, sour, bitter, or salty qualities **4** : individual preference **5** : critical appreciation of quality — taste•ful *adj* — taste•ful•ly *adv* — taste•less *adj* — taste•less•ly *adv* — tast•er *n*

**tasty** *adj* : pleasing to the sense of taste — tast•i•ness *n*

**tat•tle•tale** *n* : one that tattles

**taught** *past of* TEACH

**taunt** *n* : hurtful challenge or insult — taunt *vb* — taunt•er *n*

**taut** *adj* : tightly drawn — taut•ly *adv* — taut•ness *n*

**tax** *vb* **1** : impose a tax on **2** : charge **3** : put under stress ~ *n* **1** : charge by authority for public purposes **2** : strain — tax•able *adj* — tax•a•tion *n* — tax•pay•er *n* — tax•pay•ing *adj*

**taxi** *n* : automobile transporting passengers for a fare ~ *vb* **1** : transport or go by taxi **2** : move along the ground before takeoff or after landing

**tea** *n* : cured leaves of an Asian shrub or a drink made from these — tea•cup *n* — tea•ket•tle *n* — tea•pot *n*

**teach** *vb* (**taught; taught**) **1** : tell or show the fundamentals or skills of something **2** : cause to know the consequences **3** : impart knowledge of — teach•able *adj* — teach•er *n* — teach•ing *n*

**team** *n* **1** : draft animals harnessed together **2** : number of people organized for a game or work ~ *vb* : form or work together as a team — team *adj* — team•mate *n* — team•work *n*

**[1]tear** *n* : drop of salty liquid that moistens the eye — tear•ful *adj* — tear•ful•ly *adv*

**[2]tear** *vb* (**tore; torn**) **1** : separate or pull apart by force **2** : move or act with violence or haste ~ *n* : act or result of tearing

**tease** *vb* : annoy by goading, coaxing, or tantalizing ~ *n* **1** : act of teasing or state of being teased **2** : one that teases

**tea•spoon** *n* **1** : small spoon for stirring or sipping **2** : measuring spoon holding ⅙ fluid ounce — tea•spoon•ful *n*

**tech•ni•cal** *adj* **1** : having or relating to special mechanical or scientific knowledge **2** : by strict interpretation of rules — tech•ni•cal•ly *adv*

**tech•ni•cal•i•ty** *n* : detail meaningful only to a specialist

**tech•nique** *n* : manner of accomplishing something

**tech•nol•o•gy** *n* : applied science — tech•no•log•i•cal *adj*

**te•dious** *adj* : wearisome from length or dullness — te•dious•ly *adv* — te•dious•ness *n*

**tee** *n* : mound or peg on which a golf ball is placed before beginning play — tee *vb*

**teen•age, teen•aged** *adj* : relating to people in their teens — teen•ag•er *n*

**teens** *n pl* : years 13 to 19 in a person's life

**tee•pee** *var of* TEPEE

**teeth** *pl of* TOOTH

**teethe** *vb* : grow teeth

**tele•cast** *vb* : broadcast by television — tele•cast *n* — tele•cast•er *n*

**tele•com•mu•ni•ca•tion** *n* : communication at a distance (as by radio or telephone)

**tele•phone** *n* : instrument or system for electrical transmission of spoken words ~ *vb* : communicate with by telephone — tele•phon•er *n*

**tele•scope** *n* : tube-shaped optical instrument for viewing distant objects ~ *vb* : slide or cause to slide inside another similar section — tele•scop•ic *adj*

**tele•vise** *vb* : broadcast by television

**tele•vi•sion** *n* : transmission and reproduction of images by radio waves

**tell** *vb* (**told; told**) **1** : count **2** : relate in detail **3** : reveal **4** : give information or an order to **5** : find out by observing

**tem•per** *vb* **1** : dilute or soften **2** : toughen ~ *n* **1** : characteristic attitude or feeling **2** : toughness **3** : disposition or control over one's emotions

**tem•per•a•ment** *n* : characteristic frame of mind — tem•per•a•men•tal *adj*

**tem•per•a•ture** *n* **1** : degree of hotness or coldness **2** : fever

**[1]tem•ple** *n* : place of worship

**[2]temple** *n* : flattened space on each side of the forehead

**tem•po•rary** *adj* : lasting for a short time only — tem•po•rar•i•ly *adv*

**tempt** *vb* **1** : coax or persuade to do wrong **2** : attract or provoke — tempt•er *n* — tempt•ing•ly *adv* — tempt•ress *n*

**temp•ta•tion** *n* **1** : act of tempting **2** : something that tempts

**ten** *n* **1** : one more than 9 **2** : 10th in a set or series **3** : thing having 10 units — ten *adj or pron* — tenth *adj or adv or n*

**ten•ant** *n* : one who occupies a rented dwelling — ten•an•cy *n*

**[1]tend** *vb* : take care of or supervise something

**[2]tend** *vb* **1** : move in a particular direction **2** : show a tendency

**ten•den•cy** *n* : likelihood to move, think, or act in a particular way

**[1]ten•der** *adj* **1** : soft or delicate **2** : expressing or responsive to love or sympathy **3** : sensitive (as to touch) — ten•der•ly *adv* — ten•der•ness *n*

**[2]ten•der** *n* **1** : offer of a bid for a contract **2** : something that may be offered in payment — tender *vb*

**ten•der•ize** *vb* : make (meat) tender — ten•der•iz•er *n*

**ten•nis** *n* : racket-and-ball game played across a net

**ten•or** *n* **1** : general drift or meaning **2** : highest natural adult male voice

**[1]tense** *n* : distinct verb form that indicates time

**[2]tense** *adj* **1** : stretched tight **2** : marked by nervous tension — tense *vb* — tense•ly *adv* — tense•ness *n* — ten•si•ty *n*

**ten•sion** *n* **1** : tense condition **2** : state of mental unrest or of potential hostility or opposition

**tent** *n* : collapsible shelter

**ten•ta•tive** *adj* : subject to change or discussion — ten•ta•tive•ly *adv*

**te•pee** *n* : conical tent

**term** *n* **1** : period of time **2** : mathematical expression **3** : special word or phrase **4** *pl* : conditions **5** *pl* : relations ~ *vb* : name

**ter•min•al** *n* **1** : end **2** : device for making an electrical connection **3** : station at end of a transportation line — ter•min•al *adj*

**ter•mi•nate** *vb* : bring or come to an end — ter•mi•na•ble *adj* — ter•mi•na•tion *n*

**ter•mi•nol•o•gy** *n* : terms used in a particular subject

**ter•race** *n* **1** : balcony or patio **2** : bank with a flat top ~ *vb* : landscape in a series of banks

**ter•ri•ble** *adj* **1** : exciting terror **2** : distressing **3** : intense **4** : of very poor quality — ter•ri•bly *adv*

**ter•rif•ic** *adj* **1** : exciting terror **2** : extraordinary

**ter•ri•fy** *vb* : fill with terror — ter•ri•fy•ing•ly *adv*

**ter•ri•to•ry** *n* : particular geographical region — ter•ri•to•ri•al *adj*

**ter•ror** *n* : intense fear and panic or a cause of it

**ter•ror•ize** *vb* **1** : fill with terror **2** : coerce by threat or violence — ter•ror•ism *n* — ter•ror•ist *adj or n*

**test** *n* : examination or evaluation ~ *vb* : examine by a test — test•er *n*

**tes•ti•fy** *vb* **1** : give testimony **2** : serve as evidence

**tes•ti•mo•ni•al** *n* **1** : favorable recommendation **2** : tribute — tes•ti•mo•ni•al *adj*

**tes•ti•mo•ny** *n* : statement given as evidence in court

**text** *n* **1** : author's words **2** : main body of printed or written matter on a page **3** : textbook **4** : scriptural passage used as the theme of a sermon **5** : topic — tex•tu•al *adj*

**text·book** *n* **:** book on a school subject

**tex·tile** *n* **:** fabric

**tex·ture** *n* **1 :** feel and appearance of something **2 :** structure

**than** *conj or prep* — used in comparisons

**thank** *vb* **:** express gratitude to — **thank·ful** *adj* — **thank·ful·ly** *adv* — **thank·ful·ness** *n* — **thank·less** *adj* — **thanks** *n pl*

**Thanks·giv·ing** *n* **:** fourth Thursday in November observed as a legal holiday for giving thanks for divine goodness

**that** *pron, pl* **1 :** something indicated or understood **2 :** the one farther away ~ *adj pl* **those :** being the one mentioned or understood or farther away ~ *conj or pron* — used to introduce a clause ~ *adv* **:** to such an extent

**the** *definite article* **:** that particular one ~ *adv* — used before a comparative or superlative

**the·ater, the·atre** *n* **1 :** building or room for viewing a play or movie **2 :** dramatic arts — **the·at·ri·cal** *adj*

**theft** *n* **:** act of stealing

**their** *adj* **:** relating to them

**theirs** *pron* **:** their one or ones

**them** *pron, objective case of* THEY

**theme** *n* **1 :** subject matter **2 :** essay **3 :** melody developed in a piece of music — **the·mat·ic** *adj*

**them·selves** *pron pl* **:** they, them — used reflexively or for emphasis

**then** *adv* **1 :** at that time **2 :** soon after that **3 :** in addition **4 :** in that case **5 :** consequently ~ *n* **:** that time ~ *adj* **:** existing at that time

**the·o·ry** *n* **1 :** general principles of a subject **2 :** plausible or scientifically acceptable explanation **3 :** judgment, guess, or opinion — **the·o·ret·i·cal** *adj* — **the·o·rize** *vb* — **the·o·rist** *n*

**ther·a·py** *n* **:** treatment for mental or physical disorder — **ther·a·peu·tic** *adj* — **ther·a·peu·ti·cal·ly** *adv* — **ther·a·pist** *n*

**there** *adv* **1 :** in, at, or to that place **2 :** in that respect ~ *pron* — used to introduce a sentence or clause ~ *n* **:** that place or point

**there·fore** *adv* **:** for that reason

**there·of** *adv* **1 :** of that or it **2 :** from that

**ther·mal** *adj* **:** relating to, caused by, or conserving heat — **ther·mal·ly** *adv*

**ther·mom·e·ter** *n* **:** instrument for measuring temperature — **ther·mo·met·ric** *adj*

**ther·mo·stat** *n* **:** automatic temperature control — **ther·mo·stat·ic** *adj* — **ther·mo·stat·i·cal·ly** *adv*

**these** *pl of* THIS

**the·sis** *n* **1 :** proposition to be argued for **2 :** essay embodying results of original research

**they** *pron* **1 :** those ones **2 :** people in general

**thick** *adj* **1 :** having relatively great mass from front to back or top to bottom **2 :** having a tendency to flow very slowly ~ *n* **:** most crowded or thickest part — **thick·en** *vb* — **thick·en·er** *n* — **thick·ly** *adv* — **thick·ness** *n*

**thief** *n* **:** one that steals

**thigh** *n* **:** upper part of the leg

**thin** *adj* **1 :** having relatively little mass from front to back or top to bottom **2 :** not closely set or placed **3 :** relatively free flowing **4 :** lacking substance, fullness, or strength ~ *vb* **:** make or become thin — **thin·ly** *adv* — **thin·ness** *n*

**thing** *n* **1 :** matter of concern **2 :** event or act **3 :** object **4** *pl* **:** possessions

**think** *vb* (**thought; thought**) **1 :** form or have in the mind **2 :** have as an opinion **3 :** ponder **4 :** devise by thinking **5 :** imagine — **think·er** *n*

**third** *adj* **:** being number 3 in a countable series ~ *n* **1 :** one that is third **2 :** one of 3 equal parts — **third, third·ly** *adv*

**thirst** *n* **1 :** dryness in mouth and throat **2 :** intense desire ~ *vb* **:** feel thirst — **thirsty** *adj*

**thir·teen** *n* **:** one more than 12 — **thir·teen** *adj or pron* — **thir·teenth** *adj or n*

**thir·ty** *n* **:** 3 times 10 — **thir·ti·eth** *adj or n* — **thirty** *adj or pron*

**this** *pron, pl* **:** something close or under immediate discussion ~ *adj pl* **these :** being the one near, present, just mentioned, or more immediately under observation ~ *adv* **:** to such an extent or degree

**thorn** *n* **:** sharp spike on a plant or a plant bearing these — **thorny** *adj*

**thor·ough** *adj* **:** omitting or overlooking nothing — **thor·ough·ly** *adv* — **thor·ough·ness** *n*

**thor·ough·fare** *n* **:** a main road or route for passage

**those** *pl of* THAT

**though** *adv* **:** however ~ *conj* **1 :** despite the fact that **2 :** granting that

**thought** *past of* THINK *n* **1 :** process of thinking **2 :** serious consideration **3 :** idea

**thought·ful** *adj* **1 :** absorbed in or showing thought **2 :** considerate of others — **thought·ful·ly** *adv* — **thought·ful·ness** *n*

**thought·less** *adj* **1 :** careless or reckless **2 :** lacking concern for others — **thought·less·ly** *adv*

**thou·sand** *n* **:** 10 times 100 — **thou·sand** *adj* — **thou·sandth** *adj or n*

**thread** *n* **1 :** fine line of fibers **2 :** train of thought **3 :** ridge around a screw ~ *vb* **1 :** pass thread through **2 :** put together on a thread **3 :** make one's way through or between

**threat** *n* **1 :** expression of intention to harm **2 :** thing that threatens

**threat·en** *vb* **1 :** utter threats **2 :** show signs of being near or impending — **threat·en·ing·ly** *adv*

**three** *n* **1 :** one more than 2 **2 :** 3d in a set or series — **three** *adj or pron*

**threw** *past of* THROW

**thrift** *n* **:** careful management or saving of money — **thrift·i·ly** *adv* — **thrifty** *adj*

**thrill** *vb* **1 :** have or cause to have a sudden sharp feeling of excitement **2 :** tremble — **thrill** *n* — **thrill·er** *n* — **thrill·ing·ly** *adv*

**thrive** *vb* **1 :** grow vigorously **2 :** prosper

**throat** *n* **1 :** front part of the neck **2 :** passage to the stomach — **throat·ed** *adj* — **throaty** *adj*

**throb** *vb* **:** pulsate — **throb** *n*

**throne** *n* **:** chair representing power or sovereignty

**throt·tle** *vb* **:** choke ~ *n* **:** valve regulating volume of fuel and air delivered to engine cylinders

**through** *prep* **1 :** into at one side and out at the other side of **2 :** by way of **3 :** among, between, or all around **4 :** because of **5 :** throughout the time of ~ *adv* **1 :** from one end or side to the other **2 :** from beginning to end **3 :** to the core **4 :** into the open ~ *adj* **1 :** going directly from origin to destination **2 :** finished

**through·out** *adv* **1 :** everywhere **2 :** from beginning to end ~ *prep* **1 :** in or to every part of **2 :** during the whole of

**throw** *vb* (**threw; thrown**) **1 :** propel through the air **2 :** cause to fall or fall off **3 :** put suddenly in a certain position or condition **4 :** move quickly as if throwing **5 :** put on or off hastily — **throw** *n* — **throw·er** *n* — **throw up** *vb* **:** vomit

**thrust** *vb* (**thrust; thrust**) **1 :** shove forward **2 :** stab or pierce — **thrust** *n*

**thumb** *n* **1 :** short thick division of the hand opposing the fingers **2 :** glove part for the thumb ~ *vb* **:** leaf through with the thumb — **thumb·nail** *n*

**thun·der** *n* **:** sound following lightning — **thunder** *vb* — **thun·der·clap** *n* — **thun·der·ous** *adj* — **thun·der·ous·ly** *adv*

**Thurs·day** *n* **:** 5th day of the week

**thus** *adv* **1 :** in this or that way **2 :** to this degree or extent **3 :** because of this or that

**[1]tick** *n* **:** small 8-legged blood-sucking animal

**[2]tick** *n* **1 :** light rhythmic tap or beat **2 :** check mark ~ *vb* **1 :** make ticks **2 :** mark with a tick **3 :** operate

**tick·et** *n* **1 :** tag showing price, payment of a fee or fare, or a traffic offense **2 :** list of candidates ~ *vb* **:** put a ticket on

**tick·le** *vb* **1 :** please or amuse **2 :** touch lightly causing uneasiness, laughter, or spasmodic movements — **tickle** *n*

**tick·lish** *adj* **1 :** sensitive to tickling **2 :** requiring delicate handling — **tick·lish·ness** *n*

**tide** *n* **:** alternate rising and falling of the sea ~ *vb* **:** be enough to allow (one) to get by for a time — **tid·al** *adj* — **tide·wa·ter** *n*

**ti·dy** *adj* **1 :** well ordered and cared for **2 :** large or substantial — **ti·di·ness** *n* — **ti·dy** *vb*

**tie** *n* **1 :** line or ribbon for fastening, uniting, or closing **2 :** cross support to which railroad rails are fastened **3 :** uniting force **4 :** equality in score or tally or a deadlocked contest **5 :** necktie ~ *vb* **1 :** fasten or close by wrapping and knotting a tie **2 :** form a knot in **3 :** gain the same score or tally as an opponent

**tier** *n* **:** one of a steplike series of rows

**ti·ger** *n* **:** very large black-striped cat — **ti·ger·ish** *adj* — **ti·gress** *n*

**tight** *adj* **1 :** fitting close together esp. so as not to allow air or water in **2 :** held very firmly **3 :** taut **4 :** fitting too snugly **5 :** difficult **6 :** stingy **7 :** evenly contested **8 :** low in supply — **tight** *adv* — **tight·en** *vb* — **tight·ly** *adv* — **tight·ness** *n*

**tights** *n pl* **:** skintight garments

**tile** *n* **:** thin piece of stone or fired clay used on roofs, floors, or walls ~ *vb* **:** cover with tiles

**[1]till** *prep or conj* **:** until

**[2]till** *vb* **:** cultivate (soil) — **till·able** *adj*

**tilt** *vb* **:** cause to incline ~ *n* **:** slant

**tim·ber** *n* **1 :** cut wood for building **2 :** large squared piece of wood **3 :** wooded land or trees for timber ~ *vb* **:** cover, frame, or support with timbers — **tim·bered** *adj* — **tim·ber·land** *n*

**time** *n* **1 :** period during which something exists or continues or can be accomplished **2 :** point at which something happens **3 :** customary hour **4 :** age **5 :** rate of speed **6 :** moment, hour, day, or year as indicated by a clock or calendar **7 :** one's experience during a particular period ~ *vb* **1 :** arrange or set the time of **2 :** determine or record the time, duration, or rate of — **time·keep·er** *n* — **time·less** *adj* — **time·less·ness** *n* — **time·li·ness** *n* — **time·ly** *adv* — **tim·er** *n*

**times** *prep* **:** multiplied by

**time·ta·ble** *n* **:** table of departure and arrival times

**tim·id** *adj* **:** lacking in courage or self-confidence — **ti·mid·i·ty** *n* — **tim·id·ly** *adv*

**tin** *n* **1 :** soft white metallic chemical element **2 :** metal food can

**tine** *n* **:** one of the points of a fork

**tin·gle** *vb* **:** feel a ringing, stinging, or thrilling sensation — **tingle** *n*

**tin·kle** *vb* **:** make or cause to make a high ringing sound — **tinkle** *n*

**tint** *n* **1 :** slight or pale coloration **2 :** color shade ~ *vb* **:** give a tint to

**ti·ny** *adj* **:** very small

**[1]tip** *vb* **1 :** overturn **2 :** lean ~ *n* **:** act or state of tipping

**[2]tip** *n* **:** pointed end of something ~ *vb* **1 :** furnish with a tip **2 :** cover the tip of

**[3]tip** *n* **:** small sum given for a service performed ~ *vb* **:** give a tip to

**[4]tip** *n* **:** piece of confidential information ~ *vb* **:** give confidential information to

**tip·toe** *n* **:** the toes of the feet ~ *adv or adj* **:** supported on tiptoe ~ *vb* **:** walk quietly or on tiptoe

**tip–top** *n* **:** highest point ~ *adj* **:** excellent

**[1]tire** *vb* **1 :** make or become weary **2 :** wear out the patience of — **tire·less** *adj* — **tire·less·ly** *adv* — **tire·some** *adj* — **tire·some·ly** *adv*

**[2]tire** *n* **:** rubber cushion encircling a car wheel

**tired** *adj* **:** weary

**tis·sue** *n* **1 :** soft absorbent paper **2 :** layer of cells forming a basic structural element of an animal or plant body

**ti·tle** *n* **1 :** legal ownership **2 :** distinguishing name **3 :** designation of honor, rank, or office **4 :** championship — **ti·tled** *adj*

**TNT** *n* **:** high explosive

**to** *prep* **1 :** in the direction of **2 :** at, on, or near **3 :** resulting in **4 :** before or until **5** — used to show a relationship or object of a verb **6** — used with an infinitive ~ *adv* **1 :** forward **2 :** to a state of consciousness

**toast** *vb* **1 :** make (as a slice of bread) crisp and brown **2 :** drink in honor of someone or something **3 :** warm ~ *n* **1 :** toasted sliced bread **2 :** act of drinking in honor of someone — **toast·er** *n*

**to·bac·co** *n* **:** broad-leaved herb or its leaves prepared for smoking or chewing

**to·day** *adv* **1 :** on or for this day **2 :** at the present time ~ *n* **:** present day or time

**to–do** *n* **:** disturbance or fuss

**toe** *n* **:** one of the 5 end divisions of the foot — **toe·nail** *n*

**tof·fee, tof·fy** *n* **:** candy made of boiled sugar and butter

**to·geth·er** *adv* **1 :** in or into one place or group **2 :** in or into contact or association **3 :** at one time **4 :** as a group — **to·geth·er·ness** *n*

**toil** *vb* **:** work hard and long — **toil** *n* — **toil·er** *n* — **toil·some** *adj*

**toi·let** *n* **1 :** dressing and grooming oneself **2 :** bathroom **3 :** water basin to urinate and defecate in

**to·ken** *n* **1 :** outward sign or expression of something **2 :** small part representing the whole **3 :** piece resembling a coin

**told** *past of* TELL

**tol·er·ance** *n* **1 :** lack of opposition for beliefs or practices differing from one's own **2 :** capacity for enduring **3 :** allowable deviation — **tol·er·ant** *adj* — **tol·er·ant·ly** *adv*

**tol·er·ate** *vb* **1 :** allow to be or to be done without opposition **2 :** endure or resist the action of — **tol·er·a·ble** *adj* — **tol·er·a·bly** *adv* — **tol·er·a·tion** *n*

**toll** *n* **1 :** fee paid for a privilege or service **2 :** cost of achievement in loss or suffering — **toll·booth** *n* — **toll·gate** *n*

**to·ma·to** *n* **:** tropical American herb or its fruit

**tomb** *n* **:** house, vault, or grave for burial — **tomb·stone** *n*

**tom·boy** *n* **:** girl who behaves in a manner usu. considered boyish

**to·mor·row** *adv* **:** on or for the day after today — **tomorrow** *n*

**ton** *n* **:** unit of weight equal to 2000 pounds

**tone** *n* **1 :** vocal or musical sound **2 :** sound of definite pitch **3 :** manner of speaking that expresses an emotion or attitude **4 :** color quality **5 :** healthy condition **6 :** general character or quality ~ *vb* **:** soften or muffle — often used with *down* — **ton·al** *adj* — **to·nal·i·ty** *n*

**tongue** *n* **1 :** fleshy movable organ of the mouth **2 :** language **3 :** something long and flat and fastened at one end — **tongued** *adj* — **tongue·less** *adj*

**to·night** *adv* **:** on this night ~ *n* **:** present or coming night

**too** *adv* **1 :** in addition **2 :** excessively

**took** *past of* TAKE

**tool** *n* : device worked by hand ~ *vb* : shape or finish with a tool

**tool•bar** *n* : strip of icons on a computer display providing quick access to pictured functions

**toot** *vb* : sound or cause to sound esp. in short blasts — **toot** *n*

**tooth** *n pl* **teeth 1 :** one of the hard structures in the jaws for chewing **2 :** one of the projections on the edge of a gear wheel — **tooth•ache** *n* — **tooth•brush** *n* — **toothed** *adj* — **tooth•less** *adj* — **tooth•paste** *n* — **tooth•pick** *n*

**[1]top** *n* **1 :** highest part or level of something **2 :** lid or covering ~ *vb* **1 :** cover with a top **2 :** surpass **3 :** go over the top of ~ *adj* : being at the top — **topped** *adj* — **top•most** *adj*

**[2]top** *n* : spinning toy

**top•ic** *n* : subject for discussion or study

**top•i•cal** *adj* **1 :** relating to or arranged by topics **2 :** relating to current or local events — **top•i•cal•ly** *adv*

**top•ple** *vb* : fall or cause to fall

**torch** *n* : flaming light — **torch•bear•er** *n* — **torch•light** *n*

**tore** *past of* TEAR

**tor•ment** *n* : extreme pain or anguish or a source of this ~ *vb* **1 :** cause severe anguish to **2 :** harass — **tor•men•tor** *n*

**torn** *past part of* TEAR

**tor•na•do** *n* : violent destructive whirling wind

**tor•ti•lla** *n* : round flat cornmeal or wheat flour bread

**tor•ture** *n* **1 :** use of pain to punish or force **2 :** agony ~ *vb* : inflict torture on — **tor•tur•er** *n*

**toss** *vb* **1 :** move to and fro or up and down violently **2 :** throw with a quick light motion **3 :** move restlessly — **toss** *n*

**toss–up** *n* **1 :** a deciding by flipping a coin **2 :** even chance

**to•tal** *n* : entire amount ~ *vb* **1 :** add up **2 :** amount to — **to•tal** *adj* — **to•tal•ly** *adv*

**to•tal•i•ty** *n* : whole amount or entirety

**tote** *vb* : carry

**touch** *vb* **1 :** make contact with so as to feel **2 :** be or cause to be in contact **3 :** take into the hands or mouth **4 :** treat or mention a subject **5 :** relate or concern **6 :** move to sympathetic feeling ~ *n* **1 :** light stroke **2 :** act or fact of touching or being touched **3 :** sense of feeling **4 :** trace **5 :** state of being in contact — **touch up** *vb* : improve with minor changes

**touch•down** *n* : scoring of 6 points in football

**touchy** *adj* **1 :** easily offended **2 :** requiring tact

**tough** *adj* **1 :** strong but elastic **2 :** not easily chewed **3 :** severe or disciplined **4 :** stubborn ~ *n* : rowdy — **tough•en** *vb* — **tough•ly** *adv* — **tough•ness** *n*

**tour** *n* **1 :** period of time spent at work or on an assignment **2 :** journey with a return to the starting point ~ *vb* : travel over to see the sights — **tour•ist** *n*

**tour•na•ment** *n* **1 :** medieval jousting competition **2 :** championship series of games

**tow** *vb* : pull along behind — **tow** *n*

**to•ward, to•wards** *prep* **1 :** in the direction of **2 :** with respect to **3 :** in part payment on

**tow•el** *n* : absorbent cloth or paper for wiping or drying

**tow•er** *n* : tall structure ~ *vb* : rise to a great height — **tow•ered** *adj* — **tow•er•ing** *adj*

**town** *n* **1 :** small residential area **2 :** city — **towns•peo•ple** *n pl*

**tox•ic** *adj* : poisonous — **tox•ic•i•ty** *n*

**tox•in** *n* : poison produced by an organism

**toy** *n* : something for a child to play with ~ *vb* : amuse oneself or play with something ~ *adj* **1 :** designed as a toy **2 :** very small

**trace** *vb* **1 :** mark over the lines of (a drawing) **2 :** follow the trail or the development of ~ *n* **1 :** track **2 :** tiny amount or residue — **trace•able** *adj* — **trac•er** *n*

**track** *n* **1 :** trail left by wheels or footprints **2 :** racing course **3 :** train rails **4 :** awareness of a progression **5 :** looped belts propelling a vehicle ~ *vb* **1 :** follow the trail of **2 :** make tracks on — **track•er** *n*

**track–and–field** *adj* : relating to athletic contests of running, jumping, and throwing events

**trac•tion** *n* : gripping power to permit movement — **trac•tion•al** *adj* — **trac•tive** *adj*

**trac•tor** *n* **1 :** farm vehicle used esp. for pulling **2 :** truck for hauling a trailer

**trade** *n* **1 :** one's regular business **2 :** occupation requiring skill **3 :** the buying and selling of goods **4 :** act of trading ~ *vb* **1 :** give in exchange for something **2 :** buy and sell goods **3 :** be a regular customer — **trades•peo•ple** *n pl*

**trade•mark** *n* : word or mark identifying a manufacturer — **trade•mark** *vb*

**tra•di•tion** *n* : belief or custom passed from generation to generation — **tra•di•tion•al** *adj* — **tra•di•tion•al•ly** *adv*

**traf•fic** *n* **1 :** business dealings **2 :** movement along a route ~ *vb* : do business — **traf•fick•er** *n* — **traffic light** *n*

**trag•e•dy** *n* **1 :** serious drama describing a conflict and having a sad end **2 :** disastrous event

**trag•ic** *adj* : being a tragedy — **trag•i•cal•ly** *adv*

**trail** *vb* **1 :** hang down and drag along the ground **2 :** draw along behind **3 :** follow the track of **4 :** dwindle ~ *n* **1 :** something that trails **2 :** path or evidence left by something

**trail•er** *n* **1 :** vehicle intended to be hauled **2 :** dwelling designed to be towed to a site

**train** *n* **1 :** trailing part of a gown **2 :** connected series **3 :** group of linked railroad cars ~ *vb* **1 :** cause to grow as desired **2 :** make or become prepared or skilled **3 :** point — **train•ee** *n* — **train•er** *n* — **train•load** *n*

**trai•tor** *n* : one who betrays a trust or commits treason — **trai•tor•ous** *adj*

**tramp** *vb* **1 :** walk or hike **2 :** tread on ~ *n* : beggar or vagrant

**tram•ple** *vb* : walk or step on so as to bruise or crush — **tram•ple** *n* — **tram•pler** *n*

**trance** *n* **1 :** sleeplike condition **2 :** state of mystical absorption

**tran•quil** *adj* : quiet and undisturbed — **tran•quil•ize** *vb* — **tran•quil•iz•er** *n* — **tran•quil•li•ty, tran•quil•i•ty** *n* — **tran•quil•ly** *adv*

**trans•ac•tion** *n* **1 :** business deal **2** *pl* **:** records of proceedings — **trans•act** *vb*

**trans•fer** *vb* **1 :** move from one person, place, or situation to another **2 :** convey ownership of **3 :** print or copy by contact **4 :** change to another vehicle or transportation line ~ *n* **1 :** act or process of transferring **2 :** one that transfers or is transferred **3 :** ticket permitting one to transfer — **trans•fer•able** *adj* — **trans•fer•al** *n* — **trans•fer•ence** *n*

**trans•form** *vb* **1 :** change in structure, appearance, or character **2 :** change (an electric current) in potential or type — **trans•for•ma•tion** *n* — **trans•form•er** *n*

**tran•sit** *n* **1 :** movement over, across, or through **2 :** local and esp. public transportation **3 :** surveyor's instrument

**tran•si•tion** *n* : passage from one state, stage, or subject to another — **tran•si•tion•al** *adj*

**tran•si•to•ry** *adj* : of brief duration

**trans•late** *vb* : change into another language — **trans•lat•able** *adj* — **trans•la•tion** *n* — **trans•la•tor** *n*

**trans•lu•cent** *adj* : not transparent but clear enough to allow light to pass through — **trans•lu•cence** *n* — **trans•lu•cen•cy** *n* — **trans•lu•cent•ly** *adv*

**trans•mit** *vb* **1 :** transfer from one person or place to another **2 :** pass on by inheritance **3 :** broadcast — **trans•mis•si•ble** *adj* — **trans•mis•sion** *n* — **trans•mit•ta•ble** *adj* — **trans•mit•tal** *n* — **trans•mit•ter** *n*

**trans•par•ent** *adj* **1 :** clear enough to see through **2 :** obvious — **trans•par•en•cy** *n* — **trans•par•ent•ly** *adv*

**trans•plant** *vb* **1 :** dig up and move to another place **2 :** transfer from one body part or person to another — **transplant** *n* — **trans•plan•ta•tion** *n*

**trans•port** *vb* **1 :** carry or deliver to another place **2 :** carry away by emotion ~ *n* **1 :** act of transporting **2 :** rapture **3 :** ship or plane for carrying troops or supplies — **trans•por•ta•tion** *n* — **trans•port•er** *n*

**trans•pose** *vb* : change the position, sequence, or key — **trans•po•si•tion** *n*

**trap** *n* **1 :** device for catching animals **2 :** something by which one is caught unawares **3 :** device to allow one thing to pass through while keeping other things out ~ *vb* : catch in a trap — **trap•per** *n*

**trap•e•zoid** *n* : plane 4-sided figure with 2 parallel sides — **trap•e•zoi•dal** *adj*

**trash** *n* : something that is no good — **trashy** *adj*

**trav•el** *vb* **1 :** take a trip or tour **2 :** move or be carried from point to point ~ *n* : journey — often pl. — **trav•el•er, trav•el•ler** *n*

**trawl** *vb* : fish or catch with a trawl ~ *n* : large cone-shaped net — **trawl•er** *n*

**tray** *n* : shallow flat-bottomed receptacle for holding or carrying something

**treach•er•ous** *adj* : disloyal or dangerous — **treach•er•ous•ly** *adv*

**treach•ery** *n* : betrayal of a trust

**tread** *vb* (**trod; trod•den/trod**) **1 :** step on or over **2 :** walk **3 :** press or crush with the feet ~ *n* **1 :** way of walking **2 :** sound made in walking **3 :** part on which a thing runs

**trea•son** *n* : attempt to overthrow the government — **trea•son•able** *adj* — **trea•son•ous** *adj*

**trea•sure** *n* **1 :** wealth stored up **2 :** something of great value ~ *vb* : keep as precious

**trea•sury** *n* : place or office for keeping and distributing funds — **trea•sur•er** *n*

**treat** *vb* **1 :** have as a topic **2 :** pay for the food or entertainment of **3 :** act toward or regard in a certain way **4 :** give medical care to ~ *n* **1 :** food or entertainment paid for by another **2 :** something special and enjoyable — **treat•ment** *n*

**trea•ty** *n* : agreement between governments

**tree** *n* : tall woody plant ~ *vb* : force up a tree — **tree•less** *adj*

**trem•ble** *vb* **1 :** shake from fear or cold **2 :** move or sound as if shaken

**tre•men•dous** *adj* : amazingly large, powerful, or excellent — **tre•men•dous•ly** *adv*

**trench** *n* : long narrow cut in land

**trend** *n* : prevailing tendency, direction, or style ~ *vb* : move in a particular direction — **trendy** *adj*

**tres•pass** *n* **1 :** sin **2 :** unauthorized entry onto someone's property ~ *vb* **1 :** sin **2 :** enter illegally — **tres•pass•er** *n*

**tri•al** *n* **1 :** hearing and judgment of a matter in court **2 :** source of great annoyance **3 :** test use or experimental effort — **trial** *adj*

**tri•an•gle** *n* : plane figure with 3 sides and 3 angles — **tri•an•gu•lar** *adj*

**tribe** *n* : social group of numerous families — **trib•al** *adj* — **tribes•man** *n* — **tribes•peo•ple** *n pl*

**trib•ute** *n* **1 :** payment to acknowledge submission **2 :** tax **3 :** gift or act showing respect

**trick** *n* **1 :** scheme to deceive **2 :** prank **3 :** deceptive or ingenious feat **4 :** mannerism **5 :** knack **6 :** tour of duty ~ *vb* : deceive by cunning — **trick•ery** *n* — **trick•ster** *n*

**trick•le** *vb* : run in drops or a thin stream — **trickle** *n*

**tricky** *adj* **1 :** inclined to trickery **2 :** requiring skill or caution

**tri•cy•cle** *n* : 3-wheeled bicycle

**tri•fle** *n* : something of little value or importance ~ *vb* **1 :** speak or act in a playful or flirting way **2 :** toy — **tri•fler** *n* — **tri•fling** *adj*

**trig•ger** *n* : finger-piece of a firearm lock that fires the gun ~ *vb* : set into motion — **trig•ger** *adj* — **trig•gered** *adj*

**tril•lion** *n* : 1000 billions — **tril•lion** *adj* — **tril•lionth** *adj or n*

**trim** *vb* **1 :** decorate **2 :** make neat or reduce by cutting ~ *adj* : neat and compact ~ *n* **1 :** state or condition **2 :** ornaments — **trim•ly** *adv* — **trim•mer** *n* — **trim•ming** *n*

**Trin•i•ty** *n* : divine unity of Father, Son, and Holy Spirit

**trio** *n* **1 :** music for 3 performers **2 :** group of 3

**trip** *vb* **1 :** step lightly **2 :** stumble or cause to stumble **3 :** make or cause to make a mistake **4 :** release (as a spring or switch) ~ *n* **1 :** journey **2 :** stumble **3 :** drug-induced experience

**tri•ple** *vb* : make 3 times as great ~ *n* : group of 3 ~ *adj* **1 :** having 3 units **2 :** being 3 times as great or as many

**trip•let** *n* **1 :** group of 3 **2 :** one of 3 offspring born together

**tri•umph** *n* : victory or great success ~ *vb* : obtain or celebrate victory — **tri•um•phal** *adj* — **tri•um•phant** *adj* — **tri•um•phant•ly** *adv*

**triv•i•al** *adj* : of little importance — **triv•i•al•i•ty** *n*

**trod** *past of* TREAD

**trodden** *past part of* TREAD

**trol•ley** *n* : streetcar run by overhead electric wires

**troop** *n* **1 :** cavalry unit **2** *pl* **:** soldiers **3 :** collection of people or things ~ *vb* : move or gather in crowds

**troop•er** *n* **1 :** cavalry soldier **2 :** police officer on horseback or state police officer

**tro•phy** *n* : prize gained by a victory

**trop•ic** *n* **1 :** either of the 2 parallels of latitude one 23½ degrees north of the equator (**tropic of Cancer**) and one 23½ degrees south of the equator (**tropic of Cap•ri•corn**) **2** *pl* **:** region lying between the tropics — **tropic, trop•i•cal** *adj*

**trou•ble** *vb* **1 :** disturb **2 :** afflict **3 :** make an effort ~ *n* **1 :** cause of mental or physical distress **2 :** effort — **trou•ble•mak•er** *n* — **trou•ble•some** *adj* — **trou•ble•some•ly** *adv*

**trou•sers** *n pl* : long pants — **trouser** *adj*

**truce** *n* : agreement to halt fighting

**truck** *n* **1 :** wheeled frame for moving heavy objects **2 :** automotive vehicle for transporting heavy loads ~ *vb* : transport on a truck — **truck•er** *n* — **truck•load** *n*

**trudge** *vb* : walk or march steadily and with difficulty

**true** *adj* **1 :** loyal **2 :** in agreement with fact or reality **3 :** genuine ~ *adv* **1 :** truthfully **2 :** accurately ~ *vb* : make balanced or even — **tru•ly** *adv*

**trum•pet** *n* : tubular brass wind instrument with a flaring end ~ *vb* **1 :** blow a trumpet **2 :** proclaim loudly — **trum•pet•er** *n*

**trunk** *n* **1 :** main part (as of a body or tree) **2 :** long muscular nose of an elephant **3 :** storage chest **4 :** storage space in a car **5** *pl* **:** shorts

**trust** *n* **1 :** reliance on another **2 :** assured hope **3 :** credit **4 :** property held or managed in behalf of another **5 :** combination of firms that reduces competition **6 :** something entrusted to another's care **7** : custody ~ *vb* **1** : depend **2** : hope **3** : entrust **4** : have faith in — **trust·ful** *adj* — **trust·ful·ly** *adv* — **trust·ful·ness** *n* — **trust·worth·i·ness** *n* — **trust·wor·thy** *adj*

**truth** *n* **1** : real state of things **2** : true or accepted statement **3** : agreement with fact or reality — **truth·ful** *adj* — **truth·ful·ly** *adv* — **truth·ful·ness** *n*

**try** *vb* **1** : conduct the trial of **2** : put to a test **3** : strain **4** : make an effort at ~ *n* : act of trying

**try·out** *n* : competitive test of performance esp. for athletes or actors — **try out** *vb*

**tsar** *var of* CZAR

**T–shirt** *n* : collarless pullover shirt with short sleeves

**tub** *n* **1** : wide bucketlike vessel **2** : bathtub

**tube** *n* **1** : hollow cylinder **2** : round container from which a substance can be squeezed **3** : airtight circular tube of rubber inside a tire — **tubed** *adj* — **tube·less** *adj* — **tu·bu·lar** *adj*

**tuck** *vb* **1** : pull up into a fold **2** : put into a snug often concealing place **3** : make snug in bed — used with *in* ~ *n* : fold in a cloth

**Tues·day** *n* : 3d day of the week

**tuft** *n* : clump (as of hair or feathers) — **tuft·ed** *adj*

**tug** *vb* **1** : pull hard **2** : move by pulling ~ *n* : act of tugging

**tug–of–war** *n* (**tugs–of–war**) : pulling contest between 2 teams

**tu·ition** *n* : cost of instruction

**tu·lip** *n* : herb with cup-shaped flowers

**tum·ble** *vb* **1** : perform gymnastic feats of rolling and turning **2** : fall or cause to fall suddenly **3** : toss ~ *n* : act of tumbling

**tum·my** *n* : belly

**tu·mor** *n* : abnormal and useless growth of tissue — **tu·mor·ous** *adj*

**tu·mult** *n* **1** : uproar **2** : violent agitation of mind or feelings — **tu·mul·tu·ous** *adj*

**tu·na** *n* : large seafood fish

**tune** *n* **1** : melody **2** : correct musical pitch **3** : harmonious relationship ~ *vb* **1** : bring or come into harmony **2** : adjust in musical pitch **3** : adjust a receiver so as to receive a broadcast **4** : put in first-class working order — **tun·able** *adj* — **tune·ful** *adj* — **tun·er** *n*

**tun·nel** *n* : underground passageway ~ *vb* : make a tunnel through or under something

**tur·bine** *n* : engine turned by the force of gas or water on fan blades

**tur·bu·lent** *adj* **1** : causing violence or disturbance **2** : marked by agitation or tumult — **tur·bu·lence** *n* — **tur·bu·lent·ly** *adv*

**turf** *n* : upper layer of soil bound by grass and roots

**tur·key** *n* : large American bird raised for food

**turn** *vb* **1** : move or cause to move around an axis **2** : twist (a mechanical part) to operate **3** : wrench **4** : cause to face or move in a different direction **5** : reverse the sides or surfaces of **6** : upset **7** : go around **8** : become or cause to become **9** : seek aid from a source ~ *n* **1** : act or instance of turning **2** : change **3** : place at which something turns **4** : place, time, or opportunity to do something in order — **turn·er** *n* — **turn down** *vb* : decline to accept — **turn in** *vb* **1** : deliver or report to authorities **2** : go to bed — **turn off** *vb* : stop the functioning of — **turn out** *vb* **1** : expel **2** : produce **3** : come

together **4** : prove to be in the end — **turn over** *vb* : transfer — **turn up** *vb* **1** : discover or appear **2** : happen unexpectedly

**turn·out** *n* **1** : gathering of people for a special purpose **2** : size of a gathering

**turn·over** *n* **1** : upset or reversal **2** : filled pastry **3** : volume of business **4** : movement (as of goods or people) into, through, and out of a place

**turn·pike** *n* : expressway on which tolls are charged

**tur·tle** *n* : reptile with the trunk enclosed in a bony shell

**tur·tle·neck** *n* : high close-fitting collar that can be turned over or a sweater or shirt with this collar

**tu·tor** *n* : private teacher ~ *vb* : teach usu. individually

**TV** *n* : television

**tweak** *vb* : pinch and pull playfully — **tweak** *n*

**tweed** *n* **1** : rough woolen fabric **2** *pl* : tweed clothing — **tweedy** *adj*

**tweet** *n* : chirping note — **tweet** *vb*

**twee·zers** *n pl* : small pincerlike tool

**twelve** *n* **1** : one more than 11 **2** : 12th in a set or series **3** : something having 12 units — **twelfth** *adj or n* — **twelve** *adj or pron*

**twen·ty** *n* : 2 times 10 — **twen·ti·eth** *adj or n* — **twenty** *adj or pron*

**twen·ty–twen·ty, 20–20** *adj* : being vision of normal sharpness

**twice** *adv* **1** : on 2 occasions **2** : 2 times

**twig** *n* : small branch — **twig·gy** *adj*

**twi·light** *n* : light from the sky at dusk or dawn — **twi·light** *adj*

**twin** *n* : either of 2 offspring born together ~ *adj* **1** : born with one another or as a pair at one birth **2** : made up of 2 similar parts

**twine** *n* : strong twisted thread ~ *vb* **1**

: twist together **2** : coil about a support — **twin·er** *n* — **twiny** *adj*

**twinge** *vb* : affect with or feel a sudden sharp pain ~ *n* : sudden sharp stab (as of pain)

**twin·kle** *vb* : shine with a flickering light — *n* **1** : wink **2** : intermittent shining — **twin·kler** *n*

**twirl** *vb* : whirl round ~ *n* **1** : act of twirling **2** : coil — **twirl·er** *n*

**twist** *vb* **1** : unite by winding (threads) together **2** : wrench **3** : move in or have a spiral shape **4** : follow a winding course ~ *n* **1** : act or result of twisting **2** : unexpected development

**twist·er** *n* : tornado

**twit** *n* : fool

**twitch** *vb* : move or pull with a sudden motion — *n* : act of twitching

**twit·ter** *vb* : make chirping noises ~ *n* : small intermittent noise

**two** *n* **1** : one more than one **2** : the 2d in a set or series **3** : something having 2 units — **two** *adj or pron*

**two·fold** *adj* : double — **two·fold** *adv*

**two·some** *n* : couple

**tying** *pres part of* TIE

**type** *n* **1** : class, kind, or group set apart by common characteristics **2** : special design of printed letters ~ *vb* **1** : write with a typewriter **2** : identify or classify as a particular type

**typ·i·cal** *adj* : having the essential characteristics of a group — **typ·i·cal·i·ty** *n* — **typ·i·cal·ly** *adv* — **typ·i·cal·ness** *n*

**typ·i·fy** *vb* : be typical of

**tyr·an·ny** *n* : unjust use of absolute governmental power — **ty·ran·ni·cal** *adj* — **ty·ran·ni·cal·ly** *adv* — **tyr·an·nize** *vb*

**ty·rant** *n* : harsh ruler having absolute power

**tzar** *var of* CZAR

# U

**u** *n* : 21st letter of the alphabet

**ug·ly** *adj* **1** : offensive to look at **2** : mean or quarrelsome — **ug·li·ness** *n*

**uku·le·le** *n* : small 4-string guitar

**ul·cer** *n* : eroded sore — **ul·cer·ate** *vb* — **ul·cer·a·tion** *n* — **ul·cer·ous** *adj*

**ul·ti·mate** *adj* : final, maximum, or extreme — **ultimate** *n* — **ul·ti·mate·ly** *adv*

**ul·ti·ma·tum** *n* : final proposition or demand carrying or implying a threat

**um·brel·la** *n* : collapsible fabric device to protect from sun or rain

**um·pire** *n* **1** : arbitrator **2** : sport official — **um·pire** *vb*

**un·ac·cept·able** *adj* : not acceptable or pleasing — **un·ac·cept·ably** *adv*

**un·af·fect·ed** *adj* **1** : not influenced or changed by something **2** : natural and sincere — **un·af·fect·ed·ly** *adv*

**unan·i·mous** *adj* **1** : showing no disagreement **2** : formed with the agreement of all — **una·nim·i·ty** *n* — **unan·i·mous·ly** *adv*

**un·armed** *adj* : not armed or armored

**un·at·tached** *adj* **1** : not attached **2** : not married or engaged

**un·aware** *adv* : unawares ~ *adj* : not aware

**un·awares** *adv* **1** : without warning **2** : unintentionally

**un·bal·anced** *adj* **1** : not balanced **2** : mentally unstable

**un·beat·en** *adj* : not beaten

**un·be·liev·able** *adj* **1** : improbable **2** : superlative — **un·be·liev·ably** *adv*

**un·bro·ken** *adj* **1** : not damaged **2** : not interrupted

**un·buck·le** *vb* : unfasten the buckle of

**un·but·ton** *vb* : unfasten the buttons of

**un·called–for** *adj* : too harsh or rude for the occasion

**un·cer·tain** *adj* **1** : not determined, sure, or definitely known **2** : subject to

chance or change — **un·cer·tain·ly** *adv* — **un·cer·tain·ty** *n*

**un·cle** *n* **1** : brother of one's father or mother **2** : husband of one's aunt

**un·clean** *adj* : not clean or pure — **un·clean·ness** *n*

**un·com·mon** *adj* **1** : rare **2** : superior — **un·com·mon·ly** *adv*

**un·con·cerned** *adj* **1** : disinterested **2** : not anxious or upset — **un·con·cerned·ly** *adv*

**un·con·di·tion·al** *adj* : not limited in any way — **un·con·di·tion·al·ly** *adv*

**un·con·scious** *adj* **1** : not awake or aware of one's surroundings **2** : not consciously done ~ *n* : part of one's mental life that one is not aware of — **un·con·scious·ly** *adv* — **un·con·scious·ness** *n*

**un·con·trol·la·ble** *adj* : incapable of being controlled — **un·con·trol·la·bly** *adv*

**un·cov·er** *vb* **1** : reveal **2** : expose by removing a covering

**un·cut** *adj* **1** : not cut down, into, off, or apart **2** : not shaped by cutting **3** : not abridged

**un·de·ni·able** *adj* : plainly true — **un·de·ni·ably** *adv*

**un·der** *adv* : below or beneath something ~ *prep* **1** : lower than and sheltered by **2** : below the surface of **3** : covered or concealed by **4** : subject to the authority of **5** : less than ~ *adj* **1** : lying below or beneath **2** : subordinate **3** : less than usual, proper, or desired

**un·der·age** *adj* : of less than legal age

**un·der·clothes** *n pl* : underwear

**un·der·cloth·ing** *n* : underwear

**un·der·cov·er** *adj* : employed or engaged in secret investigation

**un·der·de·vel·oped** *adj* : not normally or adequately developed esp. economically

**un·der·dog** *n* : contestant given least chance of winning

**un·der·es·ti·mate** *vb* : estimate too low

**un·der·feed** *vb* : feed inadequately

**un·der·foot** *adv* **1** : under the feet **2** : in the way of another

**un·der·go** *vb* **1** : endure **2** : go through (as an experience)

**un·der·grad·u·ate** *n* : university or college student

**un·der·ground** *adv* **1** : beneath the surface of the earth **2** : in secret ~ *adj* **1** : being or growing under the surface of the ground **2** : secret ~ *n* : secret political movement or group

**un·der·hand** *adv or adj* **1** : with secrecy and deception **2** : with the hand kept below the waist

**un·der·line** *vb* **1** : draw a line under **2** : stress — **underline** *n*

**un·der·mine** *vb* **1** : excavate beneath **2** : weaken or wear away secretly or gradually

**un·der·neath** *prep* : directly under ~ *adv* **1** : below a surface or object **2** : on the lower side

**un·der·pants** *n pl* : short undergarment for the lower trunk

**un·der·priv·i·leged** *adj* : poor

**un·der·rate** *vb* : rate or value too low

**un·der·sea** *adj* : being, carried on, or used beneath the surface of the sea ~ *adv* **un·der·seas** : beneath the surface of the sea

**un·der·shirt** *n* : shirt worn as underwear

**un·der·shorts** *n pl* : short underpants

**un·der·side** *n* : side or surface lying underneath

**un·der·stand** *vb* **1** : be aware of the meaning of **2** : deduce **3** : have a sympathetic attitude — **un·der·stand·able** *adj* — **un·der·stand·ably** *adv*

**un·der·stand·ing** *n* **1** : intelligence **2** :

ability to comprehend and judge **3** : mutual agreement ~ *adj* : sympathetic

**un·der·stood** *adj* **1** : agreed upon **2** : implicit

**un·der·take** *vb* **1** : attempt (a task) or assume (a responsibility) **2** : guarantee — **un·der·tak·ing** *n*

**un·der·tak·er** *n* : one in the funeral business

**un·der·wa·ter** *adj* : being or used below the surface of the water — **underwater** *adv*

**under way** *adv* : in motion or in progress

**un·der·wear** *n* : clothing worn next to the skin and under ordinary clothes

**un·der·write** *vb* **1** : provide insurance for **2** : guarantee financial support of — **un·der·writ·er** *n*

**un·dies** *n pl* : underwear

**un·do** *vb* **1** : unfasten **2** : reverse **3** : ruin — **un·do·ing** *n*

**un·dress** *vb* : remove one's clothes ~ *n* : state of being naked

**un·due** *adj* : excessive — **un·du·ly** *adv*

**un·dy·ing** *adj* : immortal or perpetual

**un·earth** *vb* : dig up or discover

**un·easy** *adj* **1** : awkward or embarrassed **2** : disturbed or worried — **un·eas·i·ly** *adv* — **un·eas·i·ness** *n*

**un·em·ployed** *adj* : not having a job — **un·em·ploy·ment** *n*

**un·equal** *adj* : not equal or uniform — **un·equal·ly** *adv*

**un·equiv·o·cal** *adj* : leaving no doubt — **un·equiv·o·cal·ly** *adv*

**un·even** *adj* **1** : not smooth **2** : not regular or consistent — **un·even·ly** *adv* — **un·even·ness** *n*

**un·event·ful** *adj* : lacking interesting or noteworthy incidents — **un·event·ful·ly** *adv*

**un·ex·pect·ed** *adj* : not expected — **un·ex·pect·ed·ly** *adv*

**un·fair** *adj* : marked by injustice, partiality, or deception — **un·fair·ly** *adv*

**un·faith·ful** *adj* : not loyal — **un·faith·ful·ly** *adv* — **un·faith·ful·ness** *n*

**un·fa·mil·iar** *adj* 1 : not well known 2 : not acquainted — **un·fa·mil·iar·i·ty** *n*

**un·fas·ten** *vb* : release a catch or lock

**un·fav·or·able** *adj* : not pleasing, advantageous, or agreeable — **un·fav·or·ably** *adv*

**un·fit** *adj* : not suitable — **un·fit·ness** *n*

**un·fold** *vb* 1 : open the folds of 2 : reveal 3 : develop

**un·for·get·ta·ble** *adj* : memorable — **un·for·get·ta·bly** *adv*

**un·for·tu·nate** *adj* 1 : not lucky or successful 2 : deplorable — **un·for·tu·nate** *n* — **un·for·tu·nate·ly** *adv*

**un·found·ed** *adj* : lacking a sound basis

**un·friend·ly** *adj* : not friendly or kind — **un·friend·li·ness** *n*

**un·grate·ful** *adj* : not thankful for favors — **un·grate·ful·ly** *adv* — **un·grate·ful·ness** *n*

**un·hap·py** *adj* 1 : unfortunate 2 : sad — **un·hap·pi·ly** *adv* — **un·hap·pi·ness** *n*

**un·healthy** *adj* 1 : not wholesome 2 : not well

**un·heard–of** *adj* : not known or experienced before

**un·hinge** *vb* 1 : take from the hinges 2 : make unstable esp. mentally

**un·ho·ly** *adj* : sinister or shocking — **un·ho·li·ness** *n*

**uni·form** *adj* : not changing or showing any variation ∼ *n* : distinctive dress worn by members of a particular group — **uni·for·mi·ty** *n* — **uni·form·ly** *adv*

**uni·fy** *vb* : make into a coherent whole — **uni·fi·ca·tion** *n*

**un·in·hib·it·ed** *adj* : free of restraint — **un·in·hib·it·ed·ly** *adv*

**un·in·ten·tion·al** *adj* : not done willingly — **un·in·ten·tion·al·ly** *adv*

**un·in·ter·est·ing** *adj* : not interesting — **un·in·ter·est·ing·ly** *adv*

**union** *n* 1 : act or instance of joining two or more things into one or the state of being so joined 2 : confederation of nations or states 3 : organization of workers (**labor union, trade union**) — **union·ize** *vb* — **union·i·za·tion** *n*

**unique** *adj* 1 : being the only one of its kind 2 : very unusual — **unique·ly** *adv* — **unique·ness** *n*

**unit** *n* 1 : smallest whole number 2 : definite amount or quantity used as a standard of measurement 3 : single part of a whole — **unit** *adj*

**unite** *vb* : put or join together

**uni·ty** *n* 1 : quality or state of being united or a unit 2 : harmony

**uni·ver·sal** *adj* 1 : relating to or affecting everyone or everything 2 : present or occurring everywhere — **uni·ver·sal·ly** *adv*

**uni·verse** *n* : the complete system of all things that exist

**uni·ver·si·ty** *n* : institution of higher learning

**un·kind** *adj* : not kind or sympathetic — **un·kind·li·ness** *n* — **un·kind·ly** *adv* — **un·kind·ness** *n*

**un·law·ful** *adj* : illegal — **un·law·ful·ly** *adv*

**un·less** *conj* : except on condition that

**un·like** *adj* 1 : not similar 2 : not equal ∼ *prep* : different from — **un·like·ly** *adv* — **un·like·ness** *n* — **un·like·li·hood** *n*

**un·load** *vb* 1 : take (cargo) from a vehicle, vessel, or plane 2 : take a load from 3 : discard

**un·lock** *vb* 1 : unfasten through release of a lock 2 : release or reveal

**un·lucky** *adj* 1 : experiencing bad luck 2 : likely to bring misfortune — **un·luck·i·ly** *adv*

**un·married** *adj* : not married

**un·mis·tak·able** *adj* : not capable of being mistaken or misunderstood — **un·mis·tak·ably** *adv*

**un·nat·u·ral** *adj* 1 : not natural or spontaneous 2 : abnormal — **un·nat·u·ral·ly** *adv* — **un·nat·u·ral·ness** *n*

**un·oc·cu·pied** *adj* 1 : not busy 2 : not occupied

**un·pack** *vb* 1 : remove (things packed) from a container 2 : remove the contents of (a package)

**un·pleas·ant** *adj* : not pleasing or agreeable

**un·plug** *vb* 1 : remove a clog or plug in 2 : disconnect from an electric circuit by removing a plug

**un·re·al** *adj* : not real or genuine — **un·re·al·i·ty** *n*

**un·roll** *vb* 1 : unwind a roll of 2 : become unrolled

**un·ruly** *adj* : not readily controlled or disciplined — **un·rul·i·ness** *n*

**un·sci·en·tif·ic** *adj* : not in accord with the principles and methods of science

**un·screw** *vb* : loosen or remove by withdrawing screws or by turning

**un·self·ish** *adj* : generous — **un·self·ish·ly** *adv*

**un·set·tle** *vb* : disturb — **un·set·tled** *adj*

**un·sta·ble** *adj* 1 : not mentally or physically balanced 2 : tending to change

**un·stop·pa·ble** *adj* : not capable of being stopped

**un·tan·gle** *vb* 1 : free from a state of being tangled 2 : find a solution to

**un·think·able** *adj* : not to be thought of or considered possible

**un·tidy** *adj* : not neat or orderly

**un·tie** *vb* : open by releasing ties

**un·til** *prep* : up to the time of ∼ *conj* : to the time that

**un·to** *prep* : to

**un·used** *adj* 1 : not accustomed 2 : not used

**un·usu·al** *adj* : not usual or common — **un·usu·al·ly** *adv*

**un·well** *adj* : sick

**un·wind** *vb* 1 : undo something that is wound 2 : become unwound 3 : relax

**un·wrap** *vb* : remove the wrappings from

**un·writ·ten** *adj* : made or passed on only in speech or through tradition

**un·zip** *vb* : zip open

**up** *adv* 1 : in or to a higher position or level 2 : from beneath a surface or level 3 : in or into an upright position 4 : out of bed 5 : to or with greater intensity 6 : into existence, evidence, or knowledge 7 : away 8 — used to indicate a degree of success, completion, or finality ∼ *adj* 1 : in the state of having risen 2 : raised to or at a higher level 3 : moving, inclining, or directed upward 4 : in a state of greater intensity 5 : at an end ∼ *vb* 1 **up; upped** : act abruptly 2 **upped; upped** : move or cause to move upward ∼ *prep* 1 : to, toward, or at a higher point of 2 : along or toward the beginning of

**up·date** *vb* : bring up to date — **up·date** *n*

**up·grade** *n* 1 : upward slope 2 : increase ∼ *vb* : raise to a higher position

**up·hill** *adv* : upward on a hill or incline ∼ *adj* 1 : going up 2 : difficult

**up·hold** *vb* : support or defend — **up·hold·er** *n*

**up·keep** *n* : act or cost of keeping up or maintaining

**up·on** *prep* : on

**up·per** *adj* : higher in position, rank, or order ∼ *n* : top part of a shoe

**up·right** *adj* 1 : vertical 2 : erect in posture 3 : morally correct ∼ *n* : something that stands upright — **up·right** *adv* — **up·right·ly** *adv* — **up·right·ness** *n*

**up·ris·ing** *n* : revolt

**up·roar** *n* : state of commotion or violent disturbance

**up·roar·i·ous** *adj* 1 : marked by uproar 2 : extremely funny — **up·roar·i·ous·ly** *adv*

**up·root** *vb* : remove by or as if by pulling up by the roots

**up·set** *vb* 1 : force or be forced out of the usual position 2 : disturb emotionally or physically ∼ *n* 1 : act of throwing into disorder 2 : minor physical disorder ∼ *adj* : emotionally disturbed or agitated

**up·side down** *adv* 1 : turned so that the upper and lower parts are reversed 2 : in or into confusion or disorder — **up·side-down** *adj*

**up·stairs** *adv* : up the stairs or to the next floor ∼ *adj* : situated on the floor above ∼ *n sing or pl* : part of a building above the ground floor

**up·tight** *adj* 1 : tense 2 : angry 3 : rigidly conventional

**up–to–date** *adj* : current — **up–to–date·ness** *n*

**up·town** *n* : upper part of a town or city — **uptown** *adj or adv*

**up·ward, up·wards** *adv* 1 : in a direction from lower to higher 2 : toward a higher or greater state or number ∼ *adj* : directed toward or situated in a higher place — **up·ward·ly** *adv*

**ur·ban** *adj* : characteristic of a city

**ur·bane** *adj* : polished in manner — **ur·ban·i·ty** *n*

**ur·ban·ite** *n* : city dweller

**ur·chin** *n* : mischievous youngster

**urge** *vb* 1 : earnestly plead for or insist on (an action) 2 : try to persuade 3 : impel to a course of activity ∼ *n* : force or impulse that moves one to action

**ur·gent** *adj* 1 : calling for immediate attention 2 : urging insistently — **ur·gen·cy** *n* — **ur·gent·ly** *adv*

**urine** *n* : liquid waste material from the kidneys — **uri·nary** *adj*

**URL** *n* : address on the Internet

**urn** *n* 1 : vaselike or cuplike vessel on a pedestal 2 : large coffee pot

**us** *pron, objective case of* WE

**us·age** *n* 1 : customary practice 2 : way of doing or of using something

**use** *n* 1 : act or practice of putting something into action 2 : state of being used 3 : way of using 4 : privilege, ability, or power to use something 5 : utility or function 6 : occasion or need to use ∼ *vb* 1 : put into action or service 2 : consume 3 : behave toward 4 : to make use of 5 — used in the past tense with *to* to indicate a former practice — **us·abil·i·ty** *n* — **us·able** *adj* — **use·ful** *adj* — **use·ful·ly** *adv* — **use·ful·ness** *n* — **use·less** *adj* — **use·less·ly** *adv* — **use·less·ness** *n* — **us·er** *n*

**used** *adj* 1 : not new 2 : accustomed — used with *to*

**usu·al** *adj* : being what is expected according to custom or habit — **usu·al·ly** *adv*

**uten·sil** *n* 1 : eating or cooking tool 2 : useful tool

**util·i·ty** *n* 1 : usefulness 2 : regulated business providing a public service (as electricity)

**uti·lize** *vb* : make use of — **uti·li·za·tion** *n*

**ut·most** *adj* 1 : most distant 2 : of the greatest or highest degree or amount — **utmost** *n*

**ut·ter** *adj* : absolute ∼ *vb* : express with the voice — **ut·ter·ance** *n* — **ut·ter·er** *n* — **ut·ter·ly** *adv*

# V

**v** *n* : 22d letter of the alphabet

**va·cant** *adj* 1 : not occupied, filled, or in use 2 : devoid of thought or expression — **va·can·cy** *n* — **va·cant·ly** *adv*

**va·cate** *vb* 1 : annul 2 : leave unfilled or unoccupied

**va·ca·tion** *n* : period of rest from routine — **va·ca·tion** *vb* — **va·ca·tion·er** *n*

**vac·ci·nate** *vb* : administer a vaccine usu. by injection — **vac·ci·na·tion** *n*

**vac·cine** *n* : substance to induce immunity to a disease

**vac·u·um** *n* : empty space with no air ∼ *vb* : clean with a machine (**vacuum cleaner**) that cleans by suction

**va·gi·na** *n* : canal that leads out from the uterus — **vag·i·nal** *adj*

**vague** *adj* : not clear, definite, or distinct — **vague·ly** *adv* — **vague·ness** *n*

**vain** *adj* 1 : of no value 2 : not successful 3 : conceited — **vain·ly** *adv*

**vale·dic·to·ri·an** *n* : student giving the farewell address at commencement — **vale·dic·to·ry** *adj or n*

**val·en·tine** *n* : sweetheart or a card sent to a sweetheart or friend on St. Valentine's Day

**val·id** *adj* 1 : proper and legally binding 2 : founded on truth or fact — **va·lid·i·ty** *n* — **val·id·ly** *adv*

**val·i·date** *vb* : establish as valid — **val·i·da·tion** *n*

**val·ley** *n* : long depression between ranges of hills

**val·or** *n* : bravery or heroism — **val·or·ous** *adj*

**valu·able** *adj* 1 : worth a lot of money 2 : being of great importance or use — **valuable** *n*

**val·ue** *n* 1 : fair return or equivalent for something exchanged 2 : how much something is worth 3 : distinctive quality (as of a color or sound) 4 : guiding principle or ideal — usu. pl. ∼ *vb* 1 : estimate the worth of 2 : appreciate the importance of — **val·ue·less** *adj* — **val·u·er** *n*

**valve** *n* : structure or device to control flow of a liquid or gas — **valved** *adj* — **valve·less** *adj*

**vam·pire** *n* 1 : legendary night-wandering dead body that sucks human blood 2 : bat that feeds on the blood of animals

**van** *n* : enclosed truck

**van·dal** *n* : person who willfully defaces or destroys property — **van·dal·ism** *n* — **van·dal·ize** *vb*

**vane** *n* : bladelike device designed to be moved by force of the air or water

**van·guard** *n* 1 : troops moving at the front of an army 2 : forefront of an action or movement

**va·nil·la** *n* : a flavoring made from the pods of a tropical orchid or this orchid

**van·ish** *vb* : disappear suddenly

**van·i·ty** *n* 1 : futility or something that is futile 2 : undue pride in oneself 3 : makeup case or table

**va·por** *n* 1 : fine separated particles floating in and clouding the air 2 : gaseous form of an ordinarily liquid substance — **va·por·ize** *vb* — **va·por·i·za·tion** *n* — **va·por·iz·er** *n* — **va·por·ous** *adj*

**vari·able** *adj* : apt to vary — **vari·abil·i·ty** *n* — **vari·able** *n* — **vari·ably** *adv*

**vari·a·tion** *n* : instance or extent of varying

**var·ied** *adj* : showing variety — **var·ied·ly** *adv*

**va·ri·ety** *n* 1 : state of being different 2 : collection of different things 3 : something that differs from others of its kind

**var·i·ous** adj : being many and unlike — **var·i·ous·ly** adv

**var·nish** n : liquid that dries to a hard glossy protective coating ∼ vb : cover with varnish

**var·si·ty** n : principal team representing a school

**vary** vb 1 : alter 2 : make or be of different kinds

**vase** n : tall usu. ornamental container to hold flowers

**vast** adj : very great in size, extent, or amount — **vast·ly** adv — **vast·ness** n

¹**vault** n 1 : masonry arch 2 : usu. underground storage or burial room ∼ vb : form or cover with a vault — **vault·ed** adj — **vaulty** adj

²**vault** vb : spring over esp. with the help of the hands or a pole ∼ n : act of vaulting — **vault·er** n

**VCR** n : a device that records and plays videotapes

**veg·e·ta·ble** adj 1 : relating to or obtained from plants 2 : like that of a plant ∼ n 1 : plant 2 : plant grown for food

**veg·e·tar·i·an** n : person who eats no meat — **veg·e·tar·i·an** adj — **veg·e·tar·i·an·ism** n

**veg·e·ta·tion** n : plant life — **veg·e·ta·tion·al** adj — **veg·e·ta·tive** adj

**ve·hi·cle** n 1 : medium through which something is expressed, applied, or administered 2 : structure for transporting something esp. on wheels — **ve·hic·u·lar** adj

**veil** n 1 : sheer material to hide something or to cover the face and head 2 : something that hides ∼ vb : cover with a veil

**vein** n 1 : rock fissure filled with deposited mineral matter 2 : vessel that carries blood toward the heart 3 : sap-carrying tube in a leaf 4 : distinctive element or style of expression — **veined** adj

**vel·vet** n : fabric with a short soft pile — **vel·vet** adj — **vel·vety** adj

**vend** vb : sell — **vend·ible** adj — **ven·dor** n

**ven·geance** n : punishment in retaliation for an injury or offense

**venge·ful** adj : filled with a desire for revenge — **venge·ful·ly** adv

**ven·om** n 1 : poison secreted by certain animals 2 : ill will — **ven·om·ous** adj

**vent** vb 1 : provide with or let out at a vent 2 : give expression to ∼ n : opening for passage or for relieving pressure

**ven·ti·late** vb : allow fresh air to circulate through — **ven·ti·la·tion** n — **ven·ti·la·tor** n

**ven·ture** vb 1 : risk or take a chance on 2 : put forward (an opinion) ∼ n : speculative business enterprise

**ven·ture·some** adj : brave or daring — **ven·ture·some·ly** adv — **ven·ture·some·ness** n

**verb** n : word that expresses action or existence

**ver·bal** adj 1 : having to do with or expressed in words 2 : oral 3 : relating to or formed from a verb — **ver·bal·iza·tion** n — **ver·bal·ize** vb — **ver·bal·ly** adv

**verbal auxiliary** n : auxiliary verb

**ver·dict** n : decision of a jury

**ver·i·fy** vb : establish the truth, accuracy, or reality of — **ver·i·fi·able** adj — **ver·i·fi·ca·tion** n

**ver·min** n (**vermin**) : small animal pest

**ver·sa·tile** adj : having many abilities or uses — **ver·sa·til·i·ty** n

**verse** n 1 : line or stanza of poetry 2 : poetry 3 : short division of a chapter in the Bible

**ver·sion** n 1 : translation of the Bible 2 : account or description from a particular point of view

**ver·sus** prep : opposed to or against

**ver·te·brate** n : animal with a backbone — **verte·brate** adj

**ver·ti·cal** adj : rising straight up from a level surface — **vertical** n — **ver·ti·cal·i·ty** n — **ver·ti·cal·ly** adv

**very** adj 1 : exact 2 : exactly suitable 3 : mere or bare 4 : precisely the same ∼ adv 1 : to a high degree 2 : in actual fact

**ves·pers** n pl : late afternoon or evening worship service

**ves·sel** n 1 : a container (as a barrel, bottle, bowl, or cup) for a liquid 2 : craft for navigation esp. on water 3 : tube in which a body fluid is circulated

¹**vest** vb 1 : give a particular authority, right, or property to 2 : clothe with or as if with a garment

²**vest** n : sleeveless garment usu. worn under a suit coat

**vet·er·an** n 1 : former member of the armed forces 2 : person with long experience — **veteran** adj

**Veterans Day** n : 4th Monday in October or formerly November 11 observed as a legal holiday in commemoration of the end of war in 1918 and 1945

**vet·er·i·nar·i·an** n : doctor of animals — **vet·er·i·nary** adj

**ve·to** n 1 : power to forbid and esp. the power of a chief executive to prevent a bill from becoming law 2 : exercise of the veto ∼ vb 1 : forbid 2 : reject a legislative bill

**vex** vb : trouble, distress, or annoy — **vex·a·tion** n — **vex·a·tious** adj

**via** prep : by way of

**vi·brant** adj 1 : vibrating 2 : pulsing with vigor or activity 3 : sounding from vibration — **vi·bran·cy** n

**vi·brate** vb 1 : move or cause to move quickly back and forth or side to side 2 : respond sympathetically — **vi·bra·tion** n — **vi·bra·tor** n — **vi·bra·to·ry** adj

**vice** n 1 : immoral habit 2 : depravity

**vice ver·sa** adv : with the order reversed

**vi·cin·i·ty** n : surrounding area

**vi·cious** adj 1 : wicked 2 : savage 3 : malicious — **vi·cious·ly** adv — **vi·cious·ness** n

**vic·tim** n : person killed, hurt, or abused — **vic·tim·iza·tion** n — **vic·tim·ize** vb — **vic·tim·iz·er** n

**vic·tor** n : winner

**vic·to·ry** n : success in defeating an enemy or opponent or in overcoming difficulties — **vic·to·ri·ous** adj — **vic·to·ri·ous·ly** adv

**vid·eo** adj : relating to the television image

**vid·eo·tape** vb : make a recording of a (television production) on special tape — **videotape** n

**vie** vb : contend — **vi·er** n

**view** n 1 : process of seeing or examining 2 : opinion 3 : area of landscape that can be seen 4 : range of vision 5 : purpose or object ∼ vb 1 : look at 2 : think about or consider — **view·er** n

**view·point** n : position from which something is considered

**vigil** n 1 : day of devotion before a religious feast 2 : act or time of keeping awake 3 : long period of keeping watch (as over a sick or dying person)

**vig·i·lant** adj : alert esp. to avoid danger — **vig·i·lance** n — **vig·i·lant·ly** adv

**vig·or** n 1 : energy or strength 2 : intensity or force — **vig·or·ous** adj — **vig·or·ous·ly** adv — **vig·or·ous·ness** n

**vile** adj : thoroughly bad or contemptible — **vile·ly** adv — **vile·ness** n

**vil·la** n : country estate

**vil·lage** n : small country town — **vil·lag·er** n

**vil·lain** n : bad person — **vil·lain·ess** n — **vil·lain·ous** adj — **vil·lain·ous·ly** adv — **vil·lain·ous·ness** n — **vil·lainy** n

**vin·di·cate** vb 1 : avenge 2 : exonerate 3 : justify — **vin·di·ca·tion** n — **vin·di·ca·tor** n

**vin·dic·tive** adj : seeking or meant for revenge — **vin·dic·tive·ly** adv — **vin·dic·tive·ness** n

**vine** n : climbing or trailing plant

**vin·e·gar** n : acidic liquid obtained by fermentation — **vin·e·gary** adj

**vin·tage** n 1 : season's yield of grapes or wine 2 : period of origin ∼ adj : of enduring interest

**vi·nyl** n : strong plastic

**vi·o·late** vb 1 : act with disrespect or disregard of 2 : rape 3 : desecrate — **vi·o·la·tion** n — **vi·o·la·tor** n

**vi·o·lence** n : intense physical force that causes or is intended to cause injury or destruction — **vi·o·lent** adj — **vi·o·lent·ly** adv

**vi·o·let** n 1 : small flowering plant 2 : reddish blue

**vi·o·lin** n : bowed stringed instrument — **vi·o·lin·ist** n

**VIP** n : very important person

**vir·gin** n 1 : unmarried woman 2 : a person who has never had sexual intercourse ∼ adj 1 : chaste 2 : natural and unspoiled — **vir·gin·al** adj — **vir·gin·al·ly** adv — **vir·gin·i·ty** n

**vir·tu·al** adj : being in effect but not in fact or name — **vir·tu·al·ly** adv

**vir·tue** n 1 : moral excellence 2 : effective or commendable quality 3 : chastity — **vir·tu·ous** adj — **vir·tu·ous·ly** adv

**vi·rus** n 1 : tiny disease-causing agent 2 : a computer program that performs a malicious action (as destroying data)

**vi·sa** n : authorization to enter a foreign country

**vise** n : device for clamping something being worked on

**vis·i·ble** adj 1 : capable of being seen 2 : manifest or apparent — **vis·i·bil·i·ty** n — **vis·i·bly** adv

**vi·sion** n 1 : vivid picture seen in a dream or trance or in the imagination 2 : foresight 3 : power of seeing ∼ vb : imagine

**vis·it** vb 1 : go or come to see 2 : stay with for a time as a guest 3 : cause or be a reward, affliction, or punishment ∼ n : short stay as a guest — **vis·it·able** adj — **vis·i·tor** n

**vi·sor** n 1 : front piece of a helmet 2 : part (as on a cap or car windshield) that shades the eyes

**vis·ta** n : distant view

**vi·su·al** adj 1 : relating to sight 2 : visible — **vi·su·al·ly** adv

**vi·su·al·ize** vb : form a mental image of — **vi·su·al·iza·tion** n — **vi·su·al·iz·er** n

**vi·tal** adj 1 : relating to, necessary for, or characteristic of life 2 : full of life and vigor 3 : fatal 4 : very important — **vi·tal·ly** adv

**vi·tal·i·ty** n 1 : life force 2 : energy

**vi·ta·min** n : natural organic substance essential to health

**viv·id** adj 1 : lively 2 : brilliant 3 : intense or sharp — **viv·id·ly** adv — **viv·id·ness** n

**vo·cab·u·lary** n 1 : list or collection of words 2 : stock of words used by a person or about a subject

**vo·cal** adj 1 : relating to or produced by or for the voice 2 : speaking out freely and usu. emphatically — **vo·cal·ize** vb

**vo·ca·tion** n : regular employment — **vo·ca·tion·al** adj

**voice** n 1 : sound produced through the mouth by humans and many animals 2 : power of speaking 3 : right of choice or opinion ∼ vb : express in words — **voiced** adj

**voice mail** n : an electronic system for recording and playing back telephone messages

**void** adj 1 : containing nothing 2 : lacking — with of 3 : not legally binding ∼ n 1 : empty space 2 : feeling of hollowness ∼ vb 1 : discharge (as body waste) 2 : make (as a contract) void — **void·able** adj — **void·er** n

**vol·a·tile** adj 1 : readily vaporizing at a relatively low temperature 2 : likely to change suddenly — **vol·a·til·i·ty** n — **vol·a·til·ize** vb

**vol·ca·no** n : opening in the earth's crust from which molten rock and steam come out — **vol·ca·nic** adj

**vol·ley** n 1 : flight of missiles (as arrows) 2 : simultaneous shooting of many weapons

**vol·ley·ball** n : game of batting a large ball over a net

**volt** n : unit for measuring the force that moves an electric current — **volt·age** n

**vol·ume** n 1 : book 2 : space occupied as measured by cubic units 3 : amount 4 : loudness of a sound

**vol·un·tary** adj 1 : done, made, or given freely and without expecting compensation 2 : relating to or controlled by the will — **vol·un·tar·i·ly** adv

**vol·un·teer** n : person who offers to help or work without expecting payment or reward ∼ vb 1 : offer or give voluntarily 2 : offer oneself as a volunteer

**vom·it** vb : throw up the contents of the stomach — **vom·it** n

**vote** n 1 : individual expression of preference in choosing or reaching a decision 2 : right to indicate one's preference or the preference expressed ∼ vb 1 : cast a vote 2 : choose or defeat by vote — **vote·less** adj — **vot·er** n

**vouch·er** n : written record or receipt that serves as proof of a transaction

**vow** n : solemn promise to do something or to live or act a certain way — **vow** vb

**vow·el** n 1 : speech sound produced without obstruction or friction in the mouth 2 : letter representing such a sound

**voy·age** n : long journey esp. by water or through space ∼ vb : make a voyage — **voy·ag·er** n

**vul·gar** adj 1 : relating to the common people 2 : lacking refinement 3 : offensive in manner or language — **vul·gar·ism** n — **vul·gar·i·ty** n — **vul·gar·ize** vb — **vul·gar·ly** adv

**vul·ner·a·ble** adj : exposed to attack or damage — **vul·ner·a·bil·i·ty** n — **vul·ner·a·bly** adv

**vul·ture** n : large flesh-eating bird

**vying** pres part of VIE

# W

**w** n : 23d letter of the alphabet

**wad** n 1 : little mass 2 : soft mass of fibrous material 3 : pliable plug to retain a powder charge 4 : considerable amount ∼ vb 1 : form into a wad 2 : stuff with a wad

**wade** vb 1 : step in or through (as water) 2 : move with difficulty — **wade** n — **wad·er** n

**wa·fer** n 1 : thin crisp cake or cracker 2 : waferlike thing

**waf·fle** n : crisped cake of batter cooked in a hinged utensil (**waffle iron**) ∼ vb : hesitate in deciding

**wag** vb : sway or swing from side to side or to and fro — **wag** n

**wage** vb : engage in ∼ n 1 : payment for labor or services 2 : compensation

**wa·ger** n or vb : bet

**wag·gle** vb : wag — **waggle** n

**wag·on** n 1 : 4-wheeled vehicle drawn by animals 2 : child's 4-wheeled cart

**waist** n 1 : narrowed part of the body

between chest and hips **2 :** waistlike part — **waist•line** *n*

**wait** *vb* **1 :** remain in readiness or expectation **2 :** delay **3 :** attend as a waiter ∼ *n* **1 :** concealment **2 :** act or period of waiting

**wait•er** *n* **:** person who serves others at tables

**wait•ress** *n* **:** woman who serves others at tables

**[1]wake** *vb* (**woke; wo•ken**) **1 :** keep watch **2 :** bring or come back to consciousness after sleep ∼ *n* **1 :** state of being awake **2 :** watch held over a dead body

**[2]wake** *n* **:** track left by a ship

**wak•en** *vb* **:** wake

**walk** *vb* **1 :** move or cause to move on foot **2 :** pass over, through, or along by walking ∼ *n* **1 :** a going on foot **2 :** place or path for walking **3 :** distance to be walked **4 :** way of living **5 :** way of walking **6 :** slow 4-beat gait of a horse — **walk•er** *n*

**wall** *n* **1 :** structure for defense or for enclosing something **2 :** upright enclosing part of a building or room **3 :** something like a wall ∼ *vb* **:** provide, separate, surround, or close with a wall — **walled** *adj*

**wal•let** *n* **:** pocketbook with compartments

**wal•low** *vb* **1 :** roll about in deep mud **2 :** indulge oneself excessively ∼ *n* **:** place for wallowing

**wal•nut** *n* **1 :** nut with a furrowed shell and adherent husk **2 :** tree on which this nut grows or its brown wood

**wand** *n* **:** slender staff

**wan•der** *vb* **1 :** move about aimlessly **2 :** stray **3 :** become delirious — **wan•der•er** *n*

**wane** *vb* **1 :** grow smaller or less **2 :** lose power, prosperity, or influence — **wane** *n*

**want** *vb* **1 :** lack **2 :** need **3 :** desire earnestly ∼ *n* **1 :** deficiency **2 :** dire need **3 :** something wanted

**war** *n* **1 :** armed fighting between nations **2 :** state of hostility or conflict **3 :** struggle between opposing forces or for a particular end ∼ *vb* **:** engage in warfare — **war•less** *adj* — **war•time** *n*

**war•ble** *n* **1 :** melodious succession of low pleasing sounds **2 :** musical trill ∼ *vb* **:** sing or utter in a trilling way

**ward** *n* **1 :** a guarding or being under guard or guardianship **2 :** division of a prison or hospital **3 :** electoral or administrative division of a city **4 :** person under protection of a guardian or a law court ∼ *vb* **:** turn aside — **ward•ship** *n*

**war•den** *n* **1 :** guardian **2 :** official charged with supervisory duties or enforcement of laws **3 :** official in charge of a prison

**ward•robe** *n* **1 :** clothes closet **2 :** collection of wearing apparel

**ware•house** *n* **:** place for storage of merchandise — **ware•house** *vb* — **ware•house•man** *n* — **ware•hous•er** *n*

**war•fare** *n* **1 :** military operations between enemies **2 :** struggle

**war•like** *adj* **:** fond of, relating to, or used in war

**warm** *adj* **1 :** having or giving out moderate or adequate heat **2 :** serving to retain heat **3 :** showing strong feeling **4 :** giving a pleasant impression of warmth, cheerfulness, or friendliness ∼ *vb* **1 :** make or become warm **2 :** give warmth or energy to **3 :** experience feelings of affection **4 :** become increasingly ardent, interested, or competent — **warm•er** *n* — **warm•ly** *adv* — **warm up** *vb* **:** make ready by preliminary activity

**warmth** *n* **1 :** quality or state of being warm **2 :** enthusiasm

**warn** *vb* **1 :** put on guard **2 :** notify in advance — **warn•ing** *n or adj*

**warp** *n* **1 :** lengthwise threads in a woven fabric **2 :** twist ∼ *vb* **1 :** twist out of shape **2 :** lead astray **3 :** distort

**war•rant** *n* **1 :** authorization **2 :** legal writ authorizing action ∼ *vb* **1 :** declare or maintain positively **2 :** guarantee **3 :** approve **4 :** justify

**war•ran•ty** *n* **:** guarantee of the integrity of a product

**war•rior** *n* **:** one engaged or experienced in warfare

**wart** *n* **1 :** small projection on the skin caused by a virus **2 :** wartlike protuberance — **warty** *adj*

**wary** *adj* **:** careful in guarding against danger or deception

**was** *past 1st & 3d sing of* BE

**wash** *vb* **1 :** cleanse with or as if with a liquid (as water) **2 :** wet thoroughly with liquid **3 :** flow along the border of **4 :** flow in a stream **5 :** move or remove by or as if by the action of water **6 :** cover or daub lightly with a liquid **7 :** undergo laundering ∼ *n* **1 :** act of washing or being washed **2 :** articles to be washed **3 :** surging action of water or disturbed air — **wash•able** *adj* — **wash•cloth** *n*

**wash•er** *n* **1 :** machine for washing **2 :** ring used around a bolt or screw to ensure tightness or relieve friction

**wash•ing** *n* **:** articles to be washed

**Washington's Birthday** *n* **:** the 3d Monday in February or formerly February 22 observed as a legal holiday

**waste** *n* **1 :** sparsely settled or barren region **2 :** act or an instance of wasting **3 :** refuse (as garbage or rubbish) **4 :** material (as feces) produced but not used by a living body ∼ *vb* **1 :** ruin **2 :** spend or use carelessly **3 :** lose substance or energy ∼ *adj* **1 :** wild and uninhabited **2 :** being of no further use — **waste•bas•ket** *n* — **wast•er** *n* — **waste•ful** *adj* — **waste•ful•ly** *adv* — **waste•ful•ness** *n* — **waste•land** *n*

**watch** *vb* **1 :** be or stay awake intentionally **2 :** be on the lookout for danger **3 :** observe **4 :** keep oneself informed about ∼ *n* **1 :** act of keeping awake to guard **2 :** close observation **3 :** one that watches **4 :** period of duty on a ship or those on duty during this period **5 :** timepiece carried on the person — **watch•dog** *n* — **watch•er** *n* — **watch•ful** *adj* — **watch•ful•ly** *adv* — **watch•ful•ness** *n* — **watch•man** *n*

**wa•ter** *n* **1 :** liquid that descends as rain and forms rivers, lakes, and seas **2 :** liquid containing or resembling water ∼ *vb* **1 :** supply with or get water **2 :** dilute with or as if with water **3 :** form or secrete watery matter

**wa•ter•fall** *n* **:** steep descent of the water of a stream

**wa•ter•mel•on** *n* **:** large fruit with sweet juicy usu. red pulp

**wa•ter•proof** *adj* **:** not letting water through ∼ *vb* **:** make waterproof — **wa•ter•proof•ing** *n*

**wa•ter•tight** *adj* **1 :** so tight as not to let water in **2 :** allowing no possibility for doubt or uncertainty

**wa•tery** *adj* **1 :** containing, full of, or giving out water **2 :** being like water **3 :** soft and soggy

**watt** *n* **:** unit of electric power — **watt•age** *n*

**wave** *vb* **1 :** flutter **2 :** signal with the hands **3 :** wave to and fro with the hand **4 :** curve up and down like a wave ∼ *n* **1 :** moving swell on the surface of water **2 :** wavelike shape **3 :** waving motion **4 :** sudden temporary increase **5 :** disturbance that transfers energy from point to point — **wave•length** *n* — **wave•let** *n* — **wave•like** *adj* — **wavy** *adj*

**wa•ver** *vb* **1 :** fluctuate in opinion, allegiance, or direction **2 :** flicker **3 :** falter — **waver** *n* — **wa•ver•er** *n* — **wa•ver•ing•ly** *adv*

**[1]wax** *n* **1 :** yellowish plastic substance secreted by bees **2 :** substance like beeswax ∼ *vb* **:** treat or rub with wax esp. for polishing — **waxy** *adj*

**[2]wax** *vb* **1 :** grow larger **2 :** become

**way** *n* **1 :** thoroughfare for travel or passage **2 :** route **3 :** course of action **4 :** method **5 :** detail **6 :** usual or characteristic state of affairs **7 :** condition **8 :** distance **9 :** progress along a course — **by the way :** in a digression — **by way of 1 :** for the purpose of **2 :** by the route through — **out of the way :** remote

**way•ward** *adj* **1 :** following one's own capricious inclinations **2 :** not predictable

**we** *pron* — used of a group that includes the speaker or writer

**weak** *adj* **1 :** lacking strength or vigor **2 :** deficient in vigor of mind or character **3 :** of less than usual strength **4 :** not having or exerting authority — **weak•en** *vb* — **weak•ly** *adv* — **weak•ness** *n*

**weak•ling** *n* **:** person who is physically, mentally, or morally weak

**wealth** *n* **1 :** abundant possessions or resources **2 :** great quantity

**wealthy** *adj* **:** having wealth

**weap•on** *n* **1 :** something (as a gun) that may be used to fight with **2 :** means by which one contends against another — **weap•on•less** *adj*

**wear** *vb* (**wore; worn**) **1 :** use as an article of clothing or adornment **2 :** carry on the person **3 :** show an appearance of **4 :** decay by use or by scraping **5 :** lessen the strength of **6 :** endure use ∼ *n* **1 :** act of wearing **2 :** clothing **3 :** lasting quality **4 :** result of use — **wear•able** *adj* — **wear•er** *n* — **wear out** *vb* **1 :** make or become useless by wear **2 :** tire

**wea•ry** *adj* **1 :** worn out in strength, freshness, or patience **2 :** expressing or characteristic of weariness ∼ *vb* **:** make or become weary — **wea•ri•ly** *adv* — **wea•ri•ness** *n* — **wea•ri•some** *adj* — **wea•ri•some•ly** *adv*

**weath•er** *n* **:** state of the atmosphere ∼ *vb* **1 :** expose to or endure the action of weather **2 :** endure — **weath•er•man** *n* — **weath•er•proof** *adj or vb*

**weave** *vb* (**wove; wo•ven**) **1 :** form by interlacing strands of material **2 :** to make as if by weaving together parts **3 :** follow a winding course ∼ *n* **:** pattern or method of weaving — **weav•er** *n*

**web** *n* **1 :** cobweb **2 :** animal or plant membrane **3 :** network **4** *cap* **:** World Wide Web ∼ *vb* **:** cover or provide with a web — **webbed** *adj*

**web•bing** *n* **:** strong closely woven tape

**Web site** *n* **:** group of World Wide Web pages available online

**wed** *vb* **1 :** marry **2 :** unite

**wed•ding** *n* **:** marriage ceremony and celebration

**wedge** *n* **:** V-shaped object used for splitting, raising, forcing open, or tightening ∼ *vb* **1 :** tighten or split with a wedge **2 :** force into a narrow space

**Wednes•day** *n* **:** 4th day of the week

**wee** *adj* **:** very small

**weed** *n* **:** unwanted plant ∼ *vb* **1 :** remove weeds **2 :** get rid of — **weed•er** *n* — **weedy** *adj*

**weeds** *n pl* **:** mourning clothes

**week** *n* **1 :** 7 successive days **2 :** calendar period of 7 days beginning with Sunday and ending with Saturday **3 :** the working or school days of the calendar week

**week•day** *n* **:** any day except Sunday and often Saturday

**week•end** *n* **:** Saturday and Sunday ∼ *vb* **:** spend the weekend

**week•ly** *adj* **:** occurring, appearing, or done every week ∼ *n* **:** weekly publication — **week•ly** *adv*

**weep** *vb* (**wept; wept**) **:** shed tears — **weep•er** *n* — **weepy** *adj*

**weigh** *vb* **1 :** determine the heaviness of **2 :** have a specified weight **3 :** consider carefully **4 :** raise (an anchor) off the sea floor **5 :** press down or burden

**weight** *n* **1 :** amount that something weighs **2 :** relative heaviness **3 :** heavy object **4 :** burden or pressure **5 :** importance ∼ *vb* **1 :** load with a weight **2 :** oppress — **weight•less** *adj* — **weight•less•ness** *n* — **weighty** *adj*

**weird** *adj* **1 :** unearthly or mysterious **2 :** strange — **weird•ly** *adv* — **weird•ness** *n*

**wel•come** *vb* **:** accept or greet cordially ∼ *adj* **:** received or permitted gladly ∼ *n* **:** cordial greeting or reception

**wel•fare** *n* **1 :** prosperity **2 :** government aid for those in need

**[1]well** *n* **1 :** spring **2 :** hole sunk in the earth to obtain a natural deposit (as of oil) **3 :** source of supply **4 :** open space extending vertically through floors ∼ *vb* **:** flow forth

**[2]well** *adv* (**bet•ter; best**) **1 :** in a good or proper manner **2 :** satisfactorily **3 :** fully **4 :** intimately **5 :** considerably ∼ *adj* **1 :** satisfactory **2 :** prosperous **3 :** desirable **4 :** healthy

**well–adjusted** *adj* **:** not psychologically troubled

**well–be•ing** *n* **:** state of being happy, healthy, or prosperous

**well–known** *adj* **:** widely known or acknowledged

**well–mean•ing** *adj* **:** having good intentions

**well–off** *adj* **:** being in good condition esp. financially

**well–to–do** *adj* **:** prosperous

**went** *past of* GO

**wept** *past of* WEEP

**were** *past 2d sing, past pl, or past subjunctive of* BE

**west** *adv* **:** to or toward the west ∼ *adj* **:** situated toward or at or coming from the west ∼ *n* **1 :** direction of sunset **2** *cap* **:** regions to the west — **west•er•ly** *adv or adj* — **west•ward** *adv or adj* — **west•wards** *adv*

**west•ern** *adj* **1** *cap* **:** of a region designated West **2 :** lying toward or coming from the west — **West•ern•er** *n*

**wet** *adj* **1 :** consisting of or covered or soaked with liquid **2 :** not dry ∼ *n* **:** moisture ∼ *vb* **:** make or become moist — **wet•ly** *adv* — **wet•ness** *n*

**whack** *vb* **:** strike sharply ∼ *n* **1 :** sharp blow **2 :** proper working order **3 :** chance **4 :** try

**whale** *n* **:** large marine mammal ∼ *vb* **:** hunt for whales — **whale•boat** *n* — **whal•er** *n*

**wharf** *n* **:** structure alongside which boats lie to load or unload

**what** *pron* **1** — used to inquire the identity or nature of something **2 :** that which **3 :** whatever ∼ *adv* **:** in what respect ∼ *adj* **1** — used to inquire about the identity or nature of something **2 :** how remarkable or surprising **3 :** whatever

**what•ev•er** *pron* **1 :** anything or everything that **2 :** no matter what ∼ *adj* **:** of any kind at all

**wheat** *n* **:** cereal grain that yields flour — **wheat•en** *adj*

**wheel** *n* **1 :** disk or circular frame capable of turning on a central axis **2 :** device of which the main part is a wheel ∼ *vb* **1 :** convey or move on wheels or a wheeled vehicle **2 :** rotate **3 :** turn so as to change direction — **wheeled** *adj* — **wheel•er** *n* — **wheel•less** *adj*

**wheeze** *vb* **:** breathe with difficulty and with a whistling sound — **wheeze** *n* — **wheezy** *adj*

**when** *adv* — used to inquire about or designate a particular time ∼ *conj* **1 :** at or during the time that **2 :** every time that **3 :** if **4 :** although ∼ *pron* **:** what time

**when•ev•er** *conj or adv* **:** at whatever time

**where** *adv* **1 :** at, in, or to what place **2**

: at, in, or to what situation, position, direction, circumstances, or respect ~ *conj* 1 : at, in, or to what place, position, or circumstance 2 : at, in, or to which place ~ *n* : place

**where•abouts** *adv* : about where ~ *n sing or pl* : place where a person or thing is

**where•as** *conj* 1 : while on the contrary 2 : since

**wher•ev•er** *adv* : where ~ *conj* : at, in, or to whatever place or circumstance

**whether** *conj* 1 : if it is or was true that 2 : if it is or was better 3 : whichever is the case

**which** *adj* 1 : being what one or ones out of a group 2 : whichever ~ *pron* 1 : which one or ones 2 : whichever

**which•ev•er** *pron or adj* : no matter what one

**whiff** *n* 1 : slight gust 2 : inhalation of odor, gas, or smoke 3 : slight trace ~ *vb* : inhale an odor

**while** *n* 1 : period of time 2 : time and effort used ~ *conj* 1 : during the time that 2 : as long as 3 : although ~ *vb* : cause to pass esp. pleasantly

**whim** *n* : sudden wish, desire, or change of mind

**whim•sy, whim•sey** *n* 1 : whim 2 : fanciful creation — **whim•si•cal** *adj* — **whim•si•cal•ly** *adv*

**whine** *vb* 1 : utter a usu. high-pitched plaintive cry 2 : complain — **whine** *n* — **whin•er** *n* — **whiny** *adj*

**whip** *vb* 1 : move quickly 2 : strike with something slender and flexible 3 : defeat 4 : incite 5 : beat into a froth ~ *n* 1 : flexible device used for whipping 2 : party leader responsible for discipline 3 : beating motion — **whip•per** *n*

**whip•lash** *n* : injury from a sudden sharp movement of the neck and head

**whir** *vb* : move, fly, or revolve with a whir ~ *n* : continuous fluttering or vibratory sound

**whirl** *vb* 1 : move or drive in a circle 2 : spin 3 : move or turn quickly 4 : reel ~ *n* 1 : rapid circular movement 2 : state of commotion or confusion 3 : try

**whirl•pool** *n* : a current of water flowing in a circle

**whisk** *n* 1 : quick light sweeping or brushing motion 2 : usu. wire kitchen implement for beating ~ *vb* 1 : move or convey briskly 2 : beat 3 : brush lightly

**whis•ker** *n* 1 *pl* : beard 2 : long bristle or hair near an animal's mouth — **whis•kered** *adj*

**whis•key, whis•ky** *n* : liquor distilled from a fermented mash of grain

**whis•per** *vb* 1 : speak softly 2 : tell by whispering ~ *n* 1 : soft low sound 2 : rumor

**whis•tle** *n* 1 : device by which a shrill sound is produced 2 : shrill clear sound made by a whistle or through the lips ~ *vb* 1 : make or utter a whistle 2 : signal or call by a whistle 3 : produce by whistling — **whis•tler** *n*

**white** *adj* 1 : free from color 2 : of the color of new snow or milk 3 : having light skin ~ *n* 1 : color of maximum lightness 2 : white part or thing 3 : person who is light-skinned — **white•ness** *n* — **whit•ish** *adj*

**white–col•lar** *adj* : relating to salaried employees with duties not requiring protective or work clothing

**whit•en** *vb* : make or become white — **whit•en•er** *n*

**whit•tle** *vb* 1 : pare 2 : shape by paring 3 : reduce gradually

**whiz, whizz** *vb* : make a sound like a speeding object — **whiz, whizz** *n*

**who** *pron* 1 : what or which person or persons 2 : person or persons that 3 — used to introduce a relative clause

**who•ev•er** *pron* : no matter who

**whole** *adj* 1 : being in healthy or sound condition 2 : having all its parts or elements 3 : constituting the total sum of ~ *n* 1 : complete amount or sum 2 : something whole or entire — **on the whole** 1 : considering all circumstances 2 : in general — **whole•ness** *n*

**whole•heart•ed** *adj* : sincere

**whole•sale** *n* : sale of goods in quantity usu. for resale by a retail merchant ~ *adj* 1 : of or relating to wholesaling 2 : performed on a large scale ~ *vb* : sell at wholesale — **whole•sale** *adv* — **whole•sal•er** *n*

**whole•some** *adj* 1 : promoting mental, spiritual, or bodily health 2 : healthy — **whole•some•ness** *n*

**whol•ly** *adv* 1 : totally 2 : solely

**whom** *pron, objective case of* WHO

**whom•ev•er** *pron, objective case of* WHOEVER

**whoop** *vb* : shout loudly ~ *n* : shout

**whop•per** *n* 1 : something unusually large or extreme of its kind 2 : monstrous lie

**whose** *adj* : of or relating to whom or which ~ *pron* : whose one or ones

**why** *adv* : for what reason, cause, or purpose ~ *conj* 1 : reason for which 2 : for which ~ *n* : reason ~ *interj* — used esp. to express surprise

**wick** *n* : cord that draws up oil, tallow, or wax to be burned

**wick•ed** *adj* 1 : morally bad 2 : harmful or troublesome 3 : very unpleasant 4 : very impressive — **wick•ed•ly** *adv* — **wick•ed•ness** *n*

**wide** *adj* 1 : covering a vast area 2 : measured at right angles to the length 3 : having a great measure across 4 : opened fully 5 : far from the thing in question ~ *adv* 1 : over a great distance 2 : so as to leave considerable space between 3 : fully — **wide•ly** *adv* — **wid•en** *vb*

**wide–awake** *adj* : alert

**wides•pread** *adj* : generally known or spread out

**wid•ow** *n* : woman who has lost her husband by death and has not married again ~ *vb* : cause to become a widow — **wid•ow•hood** *n*

**wid•ow•er** *n* : man who has lost his wife by death and has not married again

**width** *n* 1 : distance from side to side 2 : largeness of extent 3 : measured and cut piece of material

**wield** *vb* 1 : use or handle esp. effectively 2 : exert — **wield•er** *n*

**wife** *n* (**wives**) : married woman — **wife•hood** *n* — **wife•less** *adj* — **wife•ly** *adj*

**wig** *n* : manufactured covering of hair for the head

**wig•gle** *vb* 1 : move with quick jerky or shaking movements 2 : wriggle — **wig•gle** *n* — **wig•gler** *n*

**wild** *adj* 1 : living or being in a state of nature and not domesticated or cultivated 2 : showing lack of restraint 3 : turbulent 4 : crazy 5 : not civilized 6 : erratic ~ *n* 1 : wilderness 2 : undomesticated state ~ *adv* : without control — **wild•ly** *adv* — **wild•ness** *n*

**wil•der•ness** *n* : uncultivated and uninhabited region

**wild•fire** *n* : sweeping and destructive fire

**wild•life** *n* : undomesticated animals

**will** *vb past* **would** 1 : wish to 2 — used as an auxiliary verb to express (1) desire or willingness, (2) customary action, (3) simple future time, (4) capability, (5) determination, (6) probability, (7) inevitability, or (8) a command 3 : dispose of by a will ~ *n* 1 : often determined wish 2 : act, process, or experience of willing 3 : power of controlling one's actions or emotions 4 : legal document disposing of property after death

**will•ful, wil•ful** *adj* 1 : governed by will without regard to reason 2 : intentional — **will•ful•ly** *adv*

**will•ing** *adj* 1 : inclined or favorably disposed in mind 2 : prompt to act 3 : done, borne, or accepted voluntarily or without reluctance — **will•ing•ly** *adv* — **will•ing•ness** *n*

**will•pow•er** *n* : energetic determination

**wilt** *vb* 1 : lose or cause to lose freshness and become limp esp. from lack of water 2 : grow weak

**win** *vb* (**won; won**) 1 : get possession of esp. by effort 2 : gain victory in battle or a contest 3 : make friendly or favorable ~ *n* : victory

**[1]wind** *n* 1 : movement of the air 2 : breath 3 : gas in the stomach or intestines 4 : air carrying a scent 5 : intimation ~ *vb* 1 : get a scent of 2 : cause to be out of breath

**[2]wind** *vb* 1 : have or follow a curving course 2 : move or lie to encircle 3 : encircle or cover with something pliable 4 : tighten the spring of ~ *n* **wound; wound** : turn or coil — **wind•er** *n*

**wind•fall** *n* 1 : thing blown down by wind 2 : unexpected benefit

**wind•mill** *n* : machine worked by the wind turning vanes

**win•dow** *n* 1 : opening in the wall of a building to let in light and air 2 : pane in a window 3 : span of time for something 4 : area of a computer display — **win•dow•less** *adj*

**wind•shield** *n* : transparent screen in front of the occupants of a vehicle

**wind•up** *n* : end — **wind up** *vb*

**wind•ward** *adj* : being in or facing the direction from which the wind is blowing ~ *n* : direction from which the wind is blowing

**windy** *adj* 1 : having wind 2 : indulging in useless talk

**wing** *n* 1 : movable paired appendage for flying 2 : winglike thing 3 *pl* : area at the side of the stage out of sight 4 : faction ~ *vb* 1 : fly 2 : propel through the air — **winged** *adj* — **wing•less** *adj* — **on the wing** : in flight — **under one's wing** : in one's charge or care

**wink** *vb* 1 : close and open the eyes quickly 2 : avoid seeing or noticing something 3 : twinkle 4 : close and open one eye quickly as a signal or hint ~ *n* 1 : brief sleep 2 : act of winking 3 : instant — **wink•er** *n*

**win•ner** *n* : one that wins

**win•ning** *n* 1 : victory 2 : money won at gambling ~ *adj* 1 : victorious 2 : charming

**win•ter** *n* : season between autumn and spring ~ *adj* : sown in autumn for harvest the next spring or summer — **win•ter•time** *n*

**wipe** *vb* 1 : clean or dry by rubbing 2 : remove by rubbing 3 : erase completely 4 : destroy 5 : pass over a surface ~ *n* : act or instance of wiping — **wip•er** *n*

**wire** *n* 1 : thread of metal 2 : work made of wire 3 : telegram or one sent through a cable under the sea ~ *vb* 1 : provide with wire 2 : bind or mount with wire — **wire•less** *adj*

**wiry** *adj* 1 : resembling wire 2 : slender yet strong and sinewy — **wir•i•ness** *n*

**wis•dom** *n* 1 : accumulated learning 2 : good sense

**wise** *adj* 1 : having or showing wisdom, good sense, or good judgment 2 : aware of what is going on — **wise•ly** *adv*

**wise•crack** *n* : clever, smart, or flippant remark ~ *vb* : make a wisecrack

**wish** *vb* 1 : have a desire 2 : express a wish concerning 3 : request ~ *n* 1 : a wishing or desire 2 : expressed will or desire

**wish•ful** *adj* 1 : expressive of a wish 2 : according with wishes rather than fact

**wit** *n* 1 : reasoning power 2 : mental soundness — *usu. pl.* 3 : quickness and cleverness in handling words and ideas 4 : talent for clever remarks or one noted for witty remarks — **wit•less** *adj* — **wit•less•ly** *adv* — **wit•less•ness** *n* — **wit•ted** *adj*

**witch** *n* 1 : person believed to have magic power 2 : ugly old woman ~ *vb* : bewitch

**witch•craft** *n* : power or practices of a witch

**with** *prep* 1 : against, to, or toward 2 : in support of 3 : because of 4 : in the company of 5 : having 6 : despite 7 : containing 8 : by means of

**with•draw** *vb* 1 : take back or away 2 : call back or retract 3 : go away 4 : terminate one's participation in or use of — **with•draw•al** *n*

**with•er** *vb* 1 : shrivel 2 : lose or cause to lose energy, force, or freshness

**with•hold** *vb* 1 : hold back 2 : refrain from giving

**with•in** *adv* 1 : in or into the interior 2 : inside oneself ~ *prep* 1 : in or to the inner part of 2 : in the limits or compass of

**with•out** *prep* 1 : outside 2 : lacking 3 : unaccompanied or unmarked by — **with•out** *adv*

**wit•ness** *n* 1 : testimony 2 : one who testifies 3 : one present at a transaction to testify that it has taken place 4 : one who has personal knowledge or experience 5 : something serving as proof ~ *vb* 1 : bear witness 2 : act as legal witness of 3 : furnish proof of 4 : be a witness of 5 : be the scene of

**wit•ty** *adj* : marked by or full of wit — **wit•ti•ly** *adv* — **wit•ti•ness** *n*

**wives** *pl of* WIFE

**wiz•ard** *n* 1 : magician 2 : very clever person — **wiz•ard•ry** *n*

**wob•ble** *vb* 1 : move or cause to move with an irregular rocking motion 2 : tremble 3 : waver — **wob•ble** *n* — **wob•bly** *adj*

**woe** *n* 1 : deep suffering 2 : misfortune

**woke** *past of* WAKE

**woken** *past part of* WAKE

**wolf** *n* (**wolves**) : large doglike predatory mammal ~ *vb* : eat greedily — **wolf•ish** *adj*

**wom•an** *n* (**wom•en**) 1 : adult female person 2 : women in general 3 : feminine nature — **wom•an•hood** *n* — **wom•an•ish** *adj* — **wom•an•li•ness** *n* — **wom•an•ly** *adv*

**won** *past of* WIN

**won•der** *n* 1 : cause of astonishment or surprise 2 : feeling (as of astonishment) aroused by something extraordinary ~ *vb* 1 : feel surprise 2 : feel curiosity or doubt

**won•der•ful** *adj* 1 : exciting wonder 2 : unusually good — **won•der•ful•ly** *adv* — **won•der•ful•ness** *n*

**won•drous** *adj* : wonderful — **won•drous•ly** *adv* — **won•drous•ness** *n*

**wood** *n* 1 : dense growth of trees usu. smaller than a forest — often pl. 2 : hard fibrous substance of trees and shrubs beneath the bark 3 : wood prepared for some use (as burning) ~ *adj* 1 : wooden 2 : suitable for working with wood 3 : living or growing in woods — **wood•chop•per** *n* — **wood•pile** *n* — **wood•shed** *n*

**wood•en** *adj* 1 : made of wood 2 : lacking resilience 3 : lacking ease, liveliness or interest — **wood•en•ly** *adv* — **wood•en•ness** *n*

**wood•work** *n* : work (as interior house fittings) made of wood

**woody** *adj* 1 : abounding with woods 2 : of, containing, or like wood fibers — **wood•i•ness** *n*

**wool** *n* 1 : soft hair of some mammals and esp. the sheep 2 : something (as a textile) made of wool — **wooled** *adj*

**wool•en, wool•len** *adj* 1 : made of wool 2 : relating to the manufacture of woolen products ~ *n* 1 : woolen fabric 2 : woolen garments — *usu. pl.*

**wool•ly** *adj* 1 : of, relating to, or bearing

**wool 2** : consisting of or resembling wool **3** : confused or turbulent

**woo•zy** *adj* **1** : confused **2** : somewhat dizzy, nauseated, or weak — **woo•zi•ness** *n*

**word** *n* **1** : brief remark **2** : speech sound or series of speech sounds that communicates a meaning **3** : written representation of a word **4** : order **5** : news **6** : promise **7** *pl* : dispute ~ *vb* : express in words — **word•less** *adj*

**word processing** *n* : production of structured and printed documents through a computer program (**word processor**) — **word process** *vb*

**wordy** *adj* : using many words — **word•i•ness** *n*

**wore** *past of* WEAR

**work** *n* **1** : labor **2** : employment **3** : task **4** : something (as an artistic production) produced by mental effort or physical labor **5** *pl* : place where industrial labor is done **6** *pl* : moving parts of a mechanism **7** : workmanship ~ *adj* **1** : suitable for wear while working **2** : used for work ~ *vb* **1** : bring to pass **2** : create by expending labor upon **3** : bring or get into a form or condition **4** : set or keep in operation **5** : solve **6** : cause to labor **7** : arrange **8** : excite **9** : labor **10** : perform work regularly for wages **11** : function according to plan or design **12** : produce a desired effect — **work•able** *adj* — **work•bench** *n* — **work•er** *n* — **work•man** *n* — **work•room** *n* — **in the works** : in preparation

**work•day** *n* **1** : day on which work is done **2** : period of time during which one is working

**work•ing** *adj* **1** : adequate to allow work to be done **2** : adopted or assumed to help further work or activity ~ *n* : operation — usu. used in pl.

**work•man•ship** *n* **1** : art or skill of a workman **2** : quality of a piece of work

**work•out** *n* : exercise to improve one's fitness

**work out** *vb* **1** : bring about by effort **2** : solve **3** : develop **4** : to be successful **5** : perform exercises

**work•shop** *n* **1** : small establishment for manufacturing or handicrafts **2** : seminar emphasizing exchange of ideas and practical methods

**world** *n* **1** : universe **2** : earth with its inhabitants and all things upon it **3** : people in general **4** : great number or quantity **5** : class of persons or their sphere of interest

**world•ly** *adj* **1** : devoted to this world and its pursuits rather than to religion **2** : sophisticated — **world•li•ness** *n*

**world•wide** *adj* : extended throughout the entire world — **worldwide** *adv*

**World Wide Web** *n* : part of the Internet accessible through a browser

**worm** *n* **1** : earthworm or a similar animal **2** *pl* : disorder caused by parasitic worms ~ *vb* **1** : move or cause to move in a slow and indirect way **2** : to free from worms — **wormy** *adj*

**worn** *past part of* WEAR

**worn–out** *adj* : exhausted or used up by or as if by wear

**wor•ry** *vb* **1** : shake and mangle with the teeth **2** : disturb **3** : feel or express anxiety ~ *n* **1** : anxiety **2** : cause of anxiety — **wor•ri•er** *n* — **wor•ri•some** *adj*

**worse** *adj, comparative of* BAD *or of* ILL **1** : bad or evil in a greater degree **2** : more unwell ~ *n* **1** : one that is worse **2** : greater degree of badness ~ *adv comparative of* BAD *or of* ILL : in a worse manner

**wors•en** *vb* : make or become worse

**wor•ship** *n* **1** : reverence toward a divine being or supernatural power **2** : expression of reverence **3** : extravagant respect or devotion ~ *vb* **1** : honor or reverence **2** : perform or take part in worship — **wor•ship•er, wor•ship•per** *n*

**worst** *adj, superlative of* BAD *or of* ILL **1** : most bad, evil, ill, or corrupt **2** : most unfavorable, unpleasant, or painful ~ *n* : one that is worst ~ *adv superlative of* ILL *or* BAD *or* BADLY : to the extreme degree of badness ~ *vb* : defeat

**worth** *prep* **1** : equal in value to **2** : deserving of ~ *n* **1** : monetary value **2** : value of something measured by its qualities **3** : moral or personal merit — **worth•less** *adj*

**worth•while** *adj* : being worth the time or effort spent

**wor•thy** *adj* **1** : having worth or value **2** : having sufficient worth ~ *n* : worthy person — **wor•thi•ly** *adv* — **wor•thi•ness** *n*

**would** *past of* WILL — used to express (1) preference, (2) intent, (3) habitual action, (4) contingency, (5) probability, or (6) a request

¹**wound** *n* **1** : injury in which the skin is broken **2** : mental hurt ~ *vb* : inflict a wound to or in

²**wound** *past of* WIND

**wove** *past of* WEAVE

**woven** *past part of* WEAVE

**wrap** *vb* **1** : cover esp. by winding or folding **2** : envelop and secure for transportation or storage **3** : enclose, surround, or conceal wholly **4** : coil, fold, draw, or twine about something ~ *n* **1** : wrapper or wrapping **2** : outer garment (as a shawl)

**wrap•per** *n* **1** : that in which something is wrapped **2** : one that wraps

**wreath** *n* : something (as boughs) intertwined into a circular shape

**wreathe** *vb* **1** : shape into or take on the shape of a wreath **2** : decorate or cover with a wreath

**wreck** *n* **1** : broken remains (as of a ship or vehicle) after heavy damage **2** : something disabled or in a state of ruin **3** : an individual who has become weak or infirm **4** : action of breaking up or destroying something ~ *vb* : ruin or damage by breaking up

**wreck•age** *n* **1** : act of wrecking **2** : remains of a wreck

**wreck•er** *n* **1** : automotive vehicle for removing disabled cars **2** : one that wrecks or tears down and removes buildings

**wrench** *vb* **1** : pull with violent twisting or force **2** : injure or disable by a violent twisting or straining ~ *n* **1** : forcible twisting **2** : tool for exerting a twisting force

**wres•tle** *vb* **1** : scuffle with and attempt to throw and pin an opponent **2** : compete against in wrestling **3** : struggle (as with a problem) ~ *n* : action or an instance of wrestling — **wres•tler** *n*

**wres•tling** *n* : sport in which 2 opponents try to throw and pin each other

**wretch•ed** *adj* **1** : deeply afflicted, dejected, or distressed **2** : grievous **3** : inferior — **wretch•ed•ly** *adv* — **wretch•ed•ness** *n*

**wrig•gle** *vb* **1** : twist and turn restlessly **2** : move along by twisting and turning — **wrig•gle** *n* — **wrig•gler** *n*

**wring** *vb* **wrung; wrung 1** : squeeze or twist out moisture **2** : get by or as if by twisting or pressing **3** : twist together in anguish **4** : pain — **wring•er** *n*

**wrin•kle** *n* : crease or small fold on a surface (as in the skin or in cloth) ~ *vb* : develop or cause to develop wrinkles — **wrin•kly** *adj*

**wrist** *n* : joint or region between the hand and the arm

**writ** *n* **1** : something written **2** : legal order in writing

**write** *vb* (**wrote; writ•ten**) **1** : form letters or words on a surface **2** : form the letters or the words of (as on paper) **3** : make up and set down for others to read **4** : write a letter to — **write off** *vb* : cancel

**writ•er** *n* : one that writes esp. as a business or occupation

**writ•ing** *n* **1** : act of one that writes **2** : handwriting **3** : something written or printed

**wrong** *n* **1** : unfair or unjust act **2** : something that is contrary to justice **3** : state of being or doing wrong ~ *adj* **1** : sinful **2** : not right according to a standard **3** : not suitable **4** : incorrect ~ *adv* **1** : in a wrong direction or manner **2** : incorrectly ~ *vb* **1** : do wrong to **2** : treat unjustly — **wrong•do•er** *n* — **wrong•do•ing** *n* — **wrong•ful** *adj* — **wrong•ful•ly** *adv* — **wrong•ful•ness** *n* — **wrong•ly** *adv*

**wrote** *past of* WRITE

**wrung** *past of* WRING

## X

**x** *n* **1** : 24th letter of the alphabet **2** : unknown quantity ~ *vb* : cancel with a series of *x*'s — usu. with *out*

**Xmas** *n* : Christmas

**x–ray** *vb* : examine, treat, or photograph with X rays

**X ray** *n* **1** : radiation of short wavelength that is able to penetrate solids **2** : photograph taken with X rays — **X–ray** *adj*

**xy•lo•phone** *n* : musical instrument with wooden bars that are struck — **xy•lo•phon•ist** *n*

## Y

**y** *n* : 25th letter of the alphabet

**yacht** *n* : luxurious pleasure boat ~ *vb* : race or cruise in a yacht

**yam** *n* **1** : edible root of a tropical vine **2** : deep orange sweet potato

**yank** *n* : strong sudden pull — **yank** *vb*

**Yan•kee** *n* : native or inhabitant of New England, the northern U.S., or the U.S.

¹**yard** *n* **1** : 3 feet **2** : long spar for supporting and spreading a sail — **yard•age** *n* — **yard•stick** *n*

²**yard** *n* **1** : enclosed roofless area **2** : grounds of a building **3** : work area

**yar•mul•ke** *n* : a small brimless cap worn by Jewish males in a synagogue

**yarn** *n* **1** : spun fiber for weaving or knitting **2** : tale

**yawn** *vb* : open the mouth wide ~ *n* : deep breath through a wide-open mouth — **yawn•er** *n*

**year** *n* **1** : period of about 365 days **2** *pl* : age

**year•book** *n* : annual report of the year's events

**year•ly** *adj* : annual — **year•ly** *adv*

**yearn** *vb* **1** : feel desire esp. for what one cannot have **2** : feel tenderness or compassion

**yearn•ing** *n* : tender or urgent desire

**yeast** *n* : froth or sediment in sugary liquids containing a tiny fungus and used in making alcoholic liquors and as a leaven in baking — **yeasty** *adj*

**yell** *vb* : utter a loud cry — **yell** *n*

**yel•low** *adj* **1** : of the color yellow **2** : sensational **3** : cowardly ~ *vb* : make or turn yellow ~ *n* **1** : color of lemons **2** : yolk of an egg — **yel•low•ish** *adj*

**yen** *n* : strong desire

**yes** *adv* — used to express consent or agreement ~ *n* : affirmative answer

**ye•shi•va, ye•shi•vah** *n* : Jewish school

**yes•ter•day** *adv* **1** : on the day preceding today **2** : only a short time ago ~ *n* **1** : day last past **2** : time not long past

**yet** *adv* **1** : in addition **2** : up to now **3** : so soon as now **4** : nevertheless ~ *conj* : but

**yield** *vb* **1** : surrender **2** : grant **3** : bear as a crop **4** : produce **5** : cease opposition or resistance ~ *n* : quantity produced or returned

**yo•ga** *n* : system of exercises for attaining bodily or mental control and well-being

**yo•gurt** *n* : fermented slightly acid soft food made from milk

**yoke** *n* **1** : neck frame for coupling draft animals or for carrying loads **2** : clamp **3** : slavery **4** : tie or link **5** : piece of a garment esp. at the shoulder ~ *vb* **1** : couple with a yoke **2** : join

**yolk** *n* : yellow part of an egg — **yolked** *adj*

**Yom Kip•pur** *n* : Jewish holiday observed in September or October with fasting and prayer as a day of atonement

**you** *pron* **1** : person or persons addressed **2** : person in general

**young** *adj* **1** : being in the first or an early stage of life, growth, or development **2** : recently come into being **3** : youthful ~ *n young* : persons or animals that are young — **young•ish** *adj*

**young•ster** *n* **1** : young person **2** : child

**your** *adj* : relating to you or yourself

**yours** *pron* : the ones belonging to you

**your•self** *pron* (**your•selves**) : you — used reflexively or for emphasis

**youth** *n* **1** : period between childhood and maturity **2** : young man **3** : young persons **4** : state or quality of being young, fresh, or vigorous

**youth•ful** *adj* **1** : relating to or appropriate to youth **2** : young **3** : vigorous and fresh — **youth•ful•ly** *adv* — **youth•ful•ness** *n*

**yo–yo** *n* : toy that falls from or rises to the hand as it unwinds and rewinds on a string

**yule** *n* : Christmas — **yule•tide** *n*

**yum•my** *adj* : highly attractive or pleasing

# Z

**z** *n* : 26th letter of the alphabet

**za•ny** *n* **1** : clown **2** : silly person ~ *adj* : crazy or foolish — **za•ni•ly** *adv* — **za•ni•ness** *n*

**zeal** *n* : enthusiasm

**ze•bra** *n* : horselike African mammal marked with light and dark stripes

**ze•nith** *n* : highest point

**ze•ro** *n* **1** : number represented by the symbol 0 or the symbol itself **2** : starting point **3** : lowest point ~ *adj* : having no size or quantity

**zest** *n* **1** : quality of enhancing enjoyment **2** : keen enjoyment — **zest•ful** *adj* — **zest•ful•ly** *adv* — **zest•ful•ness** *n*

**zig•zag** *n* : one of a series of short sharp turns or angles ~ *adj* : having zigzags ~ *adv* : in or by a zigzag path ~ *vb* : proceed along a zigzag path

**zil•lion** *n* : large indeterminate number

**¹zip** *vb* : move or act with speed ~ *n* : energy

**²zip** *vb* : close or open with a zipper

**zip code** *n* : number that identifies a U.S. postal delivery area

**zip•per** *n* : fastener consisting of 2 rows of interlocking teeth

**zip•py** *adj* : brisk

**zo•di•ac** *n* : imaginary belt in the heavens encompassing the paths of the planets and divided into 12 signs used in astrology — **zo•di•a•cal** *adj*

**zone** *n* **1** : division of the earth's surface based on latitude and climate **2** : distinctive area ~ *vb* **1** : mark off into zones **2** : reserve for special purposes — **zon•al** *adj* — **zon•al•ly** *adv* — **zo•na•tion** *n*

**zoo** *n* : collection of living animals usu. for public display — **zoo•keep•er** *n*

**zo•ol•o•gy** *n* : science of animals — **zo•o•log•i•cal** *adj* — **zo•ol•o•gist** *n*

**zoom** *vb* **1** : move with a loud hum or buzz **2** : move or increase with great speed — **zoom** *n*

# Basic English Grammar

The essence of the English language is the sentence. A sentence is a grammatically self-contained group of words that expresses a statement, a question, a command, a wish, or an exclamation. It is composed of a *subject*, about which something is said, and a *predicate*, which expresses what is said about the subject. The subject can be a single noun, a noun phrase, such as "*the strong wind*," or a noun clause, such as "*what he decides* is important to all of us." The predicate can be a single verb, a verb phrase, such as "*will be going*," a verb and all its modifiers, such as "*will be going as soon as the bus arrives*," or a verb and its complements, such as "*gave his client the bad news*."

In English, word order is important. The subject usually comes first, but not necessarily:

> **An amusement park** is across the river.
> Across the river is **an amusement park**.
> Is **an amusement park** across the river?

The grammar of English is concerned with the structure of these elements that make up a sentence. Every word in a sentence can be classified as a particular part of speech (*noun, verb, adjective,* etc.), according to its function in the sentence. The major parts of speech are briefly discussed in the following guide to basic English grammar.

## THE ADJECTIVE
The adjective gives information about a noun or pronoun, such as what kind

> the **black** cat
> a **joyful** occasion

or which one

> a **first** draft
> **that** suggestion

or how many

> **ten** players
> **few** new ideas

The adjective usually precedes the noun it modifies, but some adjectives can also follow certain verbs:

> the house is **white** (⟶ **white** house)
> the speeches seemed **long**
>   (⟶ **long** speeches)
> the chair felt **comfortable**
>   (⟶ **comfortable** chair)
> the tree grew **tall** (⟶ **tall** tree)

A few adjectives will follow their nouns, but usually only in set phrases:

> court-martial
> secretary-general

## POSITIVE, COMPARATIVE, AND SUPERLATIVE DEGREES OF ADJECTIVES
The positive degree is the basic form of the adjective. It gives basic information about the noun without reference to anything else (a *white* house). The comparative degree relates a noun to another—as having more or less of some quality (this house is *whiter* than that); the superlative degree relates the noun to all others of its class (this is the *whitest* house in the neighborhood).

When the adjective consists of a single syllable, the suffix *-er* is added to form the comparative degree, and the suffix *-est* is added to form the superlative degree. When the adjective consists of two syllables, the suffixes are often used to form the comparative (as *gentler*) and superlative (as *gentlest*), but the adverbs *more/less* can also be used to form the comparative (as *more*

*skillful* and *less skillful*), and likewise, the adverbs *most/least* can be used to form the superlative (as *most skillful* and *least skillful*). For adjectives of more than two syllables, the adverbs are usually used to form the comparative and superlative forms (as *more fortunate, most fortunate*).

There are a few adjectives that have unique comparative and superlative forms:

| Positive | Comparative | Superlative |
|---|---|---|
| good | better | best |
| bad | worse | worst |
| some | more | most |
| little (amount) | less | least |
| *but* | | |
| little (size) | littler | littlest |

There are a few adjectives that have no comparative or superlative forms:

> an **utter** failure
> the **principal** objections

## DEMONSTRATIVE ADJECTIVES
The demonstrative adjectives *this* and *that* are used to point out the one person or thing referred to (as "not *this* coat but *that* one"). The plural forms are *these* and *those*, respectively.

> **These** books are mine and **those** books are yours.

## DESCRIPTIVE ADJECTIVES
A descriptive adjective describes or indicates a quality, type, or condition:

> a **fascinating** conversation
> a **positive** attitude
> a **fast** computer

## INDEFINITE ADJECTIVES
An indefinite adjective is used to designate unspecified person(s) or thing(s):

> **some** children
> **other** projects
> **any** book

## INTERROGATIVE ADJECTIVES
An interrogative adjective is used to form a question:

> **Whose** office is this?
> **Which** book do you want?

## THE NOUN USED AS ADJECTIVE
A noun sometimes serves to modify another noun and thus functions as an adjective:

> the **Vietnam** War
> **word** processing

## POSSESSIVE ADJECTIVES
The possessive form of a personal pronoun is called a possessive adjective. Following is a list of possessive adjectives and a few examples of how they are used:

| Singular | Plural |
|---|---|
| my | our |
| your | your |
| his/her/its | their |

> Where's **my** magazine?
> **Your** cab is here.
> They can read **his** story.
> It was **her** idea.
> The box and **its** contents were inspected.
> She's **our** mother.
> **Your** photos are ready.
> We paid for **their** tickets.

## PREDICATE ADJECTIVES
A predicate adjective modifies the subject of a linking verb, such as *be, become, feel, taste, smell,* or *seem*:

> He is **lucky**.
> She became **angry**.
> They are **happy** with the outcome.
> The milk smells **bad**.
> The student seems **lonely**.

## PROPER ADJECTIVES
A proper adjective is derived from a proper noun and is capitalized:

> **Victorian** furniture
> a **Chinese** custom
> a **Shakespearean** scholar

## THE ADVERB
Adverbs, whether single words or phrases, usually give information about the verbs, such as *when*

> We arrived **yesterday**
> He woke up **late**

or *where*

> I found them **at the restaurant**
> He spent time **in [the] hospital**

or *how*

> They arose **quickly**
> She worked **hard**

Most single-word adverbs end in *-ly* and are formed by adding the suffix *-ly* to an adjective:

> **mad** ⟶ **madly**
> **wonderful** ⟶ **wonderfully**

When the adjective ends in *-y*, the adverb is formed by changing *-y* to *-i* and adding the suffix *-ly*:

> **happy** ⟶ **happily**
> **dainty** ⟶ **daintily**

When the adjective ends in *-ic*, the adverb is formed by adding the suffix *-ally*:

> **basic** ⟶ **basically**
> **numeric** ⟶ **numerically**

When an adjective ends in -ly, the adverb retains the same spelling:

> a **daily** routine (adjective)
> she calls her mother **daily** (adverb)
> an **early** meeting (adjective)
> the show started **early** (adverb)

Also, there are adverbs that do not end in -ly, for example:

> **again**
> **now**
> **soon**
> **too**
> **there**
> **how**

## POSITIVE, COMPARATIVE, AND SUPERLATIVE DEGREES OF ADVERBS

Adverbs, like adjectives, can have three degrees of comparison: the *positive* form exists without reference to anything else; the *comparative* degree relates to another—as being more or less of the adverb quality; and *superlative* relates to all members of a class. As a general rule, a single-syllable adverb ends in -er when it is comparative (as *faster*) and in -est when it is superlative (as *fastest*). For adverbs of three or more syllables, the comparative and superlative degrees are formed by using the adverbs *more/less* and *most/ least*. The comparative and superlative degrees of an adverb of two syllables are formed by following either one of these methods:

| Positive | Comparative | Superlative |
|---|---|---|
| early | earlier | earliest |
| easy | easier | easiest |
| nearly | more nearly | most nearly |
| quickly | more quickly | most quickly |
| satisfactorily | less satisfactorily | least satisfactorily |

Some adverbs, such as *only*, *quite*, and *very*, have no comparative or superlative forms.

## INTENSIVE ADVERBS

Intensive adverbs, such as *just* and *only*, are usually used only to emphasize other words. The emphasis varies according to the placement of the adverb within the sentence:

> He **just** nodded to me as he passed.
> He nodded to me **just** as he passed.
> I **only** wanted to speak with you.
> I wanted to speak **only** with you.

## INTERROGATIVE ADVERBS

Interrogative adverbs, such as *when*, *where*, and *why*, are used chiefly to introduce questions:

> **When** will he return?
> **Where** is the remote control?
> **Why** did you hide it?

## THE ARTICLE

Articles, sometimes called "determiners," are elements of a noun phrase that indicate whether the noun is "definite," that is, a specific individual, or "indefinite," that is, very general in nature.

## THE DEFINITE ARTICLE

There is only one form of the definite article: *the*.

> **The** boys were expelled.
> It was **the** best movie I have seen.

## THE INDEFINITE ARTICLE

The indefinite article *a* is used with every noun or abbreviation beginning with either a consonant or the sound of a consonant:

> **a** door
> **a** union
> **a** one-way street
> **a** B.A. degree
> **a** hat
> **a** U.S. Senator

The indefinite article *an* is used with every noun or abbreviation that begins with a vowel sound, whether or not the first letter of the noun or abbreviation is a vowel or consonant:

> **an** icicle
> **an** MP
> **an** honor
> **an** FAQ

When the first syllable of a noun beginning with *h* is not stressed or has only a slight stress, the article *a* is frequently used:

> **a** historian
> **a** heroic attempt
> **a** hilarious performance

However, the article *an* is sometimes used in these cases:

> **an** historian
> **an** heroic attempt
> **an** hilarious performance

Both forms are acceptable.

## THE CONJUNCTION

There are three main types of conjunctions: *coordinating conjunctions*, *correlative conjunctions*, and *subordinating conjunctions*.

## COORDINATING CONJUNCTIONS

Coordinating conjunctions, such as *and*, *but*, *for*, *or*, *nor*, *so*, and *yet*, are used to connect grammatical elements of the same type. These elements may be words, phrases, clauses, or complete sentences. Coordinating conjunctions are used to connect similar elements, to make exclusions or contrasts, to indicate an alternative, to indicate a cause, or to specify a result:

| | |
|---|---|
| **connecting similar elements:** | She ordered pencils, pens, **and** erasers. |
| **exclusion or contrast:** | He is a brilliant **but** arrogant man. They offered a promising plan, **but** it had not yet been tested. |
| **alternative:** | She can wait here **or** go on ahead. |
| **cause:** | The report is useless, **for** its information is no longer current. |
| **result:** | His diction is excellent, **so** every word is clear. |

## CORRELATIVE CONJUNCTIONS

Correlative conjunctions are used in groups of two to connect choices or elements of the same grammatical type:

> **Both** Rita **and** Jane attended the conference.
> **Either** you go **or** you stay.
> He had **neither** looks **nor** wit.

## SUBORDINATING CONJUNCTIONS

Subordinating conjunctions are used to connect a subordinate clause to an independent clause. These conjunctions express cause, condition or concession, manner, intention or result, time, place, or circumstance, as well as a possibility.

| | |
|---|---|
| **cause:** | **Because** she learns quickly, she is doing well in her new job. |
| **condition or concession:** | Don't call **unless** you are coming. |
| **manner:** | We'll do it **however** you tell us. |
| **intention or result:** | They burned all the bridges **so** that the enemy could not use them. |
| **time:** | She kept the meeting to a minimum **when** she could. |
| **place:** | **Wherever** he goes, he is welcomed with open arms. |

## THE NOUN

### Basic Uses

The noun may be a single word or a phrase (noun phrase). The noun phrase may consist of an article and/or adjectives and/or prepositional phrases. The noun can function as subject of a sentence, object of a verb, object of a preposition, predicate nominative, complement of an object, in apposition, and in direct discourse:

| | |
|---|---|
| **subject:** | **The office** was quiet. **The house with the green shutters** was for sale. |
| **direct object of a verb:** | He locked **the office**. |
| **indirect object of a verb:** | He gave **his client** the papers. |
| **object of a preposition:** | The business was in **bankruptcy**. The file is in **the office**. |
| **predicate nominative:** | Ms. Adams is **the managing partner**. |
| **complement of an object:** | They made Ms. Adams **managing partner**. |

| | |
|---|---|
| **in apposition:** | Ms. Adams, *the managing partner*, wrote that memo. |
| **in direct discourse:** | *Ms. Adams*, may I present Mr. Wilson. |

Nouns are often classified as proper nouns (*Eiffel Tower, White House*), common nouns (*tower, house*), abstract nouns (*honor, love*), concrete nouns (*desk, flower*), or collective nouns (*team, government*). American English typically uses a singular verb with a collective noun (the team *is*), while British English typically uses a plural verb (the government *are*).

Most nouns are neuter, showing no distinction as to whether having a masculine or feminine reference. However, a few nouns ending in *-ess* (as *empress, hostess*) are feminine in gender, and some others have a specific gender. For example: *husband, wife, father, mother, brother, sister*. The names of certain animals also have a specific gender, for example, *bull/cow, stag/doe*. When it is necessary to specify the gender of a neuter noun, the noun is usually modified with words like *male, female, man, woman* (a *male* parrot, *women* painters).

## THE NOUN AS ADJECTIVE
The noun has the function of an adjective when it precedes another noun:

> *olive* oil
> *business* management
> *emergency* room
> *dog* house

## THE FORMATION OF THE PLURAL
The plural of most nouns is formed by adding the suffix *-s* to the singular noun:

> book ⟶ books
> cat ⟶ cats

When the singular noun ends in *-s, -x, -z, -ch,* or *-sh,* the suffix *-es* is added to the singular:

> cross ⟶ crosses
> fox ⟶ foxes
> witch ⟶ witches
> wish ⟶ wishes

For a singular noun ending in *-z,* the last letter is doubled before adding the suffix *-es:*

> whiz ⟶ whizzes
> quiz ⟶ quizzes

For a singular noun ending in *-y* preceded by a consonant, the *-y* changes to *-i* and the suffix *-es* is added:

> fairy ⟶ fairies
> pony ⟶ ponies
> guppy ⟶ guppies

For a singular noun ending in *-y* preceded by a vowel, the *-y* usually does not change when the suffix *-s* is added:

> boy ⟶ boys
> attorney ⟶ attorneys

Some words that end in *-uy* sometimes change the *-y* to *-i:*

> guy ⟶ guys
> soliloquy ⟶ soliloquies

There are a few nouns that do not always change in the plural:

> fish ⟶ fish (or *fishes* when referring to more than one species)
> caribou ⟶ caribou (sometimes *caribous*)
> moose ⟶ moose

There are also some nouns that have a unique plural:

> foot ⟶ feet
> mouse ⟶ mice
> knife ⟶ knives

## THE POSSESSIVE CASE
The possessive case of most singular nouns is formed by adding an apostrophe followed by an *-s:*

> *Jackie's* passport
> This hat is *Billy's*

For plural nouns ending in *-s,* only the apostrophe is added:

> the *neighbors'* dog
> both *boys'* behavior

Proper nouns that end in *-s* often present a special case:

> *Mr. Douglas's* car
> *Socrates'* teachings

## THE PREPOSITION
The preposition is used with an object (a noun, pronoun, or the equivalent of a noun) to form a phrase that functions generally as an adjective or an adverb.

> The man *in the car* is his father. (adjective)
> The river winds *through the valley*. (adverb)
> I like *to watch sports*. (infinitive phrase used as a noun)

There are two types of prepositions: the simple preposition, which consists of a single word (for example, *against, from, near, of, on, out, in*) and the compound preposition, which consists of more than one element (for example, *according to, on account of, because of, in spite of*).

## THE CONJUNCTION VS. THE PREPOSITION
The words *after, before, but, for,* and *since* can be used as prepositions or conjunctions. Their part of speech is determined by their function in the sentence. Conjunctions are usually used to connect two elements of the same grammatical type, while prepositions are followed by an object to form a phrase.

| | |
|---|---|
| **conjunction:** | The playful *but* thoughtful youngsters did well in school. (*but* connects two adjectives) |
| **preposition:** | I was left with nothing *but* hope. (*but* followed by an object) |

| | |
|---|---|
| **conjunction:** | The device conserves fuel, *for* it is battery-powered. (*for* connects two clauses) |
| **preposition:** | The device conserves fuel *for* better mileage. (*for* followed by an object) |

## PLACE IN THE SENTENCE
A preposition comes in front of a noun or a pronoun (*under* the desk, *beside* them), after an adjective (antagonistic *to*, insufficient *for*, symbolic *of*), or after a verb as a particle (take *over*, put *on*, come *across*).

The preposition may end a sentence, especially if it is a verb particle.

> What does this all *add up to*?
> After Amy left, Sandra *took over*.

## THE PRONOUN
Pronouns are often said to stand in place of the noun or noun phrase in a sentence. Usually, the pronoun stands for something previously specified or generally understood.

Pronouns have the following characteristics: *case* (nominative, possessive, or objective); *number* (singular or plural); *person* (first, second, or third); and *gender* (masculine, feminine, or neuter). Pronouns can be classed in seven main categories, each having a specific function.

## DEMONSTRATIVE PRONOUNS
The words *this, that, these,* and *those* are demonstrative pronouns when they function as nouns. (They are classed as demonstrative adjectives when they modify a noun.) The demonstrative pronoun distinguishes a person or thing from another person or thing:

> *This* is the one I want.
> I was happy about *that*.
> *These* are the best designs.
> I picked *those* as the prettiest flowers.

The demonstrative pronoun also serves to distinguish a person or thing nearby from one that is farther away (*this* is my desk; *that* is yours).

## INDEFINITE PRONOUNS
Indefinite pronouns are used to designate a person or thing of which the identity is unknown or is not immediately evident. The indefinite pronouns include the following:

| | |
|---|---|
| all | several |
| either | anything |
| none | many |
| another | some |
| everybody | both |
| no one | much |
| any | somebody |
| everyone | each |
| one | neither |
| anybody | someone |
| everything | each one |
| other(s) | nobody |
| anyone | something |
| few | |

The indefinite pronoun and the verb that follows it should agree in number. The following pronouns are used with a singular verb: *another, anything, each one, everything, much, nobody, no one, other, someone, something*:

> **Much** is being done.
> **No one** wants to go.

The indefinite pronouns *both, few, many,* and *several* are used with plural verbs:

> **Many** are called; **few** are chosen.

Certain pronouns, such as *all, any, none,* and *some,* sometimes present difficulties, since they can be used with a singular or a plural verb. As a general rule, a pronoun that is used with a noun that cannot be counted requires a singular verb, while a pronoun that is used with a noun that can be counted requires a plural verb.

| | |
|---|---|
| **with an uncountable noun:** | All of the property is affected. None of the soup was spilled. Some of the money was spent. |
| **with a countable noun:** | All of my shoes are black. None of the clerks were available. Some of your friends were here. |

## INTERROGATIVE PRONOUNS
The interrogative pronouns *what, which, who, whom,* and *whose,* as well as those bound with the word *-ever* (*whatever, whichever,* etc.) are used to introduce a direct or an indirect question:

> **Who** is she?
> **Whoever** can that be?
> He asked me **who** she was.
> We wondered **whoever** that could be.

## PERSONAL PRONOUNS
The personal pronoun reflects the person, number, and gender of the entity it represents. Each category is made up of distinct personal pronouns:

| Person | Nominative | Possessive | Objective |
|---|---|---|---|
| **First** | | | |
| (sing.) | I | my, mine | me |
| (pl.) | we | our, ours | us |
| **Second** | | | |
| (sing.) | you | your, yours | you |
| (pl.) | you | your, yours | you |
| **Third** | | | |
| (sing.) | he | his | him |
| | she | her, hers | her |
| | it | its | it |
| (pl.) | they | their, theirs | them |

## RECIPROCAL PRONOUNS
The reciprocal pronouns *each other* and *one another* indicate a mutual action or relationship:

> Jim and Andy saw **each other** at the party.
> They do not quarrel with **one another**.

The reciprocal pronoun is also used as a possessive:

> The two companies depend on **each other's** success.
> The members enjoyed **one another's** company.

## REFLEXIVE PRONOUNS
Reflexive pronouns are formed from the personal pronouns *him, her, it, my, our, them,* and *your,* to which the combining form *-self* or *-selves* is added. The reflexive pronoun is usually used to express a reflexive action or to emphasize the subject of a sentence, clause, or phrase:

> She dressed **herself**.
> He asked **himself** if it was worth it.
> I **myself** am not involved.
> They wanted to do it **themselves**.

## RELATIVE PRONOUNS
The relative pronouns are *who, whom, whose, which,* and *that,* as well as the compounds formed by adding the ending *-ever*. These pronouns are used to introduce subordinate clauses that function as a noun or an adjective.

> a man **who** sought success
> a woman **whom** we can trust
> an author **whose** first novel was a success
> a move **which** was unforeseen
> a boy **that** behaves well
> give it to **whomever** you wish
> **whoever** thought of it
> pick **whichever** you want

In certain cases the relative pronoun may be omitted:

> The man [**whom**] I was talking to is the senator.

## THE VERB
Verbs have essentially three classes: ordinary verbs of action, such as *go*, auxiliary verbs, like *can* and *shall,* and fundamental verbs like *be, have,* and *do,* which can function as both ordinary verbs and as auxiliaries.

The verb has the following characteristics: *inflection* (for example, helps, helping, helped), *person* (first, second, third), *number* (singular, plural), *tense* (present, past, future), *aspect* (categories of time other than the simple tenses of present, past, future), *voice* (active, passive), and *mood* (indicative, subjunctive, and imperative).

## INFLECTION
Regular verbs have three inflections that are formed by adding the suffixes *-s* or *-es*, *-ed*, and *-ing* (for example, *asks, asked, asking*). Most of the irregular verbs have four inflections (for example, *sees, saw, seen, seeing*). The verb *be* has seven inflections: *is, am, are, was, were, being, been*).

Verbs ending in silent *-e* in general keep the *-e* when a consonantal suffix (such as *-s*) is added to the word, but the *-e* is dropped when the suffix begins with a vowel (such as *-ed, -ing*):

> *arrange; arranges; arranged; arranging*
> *hope; hopes; hoped; hoping*

However, certain verbs keep the *-e* in order to avoid confusion with another verb:

> *dye* (color); *dyes; dyed; dyeing*
> but
> *die* (cease to live); *dies; died; dying*
> *singe* (burn); *singes; singed; singeing*
> but
> *sing* (produce music); *sings; sang; singing*

If a single-syllable verb ends in a single consonant preceded by a single vowel, the final consonant is often doubled before the addition of *-ed* or *-ing*:

> *brag; brags; bragged; bragging*
> *grip; grips; gripped; gripping*

When a multi-syllable verb ends in the same way, and the last syllable is stressed, the final consonant is also doubled:

> *commit; commits; committed; committing*
> *occur; occurs; occurred; occurring*

It frequently happens that a verb ending in *-y* preceded by a consonant changes *-y* to *-i*, except when the suffix is *-ing*:

> *carry; carries; carried; carrying*
> *study; studies; studied; studying*

When a verb ends in *-c*, a *-k* is added to inflections if the suffix begins with *-e* or *-i*:

> *mimic; mimics; mimicked; mimicking*
> *traffic; traffics; trafficked; trafficking*

## TENSE AND ASPECT
The present and past tenses are generally formed as a single word:

> I **do**, I **did**
> we **write**, we **wrote**

The future tense is conjugated with the auxiliary verbs *shall* or *will* and the present or progressive forms:

> I **shall do** it.
> We **will come** tomorrow.
> I **shall be leaving** tomorrow.

Aspect concerns the tense of the verb other than the present, the past, or the future. Aspect has four forms: the *progressive*, the *present perfect*, the *past perfect*, and the *future perfect*.

The *progressive* is used to express an ongoing action that takes place in the present, past, or future:

> He **is reading** the paper at the moment.
> I **was studying** for the test when you called.
> I **will be going** to India next year.

The *present perfect* tense is used to express an action done in the past but which may be continuing in the present, or to express an action that occurred at an indefinite moment in the past. It is conjugated with the auxiliary verbs *has* or *have* and the past participle:

> She **has written** many books.
> They **have regretted** their mistake.

The *past perfect* expresses a completed action that occurred before another action in the past. It is conjugated with the auxiliary verb *had* and the past participle:

> She **had written** several books previously.
> We **had left** the house before they arrived.

The *future perfect* tense indicates that a future action will take place before another action or occurrence still to come. It is conjugated with the auxiliary verbs *will* or *shall* and *have* and the past participle:

> We **will have finished** the project by then.
> They **will have gone** before we will arrive.

## VOICE

The *active* voice indicates that the subject of the sentence is the doer of the action of the verb; the *passive* voice, consisting of a form of the verb *be* and a past participle, indicates that the subject of the sentence is the object of the action:

> **Active voice:** His colleagues **respect** him.
> **Passive voice:** He **is respected** by his colleagues.

## MOOD

There are three moods: the *indicative*, the *subjunctive*, and the *imperative*. The *indicative* is used to indicate a fact or to ask a question:

> He **is** here.
> **Is** he here?

The *subjunctive* is used to express a condition contrary to fact, especially in clauses introduced by *if*, and after the verb *wish*:

> If she **were** there, she could answer that.
> I wish he **were** here.

The *subjunctive* is also used in clauses beginning with the word *that* following verbs that request, demand, or recommend:

> They asked that the books **be** returned.
> She insisted that the door **remain** open.
> The law required that he **report** his earnings.

The imperative is used to express a command or a demand:

> **Come** here!
> **Pay** attention!

## TRANSITIVE AND INTRANSITIVE VERBS

A transitive verb takes a direct object:

> She **sold** her car.

An intransitive verb has no direct object:

> He **talked** all day.

# Ten General Spelling Rules

1) In general, 'i' comes before 'e' except after 'c' or in words like 'neighbor' and 'weigh'.
2) Words that end in a /seed/ sound: 'supersede' is the only word ending in 'sede'; 'exceed', 'proceed' and 'succeed' are the only three words ending in 'ceed'; all others end in 'cede'.
3) Words ending in a hard 'c' sound usually change to 'ck' before adding 'e', 'i', or 'y': picnic (r) picnicked, picnicking but picnics.
4) Words ending in a stressed single vowel + single consonant usually double the consonant before a suffix: abet (r) abetted, abetting; begin (r) beginner.
5) Words ending in silent 'e' usually drop the 'e' before a suffix that begins with a vowel but not before a suffix beginning with a consonant: bone (r) boned, boning but boneless.
6) Words ending in stressed 'ie' usually change to 'y' before a suffixal 'i': die (r) dying.
7) Words ending in a double vowel usually remain unchanged before a suffix: agree (r) agreeable; blue (r) blueness; coo (r) cooing.
8) Words ending in a consonant plus 'y' usually change the 'y' to 'i' before a suffix: beauty (r) beautiful; happy (r) happiness.
9) Words ending in a vowel plus 'y' usually do not change before a suffix: boy (r) boys; enjoy (r) enjoying.
10) Words ending in 'll' usually drop one 'l' when adding another word to form a compound: all + ready (r) already; full + fill (r) fulfill; hate + full (r) hateful.

# Ten Rules for Forming Plurals

1) Most nouns form the plural by adding 's': bag (r) bags.
2) Words that end in silent 'e' usually just add 's': college (r) colleges.
3) Nouns ending in 'x', 'z', 'ch', 'sh', and 'ss' usually add 'es': fox (r) foxes; buzz (r) buzzes; church (r) churches; bush (r) bushes; boss (r) bosses.
4) Words ending in a consonant + 'y' usually change the 'y' to 'i' and add 'es': army (r) armies; sky (r) skies.
5) Words ending in a vowel + 'y' usually add 's' with no change: day (r) days; boy (r) boys; key (r) keys.
6) Words ending in a vowel + 'o' usually add 's' with no change: duo (r) duos; studio (r) studios.
7) Words ending in a consonant + 'o': some add 's' and some add 'es': ego (r) egos; piano (r) pianos; echo (r) echoes; tomato (r) tomatoes.
8) Words ending in 'f' usually change the 'f' to 'v' and add 'es': leaf (r) leaves; self (r) selves; thief (r) thieves; but chief (r) chiefs.
9) Words ending in 'fe' usually change the 'fe' to 'v' and add 'es': knife (r) knives; life (r) lives.
10) Words that are the names of fishes, birds, and mammals usually have an unchanging form for the plural or have the unchanging form and an 's' plural, depending on meaning.